A History of the
Episcopal Church Schism
in South Carolina

A History of the Episcopal Church Schism in South Carolina

Ronald James Caldwell

WIPF & STOCK · Eugene, Oregon

A HISTORY OF THE EPISCOPAL CHURCH SCHISM IN SOUTH CAROLINA

Copyright © 2017 Ronald James Caldwell. All rights reserved. Except for brief quotations in critical publications or reviews, no part of this book may be reproduced in any manner without prior written permission from the publisher. Write: Permissions, Wipf and Stock Publishers, 199 W. 8th Ave., Suite 3, Eugene, OR 97401.

Wipf & Stock
An Imprint of Wipf and Stock Publishers
199 W. 8th Ave., Suite 3
Eugene, OR 97401

www.wipfandstock.com

PAPERBACK ISBN: 978-1-5326-1885-7
HARDCOVER ISBN: 978-1-4982-4468-8
EBOOK ISBN: 978-1-4982-4467-1

Manufactured in the U.S.A.   JULY 18, 2017

For my daughter,
Elizabeth Anne,
who weathered the storm with courage, grace, and faith

Contents

Preface | xi

1   South Carolina and the Episcopal Church before 2003 | 1

  A new Colony
  A New Church and a New Diocese
  Union and Disunion in the Nineteenth Century
  Revolution and Counter-Revolution in the Twentieth Century
    1900–1960
    The Background of the Revolution of the Episcopal Church
    Revolutionary Reforms and Bishop Gray Temple (1961–1982)
      Race
      Prayer Book
      Women's Ordination
      Homosexuality
    Counter-Revolution and Bishop Christopher FitzSimons Allison (1982–1990)
      The Roots of Counter-Revolution
      Christopher FitzSimons Allison
      Bishop Allison's Counter-Revolution, 1982–1990
      Bishop Allison after 1990
    Counter-Revolution and Bishop Edward L. Salmon, Jr., 1990–2002
      Edward Lloyd Salmon, Jr.
      The Return of the Issue of Homosexuality, 1990–1996
      The Loosening of Bonds, 1997
      Walking the Tightrope, 1998–2002
  Conclusion

2   The Crisis of 2003 in the Episcopal Church and its Immediate Aftermath | 93

The Background of the Robinson Affair
The Robinson Affair
The Aftermath of the Robinson Affair
    Reactions in the Diocese of South Carolina
    Reactions in the Anglican Communion and the Episcopal Church
    The Consecration of Bishop Robinson
    The Chapman Memo
The Diocese of South Carolina in the Late Salmon Years, 2004–2007
    The Immediate Backlash against the Episcopal Church
    The *All Saints* Case
    The Backlash against the Episcopal Church, 2004–2006
    A New Presiding Bishop
    The Search for a New Bishop
    The Election of a New Bishop
    The Failure to Gain Consents
    The Success in Gaining Consents
Four Dioceses Declare Separation from the Episcopal Church
    San Joaquin
    Pittsburgh
    Quincy
    Fort Worth

3   The Diocese of South Carolina in the Early Lawrence Years, 2008–2009 | 218

The Life of Mark Joseph Lawrence to 2008
    Bakersfield
    Finding Religion
    Ministry, 1980–2007
        McKeesport, Pennsylvania
        The Diocese of Pittsburgh and the Episcopal Church
        Life Ties
        Back to Bakersfield
        Lawrence and the Episcopal Church Issues of Homosexuality
Building Bonds, 2008
    The Ordination and Consecration of Bishop Lawrence

The Presiding Bishop's Visit to Charleston, February 24–25, 2008
Building Bonds before Lambeth 2008
Lambeth 2008
Building Bonds after Lambeth 2008
Testing Bonds, 2009
The Background of the General Convention of 2009
The General Convention of 2009
The Aftermath of the General Convention of 2009
Clergy Conference, August 13
The Background of the Special Convention of October 24, 2009
The Special Convention of October 24
The Aftermath of the Special Convention

4   Storm Clouds, 2010–2011 | 275

2010
The Logan/Tisdale Affair, January–February
The Diocesan Convention, March 26
Tensions
The Special Convention, October 15
The Aftermath of the Special Convention
2011
The Diocesan Convention, February 18–19
A Gathering Storm, March–September
The Disciplinary Board for Bishops, September–November
Quit Claim Deeds, November–December

5   The Crisis of 2012 | 328

The Background of the General Convention, January–June
The Return of the Issue of Homosexuality
The Annual Diocesan Convention, March 10
Preparations for a Crisis, March–July
The General Convention, July
The Controversial Resolutions
The Walk-Out
The Aftermath in South Carolina, July–October
The Declaration of a Crisis
The Secret Plan, August

Contents

    Outward and Inward Signs, September–October 2

The Episcopal Church and Bishop Lawrence, September–October

Schism

    October 15

    October 17

The Contest for Legitimacy, October–December

    A War of Words

    Awaiting the Special Convention

    The Special Convention

    The Renunciation and the Release and Removal of Bishop Lawrence

    The Eve of the Legal War, December 2012

6   Two Dioceses, 2013 and After | 400

Charting a New Course

To State Court, Early 2013

The Episcopal Church in South Carolina

    Rebuilding the Diocese

    The Issues of Homosexuality and Racism

The Diocese of South Carolina

    The Search for Meaning

    The Search for Identity

    Membership and Income

To Federal Court, 2013+

    vonRosenberg v. Lawrence

    Other Actions in Federal Courts

The War in State Courts, March 2013+

    The Preparation for the Circuit Court Trial

    The Circuit Court Trial, July 8–25, 2014

    The Supreme Court of South Carolina

7   Conclusion | 495

Causes

Nature

Results

Index | 513

Preface

STORMS ARE A WAY of life in the Low Country of South Carolina, always have been. Since Hurricane Hugo in 1989, however, residents of this blessed land have been unusually on edge, jittery at the appearance of any storm moving anywhere nearby. On Monday, October 15, 2012, everyone was keeping a nervous eye on Hurricane Raphael that had just crossed Puerto Rico heading northward into the warm waters of the Atlantic Ocean. If it turned northwestward, it could hit South Carolina. Its winds of ninety miles an hour would surely increase over the ocean. Its fearsome energy drawn up from the generous waters would certainly explode. To make matters worse, in the next few days, the autumnal moon-driven high tides would inevitably flood many of the streets in the low-lying peninsula that was the home to old Charleston. The local newspaper issued warnings of flooding downtown and beach erosion. Even with a passing summer shower, the old streets liked to keep their waters ankle deep. As Venice, Charleston was wedded to the sea, for better and for worse, and there had been plenty of both in its long and highly eventful history.

This time, the Low Country dodged the bullet. A cold front, always a welcomed relief after the invariably long, steamy summer, moved off the coast putting up a protective wall that forced Raphael to veer eastward out to open sea. By October 16, the storm had moved northeast of Bermuda heading off to rain itself into oblivion in the open north Atlantic.

At the same time, a storm of a different kind was about to strike South Carolina. In a way, it would be as destructive as Hugo had been. At noon on October 15, 2012, the presiding bishop of the Episcopal Church, Katharine Jefferts Schori, in New York City, made a telephone call to Mark Lawrence, the local bishop in Charleston. The Church that was long the virtual established religion of the Low Country was about to be hit by the greatest storm in its life, or at least since the Recent Unpleasantness. Jefferts Schori told Lawrence that he had been formally charged by a Church panel with abandonment of the Episcopal Church and that she was placing him under restriction. He was not to serve in any official capacity until the issue was resolved.

As soon as he hung up the phone, Lawrence called his lawyers and the dozen members of the diocesan Standing Committee, all of whom agreed that the Episcopal Diocese of South Carolina would remove itself from the Episcopal Church. They declared the moment of the phone call to be the time of the break. Two days later, they announced to the world that the Diocese of South Carolina had "disassociated" from the Episcopal Church and was now an independent Christian denomination. The old diocese split into two separate dioceses, the majority part becoming an independent unit, and the minority part adhering to the Episcopal Church.

The modern word "schism" is often defined as a formal division, or breaking apart, particularly of a religious institution. It comes from the ancient Greek word "skhizein," meaning to split. In modern English, schism means a splitting, tearing apart, division, separation, or the like.

Schisms are nothing new in the Episcopal Church, or in Christianity for that matter. The Episcopal Church has seen over fifty schisms, no one knows the real number, since the first happened in 1873 with the Reformed Episcopal Church (still a significant presence in the Low Country). In South Carolina today, there are at least ten different "Anglican/Episcopal" denominations, all claiming jurisdiction, all with their own bishops in apostolic succession. According to the authoritative *World Christian Encyclopedia: A Comparative Survey of Churches and Religions in the Modern World* (Oxford University Press, 2001), there are 168 separate "Anglican" denominations in the world. The same work declared there were 33,909 Christian denominations as of the year 2000, more than double the number of thirty years earlier, 16,075. Institutionally, Christianity is multiplying at a phenomenal rate. The number of individual Christian denominations in the world today, in 2017, may well exceed 40,000. In spite of all the high-flown efforts at ecumenicism in recent years, the fact is that Christianity is exploding, at least structurally.

The schisms derived from the differences among human interpretations of proper beliefs, practices, policies, and procedures. The Christian church was not born full-grown, quite the opposite. Jesus's close followers, at times a quarrelsome lot, had to scramble to make themselves into a coherent organization. The differences and arguments within the Christian community probably started on day one. We know from the New Testament that the first major in-house fight came very early. It was over whether the new faith should remain a Jewish sect. This was probably settled around 50 C.E. in the so-called Council of Jerusalem. The prevailing opinion was to move beyond the old bounds of Judaism, much to the chagrin of the strict traditionalists. In a way, every argument in the church since then has been basically the same, whether to keep the old ways or do things differently. That was certainly the problem that caused the schism in South Carolina.

The truth is that, in many ways, Christianity is an evolving religion. The followers of Jesus Christ held certain core Gospel beliefs but early on drew much from Judaism, the eastern mystery religions, and Greek philosophy. Over the centuries, the church grew and developed constantly. Many would argue that this is the genius of Christianity, that this why it is the most successful religion in the history of the world. All along the way, there were always differences of opinion within the church over this adaptability. It was three hundred years before the Doctrine of the Trinity was established, and that was after a major fight over the nature of Jesus. The Arians lost. The other great schisms were too numerous to name here, just to mention the East-West split in 1054 and the Protestant Reformation of 1517 and after. It seemed contradictory, but true, that the more the house of Christianity grew, the more it divided. Some would say this was a scandal because the church was the Body of Christ and schism was only rending that Body. Of course, defenders would argue the necessity of schisms. Protestantism and Anglicanism would not exist except for schisms by Martin Luther and Henry VIII.

In fact, the schism of 2012 was not the first schism in the history of the Episcopal Church in South Carolina. It was the third. The first came in 1861 when the Diocese of South Carolina joined with the other dioceses in the eleven seceding states to form the Episcopal Church in the Confederate States of America. This schism was one of necessity created by the conditions of war. At the end of the war, the schism evaporated as the dioceses of the old Confederacy simply resumed their places in the national Episcopal Church. The second "schism" was the so-called Schism of 1887. This was not really a schism, but a boycott by white racist delegates from some of the largest and most important parishes in South Carolina who walked out of a convention meeting when a black clergyman appeared. They demanded a whites-only diocese. The bishop was appalled and infuriated, but felt compelled to concede to the strikers' implacable demand. The extortion worked, at least for a long time. It was sixty-seven years later before this shameful "schism" was healed and the first historically black parish was admitted into union with the heretofore all-white convention of the Diocese of South Carolina. Interestingly enough, there was a common tie to all three schisms in South Carolina. All were directly caused by social factors, racism for the first two, and homosexuality for the third.

The purpose of the present book is to explore the 2012 schism in the Episcopal Church located in the eastern half of South Carolina. The research on this book went on for four years after the schism. As one will see, the text is heavily documented with over 2,200 footnotes citing nearly 900 sources. As much as possible, the actors' own words are given. In all, I consulted some 2,500 sources of information, primary and secondary. For the sake of space, bibliographic information is combined with the footnotes of the text. There is no separate bibliography. The first citation of a work in the footnotes gives the bibliographic detail of the item. Subsequent citations of the same work give abbreviated author/title. For a source from the Internet, the URL given is the one operative on the day it was accessed. By the time of this book's publication, some URLs may be obsolete but the item may still be found by a search of the Internet. However, some sources cited here from the Internet may no longer be available online at the time of this book's publication.

My method in this project has been in three parts: gather all the publicly available information on the topic, present it in a meaningful chronological narrative, and draw conclusions based on reasonable judgments of the sources. The first part, information, was drawn from the primary, that is, original, and secondary, or, interpretive, sources. Primary were the original documents coming from official entities as courts, church bodies and institutions, and leading officials, as the papers of the bishops. Outstanding among these sources were the 1,342 pieces of evidence introduced in the circuit court trial of July 2014. Crucial documents from the diocesan bodies, as the minutes of the trustees and the standing committee, came to light for the first time. Also important were the depositions of Bishop Lawrence, the Rev. Rickenbaker, and Nancy Armstrong. The legal proceedings, from the lowly circuit court to the U.S. Supreme Court, produced a massive wealth of documentary evidence relating to the history of the schism. Crucial too were the records of the Episcopal Church General Convention, readily available online. In the diocese, the basic source of original information was the journal of the convention, each one providing valuable material from the bishop's addresses, the bishop's diary, resolutions, and the elections to the diocesan bodies. The last few years of these were online from the diocese. In addition, *Jubilate Deo*, the diocesan newsletter, provided documents along with showing the changing attitudes of the diocesan leaders. The Church diocese, presently called the Episcopal Church in South Carolina, also offered its convention documents, and many other sources, particularly the legal ones, online at its website. This is not to say, however, that I examined all the documents relevant to the schism. Two pools of vital information remained hidden from the public, if they still existed: the records of the bishop's search committee of 2005–07, and the one thousand e-mails between Bishop Lawrence and his lawyer, Alan Runyan.

As one might imagine, there was a seemingly endless supply of secondary works about the schism. Apparently, everybody had opinions, and thanks to the Internet could freely express them. Secondary sources broke down roughly into three divisions: 1-the partisans of the diocese who defended the schism, 2-the partisans of the Episcopal Church who criticized the schism, and 3-the media trying to report the news of the events around the schism. On the whole, the pro-diocesan side dominated public relations flooding the Internet with information and often inflammatory commentary defending the diocese and denouncing the Church. One should be grateful for the diligent hard work of the diocesan staff such as Jan Pringle and Joy Hunter who kept the diocesan news sources online plentiful and up-to-date. Also invaluable were the postings of David Virtue and Mary Ann Mueller on the website Virtue Online. This was the best source of information and opinion, in general, from the "orthodox" Anglican viewpoint. More specifically on the diocese, Kendall Harmon's blog at Titus One Nine provided a host of essential material supporting the diocesan positions and decisions and criticizing the national Church. Other important Internet sites that provided helpful information and enlightening insight into the pro-diocesan views were: George Conger, the Anglican Communion Institute, the Anglican Curmudgeon, and the American Anglican Council.

On the other side, partisans of the Episcopal Church tried their best to get their message out to the public, but really did not compete evenly. They tended to be more informational and less strident in condemning the other side. Invaluable here was the Episcopal News Service, particularly the fountain of substantial articles from Mary Frances Schjonberg. The online Episcopal Café also kept readers up-to-date on events. At home in South Carolina, it was the indefatigable Steve Skardon who virtually single-handedly kept people informed of the diocesan activities on his website, South Carolina Episcopalians. Nothing passed under his radar. Partisans on both sides came to rely on his unabashed and never under-stated work. The Episcopal Forum of South Carolina also tried its best to keep local people informed by way of its website. After the schism, the diocesan office at the Episcopal Church in South Carolina began an impressive public relations effort under Holly Behre. Fortunately, she posted practically all of the relevant legal papers on the ECSC website.

Beyond the two sides, the media tried to relay the news from a neutral standpoint and did an admirable job. The hometown newspaper, the Charleston *Post and Courier*, kept up a running account of the events around the schism, mainly through the numerous articles of the evenhanded reporters Jennifer Berry Hawes and Adam Parker. Other newspapers also provided informational articles, particularly *The New York Times, Washington Post, Pittsburgh Post-Gazette,* and *Florence Morning News*. The quasi-official Episcopal Church journal, *The Living Church*, provided many articles from a balanced standpoint.

The task of the historian is to tell as truthful, complete, and reasonable a story of an historical event as he or she can. Researching and writing about a contemporary event in which nearly all of the actors are alive and well and arrayed on two opposing sides has presented special challenges. The schism was a painful event for thousands of people in South Carolina, remains so, and no doubt will continue to be for a long time to come. There was little joy on either side. The public outbursts shown in the various meetings on both sides during and right after the schism perhaps came more from emotional relief and exhaustion than from glee. Indeed, as one will see, along the way, Bishop Lawrence himself went through a great deal of personal anguish. He was not alone. Only about half the people I contacted for interviews accepted my invitations. For the others, the feelings ran too deep, the wounds remained too fresh, the suspicions lingered too strongly, or legal issues hovered too much to allow them to respond. I did not press the point. I respected their feelings. Compiling this history has not been a joyful activity for me either even though I was only an observer on the periphery of the stage. Some people asked me along the way, "Why are you doing this?" My answer was: I am a historian, this is what I do; I care about South Carolina; no one else is writing about what happened; I can make a contribution that will help both sides understand how they got to where they are. I cannot lessen the pain. I certainly cannot heal the wounds. But, as a historian, I can help people understand the reasons for their feelings. Perhaps that is enough for now.

Although this is a work of non-fiction that I believe is well documented, the judgments and conclusions I rendered were only my opinions. Two people can take the same empirical information and interpret it entirely differently, as in the famous half full/half empty glass of water. This is why there are often many widely varying, even contradictory, histories written of the same subject. Anyone who has visited the Lincoln museum at Ford's Theater in Washington has seen the jaw-dropping three-story high, and ever growing, Babel Tower of books on Abraham Lincoln. Another writer may take the schism in South Carolina and interpret it differently. Indeed, I encourage people to write about it and share their understandings of it. Actors in the schism should recount their experiences for their own sakes and for posterity. Researchers and historians should review the documents and give their interpretations of the events. This is not to say, however, that there are "alternative facts" about the schism, or any other historical event. Empirically verifiable events are indisputable facts. Only their interpretation is at issue.

Reading the following text may be upsetting to many people. Still, I think studying the schism is something important we need to do, however unpleasant, or even painful, reliving it may be. The first truth that we must reach is that a schism occurred. Denial of history is never justifiable. The leaders on both sides avoided the word "schism." Only the Episcopal Forum members used it to any extent. They did so as warnings of danger they saw ahead. The diocesan partisans used euphemisms as "disassociation," "disaffiliation," and "realignment." The Church side called their reaction "reorganization." In fact, the break was a schism, pure and simple. That is a verifiable truth. We must embrace that fundamental reality however much we may not wish to do so. The second fact both sides must recognize is that the schism was painful to a great many people and continues to be so. Many innocent victims on both sides were displaced from their church homes as a result of the schism. Since both sides claim to be Christian, it is incumbent upon them to respect the sincerity and humanity of the other. The people who made the schism did not do so lightly. They took that drastic step because they honestly and sincerely believed it was the right thing to do just as the people who stayed with the Church believed that was the right choice. One side vilifying or impugning the motives of the other is self-destructive too.

This book would not have been possible without the help and encouragement of many generous people. I count the irrepressible Steve Skardon among my good friends. For his knowledge of the diocese and his willingness to share everything he knew with me, I am grateful beyond measure. The always encouraging Dr. Joan Gundersen was my professional guide from the first. She never complained about the hours of time she contributed to reading, rereading and offering much needed advice about the manuscript. The final work is much better because of her. Peg Carpenter, of Florence, also generously read and critiqued parts of the manuscript. The attorney Thomas Tisdale, the quintessential Low Country gentleman, has been most kind and gracious. He generously shared with me his unique experiences as well as important legal documents he entered in the various courts. The intrepid lawyer Melinda Lucka likewise has been kind enough to relate her crucial roles in this story. The resourceful Barbara Mann was my guide to the work of the Episcopal Forum. The irreplaceable Rev. Dow Sanderson was a unique source of information as a leadership "insider" of the pre-schism diocese. He, too, was most kind to share his experiences with me. Three bishops generously gave me hours of their always-limited time to talk candidly of their roles in recent history of the Church: the Rt. Revs. Henry N. Parsley, Charles vonRosenberg, and Andrew Waldo. They were wise and knowledgeable men of whom every Episcopalian should be proud. In addition, the pioneering Revs. Constance Belmore and Cynthia Taylor kindly shared with me their experiences as the first women to be priests in the Diocese of South Carolina. I am grateful also for the always helpful, but under-appreciated, staffs of the libraries and courthouses I visited along the way. The duPont Library at Sewanee is one of my favorite gold mines. To my dear friends at St. Catherine's Episcopal Church in Florence, South Carolina, I say thank you for your encouragement and support.

My thanks also go out to my correspondents at my blog, "The Episcopal Church Schism in South Carolina." I started the blog in September of 2013 in order to provide updates on my research on the history of the schism as well as information and commentary regarding the ongoing events of the post-schism era. It turned out to be more popular than I had imagined, with over 180,000 "hits" in its first the three and a half years. I invited readers to e-mail me. Many did. I learned a great deal from correspondents of all three sides, pro-diocese, pro-Church, and neutral. I am most grateful for all of their comments, especially those who challenged me to reconsider my thoughts. I did so, always to my benefit. I must pay tribute also to Presiding Bishop Jefferts Schori. Soon after starting this project, I encountered her at a diocesan meeting and mentioned my work. I told her I was torn between writing a condensed version or a full one. She told me to put in the details, for, she said, "a hundred years from now, that is what people will find most interesting." I decided to follow her advice. Finally, I am grateful to my wife of fifty years, Sandra Marshall Caldwell, who long ago learned to take in cheerful stride my consuming historical projects. I could not have done this work without her.

In the end, I alone am responsible for the sins of commission and omission in the following pages. I present in this book, on the former presiding bishop's advice, as complete and thorough a history of the schism in the Episcopal Church in South Carolina as I could compile. I hope a hundred years from now people will still find it of interest.

Ronald James Caldwell
May 17, 2017

1

South Carolina and the Episcopal Church before 2003

A NEW COLONY

There is a familiar old quip about South Carolinians of long ago: They are like the Chinese. They eat rice, worship their ancestors, and speak in a foreign tongue. Beyond the superficial humor of this old witticism, there is a truth of two separate powerful strands indelibly woven throughout South Carolina history: attachment to tradition and a sense of separateness from the larger group. These traits are not necessarily complimentary or even compatible. At first glance, they may even seem contradictory. How can one revere the past and rebel against it? The colony of South Carolina was attached to the mother country then made revolution against her. The state of South Carolina helped create the United States then led the rebellion to break it up. The Episcopalians in South Carolina helped establish and guide their national church then voted to separate from it. In South Carolina, tradition and separateness were not contradictory because they were both overlain with a heavy coat of localism. Thus, tradition became what was longstanding within South Carolina and separateness became how South Carolinians saw themselves as different from others "from off" at any given moment. To old Carolinians, the world was divided into two parts, Carolina and "off."

The strength of the threads of tradition and separateness waxed and waned in South Carolina history. When both waxed together they produced dramatic, sometimes catastrophic, results. The convergence of the two gave South Carolina its experience in the American Revolution, John Calhoun's statesmanship, the Civil War, Jim Crow, Strom Thurmond's politics, and the Episcopal Church schism of 2012. The schism occurred on October 15, 2012. Two days later, the Rt. Rev. Mark Joseph Lawrence, bishop of the Diocese of South Carolina, informed the Most Rev. Katharine Jefferts Schori, the presiding bishop of the Episcopal Church, that the diocese had disaffiliated from the Episcopal Church. It is this last item that must get our attention now. Our purpose here is to address these questions: What were the causes and origins of the Episcopal Church schism of 2012 in South Carolina? What was its nature? And, what effects did it have on South Carolina, the Episcopal Church and the world beyond?

A History of the Episcopal Church Schism in South Carolina

The theme of the competing threads of tradition and separateness can be seen clearly and dramatically beginning in the early colonial period of South Carolina. The vast colony of Carolina, the land between Virginia and Spanish Florida, was created in 1663 by a cash-strapped King Charles II, mainly to pay back in land eight men who had been instrumental in placing him on the throne in 1660. The challenge was to turn a native-populated wilderness into a profitable commercial colony. That meant, first of all, to bring in population. As the proprietors handed out land grants, settlers began arriving by boatloads to the promising but dangerous land. By 1680, a permanent port city had been started, Charles Town, that became not only the point of arrival but also the heart of the new land.

The population of colonial South Carolina was remarkably diverse.[1] It was an English colony, but in many ways, was strikingly different than old England. Early settlers came from many different places speaking many different languages. Right away, the whites began enslaving thousands of indigenous peoples. As the labor supply failed to keep up with demand, landowners bought more and more slaves from the West Indies and Africa for their labor-intensive plantations and farms being carved out all along the fertile waterways of the Carolina Low Country. Nearly half of all the slaves coming to the thirteen colonies/states came through Charleston, or Sullivan's Island in Charleston harbor to be specific. Indeed, before the American Revolution, South Carolina was the only one of the thirteen colonies where slaves outnumbered white people.[2]

Religious variety mirrored the social diversity of the colony. While the Church of England, also called the Anglican church, was the choice of most of the early landed and merchant elite, it was far from being the majority religion of the population and even farther from being the only religion. Of the four thousand colonists in 1700, fewer than half were Anglicans.[3] Presbyterian churches abounded. There were also sizeable groups of Baptists, Congregationalists, Lutherans, Quakers, and French Protestants. There also grew a relatively large Jewish community drawn by the atmosphere of religious tolerance. The only people who were not given freedom to worship as they pleased were the Roman Catholics.

The structure of the Anglican church in the colonies was quite different than that of England. There were no bishops in America. The Bishop of London technically oversaw the church in the colonies, but he never ventured to America. The bishop sent commissaries as his representatives to South Carolina, but these could not function as bishops. The Anglican church in colonial South Carolina developed a distinctly parochial and independent nature as a quasi-congregational church. At least part of this phenomenon stemmed from the gradual union of the French Huguenot and English gentry. Early on, most Huguenots adhered to the Anglican church bringing with them their more austere

---

1. Edgar, Walter. *South Carolina: A History.* Columbia, SC: University of South Carolina Press, 1998, 50.

2. Slaves outnumbered whites in South Carolina throughout the eighteenth century. On the eve of the American Revolution there were 104,000 blacks and 70,000 whites in South Carolina. Edgar, *South Carolina: A History*, 78.

3. Bolton, Charles S. *Southern Anglicanism: The Church of England in Colonial South Carolina.* Westport, CT: Greenwood, 1982, 19. 1,700 Anglicans, 1,300 Presbyterians, 500 Huguenots, 400 Baptists, and 100 Quakers.

continental Calvinism. Huguenot-English family alliances became the backbone of the South Carolina colonial society. To this day, French names abound among the prominent Carolina families.[4]

The Anglican faction in the political structure of the colony struggled to make itself, and its Church, the dominant power in South Carolina. The Anglicans in the Commons House passed the Establishment Act of 1704, replaced by a milder Act in 1706, that established the Church of England in South Carolina until 1778. Supported by the state, the Anglican church settled down into a sort of comfortable home of most of the propertied elites who valued it perhaps more for its political than its religious importance. As historian Charles Bolton observed: "Anglican laymen in the South fashioned the established churches to suit their own needs and remained in control of them. Most of the Anglican clergy came to accept this situation, and they used traditional doctrines to support social and political authority within the colonies rather than on behalf of the English government."[5] Primarily through the vestry system, the Anglican church in colonial South Carolina remained a locally oriented institution.

Economically, South Carolina boomed in the eighteenth century. Indeed, it became the richest of the thirteen colonies and in some ways the one that England favored the most.[6] However, in spite of close commercial ties with England, South Carolina remained a world apart from the mother country, literally and figuratively. When crises occurred, the British government and usually the British navy were too far away to respond in time. It took several weeks to cross the Atlantic one way; often two months for a round trip. The colonists more or less had to fend for themselves. This they did time and again, all the while adding to their sense of independence.

From the first settlement to the American Revolution, the colonists of South Carolina faced many daunting challenges. Some were internal, some external, some man-made, some natural. The internal problems were mostly how to subdue the native peoples. There was a long string of wars against the Indians. There was also the question of how to control the slaves who were actually the majority of the population. The colonials responded by enacting a number of laws aimed at controlling the slave population. The external problems came mostly from how to respond to the nearby Spanish and French, usual enemies of the English and how to stop the pirates from menacing merchant shipping along the Atlantic coast. On every one of the problems, internal and external, the South Carolina colonists succeeded well. They responded to the challenges and in so doing built up a feeling of confident separateness and local independence. As historian Walter Edgar put it: "Forced to rely on its own resources, South Carolina had become used to fending for itself."[7]

While responding successfully to the powerful challenges confronting them, the colonists were not reluctant to make their own challenges to overseas authority if they

4. The French Protestant Church in Charleston continues as a proud remnant of the colonial past. Today, it is the only French Protestant church in America.

5. Bolton, *Southern Anglicanism*, 3.

6. Edgar, *South Carolina: A History*, 152. On the eve of the American Revolution, the Charleston district was by far the wealthiest region in the thirteen colonies.

7. Ibid., 107.

felt it necessary. This they did in 1719 when they united in what they saw as denials of their own rights in order to overthrow the regime of the proprietors. The government in London agreed with the colonists and in the next year sent over a governor to make it a royal colony. The revolution of 1719 "left a legacy of self-determination. South Carolinians had shown that, if need be, they could take matters into their own hands and get their way."[8]

After more than two centuries of almost continuous conflict, Great Britain won a sweeping victory over her ancient rivals for empire, Spain and France. The French and Indian War (1756–63) produced a landmark treaty that established Britain as the predominant power in North America. It was one of the ironies of modern history, however, that this astounding triumph actually turned out to be a Pyrrhic victory for Britain. The cost was arguably more than it was worth and the unforeseen consequences costlier than the wars themselves. The budgetary strain of all this expensive imperialism was more than the London government wanted to bear alone. After 1763, it decided to shift some of the cost of empire onto the shoulders of the American colonists who had, after all, greatly benefited from the British military and naval successes. Trying to make the Americans pay, even for a fraction of the costs, turned out to be the direct cause of the American Revolutionary war. Between 1763 and 1775, the British made one attempt after another to bring the colonies more in line with the overall empire not anticipating the difficulty of this. The London government had not appreciated the reality that South Carolina and the other twelve Atlantic coast colonies, two thousand miles from England, had in fact long ago developed a sense of self-sufficiency and independence. By 1775, the British government resorted to armed force and the revolutionary war began.

Of all the thirteen colonies, the British wanted to keep South Carolina the most. In the war that raged the next eight years, British military and naval forces did their best to capture and hold South Carolina. More battles were fought there than in any other colony/state. The British seized and occupied Charleston for two years. Although the colonists were torn between loyalty and rebellion, rebel forces in the Low Country held their own and were ultimately successful at driving out the British army and navy.

South Carolina declared itself an independent republic in 1776, and then joined the other twelve former Atlantic seaboard colonies to form a united nation independent of Great Britain. The South Carolina state government disestablished the Anglican church in 1778, thereby ending its old privileges and income.

A NEW CHURCH AND A NEW DIOCESE

The American Revolutionary war devastated the Anglican church in South Carolina. The colonists, especially the Anglicans, were far from united on whether to break away completely from the mother country. As Walter Edgar put it: "In 1775 there was considerable disagreement in congress, on the Council of Safety, and among the general population about breaking ties with Great Britain (. . .). From (. . .) 1759 until (. . .) 1808, there was neither good order nor harmony in South Carolina and no such thing as

---

8. Ibid., 111.

a whole community."⁹ The Anglican church, being the South Carolina branch of the state Church of England, was caught in the middle, the worst place to be. No one summarized it better than Albert Sidney Thomas in his diocesan history:

> The Revolution delivered a crushing blow to the Church in South Carolina. No other state was so completely overrun by the invader from mountain to seaboard; In no other state were the citizens so divided upon the issues, and in no other did they so generously participate in the struggle. With the war had come disestablishment (1778) of the Episcopal Church and loss of all ministerial supply and support, followed by disintegration and destruction. After the war, there were only a few churches outside of Charleston which were not practically in ruins, either burned, dilapidated, or abandoned, and mostly without clergymen.¹⁰

Although it would not regain its pre-Revolutionary prominence, the remnant of the old Anglican church in South Carolina began to rebuild slowly. The first and most urgent need was for clergy. According to the historian Frederick Dalcho, a total of fifty-seven Anglican clergymen had served in South Carolina in the period just before the Revolutionary War (1760–76) although not all at the same time.¹¹ At the time of the peace treaty in 1783, he counted just twelve Anglican/Episcopal clergymen left in all of South Carolina.¹² Rebuilding would prove to be a long and arduous process.

Shortly after the peace of 1783, former Anglicans, now calling themselves the more independent sounding term "Episcopalians," began to stir throughout the new states. Even before the peace treaty, the Rev. William White, rector of Christ Church of Philadelphia, published in 1782 his seminal work, *The Case of the Episcopal Churches in the United States Considered*, suggesting a reorganization of the Anglican religion conforming to American democratic sensibilities. The clergy of Connecticut sent Samuel Seabury to England to be ordained a bishop. On November 14, 1784, he was ordained by bishops of the Scottish Episcopal Church as the first Episcopal bishop of America.

In several states, committees began to meet as early as 1783 to seek ways to organize locally and nationally. On the 6th and 7th of October of 1784, representatives of Episcopal associations from eight states met in New York City to begin organizing a national church.¹³ South Carolina was not represented at this first meeting. The Rev. William White was elected the president of the gathering, the first convention of the Episcopal Church adopting the name Protestant Episcopal Church in the United States of America. It created the basic outline on which the Episcopal Church would build from thenceforth. It also drew up a letter to be sent to the five states not represented, including South Carolina, inviting them to form state organizations and send representatives to a general

---

9. Ibid., 225.

10. Thomas, Albert Sidney. *A Historical Account of the Protestant Episcopal Church in South Carolina, 1820–1957, being a continuation of Dalcho's account 1670–1820.* Columbia, SC: Bryan, 1957, 10–11.

11. Dalcho, Frederick. *An Historical Account of the Protestant Episcopal Church, in South Carolina, from the first settlement of the province, to the War of the Revolution.* Charleston, SC: B. Thayer, 1820, 433–35.

12. Ibid.

13. Connecticut, New York, New Jersey, Pennsylvania, Delaware, Maryland. Massachusetts, Rhode Island.

convention in Philadelphia to be held the next year, 1785: "[we] propose to those of the other states not represented, That as soon as they shall have organized or associated themselves (. . .) they unite in a general ecclesiastical constitution."[14]

White's letter went on with several other points, one of which called for a bishop in every state. In South Carolina, having a bishop presented a problem. With their Low Church tradition of power centered in the lay-controlled and virtually independent vestries, South Carolinians were wary of bishops with quasi-monarchical powers. While they tolerated the idea of bishops in general, they were decidedly against having one in their own state. The contrast to their position was the High Church tradition of New England that promoted the authority of bishops over the clergy and laity. Indeed, Connecticut had installed a bishop several years before the Episcopal Church would set up a constitutional system for itself.

White sent a copy of his letter of October 1784 to the Rev. Robert Smith, rector of St. Philip's parish, in Charleston, and the most prominent Episcopal clergyman in South Carolina. Soon after receiving White's letter, Smith and the Rev. Henry Purcell, rector of St. Michael's called a joint meeting of their vestries on February 8, 1785. Ten men attended, seven from St. Philip's and three from St. Michael's.[15] This was the initial organizational meeting of the new Episcopal Church in South Carolina. The assembly read the letter from White and resolved to send notices to the vestries of the other twenty old Anglican parishes in South Carolina requesting them to appoint deputies to meet at the state house, in Charleston, on May 12, 1785.[16]

Dalcho labeled the May 12, 1785, meeting in Charleston as the "First Convention" of the Protestant Episcopal Church in South Carolina.[17] Actually, "convention" would be an exaggeration. Only eight parishes sent representatives.[18] So few showed up that the assembly resolved to suspend the meeting. First, they agreed to postpone any consideration of White's invitation to a general convention in Philadelphia in favor of sending another notice to the South Carolina vestries not present and to advertise in the local newspapers in hopes of getting more participation. They set a new date to meet as July 12, 1785.

What Dalcho labeled as the "Second Convention" of the Protestant Episcopal Church in South Carolina met in Charleston on July 12, 1785. In spite of all the prompting, once again only eight parishes sent representatives, not the same eight.[19] This time, the assembly decided to proceed with the business at hand anyway. The letter from White was read aloud. The thirteen delegates present then elected six deputies "to represent the Pro. Epis. Church of this State, at the general Convention of Clergymen

---

14. Dalcho, *Historical Account,* 464.
15. Ibid., 463.
16. Ibid., 464.
17. Ibid., 465.
18. St. Philip's, St. Michael's, St. James of Goose Creek, St. John's of Berkeley, St. Thomas, St. Helena, St. James Santee, and St. Stephen's.
19. St. Philip's, St. Michael's, St. James of Goose Creek, St. James Santee, St. Bartholomew, St. George of Dorchester, Prince George Winyah, St. John's of Colleton.

and Lay-Deputies of the Pro. Epis. Church in the U.S.A. to be held at Philadelphia, the Tuesday before the feast of St. Michael's next."[20] The meeting then adjourned.

The South Carolina delegation: the Rev. Henry Purcell, Jacob Read, and Charles Pinckney, attended the first General Convention of the Protestant Episcopal Church in Philadelphia from September 27 to October 7, 1785. When the meeting set up a committee of fourteen to draw up an "Ecclesiastical Constitution" for the Church, Purcell and Read were included.[21] The delegates laid out an extensive basic framework for what would later become the constitution and canons of the Episcopal Church. The South Carolina delegates brought this preliminary constitution, which they had helped to write, back with them to present at the next state convention.

The session Dalcho called the "Third Convention" of the Protestant Episcopal Church in South Carolina met in Charleston on April 26, 1786. Nine parishes sent representatives.[22] Although this might be considered the third convention, it was the first to take up any substantial work, the earlier two only responding to White's invitation and choosing delegates to the Philadelphia convention. The third convention conducted two important orders of business. The first set up a committee to draw up a constitution for the Protestant Episcopal churches of the state of South Carolina. The second considered in detail the Ecclesiastical Constitution from the recent Philadelphia convention. In the whole work, only one point caused the delegates in Charleston to balk. That was the establishment of a bishop in each state: "Rule 6. Objected to; so far as relates to the establishment of a Bishop in South-Carolina."[23] This was the only rule in the document to which the delegates objected. These independent-minded South Carolinians may have been the Episcopal Church but they still did not want a bishop hovering over their parishes. Otherwise, the delegates had no problem with this new basic constitution and went on to spend most of their time discussing intricacies of the liturgy brought up in the articles.

The 1785 Ecclesiastical Constitution formed the basic structure of the Episcopal Church that would evolve into the Church's founding Constitution and Canons of 1789. It established a general convention to meet every three years composed of the clergy and laity chosen by each state. In addition to calling for a bishop in each state, it required the use of the Book of Common Prayer of the Church of England, with necessary American adaptations. To form unity, the Constitution incorporated several points. It said any state could join in the future but only after acceding to the Church's national constitution. In addition, every clergyman was to take an oath in his ordination to conform to the decisions of the general convention. Finally, Article 11 declared: "This General Ecclesiastical Constitution, when ratified by the Church in the different states, shall be considered as fundamental; and shall be unalterable by the Convention of the Church in any state."[24]

20. Dalcho, *Historical Account*, 466.

21. *Journals of the General Conventions of the Protestant Episcopal Church in the United States of America from A.D. 1785 to A.D. 1853*. Philadelphia: Raynor, 1860, 18.

22. St. Philip's, St. Michael's, St. Paul's, St. Bartholomew's, St. Thomas and St. Denis, Prince William's, St. Mark's, St. James of Goose Creek, and St. John's of Berkley.

23. Dalcho, *Historical Account*, 469.

24. Ibid.

Unalterable was the operative word as far as our story is concerned. In 1785–86, the delegates had no problem at all with this: "Rule 11. Agreed to."[25] Finally, the delegates chose four men to represent South Carolina at the general convention to be held in Philadelphia in June of 1786. In a sense of urgency, the delegates agreed to meet again in a month, before the delegates would leave for Philadelphia.

On May 29, 1786, delegates from six parishes met again in Charleston for a "Fourth Convention" of the Protestant Episcopal Church in South Carolina.[26] They resolved to establish the liturgy as approved by the 1785 general convention then gave two items for their delegates to take to the upcoming general convention in Philadelphia, a long list of detailed revisions to the liturgy and a constitution. The constitution they drew up turned out to be more for the benefit of the general convention than for South Carolina. It was a rather brief statement of just six short articles of generalities. Their only issue of contention for the general convention was their opposition to having a bishop. Therefore, in Article 4, their constitution held: "That the succession of the Ministry be agreeable to the usage which requireth the three Orders of Bishops, Priests, and Deacons (with an exception however to the establishing of Bishops in this state)."[27] The delegates in Charleston unanimously approved and adopted the constitution on May 31, 1786. Twenty-three men from thirteen parishes in the state signed it. Just before adjourning, the meeting set up a committee to draw up a detailed set of Rules and Regulations for the state association. That task turned out to be more difficult than expected. It would be twenty years before a finished set would be presented to the state convention for ratification.

Meanwhile South Carolina's delegates, the Rev. Robert Smith, Edward Mitchell, and John Parker, traveled to Philadelphia for the general convention of June 20 to 26, 1786. The main issue at hand was the development of a full constitution and canons for the Episcopal Church. The Ecclesiastical Constitution of 1785 was a preliminary document. It was at the 1786 meeting that the delegates resolved to call another general convention to finalize and establish a full constitution and canons for the Episcopal Church. On June 24, 1786, a resolution was made:

> Resolved, That it be recommended to the Convention of this Church, in the several states represented in this Convention, that they authorize and empower their deputies to the next General Convention, after we shall have obtained a Bishop or Bishops in our Church, to confirm and ratify a general Constitution, respecting both the doctrines and discipline of the Protestant Episcopal Church in the United States of America.[28]

It is important to note the wording of this resolution: *confirm and ratify*. The delegates to the convention would be empowered by their individual states to enact the constitution and canons in the course of the session in the names of their individual states. Their signatures on the documents would accomplish this. Thus, the documents

---

25. Ibid.
26. St. Philip's, St. Michael's, St. Thomas and St. Denis, Prince William's, St. James of Goose Creek, St. Bartholomew's.
27. Dalcho, *Historical Account*, 474.
28. *Journals of the General Conventions*, 42.

would not need to be submitted later to the states for ratification. They would be self-effective among the signatory states at the moment of the signatures. By contrast, the national constitutional convention in 1787 required that the federal constitution could not go into effect until nine states had ratified it.

Records showed that the state conventions in South Carolina understood and accepted the direction of the general convention that they should send deputies to compose and ratify a constitution and canons for the whole Church. At the first state convention after the resolution of June 24, 1786, held on February 22, 1787, this was the first order of business: "The Journals of the General Conventions held in Philadelphia, June 20, 1786; and at Wilmington, October 10, 1786, were read."[29] The only recorded response was to thank their deputies. There was no state convention in the year 1788. At the next one, on May 8, 1789, the last order of business was "that Deputies be elected to the General Convention to be held at Philadelphia, the last Tuesday in July next. Whereupon, the following Gentlemen were unanimously elected: The Rev. Robert Smith, William Smith, Col. Lewis Morris, William Ward Burrows, William Brisbane."[30]

Clearly the Episcopalians in South Carolina wholeheartedly resolved throughout the 1780s to be an integral part of the newly organizing national Episcopal Church, even going so far as approving a system of bishops for the whole while abstaining for themselves. By 1789, the Protestant Episcopal Church in the United States of America was ready to proceed with the full development of a formal national institutional structure. The general convention met in two sessions in Philadelphia that year, July-August and October, with delegations from nine state associations for the purpose of establishing a formal institutional structure for the national Protestant Episcopal Church. On the second day of the meeting, July 29, 1789, the resolution of June 24, 1786 was repeated.[31] This made clear, once again, the purpose of the meeting was for the several states to adopt and ratify a new Church constitution and canons immediately effective in all the signatory states.

The convention of 1789 drew up and adopted the Constitution and Canons as authoritative for the whole Church.[32] The official journal of the convention showed only cooperation from South Carolina in the daily proceedings. In fact, the Rev. Robert Smith was one of the seven committeemen charged with drafting the new constitution.[33] William Brisbane was selected as one of a committee of seven to compose the canons.[34] All of the South Carolina delegates present signed all of the appropriate documents produced

---

29. Dalcho, *Historical Account*, 475.

30. Ibid., 477.

31. *Journals of the General Conventions*, 69.

32. Delegates from nine state associations (counting Massachusetts and New Hampshire as one) signed the Constitution (Aug. 8, 1789) and Canons: New York, New Jersey, Massachusetts-New Hampshire, Connecticut, Pennsylvania, Delaware, Maryland, Virginia, and South Carolina. The nine were later to be represented in the blue field of the Episcopal Church flag by crosses arranged in a St. Andrew's pattern but in no particular order. Thus, South Carolina is one of the little crosses on the Episcopal Church flag.

33. *Journals of the General Conventions*, 70.

34. Ibid., 72.

by the convention. The Rev. Robert Smith and William Brisbane were even appointed to the Standing Committee which was to sit until the Church's next general convention.[35]

At the next state convention in South Carolina, on October 19, 1790, the first order of business was to recognize the new Episcopal Church Constitution and Canons. "The General Constitution and Canons being read, were unanimously agreed to."[36] Apparently, there was no discussion at all of the new document. Thus, it was beyond question that the Episcopal Church in South Carolina adopted the national Church's Constitution and Canons by the signatures on the documents by the representatives of South Carolina at the general conventions of 1789. This was affirmed by the unanimous vote of the state convention on October 19, 1790, some sixteen years before South Carolina would enact its own full constitution and canons called the Rules and Regulations. In fact, a review by the state convention years later, in 1807, declared that the deputies to the general convention of 1789 had indeed ratified the constitution and canons on behalf of the Church in South Carolina: "[the deputies] attended the convention, and, on behalf of the Protestant Episcopal Church of this state, subscribed the constitution."[37] It is important to note the term "on behalf." Even eighteen years afterwards, the understanding in South Carolina remained that the state had ratified the Episcopal Church's constitution and canons in 1789 as the deputies from South Carolina had signed the documents.

The one lingering problem for the South Carolina Episcopalians was the issue of bishops. The national Church had clearly called for bishops and had incorporated them into its core structure. As part of the agreements of 1789, a powerful House of Bishops had been established separate from the Lay and Clerical House of Deputies in the general convention. South Carolina had protested, but only mildly and evidently did little if anything to oppose the concept of bishops in the general conventions in what was after all an episcopal church. Whether South Carolina itself would have a bishop was the only contentious issue at hand after 1789. For a few years, the delegates to the state conventions ignored the issue, no doubt content to let local matters alone. It could not be ignored indefinitely, however. At the state convention in Charleston on the Sixteenth of October of 1794, the subject arose again: "The subject of the Bishops claiming a negative on all the Proceedings of the Clergy and Laity in Convention assembled, came before them; and the unanimous opinion was, that no such power should be granted."[38] Apparently prejudice against bishops had not changed at all in the nine years since the first meeting of the Episcopal Church in South Carolina. The delegates appeared to be just as opposed as ever to having a bishop. However, following this seemingly immovable show of opinion, a truly astonishing event occurred. An unidentified person arose in the meeting to offer reconsideration of the issue suggesting that further refusal of South Carolina to have a bishop would cause a schism in the Episcopal Church. As Dalcho described it: "It was then suggested, that as such an opposition would probably occasion a schism, and that we should be separated from the general Association (. . .) whether it would not be expedient, prior to any secession taking place, to delegate some person

35. Ibid., 112.
36. Dalcho, *Historical Account*, 478.
37. Ibid., 500.
38. Ibid., 480.

from this place to obtain the Episcopate."[39] Apparently the delegates discussed the issue anew after which they reversed themselves and voted to set up a committee to choose a bishop for South Carolina. Within a short time, perhaps a few minutes, the delegates had gone from unanimous opposition against a bishop to setting up a committee to select one, all because they did not want to break up the Episcopal Church. For once, South Carolinians, so often accused of being stubbornly independent and provincial, put consideration of the nation above themselves. For the sake of unity in the fledgling national Episcopal Church, the South Carolina Episcopalians swallowed their pride and, however reluctantly, agreed to have a bishop and become a diocese.

At the next state convention, in Charleston, on February 10, 1795, the delegates unanimously elected as their bishop the only logical choice, the Rev. Robert Smith, the longtime rector of St. Philip's and universally acclaimed leader of Episcopalians in the state. There was simply no competing candidate. Smith became the first bishop of the Protestant Episcopal Church in the Diocese of South Carolina. He was consecrated in Christ Church of Philadelphia on September 13, 1795, by four bishops of the Episcopal Church. After he died just six years later at the age of seventy, the annual conventions were in no rush to find a new bishop. In fact, it took eleven years before they would get around to installing a second one, Theodore Dehon (1812–17).[40] Nevertheless, South Carolina had taken its place as a loyal diocese firmly united with the Episcopal Church.

Church growth in South Carolina was to prove to be difficult in the early years. For the five years between 1799 and 1803, there was no diocesan convention. When the Church did revive in 1804, it proceeded to complete its diocesan constitution in a detailed set of Rules and Regulations it adopted in 1806. In the following diocesan convention, in 1807, a question was raised as to whether the diocese had ever adopted the Constitution and Canons of the Episcopal Church and a committee was set up to report on it.[41] The committee reported the next day that three delegates from South Carolina had attended the general convention of 1789 "and, on behalf of the Protestant Episcopal Church of this state, subscribed the constitution."[42] Moreover, "On the 19th of October 1790, a convention of the Episcopal Churches of this state, was held in Charleston (. . .) at which convention the general constitution and canons were unanimously agreed to."[43] Upon this report, a motion was made and a unanimous vote cast "That the general constitution and canons of 1789, had been adopted by the convention of this state."[44] As they had always been, the following diocesan conventions remained scrupulously cognizant of adhering faithfully to the Episcopal Church's Constitutions and Canons as well as their own.

The establishment of the Episcopal Church Constitution and Canons in 1789 raised the question of the constitutional relationship between the Church and the individual dioceses. The issue played prominently in the litigation of the five incidents in which

39. Ibid.
40. In 1804, the Rev. Edward Jenkins was elected bishop, but declined.
41. Dalcho, *Historical Account*, 499.
42. Ibid.
43. Ibid., 500.
44. Ibid.

the majorities of dioceses proclaimed their dioceses' legal secession from the Episcopal Church. Proponents of diocesan sovereignty argued that the Episcopal Church Constitution and Canons did not explicitly forbid diocesan secession from the Church. They also pointed out there was no supremacy clause, such as in the U.S. Constitution (Article 6, Clause 2), that would give decisions of General Convention precedence over those of the individual dioceses. On the other side, partisans of the supremacy of the national Church insisted that the illegality of secession was implied just as it was in the U.S. Constitution that also had no explicit ban on a state leaving the Union. They said the same about a supremacy clause as the Constitution and Canons time and again gave power to the General Convention to make decisions for the whole Church while vows at ordination required clerical submission to the national Church. A great deal has been written on both sides of the issue of sovereignty in the Episcopal Church, but the most thoughtful and objective study of the Episcopal Church constitutional structure is that of James Dator who published *Many Parts, One Body: How the Episcopal Church Works* in 2010. It was based on his 1959 doctoral dissertation at American University, the most thorough academic study of the issue. Dator described the Episcopal Church government as a union. In ways, he said, it seems a confederation but is not, in ways a federation but is not. It is like neither the Articles of Confederation arrangement nor the federal Constitution government. "There is no essential division of power between the General Convention and the dioceses. In fact, there is no limit at all upon the Convention's governing powers (. . .). Thus, the government is unitary."[45] If the Church government were unitary, then it was logical to see the whole structure of the dioceses and general convention as one body. If it existed only as a union, it is not reasonable to say a diocese existed separately or independently of the general convention. Once it gave accession to the Constitution and Canons, as South Carolina did right away in signing the documents in 1789, and repeatedly reaffirmed many times afterwards, a diocese was not an independent and self-sufficient entity apart from the Episcopal Church.

However slowly, the remnant of the devastated old Anglican church in the colonies reassembled, reorganized, and resolved to build a new church in the new nation. Under the name of the Protestant Episcopal Church, it unified and established a remarkable new institutional structure in the same year the new government under the new United States Constitution started, 1789. In South Carolina, the newly styled Episcopalians reorganized too, eagerly bound themselves to the new national Church, helped devise the institutional structure of the new Church, set aside their prejudice against bishops, and resolved to promote the national Church in the state of South Carolina. The state of South Carolina could proudly call itself a founder of both the United States of America and the Protestant Episcopal Church in the United States of America. How strongly attached South Carolinians would remain to both of these, only time would tell.

---

45. Dator, James and Jan Nunley, *Many Parts, One Body, How the Episcopal Church Works*. New York: Church Publishing, 2010, 144.

UNION AND DISUNION IN THE NINETEENTH CENTURY

The nineteenth century began inauspiciously for the fledgling Episcopal Diocese of South Carolina. While it had played an important role in the creation of the Episcopal Church in the 1780s, the diocese itself had struggled to survive in the early national period. It could round only up a dozen or so clergy and a handful of parishes for conventions. It had drawn up only a brief preliminary constitution. It had obtained its first bishop, but one who respected the traditional parochial independence and held no confirmations. As Bishop Christopher Gadsden would put it years later: "'In 1804 the Diocese was reduced we may say, to its original elements. The Bishop was gone to his rest, no Convention had been held for five years, and there was no Standing Committee in existence.'"[46] In the first years of the new century, the Episcopal Church in South Carolina had nowhere to go but up, and this it did and did so spectacularly in the six decades before the great cataclysm of 1861 turning itself into perhaps the most important religious institution in the state.

In 1810, there were 23 parishes, 11 clergymen, and perhaps one thousand communicants in the diocese of South Carolina.[47] Fifty years later, on the eve of the Civil War there were 73 parishes and missions served by 72 clergymen[48] and about ten thousand baptized members.[49] Between 1810 and 1860, 46 new parishes and 3 missions were established, with 18 of those appearing in the decade of the 1850s.[50]

The rebirth of the diocese began in 1810 with the establishment of The Society for the Advancement of Christianity in South Carolina. According to the historian Albert Thomas, it "immediately began its great work—the promotion of Christian knowledge, encouragement of candidates for the ministry and, above all, missionary work. Few new churches in the diocese for the next century were established without the fostering care of this Society."[51] Two years later, Bishop Dehon began his episcopate which in ways set the pattern for his successors. He held the first confirmations in South Carolina, in 1813. While laboring hard to build up and unify the diocese of South Carolina, he also worked for the national Church. Historian Thomas declared "It was through him that the General Theological Seminary in New York was established."[52] For many years to come, South Carolina was to be the main stay of the Seminary, donating a total of $11,494 by 1835, about two-thirds of its cost to operate.[53] In addition, Frederick Kohne, a pew-holder of St. Michael's in Charleston bequeathed a legacy to the Seminary of $100,000 in the 1840s, giving South Carolina a strong presence on the school's board of

---

46. Thomas, *Historical Account*, 14.

47. Dalcho, *Historical Account*, 509–10.

48. *Journal of the Proceedings of the Seventy-Second Annual Convention of The Protestant Episcopal Church in South-Carolina held in Trinity Church, Abbeville, on the 19th and 20th of June 1861*. Charleston, SC: Miller, 1861, 7–8.

49. Ibid., 57.

50. Ibid., 7–8.

51. Thomas, *Historical Account*, 14.

52. Ibid., 15.

53. Ibid., 19.

trustees.[54] South Carolina's support for the school in New York City remained firm even though the diocese of South Carolina opened its own seminary, in Camden, in 1859.[55]

At the same time the Episcopal Church in South Carolina grew numerically, it gradually bonded as a true diocese retaining its Low Church sensibilities but leaving behind the colonial localism that had been slow to decline after the Revolutionary War. The brief preliminary constitution adopted by the state convention in 1786 had provided no specifics on how the church would regulate itself in the state. In 1806, the diocesan convention finally adopted its first detailed constitution in "Rules and Regulations for the Government of the Protestant Episcopal Church in the State of South-Carolina." The preamble read: "Whereas, by General Conventions of the Protestant Episcopal Churches in the U.S.A. a constitution and canons have been formed for the government and discipline of the same."[56] The document went on to list seventeen rules, all of which followed the directions outlined in the national Church's Constitution and Canons. The adoption of the new detailed Rules and Regulations in 1806 brought an end to the quasi-congregationalism common among the colonial parishes in South Carolina and enforced a uniformity that had originated in the Episcopal Church's Constitution and Canons.

The constitution of 1786 and Rules and Regulations of 1806 remained the governing charters of the Diocese of South Carolina until 1840. The diocesan convention of 1839 set up a committee to draw up a new version of the governing documents that would follow more closely the pattern of the national Church's Constitution and Canons. The committee was composed of some of the finest theological and legal minds of the South Carolina diocese: Bishop Nathaniel Bowen, Paul T. Gervais, Christopher Gadsden (future bishop), Thomas J. Young, Samuel Wragg, James L. Petigru[57], N. Russell Middleton, and Allard H. Belin.[58] The committee worked for many weeks, until July of 1839, preparing their proposal for the next convention. When the committee presented its new Constitution and Canons to the convention of 1840, it gave as "Article 1. Of Acceding to the Constitution and Canons of the Protestant Episcopal Church of the General Convention. The Protestant Episcopal Church in South Carolina accedes to, recognizes and adopts the general Constitution and Canons of the Protestant Episcopal Church in the U.S.A., and acknowledges their authority accordingly."[59] The rest of the new diocesan constitution and canons followed closely the model of the national Church's. It was clear the diocesan leaders were endeavoring to bond the diocese ever closer to the Episcopal Church.

All indications were that the diocese of South Carolina considered itself an integral part of the national Episcopal Church in the antebellum period. The bishops, clergy, and

54. Ibid., 44.

55. Ibid., 50.

56. Dalcho, *Historical Account*, 499.

57. James Lewis Petigru (1789–1863) was a prominent lawyer and statesman and a leading unionist. On hearing the state convention had voted on secession in December of 1860, he reportedly quipped that South Carolina was too small to be a republic and too large to be an insane asylum.

58. *Journal of the Proceedings of the Fifty-First Annual Convention of the Protestant Episcopal Church, in South-Carolina: Held in the City of Charleston, on the 12th, 13th, 14th, and 15th of February, 1840.* Charleston, SC: Miller, 1840, 37.

59. Ibid.

laity participated fully in the general conventions and other aspects of the life of the national Church. In fact, the Episcopal Church was the only major Protestant denomination that did not split north/south before the Civil War. The Methodists, Presbyterians, and Baptists all divided along the fault line. Why did the national Episcopal Church not take up the issue of slavery? As historian David L. Holmes put it: "Abhorring schism above all else, and realizing that resolutions on slavery would inevitably bring disputes, the church avoided an official stand on human bondage."[60] As far as South Carolina was concerned, avoiding the issue of slavery was preferable, indeed essential. The Episcopal Church was the established church among most of the great planter families of the South Carolina Low Country, many of whom owned slave populations numbered in the hundreds. Before the Civil War they dominated Episcopal Church business just as they did the state government in South Carolina.

Avoidance of the issue of slavery was not the only reason for the unity within the Episcopal Church before the Civil War. Religious sensibilities, personal friendships, and political attitudes also played parts. Anglicanism had always valued calm reason, compromise, and toleration of different views and eschewed the volatile emotionalism common in some other Protestant denominations. This guide of reason prevailed in antebellum America just as it had in Elizabethan England. And, what bound the country together in this refined religion was the universal *Book of Common Prayer* with its standard liturgy repeated in every Episcopal Church in every part of America on every Sunday. Moreover, there were many personal ties between the clergy and lay people of South Carolina and those of the northern states. South Carolina's bishops counted many close friends among their peers above the Mason-Dixon line just as did many of the priests. Too, numerous planter families of the Low Country, enjoying fabulous wealth, spent summers in the more pleasant climates of the north congregating in elite places such as Newport, Rhode Island. Also, Episcopalians in general were mindful of the separation of church and state. They preferred to see slavery as a purely political issue and not a matter for church attention. Therefore, Episcopalians from all over America were perfectly content to meet in pleasant national conventions without ever addressing the overriding public issue of the day that was about to bring down a cataclysm on the country. Indeed, the Episcopal Church was even more united in 1860 than it had been when it was created in 1789.

The decade of the 1850s saw an intense prelude to strife as one event after another added to the great looming national crisis. All the while, South Carolina was the heart of the anti-union movement and many men who were prominent in the Episcopal Diocese of South Carolina were also leaders of the secession movement. Finally, the election of Abraham Lincoln in 1860 cinched the secession movement. Southern whites commonly believed the Republican Party's stand against the extension of slavery into the territories would mean the eventual end of slavery itself and with it their way of life. Once again, South Carolina led the way. The state legislature called for a state convention to vote on whether to leave the Union. On December 20, 1860, the secession convention in Charleston voted unanimously to remove the state of South Carolina from the United States. In time, ten other slave states followed as the Confederate States of America was

---

60. Holmes, David L. *A Brief History of the Episcopal Church*. Valley Forge, PA: Trinity, 1993, 80.

established. The United States government refused to recognize the secession and considered the acts rebellion. War could not be avoided. It started on April 12, 1861, with the Confederate firing on the U.S. Fort Sumter, in Charleston harbor.

The split of the United States and the ensuing war necessitated the division of the Episcopal Church. The Union states maintained the pre-War Church structure, holding regular general conventions during the war in which the southern dioceses were simply counted as absent and their places held vacant. Given the wartime conditions of the day, the dioceses in the Confederate states had no choice but to form a separate Church organization for themselves. Bishop Thomas F. Davis led an illustrious committee of South Carolinians to a preliminary meeting of the Confederate Episcopal Church, in Montgomery, Alabama, on July 3, 1861, long after the fighting had begun.[61] Following this, a convention met in Columbia, South Carolina, in October of 1861, to draw up the governing documents of the Episcopal Church in the Confederacy. The new constitution, canons, and prayer book followed very closely those of the parent church and were adopted by the Diocese of South Carolina as well the other dioceses across the Confederacy.

At the end of the Civil War, there were voices in the South urging the continuation of the separate Episcopal Church but they found little response. Perhaps the devastation and exhaustion overwhelmed any further will to press on for separation from the larger union. The national Church leaders were anxious to heal the wounds, reunify the Church and get on with its life. Sometime before the general convention in Philadelphia, in October of 1865, the Presiding Bishop, John Henry Hopkins, of Vermont, wrote to all the southern bishops urging them to attend and promising a warm welcome.[62] Several southern bishops and diocesan delegations did attend the general convention of 1865 and reclaimed their vacant seats. In South Carolina, however, Bishop Davis waited until the next diocesan convention, on February 14, 1866, to recommend, somewhat reluctantly, the return of the Diocese of South Carolina to the national Church: "Let us rise to our new responsibility, not sluggishly, reluctantly or opposingly, but with clear judgments, the spirit of alacrity, and Christian confidence. I advise the immediate return of the diocese into union with the Church of the United States."[63] The convention agreed. The Diocese of South Carolina quietly resumed its place in the Episcopal Church almost as if nothing had happened.

Unfortunately for the Church in South Carolina plenty had happened since 1860 and the terrible effects of defeat in war were all around. In 1865, and for years thereafter, devastation, ruin, poverty, hunger, even desolation stood across what was once the richest of all the thirteen colonies. The scene was reminiscent of the grievous condition of the Church at the end of the Revolutionary War, only worse. Once again, the Church would have to rebuild from the ashes, but this time it would have to do so in a society boiling in post-war turmoil. As it rebuilt, the diocese would have to address how it would

---

61. *Journal of the Proceedings of the Seventy-Second* (. . .) 1861, 72. Delegates from South Carolina at the Convention in Montgomery: the Rev. P.J. Shand, the Rev. Paul Trapier, C.C. Pinckney, Robert Francis Withers Allston (Governor of South Carolina 1856–58), Edward McCrady, and Gen. William E. Martin.

62. Thomas, *Historical Account*, 60.

63. Ibid., 64.

handle the race issue, particularly what role the newly freed African Americans would play in the diocese. Race relations would hang over the diocese of South Carolina like a threatening cloud for decades to come, in fact for nearly a century after the Civil War. As time would tell, it was much easier to rebuild the buildings than to rebuild a social structure upended after its construction of almost two centuries.

One immediate effect of the Civil War was the drastic fall in the number of "colored communicants," down ninety percent, from about three thousand just before the War to three hundred just after. Congregations of African Americans were reduced to two in Charleston, Calvary and St. Marks, and a few rural missions. Where did the majority of pre-war "colored communicants" go? Perhaps to the newly booming African American churches of other denominations such as the African Methodist Episcopal Church. Some of them moved into the Reformed Episcopal Church which developed in the early 1870s and still thrives in the South Carolina Low Country. Gradually, however, communicant numbers began to edge up in the Episcopal diocese. By 1873, it listed 3,133 white communicants and 657 "colored."[64]

It was not the number of communicants, however, that produced so much of a problem as the relationship of whites and blacks in the structure of the Diocese of South Carolina. This issue came to the forefront when St. Mark's Church, established in Charleston in 1865, applied to be admitted into union with the convention in 1875.[65] If admitted, it would be the first African American parish in the diocese and would be treated equally with the other parishes. This created a storm of protest that lasted twelve years, mainly from the lay delegates to the diocesan conventions. The bishop and most of the clergy were in favor, but the majority of the all-white laity were not. When black clergymen presented themselves in the convention, they found the same hostile reception from laymen. Most white lay delegates adamantly opposed equal treatment for African Americans in the Diocese of South Carolina.

In the diocesan convention of 1887, a black clergyman appeared for admission whereupon the delegates from St. Paul's of Charleston walked out followed by those of twelve other parishes including St. Philip's, St. Michael's, Grace Church all of Charleston, St. Andrew's, St. John's Berkeley, Prince Frederick's, All Saints, Black Oak, Grahamville, Abbeville, and Aiken.[66] One of the most important leaders of this rebellion was Edward McCrady, Jr., a lay deputy representing St. Philip's. He was a member of the state legislature and "played a prominent role in the post-Reconstruction disenfranchisement of African Americans."[67] Twenty-six clergy and deputies remained in the meeting representing fifteen parishes. A quorum was declared and business proceeded. Bishop William Howe had tried his best to promote the rights of African Americans in the diocese

64. Ibid., 85.

65. "Reformed Episcopal Church," Wikipedia, accessed November 8, 2015, https://en.wikipedia.org/wiki/Reformed_Episcopal_Church. Not coincidentally, in 1875, five hundred African-American members of the Diocese of South Carolina joined the Reformed Episcopal Church.

66. *Journal of the Ninety-Seventy Annual Convention of the Protestant Episcopal Church in the Diocese of South Carolina, held in St. Philip's Church, Charleston, on the 12th, 13th, and 14th of May A.D. 1887.* Charleston, SC: Walker Evans, 1887, 23.

67. Helsley, Alexia Jones. "McCrady, Edward, Jr." In *The South Carolina Encyclopedia*, edited by Walter Edgar, 607–8. Columbia, SC: University of South Carolina Press, 2006.

since the start of his episcopacy in 1871 and counted the support of most of the priests. Now he seemed to struggle to control his own anger and frustration at this defiant rebellion, led mostly by prominent laymen. He cut business in the session as short as possible. On ending the abbreviated convention, he told the assembly: "I trust that our brethren will reconsider the case and see whether it is sufficient ground for these old Parishes to go out because one colored clergyman, who has sat in Convention in Virginia, for *eight* years, I am informed, is here with us."[68]

When the "brethren" made it clear they would not "reconsider," Bishop Howe had little choice but to deal with these rebels who were some of the most powerful communicants of the diocese representing at least the great parishes of Charleston. It was unimaginable that the diocese could go on without them. Before the next annual diocesan convention, a settlement was drawn up giving in to the rebels' demands. Amendments were composed and presented to the convention of 1889 allowing the entry of clergymen only from parishes in union with the convention. Not one of the three African American parishes, St. Mark's and Calvary in Charleston and St. Luke's in Columbia, had been admitted into union with the convention. Moreover, a commission was set up under the bishop "to effect the complete separation into two complete organizations, under the Bishop of the Diocese."[69] Having won the day after a thirteen year fight, the segregationist rebels returned triumphantly to the convention sessions.

The diocese set up a "missionary district" as a separate organization for the African American members of the diocese with a legislative body called a Convocation. This completely segregated the diocesan institutional structure by race and reduced the African Americans to second-class citizenship. In time, an archdeacon would be appointed to serve the African American communicants. Most white delegates saw this as a "compromise." Evidently, most blacks did not see it that way. Those who remained in the Episcopal diocese of South Carolina would have to be content with segregation and second-tier treatment. The racial separation established in the diocese in the 1870s and 1880s stayed in place until the Civil Rights movement of the 1960s.

The event of 1887–88 is sometimes called the Schism of 1887. Actually, schism is not an accurate term for what happened. The withdrawing parties left only the meeting in 1887. Their parishes did not withdraw from union with the convention. There was no serious effort to split the old diocese. The white racist rebels were only using extortion to get what they wanted from the rest of the diocese. It worked. Once they got what they demanded, they resumed their places as if nothing had happened. They forced the segregation of the diocese by race, subjecting the African Americans to inferior status.

It is fair to ask, how did the Schism of 1887 in South Carolina compare with that of 2012? The great similarity was that both were directly caused primarily by social factors, race in 1887 and homosexuality in 2012. 1887 was related to the "Redeemer" movement underway in South Carolina, indeed all of the lower South, a severe white political backlash against the defeat in the war, the end of slavery, and the Union-imposed

---

68. *Journal of the Ninety-Seventh Annual Convention (. . .)* 1887, 32.

69. *Journal of the Ninety-Eighth Annual Convention of The Protestant Episcopal Church in the Diocese of South Carolina, held in Grace Church, Anderson, on the 2d and 3d of May, A.D. 1888.* Charleston, SC: Walker Evans, 1888, 19.

Reconstruction. African American equality, or even civil rights, fell victim across the board. A harsh, virulent racism gripped the state for decades to come. Under unabashed racist governor "Pitchfork Ben" Tillman, a new state constitution in 1895 disenfranchised the vast majority of African American citizens of the state. Jim Crow laws beyond count became the order of the day as did lynchings, of which 156 occurred in South Carolina between 1882 and 1930.[70] As one will see, the schism of 2012 was also a social reaction, the direct reaction to the Episcopal Church's policies promoting equality for homosexuals in the Church. That is about as far as the similarities between 1887 and 2012 went.

As the nineteenth century ended, the Episcopal Church in South Carolina showed widespread, if slow, growth, at least among whites. The total number of congregations had risen to 92:62 parishes, the rest missions. Eighty clergy served about ten thousand baptized members including 5,555 white communicants, and 667 black communicants.[71] The fact that the number of "colored" communicants in 1899 had scarcely changed from that of 1873 revealed, unsurprisingly, that the diocesan racial policies of discrimination did not attract new African American members.

REVOLUTION AND COUNTER-REVOLUTION IN THE TWENTIETH CENTURY

1900–1960

As the new century began, the Diocese of South Carolina remained strongly attached to the national Episcopal Church and preoccupied with its own internal conditions. No one could have foreseen in the year 1900 what vast and revolutionary changes would occur in the world, in the nation, in the Episcopal Church, and in the Diocese of South Carolina over the next hundred years. When the tumultuous twentieth century would come to an end, the world would be fundamentally different in many important aspects and the effects of those differences would impact life in South Carolina in ways unimaginable in the year 1900.

Bishop William Alexander Guerry began his episcopate in 1908 on a strong note. The diocese adopted its official seal and women were allowed to vote in parishes for the first time.[72] Numbers were stronger than ever: 8,747 communicants in 101 churches with 60 clergymen.[73] Yet, not surprisingly, race was still an overriding issue in his early years. Southern dioceses continued debating how to deal with their "colored" communicants in the institutional structures.

---

70. Durocher, Kristina Anne. "Lynching." In *The South Carolina Encyclopedia*, edited by Walter Edgar, 579–80. Columbia, SC: University of South Carolina Press, 2006.

71. *Journal of the One Hundred and Ninth Annual Council of the Protestant Episcopal Church in the Diocese of South Carolina held in St. David's Church, Cheraw, May 3rd, 4th, 5th 1899*. Charleston, SC: Walker Evans, 1899, 1–4.

72. Thomas, *Historical Account*, 130.

73. Ibid.

General Convention, meeting in Boston in 1904, discussed creating the office of bishop suffragan. By 1910, Church canon law had been changed to allow suffragan bishops in the dioceses. Across the south, diocesan conventions began considering whether to create new positions of suffragan specifically for their "Negro" members. Another suggestion was to have a missionary district across the south with its own "colored" bishop. While the suffragan scheme might appear to be progressive, in fact it would leave the dioceses as segregated as ever. Not surprisingly, the "Negroes" themselves were not supportive of this movement which did nothing to promote their integration into the dioceses.[74] Two southern dioceses did install suffragan bishops "for Colored Work." In December of 1917, Arkansas elected the Rev. Thomas Demby (d. 1957). In May of 1918, North Carolina unanimously elected the Rev. Henry B. Delany (d. 1928).

In South Carolina, Bishop Guerry was a strong advocate of the "Negro" suffragan bishop idea that he believed would alleviate the hitherto shamefully unfair status of African Americans in the diocese. In the annual convention of 1911, he spoke passionately at length in favor of creating a new office of suffragan which would replace the old racist scheme of division that had resulted from the "Schism of 1887." The convention exploded. As historian Albert S. Thomas put it mildly: "There was much agitation in the diocese over this question."[75] The next year, 1912, Bishop Guerry made another spirited request to the convention for a suffragan. The assembled delegates (all white) had had enough of the bishop's social progressivism. The Rev. W.H. Barnwell made a resolution that was adopted: "'This council is not in favor of the election of a Negro Suffragan Bishop *at this time.*'"[76] Stung by this bold rebuke, the bishop was forced to abandon his request. Instead, he proceeded to use an archdeacon for "Colored Work." Perhaps one priest spoke for the majority when he wrote of the doomed suffragan plan: "'a nefarious scheme against the social order of the South.'"[77]

Blocked on the suffragan front, Bishop Guerry went ahead with many other works in the diocese. In 1922, he guided the diocese into a division, Upper South Carolina and South Carolina. Afterwards, the Diocese of South Carolina was really only the eastern half of the state. He did not give up entirely on improving the lot of the "colored" communicants. He often employed Bishop Delany, of North Carolina, for visits to South Carolina. Delany would be the first African American bishop that the "colored" communicants of South Carolina had ever seen, something that must have given them at least a little satisfaction. Too, Guerry began diocesan support for Voorhees College, in Denmark, South Carolina, in 1924, a school for African Americans that had begun in 1897.

On June 5, 1928, Bishop Guerry was shot in his office at St. Philip's Church in Charleston by the Rev. James Herbert Woodward. With two bullets, Woodward discharged one into Guerry and one into himself taking his own life. Bishop Guerry died four days later. The Rev. Woodward, as it turned out, had been a priest in the diocese of

---

74. Reimers, David M. "Negro Bishops and Diocesan Segregation in the Protestant Episcopal Church: 1870–1954." *Historical Magazine of the Protestant Episcopal Church* 31 (1962) 231–42.

75. Thomas, *Historical Account*, 131.

76. Ibid., 132.

77. Reimers, "Negro Bishops," 235.

South Carolina in 1915 serving four small churches near Bluffton.[78] That year he published a forty-five-page essay entitled "The Negro Bishop Movement in the Episcopal Diocese of South Carolina" and sold it by mail from his home in McPhersonville for twenty-five cents a copy.[79] It was a blatantly racist diatribe: "The bestial nature, the ape, the sarx, the satyr, that lurks in all men, is, relatively, larger and stronger and more dominating, in the Negro, than in the white man."[80] His point was to oppose strongly and at length Bishop Guerry's plan for an African American suffragan bishop and any other idea of making "Negro" bishops.[81] Guerry was another victim in the long history of virulent and violent racism from which South Carolina could not seem to escape.

The Great Depression and the Second World War dominated the years of the 1930s and early 1940s. The Episcopal Church in South Carolina, as almost everywhere else, was preoccupied with the economic hardships and social disruptions caused by these sweeping events. Once the war ended in 1945 and economic prosperity began to soar, the church in the nation and in the Diocese of South Carolina was free to return to its own matters of institutional development.

Racial integration was already emerging as a national issue by the end of the War. In the churches and in the federal government, movements gained ground in the late 1940s to remove racial barriers. Most famously, President Truman integrated the U.S. armed forces in 1948. In the Episcopal Church, there were gradual but important steps in integration. After ignoring race for more than a century and a half, with only a few small exceptions, the Church finally adopted a significant position on race relations in its general convention of 1952. It condemned racial discrimination and resolved to combat

---

78. *The American Church Almanac and Year Book for 1915.* New York: Edwin and Gorham, 1914, 335. Holy Trinity, Grahamville; St. Edmund, Hardeeville; Okatee, and Sheldon Church, McPhersonville.

79. Woodward, (the Rev.) James Herbert. *The Negro Bishop Movement in The Episcopal Church of South Carolina.* McPhersonville, SC: the author, 1915; Savannah GA: Braid and Hutton, 1916.

80. Ibid., 36.

81. Diocesan news at the time downplayed racism as Woodward's motivation for Guerry's murder favoring the official version that the gunman was simply deranged. However, the Rev. Calhoun Walpole and Thomas S. Tisdale, former chancellor of the diocese, conducted new research in the early 2000s that revived the racist background of the crime. With this information, Tisdale wrote a play, "Truth in Cold Blood," that was performed at the Dock Street Theater, in Charleston, in July of 2014, emphasizing racism as the motivation for the murder. See: Stephanie Harvin, "Play about Bishop William A. Guerry's Murder Highlights the Search for Truth," *The Post and Courier,* (Charleston, SC), July 9, 2014.

Not everyone accepted the revisionist work of Guerry's life. Shortly after the schism, the Rev. Gregory Snyder, rector of St. John's on Johns Island, and follower of Bishop Lawrence, took issue with the Episcopalians' interpretation in: "Comprehensive Identity Theft, Misrepresenting the Rt. Rev. William Alexander Guerry," January 16, 2013, www.diosc.com/sys/images/documents/tec/snyder_guerry_identity_theft.pdf.

In 2013, a writer to the Charleston *Post and Courier,* protested the recent "politically correct" explanation in favor of the conventional narrative of the gunman's tragic personal problems: Dorothy M. Anderson, "Clarifying the Sad Story of Bishop William Guerry," *The Post and Courier* (Charleston, SC), June 26, 2013. See also: Hawes, Jennifer Berry, "Church Honors S.C. Bishop Killed in his Charleston Office," *The Post and Courier* (Charleston, SC), June 9, 2013.

In 2015, Bishop Guerry, "Bishop, Reformer, Martyr," was added to the list of martyrs in Canterbury Cathedral. The first feast day of Bishop Guerry was celebrated at Grace Church Cathedral, in Charleston, on June 8, 2016. See: "William Alexander Guerry, Bishop, Reformer and Martyr, 1861–1928," The Episcopal Church in South Carolina, www.episcopalchurchsc.org/bishop-guerry.html.

it wherever it may be found. This was a small first step in what would develop as a strong movement of social justice in the Episcopal Church. Moreover, all ten Church seminaries integrated except one, the University of the South, at Sewanee, Tennessee. It too finally agreed to admit black students in 1953. Also, soon after the war, the remaining few southern dioceses that still barred blacks from their conventions, integrated one by one. When the Upper South Carolina convention agreed to admit African Americans in 1947, South Carolina was left as the only diocese in the Episcopal Church still refusing to integrate its convention.

The mood and trend in the country did not go unnoticed in the diocese. Indeed, one of the first issues to resurface there after the Second World War was the ever-present problem of race relations in the diocesan structure. To address this, the diocesan convention of 1945 set up a committee to make a recommendation on African American representation.[82] The committee proposed to amend the diocesan constitution to open the convention to any church. In 1946, this was first given preliminary approval then voted down by the lay delegates. The proposal was reintroduced in the convention of 1949, only to be deferred until 1951 when the lay delegates defeated it a second time. In the annual convention of 1953, the resolution was submitted for a third time. Perhaps facing embarrassing defeat yet again, the Rev. Louis A. Haskell offered a substitute resolution that the "Negro" churches simply be invited to apply for admission to the convention. This passed 85–31. Under this resolution, St. Mark's parish, of Charleston, was admitted into union with the convention in 1954, the first historically African American parish united with the Diocese of South Carolina.[83] Also, in 1954, Calvary Church, in Charleston, and St. Paul's of Orangeburg, were admitted as organized missions. At the same time, the diocesan constitution was changed to remove the provision that the convention was limited to persons of the white race.[84] The next year, African American delegates appeared in the convention were seated and given vote for the first time in the 170-year history of the diocese. It had been eighty years since St. Mark's had applied for admission to the convention. The Schism of 1887 was finally settled.

At long last, the Diocese of South Carolina brought racial equality to its convention, eighty-nine years after the Civil War, the last diocese in the nation to integrate its annual assembly. Yet, there were important aspects of diocesan life that remained segregated in the spirit of Jim Crow, and would continue so for another decade. As if to reaffirm its lingering racism, the diocesan convention of 1956 voted 94–43 for a resolution stating "'there is nothing morally wrong in voluntary recognition of racial differences (. . .) voluntary alignments can be both natural and Christian.'"[85] Old feelings died hard in South Carolina even as the diocese boomed from 9,907 communicants in 1944, to 12,353 in

---

82. Thomas, *Historical Account*, 159.

83. *Journal of the One Hundred and Sixty-Fourth Annual Convention of the Protestant Episcopal Church in the Diocese of South Carolina, held in the Church of St. Luke and St. Paul, Charleston, S.C. May 4, 5, 1954*. Charleston, SC: the diocese, 1954, 14. Although they were admitted in 1954, the delegates of St. Mark's, Calvary, and St. Paul's of Orangeburg were not allowed to vote until the next year.

84. Sumner, David E. *The Episcopal Church's History: 1945–1985*. Wilton, CT: Morehouse-Barlow, 1987, 36.

85. Thomas, *Historical Account*, 163.

1955, and the budget more than doubled, to $114,429.[86] The old diocesan Convocation of Negro Churchmen with its archdeacon continued to function as a separate body in the diocese. In 1955 it listed 1,309 communicants, slightly more than 10 percent of all communicants of the diocese, about the same percentage since Reconstruction.[87]

Bishop Thomas Carruthers thought it was time for the diocese to move on beyond its debilitating racial segregation. In 1960, the annual convention passed a resolution to set up a "Committee on Negro Work" to "plan more effective work" in incorporating blacks into the diocese. Data showed that between 1930 and 1957, "Negro" membership in the diocese had fallen 18 percent while overall membership had increased 50 percent. The Committee on Negro Work would be one of Carruthers's last accomplishments.[88] He died a few weeks after the convention of 1960 leaving a diocese that was still essentially segregated. Only the annual convention had ended its racial discrimination.

The Background of the Revolution of the Episcopal Church

By the time of Carruthers's death in 1960, the Episcopal Church was already starting on the greatest revolution in its history. By the end of the next half-century, the Church would be a strikingly different institution in many important respects. The foundational transformation came in a dramatic reversal in its view of its place in the greater society, both in America and the world. The old view, lasting from the 1780s until the end of the Second World War in 1945, was to avoid social and cultural issues and to concern itself almost completely with internal matters of faith and administration. With rare exceptions, for a century and a half the Episcopal Church had continued its antebellum policy of the avoidance of any controversial issues such as race. While the early policy succeeded in keeping the Church remarkably united, in the long run it also produced a rising guilt among many Episcopalians that through its long history the Church's indifference to the wrongs all around it was at least the sin of omission. This change of heart was to flower along with the post-war Civil Rights movement in America.

The early twentieth century was one of the greatest liberation movements in world history. The colossal Great War of 1914–18 devastated the old monarchical systems of Europe and diminished their attendant social orders of class based on birth. America, or at least President Wilson, saw the war as a great crusade to make the world safe for democracy. While it did end in the triumph of the great western democracies, it also created the conditions for the rise of the worst totalitarian forces known to modern history, the Nazis, the Soviets, and the fascists.

A decade after the First World War, the world began to spiral downward economically into the worst economic collapse in modern history, the Great Depression. In

---

86. Ibid., 162.

87. *Journal of the One Hundred and Sixty-Fourth (. . .)* 1954, 39. The Convocation included: St. Marks's, Calvary, St. Philip's of Denmark, St. Paul's of Orangeburg, Holy Cross Faith Memorial of Pawleys Island, Redeemer of Pineville, Good Shepherd of Sumter, St. Augustine's of Sumter County, and Atonement of Walterboro.

88. *Journal of the One Hundred and Seventieth Annual Meeting of the Convention, May 3, 4, 1960, at St. Philip's Church, Charleston, S.C.* Charleston, SC: the diocese, 1960, 36.

America, the New Deal of the 1930s ingrained a new fundamental principle of political life, the responsibility of the government to care for all of its citizens. This replaced for good the limited government idea that had dominated the government since 1789. The public began to look more and more to national institutions for ways to make life better for everyone.

The Second World War, 1939–45, a conflict so vast, destructive, and deadly it made the First World War look pale in comparison, brought the total defeat of the totalitarian regimes of Nazism and fascism and the Japanese authoritarian militarism in the name of freedom, justice, and equality. The Soviet Union, that just happened to be on the winning side because of Hitler's maniacal delusion he could conquer Russia, something the greatest military genius of modern history, Napoleon, learned the hard way he could not do, lumbered on until it collapsed under the crushing weight of its own internal contradictions in the 1980s. Then, Soviet totalitarianism too succumbed to the great democratic revolution of modern history.

Thus, the twentieth century changed the world in a way no earlier century had ever done. In the first half of the century the most destructive wars in all of history and the worst economic depression ever known changed life forever. Out of those events came two transforming movements of history. The first was the victory of the principles of western democracy, the legacy of the great American and French revolutions of the late eighteenth century, with their rule of the people in freedom, equality, and justice. Democracy crushed totalitarianism and spread to every continent in the world as the prevailing political order. The second great change of the early twentieth century was the new understanding of national institutions that came out of the New Deal. The underlying principle of the New Deal was the idea it was the responsibility of the government to use all its powers to improve life for all of the people. Both movements impacted on the Episcopal Church as on every other national institution after the end of the Second World War in 1945. The world the Episcopal Church faced in 1945 was vastly different than any it had ever known in its 160 years.

This surging combination of democratic and proactive populist government produced a powerful new reform wave in America to extend rights to all citizens in American society. The remainder of the twentieth century would see the effects of this ever-rising tsunami. The most urgent need for reform concerned racism. African Americans had first been held in slavery in America for nearly two and a half centuries, then had been systematically deprived of their rights and discriminated against in almost every way in the country, but especially in the south, and nowhere more than in South Carolina. It had all been a gross violation of human rights and a contradiction of the principles on which the United States had been founded. After 1945, this discrimination slowly and surely began to change. By the mid-1950s, the Civil Rights movement exploded; and when this occurred the dam broke for reforms for every other mistreated element of American society that now could not be denied fair treatment in a democratic and just society.

Revolutionary Reforms and Bishop Gray Temple (1961–1982)

Race

The issue of racial justice had already been making tentative steps in both the national Church and the Diocese of South Carolina when Bishop Carruthers died suddenly on June 12, 1960, at the age of sixty. On September 27, 1960, a special convention for the election of a bishop met at the Church of the Holy Comforter in Sumter. Fourteen names were placed in nomination. On the fifth ballot, the assembly chose the Rev. Gray Temple.[89] The Rev. Louis A. Haskell came in second place.[90] Temple was ordained and consecrated bishop of the Diocese of South Carolina on January 11, 1961, at the Church of St. Luke and St. Paul in Charleston. The Rt. Rev. Arthur Lichtenberger, presiding bishop of the Episcopal Church led the service assisted by eleven other bishops. Temple had served as rector of Trinity Episcopal Church in Columbia, South Carolina, from 1955 to 1960.[91] He would serve as bishop of South Carolina until his retirement in 1982. As in the national Church, Temple's years of 1961–82 were to see revolutionary reforms in the diocese, the first and most important concerning race.

The national Episcopal Church enacted a slowly evolving but firm devotion to racial justice starting in the midst of the Second World War. In 1943, General Convention resolved "'We dare not break our Christian fellowship by any attitude or act in the House of God which marks our brethren of other races as unequal or inferior.'"[92] This officially reversed the hitherto *laissez-faire* policy on race the Church had followed since its beginning in the 1780s. For the next two decades, the Church gradually incorporated ways of improving conditions for the African American minority in the country. The 1955 General Convention resolved to support the 1954 Supreme Court decision that struck down racially separate public schools and to work for school integration: "'[We] accept and support the ruling of the Supreme Court and (. . .) anticipate constructively the local implementation of this ruling as the law of the land.'"[93] It continued, "discrimination and segregation are contrary to the mind of Christ and the will of God.'"[94] In 1958, General Convention elected as the new presiding bishop, Arthur C. Lichtenberger, who was to lead the Episcopal Church in ever greater commitment to racial justice. At the same time, the Church set up the Episcopal Society for Cultural and Racial Unity the goals of which were the complete integration of the Episcopal Church and direct involvement in

---

89. "Bishop Temple of South Carolina Dies." *The Living* Church, November 21, 1999, The Living Church 1995–2001, The Archives of the Episcopal Church, http://www.episcopalarchives.org/cgi-bin/the_living_church/TLCarticle.pl?volume=219&issue=21&article_id=10. Temple was born in 1914 in Lewiston, Maine. He was graduated from Brown University and the Virginia Theological Seminary; was ordained a deacon in 1938, and priest in 1939; and served churches in Virginia and North Carolina before moving to Columbia.

90. *Journal of the One Hundred and Seventy-First Annual Meeting of the Convention, April 18, 19, 1961, at Grace Church, Charleston, S.C.* Charleston, SC: the diocese, 1961, 148.

91. "Gray Temple Elevated to Office of Bishop." *The State* (Columbia, SC), January 12, 1961.

92. Sumner, *Episcopal Church's History*, 33.

93. Ibid., 37.

94. Ibid.

local and national campaigns for racial justice. In 1963, the House of Bishops issued a statement urging support of the pending civil rights bill (Civil Rights Act of 1964). Then, in 1964, General Convention elected as presiding bishop, John E. Hines, a man "firmly committed to social and racial justice."[95] Thus, by the mid-1960s, the Episcopal Church developed a resolute activism of social justice for African Americans. This transformation was to propel the Episcopal Church from this point on, at least well into the twenty-first century. A heretofore aloof, stodgy, conservative, socially indifferent church turned into a boldly activist one ready to right the wrongs of the community of which it was a historically essential part. In time this reversal of attitude would reap both sweeping accomplishments and grievous problems.

In the Diocese of South Carolina, this same commitment to social reform carried over into the episcopate of Gray Temple (1961–82). As the national Church's, his first reform program was for African Americans. His first address as bishop to the diocesan convention set the tone for his term. He declared that race was the main dividing point between liberals and conservatives in the diocese and said that while he encouraged differences of opinion and toleration, "I would hope that we Christians can disagree in Christian *love* [sic]."[96] Temple maintained the old Negro Convocation for the moment but asked the convention to prepare to abolish it. The Committee on Negro Work, that Bishop Carruthers had established in 1960, reported in 1961 that there were thirteen black churches, five black priests (two of which Temple ordained in 1961), and ten lay-readers.[97] If anyone had any doubt about African American feelings in the Diocese, this would end in the Negro Committee's report to the meeting of the convention in 1962: "We find a complete lack of any sense of being part of the Diocese by all the Negro Parishes and Missions."[98]

Temple resolved to end completely the long embedded racial segregation of the diocese. In the 1965 annual diocesan meeting, he declared: "All conferences in the Diocese (with the exception of the E.Y.C.) are open to all people."[99] He saw to it that E.Y.C. integrated that year. He also reminded the delegates that the national Episcopal Church had resolved that the church must not be a respecter of persons and called on the convention "to plan so that the Diocese can be more efficient in meeting the needs of all of our people, regardless of economic status or ethnic origin."[100] In the next convention, 1966, Temple announced: "The Diocese of South Carolina has now reached the point in its history where it is no longer necessary to have a separate Archdeaconry for Negro

---

95. Ibid., 42.

96. *Journal of the One Hundred and Seventy-First (. . .)* 1961, 42.

97. Priests: the Rev. W.E. Forsythe, Holy Cross/Faith Memorial, Pawleys Island; the Rev. Henry L. Grant, Voorhees and St. Philip's, Denmark; the Rev. Edward Johnson, St. Mark's and St. Stephen's, Charleston; the Rev. Stephen Mackey, Calvary, Charleston; the Rev. William C. Weaver, St. Paul's, Orangeburg. Temple ordained Johnson and Weaver in 1961.

98. *Journal of the One Hundred and Seventy-Second Annual Meeting of the Convention, May 8, 9, 1962, at St. Helena's Church, Beaufort, S.C.* Charleston, SC: the diocese, 1962, 102.

99. *Journal of the One Hundred and Seventy-Fifth Annual Meeting of the Convention, May 4–5, 1965, at St. James Church, James Island, Rt. 5, Charleston, S.C.* Charleston, SC: the diocese, 1965, 40.

100. Ibid.

Work."[101] He announced he had abolished at long last the old office that had segregated blacks in the diocese. He added that both camps, St. Christopher and Baskerville, were now open to both races. With this, the institution of the Diocese of South Carolina became truly and completely integrated. All racial barriers were gone. It had been a long and hard course to reverse the deep-seated racism that had gripped the diocese at least since the Schism of 1887. What Bishop Temple had accomplished would have been unimaginable a century earlier. He finished what virtually every South Carolina bishop in that hundred years had wanted but failed to do. He was their heir. He was also the devoted son of the national Church.

The first half of the decade of the 1960s saw a civil rights movement in America characterized generally by peaceful protests and demonstrations, desegregations, and the passage of laws for civil and voting rights. The second half of this decade, however, was marked by increasingly strident movements and more violent expressions of racial tensions both in the nation and in South Carolina. Widespread destructive and deadly riots occurred in many big cities across the U.S. Although South Carolina remained relative calm at this time, it too experienced examples of racially motivated violence; and, these were to impact the Diocese.

The changing mood in mid-decade America directly affected life in the national Church and the diocese. The rather mild Episcopal Society for Cultural and Racial Unity was replaced under Presiding Bishop Hines's leadership by the General Convention Special Program (GCSP), established in 1967. This was created to be a directly active body for "the empowerment of blacks and minority groups through grants to help these groups achieve their purposes."[102] At the General Convention of 1967, Hines delivered "one of the most radical proposals ever presented to the Episcopal Church."[103] He asked the Church to "'take its place humbly and boldly alongside of, and in support of, the dispossessed and oppressed peoples of this country.'"[104] He called for a funding of three million dollars a year, part from the general budget, part from the Episcopal Church Women's United Thank Offering. The convention approved this. Subsequently, "GCSP enacted its drama over the next six years in perhaps the Episcopal Church's most controversial era. The history of civil rights between 1967 and 1973 is in large measure the history of the General Convention Special Program."[105] As grants began to flow from GCSP to various minority-based community programs, backlash also flowed, particularly from the historically racist southern dioceses, including South Carolina.

There were two outstanding civil rights events in South Carolina, the Orangeburg Massacre of 1968 and the Charleston hospital workers' strike of 1969. The first occurred in the town of Orangeburg, the home of the historically black South Carolina State College. There, a force of sixty-five patrolmen fired on an unarmed crowd killing three and

---

101. *Journal of the One Hundred Seventy-Sixth Annual Meeting of the Convention, April* 29–30, 1966, *at St. John's Church, Florence, S.C.* Charleston, SC: the diocese, 1966, 41.

102. Sumner, *Episcopal Church's History,* 44.

103. Ibid., 47.

104. Ibid.

105. Ibid., 48.

wounding twenty-seven people on February 8, 1968.[106] In the second, four hundred African American workers went on strike at two Charleston hospitals, both controlled entirely by whites.[107] After several months of demonstrations and rising tensions, the strike was settled in a compromise made by the strikers and William Huff, vice president of the Medical College Hospital.[108] The workers received most of their demands. The white authorities grudgingly accepted the arrangement.

While the state of South Carolina remained relatively calm in the civil rights era, the same could not be said of the attitude of the diocese towards the national Church. Two events in 1969–70 relating to the diocese and the national Church caused an enormous storm of protest in South Carolina against the central authorities of the Episcopal Church. The first was an incident at Voorhees College, the historically black Episcopal Church-supported school in the town of Denmark, in the Diocese of South Carolina. After various resentments and protests built up among the student body, a group including the Black Awareness Coordinating Committee (BACC), armed themselves and took over buildings of Voorhees including the library in April of 1969, less than a year after the Orangeburg Massacre. Alarmed officials called in the National Guard which quickly ended the occupation as some protesters were arrested. A court trial ensued and eight members of BACC were convicted of rioting and violence by a majority-black jury and sentenced to jail.[109] The flash point for the diocese was that in 1970, the GCSP had given the criminally-charged BACC at Voorhees a grant of $25,000 and had done so over the strong protests of the two diocesan bishops of South Carolina.[110]

The second incident to generate fury against the national Church occurred, shortly after the Voorhees arrests, at the General Convention session of August 31–September 5, 1969, at Notre Dame University in South Bend, Indiana. There, the deputies approved a resolution to grant $200,000 to the Black Economic Development Conference which had adopted the black power movement's Black Manifesto, a demand for hundreds of millions in dollars in reparations to blacks from the white churches. The resolution stated: "'the Black Economic Development Conference is a movement which is an expression of self-determination for the organizing of the black community in America.'"[111] Parishes across the country exploded in protest, no more so than in South Carolina. The consistently conservative mouthpiece of the Low Country, the Charleston *News and Courier* could hardly control its rage. On September 4, it published articles, "Churchmen Finance Black Revolution," and "Accepting the Extremists"[112] suggesting

---

106. Bass, Jack. "Orangeburg Massacre." In *The South Carolina Encyclopedia*, edited by Walter Edgar, 288–89. Columbia, SC: University of South Carolina Press, 2006.

107. Hopkins, George W. "Charleston hospital Workers' Strike." In *The South Carolina Encyclopedia*, edited by Walter Edgar, 151–52. Columbia, SC: University of South Carolina Press, 2006.

108. Father of the Rev. Christopher M. Huff, a priest in the Episcopal Church in South Carolina.

109. *Journal of the One Hundred Eightieth Annual Meeting of the Convention, First Session—April 18, 19, 1970 at St. Philip's Church, Charleston, S.C. Second Session—October 31, 1970, Church of the Good Shepherd, North Charleston, S.C.* Charleston, SC: the diocese, 1970, 58.

110. Sumner, *Episcopal Church's History*, 58.

111. Ibid., 53.

112. Way, William and Virginia Kirkland Donehue. *By Grace, Through Faith: A History of Grace Church, Charleston, 1846–1999.* Charleston, SC: Grace Church, 2000, 115.

the Episcopal Church had fallen under the control of black extremists. On the editorial page, the editors declared: "'We are shocked and astonished that a church group would take such an irresponsible position. It should be repudiated both inside and outside the denomination.'"[113]

Many parishes in South Carolina were of the same mind as the editors, that the local church should repudiate the Episcopal Church. Bishop Temple walked a tightrope of criticizing the Church's actions while calling for calm and loyalty.[114] He immediately sent out a pastoral letter to all local churches that was read from pulpits on Sunday, September 14. In it he addressed both sides, "'misunderstandings and concerns,'" of the South Bend convention.[115] No doubt reflecting the bishop's attitude, the Rev. Howard Cutler told his congregation in Saint Andrew's of West Ashley: "'My plea is not to give way to emotionalism. As Christians we are called to act with sanity and not insanity, keep our feet on the ground, to be calm as one can, in the vernacular of the day to keep our cool.'"[116] It was hard for the diocesan Executive Council to keep its cool. It met shortly thereafter at Kanuga, in North Carolina, to blast the Black Manifesto as anti-Christian and anti-democratic and to plan protests against the national Church.

The first impulse in the diocese was to lash back against the Episcopal Church by cutting funding to it. By the opening of the annual diocesan convention on April 18, 1970, the Council had already voted to remove the quota payment to the Episcopal Church from the annual diocesan budget, but the quota itself remained an issue before the convention delegates.[117] In discussion, Donald White, the treasurer, asked to make the quota part of the diocesan budget, thereby guaranteeing support of the national Church. The amount for 1971 was $89,000. In opposition, the Rev. Edward Guerry, of St. John's on Johns Island, asked that parishes be allowed to pledge separately between diocese and Church while communicants be allowed the same. This would certainly reduce the diocesan contribution to the Episcopal Church. A "compromise" was then passed 106–73, allowing each vestry to decide whether to separate the amounts. This was really a win for the national Church critics. The diocesan budget was adopted without the quota to the Church. This was the first significant rift between the diocese and the Episcopal Church since the Civil War.[118] For the moment, a stunned Bishop Temple could only look on.[119]

As the April session proceeded, delegate B. Allston Moore moved to demand cancellation of the funding of the GCSP grant to the BACC at Voorhees. The resolution passed. Even Bishop Temple, usually reliably defensive of the Episcopal Church, could

---

113. Ibid., 116.

114. Bishop Temple served on the Executive Council of the Episcopal Church from 1967 to 1973.

115. Porwoll, Paul. *Against All Odds: History of Saint Andrew's Parish Church, Charleston, 1706-2013*. Bloomington, IN: WestBow, 2014, 254.

116. Ibid.

117. *Journal of the One Hundred Eightieth (. . .)* 1970, 34.

118. Ibid., 34-35.

119. In Grace Church of Charleston, the vestry voted in 1970 to stop all money to the national Church holding it instead in a vestry-controlled trust fund. Way and Donehue, *By Grace, Through Faith*, 116.

not resist a rare jab at it on this issue. He told the convention the General Convention in Seattle had taken too much authority from the dioceses and the Church's Executive Council was now making policy and directing it to the dioceses. With this, for the first time in a century, the diocese came dangerously close to open hostility to the Episcopal Church. This mood might have escalated to something much more consequential if Bishop Temple had wished, but he did not. He was soon to backtrack and return to loyal defense of the Church.[120] Nevertheless, he could not erase this 1970 episode of widespread resentment in the diocese against what many South Carolinians saw as a too-liberal national Church.

Perhaps to temper the escalating race-based animosity in the diocese, Temple went out of his way in his first address to the 1970 convention to show how much the diocese was doing for racial justice. On the heels of the Orangeburg Massacre, the Voorhees riot, and the Charleston hospital strike, Temple announced astonishing programs targeted poor blacks. In one, he said the estate of Eleanor Gibson had given $150,000 "'to relieve the needs of the poor," the donations to be allocated by the bishop. In another gift, someone had donated $15,000 a year for five years to the St. John's mission community center. Too, another anonymous donor had given $10,000 a year "for use in helping resolve some of the racial tensions in Charleston," something this source had done for the last ten years.[121]

By the time the second session of the 1970 convention met, on 31 October, Temple was ready to return to defense of the Episcopal Church. In his bishop's address, he called on the delegates to reinstate full financial support of the national Church because it was the right thing to do. He criticized the split pledging scheme that had already reduced the payment to the church from $80,000 to $35,000.[122] Nevertheless, the delegates passed a resolution allowing parishes to donate separately to the diocese and the Church.[123] Dismayed but undeterred, Temple return to the issue at the next convention, in 1971, after racially-fired tempers had cooled a bit. He declared to the delegates: "I strongly recommend we make our pledge to the Program of the National Church as a Diocese in convention assembled and not as individuals, as we've done the past two years."[124] This time the delegates agreed. The diocese returned to the previous system of annual diocesan quota payment to the Episcopal Church. Temple also announced with pride and satisfaction that he had drawn from the Eleanor Gibson fund to aid the poor in the Charleston Day Care Center, Charleston Urban Ministry, Rural Missions, Pineville Day Care Center, Church Home for Children, and the Committee on Better Racial Assurance.[125]

120. A theory appeared later that the 2012 schism really resulted from racism, that it was a delayed reaction to the Episcopal Church's activist policies in the 1960s in favor of blacks, a reaction that boiled up for several decades. If this were true, the later "causes," such as homosexuality, were only superficial covers for the deeper resentment against the national Church because of its racial policies. This author discovered no documentary evidence to support this theory.

121. *Journal of the One Hundred Eightieth (. . .) 1970*, 39.

122. Ibid., 46.

123. Ibid., 59.

124. *Journal of the One Hundred Eighty-First Annual Meeting of the Convention, September 24–25, 1971, St. Helena's Church, Beaufort, South Carolina*. Charleston, SC: the diocese, 1971, 43.

125. *Journal of the One Hundred Eightieth (. . .) 1970*, 44.

With that, racial issues began to fade in the diocese, at least overtly. In the national Church, the GCSP wound down and out and racial issues declined as other matters came to the forefront.[126] By the early 1970s, the great crusade for racial justice in the Episcopal Church, while still there, was increasingly falling in importance to the other rising issues of the day such as a new prayer book, women's ordination, and the place of homosexual persons in the life of the church. All things considered, the Diocese of South Carolina, heretofore the most racist of all dioceses of the Episcopal Church, progressed through the Civil Rights period well. It had gone from outright rigid segregationism all the way to racial justice and equality, an astonishing reversal in a rather brief period of time; and this was mostly the result of the hard and resolute work of Bishop Temple. Against enormous pressure from well-established parishes, he had managed to hold down racism, reverse discrimination, and keep loyalty to the national Church, all at the same time. Perhaps as good evidence of progress on racism, Calvary Church, an historically black parish in Charleston, hosted the diocesan convention in 1980. This was the first time an African American parish hosted a diocesan convention, something unthinkable even a half century earlier. What Bishop Temple managed in the Diocese of South Carolina was no mean feat. Indeed, it could be argued well that no bishop in the history of the diocese accomplished more.

Prayer Book

While astonishing racial reforms occupied center stage, another issue quietly developed, at the same time, that for many Episcopalians of South Carolina would prove to be even more unsettling than racial integration. It was the revision of *The Book of Common Prayer*. It is often difficult for outsiders to understand just how important "The Prayer Book" is to Episcopalians, and Anglicans in general, who hold it as almost sacrosanct and only slightly lower than the Bible. The Prayer Book is not just a book of prayers, it contains the very heart and voice of Episcopalian worship. It defines meaning and structure to almost all of the Church. The Episcopal Church as we know it would simply not exist without the Prayer Book whose dignified, lofty, and comforting liturgies are intoned everywhere repeatedly on Sunday after Sunday. Thus, it was not surprising that Church people would be naturally resistant to alter what they saw as the constant rock of the faith. Yet, the truth was that the prayer book had been revised many times since the first one was compiled by Archbishop of Canterbury, Thomas Cranmer, in 1549, to unify the newly independent Church of England in an "Anglican" identity. That towering work was revised in 1552, 1559, and again in 1662. In America, the first prayer book, adapted from the 1662 edition, was established in 1789 as the Episcopal Church itself was formed. That book was revised in 1892 and again in 1928. The so-called "1928 Book" remained essentially the old Elizabethan-era service book whose stilted forms and archaic language seemed ever more archaic in the rapidly changing twentieth century world. Soon after the Second World War, appeals for modernization of the old prayer book began to rise.

---

126. In 1973, the GCSP was replaced by the Committee for Continuing Action and Development whose programs were meant to benefit blacks, Indians, and Hispanics.

In the Episcopal Church, the prayer book came under the jurisdiction of the Standing Liturgical Commission which by 1950 began to issue various trial liturgies for experimental use in the churches. In 1964, the General Convention directed the Commission to draw up a plan to revise the 1928 prayer book. In 1967, while the Convention was preoccupied with racial issues, the Commission presented its plan that was promptly approved by the Convention with rather little attention. In 1970, the Church published the first prayer book for trial use entitled *Services for Trial Use* and commonly called "The Green Book" after its soft-back cover. This was replaced in 1973 by *Authorized Services 1973*. That in turn was replaced in 1976 by *The Proposed Book of Common Prayer*. Finally, in 1979, the General Convention overwhelmingly adopted the new prayer book. The revisions turned out to be extensive, too much so to the critics. It changed the essential Sunday service to the Eucharist, included more lay participation, gave more choices in liturgies, emphasized common life, and modernized the language. Although eventually the revisions proved popular, the road getting there was long and tortuous. Along the way, a small minority of communicants refused to go along and left the Episcopal Church to form independent "1928 Prayer Book" churches.

In a state as innately conservative and traditional as South Carolina, one might expect a strong opposition to changing the venerable old prayer book and one would be right. But, once again, as with race, a resolute bishop led the diocese to make reform with relatively little serious resistance. It took him eleven years to do this, but he did it with only a minimal loss in the diocese. In 1968, Bishop Temple first issued a directive to the diocese to use the new proposed trial liturgy.[127] Initial results were mixed, as Temple reported to the convention of 1969: "After an immediate feeling of consternation, we settled down to give it an honest try."[128] He then directed the diocese to use the Proposed Liturgy from Ash Wednesday to Trinity Sunday of 1970.[129] At the same time, the Diocesan Liturgical Committee reported the results of its survey of trial use in the diocese: 74 percent of clergy welcomed the new liturgy while 60 percent of the laity opposed it.[130] It was clear the clergy had their work cut out to wean the majority of churchgoers from the old 1928 prayer book. Undeterred as usual, Temple moved right along ordering mandatory use of the trial liturgy from the Spring of 1971 to Palm Sunday of 1972. He later reported the response to this as "varied."[131] Apparently, many communicants were slow to adapt to the liturgical changes. Temple persevered, ordering use of the final version of the trial liturgies in 1975–76.[132]

After years of trial use, the diocesan convention voted on the new proposed prayer book in 1976, one year before the Church's General Convention would take up the issue

---

127. *Journal of the One Hundred Seventy-Ninth Annual Meeting of the Convention, April 18, 19, 1969, at the Church of the Holy Communion, Charleston, S.C.* Charleston, SC: the diocese, 1969, 42.

128. Ibid.

129. Ibid.

130. Ibid., 126–27.

131. *Journal of the One Hundred Eighty-Second Annual Meeting of the Convention, September 22–24, 1972, Grace Church, Charleston, South Carolina.* Charleston, SC: the diocese, 1972, 162.

132. *Journal of the One Hundred Eighty-Fifth Annual Meeting of the Convention, September 12–13, 1975, St. Michael's Church, Charleston, Volume II.* Charleston, SC: the diocese, 1975, 124.

again. The diocesan convention broke down its voting into three choices: 1—To accept the proposed prayer book, clergy 49, laity 71; 2—to reject the proposed book and keep the 1928 book, clergy 3, laity 31; 3—to refer the proposed book for more revision closer to the 1928 book, clergy 9, laity 56.[133] Thus, the convention approved the trial liturgy, overwhelmingly among the clergy but only by plurality among the laity. This brought the effective end of the issue. In the 1979 diocesan convention, Temple appealed for the approval of the new prayer book and the delegates easily passed a resolution to adopt the new revised prayer book of 1979.[134]

Women's Ordination

While reforms on race and the prayer book moved along in the post-Second World War era, yet another controversial issue gradually developed in the Episcopal Church, that of the role of women, particularly the ordination of women. Since its start in the 1780s, the Episcopal Church, as practically all denominations, was a male bastion. Women were barred from positions of leadership and authority. By around 1960, however, a women's liberation movement swept the country as the earlier civil rights crusade moved into high gear. In the Episcopal Church too, demands began to arise for equal treatment for women in the structure of the Church. As with civil rights and prayer book, this issue too was to follow a long and tortuous road before completion; and, once again, it was South Carolina that lagged along. And, once again, as with race and prayer book, it was the resolute leadership of Bishop Temple that made reforms for women happen in the Diocese of South Carolina. He was as committed to this as he was to racial justice and liturgical reform.

The movement for women's equality in the Episcopal Church had two parts, the opening of positions of leadership and authority to females, and the admission of women to Holy Orders. The first part occurred on the diocesan level then on the national. The second was a matter of decision on the national level to be applied to the dioceses. On the first part, the removal of gender barriers to offices, various dioceses dealt with this in various ways increasing in the 1950s and early 1960s. By 1964, approximately half of the dioceses had removed all gender-based barriers on the parish and diocesan levels.[135] By 1971, South Carolina was the only diocese in the entire Episcopal Church that still barred women from being elected as delegates to the diocesan convention.[136] As the diocese had been the last in the Episcopal Church to integrate racially, it was also the last to grant equal rights to women.

On the national level, the General Convention finally voted to remove gender-based barriers in 1967 as "laymen" became "laypersons." The first women deputies to

---

133. *Journal of the One Hundred Eighty-Sixth Annual Meeting of the Convention, August 27–28, 1976, All Saints' Church, Florence, Volume II.* Charleston, SC: the diocese, 1975, 160.

134. *Journal of the One Hundred Eighty-Ninth Annual Meeting of the Convention, August 31–September 1, 1979, The Church of the Holy Communion, Charleston, Volume II.* Charleston, SC: the diocese, 1979, 168.

135. Sumner, *Episcopal Church's History*, 10.

136. *Journal of the One Hundred Eighty-First (. . .) 1971*, 43.

the General Convention were admitted in 1970 as women were granted equal access to offices of the Episcopal Church. Thirty-six years later, the first woman was to be elected Presiding Bishop of the Episcopal Church, the first branch of the Anglican Communion to be led by a female.

By 1967, Bishop Temple was completely committed to equal rights for women in the diocese.[137] He told the diocesan convention that spring, just a few months before the vote in the General Convention, that the proposal to allow women to serve in the national House of Deputies would be approved. He then called for all gender-based barriers to be removed in the Diocese of South Carolina. While vestries were already open to women, many other offices remained closed. Pointing out how much the diocese lagged in this, he said: *"The time has come for this Diocese to face up to the place of women in the life of our Church."* (sic). He went on to propose changing Canon VII, Section 1 from "layman" to "lay persons" and replacing all references to males to that of lay persons. The convention approved his requests.[138]

As part of this reform, Temple called on the convention to allow women to serve as delegates to the annual diocesan conventions. When this came up for a final vote in 1971, he lamented: "The Diocese of South Carolina is the only Diocese of the whole Church which now has such a restriction." He declared: "I strongly favor the passage of this change to our Constitution and ask you to support it." The delegates complied. With this, South Carolina became the last diocese in the Episcopal Church to grant full equality to women in all lay offices on the parish and diocesan level.[139]

The question of women's ordination was an aspect of the larger issue of women's equality in the Episcopal Church. The movement for women's ordination in the Episcopal Church gained force in the 1960s to reach a milestone in 1970. That year, the General Convention approved the ordination of women as deacons. At the same time, it rejected the ordination of women to the priesthood. The next General Convention, in 1973, also rejected it. Bishop Temple supported women's ordination and told the 1974 diocesan convention: "I find no reason to believe that the Church may not choose to ordain women as well as men."[140]

In spite of the General Convention's rejections, activists for women's ordination forged ahead. First occurred the case of "the Philadelphia 11." On July 29, 1974, two retired and one resigned bishop conducted a service of ordination to the priesthood for eleven women. The House of Bishops met immediately and declared the ordinations

---

137. Grace Church of Charleston (one of the parishes that remained with the Episcopal Church in the schism) was perhaps typical of parochial attitudes to women's roles. The annual parish meeting in 1968 voted down a resolution to allow women to be elected to the vestry. That same year the Board of the Women of the Church declared they were "adamant that the church affairs be left to the men." A resolution to allow women on the vestry passed in the parish meeting of 1969, but it was another five years before a woman could be persuaded to sit on the vestry. The first female warden of Grace served in 1980. Way and Donehue, *By Grace Through Faith*, 116.

138. *Journal of the One Hundred Seventy-Seventh Annual Meeting of the Convention, April 21, 22, 1967 at St. Philip's Church, Charleston, S.C.* Charleston, SC: the diocese, 1967, 39.

139. *Journal of the One Hundred Eighty First (. . .) 1971*, 43.

140. *Journal of the One Hundred Eighty-Fourth Annual Meeting of the Convention, September 20–21, 1974.* Charleston, SC: the diocese, 1974, 152.

invalid. At the same time, the bishops also said they approved in principle of women's ordination. This only added to the confusion. Then, on September 7, 1975, a retired bishop conducted a service in Washington D.C. to ordain four women to the priesthood. The issue was now a crisis that everyone knew would come to a head at the next General Convention.

At the diocesan convention of 1975, Bishop Temple criticized the "'lawless acts'" of the irregular ordinations of 1974 but reaffirmed his support for women's ordination. He said he would vote favorably at the General Convention of 1976 to be held in Minneapolis. He asked the convention to support a resolution in favor of women's ordination. It complied.[141]

The Minneapolis convention of 1976 brought an end to the issue of women's ordination by voting to approve it. The House of Bishops set aside its earlier vote and agreed to recognize the validity of the ordinations of 1974 and 1975. Women were now freely allowed to serve as priests of the Episcopal Church.[142] A few years later, the barrier against women as bishops fell. In 1988, a woman was consecrated a bishop of the Episcopal Church.

While the Diocese of South Carolina and most of the Episcopal Church supported the ordination of women, a resolute, if small, minority refused to accept it. As some who would not follow the new prayer book left the Church, some who rejected the ordination of women also left to form independent denominations. To Bishop Temple, schism was a scandal. In his address to the 1977 diocesan convention, he lamented at length the "schismatic movement" that followed women's ordination. He had no patience for such actions:

> I say to you that this new movement is wrong because it is schismatic and divides the Body. Anyone who joins this movement is leaving The Church and starting a new one, whatever language is used to define the action. I cannot believe this is the will of God, who wills unity not division; love not separation; obedience and not self-gratification.[143]

Bishop Temple's prophetic words of 1977 soon faded from memory to be completely forgotten in his successors' rush to denounce the Episcopal Church. In time, one of his heirs would reverse Temple's sentiment entirely and create a schism the likes of which the old bishop could not have imagined. As we will see, the Diocese of South Carolina would change dramatically between 1977 and 2012.

---

141. *Journal of the One Hundred Eighty-Fifth (. . .) . . . 1975*, 124.

142. At first, women's ordination was left up to the dioceses. In 2003, three still refused ordination to women to the priesthood: San Joaquin, Quincy, and Ft. Worth.

143. *Journal of the One Hundred Eighty-Seventh Annual Meeting of the Convention, September 16–17, 1977, The Cathedral Church of St. Luke and St. Paul, Charleston, Volume II*. Charleston, SC: the diocese, 1977, 131.

Homosexuality

The post-Second World War social reform movement in America was most conspicuous first for African Americans and then for women. As these great elements came to the national forefront and won significant victories of freedom and equality in American life, other less visible minorities followed along to challenge the old status quo and demand the same sort of egalitarian reforms. These would include Native Americans, disabled Americans, Hispanics, and homosexual persons. It was this last group that was to impact most strongly on the life of the Episcopal Church, and particularly the Diocese of South Carolina in the 1970s and for decades thereafter.

The issue of rights for homosexual persons was not just another social reform movement along the lines of equality for blacks and women. It was structurally different than the matters of civil rights and women's ordination. A much larger and more complicated subject, it involved two different but interrelated profound aspects confronting the Episcopal Church: morality and ordination. The first involved the question of whether same-gender sexual acts were inherently immoral and sinful. The second involved the question of whether partnered homosexual persons should have the right to be ordained in the Church. Of course, everyone knew that homosexuals who were not open, that is, who were closeted or celibate, had been ordained for years, most likely forever in the life of the Christian church. The first aspect, morality, was so difficult and contentious that the first tendency in the Church was to avoid it. The second aspect of ordination, controversial enough, was really much easier to approach on an institutional level. Thus, over the years the Episcopal Church preferred to lean away from the morality issue and concentrate on the institutional side.

The General Convention of 1976 took up the matter of homosexuality, however reluctantly, the first Church General Convention to do so. The Committee on Ministry offered a resolution calling for an in-depth study of the question of the ordination of homosexuals and a report at the next General Convention. The opponents were prepared. Deputy Meredith, of Southern Virginia, offered a substitute resolution that would, at least momentarily, prevent the ordinations of open homosexuals: "the House of Deputies respectfully request the Bishops of the Episcopal Church to refrain from ordaining practicing homosexuals until such time as this Church, by vote of the General Convention, officially approve the same."[144] A vote by orders was called. Everyone understood the significance of the moment. The assembly was going to vote on whether to stop or continue the ordinations of openly homosexual persons. The vote was agonizingly close. In the Clergy order, 50 delegations voted yes, that is, to stop the ordinations, 43 voted no, and 16 were divided. In the Lay order, 56 delegations voted yes, 42 no, and 10 remained divided.[145] Meredith's substitute resolution lost, narrowly defeated among the clergy. As it turned out, the lay deputies were more in favor of banning gay ordinations than were the clergy. The narrowness of the decision, almost 50/50, reflected the deep division in

---

144. "1976-B102." The Acts of Convention 1976–2012, The Archives of the Episcopal Church, http://www.episcopalarchives.org/cgi-bin/acts/acts_resolution-complete.pl?resolution=1976-B102.

145. Ibid.

the Episcopal Church and would be a harbinger of the highly contentious and difficult days to come. Race and gender were simple issues compared with that of homosexuality.

Bishop Temple had little to say publicly about homosexuality. Perhaps by this point in his tenure, he was nearly exhausted from the long struggles for racial justice and women's rights. Besides, he had to deal with many other contentious problems of internal interest to the diocese beyond the scope of the present narrative. By the late 1970s, Temple seemed reluctant to take on any more problems. He made only two simple public statements on homosexuality. In his address to the 1977 diocesan convention he said, "I would not knowingly ordain a homosexual."[146] On the eve of the General Convention of 1979, at which the report on homosexuality would be presented, he told the diocesan convention once again that he would not ordain a homosexual and would not "permit the marriage of homosexuals."[147] Temple's lack of interest in the issue of homosexuality suggested he did not see it as an important problem in the diocese or the national Church. It was on this matter that his successive bishops would stand in stark contrast to him.

Perhaps Temple downplayed homosexuality in the diocese because he knew the 1979 General Convention would also set aside the issue. As the nearly 50/50 split in the last General Convention showed, the issue of homosexuality was much too divisive, difficult, and complicated for the Church to resolve at this early stage. The Convention did receive the report on homosexuality it had commissioned in 1976. What to do next was the problem at hand. The deputies arrived at a sort of compromise as it passed Resolution A053, "Recommended Guidelines on the Ordination of Homosexuals." On one hand, it said: "There should be no barrier to the ordination of qualified persons of either heterosexual or homosexual orientation whose behavior the Church considers wholesome."[148] On the other hand, it slammed the door: "We believe it is not appropriate for this Church to ordain a practicing homosexual."[149] At first glance, this resolution appeared contradictory as both for and against ordination of homosexuals. On closer reading, the difference was in one word, "practicing." Homosexuals could be ordained but "practicing" ones could not. No effort was made to describe what the word "practicing" meant. At the end of the Denver Convention of 1979, the conservative opponents of the ordination of open homosexuals breathed a great sigh of relief believing they had put away the problem. As it turned out, they did set the issue aside for several years, but this was only temporary. As society moved toward greater acceptance of homosexuality, the Episcopal Church would have to return to the issue and grapple with the conundrum of ordaining some homosexuals and not others. Nevertheless, at the moment, as far as Bishop Temple was concerned, the problem of homosexuality was over. He could wind down his episcopacy without ever having to deal with it again.

Bishop Temple succeeded well in leading the diocese through the minefield of racial integration, new prayer book, and women's equality in the 1960s and 1970s. Difficult

146. *Journal of the One Hundred Eighty-Seventh (. . .)* 1977, 131.
147. *Journal of the One Hundred Eighty-Ninth (. . .)* 1979, 144.
148. "1979–A053." The Acts of Convention 1976–2012, The Archives of the Episcopal Church, http://www.episcopalarchives.org/cgi-bin/acts/acts_resolution.pl?resolution=1979–A053.
149. Ibid.

in themselves, these were made even harder by some of the largest and most influential parishes in the diocese that were also strongly conservative and resistant to change. For instance, St. Philip's of Charleston, the oldest church in South Carolina, perennially denounced the National Council of Churches and the World Council of Churches and frequently criticizing the national Church for its supposedly radical stands.[150] In 1979, delegates from St. Philip's went so far as to introduce a resolution in the diocesan convention demanding the Presiding Bishop stop all funds to the World Council of Churches and the General Convention to withdraw the Episcopal Church's membership from the World Council. Bishop Temple refused to support it and the convention voted down the proposed resolution. St. Philip's was also a leader in the movement to cut off funds to the national Church in the wake of its racial programs of the late 1960s. As we have seen, at that time Temple narrowly escaped a racially-inspired parochial revolt against the diocese and the national church and only belatedly guided the diocese to restore its full contribution to the Church. More than once, Temple had to remind quarrelsome communicants that, after all, the diocese was part and parcel of the Episcopal Church, and the Church was governed by the General Convention. To the diocesan convention of 1967 he said: "The General Convention is to the Dioceses what Congress is to the State legislature. Each Diocese governs its own affairs through its annual convention, but only under over-all policy and law set by the General Convention."[151] As one will see, Temple's successors would disagree with this view.

By 1973, it was time for the diocese to be officially registered with the state of South Carolina as a non-profit corporation under state law. In the October diocesan convention, a resolution passed called "Concerning Incorporation." It stated: "The Protestant Episcopal Diocese of South Carolina appoints the Rt. Rev. Gray Temple and the Rev. Canon George I. Chassey, Jr. to apply to the South Carolina Secretary of State for a certificate of incorporation."[152] They did so; and on November 14, 1973, the State of South Carolina issued a Certificate of Incorporation to The Protestant Episcopal Diocese of South Carolina. Inscribed on the single-page document was this: "The purpose of the said proposed Corporation is to continue the operation of an Episcopal Diocese under the Constitution and Canons of The Protestant Episcopal Church in the United States of America."[153] This document was to play a key role in the post-schism litigation.

It should also be pointed out that while Bishop Temple juggled all the various problems already described, and usually did so against the resistance of the most powerful parishes, he also managed to deal with a host of other diocesan problems and projects

---

150. For a recent parish history, see McIntosh, William, III. *Spiritual Journey of St. Philip's Church, Charleston, S.C., 1906–2012.* Charleston, SC: William McIntosh, 2013.

151. *Journal of the One Hundred Seventy-Seventh (. . .)* 1967, 38.

152. *Journal of the One Hundred Eighty-Third Annual Meeting of the Convention, October 26–27, 1973, Holy Trinity Church, Charleston, Volume II.* Charleston, SC: the diocese, 1973, 179.

153. Certificate of Incorporation, State of South Carolina, Secretary of State, November 14, 1973. On October 15, 2010, the reconvened diocesan convention passed a resolution to amend the 1973 corporate charter by removing the reference to the Episcopal Church. On October 19, 2010, the charter was changed to delete the Episcopal Church. In the legal maneuverings after the schism in 2012, this became a major issue of contention. The diocesan side argued the 2010 revision of the corporate charter was entirely legal. The Church side argued in court that the revision was illegal and therefore null and void.

of internal interest. Space here does not permit a full accounting of these, only to point out some of the most important ones: designation of the Cathedral Church of St. Luke and St. Paul in Charleston, division of the diocese into five deaneries, the construction of Canterbury House in Charleston, the building of a new diocesan headquarters, the development of St. Christopher's Camp and Conference Center, and aid in founding the retirement communities of Bishop Gadsden on James Island and Still Hopes in West Columbia, SC. The camp was perhaps the most controversial. Temple led the diocese to sell 1,200 acres of Seabrook Island for two million dollars, the money used to construct a first-class camp and conference center on the remaining 200 acres.[154] Camp St. Christopher became the envy of many a diocese.

By the late 1970s, Bishop Temple was ready to begin phasing out his episcopacy. In 1979, he asked the diocesan convention to pass a resolution calling for the election of a bishop coadjutor for the diocese.[155] When Temple retired in 1982 after twenty-one years in office, he could look back in satisfaction in many ways. He had succeeded at bringing the diocese well through four major crises in the national Church: civil rights, new prayer book, women's ordination, and homosexuality. Even at great difficulty, he had steadfastly kept the diocese loyal to the Church. In addition, he had accomplished an impressive list of internal works. Moreover, while managing all these, he guided the diocese to remarkable growth. When he arrived in 1961, the diocese had 20,133 baptized members and 13,995 communicants with a budget of $1,265,511.[156] When he retired, in 1982, the diocese had 25,096 baptized members, 19,188 communicants, and a budget of $2,400,064.[157] Thus, in Temple's two decades, the diocese grew 17 percent in membership, 29 percent in communicants, and nearly one hundred percent in budget. A strong case can be made that Gray Temple was the greatest bishop in the history of the Diocese of South Carolina.[158]

Counter-Revolution and Bishop Christopher FitzSimons Allison (1982–1990)

The Roots of Counter-Revolution

On the surface and in general, all appeared well with the Episcopal Church and the Diocese of South Carolina when Bishop Temple retired after two remarkable decades. Major reforms, unity, and prosperity seemed secure, and the future looked nothing but bright in 1982. Beneath the impressive outward appearance, however, a different picture was emerging. A closer look at the unity, peace and growth would reveal ominous fissures and other hidden dangers that, though small at first, had the potential to get worse, much worse in time. In general, there were two major problem areas, each one a danger

---

154. *Journal of the One Hundred Eightieth* (. . .) 1970, 39.

155. *Journal of the One Hundred Eighty-Ninth* (. . .) 1979, 168.

156. *Journal of the One Hundred and Seventy-First* (. . .) 1961, 121–22.

157. *Journal of the One Hundred Ninety-Third Annual Meeting of the Convention, September* 22–24, 1983, *Grace Church, Charleston, S.C., Vol.* 1. Charleston, SC: the diocese, 1983, 89, 10.

158. Temple and his wife Maria Drane retired to Edisto Island, then to Still Hopes in West Columbia, SC. He died there on October 27, 1999, aged 85.

in itself, but combined could be disastrous for the Episcopal Church in the years to come. One was the growth of an adversarial minority, the other was the issue of homosexuality. At the time, in 1982, neither one seemed to be very dangerous to the Church. Indeed, the ordination of open homosexuals appeared to be off the table since the General Convention of 1979. Little was to be said about that issue for years afterward. Momentary calm prevailed in the Episcopal Church and the diocese in the early 1980s as leadership passed from Temple to Allison.

On the first problem, there was in fact a growing minority of disaffected Episcopalians in the 1970s and early 1980s. The church "wings" in particular grew alarmed by the reforms of the day, Anglo-Catholics most upset by the ordination of women, and evangelicals disturbed by the revisions of the prayer book. Both groups shared the tendency to feel that the Episcopal Church had gone too far in its radical changes to worship and social policy. These conservative elements in general believed the purpose of religion was to unite man and God, the Catholics through the sacraments, the evangelicals through the Scriptures. The goal was to build a bond of one person and one God, a "vertical" relationship. Holding individual salvation to be all that really mattered, the conservatives regarded the Church's social reforms as scarcely relevant at best and destructive at worst. They wanted to keep the religion of the past, "the faith once delivered," as they often said, as intact as possible. Among this group there was universal agreement that same-gender sexual acts were sinful and should never be even implicitly condoned by the Church. Moreover, they believed overwhelmingly that homosexuality was a matter of choice and not inborn.[159] Therefore, to them, the ordination of non-celibate homosexual persons was out of the question; and it was they who had gotten the General Convention to reject ordination of "practicing" homosexuals in 1979.

Conservatives then became increasingly critical of the social gospel movement the Episcopal Church had adopted in the 1950s and reinforced and expanded in the 1960s and 70s. In contrast to the conservative vertical attitude, the social gospelers may be called "horizontal" Christians because they believed the Church should now focus its energies in making beneficial changes in society. As the reforms grew over the years, the rift between those who wanted to promote faith and those who wanted to push social reform gradually widened. As for homosexuality, while the "verticalists" saw it as a moral issue, the "horizontalists" regarded it as a matter of human rights. They saw homosexuals as another oppressed minority in need of liberation. The differing views on homosexuality, while masked by the temporary respite of the early 1980s, would soon explode into the most serious crisis to shake the Episcopal Church since the Civil War.

Concerning the first problem, the dissidents, small but ominous signs began appearing in the Episcopal Church in reaction to its reform movements of the 1960s and 1970s. It was in the Civil Rights period of the late 1950s and early 1960s that conservatives raised the first widespread criticisms of the supposedly too-liberal policies of the Episcopal Church. The number of individual defections from the Church because of its racial reforms has not been quantified, but it could not have been large in the 1950s and early 1960s. The Diocese of South Carolina gained members continually throughout this

---

159. Greeley, Andrew and Michael Hout. *The Truth about Conservative Christians: What They Think and What They Believe,* Chicago: University of Chicago Press, 2006, 119.

period. The Episcopal Church swelled in numbers until 1966, well into the time of the Civil Rights era.

Conservative opposition began to coalesce into organized groups in the early 1970s, the same time that women's ordination and prayer book reform gained forceful momentum. The first broad coalition of conservative Church people formed in 1973 as the Fellowship of Concerned Churchmen. It issued a statement rejecting women's ordination and, refusing to recognize the Church's actions on it, called a meeting in Nashville in November of 1976.[160] In turn, that assembly called the St. Louis Congress in September of 1977. This Congress may be fairly regarded as the effective beginning of the movement to replace the Episcopal Church as the legitimate body of Anglicanism in the U.S. The so-called "Continuing Anglican Movement" came from the belief that the Episcopal Church had abandoned true Anglicanism by its too-radical reforms; and, therefore, the legitimate Anglicans would "continue" the old faith in separate institutions. The Congress's Affirmation of St. Louis was the foundation document of the anti-Episcopal Church movement. It declared that the Episcopal Church had abandoned Anglicanism by agreeing to ordain women, true Anglicanism would continue in the U.S. outside the Episcopal Church, the Episcopal Church had created schism through its erroneous actions, and continuing Anglicans would recognize the Archbishop of Canterbury.[161] The Congress also called for the formation of a "continuing Anglican" church to be called the Anglican Church in North America (Episcopal). Unity, however, did not happen, as groups agreed only on forming numerous independent bodies with names such as Anglican Catholic Church, American Episcopal Church, Anglican Jurisdiction of the Americas, Anglican Diocese (later Province) of Christ the King, United Episcopal Church, and Anglican Catholic Church of Canada.[162] In the 1990s, the "Continuing Anglican Movement" world morph into the "Anglican Realignment" movement.

Conservative, or "vertical," Episcopalians split into two factions, one, the minority, leaving the Episcopal Church to form new independent churches, and the other, the majority remaining in the Church to oppose the hated reforms. Although conservatives were a minority in the Episcopal Church they were a relatively strong and committed one, strong enough to defeat ordination of open homosexuals in the 1979 General Convention. Still seething over the GCSP, liturgical changes, the ordination of women, and what they considered the loosening of morals and a turning away from "orthodox" faith, conservative elements in the Church, particularly the committed Anglo-Catholics and evangelicals were resolved to stop the bleeding and cauterize the wound at homosexuality. It would be their last-ditch stand to protect what they believed was left of true religion in the suspect Episcopal Church. On the evangelical side, the Fellowship of Witness coalesced the faithful to oppose the supposedly too-liberal trends in the Church.[163]

In the Diocese of South Carolina, the number of individual communicants who left the Episcopal Church in the 1960s and 1970s cannot be determined, but it is known

---

160. Sumner, *Episcopal Church's History*, 155.

161. "Affirmation of St. Louis," Wikipedia, http://en.wikipedia.org/wiki/Affirmation_of_St._Louis.

162. For details on these groups, see Sumner, *Episcopal Church's History*, 160.

163. Ibid., 127. This group was later called the Evangelical Fellowship of the Anglican Communion-USA.

that at least two "continuing Anglican" congregations formed, both in the new Anglican Catholic Church. Apparently the main complaint in both groups was against the new prayer book; they advertised as "1928 Prayer Book" churches. One was the Anglican Church of Our Saviour, formed in Florence in 1977. The other was St. Timothy's Anglican Catholic Church, formed in 1977. It eventually settled in the West Ashley area of Charleston and drew some dissident Episcopalians from old St. Andrew's of West Ashley.[164]

The loss of communicants in the Diocese of South Carolina to splinter churches was relatively small and did not affect the steady rise in membership until the end of Bishop Temple's tenure. In the Episcopal Church, however, by 1982 there were ominous signs of numerical decline. The height of the membership in the Church occurred in 1966 at 3,429,153. After that, church membership figures fell steadily except for brief up-ticks in 1979, 1982–83, and 1990–95.[165] By the time Temple retired in 1982, the national Church had lost approximately 20 percent of its membership. In the context of the growing divisions in the Episcopal Church, the minority groups blamed the losses on the disruptive reforms; and, in the years to come would continue doing so. The actual reasons for the membership decline remained a matter of conjecture as some people believed it had to do less with liberal reforms and more with demography, birth rates, lack of evangelism, low retention, and immigration factors.[166] At any rate, the numbers of people joining splinter groups was only a small fraction of the declining figures of the Episcopal Church.

By the late 1970s, the Episcopal Church needed to adopt a clear-cut policy on property ownership. This was caused by two factors: several congregations had tried to leave the Church with their properties, and the 1979 Supreme Court decision *Jones v. Wolf*. The First Amendment to the U.S. Constitution explicitly forbade the civil state from interfering in the internal matters of a religious body. However, *Jones* said that courts could follow "neutral principles" of law in adjudicating property disputes between church factions. The court said: "'The [neutrality] method relies exclusively on objective, well established concepts of trust and property law familiar to lawyers and judges. It thereby promises to free courts completely from entanglement in questions of religious doctrine, polity and practice.'"[167] The Court went on to explain that national churches could form express trusts in properties: "'The constitution of the general church can be made to recite an express trust in favor of the denominational church. The burden involved in taking such steps will be minimal. And the civil courts will be bound to give effect to the result indicated by the parties, provided it is embodied in some legally cognizable form.'"[168] With the need for a policy on property and the direction of the Supreme Court

---

164. Porwoll, *Against All Odds*, 268.

165. "Episcopal Church," The Association of Religion Data Archives, http://www.thearda.com/Denoms/D_849.asp. By 2012, the time of the schism in South Carolina, the Episcopal Church membership had declined 45 percent from its 1966 high and stood at 1,894,181.

166. Coats, William R. "Who (or What) Caused the Decline in Membership in the Episcopal Church?" http://www.rci.rutgers.edu/~lcrew/dojustice/j325.html.

167. "Dennis Canon," Wikipedia, http://en.wikipedia.org/wiki/Dennis_canon.

168. Ibid.

in *Jones*, the General Convention of 1979 passed Resolution D024, commonly called the Dennis Canon after its author. It stated: "'All real and personal property held by or for the benefit of any Parish, Mission, or Congregation is held in trust for this Church and the Diocese thereof in which such Parish, Mission or Congregation is located.'"[169] The Dennis Canon became the explicit law of the Episcopal Church regarding all properties held by local churches. Even if a parish owned actual title to the property, it did so for the trustees, the Episcopal Church and the local diocese. Thus, if a congregation decided to leave the Episcopal Church, even if it held the title, it could not take the parish property without permission of the Church and the diocese.

Christopher FitzSimons Allison

The Rev. Christopher FitzSimons Allison was chosen bishop coadjutor of the Diocese of South Carolina on May 17, 1980, in an election that, in retrospect, did not bode well for the future of the diocese. There were seventeen candidates on the ballot. The vote necessary to elect was 37 of the 71 clergy present and 27 of the 51 and 1/2 lay votes present. On the first ballot, Allison led but did not reach the necessary counts. Another five ballots passed to the same effect as none of the other sixteen candidates could rally a coalition to reach a majority. Finally, on the seventh ballot, Allison won 37 of the clergy and 37 of the laity thus clinching the election. While he had carried a clear majority of the laity, he had won just the bare minimum among the clergy. In fact, 34 of the diocesan clergy, nearly half, did not vote for Allison even after six ballots.[170]

Allison was consecrated Bishop Coadjutor of the Diocese of South Carolina on September 25, 1980, the day before the annual diocesan convention, in the Gailliard Auditorium of Charleston with an audience of 2,500 people. The Rt. Rev. John M. Allin, the Presiding Bishop of the Episcopal Church, served as chief consecrator. The preacher of the day was the Very Rev. John H. Rodgers, Jr., dean of the Trinity Episcopal School for Ministry who set an evangelical tone for this new episcopacy as "he charged the new bishop to be attentive to Scripture, to continue to preach repentance and forgiveness of sin, and to rely on the promise of the Holy Spirit for power to serve."[171] Actually, Allison himself had already enunciated a new course of criticism of the Episcopal Church as he said after his election: "Our direction should be one that would be more open to the guidance of the Holy Spirit, more a word to, than an echo of, our culture, and a more complete manifestation of the church, lay and clerical."[172]

Once Bishop Temple retired on January 1, 1982, and Allison took over the next day as the diocesan bishop, this different course would become increasingly clear. Under

169. Ibid.

170. *Journal of the One Hundred Ninetieth Annual Meeting of the Convention, September 26–27, 1980, Cathedral Church of St. Luke and Saint Paul, Host Parish Calvary Church, Charleston, Volume I.* Charleston, SC: the diocese, 1980, 105.

171. "C. Fitzsimons Allison Consecrated in South Carolina." Episcopal News Service, October 2, 1980, Episcopal Press and News 1962–2006, The Archives of the Episcopal Church, http://episcopalarchives.org/cgi-bin/ENS/ENSpress_release.pl?pr_number=80346.

172. Ibid.

Allison, the tone, attitude, and direction of the diocese would take a decidedly rightward turn. Much of what Bishop Temple had worked so hard to accomplish would begin to be ignored by the new leadership as the decade of the 1980s moved along.

Allison was born on March 5, 1927, in Columbia, South Carolina, to James Richard and Susan Milliken FitzSimons Allison. He said one time he had been baptized, confirmed and ordained in Trinity Church of Columbia.[173] He finished a B.A. degree at the University of the South (Sewanee) in 1949. The next year he married Martha Allston Parker of Georgetown, South Carolina. He studied at Virginia Theological Seminary where he earned a Bachelor of Divinity degree in 1952 and gained ordination to the diaconate in June 1952 and the priesthood in May 1953. From 1954 to 1956, Allison studied at Christ Church, Oxford; and was awarded the degree of Doctor of Philosophy. He taught in the School of Theology at Sewanee from 1956 to 1967, then the Virginia Theological Seminary until 1975. As a career academic theologian for nearly twenty years, and author of several publications, Allison made a notable name for himself, particularly among evangelical Episcopalians. In 1975, he resigned from VTS to become rector of Grace Church in New York City where he was to remain for five years.

It was in 1975 that events in Allison's life began to turn in ways fateful to the Diocese of South Carolina. According to a 2009 memoir of the Rev. Benjamin Bosworth Smith:

> The Board of Trustees [of VTS] elected Dr. Charles Price, Harvard University Chaplain, as Professor of Theology, overlooking the interim acting professor, Dr. John Rodgers, for the chair. Fitz Allison, in a pique with the Board of Trustees' decision, promptly resigned as Professor of Church History, and accepted a call to serve as Rector of Grace Church, New York City. A few months later he joined with a retired Australian Bishop, Bishop Alfred Stanway, to found a new seminary to provide a theological professorship for his friend, John Rodgers. That was the beginning of an astonishing upstart school, The Trinity Episcopal School for Ministry, to give both John Rodgers and Fitz Allison a chance to teach on their own terms.[174]

According to Smith, Allison was highly instrumental in creating the Trinity Episcopal School for Ministry, later Trinity School for Ministry. It was meant to be an "orthodox" alternative to the established Episcopal seminaries that many evangelicals like Allison felt had become infused with modernist, relativist, and weak non-orthodox theology. Trinity set the stage for Rodgers to teach the neo-orthodox views that he had inherited from his mentor, the great twentieth century Swiss theologian, Karl Barth. Barth was the leading academic advocate of the revival of traditional orthodoxy in the face of the post-Second World War new wave of theology that so often advanced critical reinterpretations of old beliefs and concepts. Evangelicals in the Episcopal Church, and other denominations, revered Barth for his influential reiteration of traditional theology,

---

173. *Journal of the One Hundred Ninety-Ninth Annual Meeting of the Convention, February 23–25, 1989, All Saints' Church, Waccamaw, Pawleys Island, Proceedings of the Convention.* Charleston, SC: the diocese, 1989, 41.

174. Smith, (the Rev.) Benjamin Bosworth. "My Analysis of The Fix We're In." http://www.episcopalforumofsc.org/Overview%20Documents/My%20analysis%20of%20the%20we%20are%20in.pdf. Smith was rector of Grace Church, Charleston, 1977–1992.

sometimes called neo-conservative, or neo-orthodox. Many of his admirers simply called themselves the "orthodox."

By the mid-1970s, the evangelical minority, who wished to promote the conservative "vertical" posture of religion, were growing increasingly critical of the trajectory of the Episcopal Church in its decidedly "horizontal" policies of social reform. According to historian David Sumner, "Trinity was founded in 1975 by the Fellowship of Witness, an organization devoted to promoting the evangelical tradition in the Episcopal Church. Like the Fellowship of Witness, the goal of the seminary was to provide an evangelical, biblically-based education, within the context of the Anglican tradition."[175] When the new seminary opened for classes in 1976, Allison's good friend John Rodgers was in place as the senior professor. Two years later he was named dean and president as the school moved to its permanent locating in Ambridge, Pennsylvania, near Pittsburgh. It was this John Rodgers who preached at Allison's consecration as bishop coadjutor in 1980.

Outside of the Diocese of Pittsburgh, the new seminary developed its strongest ties with the Diocese of South Carolina. These bonds have strengthened over the years. The 2013 listing of TSM's Board of Trustees showed that six of the twenty-eight names were in South Carolina, most notably Mark Lawrence. Among the "Trustees Emeritus" were Allison and several others from South Carolina or with strong ties there. A glance over the trustees shows numerous names not in the Episcopal Church and several names prominent in the secessionist movement from the Church. In 2007, the seminary dropped the word "Episcopal" from its public title as more and more of its teachers and students identified with non-Episcopal "Anglican" bodies.

Meanwhile, after Allison became bishop of South Carolina, he was a tireless advocate of hiring graduates of TSM. Once when asked how he managed to get so many conservative evangelical clergy in the diocese, Allison said: "'I would guide search committees to consider those ministers who graduated from Trinity or were otherwise orthodox but it was hard and I made some mistakes.'"[176] Allison made it known he wanted clergy from the conservative seminaries, TSM and Nashotah House. Gradually, one by one, many vacancies in the diocese were filled by TSM graduates as the diocese became ever more conservative, or "orthodox" as Allison would say, between 1982 and 1990. This trend only increased after Allison so that by the time of the schism, clergy tied to TSM held the rectorships of some prominent parishes and dominated the organs of power in the Diocese of South Carolina. Thus, one cannot overestimate the effect of TSM on the conservative turn of the Diocese of South Carolina after 1982. In a sense, Trinity School for Ministry was the "school" that bred the 2012 schism in South Carolina.

---

175. Sumner, *Episcopal Church's History*, 103.
176. McIntosh, *Spiritual Journey of St. Philip's*, 179.

Bishop Allison's Counter-Revolution, 1982–1990

Bishop Temple juggled four major reform movements coming from the Episcopal Church, race, prayer book, women's ordination, and homosexuality, along with numerous internal developmental issues in the diocese. By the time Allison's episcopate started in 1982, the first three were practically settled in both the national Church and the diocese. Race was no longer an issue, at least overtly.[177] A new prayer book had been put in place in 1979. Women's ordination to the priesthood had been settled in 1976. Most conservative Episcopalians remained in the Church, however unhappily, as only small groups of schismatics peeled off over one controversial issue or another. They could even feel a slight sense of victory having forced the issue of homosexuality off the table in the 1979 General Convention. Thus, the mood among the more "vertical" elements of the church, the evangelicals and the Anglo-Catholics, was the calm after the storm. They could only hope that the "horizontal" reform movement has run its course to be replaced by stability.

To Bishop Allison, the first two of the four issues, race and prayer book were moot points. He scarcely if ever referred to them as there was no need to do so. However, the third issue was different. Women's ordination could not be avoided. Temple had been very much in favor of women's ordination and had set the approval policy for the diocese but no female had come forth for ordination in the diocese during his tenure. By the early 1980s, that was to change and Allison would have to deal with the issue. It is instructive at this point to look at Allison's bishop's addresses to the diocesan conventions and contrast them to those of Bishop Temple. Temple had spent most of his time on the issues of the day, on internal programs and developments in the diocese, and following the reforms of the national Church. Former professor Allison's addresses, on the other hand, tended to be theological discourses. They were "vertically" oriented morality sermons on sin and salvation with lots of Biblical and literary references and with relatively little attention to the internal institutional development of the diocese. Apparently, he did not publicly comment on women's ordination.

Meanwhile, women began moving toward ordination in the Diocese of South Carolina, however unenthusiastic they found the bishop. The first woman to be ordained to the priesthood in the diocese was Constance D. S. Belmore. The service was held on April 25, 1984, at Grace Church in Charleston and was conducted by the Rt. Rev. William Moultrie Moore, Jr., the retired bishop of Easton, in Maryland, for the Diocese of East Carolina. Allison and Temple attended but did not participate. The event garnered tremendous interest and publicity, even an article in the local newspaper. Grace Church was packed with an overwhelmingly enthusiastic congregation. A huge and joyous reception followed in the parish hall.[178] A barrier fell. The next year, Belmore's name appeared on the official clergy list of the diocese.

---

177. Effective incorporation of blacks into the structure of the diocese continued slowly. In 1998, the first African-American was placed on the diocesan Standing Committee. *Journal of the Two Hundred and Ninth Annual Meeting of the Convention, March 5–6, 1999, Church of the Cross, Bluffton, S.C., the Westin Resort, Hilton Head, S.C., Proceedings of the Convention.* Charleston, SC: the diocese, 1999, 63.

178. Belmore, Constance. Telephone interview with author, June 24, 2015. Belmore was born in

With Belmore's ordination, other women began to appear to be considered for ordination in the Diocese of South Carolina. In 1986, the Standing Committee recommended the ordination to the diaconate of Cynthia Nan Taylor, the first woman to be ordained a deacon in the diocese. She served as assistant to the Rev. J. Edwin Pippin at All Saints in Florence.[179] In 1987, the committee approved her ordination to the priesthood. Taylor[180] was ordained to the priesthood by Bishop Allison at All Saints in Florence on May 16, 1987, the first woman ordained a priest in the Diocese of South Carolina for the diocese (Belmore had been ordained for East Carolina).[181] The next year, 1988, Jennie C. Olbrych was ordained a deacon and became an assistant at St. Paul's in Summerville.[182] On April 6, 1989, the committee recommended that Olbrych be ordained a priest.[183] Thus, three women were ordained priests in the Diocese of South Carolina during Allison's tenure of 1982–90. In addition to ordination, women were slowly being admitted to offices of leadership in the diocese. In 1987, the first woman was elected to serve on the diocesan Standing Committee, Doris E. Hane (1987–90); incidentally, 1987 was also the year the Committee first approved the ordination of a woman to the priesthood. The next year a second female was chosen for the Standing Committee, Mrs. Norman S. Walsh (1988–91).[184]

Although the Diocese of South Carolina was not overtly hostile to the ordination of women, as it was to the acceptance of homosexuals, and gradually allowed women to be ordained, it remained a male-oriented bastion ranking well below the national averages

---

Charlotte, North Carolina. She attended General Theological Seminary in New York City where her faculty advisor was Philip Turner. In 1983, she was ordained a deacon in East Carolina and served Trinity Church in Lumberton. She moved to Charleston after her husband, the Rev. Kent Belmore, became assistant at the Church of the Holy Communion in 1983. Constance Belmore joined the staff of Grace Church and served as chaplain at the College of Charleston where she remained for five years. Afterwards, she was associate director of community ministries in the Diocese of Atlanta for sixteen years. As of June 2015, Belmore was a hospital chaplain in Las Vegas where her husband was retired.

179. *Journal of the One Hundred Ninety-Seventh Annual Meeting of the Convention, February 19–21, 1987, Cathedral of St. Luke and St. Paul, Charleston, Host Church: St. James' James Island, Proceedings of the Convention.* Charleston, SC: the diocese, 1987, 17.

180. Taylor, Cynthia. Telephone interview with author, March 1, 2016. Cynthia Nan Taylor, from Sumter SC, was graduated from the Virginia Theological Seminary which she attended 1983–86. She served as assistant at All Saints of Florence from June 1986 to December of 1987. From 1988 to 1991 she was an assistant at the American Cathedral in Paris; from 1991 to 1999 an assistant at St. Paul's of Augusta, Georgia. In 1999, she established a church plant, Holy Comforter in Martinez, Georgia, where she remained as pastor as of March, 2016.

181. *Journal of the One Hundred Ninety-Eighth Annual Meeting of the Convention, February 25–27, 1988, Cathedral of St. Luke and St. Paul, Charleston, Proceedings of the Convention.* Charleston, SC: the diocese, 1988, 41.

182. *Journal of the One Hundred Ninety-Ninth (. . .)* 1989, 17.

183. *Journal of the Two Hundreth Annual Meeting of the Convention, St. Philip's Church, Charleston, Proceedings of the Convention, February 22–24, 1990, Proceedings of the Special Convention, September 9, 1989.* Charleston, SC: the diocese, 1990, 37. Olbrych was the only one of the four still in the diocese at the time of the schism. After 2006, she was vicar of St. James Santee, McClellanville, a mission that remained with the Episcopal Church after the schism. She also served as associate chaplain to the lower school of Porter-Gaud in Charleston. She was listed among the "Clergy in Good Standing" of the Episcopal Church in South Carolina and the clergy of the Diocese of South Carolina in 2016.

184. *Journal of the One Hundred Ninety-Eighth (. . .)* 1988, 17.

for women clergy in the Episcopal Church. A diocesan survey conducted in 2002, eighteen years after the first woman was ordained a priest in the diocese, showed a continuing strong bias against women in positions of leadership and authority. Thirty-eight per-cent of the men surveyed said that women should not be allowed in positions of leadership in the parish or diocese.[185] Two-thirds of women surveyed, and three-fourths of men, disapproved of more women clergy. Most men and women were opposed to having women clergy in their parishes and to having female bishops. Most parishes had at most a few women on vestries. Only a quarter of parishes had ever had female wardens. The evidence showed that this anti-female attitude changed hardly at all over the years in South Carolina. Allison's indifference continued in the Salmon tenure. By the time Mark Lawrence arrived in 2008, women still accounted for only a handful of the priests and deacons in the diocese and a small sprinkling among the diocesan power committees. Lawrence came from a diocese that had never ordained a woman to the priesthood. In the next seven years, he ordained two women to the diaconate and one of these to the priesthood. As one will see, the Episcopal Church's election of the first woman to serve as presiding bishop, in 2006, was followed by a tremendous backlash in South Carolina. A case can be made that diocesan prejudice against women in positions of power was part of the mixture of factors that propelled the male-oriented majority in the diocese toward schism from the Church.

While Allison showed little interest in women's ordination and the role of women in the diocese, the same could not be said of the fourth controversial issue, homosexuality. In fact, he seemed to become preoccupied with the matter. From 1985 to 1990, he made it the constantly recurring overriding theme of all his addresses. At first, however, there was little news about homosexuality. After the 1979 General Convention rejected the ordination of "practicing" homosexuals, the next two General Conventions were reluctant to deal with the controversial topic. The 1982 Convention changed nothing and only reiterated its inconsequential stand "affirming that homosexual persons are children of God and are entitled to full civil rights."[186] Conservatives breathed a sigh of relief. At the 1985 General Convention, it was much the same as the deputies once again rejected moves to open ordination to open homosexuals. They passed only one vague and weak resolution on homosexuality calling on dioceses to have a "better understanding" of homosexual persons.[187] By now, the conservatives must have been feeling triumphant that the issue of ordaining open homosexuals was dead. Three successive General Conventions had defeated or ignored it. Yet, the conservatives in the Diocese of South Carolina were not content to drop the subject. When the diocesan convention met in September of 1985, a few weeks after the General Convention, the Rev. Samuel

---

185. Diocese of South Carolina Committee on the Status of Women Survey, July 2002.

186. "1982–B061, Reaffirm the Civil Rights of Homosexuals." The Acts of Convention, 1976–2012, The Archives of the Episcopal Church, http://www.episcopalarchives.org/cgi-bin/acts/acts_resolution.pl?resolution=1982-B061.

187. "1985–D082, Urges Dioceses to Reach a Better Understanding of Homosexuality." The Acts of Convention, 1976–2012, The Archives of the Episcopal Church, http://www.episcopalarchives.org/cgi-bin/acts/acts_resolution.pl?resolution=1985-D082.

C.W. Fleming[188] offered a resolution, R–15, entitled "Homosexuality and Ordination." It proclaimed: "that the 1985 meeting of the Convention of the Diocese of South Carolina respectfully notify the Presiding Bishop Elect [Browning] that we do not approve the ordination of practicing homosexuals."[189] The delegates approved the resolution. This officially began a three-decade long obsession in the Diocese of South Carolina with the issue of homosexuality.

Even then, Bishop Allison and other leading conservatives in the diocese were not ready to leave the issue of homosexuality even if the General Convention had already set it aside. They were just warming up. At the diocesan convention in February of 1987, Allison went on at length in his bishop's address about the Scriptures, sin, and moral behavior, as usual, but this time added a pointed denunciation of the Rt. Rev. John S. Spong[190]: "The publicity surrounding the endeavor of the Bishop of Newark for our Church to consider different teachings regarding homosexual and heterosexual activity has caused a great deal of concern over our whole Church. On a negative note, I must in all candor tell you that I believe this issue to be one capable of doing great harm to our Church."[191] He then called for himself and the Diocesan Council to set up a special commission "for the purpose of informing our General Convention delegates and recommending action for this Diocese to take."[192] The Rev. Fleming then introduced a resolution, R–9, "Christian Morality Concerning Sexual Behavior": "neither the Clergy nor the Laity of this Church should encourage any attempt to legitimize any sexual behavior other than that which is appropriate between a man and a woman united in Holy Matrimony."[193] It passed, as did resolution R–13, "The Church's Teaching Regarding Homosexual and Heterosexual Activity," that set up a commission, on Allison's wish, to advise deputies of the diocese to the General Convention of 1988. The Rev. Philip Turner, a well-known conservative academic at General Theological Seminary, was to be a consultant.[194] The

---

188. Fleming was rector of the Church of the Holy Communion, the flagship Anglo-Catholic parish of the diocese, Charleston, from 1967 to his retirement 1985. Afterwards, he served as interim rector of Holy Cross, Sullivans Island. He was one of seventy clergymen to send a letter on April 8, 1976, opposing the election of the Rev. John S. Spong as bishop coadjutor of Newark on the grounds his views and writings were "unorthodox." See: www.episcopalarchives.org/cgi-bin/ENS/ENSpress_release.pl?pr_number=76124.

189. *Journal of the One Hundred Ninety-Fifth Annual Meeting of the Convention, September 26–28, 1985, Cathedral of St. Luke and St. Paul, Charleston, Host Church, St. Andrew's, Mt. Pleasant, Volume II.* Charleston, SC: the diocese, 1985, 167.

190. Spong, a native of Charlotte, North Carolina, served for years as a priest in North Carolina. In 1976 he was elected bishop coadjutor of Newark and was diocesan bishop from 1979 to 2000. He was a prolific writer who challenged old ways of thinking. He advocated equal rights for homosexuals in the Episcopal Church. Conservative Episcopalians came to see Spong as an arch-enemy. Allison became an outspoken critic of Spong's views on homosexuality and theology.

191. *Journal of the One Hundred Ninety-Seventh (. . .) 1987,* 68.

192. Ibid.

193. Ibid., 97.

194. Ibid., 98–99. Bishop Temple had made a point of leaving the diocesan deputies to General Convention to vote their own consciences.

commission was created with the title, "Diocesan Commission on Human Sexuality," under the chairmanship of the Rev. Rick Belser.[195]

Then, in 1987 appeared a document that, as Allison put it, "'lit my fuse.'"[196] The explosion that came from that fuse was like nothing that had yet appeared in his episcopacy. In September of that year, the attendants in the meeting of the House of Bishops were handed copies of a new report entitled *Sexuality: A Divine Gift, A Sacramental Approach to Human Sexuality and Family Life*. Upon examining the book, Allison instantly erupted in furious outrage and conveyed his extreme displeasure immediately to the diocese which became almost completely engulfed in reaction to the book for a year or more. Allison's frank admission that the book lit his fuse would turn out to be an understatement.

Sexuality had begun as a resolution of the 1982 General Convention calling for the development of "'ways by which the Church can assist its people in their formative years (children through adults) to develop moral and spiritual perspectives in matters relating to sexuality and family life.'"[197] A committee of eleven members was set up called the Task Force on Human Sexuality[198] "assembled from Episcopal parishes, schools and national church staff in cooperation with the National Association of Episcopal Schools."[199] After meeting seven times over three years, they produced the 110-page book, *Sexuality*, along with a twenty-one-page "Leader's Guide" presenting "a teaching process based on dialogue, information and theological reflection; a suggested method for deciding when and what to teach; a guide to help select a leader/teacher for exploring issues of human sexuality and an extensive list of both print and audio-visual resources."[200] The book did affirm that "'lifelong, monogamous marriage is the normal or ideal context for intimate sexual expression between Christians' and says extramarital sex is immoral because it violates the marital bond."[201] However, it added "that some premarital and post-marital 'sexual relationships intend to mirror, at a significant level, the faithfulness of marriage.'"[202] It also asked for people to drop the traditional condemnation of homosexuality. While the book condemned sexual promiscuity and abortion, it called on the Episcopal Church "'to begin a process that will enable Christians to think through new moral and sexual options in the light of new realities.'"[203] The whole idea of the new materials was to open up the Church, particularly young people, to exploring and

---

195. *Journal of the One Hundred Ninety-Eighth (. . .)* 1988, 66.

196. Mattingly, Terry. "Liberal Book on Sexuality Quietly Buried at Episcopal Convention." *The Telegraph* (Nashua NH), July 9, 1988. Mattingly, a reporter for the *Rocky Mountain News*, contributed columns for the Scripps-Howard News Service.

197. "Training Sessions Held on Curriculum." August 6, 1987, Episcopal Press and News, 1962–2006, The Archives of the Episcopal Church, http://www.episcopalarchives.org/cgi-bin/ENS/ENSpress_release.pl?pr_number=87167.

198. For a list of members see: "Training Sessions."

199. "Training Sessions."

200. Ibid.

201. Cornell, George W. "Face Declining Membership: Episcopalians Grapple with Sexuality Stand." Associated Press, July 2, 1988, http://articles.latimes.com/1988-07-02/local/me-5221_1_sexual-activity.

202. Ibid.

203. Ibid.

discussing issues of sexuality in a Christian context. They presented extensive suggested programs and activities along with a long list of print and audio-visual resources that could be used.

Among conservative evangelicals and Anglo-Catholics, the subject of sex was closed. They saw religion, and its accompanying moral standards, as absolute truths handed down through the ages that must be passed intact to future generations. As far as sexuality was concerned, a simple rule applied, sexual relations were acceptable only between a married couple, male and female. All sexual activity outside the heterosexual marriage bond was unchristian and immoral. Therefore, hard line conservatives saw the new *Sexuality* curricula as wasteful at best and downright sinful at worst. They demanded it be withdrawn at once. And, no one was more active in this demand than the feisty bishop of South Carolina.

Allison immediately launched a campaign against *Sexuality* claiming it ignored the Scriptures and the stated policies of the Episcopal Church on sexuality, and presented only the pro-homosexual and liberal sources while omitting viewpoints and writings of traditionally aligned authorities. He said, "This document teaches what is precisely against the traditional moral principles and the stated positions of the Episcopal Church."[204] He was particularly upset by one recommended source, a sound filmstrip called "About Your Sexuality," which showed, critics said, "actors masturbating and performing explicit acts of heterosexual, gay, and lesbian sex."[205] Allison called the filmstrip "'hard-core pornography.'"[206] Labeling the new book "a work of outrageous incompetence and deliberate deceit," Allison banned it from his diocese.[207] At the next Province IV conference of bishops, Allison lobbied for a resolution to ask Presiding Bishop Browning to withdraw the book but was voted down.[208] He was not deterred.

A resolute Allison united the diocesan leadership behind him. The next convention, in Charleston, in February of 1988, was overwhelmingly concerned with *Sexuality*. Allison showed little interest in anything else in his bishop's address railing at length against any attempt to question traditional views on sex. Any change in the old views, he said, would be "a world turned upside down" where we create God in our own image "to turn our 'flesh into the word' of redemption; to close our minds to truth by practicing a false 'openness' and to be seduced into another religion—a religion of our own perceived 'needs.'"[209] Four proposed resolutions were ready for approval backing up the bishop's immovable stand; all passed easily. One, R–5, offered by the Rev. Dow Sanderson, called "Human Sexuality," "implore[d] the Presiding Bishop to cease publishing *Sexuality*:

---

204. Hyer, Marjorie. "Clerical 'Dr. Ruth' Spurs Uproar." *The Bulletin* (Bend, OR), June 24, 1988, A-10.

205. Mattingly, "Liberal Book."

206. McManus, Mike. "Is Sexual Sin Accepted by Episcopalians?" *Times-News* (Hendersonville, NC), April 16, 1988, 20. McManus's columns were syndicated in hundreds of newspapers.

207. Hyer, "Clerical 'Dr. Ruth.'"

208. Virtue, David. "How the House of Bishops Was Used as a Tool of the Gay Lobby." Virtueonline, December 9, 2003, http://listserv.virtueonline.org/pipermail/virtueonline_listserv.virtueonline.org/2003-December/006333.html.

209. *Journal of the One Hundred Ninety-Eighth (. . .)* 1988, 70.

A Divine Gift and withdraw it from circulation."²¹⁰ Another, R–8, "Christian Morality Concerning Sexual Behavior," asked the convention to make a standing resolution of Fleming's R–9 from the 1987 diocesan convention that endorsed sexual relations only for a heterosexual married couple. Two other resolutions bolstered Allison's stand: R–12, "Support for Bishop Allison's Leadership in the Church's Discussion in the Area of Human Sexuality," and R–13, "Publication of 'A World Turned Upside Down,'" in which the sections of the bishop's address on sexuality were to be published for everyone to read in the diocesan newspaper, *Jubilate Deo*.

Allison carried on his campaign as publicly as he could throughout the spring of 1988 being singled out in numerous newspaper articles across the country as a leading spokesman for the conservative opposition. To one reporter he elaborated on his world-turned-upside-down theme: "'The material views the world upside down. The Christian faith teaches that the Word became flesh. They are saying that the flesh IS the word. This publication is portraying sex as the agency of redemption, rather than the object of redemption.'"²¹¹ He did not elaborate on exactly what parts of the book said sex was the agency of redemption. Some of his attention-grabbing remarks were even more puzzling, for instance, "'The publication eliminates guilt as any kind of guardian for innocent people being misused sexually. If we are not going to have guilt, there are not enough police to defend against gang rape and child molestation.'"²¹² One could only wonder at the connection between the new book and gang rape and child molestation.

In fact, *Sexuality* was only meant to be a guide for interested parties to use as they discussed issues of sexuality, particularly among young people. It was offered by the Task Force and the school association. It was not an official publication of the Episcopal Church; it had not been endorsed or accepted in any way by the Episcopal Church as a whole. Even so, conservatives saw this book as an enormous threat, a sort of Trojan horse, that once accepted would corrupt the church from within. They had beaten down the move to extend ordination to "practicing" homosexuals. They could beat this too. They put up a fierce fight that paid off for them. By the spring of 1988, national Church leaders were already backing away from the controversial book. When the Executive Council of the Episcopal Church met in May of 1988, just a few weeks before the General Convention, it reeled under the furious onslaught. It caved to conservative demands and issued a supplemental list of resources more to their liking called *Continuing the Dialogue*. Perhaps trying to head off a showdown that everyone knew was coming in the General Convention, the Council tried to soothe ruffled feathers in conciliatory language: "We the members of the Executive Council of the Episcopal Church do hereby acknowledge and regret the confusion and distress surrounding the publication and distribution of the study document. We further wish to assure the Church that no change has been made in the official policies of the Episcopal Church regarding sexuality."²¹³

210. Ibid., 95–96.
211. McManus, "Is Sexual Sin."
212. Ibid.
213. "Council Addresses World and Church Issues," May 26, 1988, Episcopal Press and News, 1962–2006, The Archives of the Episcopal Church, http://www.episcopalarchives.org/cgi-Bin/ENS/ENSpress_release.pl?pr_number=88106.

Whatever their intention, these words did nothing to deter the conservative critics. Indeed, the Council's wavering on the new book may even have served to encourage the attackers in their resolve to kill it.

A crucial player in Allison's war against *Sexuality* in 1987–88 was a young man newly arrived in the diocese, Kendall S. Harmon. According to his online biography, Harmon was born in Illinois in 1960, grew up in central New Jersey, and "experienced meeting Jesus Christ personally at age eighteen."[214] He was graduated from Bowdoin College summa cum laude, Phi Beta Kappa, with a degree in chemistry, in 1982. He took seminary courses at Regent College, Vancouver, then graduated from Trinity Episcopal School for Ministry in 1987. At that time, he moved to the Diocese of South Carolina to serve as an assistant at Holy Comforter in Sumter. No doubt impressed by the twenty-seven-year-old's zeal, intelligence, and clear-cut evangelical credentials, Bishop Allison enlisted him right away in his crusade against *Sexuality*. The young deacon Harmon took the challenge and apparently eagerly devoted himself to it with all his considerable intellectual powers.

Right away, Harmon threw himself energetically into his new project of attacking *Sexuality*. Within a few weeks, and before the end of the year 1987, he issued a fifty-five-page booklet entitled "A Deeply Disturbing Document: A Comprehensive Critique of the Episcopal Church Curriculum, 'Sexuality: A Divine Gift.'" The title summarized his booklet well. One author called it "a slashing 52-page critique of the document."[215] As Allison, Harmon seemed to think *Sexuality* would encourage perverse sexual behavior: "'In his critique, he writes, suppose one is struggling with his or her 'sexual orientation which is a desire to be involved with young children. You enjoy Holy Communion each week, an experience in which you relate intimately with God, and now you are being told you can enjoy this same intimacy through the sacrament of sexuality.'"[216] The logical conclusion, he suggested, would be to "'encourage you to go out and fulfill your sexual desires. Do we want to be in a church which promotes pedophilia by implying that sexual activity of any sort is a sacrament?'"[217] Exactly how the Episcopal Church would be promoting pedophilia through the new book was left unaddressed. Nevertheless, with the bishop's blessing, Harmon sent out dozens of copies of his "slashing" booklet to Episcopal Church leaders nationwide as part of the campaign to kill *Sexuality*.

As Allison, Harmon gained prominence as a spokesman in the nation-wide anti-*Sexuality* crusade and was soon being quoted in widespread newspaper columns about the controversy. He blasted *Sexuality* as nothing less than "'the most controversial document in the history of the Episcopal Church.'"[218] That caught everyone's attention, and is still doing so. He was quoted in another article being shocked by the filmstrip "About Your Sexuality," saying he was concerned it would cause "'systematic desensitization'" to

---

214. "Kendall: A Brief Biography." April 13, 2010, http://www.kendallharmon.net/t19/index.php/t19/article/29445/.

215. Hyer, "Clerical 'Dr. Ruth.'"

216. Ibid.

217. Ibid.

218. Ibid.

young teenagers.[219] He was quoted elsewhere as saying, "It never mentions sin (. . .). It doesn't mention adultery, child molestation or incest."[220]

As it turned out, the indignant conservatives did not need any sort of great cataclysmic confrontation in the General Convention to get rid of the hated book. The end came as a whimper, not a bang. In the course of the business of the Convention, *Sexuality* was quietly set aside without the least bit of fanfare. Even so, there was no mistaking that the withdrawal of the book was a major victory of the "vertically" inclined conservative minority over the "horizontally" oriented majority in the Episcopal Church. Allison, Harmon, and dozens of other like-minded Churchmen had gained a rare triumph and they did not hesitate to boast of the fact. Allison told the next diocesan convention, "We caused the study to be withdrawn after thousands of dollars had been spent on it."[221] He took full credit for the Diocese of South Carolina. Yet, even then he could not leave the dead horse alone. In his bishop's address to that convention, he once again denounced at great length the book that was now long-gone. Even a year later, Allison was still at it, delivering yet another lengthy diatribe on *Sexuality*, a book he was resolved the diocese would never forget. Nor would he allow them to forget who had led the successful fight. He heaped praise, perhaps a bit belatedly, on Harmon: "Our Diocese has benefited from the considerable labor of Kendall Harmon, whom I have asked to review the contents of the recommended bibliography for our information and judgement. Kendall performed this task diligently and conscientiously."[222] Allison retired as bishop of the diocese in 1990, perhaps still beating his breast at what he saw as a crucial victory in the war of evangelical conservatism against the menacing adversary of liberal modernism in the Episcopal Church. If so, the victory lap was premature. The death of *Sexuality* would soon fade into insignificance as much more important issues gradually built up to produce more serious conflicts in the Church and give the conservatives the fight of their lives. Afterwards, they could only look back nostalgically to relish that fleeting moment of triumph in 1988 when they destroyed *Sexuality: A Divine Gift*.

To be sure, Episcopalian conservatives did not win every battle in the 1980s, far from it. One high-profile fight they lost was their effort to prevent the Rev. Barbara Harris from being ordained a bishop of the Episcopal Church. Harris, an African American woman, was elected by the Diocese of Massachusetts in 1988 to be its next bishop suffragan. She had been a priest for eight years and had served several churches, but was best known, at least among conservatives, as the editor of *Witness*, a publication advocating a strongly "horizontal" religion of social activism. If approved, she would be the first woman bishop of the Episcopal Church and of the Anglican Communion. Since she could become bishop only by gaining consent of the majority of diocesan standing committees in the entire Episcopal Church, conservatives coalesced to block her approval. Fresh off its victory against *Sexuality*, Episcopalians United went to work. A new

---

219. McManus, "Is Sexual Sin."
220. Hyer, "Clerical 'Dr. Ruth.'"
221. *Journal of the One Hundred Ninety-Ninth (. . .)* 1989, 56.
222. *Journal of the Two Hundreth (. . .)* 1990, 66.

group formed to oppose her acceptance called the Episcopal Synod of America.[223] In the Diocese of South Carolina, Kendall Harmon, also fresh off his victory in the *Sexuality* affair, arose to lead the charge against Harris. As the standing committees were considering their consent, Harmon sent a seven-page detailed letter out across the Church entitled, "Hard Questions about Ms. Harris." He listed four questions challenging her fitness to be a bishop: experience (only eight years as a priest), education (no college or seminary degree), "extremist" views (as editor of *Witness* she supported LGBT equality and rights), and attitude (angry, vitriolic).[224] Note that within the four questions, the only policy that Harmon singled out was Harris's stand for homosexual rights. This time, Harmon and the right-wing coalition failed. A majority of standing committees voted to approve Harris's election. Conservatives could only look on with chagrin as Barbara Harris was ordained bishop suffragan of Massachusetts on February 11, 1989. Another barrier had fallen but also another reason arose for evermore disgruntled conservatives to oppose the trajectory of the Episcopal Church.

Even though they lost the fight on "Ms. Harris," Episcopalian conservatives could still feel confident they were upholding the wall of "orthodoxy" in the Church against the flood of dangerous "reappraisers" as they liked to call their liberal-minded adversaries. Keeping the ordination of "practicing" homosexuals off the table and killing the book on sexuality were not small accomplishments. Nevertheless, they must have sensed a rising threat of dangers all around them. Allison certainly did. In his swansong address to the annual diocesan convention, in 1990, he directed his attention once again to his favorite theological nemesis, Bishop John Spong of Newark, who had just hit the news for ordaining an openly homosexual man. "Bishop Spong's action in ordaining a practicing homosexual has brought great discredit to the Episcopal Church," Allison opined.[225] Moreover, the retiring bishop worried that something was substantially wrong in the very heart of the Church: "Serious theological errors involving the doctrine of the Trinity are implied by some misuse of 'inclusive language.' The essential uniqueness of Jesus Christ is increasingly denied. Perhaps the most serious symptom of the neglect of doctrine can be seen in the way we as a Church have dealt with the matter of sexual ethics."[226] One could only wonder what he meant by the last line considering that the Church had denied ordination of open homosexuals and had withdrawn the book on sexuality, in no small part on his demand. Moreover, while well-publicized liberals, as Spong, grabbed headlines, they spoke only for themselves and not the Episcopal Church. Any change in the official doctrines and dogma of the Episcopal Church would have to go through the General Convention. In fact, there was no change in beliefs about the Trinity or Jesus Christ or in any other doctrine of the Episcopal Church.[227]

---

223. "Forward in Faith North America," Wikipedia, http://eb.wikipedia.org/wiki/Forward_in_Faith _North_America.

224. McManus, Mike. "Episcopalians Choose Wrong Woman for Job." *Spartanburg Herald-Journal* (Spartanburg, SC), December 10, 1988.

225. *Journal of the Two Hundreth (. . .)* 1990, 66.

226. Ibid., 64.

227. Allison's implication that liberals were redefining basic doctrines of the Episcopal Church along heretical lines would reverberate through the schism. After the schism, this became the official

Allison retired in 1990, at the relatively young age of sixty-three to have more time to read, contemplate, research and write about the academic theology that had always been his first love. Despite his rather somber mood in his last diocesan convention, he must have felt a sense of satisfaction at having guided the diocese for eight years and waging well the good fight for his deeply-held convictions against the stronger forces of those he believed were foolishly diminishing the old religion of the Episcopal Church. Administration and internal development, however, were not theologian Allison's strong points, much in contrast to his predecessor. Allison seemed to be more concerned with promoting ideological purity than running the everyday affairs of the diocese. The diocesan statistics suggested this. For the first time since the Civil War, the Diocese of South Carolina sustained a significant decline in membership and income. Baptized membership in the Diocese fell three percent in Allison's tenure, 1982–1990, from 25,096 to 24,221. Communicant numbers declined 4 percent, 19,188 to 18,418. Income fell a drastic 22 percent, from $2,400,064 to $1,865,338.[228]

It is fair at this point to ask, what difference did Bishop Allison make in the history of the Diocese of South Carolina? What was his legacy for the diocese? What role did he play in the history of the schism in South Carolina? Before addressing these, it is useful to review the general divisions in the make-up of the Episcopal Church, indeed in Anglicanism as a whole. There were three roughly defined parties: evangelicals, Anglo-Catholics, and, for want of a better term, "generalists." The first two tended to be ideological, that is, with sharply defined and held views of religion. Both emphasized personal redemption theology but in different approaches. The generalists, who were the majority of the Episcopal Church, in contrast, tended to be non-dogmatic, tolerant of different views, and blended personal redemption and social outreach. As we have seen it was this faction that carried the Episcopal Church into and through its great period of social reform after the Second World War and made it a strongly "horizontal" church committed to activism for social reform, for African Americans, women, homosexuals, and others.

Bishop Temple was of the broad middle generalist school. He was a practical-minded consensus builder who focused on developing the diocese by internal improvements while keeping it comfortably in the mainstream of the Episcopal Church. As we have seen, he did this with great difficulty but also with great success. He left the diocese larger, stronger, more unified, and well-identified as a diocese of the Episcopal Church. Bishop Allison, on the other hand, was an ideologist, an ardent evangelical who had already defined himself as a distinctly conservative academic theologian. His main concern as bishop seemed to be to promote his concept of theological and moral purity in the Episcopal Church. As bishop, he could use the diocese as a platform to do that in the wider Church. By the time of his episcopacy, race, women and prayer book were dying issues. The only one left unresolved in the Episcopal Church was homosexuality. Thus, evangelicals as Allison, with their socially conservative Anglo-Catholic allies, made the

---

explanation of the cause of the schism issued by the independent diocese.

228. *Journal of the Two Hundred and First Annual Meeting of the Convention, Cathedral Church, Charleston, Proceedings of the Convention, February 21–23, 1991.* Charleston, SC: the diocese, 1991, 247, 126–127.

issue of homosexuality their last stand for "orthodoxy" as they called it. They poured all their energy into the effort to preserve whatever they believed remained of moral purity in the Episcopal Church. In his zeal, Bishop Allison guided the Diocese of South Carolina on a decidedly right-wing turn, defining the diocese as a bulwark against the encroachment of what conservatives saw as sinful homosexuality. He brought in all the clergy he could from Trinity seminary leaving behind him an indelible and permanent ideologically conservative phalanx in the diocese. Allison won enough victories to feel he had accomplished much in his goal, even if the internal state of the diocese declined and weakened. Overall, he left the diocese with one great legacy: Ideological purity takes precedence over institutional loyalty. He firmly established this as the ongoing underlying principle to guide the Diocese of South Carolina after him; and it would be the one that would increasingly propel the diocese all the way to the schism, twenty-two years later.

Bishop Allison after 1990

Allison ended his episcopacy in 1990 as his bright young protégé Kendall Harmon headed off in his mentor's footsteps for a three-year sojourn in Oxford to pursue a doctor's degree in theology.[229] Once asked why he retired so soon, Allison said: "'the reason for my early retirement was, and has been, to devote myself to writing, teaching, speaking, publishing and debating in an attempt to turn the Episcopal Church's teaching towards a more classical Christianity.'"[230] Already a prolific writer of books and articles, Allison published numerous works after 1990 including *The Cruelty of Heresy: An Affirmation of Christian Orthodoxy* in 1994 and *Trust in an Age of Arrogance* in 2009. "Allison's books argue strongly for Christian orthodoxy, and specifically for Christian pastors and teachers to be focused upon grace and justification by faith alone as the key doctrines of the Christian Church."[231] *Cruelty* has been summarized as: "Ancient heresies have modern expressions that influence our churches and culture, creating cruel dilemmas for today's Christian in the form of error, sin, and various distortions on orthodox faith."[232]

However much he wrote, Allison became known after 1990 not so much for what he said but for what he did to challenge the structure of the Episcopal Church. The beginnings of Allison's controversial actions can be traced back at least to 1992. At that time, he attended a meeting of the House of Bishops at Kanuga, North Carolina, when a question arose for discussion, "Why are we dysfunctional?" Allison shot back the answer was simple: *apostasy*. He went on to denounce the work of Episcopalian writers such as the "lesbian priest" Carter Heyward. When it came time for Communion, Allison

---

229. "In 1993 Kendall was awarded his Doctor of Philosophy from Oxford University, defending a dissertation on some twentieth-century explorations of the doctrine of hell." "Kendall: A Brief Biography."

230. McIntosh, *Spiritual Journal of St. Philip's*, 179.

231. "C. FitzSimons Allison," http://en.wikipedia.org/wiki/C._FitzSimons_Allison.

232. "Christopher Fitzsimons Allison," Prabook, http://prabook.org/web/person-view.Html?profiled=583227.

showed his displeasure at the church's "apostasy" by refusing the bread and wine. From there his acts of personal defiance against the Episcopal Church only escalated.[233]

After his retirement, Allison continued living in the diocese of South Carolina and giving encouragement to conservative Episcopalian groups. On September 8, 1997, he attended the "First Promise" conference at All Saints' Church, Pawleys Island, hosted by the rector Charles H. Murphy III, which issued a statement declaring that the Episcopal Church had departed from the doctrine, discipline, and worship of the Christ and appealed to overseas Anglican bishops for aid.[234] For years thereafter, Allison served as one of the three "episcopal advisors" of First Promise.[235] Some of the leading participants later formed the Anglican Mission in America, a dissident group of Episcopalians that soon left the Church to form a separate denomination. In 1997, however, First Promise did not present much of a platform for Allison.

Two years later, Allison was in the news again, this time actively seeking a highly visible showdown with Episcopal Church officials. In May of 1999, he went to Brocton, Massachusetts, to conduct a service for dissident congregants of St. Paul's Church and he did so without the permission of the local bishop, M. Thomas Shaw, in disregard of the canons of the Episcopal Church. After the unauthorized service, Shaw let it be known he would not pursue the matter and Allison returned home. It might have been that Allison's ultimate goal was to gain a public forum to denounce not Shaw but his favorite adversary, John Spong, who had recently published his "Twelve Theses" that Allison opposed. If so, Allison was to be disappointed doubly. Indeed, he never got his great debate with Spong which must have been frustrating. In fact, this author has seen no evidence to suggest that Spong ever paid any attention to Allison.

Unable to generate much publicity by flaunting Church law in Massachusetts, Allison charged headlong into a move he knew would be guaranteed to bring him plenty of news coverage. In January of 2000, he journeyed to Singapore, in the Anglican province of South East Asia, to participate in what he knew would be an earthquake event. On January 29, he was one of six bishops[236] to consecrate as bishops for South East Asia and Rwanda, two Episcopal priests, his new friend, Charles H. Murphy, III, the rector of All Saints of Pawleys Island and head of First Promise, and his old friend, John H. Rodgers, Jr., dean emeritus of Trinity seminary. The event occurred at St. Andrew's Cathedral in Singapore. If Allison expected this highly visible provocation to give him the great public platform for him to make his case for orthodoxy, he was to be disappointed, again. While there was an abundance of reaction to these "irregular" consecrations, there was no retribution against Allison. No move meant no platform.

233. Mattingly, Terry. "The Time for Broken Communion?" www.patheos.com/blogs/tmatt/1999/05/the-time-for-broken-communion/.

234. "First Promise." http://theroadtoemmaus.org/RdLb/32Ang/Epis/AmiA/1stProm.htm.

235. "Pivotal Moment Bishop Charles Murphy Talks about his Consecration in Singapore." *The Living Church*, March 26, 2000, The Living Church, 1995–2001, The Archives of the Episcopal Church, http://www.episcopalarchives.org/cgi-bin/the_living_church/TLCarticle.pl?volume=2208&issue=13&article_id=1.

236. Two primates: Moses Tay, Archbishop of South East Asia, and Emmanuel Kolini, Archbishop of Rwanda; one active bishop, John Ruchyahana, of Rwanda; and three retired bishops, Allison, Alex Dickson, former bishop of West Tennessee, and David Pytches, former bishop of Chile, Bolivia and Peru.

Meanwhile the two new "irregular" bishops, Murphy and Rodgers, moved ahead and by August of 2000 formed the "Anglican Mission in America" under the auspices of the Anglican provinces of South East Asia and Rwanda. They gave as their impetus for this the pro-homosexual agenda of the Episcopal Church's General Convention of 2000.[237] In an effort to serve the numerous disgruntled conservative Episcopal parishes around the country, they decided they needed more missionary bishops. In June of 2001, Allison went to Denver to serve as one of eight bishops[238] to consecrate four more bishops for the new Anglican Mission in America. One of the four was Thaddeus R. Barnum from All Saints of Pawleys Island. To no one's surprise, the new consecrations "attracted considerable media attention."[239] Once again, as the year before, all the flurry of media reports did not produce an opportunity for Allison personally to gain his long-sought spotlight. The Episcopal Church's Executive Council met in February of 2002 and passed a resolution unanimously decrying the consecrations as potentially schismatic. As far as retired Episcopal bishops who had participated in the consecrations were concerned, the Council refused to call names and reprimanded them only mildly: "We consider bishops of our church [Allison and Dickson] who participate in any irregular ordinations to the episcopate to be in direct violation of their ordination vows (. . .) as well as its constitutions and canons."[240] No action was taken against Allison for any of these irregular consecrations. But alas, yet once again, no action meant no platform.

If Allison's goal upon his retirement in 1990 had been to turn the Episcopal Church back toward "orthodoxy," he must have been disappointed after a dozen years of trying his best. In fact, he never got a great opportunity to make his case to the church and the world. Although aging, he remained apparently as youthful, energetic, and sharp as ever. He tried no more overtly provocative acts as the irregular consecrations, but he did continue in quieter ways encouraging "orthodox" groups and joining with like-minded bishops regularly to protest the policies and procedures of the Episcopal Church they found objectionable. For instance, on March 12, 2002, he was one of nineteen at the House of Bishops meeting in Camp Allen, Texas, to sign a rather poignant appeal to the majority: "We solemnly plead that this House not leave this gathering without an agreement (. . .) protecting the sensibilities, integrity and place of those whose 'traditional orthodox faith' renders them unable to accept the innovations of the past three decades."[241]

---

237. "Murphy and Rodgers Launch Traditionalist Anglican Mission in America." Episcopal News Service, August 22, 2000, Episcopal Press and News 1962–2006, The Archives of the Episcopal Church, http://www.episcopalarchives.org/cgi-bin/ENS/ENSpress_release.pl?pr_number=2000-117.

238. Datuk Yong Ping Chung, Archbishop of South East Asia; Emmanuel M. Kolini, Archbishop of Rwanda; John Rucyahana and Venuste Mutiganda, bishops of Rwanda; Charles Murphy; John Rodgers; and retired bishops Allison and Alex Dickson.

239. Totman, Schuyler. "AMiA Consecrates Four More Bishops." *The Living Church*, July 15, 2001, The Living Church 1995–2001, The Archives of the Episcopal Church, http://www.episcopalarchives.org/cgi-bin/the_living_church/TLCarticle.pl?volume=223&issue=3&article_id=11.

240. "Executive Council Calls AMiA Schismatic, 'Untenable.'" Anglican News Service, March 5, 2002, http://www.anglicannews.org/news/2002/03/executive-council-calls-amia-schismatic-untenable.aspx.

241. "An Appeal for the Preservation of Godly Union." March 12, 2002, http://www.americananglican.org/an-appeal-for-the-preservation-of-godly-union.

The Episcopal Church did not completely ignore Allison's provocative actions. In March of 2004, the House of Bishops censured Allison along with Maurice Benitez, William Cox, Alex Dickson, and William Wantland.[242] In response, Allison and the other four issued a blistering statement telling the bishops they "cannot tell the difference between heretical teaching and the Nicene Creed."[243] Finally, in defiance they told the bishops: "We stand in solidarity with the 21 global Anglican provinces who have either, 'impaired or broken communion' with the Episcopal Church" and promised to go right ahead with their chosen actions.[244] The breach between Allison and the majority of Episcopal bishops remained.

Allison continued living in the Diocese of South Carolina and participating in the various diocesan events. His wife Martha had inherited a former rice plantation, "Rosemont," near Georgetown.[245] This gave Allison easy access to Charleston. Also, for several years after his retirement in 1990, Allison kept a home on Water Street in Charleston.[246] In the run-up to the schism of 2012 he was not in the inner circle of the ruling clique, but he remained an influential and generally well-respected "elder statesman" speaking his ever-sharp mind whenever the occasion allowed. He was an enthusiastic backer of Mark Lawrence in the election controversies of 2006–07 and remained one of his most vocal supporters thereafter. At diocesan clergy meetings, he could be counted on to give the first ringing endorsement after every address of Bishop Lawrence. He remained a stalwart apologist for the majority side of the diocese during and after the schism of 2012 never holding back his thoughts, even well into his 80s, and apparently never changing the views he had held so firmly for so many decades.

Counter-Revolution and Bishop Edward L. Salmon, Jr., 1990–2002

Edward Lloyd Salmon, Jr.

Edward Lloyd Salmon, Jr., followed Allison as bishop of the Diocese of South Carolina and served until Mark Lawrence arrived in 2008. He was born in Natchez, Mississippi, on January 30, 1934. Salmon was graduated from the University of the South (Sewanee) in 1956 and from the Virginia Theological Seminary in 1960. He was ordained a deacon in June of 1960 and a priest in March of 1961 in the Diocese of Arkansas. From 1960 to 1989, he was a parochial priest in several churches in Arkansas and Missouri, last at St. Michael and St. George in Clayton, Missouri, 1978–89. He made a reputation for himself as an outstanding preacher and a reasonably-minded conservative effective at parish leadership. With his background of practical local administration, Salmon stood in stark contrast to his predecessor who was an academic theologian with limited parochial experience.

242. "5 Senior Bishops Respond to House of Bishops' Censure." American Anglican Council, March 25, 2004, http:www.freerepublic.com/focus/f-religion/1105180/posts.

243. Ibid.

244. Ibid.

245. Zeigler, Eugene N., Jr. *When Conscience and Power Meet, A Memoir.* Columbia, SC: University of South Carolina Press, 2008, 310.

246. Ibid., 311.

Although he had no previous connection to South Carolina, Salmon was the clear first choice to follow Allison. He made a remarkably positive impression in the preliminaries to the voting. He was elected by a special diocesan convention on September 9, 1989, winning easily on the first ballot. He won 61 clergy votes (48 needed) and 30 and 1/2 lay votes (29 and 1/2 needed). Obviously, Salmon had already been selected as the next bishop beforehand by the clergy.[247] He was consecrated bishop on February 24, 1990, at the conclusion of the annual diocesan convention, with the Most Rev. Edmond Lee Browning, Presiding Bishop of the Episcopal Church, serving as chief consecrator and former Presiding Bishop, John M. Allin, as preacher. The service was held before one thousand and four hundred people in the Citadel Square Baptist Church, in Charleston, the cathedral being unavailable following Hurricane Hugo damage.

According to the chancellor at the time, Nick Zeigler, Allison and Salmon could not have been more different in personality. He wrote: "Whereas Fitz is mercurial, energetic, and combative, Salmon is deliberate, contemplative, and conciliatory. Fitz has the jocular manner of an extrovert: Salmon's bearing has an aspect of old-fashioned gravitas."[248]

Allison and Salmon were the diocesan bishops but they were not the only bishops in the Diocese of South Carolina at this time. George Edward Haynsworth served as Assistant Bishop from December 1, 1985, to December 31, 1990. A few years after Haynsworth retired, the diocese decided to establish, for the first time, the position of bishop suffragan. William J. Skilton was elected, serving from March 2, 1996, to December 31, 2006. His service of consecration at the Cathedral of St. Luke and St. Paul in Charleston was conducted by the Presiding Bishop, Browning, who was chief consecrator. Skilton was born in Cuba in 1940, and served churches in the Dominican Republic for years. As rector of St. Thomas's Church in North Charleston, he became "known throughout the diocese for his emphasis on mission and the need for unity among Christians of all races."[249]

The Return of the Issue of Homosexuality, 1990–1996

Although the 1979 General Convention of the Episcopal Church passed a resolution disapproving of the ordination of "practicing" homosexuals, the issue of homosexuality did not go away. In fact, the wording of that resolution left some people wondering if the Church had really outlawed the ordination of homosexuals at all. The resolution read: "We believe it is not appropriate for this Church to ordain a practicing homosexual." What did "not appropriate" mean? Was this a ban or not? People could interpret the language of the resolution in different ways and they did. Bishop Spong was one who interpreted it only as advisory rather than mandatory. Besides, the resolution was not canon law and was never made into canon law. The General Conventions through the 1980s did not reverse the 1979 resolution, but they kept discussing the issue of homosexuality and passing numerous resolutions supporting homosexuals in general. Even

---

247. *Journal of the Two Hundreth* (. . .) 1990, 154.
248. Zeigler, *When Conscience*, 311.
249. Harmon, Kendall. "First Suffragan for South Carolina." *The Living Church*, March 24, 1996, The Living Church 1995–2001, The Archives of the Episcopal Church, http://www.episcopalarchives.org/cgi-bin/the_living_church/TLCarticle.pl?volume=212&issue=12&article_id=12.

so, everyone had to recognize that the "anti" forces had the upper hand under the 1979 resolution. This sort of uneasy stalemate continued until 1989 when events began to occur to force the unresolved issue front and center again.

The question of whether non-celibate homosexuals should be allowed into the Holy Orders of the Episcopal Church started toward resolution much in the same way women's ordination had done, by proponents employing civil disobedience, that is, by defiantly staging "illegal," or at least "irregular" ordinations to force the issue. Just as numerous church leaders had refused to accept the majority's early opposition to women's ordination, once again, many leaders refused to agree that the Church should forbid the ordination of "practicing" homosexuals. A new Presiding Bishop, Edmond Browning, arrived in 1986 declaring: "'I want to be very clear: this church of ours is open to all—there shall be no outcasts—the convictions and the hopes of all will be honored.'"[250] Bishop Spong of Newark, Allison's *bête noire*, took the lead in challenging the status quo on homosexuality. In February of 1988, he approved a policy of offering church blessings for same-sex unions, the first Episcopal bishop to do so.[251] At the same time, eagle-eyes in the Diocese of South Carolina's annual meeting reported that the Episcopal Divinity School in Cambridge, Massachusetts, was about to graduate a man, Robert Williams, listing a "'male spouse.'"[252]

The next year, 1989, marked the beginning of a chain of events that would eventually produce resolution of the issue of ordination for non-celibate homosexuals. On December 16, 1989, in Hoboken, New Jersey, Spong ordained Robert Williams (the one who had listed a male spouse), an open homosexual.[253] The Diocese of South Carolina, led by its righteously indignant bishop, immediately exploded in rage. When the diocesan convention met two months later, Allison had plenty of harsh words for Spong and called on the presiding bishop and the House of Bishops to censure the renegade bishop of Newark.[254] Two resolutions were ready to be presented to the diocesan convention; both passed. One, R-2, "The Recent Ordination of a Practicing Homosexual in the Diocese of Newark," was presented by Richard Archer, Richard Belser, Holland Clark, Terrell Glenn, Kendall Harmon, and Charles Murphy III.[255] It "deplore[d] the ordination of Robert Williams by Bishop Spong as a violation of the teaching of scripture and the Episcopal Church," and went on to plead with "the House of Bishops to take the necessary disciplinary action in responding to Bishop Spong's willful misuse of his Episcopal authority."[256] Another resolution, R-9 carried the same title as the earlier one. It said "The Diocese of South Carolina call[s] upon the Presiding Bishop to issue a clear

---

250. Sumner, *Episcopal Church's History*, 177.

251. "The Episcopal Church and Homosexuality in the U.S.: Timeline." Outhistory, http://outhistory.org/exhibits/show/religion_homosex/episcopal.

252. *Journal of the Two Hundreth (. . .)* 1990, 66.

253. Williams was ordained a deacon and a priest but had a rocky relationship with Spong. Williams died in December of 1992 of an AIDS-related illness. "The Episcopal Church and Homosexuality in the U.S."

254. *Journal of the Two Hundreth (. . .)* 1990, 96. Several times, people made complaints against Spong to the House of Bishops, but the bishops refused to take any official action against Spong.

255. Ibid.

256. Ibid., 97.

and unambiguous statement of the official position of the Church regarding the ordination of practicing homosexuals," and went on to "call upon the Presiding Bishop and House of Bishops to censure the Bishop of Newark."[257] In their outrage, apparently the convention delegates missed the inconsistency in these two resolutions, one declaring a teaching of the Church and the other calling on the Church to declare a teaching. At any rate, South Carolina registered its displeasure loudly and clearly.

Kendall Harmon, assistant at Holy Comforter in Sumter, arose as one of the most outspoken critics in the diocese of the ordination of non-celibate homosexuals. In February of 1990, before the annual meeting of the convention, he posted in *Jubilate Deo*, the diocesan newspaper, an editorial entitled "Should a Practicing Homosexual Be Ordained?" in which he strongly denounced Williams's ordination and the Presiding Bishop's failure to intervene.[258] Harmon declared Bishop Spong had "grievously violated" the Church's teaching on sexuality.[259] In April, he posted in the same publication a book review of *Dirt, Greed, and Sex* by L. William Countryman, a professor at the Divinity School of the Pacific. The book questioned numerous scriptural references to sexuality; and Harmon denounced it as "dangerous since its deeply flawed thesis leads to several modern applications which would further damage the church's witness in a sexually confused society."[260]

The Williams affair was just the beginning of a new crisis on the issue of homosexuality. On September 30, 1990, the Rt. Rev. Walter Cameron Righter, Assistant Bishop of Newark, ordained to the diaconate Barry Stopfel "a practicing homosexual, living in a sexual partnership with a person of the same sex prior to ordination and intending to continue in that relationship after ordination."[261] The next year, Spong ordained to the priesthood Stopfel who went on to serve St. George's in Maplewood, New Jersey. Also in 1991, the Rt. Rev. Ronald H. Haines, bishop of Washington, reportedly ordained an open lesbian.[262] In 1993, Integrity, the Episcopal gay-rights group estimated that more than fifty homosexuals had been ordained in the Episcopal Church since 1977, more than in any other denomination.[263]

The highly-publicized ordinations of open homosexuals guaranteed that the next General Convention, meeting in Phoenix in 1991, would have to face the crisis head on whether the delegates wanted to or not. Attendees reported it was the most raucous and acrimonious meeting of the Convention in memory. Reports from the closed House of Bishops described shouting matches and time-outs. As one report put it, "Sometimes the temperature of the debate inside the Phoenix Civic Plaza during the

257. Ibid., 100.
258. Harmon, Kendall. "Should a Practicing Homosexual Be Ordained?" *Jubilate Deo* (Diocese of South Carolina), February 1990.
259. Ibid.
260. Harmon, Kendall. "Book Review: Dirt Greed, and Sex." *Jubilate Deo* (Diocese of South Carolina), April 1990.
261. "The Protestant Episcopal Church in the United States of America, in the Court for the Trial of a Bishop." May 16, 1996, http://www.rci.rutgers.edu/~lcrew/decision.html.
262. "The Episcopal Church and Homosexuality in the U.S."
263. Ibid.

10-day meeting matched the sizzling heat outside—particularly as the church turned to sexuality issues."[264] Conservatives were well-prepared. They complained in the House of Bishops against Spong, Righter, and Haines, but, to their disappointment, no censures were forthcoming. Instead the bishops and the deputies hammered out a rather tortured resolution trying to satisfy both sides and really settling nothing. Resolution A104 was a lengthy and strange patchwork of initiatives. First it declared "that the teaching of the Episcopal Church is that physical sexual expression is appropriate only within the lifelong monogamous 'union of husband and wife in heart, body, and mind.'"[265] The second part called on the church to work to "reconcile the discontinuity between this teaching and the experience of many members of this body."[266] This implied that homosexuals could not agree with part one, but the exact meaning of this part was not clarified. The next part was an odd lament that General Convention "confesses our failure to lead and to resolve this discontinuity."[267] This implied that the convention could not find a consensus on homosexuality. This was stating the obvious. The next part called on dioceses and congregations to "enter into dialogue" on sexuality and submit reports. The last part called on the House of Bishops for help. It asked the bishops to prepare a pastoral teaching on homosexuality by the next triennial convention. In the end, the General Convention of 1991 reaffirmed traditional marriage but settled nothing else. In fact, nothing in the peculiar resolution, A104, really addressed the overriding issue of the day, that is: Should non-celibate homosexuals be allowed ordination in the Episcopal Church?

The reality of the situation at the end of the General Convention of 1991 was that the "anti" forces had lost their edge, and the momentum was beginning to shift to the "pro" side. The House of Bishops adjourned without either censuring the three defiant bishops or declaring the controversial ordinations invalid, as they had done in 1974 in reaction to the first "irregular" ordinations of women. By default, the bishops, and by extension the Convention, had given de facto recognition of the ordinations of non-celibate homosexuals. There was nothing at that point to stop more ordinations of openly homosexual clergy. This new reality was not lost on the conservative forces which now sought ways to respond to what they could only see as a most disappointing if not alarming turn of events.

Perhaps the best organized and strongest "anti" organization at that point was the Episcopal Synod of America which met on November 8, 1991, in Fresno, California, in the Diocese of San Joaquin and set up a "missionary diocese" in the Episcopal Church. Its goal was to unite the conservative and dissident parishes across the country into a non-geographic diocese. Such a thing, naturally, would be in flagrant disregard of the Constitution and Canons of the Episcopal Church and therefore completely unacceptable to Church leaders. Presiding Bishop Browning traveled to Ft. Worth on November

264. "Highlights of Convention." *Jubilate Deo* (Diocese of South Carolina), September 1991.

265. "1991–A104, Affirm the Church's Teaching on Sexual Expression, Commission Congregational Dialogue, and Direct Bishops to Prepare a Pastoral Teaching." The Acts of Convention, The Archives of the Episcopal Church, http://www.episcopalarchives.org/cgi-bin/acts/acts_resolution.pl?resolution=1991-A104.

266. Ibid.

267. Ibid.

18 and asked the ESA officials not to implement the plan, telling them it was "'uncanonical and anyone identifying with it would be outside the Episcopal Church.'"[268] George Carey, the Archbishop of Canterbury, said it was "'potentially schismatic.'"[269]

The South Carolina diocesan convention meeting of March 1992, was the first after the emotional General Convention of 1991, and was to be almost as tumultuous as the Phoenix meeting itself. It was described by Nick Zeigler, the chancellor.[270] The Rev. Charles Murphy, of All Saints, Pawleys Island, was chair of the Resolutions Committee. He was well-known as a highly vocal critic of the Church's actions on homosexuality. Bishop Salmon did not want any resolution at that time on sexuality. In Zeigler's words, "Bishop Salmon had tried to prevent the diocesan conventions from considering and debating resolutions of a political nature."[271] In his address to the convention, Salmon had stressed how much the House of Bishops was working to heal the rifts in the Church. The Resolutions Committee had nine proposed resolutions to present to the convention. "It was the understanding that all nine would be tabled in order to prevent what the newspapers called a 'shootout at the OK Corral.'"[272] The first eight proposed resolutions came up and, sure enough, each was tabled. Then, the ninth arrived. It was a scarcely veiled denunciation of homosexuality. One motion to table was voted down. Another motion to table was voted down. Then chaos broke out: "the delegates got more emotional and began shouting out their votes on various motions and shouting at each other as the debate continued."[273] An exasperated Salmon chastised the assembly: "'It makes enemies of people and it has just done that in this room. The amount of feeling people have about this has totally transformed this convention.'"[274] After much discussion on what to do, the Resolutions Committee presented its proposed resolutions and the ninth one passed. It was resolution, R-10, "House of Bishops' Dialogue," declaring: "The Diocese of South Carolina urges affirmation of the following points (. . .) 4. Genital sexual expression is to be understood and taught as God's gift exclusively for men and women united in Holy Matrimony."[275] The resolution really had no significance except to express the majority opinion of the diocese. Chancellor Zeigler wrote later that the bad blood between Salmon and Murphy had actually started at the Phoenix Convention of 1991 when the two broke into arguments.[276] As one will see, Murphy became an ever more prickly thorn in Salmon's flesh from then on.

With the memory of the tumultuous 1991 Phoenix Convention still fresh in mind, Church people could only look on in uneasy anticipation at the approaching 1994 Convention to meet in Indianapolis. Once again, the interface of the Episcopal Church and

268. "ESA Establishes Missionary Diocese." *Jubilate Deo* (Diocese of South Carolina), January 1992.
269. Ibid.
270. Zeigler, *When Conscience*, 313-15.
271. Ibid., 313.
272. Ibid., 314.
273. Ibid.
274. Ibid., 314.
275. *Journal of the Two Hundred and Second Annual Meeting of the Convention, Grace Church, Charleston, Proceedings of the Convention, March* 13-14, 1992. Charleston, SC: the diocese, 1992, 155.
276. Zeigler, *When Conscience*, 319.

homosexuality was bound to be overriding issue of the day. Would this meeting handle this explosive issue any more effectively? Had the Church really become dysfunctional as the bishops had mused in their 1992 conference? Was it too much to hope the Convention could finally agree on a definitive policy on the ordination of non-celibate homosexual persons? Had indeed the momentum shifted from the "anti" to the "pro" side?

The most highly anticipated item everyone expected to appear in the Indianapolis convention was the House of Bishops' pastoral teaching on human sexuality that had been commissioned by the last General Convention. It was developed over three years in numerous private meetings going through several drafts, all in secrecy.[277] Several weeks before the convention, however, Episcopalians United leaked the last two drafts of the pastoral.[278] The conservatives arrived in Indianapolis well-prepared to launch a counter-attack brandishing a fresh one-page document entitled, "An Affirmation In Response to the Proposed Pastoral of the House of Bishops Concerning Human Sexuality," and signed by 106 bishops including three from South Carolina (Salmon, Haynsworth, Allison). "Affirmation" made three points: 1-"Marriage is a union of husband and wife, one man and one woman," 2-"Sexual relationships between members of the same sex are also a denial of God's plan, and cannot be condoned by the Church," and 3-"Neither the Church nor its bishops have the authority to compromise in principle, or give approval in practice, to standards less or other than our God has given us."[279] The conservative bishops "claimed the pastoral was a substantial departure from traditional biblical Christianity.[280] Thus, approximately a third of all bishops denounced the pastoral in advance, made it clear they flatly rejected homosexual behavior, and announced their views were not open to "compromise." The "Affirmation" document did not explicitly oppose the ordination of homosexuals although it did imply such in its three articles. The question at hand: Would the conservatives be able to kill this new pastoral teaching as they had *Sexuality* in 1988?

The situation had changed in the six years since Allison and his allies had been able to force out a book on human sexuality. Now, the advocates of homosexual rights were better organized and resolved to go to the mat against their adversaries. The left wing scrambled to fight back with their own position statement. This one was written by Bishop Spong, dated August 25, the second day of the convention and signed by 55 bishops at the General Convention. It came to be known as "A Statement in Koinonia," and was eventually endorsed by 90 bishops and 144 deputies. It made three major points: 1-that homosexuality is "morally neutral," 2-that gays and lesbians in committed relationships should be honored, and 3-that ordination should be open to homosexuals.[281] The opposing documents of 1994, the right-wing "Affirmation" and the left-wing "Koinonia,"

---

277. Thrall, James. "Sexuality Issues Continue to Provoke Debate." Episcopal News Service, Episcopal Press and News 1962–2006, The Archives of the Episcopal Church, http://www.episcopalarchives.org/cgi-bin/ENS/ENSpress_release.pl?pr_number=94136.

278. Ibid.

279. "An Affirmation." *Jubilate Deo* (Diocese of South Carolina), October/November 1994.

280. Thrall, "Sexuality Issues."

281. "A Statement in Koinonia." August 25, 1994, http://www.integrityusa.org/archive/samesexblessings/a_statement_in_koinonia.htm.

summarized well the polar opposite positions on the issue of homosexuality and did so really for the first time. Judging from the numbers of bishops signing the two "wing" documents, the Episcopal Church at that point was divided roughly in thirds, one-third opposing rights for homosexuals, one-third favoring, and one-third neutral. Rather than try to mediate between the opposing sides and find a consensus, which at that moment was probably impossible given the rigidity of the views, the House of Bishops resolved to present its original document that it now called a "pastoral study document" rather than a pastoral teaching, and to do so without appending either "Affirmation" or "Koinonia" to it.[282] The upshot was that the Convention set up a twelve-member committee to continue dialogue on human sexuality.

While the bishop's "pastoral study document" settled nothing, and led only to more seemingly endless "dialogue" on sexuality, the Convention moved to several proposed resolutions that did deal directly with the issue of homosexuality. The most important were D007 and C020 that revised the canons of the Church to open ordination to homosexuals. As C020 put it, Church law would now read: "No person shall be denied rights, status, or an equal place in the life, worship, and governance of this Church because of race, color, ethnic origin, national origin, marital status, sex, sexual orientation, disabilities or age, except as otherwise specified by Canon."[283] These were easily adopted with amazingly little debate.[284] Suddenly, there it was. Sexual orientation was added to the list under which no one could be denied ordination in the Episcopal Church. In a quiet if backhanded manner, the Church had officially opened its Holy Orders to homosexual persons and, moreover, did so without comment on celibacy.

Apparently, it happened so subtly that the large and loud conservative minority was caught unawares. Back home, Bishop Salmon published a long and detailed report on the Convention in the diocesan newspaper describing what he saw as the ten most important accomplishments of the Convention without ever once mentioning the revision of the canon to open ordination to homosexuals.[285] Since Salmon was certainly knowledgeable of the canonical change, one can only assume he did not recognize its significance. It would not be long, however, before that significance fell hard on Salmon and the whole array of conservative Episcopalians.

Other than the canonical change removing the barrier to the ordination of homosexuals, the next most important work of the 1994 Convention was C042 that called for a study of the foundations involved in the development of rites for the blessing of same-sex unions. Resolution C042 called for "a report addressing the theological foundations and pastoral considerations involved in the development of rites honoring love and commitment between persons of the same sex."[286] Once again, as with the canonical

---

282. Thrall, "Sexuality Issues."

283. "1994–C020, Amend Canon 1.17.5." The Acts of Convention, The Archives of the Episcopal Church, http://www.episcopalarchives.org/cgi-bin/acts/acts_resolution.pl?resolution=1994-C020.

284. Thrall, "Sexuality Issues."

285. "Bishop Reports on General Convention." *Jubilate Deo* (Diocese of South Carolina), October/November 1994.

286. "1994–C042, Prepare Report Concerning Rites for Same-Sex Commitments." The Acts of Convention, The Archives of the Episcopal Church, http://www.episcopalarchives.org/cgi-bin/acts/

change, the Convention approved this with surprisingly little debate.[287] Apparently, yet again, most conservatives did not appreciate the significance of the potential outcome of this resolution. It was not long, however, before that would change.

The General Convention of 1994 left the Episcopal Church with a changed policy on the issue of homosexuality that was not commonly recognized at the time. The new canon law banning discrimination against gays superseded the 1979 "not appropriate" resolution as the new rule of the church. Homosexuals' rights to ordination in the Episcopal Church were now cemented in Church law for the first time. Moreover, it put into place a process that would eventually lead to the Church's adoption of the blessing of same-sex unions. At the same time, it gave expression to the rights and equality of homosexuals in the Church and in society as a whole. Whether the right-wing minority recognized it or not, in reality, the 1994 General Convention accelerated the momentum in the church favoring homosexuals' rights. Since 1976, the "anti" side had had the upper hand at least until the 1991 General Convention. After 1994, the pro-homosexual rights side would have the stronger voice. Although it would take a while to become clear, Spong's left "wing" would win this long fight and would do so by capturing enough of the neutral middle ground. In time, the Episcopal Church would come to accept all three points of Spong's "Koinonia" statement of 1994 thereby rejecting the conservatives' "Affirmation." In so doing, it would give tacit recognition that homosexuality was morally neutral.

The Episcopalian "anti" forces, while back on their heels, were not willing to give up on the issue. Now they had to decide how they would promote their self-declared non-negotiable view of homosexuality given the substantive changes brought about by the 1994 convention which they soon began to regard with alarm. Having failed to carry the day in the General Convention, leading conservative bishops turned to a new strategy. They charged a prominent liberal bishop with heresy and forced the Church to call him into court. If they could not get "Congress" to back them up, perhaps they could get the "Supreme Court" to do so.

On January 27, 1995, ten of the most conservative bishops[288] of the Episcopal Church delivered to Presiding Bishop Browning, a "Presentment," or accusation calling for ecclesiastical legal action against Assistant Bishop Walter C. Righter, of Newark.[289] It is interesting to note that the "presenters" chose to take action against Righter rather than the more visible Bishop John Spong who had actually been the mastermind of the controversial ordinations. In order to have a trial for heresy, the presenters had to collect the endorsements of at least 25 percent of the church's bishops. That would have been 75. They secured 76 signatures, including 44 retired bishops. Thus, 32 active bishops signed

---

acts_resolution.pl?resolution=1994-C042.

287. Thrall, "Sexuality Issues."

288. James M. Stanton, of Dallas; Stephen H. Jecko, of Florida; John David Schofield, of San Joaquin; John W. Howe, of Central Florida; Maurice M. Benitez, of Texas; William C. Wantland, of Eau Clair; Jack L. Iker, of Ft. Worth; Keith L. Ackerman, of Quincy; James M. Coleman, of West Tennessee; and Terence Kelshaw, of Rio Grande.

289. Righter was born in Philadelphia in 1923; educated at the University of Pittsburgh and the Berkeley Divinity School of Yale University; ordained deacon and priest in 1951; Bishop of Iowa, 1972–88; Assistant Bishop of Newark. See: LeBlanc, Douglas, "Barry Stpofel: Righter 'Chose Love over Doctrine.'" *The Living Church*, November 15, 2011.

signifying the approximate one-third of diocesan bishops on the "anti" side of the homosexual issue.[290] The numbers may have been higher except for Browning's opposition. He announced, "'This presentment is not the way to go (. . .) [it] will not solve anything,'" and "'can only disrupt us from the path we are on.'"[291] The accusers charged that Righter had violated canon law on two counts, having taught a doctrine that was contrary to the church's, and having broken his ordination vows by not conforming to the doctrine of the Church. Both resulted from his having ordained a "practicing" homosexual man (Barry Stopfel) to the diaconate. The case essentially rested on the strength of the 1979 General Convention resolution holding it was "not appropriate" to ordain a practicing homosexual. Righter did not contest the facts in the case, instead fought back in his own defense in a response brief of May 10, 1995. In the pre-trial hearing on December 8, 1995, both sides agreed the issue at stake was the doctrine of the Episcopal Church. The Presenters said the Church doctrine clearly forbade the ordination of practicing homosexuals. The Respondent said it did not. The Court for the Trial of a Bishop considered the arguments in the first session of the trial, held in Wilmington, Delaware, on February 27, 1996.[292]

On May 15, 1996, the court issued a thirty-three-page written decision dismissing the case. Only one judge among the eight, Fairfield of North Dakota, dissented to write his own opinion. In summary, the judges concluded that there was no doctrine in the Episcopal Church forbidding the ordination of non-celibate homosexuals. As for the touted 1979 "not appropriate" General Convention resolution, they said it was only advisory, not binding, and not a doctrine of the Church. This vindicated Bishop Spong's position on the resolution in the 1980s. The judges continued that only General Convention could determine the doctrine and discipline of the Episcopal Church, and that had not happened in regard to the ordination of homosexuals. In short, Righter could not be in violation of a non-existent doctrine. The court dismissed both charges. Righter was spared a formal trial for heresy.

The court's decision was a staggering blow to the conservative opposition to homosexual rights in the Episcopal Church. Their ploy had backfired. They were in a weaker position now than they had ever been. Righter, and by extension, Spong had been exonerated. These two liberal bishops and their "pro" side had prevailed in a sweeping and stunning victory. Following the clear direction of the court's decision, the only hope left for the conservative opposition in the Episcopal Church was to get the General Convention to establish a doctrine forbidding the ordination of practicing homosexuals. At that point, everyone knew it was a longshot. It was possible, but not probable. The

---

290. "The Episcopal Church and Homosexuality, Activities during 1996." http://www.religioustolerance.org/hom_epis2.htm.

291. "House of Bishops Meets to Discuss Difference." Episcopal News Service, as quoted in *Jubilate Deo* (Diocese of South Carolina), June/July 1995.

292. The bishops who served as judges on the court were: Edward W. Jones, chair, of Indianapolis; Robert C. Johnson, Jr., of North Carolina; Donis D. Patterson, retired of Dallas; Cabell Tennis, of Delaware; Douglas E. Theuner, of New Hampshire; Arthur E. Walmsley, retired of Connecticut; Roger J. White, of Milwaukee; and Andrew Fairfield, of North Dakota. In the final decision, of May 15, 1996, only Fairfield dissented; he wrote a separate opinion.

only question at hand was whether the conservatives had the strength to push through a canonical change to block homosexual ordinations.

In South Carolina, Bishop Salmon lost no time in denouncing the court ruling. In fact, the day after the decision hit the news, he wrote a long opinion piece criticizing the court as too narrow-minded.[293] Salmon insisted that Church doctrine could be found in the collected "teaching" of the Church without having to be spelled out in detail in the canons. The presenting bishops lost little time too in responding. Nine of them held a press conference in an airport hotel in Dallas, Texas, on May 28, to call the decision, not surprisingly, "'flawed and erroneous.'"[294] They went on to announce they would be proposing that a canon be adopted by the General Convention to oblige the clergy to abstain in all sexual relations outside of marriage between one man and one woman.[295] This canon, presumably, would satisfy the court's requirement of an explicit doctrine banning the ordination of non-celibate homosexuals. Of course, such a sweeping law could be used against anyone engaging in any sex outside of traditional marriage, and that could be a sort of Pandora's box.

As the Episcopal Church prepared for another contentious General Convention, the leaders of the Diocese of South Carolina continued to dig in their heels on homosexuality. Indeed, in 1994, Bishop Salmon had issued a directive for the diocese under which all the clergy had to sign a statement: "We expect Holy Matrimony to be the context for sexual relations."[296] All new clergy were required to sign the statement as they entered the diocese. The implication in that pledge was the denunciation of same-gender sexual relations. As delegates prepared to go to the General Convention, Bishop Salmon reminded everyone again, as if it were necessary, "We do not support any actions nationally which reject the orthodox teachings of the church, or which attack the Holy Scripture. All of the South Carolina bishops signed the presentment against Bishop Righter."[297]

The Loosening of Bonds, 1997

Although by the start of 1997 the momentum in the Church's ongoing discussion of homosexuality had clearly shifted to the proponents' side, it would be untrue to say they had won the war. It was too important an issue. The opponents knew they had too much at stake to leave the field of combat now to the likes of John Spong. Although they had lost a battle in the court, they had not yet lost the cause. The next moment of

---

293. "Bishop Salmon Responds to Righter Court Opinion." *Jubilate Deo* (Diocese of South Carolina), June/July 1996.

294. Parmley, Helen. "Bishops Propose Canonical Change Forbidding Ordination of Non-Celibate Homosexuals." Episcopal News Service, as quoted in *Jubilate Deo* (Diocese of South Carolina), August/September 1996.

295. Ibid.

296. *Journal of the Two Hundred and Seventh Annual Meeting of the Convention, February 28–March 1, 1997, All Saints Church, Pawleys Island, S.C., Proceedings of the Convention*. Charleston, SC: the diocese, 1997, 33.

297. Ibid.

engagement, the General Convention of 1997, could possibly turn the momentum back to their side.

Before the Convention, conservative groups maneuvered to prepare for battle. The established opposition groups, as Episcopal Synod America and Episcopalians United were at work. Too, a new conservative organization formed in 1996 on the eve of the Convention, called the American Anglican Council,[298] a gathering of hard-liners bonded by opposition to the ordination of practicing homosexuals and the blessing of same-sex unions. While earlier protest organizations, as ESA, opposed the ordination of women, the AAC did not. It focused on homosexuality. According to the AAC website, "Homosexuality is condemned in Scripture as sinful regardless of the context (. . .) The Church is called to lovingly lead sinners toward repentance and transformation (if they are willing) rather than embrace sinful behavior."[299] No right-wing group was better prepared for battle in 1997 than the AAC. Bishop Salmon said later that "A collection of orthodox Episcopalian groups led by Bishop James Stanton of Dallas got together before the convention and provided behind-the-scenes leadership on many issues (. . .) many items on the revisionist agenda."[300]

While several Episcopalian dissident groups opposed the Church's reforms for homosexuals, the American Anglican Council (AAC) was to prove to be by far the most effective. It was incorporated in 1996 by Diane Knippers and two others in order to oppose pro-homosexual movements in the Episcopal Church. It quickly became the power center among the most conservative elements of the Church and would remain so for many years. Knippers was head of the Institute on Religion and Democracy (IRD). She had joined the IRD in 1982 and had become its president in 1992 a post she would hold until her death in 2005.[301] IRD had been formed in 1981 as a political action committee to promote a conservative agenda, such as President Reagan's anti-Communist policies in the Western Hemisphere.[302] According to one observer, "'IRD's conservative social policy goals include increasing military spending and foreign interventions, opposing environmental protection efforts, and eliminating social welfare programs' and that the organization is non-religious in nature and a front for conservative political groups that hope to undermine Christian voices opposed to conservative public policies."[303]

IRD and its off-shoot, American Anglican Council, were not popular or grassroots organizations. They were small organizations funded largely by wealthy right-wing foundations and individuals all of whom had socially conservative agendas. The best description of the background, aims, ties, and funding of AAC was in Jim Naughton's

---

298. Incorporated 19 August 1996 in the District of Columbia. See: "Our History," American Anglican Council, www.americananglican.org/our~history.

299. "Frequently Asked Questions, American Anglican Council." https://americananglican.org/about-us/aac-faq.

300. "The 72nd General Convention, Report to the Diocese from our Bishops." *Jubilate Deo* (Diocese of South Carolina), September 1997.

301. Newman, Andy. "Diane Knippers Dies at 53: Strategist for Christian Right." *The New York Times*, April 23, 2005.

302. "Institute on Religion and Democracy," Wikipedia, https://en.wikipedia.org/wiki/Institute_on_Religion_and_Democracy.

303. Ibid.

landmark work, "Following the Money" published in the Diocese of Washington's newsletter, *Washington Window*, in April of 2006.[304] Another source reported: "Between 1985 and 2005, IRD received more than $4.75 million from the Lynde and Harry Bradley, Sarah Scaife, John M. Olin, Carthage, and the JM Foundations. IRD has also reportedly received generous funding from the right-wing Ahmanson Foundation."[305] After the end of the Cold War, around 1990, the IRD changed its focus to social issues at home as reflected in the liberal trending churches such as Presbyterian, Methodist, United Church of Christ, and Episcopal. Fundamentalists had already taken over the Southern Baptist Convention in 1989. IRD identified feminism and homosexuality as the liberally-driven issues that had to be targeted.[306] Thus, in its program to stem the tide of liberalism in mainline churches, IRD set up AAC for the Episcopal Church. The first head of AAC was to be Bishop James Stanton, of Dallas, also on the board of IRD. Knippers, the head of IRD, was to serve on the board of AAC. She was also an active layperson at Truro Church in Fairfax, Virginia, a center for Episcopalian ultra-conservativism.

As IRD, AAC was apparently funded largely by right-wing foundations and individuals, perhaps most notably Howard and Roberta Ahmanson, who may have made a secret agreement with AAC to contribute $200,000 a year in matching funds.[307] In 2000, the Ahmansons provided half of the million dollar budget of the AAC.[308] One observer wrote, "He [Ahmanson] is an ultra-conservative heir of a savings and loan fortune who has long supported religious right extremists and fundamentalist Christian causes."[309] Howard Ahmanson was a communicant of St. James Episcopal Church, Newport Beach CA, whose rector, David C. Anderson, became the president of AAC. In 2005 *Time* magazine called the Ahmansons "the financiers" of the Evangelical movement in America.[310] In 2008 he contributed $1,395,000 in support of Proposition 8 on the California ballot, an initiative that passed.[311] It denied same-sex couples the right to marry. Ahmanson was also a crucial supporter of IRD, listing as his first cause, the Episcopal Action program.[312] The Ahmansons gave IRD nearly half a million dollars in 2001 just as IRD and AAC were stepping up efforts to promote anti-homosexual movements in the Episcopal

---

304. Naughton, Jim. "Following the Money." *The Washington Window* (Diocese of Washington), April 2006.

305. "Institute on Religion and Democracy," Institute for Policy Studies, August 1, 2013. http://rightweb.ird-online.org/profile/Institute-on-Religion-and-Democracy.

306. Goodstein, Laurie and Kirkpatrick, David D. "Conservative Group Amplifies Voice of Protestant Orthodoxy." *The New York Times*, May 22, 2004, http://www.nytimes.com/2004/05/22/us/conservative-group-amplifies-voice-of-protestant-orthodoxy.

307. Taylor, Jack H. "American Anglican Council and Institute for Religion and Democracy." September 18, 2003, http://www.rci.rutgers.edu/~lcrew/dojustice/j111.html.

308. Naughton, "Following the Money."

309. Taylor, "American Anglican."

310. "Howard Ahmanson, Jr." Wikipedia, https://en.wikipedia.org/wiki/Howard_Ahmanson-Jr.

311. Ibid.

312. "Fieldstead and Company." http://fieldstead.com/philanthropy/justice-and-public-policy.html.

Church.[313] Between 2001 and 2004, IRD spent $449,182 on its activities concerning the Episcopal Church.[314]

The Diocese of South Carolina did its part in organizing a conservative resistance at this time. Thanks to the influence of retired bishop Allison, the annual conference of SEAD, Scholarly Engagement with Anglican Doctrine, moved from the Virginia Theological Seminary to the cathedral in Charleston for its eighth annual meeting in January of 1997. Counterattack against the liberals was the theme, as one source said: "If 1996 has been an *annus hereticus* in terms of widely reported questioning of orthodox Christian faith in academic circles and even Church circles, 1997 may prove to be the year of counterattack."[315]

Also, early in 1997, "the Second Anglican Encounter in the South" met in Kuala Lumpur, Malaysia, February 10–15. This group later changed its name to Global South. On February 15, the conference of Anglican bishops and leaders, mostly from Africa and Asia, adopted a formal statement entitled "The Kuala Lumpur Statement on Human Sexuality."[316] Among its eleven provisions, one said human sexuality should be expressed only in marriage between a man and a woman. Another declared homosexual practices to be sin. Yet another held that the ordination of practicing homosexuals and the blessing of same-sex unions were against Holy Scriptures. Conservative bishops held the "Kuala Lumpur Statement" in hand when they arrived at the General Convention.

The South Carolina diocesan meeting at All Saints Church, Pawleys Island, from February 28 to March 1, 1997, showed the strains of tension concerning the issue of homosexuality. The rector of All Saints, Charles Murphy, wanted the diocese to take a stronger stance against the Church's pro-homosexual policies. Bishop Salmon had already established the requirement that all clergy of the diocese sign a pledge recognizing Holy Matrimony as the context for sexual relations. Salmon considered this satisfactory enough to close the issue. However, a clergyman offered a resolution in the convention to revise the diocesan canons to say that all clergy and lay leaders of the diocese were obliged to refrain from sexual relations outside of heterosexual marriage. Salmon opposed the resolution saying it was unnecessary in view of the pledge that all clergy had signed. Nick Zeigler, the chancellor described the following scene in his memoir. As Salmon stood to explain his reasons to the assembly:

> Suddenly there was a commotion on the floor of the convention, and I saw the Reverend [Charles] Murphy striding down the center aisle shouting at Bishop Salmon. A bitter exchange took place between them with regard to what had been said while they were attending the [1991] convention in Phoenix (. . .). At one point the Reverend Murphy said in a loud voice that reverberated throughout

---

313. Naughton, "Following the Money."

314. Ibid.

315. McKeachie, William. "Cathedral to Host SEAD Conference." *Jubilate Deo* (Diocese of South Carolina), December 1996/January 1997.

316. "The Kuala Lumpur Statement on Human Sexuality—2nd Encounter in the South, 10 to 15 Feb 97." Global South Anglican. http://www.globalsouthanglican.org/index.php/blog/comments/the_kuala_lumpur_statement.

the church, 'That's a lie!' The acrimonious exchange went on for several minutes before three hundred startled delegates.[317]

Salmon and Murphy both left the room. Salmon returned after twenty minutes. The shaken delegates quickly voted to table, that is to kill, the proposed resolution. The bishop finally had his way but "was deeply hurt by the incident."[318] Relations between Salmon and Murphy were only to get worse.

Tensions elsewhere mounted as time neared for the Philadelphia General Convention of July 16–25, 1997. The recent Convention resolutions and the court ruling of 1996 had set the stage for the biggest confrontation yet between the proponents and the opponents of homosexual rights in the Episcopal Church. Would this turn out to be the defining moment in which the Church would finally resolve the issue of homosexuality? Or, would the Convention collapse, again, into acrimonious disharmony? The only thing certain was it could not avoid the issue.

The greatest question at hand was, Would the conservative bishops be able to establish a doctrine banning the ordination of practicing homosexuals? The Righter court had made it clear such ordinations could not be stopped unless the Church adopted a clear doctrine to do so. That meant changing canon law, a tall order. Conservative bishops brandished the Kuala Lumpur Statement which not only rejected the ordination of practicing homosexuals and the blessing of same-sex unions, but also declared homosexual practices to be sin. That was about as clear and strong a statement against homosexuality that they could make at that time. In the House of Bishops, retired bishop Alex Dickson, of West Tennessee, moved that the House adopt the Kuala Lumpur statement. That would set it on the road to becoming the doctrine of the Episcopal Church. A roll call vote followed and ended with 94 bishops voting "No," 42 voting "Yes," and 2 abstaining.[319] In a stunning moment, the bishops spurned the Kuala Lumpur Statement by more than two to one. Apparently, only the approximate one-third of the bishops who were "anti" supported it. The two-thirds who were "pro" and neutral bishops had combined to reject it.

However much it may look in retrospect that the conservative campaign against homosexuality had been crushed for good by the landslide defeat of the Kuala Lumpur resolution, this was not quite the case. The conservatives still had a powerful coalition and could perhaps reach the same objective of blocking gay rights through other means and maneuvers. In fact, in spite of the Kuala Lumpur vote, they won three major victories against homosexuality in the 1997 Convention, altogether a significant achievement. The most important one was to block a resolution to develop a rite for the blessing of same-sex unions. Resolution C002 in the House of Deputies called on the Standing Liturgical Commission "to develop (. . .) a rite or rites for the blessing of committed relationships between persons of the same sex and to present such forms to the 73rd

---

317. Zeigler, *When Conscience*, 320.

318. Ibid.

319. "1997-B032, Refer a Resolution on the Kuala Lumpur Statement on Human Sexuality." The Acts of Convention 1976–2012, The Archives of the Episcopal Church, http://www.episcopalarchives.org/cgi-bin/acts/acts_resolution-complete.pl?resolution=1997-B032.

General Convention for inclusion in *The Book of Occasional Services*."[320] The conservatives were well prepared. A roll call vote was taken by orders: lay order, 56 "Yes," 41 "No," and 15 divided; clerical order, 56 "Yes," 37 "No," and 20 divided.[321] The necessary number to pass in each order was 57. The resolution failed by one vote in each order although more deputies supported it than opposed it. Afterwards, Bishop Salmon said the defeat happened because of the "effective networking and strong work of the American Anglican Council."[322]

The conservative coalition also prevailed on a measure calling on the Church Pension Fund to extend benefits to same-sex partners. Resolution C005 was defeated in the House of Deputies. In the lay order, there were 45 "Yes" votes, 46 "No," and 18 divided (55 necessary to pass). In the clerical order, there were 50 "yes" votes, 40 "No," and 20 divided (56 necessary to pass).[323] Moreover, the traditionalists got the Convention to reaffirm marriage as the union of a man and a woman. This came in Resolution C003 which stated: "[We] affirm the sacredness of Christian marriage between one man and one woman with intent of life-long relationship."[324] Conservatives had every reason to feel a certain high satisfaction at having defeated the hated rites for same-sex blessings and benefits for same-sex partners, while reaffirming the Church's traditional teaching on marriage. Apparently, the clerical delegates from South Carolina played significant roles in these measures, at least from the report to the diocese that commended Dow Sanderson, John Burwell, Kendall Harmon, and Terrell Glenn.[325]

Yet, conservatives had good reason to worry about the future. In addition to the failure to enunciate a Church doctrine on the ordination of homosexuals, there were three other events in the Convention to give them concern. In the first place, the resolution that passed reaffirming traditional marriage had a second part that could possibly have, in their view, dire consequences. It called on the Standing Liturgical Commission to continue its study of same-sex relationships and to issue a report before the next General Convention recommending future steps "for the resolution of issues related to such committed relationships."[326] This sounded suspiciously close to encouraging the

---

320. "1997–C002, On the Topic of Rites for the Blessing of Same-Sex Relationships." The Acts of Convention 1976-2012, The Archives of the Episcopal Church, http://www.episcopalarchives.org/cgi-bin/acts/acts_resolution-complete.pl?resolution=1997-C002.

321. Ibid.

322. "The 72nd General Convention."

323. "1997–C005, On the Topic of CPF Benefits for Same Sex Partners." The Acts of Convention 1976–2012, The Archives of the Episcopal Church, http://www.episcopalarchives.org/cgi-bin/acts/acts_resolution-complete.pl?resolution=1997-C005.

324. "1997–C003, Affirm Traditional Marriage and Request Study of Same-Sex Relationships." The Acts of Convention 1976–2012, The Archives of the Episcopal Church, http://www.episcopalarchives.org/cgi-bin/acts/acts_resolution.pl?resolution=1997-C003.

325. "The 72nd General Convention."
Of the four clerical deputies in 1997, only one remained with the Episcopal Church in the schism of 2012, Dow Sanderson. Kendall Harmon and John Burwell remained as prominent conservative leaders in DSC. They abandoned TEC in the schism of 2012. Terrell Glenn joined the Province of Rwanda for the Anglican Mission in America. He became rector of All Saints in Pawleys Island and a bishop under Rwanda. He later resigned from AMiA. See: www.zoominfo.com/p/TerrellGlenn/507044587.

326. "1997–C003."

commission to favor homosexuality. Another Resolution, D011, apologized to gays and lesbians "for years of rejection and maltreatment by the Church."[327] That same resolution declared that there was a diversity of opinion on the morality of homosexual practices thereby overriding the conservative attitude of absolute rejection of homosexual behavior as innately sinful.

In one other important item of business, the Convention chose Frank Tracy Griswold, the bishop of Chicago, to be the next Presiding Bishop to serve until 2006. He was considered a moderate although some conservatives soon began to criticize him for being too favorable to homosexuals.[328] The 1997 General Convention concluded without, once again, reaching a definitive position on the ordination of homosexuals. The failure to do this really was a victory for the "pro" side because by default it left in place the canon law and the court decision removing the obstacles to the ordination of homosexuals and the Convention of 1997 had done nothing to alter this. In the end, what the Convention settled was that the conservatives could not get a doctrine banning open homosexuals from ordination. The two-to-one defeat in the House of Bishops ended that idea forever. Moreover, the Convention left open the real possibility that a rite for the blessing of same-sex unions would be approved in the near future. Thus, while the conservatives could tout some important victories in 1997, in actuality they lost more than they gained. Perhaps more importantly, they came to see that the momentum in the Church was moving against them. This new reality was not lost on the rising bodies of far-right wing Episcopalians who increasingly viewed the Episcopal Church as hopelessly lost in left-wing sin and heresy.

Fired up by the backlash against General Convention's supposed direction favoring homosexual rights in the Episcopal Church, Episcopalian dissidents moved with a sense of urgency. The Lambeth Conference would be meeting in the next year, 1998. If the anti-homosexual coalition could not stop the Church from a pro-gay agenda, perhaps they could leap over the Episcopal Church to get the Anglican Communion to force the church back. The American Anglican Council had already been building ties with socially conservative foreign bishops. Another organization was doing the same, the Ekklesia Society, founded in 1995 and led by the Rev. Bill Atwood, of Texas. "Atwood's work linking Southern bishops with one another and with Northern conservatives played a central role in the development of conservative Anglican global relationships. A significant catalyst for the rapid development of these relationships was the approach of the 1998 Lambeth Conference."[329]

In order to educate and energize conservative foreign bishops to take the anti-homosexual crusade to Lambeth, the American Anglican Council, Ekklesia and allied groups organized a conference at Flower Mound, Texas, twenty miles northwest of Dallas, from

---

327. "1997–D011, Apologize for the Church's Rejection of Gays and Lesbians." The Acts of Convention 1976–2012, The Archives of the Episcopal Church, http://www.episcopalarchives.org/GC2009/08_wms/2009-C010.pdf.

328. He had signed the "Koinonia Statement" of 1994.

329. Hassett, Miranda K. *Anglican Communion in Crisis: How Episcopal Dissidents and their African Allies are Reshaping Anglicanism.* Princeton, NJ: Princeton University Press, 2007, 52.

September 20 to 24, 1997, called the Anglican Life and Witness Conference.[330] It brought together Episcopalian conservatives and fifty bishops from sixteen countries of Africa, Asia, and the Americas. Small study groups were set up to educate the foreign bishops on the need to appeal to Lambeth even though in most of their nations homosexuality was not an issue of public note. One of the speakers was Stephen Noll,[331] of Trinity School for Ministry, who gave a talk, "the Handwriting on the Wall: Why the Sexuality Conflict in the Episcopal Church Is God's Word to the Anglican Communion."[332] Noll told the foreign bishops "that although homosexuality was not a matter of current public debate in most of their home contexts, they must engage with the issue in order to help beleaguered Northern brethren and to protect their own churches from the spread of negative Northern influences."[333] In order to strengthen the impetus against homosexuality, the conference drew up a declaration, called the Dallas Statement, linking international debt and homosexuality. The gambit worked very well. This conference was to prove to be the effective starting place of the convergence of Episcopalian ultra-conservatives and Third World, particularly African, bishops.[334] Atwood[335] left the meeting saying he was "convinced that the bishops of the South will have a significant impact on next summer's [Lambeth] meeting."[336] Events would prove his conviction to be correct. It is doubtful that the enormously divisive issue of homosexuality in the Anglican Communion would have developed without the work of the small but well-organized, well-motivated, and well-funded counter-revolutionary factions in America.

As for South Carolina, the delegation returned home from the Philadelphia Convention to lament too the direction of error they saw coming out of the Convention. In their published report, the bishops had little good to say about the meeting, mostly to applaud the conservative forces. Clerical deputies Glenn and Harmon published dark reviews sensing great trouble ahead. Glenn wrote, "I was tremendously disappointed in the Convention. We have elected a Presiding Bishop who has knowingly ordained practicing homosexuals." Moreover, he said, "We have replaced scripture with the canons of the Church as the supreme authority for faith and practice." Glenn would renounce his Holy Orders in the Episcopal Church three years later. Harmon issued an ominous warning of division ahead: "We are closer than ever to the emergence of an orthodox resistance movement within the Episcopal Church."[337]

---

330. "Anglican Bishops Address Issues of Sexuality and International Debt at Dallas Meeting." Episcopal News Service, October 17, 1997. http://www.episcopalarchives.org/cgi-bin/ENS/ENSpress_release.pl?pr_number=97-1973.

331. Noll served as vice chancellor of Uganda Christian University 2000–2010.

332. Hassett, *Anglican Communion in Crisis*, 59.

333. Ibid., 60.

334. Ibid., 61.

335. Atwood left the Episcopal Church in 2006 and became a bishop suffragan in Kenya then bishop of the International Diocese, Anglican Church in North America.

336. "Anglican Bishops Address Issues."

337. "The 72nd General Convention."

Bishop Salmon said it best, "There was considerable unrest in the diocese when our deputies returned from General Convention."[338] Angry demands arose from numerous parishes to cut funding to the national Church in protest of its supposedly "revisionist agenda" as conservatives like to call the recent resolutions favoring women and homosexuals. The five deans of the diocese drew up three resolutions to present to the October 1997 meeting of the Diocesan Council which was presided over by Bishop Salmon. All passed by majority vote. The most important one allowed congregations to designate that part of their contribution to the diocese that would go to the national Church to be directed instead to missions. A second one advocated associating with and supporting conservative resistance groups, namely the American Anglican Council and Ekklesia. The third would show solidarity with the Episcopal Synod of America in opposing the mandatory ordination of women. Dow Sanderson, one of the deans, said the resolutions were "a first step in assuring that those parishes which in good conscience support the revisionist agenda of '815' could exercise that conscience."[339] A few months later, Bishop Salmon told the diocesan convention they should keep the 10-10-10 solution on tithing, but the 10 percent that would go to the national Church could be redirected. He said any vestry could end its contribution to the Episcopal Church and that four vestries had already done so.[340] It should be recalled that a diocesan movement to cut funding to the national Church had already appeared in reaction to racial policies but that Bishop Temple had soon restored normal diocesan funding to the Episcopal Church in the 1970s. This time, the cuts would continue and would even accelerate. As we will see, by 2012, the Diocese of South Carolina was to reduce its contribution to the Episcopal Church to a barely discernable nominal amount.

Meanwhile, inspired by the calls for an orthodox province coming from AAC and ESA, a collection of some of the most conservative Episcopal clergy in South Carolina, and in the southeast, met in Pawleys Island to plan a concerted reaction against the supposedly errant Episcopal Church. The Rev. Charles (Chuck) Murphy III,[341] rector of All Saints of Pawleys Island, and Jon Shuler[342] co-hosted the meeting of some thirty clergy on September 8-9, 1997. There were notable connections to AAC and ESA. From ESA came Pete

---

338. *Journal of the Two Hundred Eighth Annual Meeting of the Convention, February 27-28, 1998, St. Andrew's Church, Mt. Pleasant, S.C., Proceedings of the Convention.* Charleston, SC: the diocese, 1998, 33.

339. "Matters of Conscience in South Carolina." *The Living Church*, October 26, 1997, The Living Church 1995-2001, The Archives of the Episcopal Church, http://www.episcopalarchives.org/cgi-bin/the_living_church/TLCarticle.pl?volume=215&issue=17&article_id=14.

340. *Journal of the Two Hundred Eighth . . . 1998*, 34.

341. "Two American Priests Become Bishops in Singapore, Then Return to U.S." *The Living Church*, February 20, 2000, The Living Church 1995-2001, The Archives of the Episcopal Church, http://www.episcopalarchives.org/cgi-bin/the_living_church/TLCarticle.pl?volume=220&issue=article_id=2. Murphy was born in Decatur AL in 1947. He was graduated from the University of Alabama and the School of Theology of the University of the South (Sewanee). He was ordained to the diaconate and priesthood in Alabama in 1975 and served as curate at St. Paul's of Selma 1975-77, rector of St. Thomas of Greenville AL 1977-80, and canon of Trinity Cathedral in Columbia SC 1980-82. He had been rector of All Saints, Pawleys Island, since 1982 and had overseen an energetic expansion of the parish. In the Diocese of South Carolina, he had served as deputy to General Convention and member of the standing committee and the diocesan council.

342. Of NAMS, the New Anglican Missionary Society, established in 1994.

Moriarty, the president, Dow Sanderson, and Jeffrey Steenson.[343] Present also was retired bishop Alex Dickson, on the board of the AAC. Retired bishops Allison and Benitez were also in attendance.[344] The meeting came to be called the First Promise conference. It was also the birth of what would later be known as the Anglican Mission in the Americas.

The motivation for the meeting was clearly stated at the start: "to take a definitive stand in rejection of ECUSA pronouncements at General Convention."[345] In particular, the group denounced three hated actions of the 1997 Convention: "the election of a primate [Griswold] who has departed from the teaching of the apostles; the mandatory and coercive enforcement of the ordination of women; and the failure to uphold and require a biblical sexual ethic [on homosexuality] for this church's clergy and people."[346] Following closely on the ESA letter of July 29, the meeting issued the First Promise Statement on September 9, declaring the Episcopal Church to have departed from the true doctrine, discipline, and worship of the historic church, and as a result to have its authority "fundamentally impaired."[347] "First Promise" referred to the prayer book ordination vow that first required a promise to be loyal to the doctrine, discipline, and worship as the church has received them. While the Statement stopped just short of establishing a separate entity for "orthodox" Episcopalians, many of its nine provisions implied such. One said they would not be bound by geographical boundaries. Another said they would recognize only "faithful bishops." One point held that they would recognize only the Kuala Lumpur Statement on sexuality and would reject communion with anyone who did not accept it. The most ominous of the provisions called on overseas Anglican bishops to "support" the "orthodox" in America and most seriously of all, "to discipline those members [the Episcopal Church] who have departed from it.[348] This was an undisguised appeal for outside intervention by foreign Anglican prelates into the Episcopal Church to stop the supposed heresy. As with the ESA and AAC statements of July, the tone of the First Promise Statement was resignation at reforming the Episcopal Church from within. The apparent goal at this point of First Promise, ESA, AAC, and allied groups was to form a separate entity within the Episcopal Church free from the "revisionist agenda," i.e., equal rights for homosexuals and mandatory rights for women. This goal, however, was not certain; the exact structure of this entity was never clearly defined by the "orthodox" parties that sought it. There can be a certain amount of doubt that the old goal of an orthodox church-within-a-church was still the actual aim of the resistance movement after the Convention of 1997. As we will see, it would not be long before some of the reactionary Episcopalian leaders of 1997 started leaving the Church.[349] Perhaps a telling clue of where First Promise was leading came in

343. Steenson served as bishop of Rio Grande from 2005 to 2007. He converted to Catholicism and served as the first ordinary in the Roman Catholic Ordinariate 2012–15.

344. "First Promise."

345. Ibid.

346. Ibid.

347. Ibid.

348. Ibid.

349. Twenty-six, all clergymen, signed the First Promise Statement of Sept. 9, 1997. Terrell Glenn and Chuck Murphy later left the Episcopal Church for the Province of Rwanda bringing along All Saints

a statement of purpose adopted at the group's annual meeting on September 21, 1998, to prepare "an orthodox Anglican Province in the United States by either the reformation of the Episcopal Church or by the emergence of an alternative."[350] Only a year old, First Promise was now publicly suggesting forming a separate church as an "alternative" to the supposedly fatally corrupt Episcopal Church.

Walking the Tightrope, 1998–2002

Following the First Promise statement with its implication of schism from the Episcopal Church, there was a change in tone coming from the bishop of the Diocese of South Carolina toward the national Church. Salmon did not attend the First Promise conference and did not support it afterwards, as opposed to retired bishop Allison. Salmon did not advocate secession from the Episcopal Church. On one hand, he kept his conservative beliefs, but on the other hand he had to deal with elements in his diocese that were moving toward division that he would not condone. How to handle the secessionists in his own diocese would soon become Salmon's problem. Nick Zeigler wrote in his memoir that at this time: "Bishop Salmon counseled patience while trying to find some means of holding the diocese together and opposing the actions of the national church."[351]

In 1998, 1999, and 2000, Salmon faced three issues that he could have made into occasions to differentiate the diocese farther from the national Church: Spong's Twelve Theses, the Lambeth Conference statement on sexuality, and the General Convention of 2000. Before First Promise, he might have used these to step up his denunciations of the Episcopal Church. Now he seemed to go out of his way to reduce his criticism of the national Church. He was walking a tightrope. He could not go too far to one side or the other.

In the case of Spong, Salmon published "A Pastoral Letter to the People and Clergy of the Diocese of South Carolina," in the August/September 1998 issue of *Jubilate Deo*, the diocesan newspaper.[352] This was a denunciation of Spong's so-called Twelve Theses, or Twelve Points of Reform, taken from his new book, *A New Christianity for a New World*. The Twelve Theses were given in a list of points calling for new ways of looking at the traditional Christian assumptions about God, man, the scriptures, moral and ethical behavior, and pre-scientific concepts of supernatural life. In Number 12, Spong insisted that sexual orientation should not be used to judge people.[353] To conservatives, particularly staunch evangelicals and Anglo-Catholics, these twelve points were nothing short of heresy. Salmon was in this group: "These Theses are, in my view, a denial of the

---

of Pawleys Island. Jeffrey Steeson later became the head of the Roman Catholic Ordinariate in America. Geoffrey Chapman authored the landmark Chapman Memo in 2003 outlining a blueprint for leaving the Episcopal Church. One of the few signatories to remain in the Episcopal Church was Dow Sanderson. Eventually 127 people signed the First Promise Statement.

350. Zabriskie, Marek P. "Breaking Away." *The Living Church*, November 26, 2000, http://www.episcopalarchives.org/cgi-bin/the_living_church/TLCarticle.pl?volume=221&issue=22&article_id=18.

351. Zeigler, *When Conscience*, 321.

352. Salmon, (the Rt. Rev.) Edward L., Jr. "A Pastoral Letter to the People and Clergy of the Diocese of South Carolina." *Jubilate Deo* (Diocese of South Carolina), August/September 1998.

353. "John Shelby Spong," Wikipedia, https://en.wikipedia.org/wiki/John_Shelby_Spong.

Christian faith and not the basis of any reformation of the Church. They are heretical."[354] He went on that he had signed a statement called the "Declaration to the Church," along with thirty other like-minded bishops discarding the theses that "in no way represent the doctrine, discipline, and worship of the Episcopal Church."[355] Salmon exercised great care in separating Spong's ideas from the Episcopal Church. In his long "Pastoral Letter" he used the term "the Church" six times, but "the Episcopal Church," just once. He refused to use the Theses as an excuse to belittle the Episcopal Church again. A decade later, diocesan leaders would not be so reluctant to superimpose the unconventional ideas of some Church officials onto the whole Episcopal Church.

The Lambeth Conference of 1998 was another case in point in which Salmon downplayed criticism of the national Church. The Conference was the Archbishop of Canterbury's once-a-decade meeting of the bishops of all the thirty-eight provinces of the worldwide Anglican Communion. The 1998 assembly was attended by 749 bishops led by Archbishop George Carey. Conservative bishops led the conference to adopt Resolution 1.10 "Human Sexuality." It made three points: to condemn homosexual behavior, oppose the blessing of same-sex unions, and advise against the ordination of non-celibate homosexuals: "rejecting homosexual practices as incompatible with Scripture (. . .) cannot advise the legitimising or blessing of same sex unions nor ordaining those involved in same gender unions."[356] There was an immediate backlash from the bishops of the developed countries. They drew up a letter of apology to homosexual persons that was eventually signed by 185 bishops representing fourteen Anglican provinces. From the U.S., seventy-five bishops signed including many from the southeast: Upper South Carolina, North Carolina, East Carolina, Atlanta, Alabama, Mississippi, and Southern Virginia.[357] In the months thereafter, Salmon had little to say about Lambeth or its controversial resolution. In the next diocesan convention, a mild resolution passed supporting the Lambeth statement on sexuality. That was about the extent of the reaction in South Carolina.

The year 2000 would bring the next triennial session of the General Convention where once again homosexuality was certain to be a hot topic. Bishop Salmon paid little attention to this convention, again in stark contrast to his attitudes to the conventions of 1991, 1994, and 1997, which had all produced crises in the diocese. In the diocesan conventions of 2000 and 2001, Salmon barely mentioned the General Convention. The General Convention of 2000 passed a landmark resolution, D039, in direct reaction to the Lambeth Statement. While "acknowledging the Church's teaching on the sanctity of marriage," it recognized couples "living in other life-long committed relationships."[358]

354. Salmon, "A Pastoral Letter to the People."

355. Ibid.

356. "Section 1.10"; 749 bishops attended, 389 voting in favor (52%), 190 against, the rest abstaining. "Lambeth Conferences," Wikipedia, https://en.wikipedia.org/wiki/Lambeth_Conferences.

357. "A Pastoral Statement to Lesbian and Gay Anglicans from Some Member Bishops of the Lambeth Conference." August 5, 1998, http://justus.anglican.org/resources/Lambeth1998/paststmt.html.

358. "2000–D039, Acknowledge Relationships other than Marriage and Existence of Disagreement on the Church's Teaching." The Acts of Convention 1976–2006, http://www.episcopalarchives.org/GC2009/08_wms/2009-C010.

In effect, it rejected the Lambeth Statement idea that homosexuality was immoral and accepted it as morally neutral. The Convention went on to pass three more resolutions that were "gay friendly." One also moved close to the morally neutral idea, resolution C043 that affirmed and endorsed the Cambridge Accord. The Accord had been drawn up on October 1, 1999, as a pro-homosexual response to the Lambeth Statement. It declared "that every human being is created equal in the eyes of God."[359] One potentially highly important pro-homosexual proposed resolution one died with adjournment. It was C021, "On the Topic of a Definition of 'Sexual Equality.'" Although it was aimed at promoting equality between the genders, it contained a provision that could potentially end the issue of the ordination of homosexuals once and for all: "That every member of the Church is eligible to seek and hold ecclesiastical office in accordance with canonical and diocesan requirements."[360] It should be recalled that before 2003, the General Convention had not passed a resolution explicitly opening up ordination to non-celibate homosexuals although one could argue that the collected body of the various resolutions on homosexuality of the 1990s had meant the same.

Immediately after the General Convention, the American Anglican Council organized a reaction. It should be recalled that AAC staged its first conservative conference soon after the General Convention of 1997 to unite dissident Episcopalians with certain African bishops, an alliance that led to the Lambeth statement of 1998 on homosexuality. Likewise, AAC called another conservative rally on the heels of the 2000 General Convention and, as one will see, would do so again following the Convention of 2003. The meeting in 2000 was in Nassau, Bahamas, on 21–22 August. The Board of the AAC, under the chairmanship of Bishop Stanton of Dallas, met and adopted five resolutions to: recognize consecrations of Charles Murphy and John Rodgers, condemn General Convention's resolution enforcing the ordination of women, call for the creation of a new structure "parallel to the existing structures of the Episcopal Church" for the "orthodox," and condemn the General Convention's support of homosexuality.[361]

To Nassau went a wide array of conservative elements. AAC allied societies were there: Ekklesia, Forward in Faith North America, SEAD, and the Prayer Book Society. Three Anglican primates attended: West Indies, Kenya, and Southern Cone. From the US were Bishops Salmon, Ackerman of Quincy, Iker of Ft. Worth, Stanton of Dallas, and Herzog of Albany. This "Nassau Coalition" declared a pastoral emergency in the Episcopal Church and sent out letters to the Archbishop of Canterbury, the U.S. presiding bishop, and the primates of the Anglican Communion summarizing what the AAC had adopted. The meeting was another step toward creating a replacement church for the Episcopal Church, what the AAC called at this time "parallel."[362]

359. "Cambridge Accord," Wikipedia, http://en.wikipedia.org/wiki/Cambridge_Accord.

360. "2000-C021, On the Topic of a Definition of 'Sexual Equality.'" The Acts of Convention 1976–2012, The Archives of the Episcopal Church, http://www.episcopalarchives.org/cgi-bin/acts/acts_resolution-complete.pl?resolution=2000-C021.

361. "AAC Nassau Resolutions," Virtueonline, August 29, 2000, http://listserv.virtueonline.org/pipermail/virtueonline_listserv.virtueonline.org/2000-August/001591.html.

362. "Primates and Others Gather in Reaction to General Convention Discussions." *The Living Church*, September 17, 2000, The Living Church 1995–2001, The Archives of the Episcopal Church, http://episcopalarchives.org/cgi-bin/the_living_church/TLCarticle.pl?volume=221&issue=12&article_id=4.

Bishop Salmon was so consumed by a more immediate problem that he paid little attention to the resolutions of the General Convention and the Nassau Coalition. However, a highly significant event occurred in the first diocesan convention after the General Convention of 2000. The Rev. Richard Belser[363] and some of his conservative cohorts drew up a stunning proposed resolution they presented without warning to the 2001 meeting of the diocesan convention:

> The Presiding Bishop of the Protestant Episcopal Church is hereby placed on notice of the Diocese of South Carolina's strong objections to the actions of the House of Bishops and the General Convention of 2000 and warns that if further action is taken to implement the proposed changing of the Book of Common Prayer to include a 'marriage' service for same-sex couples, the blessing of same-sex couples and authorizing of ordination of non-celibate homosexual persons (. . .) the Diocese of South Carolina will be forced to reconsider its relationship with the Episcopal Church in the United States of America.[364]

This resolution clearly threatened schism from the Episcopal Church. This was the first such statement in the history of the Diocese of South Carolina since the Civil War. It reflected the feeling of a considerable number of people in the diocese in 2001, but apparently not yet a majority. Salmon did not support it. Dow Sanderson, heretofore prominent among the diocesan conservatives (an original signatory of the First Promise statement) spoke out spontaneously to table the resolution. He reasoned there were already enough diocesan resolutions on record about sexuality.[365] With his high reputation on the right, Sanderson's heartfelt reservation may well have tilted the balance against the surprise proposed resolution. The convention voted to table. It was not brought up again. Although the resolution failed to pull a majority in 2001, it established a sort of template for the diocese for more than a decade. The three objections it raised: ordination of practicing homosexuals, blessing of same-sex unions, and marriage service for homosexuals would indeed become the very crises around which the conservatives would rally the diocese finally to the point they had explicitly raised in 2001, schism. It would take eleven years for the anti-Church party in the diocese who supported the failed resolution of 2001 to bring it to fruition. How this came about is the story recounted in the next few chapters of this book.

The reality of the deep and growing divisions in the diocese was not lost on Bishop Salmon who was shaken if not alarmed by the shocking proposed resolution of 2001. As a consequence, Salmon asked Dow Sanderson, the esteemed conservative who had spoken out against the proposed resolution, to chair a reconciliation committee in the diocese. The purpose would be to find common ground to preserve cohesion in the diocese. The committee met several times at the Church of the Holy Communion, in Charleston,

---

363. Sanderson, (the Rev.) Dow. Telephone conversation with author, December 10, 2015.

364. *Journal of the Two Hundred and Eleventh Annual Meeting of the Convention, March 8, 9, & 10, 2001, Cathedral of St. Luke and St. Paul, Charleston, S.C., Porter-Gaud School, Charleston, S.C., Proceedings of the Convention.* Charleston, SC: the diocese, 2001, 68.

365. Sanderson, telephone conversation.

and produced a report for the meeting of the diocesan convention. The committee urged a broad enough church to make room for differing views.[366]

If Salmon were rattled in the diocesan convention of 2001, he was no less so in the annual meeting of 2002 which convened at Trinity Church, Myrtle Beach on 1–2 March. No doubt with events in All Saints, Pawleys Island, last year's failed proposed resolution, and growing unrest among the conservatives in the diocese against the national Church, Salmon went on at length about disruptions in the local churches: "I have seen more destructive conflict within our congregations in 2001 than in any year in my memory."[367] He continued, "We have had six congregations recently disrupted by conflict, some to the point of significant damage."[368] Salmon also pointed out at length the impressive growth and development of the diocese, perhaps another way of appealing for cohesiveness. He did not mention two controversial proposed resolutions about to be presented in the convention, both of which would work against institutional stability.

Substitute Resolution R–1 was offered by Dow Sanderson, Patrick Allen, Tom Murray, Daniel Clark, Frank Limehouse, Charlie Walton, and Jeffrey Miller. It opened by declaring the oft-repeated conservative mantra of the faith once delivered: "The Episcopal Church in the Diocese of South Carolina affirms that we have received as a sacred trust the Faith once delivered to the saints."[369] The resolution had three parts. Number One said "We will not use liturgies that depart from the Historic Faith."[370] Number Two stated, "We will not accept General Convention Resolutions condoning an unbiblical morality."[371] It condemned all sexual relations, e.g., homosexual, outside of traditional, i.e., heterosexual, Christian marriage. "Not accept" meant the diocese would nullify any resolution of the Episcopal Church that it considered to be outside of its view of marriage. The third part said, "We will not accept coercive canons, which contradict the mind of the Anglican Communion."[372] This referred to the recent General Convention resolution enforcing the right of women to ordination in the dioceses. Once again, "not accept" meant nullification of national Church decisions. Finally, the resolution declared loyalty to the Episcopal Church, but only on condition: "We are committed in every way to remaining a part of the Episcopal Church. We will witness in unity even as we witness to the higher calling of the Truth we have received."[373] In this view, the diocesan understanding of revealed truth would trump loyalty to the Episcopal Church. In other words, local would prevail over national sovereignty. No doubt at the time, this resolution, which passed overwhelmingly, was seen as a unifying force to appease

366. Ibid.

367. Salmon, (the Rt. Rev.) Edrard L., Jr. "Bishop's Address 2002." As quoted in Virtueonline, March 6, 2002, http://listserv.virtueonline.org/pipermail/virtueonline.listserv.virtueonline.org/2002-March.

368. Ibid.

369. "Diocese Passes Resolution Upholding Historic Faith, Condemns Unbiblical Morality." Virtueonline, March 6, 2002, http://listserv.virtueonline.org/pipermail/virtueonline_listserv.virtueonline.org/2002-March.

370. Ibid.

371. Ibid.

372. Ibid.

373. Ibid.

various factions in the diocese. However, in hindsight it contributed significantly to the anti-Episcopal Church stance. It incorporated repeatedly the idea of nullification; and, at the same time placed the diocesan interpretation of truth above loyalty to the national Church. In time, these ideas became so ingrained in the diocese that, as events occurred, the diocese naturally proceeded on the principles that it had so easily assumed in March of 2002. Although the Diocese of South Carolina did not repeat the threat of secession in the failed resolution of 2001, in effect, it returned the same hostility to the Episcopal Church, in different guise, the successful resolution of 2002.

Although the diocese clearly and increasingly opposed the direction of the Episcopal Church on social issues, it still had a long way to go before this would become schism. Indeed, the same convention that breezily passed R–1 also took up another, and more controversial resolution that would have given the local parishes ownership of their properties if they wanted to leave the diocese and affiliate with an Anglican body other than the Episcopal Church. The assembly overwhelmingly rejected this proposed resolution without discussion.[374] No doubt everyone held in mind All Saints of Pawleys Island that was showing signs of preparing to leave the diocese.

As we have seen, the Rev. Chuck Murphy, one of the most conservative voices of the diocese was rector of All Saints, from 1982, and head of First Promise. In 1998, at the same time First Promise raised the suggestion of leaving the Episcopal Church, a local newspaper reported that Murphy had consulted attorneys about whether All Saints could keep its property if it left the diocese.[375] In January, Salmon learned that Allison and Murphy were going to Singapore for the purpose of Murphy's consecration as a bishop. He contacted Allison and Murphy and expressed his objections only to be informed curtly by the two "that any decision regarding consecrations would belong to the archbishops and not to them."[376] This rather impertinent rebuff certainly did not endear Salmon to Allison or Murphy.

A few days after the Singapore consecrations, Bishop Salmon sent out a pastoral letter to his diocese relaying his disappointment and frustration. He gave his side of the background of the consecrations and added while a bishop, Murphy could not function as a priest of the Diocese of South Carolina. Salmon said he expected to meet shortly with Murphy and the vestry of All Saints to work out a road to the future.[377] A few days later, Salmon told the annual meeting of the diocesan convention Murphy was not a priest of the diocese and could not vote in the convention. He added that he had met with the vestry of All Saints and told them they must get a new rector. Thaddeus Barnum became the interim rector of All Saints. Murphy's name did not appear on the official list

---

374. Harmon, (the Rev.) Kendall. "South Carolina Diocesan Convention Affirms Church Growth, Orthodoxy." As quoted in Virtueonline, March 6, 2002, http://listserv.virtueonline.org/pipermail/virtueonline_listserv.virtueonline.org/2002-March.

375. Salmon, (the Rt. Rev.) Edward L., Jr. "USA: A Pastoral Letter to the Congregations of the Diocese of South Carolina." Anglican News Service, http://www.anglicannews.org/news/2000/02/usa-a-pastoral-letter-to-the-congregations-of-the-diocese-of-south-carolina.aspx.

376. Ibid.

377. Ibid.

of the clergy of the diocese in the journal of 2000.[378] However, Salmon could not go too far in his remarks and actions against Murphy who had many friends and philosophical allies in the diocese ready to come to his defense. In his remarks to the diocesan convention Salmon had plenty of good things to say about Murphy. He said he would be willing to license Murphy to function sacramentally as a missionary bishop.[379] Moreover, Salmon went out of his way to blame the whole mess on a supposed crisis of authority in the Episcopal Church as shown in events such as the illegal ordinations of the women in 1974 and 1975 that were regularized in 1976, and Bishop Spong's promotion of radical ideas and policies without reprimand from the Church. Thus, Salmon blamed the present crisis not on Murphy but on a breakdown or order in the Episcopal Church that has produced "'a state of warfare that has given us this prize.'"[380] It appeared that Salmon's balancing act of pleasing the powerful conservative coalition in his diocese and staying in the Episcopal Church was getting more difficult by the day.

One factor that made it more difficult was the creation of the Anglican Mission in America in 2000. Murphy and Rodgers met the archbishops of Rwanda and South East Asia and several other bishops at the Amsterdam Consultation, July 27–29, 2000, and agreed to set up the Anglican Mission in America as a missionary outreach of Rwanda and South East Asia. As Murphy said, "We were authorized to plant churches and receive those that could not in good conscience remain within the Episcopal Church."[381] He cited the actions of the 2000 General Convention on homosexuality as the cause of the new mission.[382] The AMiA meant a de facto schism in the Episcopal Church because parishes that adhered to it would follow the primate of a foreign church and his bishops. Murphy and Rodgers claimed at the start they had seventeen Episcopal parishes in AMiA and expected many more soon.[383]

At the same time, Salmon tried to deal with the complications following Murphy's consecration and the growing possibility of All Saints parish leaving the diocese, he addressed the issue of property ownership of All Saints. The Dennis Canon had been formally incorporated into the diocesan canons in 1987. Under this church law, all parish property ultimately belonged to the Episcopal Church and the diocese, even if the local parish held the deeds. The problem with All Saints was that the diocese had issued a quit claim deed of the property to the parish in 1903, long before the Dennis Canon appeared. A quit claim deed would "quit" or surrender any legal claim the diocese would have to the local properties.

378. *Journal of the Two Hundred and Tenth Annual Meeting of the Convention, February 11–12, 2000, St. Philip's Church, Charleston, SC, Charleston Place, Charleston SC, Proceedings of the Convention.* Charleston, SC: the diocese, 2000, 33–34.

379. Munday, Dave. "Bishop Edward Salmon of South Carolina Backs Chuck Murphy." *The Post and Courier* (Charleston, SC), as quoted in Virtueonline, February 13, 2000, http://listserv.virtueonline.org/pipermail/virtueonline_listserv.virtueonline.org/2000-February/001035.html.

380. "Excerpt from the Address Given by the Rt. Revd Edward L. Salmon, Jr., Bishop of South Carolina." Anglicans Online, February 11, 2000, http://www.anglicansonline.org/archive/news/articles/2000/000211a.html.

381. Brust, Cynthia. "A Look Back." *Wave*, November 2007, http://www.thesocietyofmission.com.

382. "Murphy and Rodgers."

383. Ibid.

Soon after Murphy's ordination as bishop and about the time of the establishment of the Anglican Mission in America, which was in August of 2000, All Saints hired a major law firm to make an exhaustive title search in the courthouse records of Georgetown County.[384] Chancellor Zeigler surmised from this that All Saints was planning to leave the diocese with property in hand.[385] The title search discovered that the original 1745 trust deed and the 1903 quit claim deed were the only deeds recorded for the property in question. Zeigler, alarmed at All Saints' action, recommended to Bishop Salmon that the diocese record the Dennis Canon in the courthouse of each county.[386] This would ensure no parish could leave with the property because the county record would show the property was held in trust for the diocese and the national Church. Salmon agreed; and on September 11, 2000, the Dennis Canon was recorded in the clerk of the court's office in Georgetown County.[387] In response to this, in October of 2000, All Saints brought suit in the circuit court of Georgetown County, Judge John Breeden, Jr., asking for a declaratory judgment that it alone owned the property. All Saints also invited the dozen or so other colonial churches to join the lawsuit, but none accepted.[388] In a curious twist, on August 31, 2001, All Saints filed motion in court that it did not own the property after all but rather it belonged to the heirs of the original 1745 Pawley trust and to the inhabitants of Waccamaw. After a trial on September 4, 2001, Judge Breeden ruled, on October 15, 2001, that the property did indeed belong to the heirs of the 1745 trust and the inhabitants of Waccamaw and to neither the parish nor the diocese. In effect, this left the property to the parish. The diocese appealed the decision to the South Carolina Court of Appeals.[389]

Bishop Salmon had good reason to fear All Saints was in the process of trying to leave the diocese with its property in hand when the delegates from All Saints arrived at the 2001 annual diocesan convention claiming they had rejected a part of the diocesan constitution and canons but were still in union with the diocese and asking for seats and voice. Their conservative allies in the diocese were ready to help. The Revs. Burwell, Belser, McCormick, and Limehouse presented a proposed resolution entitled "Seating for All Saints' Waccamaw."[390] It said, "All Saints Parish, Waccamaw currently finds itself unwilling to conform with Article VIII, Section 2."[391] It continued, "This Diocese will nevertheless admit all lay delegates from All Saints' Parish, Waccamaw, at this 211th Annual Convention of the Diocese of South Carolina, giving them seat and voice."[392] After

384. Zeigler, *When Conscience*, 322.

385. Ibid.

386. Ibid.

387. Ibid.

388. Ibid.

389. "26724–All Saints v. Campbell." South Carolina, Judicial Department, http://www.judicial.state.sc.us/opinions/displayOpinion.cfm?caseNo=26724.

The Court of Appeals held a hearing on September 10, 2003, and issued a written opinion on March 8, 2004, reversing part of the circuit court decision and remanding the case to the lower court.

390. *Journal of the Two Hundred and Eleventh (. . .)* 2001, 68.

391. Ibid.

392. Ibid.

protracted discussion, the delegates adopted the resolution and the delegates from All Saints were seated, although the parish was deemed not in union with the diocese.[393]

On June 24, 2001, came more shocking news from the Anglican Mission in America. Eight bishops, including Allison, ordained four new bishops for the AMiA, in Denver. One of the four was Thaddeus Barnum, the one who had been appointed interim rector of All Saints after Murphy. As Murphy and Rodgers, the four new bishops were to serve as "missionary" bishops in the U.S. under the archbishops of Rwanda and South East Asia. The fact that one third of the six AMiA bishops had come from the Diocese of South Carolina was not ignored by Bishop Salmon in a special message published on the front page of *Jubilate Deo*. As the year before, he showed his disapproval: "I profoundly regret the decision of the Anglican Mission in America leadership to take such a step."[394] This time he threw doubt on their validity: "The consecrations in Denver are not under the authority of the canons of the American Church (. . .). The Archbishop of Canterbury (. . .) did declare them irregular and has refused to accept the new bishops in a relationship with Canterbury."[395] As Salmon, the national Church leadership was growing alarmed at the continuing consecrations. It had more or less ignored the first round, in 2000, but could hardly do so again. When the Church's Executive Council met in San Antonio, February 22–25, 2002, it strongly condemned the AMiA and its consecrations, but took no direct action against the persons involved.

CONCLUSION

The year 2002 was the calm before the storm. As it came to a close, the Episcopal Church and the Diocese of South Carolina could look back at a half-century of transformative change. The Church and the diocese were vastly different than they had been five decades earlier when they were rather quiet, even staid, largely inward-directed bastions of the educated, cultured, comfortable people in America whose aim seemed to be to maintain a genteel status quo by endlessly repeating the lofty liturgies in the prayer book. From a vertically directed religion of man and God, the Episcopal Church turned to a horizontally oriented religion directed to reforming the ills in society all around it. Racial justice and a democratized prayer book were almost entirely completed before 1980. Equality for women took longer, but the ordination of women was settled in 1976 even though holdouts remained for the next few decades.

The fourth great reform movement, equal rights for homosexuals, was by far the most difficult and complicated one the Church faced. Conservatives saw a problem of morality while liberals saw one of human rights. Thus, the two sides fought two different campaigns in the same overall war. They never met on the same battlefield. And, along the way, the Episcopal Church never had a great debate on homosexuality. It wound up

---

393. Zeigler, *When Conscience*, 324.

394. Salmon, (the Rt. Rev.) Edward L., Jr. "A Message from Bishop Salmon to the Clergy and People of the Diocese of South Carolina." *Jubilate Deo* (Diocese of South Carolina), August/September 2001.

395. Ibid.

settling the issue by default, in the end making a de facto resolution of the question of the interface between the Church and homosexuality.

Conservative Episcopalians viewed the sexual practices of homosexuals as sinful and immoral and defended their stand by quoting the half-dozen verses in the Bible they said condemned homosexuality. They also declared their position to be absolute and non-negotiable, not open to compromise. In 1979, they got the Church to oppose the ordination of open homosexuals. From the 1970s to the 1990s they moved through the General Conventions a long list of resolutions affirming that sexual relations were appropriate only in the context of heterosexual marriage. The implication in the resolutions was that sexual activities between persons of the same gender were immoral; and, therefore, it should go without saying that the Church should not ordain openly sinful and immoral persons. Conservative Episcopalians held the upper hand on this issue in the Church from 1976 to 1991. In the course of events, they came to believe they had settled on their terms the Episcopal Church's policy on the ordination of open homosexuals. They believed they had won the war.

Their opposite force in the Episcopal Church we can call for simplicity's sake, the liberals. They interpreted the problem at hand almost entirely differently. Viewing the oft-quoted Bible verses as unclear and debatable, they interpreted homosexual behavior as morally neutral, neither good nor bad. From 1976 onward, they fought their campaign to get the Episcopal Church to recognize full equality of homosexuals in the life of the Church. One by one, they pushed through resolutions in General Conventions to defend and promote rights for homosexuals. Thus, while the Episcopal Church resolved time and again to defend heterosexual marriage, it also adopted one resolution after another favoring homosexuals. This allowed the two sides, fighting different campaigns, to believe they were winning the war.

The war over homosexuality went through three periods in the life of the Episcopal Church. In the first, 1976 to 1991, the conservatives predominated. The second, 1991 to 1997, was the time of conflict. The Church was divided into thirds, conservative, liberal, and neutral. The right and left engaged in a tug-of-war over the uncommitted neutrals. It started with the dangerously acrimonious session of the House of Bishops in 1991 and ended with the General Convention of 1997 which made the strange settlement of rejecting the establishment of the blessing of same-sex unions while setting up an exploration of that very same subject for the future. By 1997, the liberals won the upper hand. The third period, 1997 to 2002, was the aftermath of the liberals' victory.

The liberals' success, however, was so subtle that many Episcopalians did not recognize it, let alone accept it. By 1997, the Church actually arrived at a de facto resolution of the question of the ordination of homosexuals. The House of Bishops failed to take action against Spong or Righter and to repudiate their ordinations of open homosexuals. General Convention quietly changed the Church canons to remove sexual orientation as a barrier to ordination. It also rejected any canonical change to block the ordination of homosexuals. An ecclesiastical court sided with the liberals and declared the teachings of the Episcopal Church did not preclude the ordination of homosexuals. The effectual accumulation of all these back-door changes was to open ordination to homosexuals without qualification. This was the largely unappreciated reality of 1997.

The liberals won over the majority of the Episcopal Church in the period of conflict, 1991 to 1997. Why was this so? Why did they eventually prevail over the conservatives on the issue of homosexuality? There were several reasons for this. In the first place, Anglicanism/Episcopalianism was historically non-doctrinaire and non-ideological. When the Church of England declared its independence from Rome in the sixteenth century, it deliberately adopted a very broad and tolerant policy as a church for the entire nation. Accepting widely different viewpoints meant it could not take sides. Thereafter, Anglicanism as a whole avoided taking doctrinaire positions. What the conservatives in the Episcopal Church from the 1970s to the 1990s wanted was for the Church to take a doctrinaire position condemning homosexuality. This went against the grain of Church history. Moreover, the fact that conservatives announced that their position was non-negotiable made the liberals appear to be the reasonable side to the people in the uncommitted middle ground. Also, one should bear in mind the big picture of the Episcopal Church after the Second World War. It redefined itself as the Church of the social gospel committed to righting the wrongs of society all around it. The liberals' argument that homosexuals deserved the same liberation and equal rights as everyone else rang true to the majority. How could they deny equality within the Church to homosexuals when they had already fought so hard for the rights of blacks and women? Of course, opening ordination carried, by default, the unspoken rejection of the conservatives' view on morality and validation of the liberals' idea of moral neutrality.

Owing to the way in which the Episcopal Church had made its resolution of the issue of homosexuality by default, most conservatives, indeed perhaps most Episcopalians, did not appreciate the reality of what had happened. Most conservative Episcopalians did not understand just what had happened in the Church to settle the issue. They preferred to cling to the myth that the Church's resolutions on marriage meant the condemnation of homosexual ordination. Thus, as the year 2002 came to an end, conservative and liberal viewpoints were as far apart as ever on the subject of homosexuality. As we will see, given this background, the events of 2003 were immensely shocking to the conservatives. Suddenly, their fondly held illusion of moral victory vanished and the reality of what had actually happened a few years earlier in the Episcopal Church came crashing down on them as a bolt of lightning. It should not be surprising then that the reactions in the Church to the fourth great reform movement would be vastly different than those of the earlier three.

The Diocese of South Carolina underwent an equally dramatic change in these decades. Until his retirement in 1982, Bishop Temple had worked hard to keep the diocese in the mainstream of the national Church. In this he succeeded even against significant internal resistance and while making great institutional developments for the diocese. This was to change swiftly after Bishop Allison took over. A contentious theologian of resolute evangelical bent, Allison saw the diocese as a bulwark of "orthodoxy" to resist the heretical radicalism he believed emanated from the far-left leaders such as John Spong. He was there to get the diocese to fight the good fight, and he succeeded, at least to some degree such as demolishing the book on sexuality. At the same time, he did all he could to pack the local churches with like-minded clergy, particularly those from his partisan creation, Trinity School for Ministry. When Allison retired in 1990, the diocese was decidedly conservative even if it had lost members and income. Ideology was more important than institutional development. Salmon, his successor, by contrast was not ideological, but a fairly conservative man who was committed to institutional cohesion. He seemed to want to please everyone. From 1990 to 1997, he leaned congenially to the predominant conservative side of the diocese and frequently criticized the Episcopal Church for its reforms, particularly those concerning homosexuality. With the appearance of a probable schism within his own diocese from All Saints of Pawleys Island and its Anglican Mission in America creation, his attitude changed and became less critical of the national Church and more concerned about the home-grown danger at hand. He went to court to enforce the Dennis Canon and protect the property claims of the diocese. Yet, at the same time, he had to live with the large and powerful conservative coalition in his diocese that came close to passing a resolution threatening secession from the Episcopal Church. For the moment, Salmon managed to balance opposition to reforms of the national Church with the institutional integrity of the diocese and Church. The driving issues for the diocese in the next decade were clear by 2002: opposition to the ordination of practicing homosexuals, the blessing of same-sex unions, and homosexual marriage, and local property ownership.

Before moving on to the crisis of 2003, it is useful to stop for a moment and look at the context in which the Diocese of South Carolina existed then. The diocese moved from the mainstream of the Episcopal Church to consistent criticism, if not hostility, against the national Church in the 1980s and 1990s. Although detailed histories of the neighboring Episcopal dioceses were beyond the scope of the present work, cursory reviews of them revealed South Carolina to be the unique case in the region. Not one other diocese in the southeastern U.S. duplicated the sudden rightward turn. Not one other diocese overtly supported South Carolina. The closest to an ally was Bishop John Howe, of Central Florida (1990–2012), but his diocese did not exhibit the organized tendencies and examples of schism that South Carolina showed even before 2003. Not one of the adjacent dioceses even came close to paralleling South Carolina in its rightward move. Indeed, most of the neighboring bishops signed the Cambridge Accord of 1999 that was directly opposed to the anti-homosexual stand of the Lambeth Statement of 1998. South Carolina became an outlier in the province as it was also becoming such in the national Church. This begs the question of why this happened. Why did South Carolina become the region's diocese most hostile to the Episcopal Church? Was this because the Low Country had always been more conservative, inward-directed, and separatist-minded than any other part of the southeast? It is dubious that this is the explanation because this was the same region that had been in the mainstream of the Episcopal Church up to 1982. Political scientists would tell us that as far as political patterns go, the Low Country is not as conservative as the Upstate of South Carolina where voting is historically more to the right. Yet, throughout all of this, the Diocese of Upper South Carolina remained in the mainstream of the national Church. The Low Country had always been a traditional place steeped in history, but this did not explain what happened in the diocese in the late twentieth century.

The existing public records and documents of the Diocese of South Carolina suggested the counter-revolution of the 1980s and 1990s there came from the leading clergy, many of whom were not natives of South Carolina. The bishops, and many of their priests and deacons were the ones leading the campaign of criticism, resistance, and hostility to the trends and events in the national Church. This was a conservative counter-revolution from the top down. It did not originate from the ordinary communicants in the pews who remained the same. This evangelical conservatism clearly appeared with Bishop Allison in the early 1980s and was greatly bolstered by an influx of young graduates of Trinity School for Ministry. By the time Bishop Salmon arrived in 1990, a distinct conservative presence exhibited itself among the parish clergy. At the same time, there was no organized counterforce in the diocese defending the national Church. An informal coalition of like-minded clergy on the right formed but none on the left. This threw the balance in the diocese far to the right. Basically, what the conservatives wanted was an end to the "horizontal" religion of social activism and a return to the old "vertical" religion of personal salvation. This put the diocese at odds with the well-entrenched "horizontal" character of the national Church. Bishop Salmon, trying to keep institutional cohesion, sided with the conservatives but then had to draw back as he saw the most extreme local elements moving to schism from the diocese and the Church. It was no accident that the first significant separatist movement from the Episcopal Church in many years happened in the Low Country and occurred on the heels of the anti-homosexual crusade in the Episcopal Church.

Thus, between 1982 and 2003, the Episcopal Diocese of South Carolina moved to the far-right edge of the Episcopal Church. Its tie to the Church increasingly weakened. Many of its clergy were openly hostile to the policies and procedures of the national Church and were actively involved in various Episcopalian resistance organizations. Talk of secession from the Episcopal Church had broken out but had not quite taken hold. While they did not quite comprehend the liberals' victory on homosexuality, the conservative clergy of South Carolina grew ever more suspicious of the national Church. A small number went off with the Chuck Murphy's Anglican Mission in America, but the majority remained in the Church, however unhappily, for the time being. This was the uneasy state of the diocese when the explosion of 2003 occurred.

2

The Crisis of 2003 in the Episcopal Church and its Immediate Aftermath

THE BACKGROUND OF THE ROBINSON AFFAIR

THE YEAR 2003 STARTED calmly enough. At that moment, no one could have foreseen how differently the Episcopal Church and the Diocese of South Carolina would appear one year later. The year 2003 would prove to be a pivotal one in the life of the modern Episcopal Church, the moment when the conservative minority was suddenly jolted into the reality that the Church had rejected their stand on the issue of homosexuality. For the Diocese of South Carolina, the crisis of 2003 was to present the irresistible moment of decision. The conservatives, the unchallenged prevailing party in the diocese, had to choose between joining the dioceses that were moving toward secession and remaining in the Episcopal Church. This was not to be simple and easy though because, in the midst of it all arose the complication that Bishop Salmon faced mandatory retirement and a new diocesan bishop had to be elected, approved and installed.

Although the Episcopal Church never explicitly resolved the conflict on the issue of the morality of homosexuality, it did settle it in a backward and subtle manner by default, the same way it dealt with the question of the ordination of homosexuals. In 2001, when the conservative leaders in South Carolina drew up their unsuccessful resolution for the diocesan convention, they listed banning ordination of homosexuals, something that was impossible under Episcopal Church law at that time. They did not understand this issue had already been settled in the Church for years. Indeed, the Church had started moving beyond that into the sub-issue of whether to allow the liturgical blessings of same-sex couples. Thus, although the Episcopal Church actually resolved the issue of homosexuality in the period of conflict 1990–1997, the Diocese of South Carolina had refused to accept it, indeed, even to recognize that it had happened. They preferred to cling to their longstanding comfortable belief that "the teaching" of the Episcopal Church condemned homosexuality and they could still use this to block the ordination of non-celibate homosexuals. The problem was that the majority of the Church did not believe that in 2003. In reality, whether people in South Carolina recognized it or not, the Church as a whole no longer regarded homosexual behavior as essentially immoral or saw it as a reason to prevent the ordination of non-celibate homosexuals. Thus, when the crisis of 2003 occurred, the Episcopal Church and the Diocese of South Carolina would react very differently. What only rattled the national Church turned out to be a major cataclysm in the diocese. The reason for this was that the Church and the diocese were far apart in their understandings of the role of homosexuality in the Church at the start of the year 2003. Part of the fault for this gulf lay with the national Church, in its inability to articulate a clear-cut policy on homosexuality, and part with the diocese, in its failure to recognize the reality of the Church's evolving liberal attitude toward homosexuality.

The closest the Church came to reaching a consensus on homosexuality before the Robinson affair was a bishops' report on sexuality issued in early 2003. "The Gift of Sexuality: A Theological Perspective," was adopted by the House of Bishops in a meeting at Kanuga, North Carolina, on March 18, 2003. It had been drawn up by the Theology Committee of the House of Bishops which was chaired by the universally esteemed even-handed moderate, Henry N. Parsley, bishop of Alabama. Parsley brought together a widely varying collection of six bishops and seven academics representing the different perspectives on the issue of the interface of the Episcopal Church and homosexuality.[1] For eighteen months the members had worked preparing papers which were edited into one report that was unanimously approved by the committee for presentation to the House of Bishops and, by extension, the Church. This in itself, was a remarkable accomplishment.

In retrospect, the Theology Committee's report (hereafter "the Parsley Report") unknowingly summarized well the status of the issue of homosexuality in the Episcopal Church on the eve of the Robinson crisis of 2003, which early in that year no one could have foreseen. The effects of the liberal trending movement of the Church in the 1990s were evident in its tone and content. Instead of defining the issue as it had been originally seen in the 1970s and 1980s as the two sub-texts of 1-the conservative demand for the condemnation of sexual relations of homosexuals and 2-the liberal push for ordination as a human right for homosexuals, the Parsley Report defined the sub-issues as 1-the blessing of same-sex unions and 2-the ordination of homosexuals. The conservative view on morality was relegated to the historical context. On the first point, the blessing of same-sex unions, it presented the arguments of both sides then concluded "Because at this time we are nowhere near consensus in the Church regarding the blessing of homosexual relationships, we cannot recommend authorizing the development of new rites for such blessings."[2] It should be recalled that the 1997 General Convention had rejected a resolution to move to the blessing of same-sex unions while accepting a resolution to study the matter for the future. The Parsley Report was clear in opposing the blessing of same-sex unions, at least for the time being. On the second point, it was not so clear. Concerning the ordination of homosexuals, it recognized that ordination

1. Parsley, (the Rt. Rev.) Henry N. Interview with author, December 12, 2013. Bishops: Parsley, Theodore A. Daniels, William O. Gregg, John W. Howe, Robert W. Ihloff, and Catherine S. Roskam; academics: Michael Battle, Ellen Charry, Ian T. Douglas, James E. Grifiss, Mark McIntosh, Russell Reno, and Kathryn Tanner.

2. "The Gift of Sexuality: A Theological Perspective." Report of the Theology Committee of the House of Bishops of the Episcopal Church, http://arc.episcopalchurch.org/presiding-bishop/theologycommreport.pdf.

was the prerogative of the local bishops then concluded: "We call on bishops and Standing Committees to be respectful of the ways in which decisions made in one Diocese have ramifications on others. We remind all that ordination is for the whole Church."³ This was a position that took no position, thus leaving tacit recognition of the liberals' controversial ordinations.

The Parsley Report, in effect, recognized the ordination of homosexuals without qualification, at least in the dioceses that approved of such. It optimistically called for a continuation of the discussion of the broad issue of homosexuality in hopes that the Church could reach a consensus before establishing a clear-cut position on the issue. It concluded: "we believe it is imperative that the Episcopal Church refrain from any attempt to 'settle' the matter legislatively. For a season at least, we must acknowledge and live with the great pain and discomfort of our disagreements."⁴ In short, the Report called on the Church to agree to disagree and to refrain for the time being from passing resolutions regarding homosexuality.⁵

Looking back, what the Theology Committee effectively did in the spring of 2003 was to give credence to the liberal position on the ordination of homosexuals on the eve of the very moment when this was to be put to its greatest test ever. To strengthen the liberals' hand was certainly not the Committee's intention, but it was the historic outcome nevertheless. In a sense, the Theology Committee's report unwittingly helped pave the way for the approval of the first practicing homosexual as a bishop of the Episcopal Church.

THE ROBINSON AFFAIR

On June 7, 2003, the Diocese of New Hampshire, meeting in St. Paul's Church, Concord, elected Vicky Gene Robinson, the diocesan canon to the ordinary, as bishop coadjutor. He was an openly homosexual man living with a same-gender partner. Robinson's choice was clearly the wish of the majority of the diocesan convention. He carried 58 clergy votes (39 necessary), and 96 lay votes (83 necessary).⁶ This election forced the issue onto the General Convention because canon law held that an election for a bishop within three months of a meeting of the General Convention required a vote in the House of Deputies and the House of Bishops in the upcoming Convention: "if the election shall have taken place within three months next before the meeting of the General Convention, the consent of the House of Deputies shall be required in place of that of a majority of the Standing Committees."⁷ There was no way the 2003 Convention could

---

3. Ibid.

4. Ibid.

5. The Report did not describe the difference between a majority vote to pass a resolution and "consensus."

6. Adams, Elizabeth. *Going to Heaven: The Life and Election of Bishop Gene Robinson.* Brooklyn, NY: Soft Skull, 2006, 98. Robinson was elected on the second ballot. His vote on the first ballot had been 51 clergy and 77 lay, 6 votes short on the lay side. The vote indicated Robinson's support was stronger among the clergy than among the laity.

7. *Constitution and Canons, The Episcopal Church.* New York: the Church, 2003. http://www.

avoid the issue. It would have to vote to accept or to reject a non-celibate homosexual as a bishop. If it consented, Robinson would become the first openly homosexual bishop in the Episcopal Church, the Anglican Communion, and in any major denomination claiming apostolic succession. After twenty-seven years of maneuvering over, under, and around the issue of homosexuality and its complex set of sub-texts, the Episcopal Church would finally have to stand and make a bold decision on the issue of homosexuality. Robinson's election meant the recommendations of the recent Parsley Report would have to be discarded. There was no choice. The issue would have to be settled in 2003 by legislation.

Why should this produce a crisis in the Episcopal Church? After all, open and non-celibate homosexual clergy had been ordained for years, at least fourteen. Moreover, since 1991, there had been a long list of resolutions, canonical changes, and reports in the Church giving tacit acceptance of the ordination of homosexuals, the Parsley Report being only the most recent. It had recognized, if not quite promoted, such ordinations in various dioceses of the Church. Since 1989, some Episcopal dioceses had ordained openly gay deacons and priests.

So, why the fuss now that a practicing homosexual was up to be approved as a bishop? The answer was that it was one thing to ordain a deacon or a priest, but something different for a bishop. In the first place, a bishop would have apostolic succession, that is, authority conveyed all the way from the first bishops of the early church. No openly partnered homosexual had ever been given apostolic succession. Bestowing it to one would be tantamount to the approval of the sexual acts of homosexual persons. This would end the historic teaching that sexual relations outside of traditional marriage were immoral. Too, a bishop was an office of authority in the whole church even if he is in only one diocese. Also, a bishop had to be approved by a majority of the Church either in General Convention or the diocesan standing committees. Approval of an openly gay bishop would set a precedence for the whole Church, not the least of which would be to end the conservative view of the immorality of homosexual acts.

Conservatives preferred to believe they had held the fort on this by passing numerous resolutions in General Convention defending traditional marriage and getting the Lambeth Conference of 1998 to agree. Liberals, on the other hand, believed they had made a de facto settlement for moral neutrality through the gradual acceptance of homosexual ordination without qualification. After more than a quarter of a century in which the Episcopal Church had avoided directly confronting the question of morality, it could not be avoided any longer. Either homosexuality was immoral and sinful and Robinson should be rejected, or it was morally neutral and Robinson should be approved. The Church would reach a resolution in 2003, but did so in its too familiar method of decision by default and de facto settlement.

The General Convention was to meet in Minneapolis from July 30 to August 8. The fifty-three days between Robinson's election and the opening of the Convention witnessed a whirlwind of highly publicized activities, to no one's surprise. The conservatives, shocked and appalled, arose in loud and angry fury trumpeting dire warnings of disaster if the Church approved of a gay bishop. Again to no one's surprise, the diocesan

episcopalarchives.org?C_and_C_2003.pdf.

leaders of South Carolina were in the thick of it. Robinson's election occurred just before noon on the 7th. Within a few hours, bishops Salmon and Skilton issued a lengthy statement denouncing the election and calling on the Church to reject it. It was disseminated widely by Kendall Harmon who claimed the title, "Communications Director, Diocese of South Carolina" and was reprinted in the next issue of *Jubilate Deo*, the diocesan newspaper.[8] Following the diocesan fondness for drama, the statement began by declaring that the Anglican Communion was in one of its greatest crises ever. True to the longstanding conservative viewpoint, Salmon and Skilton said the issue at hand was one of sin and morality: "[the] official position of the Episcopal Church is that the only proper context for the expression of sexual intimacy is between a man and a woman who are married to each other."[9] The statement continued, "If Gene Robinson's election is confirmed by General Convention, it would bring through the back door a practice that the Episcopal Church has never agreed to approve through the front door."[10] It was on this the bishops showed they missed the reality of what had been happening in the Episcopal Church for at least a decade. Approval of the ordination of homosexuals, and the concurrent disregard of the conservatives' view of morality had gradually and subtly crept into the Church through the back door. It was already there. This is why conservatives such as Salmon and Skilton were so shocked by Robinson's election and why they misunderstood the status of homosexuality in the Church as of 2003. They doggedly denounced homosexuality as sinful and immoral, but the general feeling in the Church had moved beyond that into at least moral neutrality. Bishops with rigidly dogmatic views as Salmon and Skilton were in fact an ever-shrinking minority well before the Robinson affair of 2003.

On July 9, Salmon joined Robert Duncan, bishop of Pittsburgh, in publishing another statement warning of dire consequences. They reiterated the standard conservative ideology that homosexual practices were sinful and immoral: "The Church of Jesus Christ has carefully taught that the only proper context for the expression of sexual intimacy is between a man and a woman who are married to each other."[11] They continued, "In the vote on Gene Robinson a 'basic issue is at stake,' the church's teaching on human sexuality and relationships (. . .). If the General Convention votes to approve Bishop-elect Robinson the Convention will vote to do something the Episcopal Church has never agreed to do."[12] As we have seen, it was literally true that the Episcopal Church had never overtly denied its oft-repeated stand that sexual relations belong in heterosexual marriage. This is what the conservatives insisted upon, and they were right superficially.

Despite their protestations, there were signs that the conservatives knew well ahead of time they were doomed to fail in the upcoming General Convention. Deep down they

---

8. Kendall Harmon was editor of *Jubilate Deo* from 2002 to 2008. The diocesan newspaper at this time became consistently conservative and increasingly critical of the national Church.

9. "Grave Concern over a Great Crisis—Statement of South Carolina Bishops in the Episcopal Election in New Hampshire." June 7, 2003, http://www.americananglican.org/grave-concern-over-a-great-crisis.

10. Ibid.

11. "A Joint Statement from the Bishop of Pittsburgh and the Bishop of South Carolina." July 9, 2003, http://www.americananglican.org/a-joint-statement-from-the-bishop-of-pittsburgh.

12. Ibid.

may well have known the game was lost. Sensing their weakness within the structure of the Episcopal Church, conservatives reached out to foreign allies who were also resolved to defeat homosexual rights in their own localities. In the critical weeks leading up to the General Convention, conservatives appealed as much as they could for support from their overseas comrades in arms. On July 15, twenty-four bishops, eighteen of whom were diocesan, published an open letter to the primates of the Anglican Communion asking for their help, not in defeating the impending pro-homosexual measures which they said were likely to pass, but in rescuing the remnant orthodox factions from the heretical majority of the Episcopal Church.[13] The details of how the overseas primates would rescue them were left unstated. In their poignant, if desperate, appeal, the distressed bishops said: "We do hereby affirm the moral and spiritual authority of you, the "Concerned Primates' of the Anglican Communion, and do join in commitment with you to address the situation under your leadership. We desire to act in concert with you, and are ready to take counsel from you. We pledge solidarity with you."[14] It is interesting to note than twenty-four bishops signed this letter. That would amount to less than 10 percent of Episcopal bishops. Just nine years earlier, conservatives had drawn up a strong statement called "An Affirmation" that defended traditional marriage, condemned homosexuality, and declared no compromise. That document had been signed by 106 bishops, roughly a third of all Episcopal bishops. The drop from 106 bishops in 1994 to 24 in 2003 reflected the reality of what had happened to views on homosexuality in the Episcopal Church.

The most serious move of the conservative minority in the run-up to General Convention was to convene a meeting of their leaders and seven of the most conservative primates of the Anglican Communion: Peter Akinola of Nigeria, Emmanuel Kolini of Rwanda, Bernard Melango of Central Africa, Drexel Gomez of West Indies, Gregory Venables of Southern Cone, and Yong Ping Chung of Southeast Asia.[15] Forty-eight prominent Episcopalian conservatives attended including fifteen bishops (ten were diocesan bishops).[16] In all, sixty-two people joined in the two-day secret meeting at Truro Episcopal Church in Fairfax, Virginia.[17] Four came from South Carolina: Bishops Salmon and Skilton, the Rev. Kendall Harmon, and the Rev. Al Zadig. The conference issued the "Truro Statement" on July 23, 2003. It was blunt, vaguely threatening and obviously

---

13. "Twenty-Four Episcopal Bishops Declare 'Impaired Communion' with Canadian Diocese of New Westminster." July 15, 2002, http://www.americananglican.org/twenty-four-episcopal-bishops-declare-impaired-communion.

14. Ibid.

15. "A Statement from the Gathering of Worldwide Anglican Mainstream Leaders." July 23, 2003, http://www.americananglican.org/a-statement-from-the-gathering-of-worldwide-anglican-mainstream.

16. The meeting brought together a who's who of the Episcopal Church conservatives at that time. Among the dioceses well represented were 4 of the 5 that eventually voted to leave the Church (Keith Ackerman of Quincy, Robert Duncan of Pittsburgh, Jack Iker of Ft. Worth, and Edward Salmon of South Carolina). Salmon remained in the Episcopal Church after the schism in South Carolina. In the list of the 48 clergy and laity present were familiar names such as Don Armstrong, Alison Barfoot, Gregory Brewer, Geoffrey Chapman, Martyn Minns, Ephraim Radner, Christopher Seitz, Philip Turner, and Diane Knippers. South Carolina had perhaps the most representatives at four (Salmon, Skilton, Harmon, and Zadig). "A Statement from the Gathering."

17. Nunley, Jan. "Episcopalians: Group Prepared to Respond if General Convention Affirms Robinson." Episcopal News Service, http://arc.episcopalchurch.org/ens/2003-167.html.

mean to impress the General Convention which was set to open a week later. Right off, it predicted cataclysm: "The proposed actions by General Convention to confirm a non-celibate homosexual as a bishop of this Communion or to approve the creation of liturgies for the blessing of relationships outside of marriage would shatter the church."[18] It went on, "The proposed actions will precipitate a dramatic realignment of the Church."[19] Then it ended with a dark but ambiguous warning: "Should these events occur, the majority of the Primates anticipate convening an extraordinary meeting at which they too will respond to the actions of General Convention."[20] No explanation followed, so the meaning of this scarcely veiled threat was anyone's guess. When reporters asked Harmon what it meant, he said, cryptically, "'We are trying to preserve an element of surprise. That is part of the strategy here.'"[21] A few days later, Harmon said in a discussion on PBS News Hour, 1 August: "We do not know what is going to happen. But we are going to wait and see what happens, but when it happens and if it happens, we wish not to spell out all the specifics, because this is a strategy and it involves an element of surprise."[22]

If the purpose of the Truro Statement were to put pressure on the Episcopal Church to back off approving Robinson and the blessing of same-sex unions, there is no evidence that it worked. Perhaps the purpose was to unify a coalition to make a secession of conservative dioceses from the Episcopal Church that would be aided and abetted by prominent Third World Anglican prelates. Evidence seems to indicate that on the eve of the 2003 General Convention, the ultra-conservative faction of the Episcopal Church knew they had lost the internal war on homosexuality and were already looking beyond their own Church's institutional structure. They were coalescing and building ties with powerful primates in the Third World who were their ideological allies as if they were preparing for the post-Convention. Exactly where all of this was taking the far-right was unclear before the Convention. It would become much clearer in the months afterwards.

To say that excitement surrounded the opening of the 74th General Convention of the Episcopal Church would be a simplistic understatement. It was the most important General Convention since the Civil War and everyone knew it, not just in the Episcopal Church, but in churches beyond, in America as a whole, and to a great extent the entire world. The Episcopal Church was about to do what no major Christian church had ever done in recorded history. The significance of this was apparently not lost on anyone. It seemed the eyes of the world turned to Minneapolis and media beyond count showed up to report the news. The focus of it all was a fifty-three-year-old humble little man, the son of a Kentucky sharecropper.

The overshadowing thought on everyone's mind, the vote on Robinson, proved agonizingly slow to occur. It was a week before it came to conclusion on August 5. If the conservative opposition knew that they were about to lose, as the bishops admitted in their July 15 letter, they did not show it in the run-up to the vote. On the contrary,

18. "A Statement from the Gathering."
19. Ibid.
20. Ibid.
21. Nunley, "Episcopalians."
22. "A Church's Choice: First Openly Gay Bishop." PBS News Hour, August 1, 2003, http://www.pbs.org/newshour/bb/religion-july-dec03-episcopalian.

they fought as hard as they could to forestall the approval presenting allegations against Robinson that had to be investigated and cleared before the vote. Finally, the time for voting arrived as the Committee on Consecration of Bishops of the House of Deputies presented its report favoring the approval of Robinson. The Committee was not unanimous, however. The minority, led by Deputy the Very Rev. Mark J. Lawrence, of San Joaquin, and including Anthony J. Clark and John E. Masters, presented their dissent to the assembly which astutely focused on the essential issue at hand, the change in the Church's regard to homosexuality from immoral to amoral: "The approval of a bishop in said lifestyle would become a pretext upon which the church would de facto resolve the question of the appropriateness of homosexual behavior without due reordering of the church's teaching."[23] This was exactly the great issue of the day. However, what Lawrence and his allies did not recognize was that the issue had really already been resolved in the 1990s when the Church recognized the ordination of homosexuals. In a sense, the approval of Robinson had already been made the decade earlier. Lawrence was right to identify the problem but he was wrong in its timing. The attitude of the Church had in fact long shifted to the liberal position of moral neutrality.

As everyone expected, the pre-vote back and forth in the House of Deputies on August 3 was intense. After thirty minutes of open debate, Wade Logan of South Carolina[24] asked for another fifteen minutes, then someone else for another fifteen. When an hour had gone by, the president ended the debate period and called for voting. There were 108 delegations representing the dioceses, and each was sub-divided into clerical and lay orders. A roll call vote by order was held. A simple majority required 55 votes for approval. When the votes were counted, the lay sections of the delegations voted 63 in favor, 32 against, and 13 divided. The clerical units voted 65 in favor, 31 opposed, and 12 divided. About two-thirds of the House, both clerical and lay, approved of the selection of Gene Robinson. The split in the Episcopal Church in 1994 on the issue of homosexuality was generally into thirds, one third opposed, one third in favor, and the other neutral or non-committed. By 2003, that had changed as the liberals gained a clear majority in the Episcopal Church, much to the pain and chagrin of the conservatives who remained at their one-third level. Kendall Harmon railed out against the vote in immoderate rhetoric: "'It is a shattering event. It is a watershed. It is a crossing of the line.'"[25] Then he went on to imply the vote was close: "'If nine votes had been different, his confirmation would have been defeated 54 to 54.'"[26] In fact, the vote was not close.

In the House of Bishops, the discussion on August 4 lasted an hour starting off with statements of fourteen bishops favoring and seven opposing consent before opening up

---

23. "2003-C045." The Acts of Convention 1976–2009, The Archives of the Episcopal Church, http://www.episcopalarchives.org/cgi-bin/acts/acts_resolution-complete.pl?resolution=2003-C045.

24. The South Carolina deputies to the 2003 General Convention were—lay: Robert S. Bell, Lydia Evans, Lonnie Hamilton III, and Wade H. Logan, III; clerical: John B. Burwell, Kendall Harmon, Jennie C. Olbrych, Michael T. Malone.

25. Levin, Steve. "Gay Cleric Wins Initial Vote for Bishop." *Pittsburgh Post-Gazette* (Pittsburgh, PA), August 4, 2003.

26. Ibid.

a debate.[27] Finally, the chaplain said a prayer and the House remained in silence for the fifteen minutes. In this matter, 107 bishops were eligible to vote. When the numbers were tallied, 62 bishops voted in favor, 43 opposed and 2 abstained.[28] Of those voting to approve or disapprove, 59 percent voted for Robinson. In political terms, a vote of 60 percent is considered a landslide. The bishops' approval of Robinson was a virtual landslide. When the final votes were known, the cumulative decision of the Church was around three-fifths to approve the first non-celibate homosexual bishop in history. The decision was clear to all: the Episcopal Church had resolved the issue of homosexuality and had done so on the side of the liberals. Homosexuals were now to have access to ordination without qualification. Homosexuality was no longer to be condemned as sinful but accepted as morally neutral. This was truly a stunning and towering moment in the history of the Episcopal Church and of Christianity.

The significance of it all was as clear to the conservatives as to everyone else. After decades of fighting, they finally came to understand they had lost the war on homosexuality in the Episcopal Church. However, recognizing defeat did not necessarily mean surrender. The ultra-conservatives in the Episcopal Church refused to accept the Church's decision on homosexuality. Bishop Salmon, for one, was reported to have said, "'We are not going to accept this.'"[29] It should be recalled that the conservatives had declared in 1994 that their position on homosexuality was non-negotiable and non-compromising. In the House of Bishops, Robert Duncan, the bishop of Pittsburgh, led a group of stunned cohorts to present a statement of regret to their fellow bishops in "grief too deep for words."[30] They said they refused to accept the action of the Convention and instead declared an emergency: "We are calling upon the Primates of the Anglican Communion, under the presidency of the Archbishop of Canterbury (...) to intervene in the pastoral emergency that has overtaken us."[31] Over in the House of Deputies, South Carolinian Kendall Harmon addressed the assembly for the defeated minority surrounded by some twenty friends. One source said, "Harmon was nearly breathless with anger as he outlined what he saw as the danger to the church."[32] He too said his side, as the dissenting bishops', "reject this action and dissociate ourselves from it."[33] He proclaimed: "This

27. Skidmore, David. "Episcopal Bishops Approve Robinson." August 6, 2003, http://www.episcopalchurch.org/library/article/bishops-approve-Robinson.

28. The individual votes were given in the Journal of the General Convention of 2003. Another useful source gives the votes and the opinions of the individual bishops: "Positions on the Election of V. Gene Robinson," www.deimel.org/church_resources/vgr.htm. In the southeast U.S. about two-thirds of the bishops voted against Robinson. Those voting for were the diocesan bishops of: Atlanta, East Carolina, North Carolina (Michael Curry, the future Presiding Bishop), Southeast Florida, Southwestern Virginia, Virginia, and Western North Carolina.

29. "Positions on the Election of V. Gene Robinson." http://www.deimel.org/church_resources/vgr.htm.

30. "Appendix J, Day 7, Statement of Bishops upon the Confirmation of Gene Robinson." Journal of the General Convention of 2003, http://www.episcopalarchives.org/webdav/GCminutes/Journal_2003/2003gcjournal-index2.pdf.

31. Ibid.

32. Zoll, Rachel. "Episcopalians Protesting Gay Bishop." Associated Press, August 7, 2003, http://www.desertnews.com/article/1001749/Episcopalians-protesting-gay-bishop.html.

33. Harmon, (the Rev. Dr.) Kendall S. (August 6, 2003), http://www.holycross.net/index.cfm?sectio

unilateral action on our part is catastrophic (. . .). We have made a terrible mistake."[34] Harmon too called on the Archbishop of Canterbury to intervene: "In overturning the unambiguous moral teaching of the Church universal, this Church has erred and must be corrected by the Anglican Communion."[35] Neither Duncan nor Harmon gave any explanation of how they thought the Archbishop was going "to intervene" "to correct" the Episcopal Church given the fact that the Episcopal Church was an independent institution in which the Archbishop of Canterbury had no right to interfere. However, the ultra-conservatives showed the direction they would move in the future by going beyond the Episcopal Church to link up with other parts of the Anglican Communion.

Compared with the Robinson vote, every other resolution seemed anticlimactic. However, there were several other important resolutions, one of which was the critical issue of the blessing of same sex-unions. One should recall that the 1997 General Convention had defeated a resolution to prepare liturgies for the blessing of same-sex unions, although by the smallest majority possible. Another resolution was offered on August 6, 2003, C051, "Consider Blessing Committed, Same-Gender Relationships" and it came up for consideration after Robinson's affirmation. The original proposed resolution offered to the House of Bishops said: "That the 74th General Convention approve the liturgical blessing of the committed relationship of two adults of the same gender."[36] If the liberals thought the approval of Robinson broke the logjam and all sorts of attendant reforms would swiftly flow behind it, they were in for a surprise. The House of Bishops balked. On the face of it, it was illogical to approve of an openly gay bishop then disapprove of the blessings of gay unions, but this is what the bishops did. Perhaps they thought two major liberal reforms at once would destroy the delicate balance in the Church between the polar wings. Perhaps they were trying to appease the ultra-conservative and stave off schism. Perhaps they were trying to be typical Anglican tolerant moderates and show their acceptance of divergent views.

Bishop Lee, of Virginia, who had voted for Robinson, spoke out against C051 and offered a revision that removed the language directing the drawing up of the liturgies for the blessing of same-sex unions.[37] The House of Bishops agreed and passed a substitute resolution that only vaguely supported a continued study of the issue of the liturgies although it recognized the existence of services for the blessing of same-sex unions used in some dioceses. The vote to pass the revised resolution was 62 yes, 43 no, and 2 abstentions. Bishop Salmon said later he voted against this resolution.[38] He said at the time he had no major objection to the revised resolution, but observed sensibly that the whole resolution was pointless since the Convention had already voted to approve a man who

---

n=1&page=56&Obj=226.

34. Ibid.

35. Ibid.

36. "2003–C051." The Acts of Convention 1976–2012, The Archives of the Episcopal Church, http://www.episcopalarchives.org/cgi-bin/acts/acts_resolution-complete.pl?resolution=2003-C051.

37. Ibid.

38. *The Journal of the Two Hundred and Fourteenth Annual Meeting of the Convention of the Diocese of South Carolina, North Charleston Convention Center, and the Proceedings of the Special Convention, October 2, 2003, St. Paul's Summerville.* Charleston, SC: the diocese, 2004, 159.

was in fact living in a same-sex relationship.[39] In effect, the Church had already approved of same-sex relationships. Bishop Skilton seemed a bit happier with the resolution. He said, "'I think it is something we can go home with.'"[40] He said he was willing to live with the compromise: "'It is certainly better than what was originally proposed.'"[41] Bishop Lee's public remarks give us some clues on why the bishops backed away from the blessings. He said in view of the Robinson vote, the Church needed to exercise restraint and consider the feelings of the forty-three bishops who were sincerely grieving.[42] When the House of Deputies voted, they approved the revised resolution by 58 among the laity (55 needed) and 62 of the clergy (55 needed). Thus, the General Convention of 2003 wound up with the same sort of solution that the Convention of 1997 had made, to reject for the moment the formulation of liturgies for the blessing of same-sex unions while leaving the door wide open for the future.

Another resolution came up in the Convention to change canon law in favor of homosexuals. A111 revised the wording of Title III, Canon 1, Section 2 to read "No person shall be denied access to the discernment process for any ministry, lay or ordained, in this Church because of race (. . .) sexual orientation."[43] This was an elaboration on the 1994 canonical change removing barriers against the ordination of homosexuals.

The historic 74th General Convention came to an end on August 8, 2003. In sum, the Episcopal Church solidified its stand on homosexuality by clearly accepting the liberal viewpoint that ordination in the Church should be open to gays without qualification and, by extension, homosexuality should be viewed as morally neutral. As we have seen, the Church was actually capping off what it had already subtly decided in the 1990s. From this point on, dioceses would be free to confer Holy Orders on non-celibate homosexuals on every level. Although the blessing of same-sex unions had been rejected, it had really only been deferred for the future. It was just a matter of time.

One may note that this author used the term "Robinson Affair," rather than Robinson Crisis. To describe what happened in 2003 as a crisis would be to exaggerate beyond reason what actually occurred. As we have seen the fundamental issues involved had been decided years earlier, in the cumulative acts of General Convention of the 1990s, the work of the House of Bishops, the Righter trial of 1996, and measures in some of the dioceses. The affirmation of Gene Robinson was really the aftermath of this. In spite of all the intense media attention and the doomsday hyperbole of the jeremiad ultra-conservatives, there really was no crisis in 2003. Even the conservative bishops admitted beforehand the outcome would be against them. Looking back, the amazing thing was just how little disruption there was in the summer of 2003. The opposition to Robinson

---

39. Thompson, Richelle. "Bishops Turn Down Development of Same-Sex Liturgies." Episcopal News Service, August 6, 2003, http://www.episcopalchurch.org/library/article/bishops-turn-down-development-same-sex-liturgies.

40. Ibid.

41. Ibid.

42. Ibid.

43. "2003–A111, Revise Title III Canons." The Acts of Convention 1976–2012, The Archives of the Episcopal Church, http://www.episcopalarchives.org/cgi-bin/acts/acts_resolution-complete.pl?resolution=2003-A111.

was not even close to the support. He was approved by near-landslide levels across the board, in every part of the Church structure. The opposition to Robinson was in fact remarkably limited. As we have seen, relatively few bishops signed the protest statements before the Convention.[44] In the Convention itself, the protest was much smaller in size than in decibel level. Only seven bishops took the microphone to make statements of opposition before the vote in the House of Bishops.[45] The eighteen bishops who stood with Duncan as he read his protest following the vote in the House of Bishops represented a small percentage of the bishops present.[46] They unwittingly displayed how few bishops really opposed Robinson. After the vote, three bishops (of about three hundred present) were seen leaving the meeting in protest.[47] In the House of Deputies, Harmon spoke accompanied by twenty deputies.[48] Of the eight hundred deputies present, they counted for less than 3 percent of the House. Once again, Harmon's party unintentionally showed just how large the support was for Robinson among the deputies A few devastated delegates fell on their knees and wept as Harmon spoke. About a dozen delegates were seen walking about with ashes of penance on their foreheads.[49] A handful of delegates turned in their badges and quit the meeting. The American Anglican Council, the primary union of conservative dissidents, held a protest worship service attended by 300 people,[50] at most 20 percent of the number of people present for the Convention in Minneapolis. Thus, the vision of crisis was largely the construct of the ultra-conservatives who were projecting their own feelings onto the Convention. The vast majority of the people at the 2003 Convention displayed no sense of crisis.

THE AFTERMATH OF THE ROBINSON AFFAIR

Reactions in the Diocese of South Carolina

Having lost the war against homosexuality in the Episcopal Church, the irreconcilable ultra-conservatives banded together to appeal for overseas intervention. As we have seen, the conservatives composed about a third of the Episcopal Church as reflected in the voting patterns of the 1990s and early 2000s. Of that group, about a third, or 10 percent of the whole Episcopal Church, can be called the ultra-conservatives. These were the ones who refused to accept in any way the two decisions of the 2003 Convention, an openly homosexual bishop and recognition of the blessing of same-sex unions. The ultra-conservatives did not specify exactly what they expected the foreign intervention

---

44. The primates who signed the Truro Statement represented 26 percent of the membership of the Anglican Communion. The American bishops who signed represented 9 percent of the Episcopal Church. Nunley, "Episcopalians."

45. Skidmore, "Episcopal Bishops." About 300 diocesan, assistant, and retired bishops made up the House of Bishops, but only the 107 diocesan bishops were allowed to vote on Robinson.

46. Ibid.

47. Zoll, "Episcopalians."

48. Ibid.

49. Ibid.

50. Ibid.

to be or how it would impact on the Episcopal Church, however. Did they mean to use foreign pressure to force the Episcopal Church to repeal its measures favoring homosexuals? Did they mean to get the foreign primates to ostracize the Episcopal Church from the Anglican Communion? Anyway, how would this help them in the Episcopal Church? Did they mean to form a sub-church under foreign primatial authority? Did they mean to break away from the Episcopal Church and make a separate "orthodox" Anglican church under foreign primates? In the immediate aftermath of the Robinson Affair, none of this was clear. All that was obvious was that the far-right refused to accept what had happened in General Convention, were banding together, and were appealing to like-minded foreign authorities in the Anglican Communion for some kind of extraterritorial help.

What was South Carolina to do? Immediately after the vote on Robinson, Kendall Harmon told reporters the Diocese of South Carolina was planning to call a special convention.[51] The public records did not reveal where this idea originated, only that Harmon announced it to the press. The delegation from South Carolina went home from the Convention with counter-revolution in mind. Salmon returned home ready to move forward with the ultra-conservatives in appealing to foreign authorities. If he had been consciously reticent to criticize the Episcopal Church in the few years before 2003, that suddenly vanished in August of 2003. The public documents did not reveal his motivation, whether he was sincerely acting on his own or was merely following the prevailing opinion strongly evident in the words of diocesan spokespeople such as Harmon. At any rate, he energetically threw himself into the ultra-conservatives' campaign to link up with foreign Anglican primates.

Salmon began action right away. Nine days after the Convention adjourned, he hosted two prominent conservative bishops, Don Wimberly, bishop of Texas, and James Stanton, bishop of Dallas, in Charleston.[52] The next day, August 18, Salmon met the diocesan Standing Committee. The entire committee[53] was present, and included three[54] of the deputies to the Convention. Also attending were non-members canon theologian Kendall Harmon, bishop suffragan William Skilton, and chancellor Nick Ziegler. Salmon and Harmon seemed to be prepared to guide the meeting. Up to this time, the diocesan Standing Committee had busied itself entirely with routine and non-controversial business, accepting new clergy for ordination, giving consent to bishops' elections across the national Church, approving financial and property arrangements for local parishes and the like. This changed on August 18, 2003, for good. The Standing Committee became intimately involved with the bishop(s), Harmon, and the chancellor (and later other lawyers) and became directly tied into a top-down decision making structure. An ar-

---

51. "Episcopalian Meeting Leaves Many Clergy in Doubt." *Lubbock Avalanche-Journal* (Lubbock, TX), August 10, 2003, http://lubbockonline.com/stories/081003/rel_080103069.shtml.

52. "Minutes of the Standing Committee Meeting." The Standing Committee of the Episcopal Diocese of South Carolina. [August 18, 2003]. Stanton had been the lead bishop in the presentment against Bishop Righter in 1995.

53. Clergy: Craige Borrett, Rick Belser, Frank Limehouse, Jennie Olbrych, Dow Sanderson, Mike Lumpkin; Laity: Lydia Evans, Barbara Gilchrist, Robert Bell, Thomas Heyward, Herbert Fielding.

54. Evans, Bell, and Olbrych.

rangement was established that remained in place through the schism of 2012 in which the bishop-canon theologian-lawyer(s) apparently routinely met in closed sessions with the Standing Committee which ratified proposals secretly, most often unanimously, then made the decisions known when they chose by sending them to the clergy, the diocesan conventions when necessary, and finally the public. The diocesan conventions after this would quickly turn into Dumas routinely approving with little or no debate or revision whatever was presented to them. This authoritarian decision making structure began on August 18, 2003, grew to maturity in the next few years and continued indefinitely. Well before 2012 the system was entrenched and would prove crucial in the run-up to the schism that year.

Salmon started off the meeting of 18 August by declaring the diocese's role in the conservatives' appeal to foreign authorities:

> Bishop Salmon added, this is not a local American struggle between liberals and conservatives or a struggle between Dioceses. The events unfolding at this stage are out of our hands. The October meeting of the Primates at Anglican Communion is where the focus of attention has moved. This is coming from the top down, not the bottom up at this point.[55]

This is coming from the top down, not the bottom up could be used to describe the new decision making process in the diocese, and arguably the whole history of the schism. Salmon then proceeded with his real business of bonding the committee into the diocesan power structure. He made several crucial proposals, all of which the committee approved unanimously. In the first he called for a special diocesan convention presumably for the purpose of unifying the diocese behind its leaders' decision to denounce the Episcopal Church and seek help from foreign primates. In the talk that followed Salmon's proposal, Jennie Olbrych made a resolution to call a special convention following the primates' meeting that was scheduled for 15 October. Kendall Harmon spoke up and said the special convention should be before the primates' meeting, "to encourage the Church of South Carolina, to repudiate the actions of General Convention, to appeal to the Primates to assist us and to reaffirm our faithful membership in the Anglican Communion."[56] Once Harmon had spoken, Olbrych's motion was withdrawn and Olbrych herself made a new motion to adopt Harmon's suggestion and call a special convention before the primates' meeting, just as Harmon wished. The motion passed unanimously. According to the committee minutes, the resolution that was ratified said exactly what Harmon had offered beforehand. Then, Olbrych presented a second motion that appeared to have been prepared ahead of time (it strains credibility that this resolution was written on the spot by the committee). If anyone had any doubt about the attitude of the leadership of the Diocese of South Carolina toward the Episcopal Church, he or she could not have after this. For the first time, the Diocese officially set itself apart from the national Church:

> The Standing Committee of the Episcopal Diocese of South Carolina, holds that the 74th General Convention of the Episcopal Church has exceeded its authority

55. "Minutes of the Standing Committee." [August 18, 2003].
56. Ibid.

and departed from its constitution, in confirming the election as bishop of a non-celibate homosexual man and in permitting same-sex blessings, separating itself from the Anglican Communion and from the One Holy Catholic and Apostolic Church, directly rejecting its solemn responsibility to uphold and propagate the historic Faith and Order, as set forth in Holy Scripture and in the Book of Common Prayer. These acts are held to be in conflict with the Canons of the Diocese of South Carolina and have no binding effect in the Diocese.[57]

The key phrase was the last *no binding effect in the Diocese*. In effect, this declared local sovereignty, only a short step away from independence, or schism from the national Church. The 2001 diocesan convention had defeated a resolution that only threatened to consider schism. This resolution of August 18, 2003, was much stronger and it passed the committee unanimously. To press the point of urgency, the committee directed both resolutions to be published immediately on the diocesan website and e-mailed to every parish. Thus ended what was arguably the most important meeting of the Standing Committee before 2012. Apparently without any difference of opinion, let alone debate, the like-minded committee had passed through fateful decisions that set the stage for an adversarial relationship between diocese and national Church. One could make the case that the chain of events that eventually produced the schism of 2012 actually began in earnest nine years earlier, on August 18, 2003.

The Standing Committee meeting of August 18 proved crucial for several reasons. First, it established the diocesan posture that the Episcopal Church was in error. Secondly, it declared the right of the diocese to nullify the decisions of the national Church. Thirdly, it began the practice of calling special conventions to validate the decisions of the diocesan leadership. And finally, it formulated a mechanism by which the diocese would be governed from then on. Policy and procedure positions came from the bishop and a small core of advisors who met secretly with the Standing Committee that would ratify the decisions, typically unanimously.

Between 2003 and the schism of 2012, bishops departed and arrived, Standing Committee membership revolved, lawyers came and went, delegates to the special and annual meetings of the conventions changed, but one person remained constant throughout: Kendall Harmon. Harmon had completed his doctoral thesis on Hell[58] and had been awarded a doctor's degree at Oxford University in 1993 before returning to South Carolina and taking a post at St. Paul's of Summerville where he held the title of Theologian-in-Residence from 1996 to 2001.[59] He had already made a name for himself in the 1980s as an forceful, intelligent, outspoken conservative activist when he supported Bishop Allison's campaign against the book on sexuality and argued publicly against homosexual ordination and the confirmation of Barbara Harris as bishop. Following his return from Oxford, he quickly moved into positions of influence in the diocese serving on the Standing Committee and acting as deputy to the General Conventions of 1997, 2000, 2003, 2006, and 2009.[60] He was

57. Ibid.
58. *Finally Excluded from God?: Some Twentieth Century Theological Explorations of the Problem of Hell and Universalism with reference to the Historical Development of these Doctrines.*
59. "Kendall: A Brief Biography."
60. Ibid.

on the editorial advisory board of *Jubilate Deo*, the diocesan newspaper from 1996 to 2001; and served as editor from 2002 to 2008. He was also editor of *Anglican Digest* a prominent conservative periodical publication based in Arkansas. In March of 2002, Bishop Salmon announced that he had appointed Harmon to be Canon Theologian of the Diocese. This title was created for him; such a term had not existed before. It carried no constitutional function such as bishop, chancellor, or standing committee. Records showed that he attended some sessions of the diocesan Standing Committee. In addition, after 2003, Harmon was Communications Director of the Diocese. He also eventually became assistant rector at Christ/St. Paul's of Yonges Island. A useful summary of his viewpoint comes from Wikipedia: "Harmon has espoused a traditional/conservative position he describes as 're-asserting' the historical Christian position on same-sex erotic activity."[61] After January of 2004, Harmon became well known for his popular online blog "Titus One Nine"[62] which reprinted conservative sources and allowed a like-minded public forum. It became the quasi-official voice of the diocese and played an important role in influencing local public opinion by conveying selective information to communicants in the run-up to the schism. One should not underestimate the role Harmon played in the diocese in the twenty-two years before the schism.

Soon after the fateful August 18 Standing Committee meeting, three resolutions were drawn up to be presented for approval at the special meeting of the convention of the diocese which was set for October 2, a week before the primates meeting. On September 10, the Standing Committee met again. The public record did not reveal who wrote the three proposed resolutions, but the Standing Committee minutes did show that Harmon brought them alone to the committee meeting on the 10th. He was accompanied by neither the bishop nor the chancellor, as he had been on August 18. One can only assume Salmon had approved of these in advance. It would be unimaginable to have proposed resolutions without the bishop's prior approval. Ten of the twelve committee members were present on the 10th. The committee minutes stated: "The purpose of the meeting was to go over the 3 resolutions prepared for the Diocesan Special Convention."[63] It was clear that someone(s) had prepared them before the 10th. The committee made some amendments to each, then adopted them unanimously. It was announced that Craige Borrett, the chair of the committee, would present the resolutions to the convention and Kendall Harmon would "speak to the Resolutions."[64] The texts of the three resolutions were then set to be published so that everyone would know their full contents ahead of the special convention. They were printed in the next issue of the diocesan newspaper, *Jubilate Deo*. With their no-holds-barred denunciation of the national Church and the presiding bishop and their call for foreign intervention, these dramatic proposed resolutions instantly became the talk of the diocese inflaming both critics and defenders of the Episcopal Church.

---

61. "Kendall Harmon," Wikipedia, http://en.wikipedia.org/wiki/Kendall_Harmon.

62. New International Version: "He must hold firmly to the trustworthy message as it has been taught, so that he can encourage others by sound doctrine and refute those who oppose it."

63. "Minutes of the Standing Committee." [September 10, 2003].

64. Ibid.

On the day of the special convention, October 2, the Standing Committee met separately at 1:00 p.m. to go over the last-minute details of the three resolutions.[65] Borrett told the committee that they were serving as the resolutions committee of the special convention. The committee refused last minute changes to resolutions number one (the most important) and three, but did agree to a substitute for number two. Finally, the resolutions were ready for presentation to the special convention for vote.

The special convention of October 2, 2003, was the most important meeting of the diocese for several years, perhaps until 2009. Everyone knew the proposed resolutions. Everyone knew the issues. Everyone understood the gravity of the moment. Everyone knew too the majority of the delegates would be on the side of the conservative diocesan leaders. The minority pro-Episcopal Church side knew this as well as anyone, but they came prepared to make a stand, perhaps their last, to defend the fading bond between the diocese and the Episcopal Church. They would not go down without a fight. They would not be silenced, at least not yet. Tensions ran high as 316 delegates (90 clergy and 226 lay) assembled at St. Paul's Church in Summerville.

Bishop Salmon started the meeting with a leaden bishop's address, somber, serious and grave. He made some sweeping condemnations of the Episcopal Church summarized in, "The General Convention has endorsed a new religion."[66] He said the General Convention in Minneapolis had changed the Episcopal Church by violating its own constitution and violating "the historic teaching of the church covering human sexuality."[67] After a long list of negative fallout from the Robinson affirmation and a rehash of the Bible verses supposedly condemning homosexuality, Salmon concluded by asking the convention to reject the decisions of the 2003 General Convention and support him in appealing to the Archbishop of Canterbury. The assembly responded by giving him a standing ovation.

The marginalized pro-Church minority, who knew they were about to lose the votes on the resolutions, arose to make a public stand. The Rev. Tommy Tipton, of Holy Cross/Faith Memorial of Pawleys Island, read to the assembly a statement drawn up by a group of nineteen clergy[68] essentially asking for continued dialogue on the difficult questions facing the Church. "We rise to the fact that the people who are the Diocese of SC are not of one mind as it is being presented to the rest of the world," they said.[69] They continued, "We call upon this Diocese to enter into the conversation pertaining to the issues surrounding our Church with greater mutual respect of those who hold opposing

---

65. "Minutes of the Standing Committee." [October 2, 2003].

66. *Journal of the Two Hundred and Fourteenth* (. . .) 2003, 162.

67. Ibid.

68. Active: Tommy Tipton, of Holy Cross/Faith Memorial; Michael Cole, HC/FM; Donald McPhail, Grace Church of Charleston; Gregory Hodgson, Grace; Joel Hafer, All Saints of Florence; Richard Thompson, St. James Santee; Richard Lindsay, All Saints of Hilton Head; George Tompkins, Old Saint Andrew's of West Ashley; Jim Bills, St. Stephen's of Charleston; Jack Nietert, All Saints of Hampton; Roy Hills, St. Mary's of Goose Creek; Byron Tindall, Christ Church of Denmark; and Marilyn Powell. Retired: Alanson Houghton, Benjamin Smith, Colton Smith, James Cantier, Joseph Stoudenmire, and Philip Porcher.

69. *Journal of the Two Hundred and Fourteenth* (. . .) 2003, 156.

views rather than the simple condemnation of those with whom we may disagree."[70] Finally, they appealed to the assembly: "Because of our hearts, our minds, our consciences and our beliefs we stand in opposition to the spirit of these resolutions and invite all those who share our struggle and our discomfort with these resolutions to stand and to vote no."[71] For the most part, these words fell on deaf ears. The agenda then moved to the resolutions in question.

The first resolution, R-1, was the most important. Part of it was the statement the Standing Committee had passed unanimously in its August 18 meeting. However, it contained additional sections. In one, the resolution called "for intervention in the pastoral and ideological emergency created by the apostasy of the 74th General Convention."[72] Steve Skardon offered a substitute resolution for R-1. It was put to a vote and defeated 215 to 50.[73] This 81 to 19 percent split in the assembly reflected both the confident control the conservatives held and the divide in the diocese. Having failed to replace the resolution, the Rev. Mark Goodman proposed that the paragraph containing the word "apostasy" be rewritten. This was put to a vote and defeated 192 to 56.[74] Finally, Michael Lumpkin made a motion to change one word, that is, to replace the "apostasy" with "action." It passed 162 to 109.[75] The original language: *emergency created by the apostasy of the 74th General Convention* read *emergency created by the actions of the 74th General Convention* in the final resolution. This conveyed the same meaning in less extreme terms. With a one-word change, the original resolution was brought up for vote. The clergy approved it 72 to 17; the parishes 40 for, 4 against, and 4 divided; the missions 13 for, 2 opposed, and 2 divided.[76] Thus entered the official record one of the most fateful resolutions the Diocese of South Carolina ever approved. By this, the diocese unilaterally declared that the Episcopal Church had acted unconstitutionally, that the diocese nullified within its bounds both the national Church's affirmation of a non-celibate bishop and recognition of the blessing of same-sex unions, and that it appealed to the "International Primates" to recognize the "orthodox dioceses and parishes" in America as the true body of the Anglican Communion in the United States.[77] Only two years earlier, the diocese had voted down a weaker proposed resolution to threaten a schism. The overwhelming approval of R-1 on October 3, 2003, first showed how far the diocese had moved in two years and second revealed the philosophical support in the diocese for the ultra-conservative faction in the Episcopal Church. The mainstream diocese that Temple had left in 1982 was now on the far-right edge of the national Church and hinting it would go ever farther. The conservative leadership of the diocese had won

70. Ibid.

71. Ibid.

72. [Special Convention, October 2, 2003]. *Jubilate Deo* (Diocese of South Carolina), October/November 2003.

73. *Journal of the Two Hundred and Fourteenth (. . .)* 2003, 157.

74. Ibid.

75. Ibid.

76. Ibid.

77. Ibid., 163.

a monumental and stunning victory leaving the small pro-Church minority, that had been excluded from the power structure, in frustration and despair.

The meeting then proceeded to the second proposed resolution which was a denunciation of Presiding Bishop Frank Griswold whom conservatives believed had swayed the General Convention to favor Robinson. It really had no point except to demonize a convenient scapegoat and to diminish respect for the Episcopal Church in a receptive diocese. The original resolution used some harsh language: "the Presiding Bishop used his office strongly to support the ratification of the radically divisive election of the bishop of New Hampshire before the vote took place at General Convention."[78] It went on, "the Presiding Bishop has by his own leadership left the Episcopal Church and the Anglican Communion more shattered than when he entered his office."[79] The wild assertions in this resolution ignored vital truths such as Robinson had been approved by near-landslide levels in both houses of the Convention and the ultra-conservatives were the ones appealing to foreign primates to break up the Episcopal Church. The obvious purpose of this extraordinary resolution was to fan the flames of resentment against the Episcopal Church. As with the recoil from the word "apostasy" in R–1, there was also reaction against the original proposal of R–2. St. Paul's of Orangeburg had offered a substitute in the standing committee which the committee had approved. The substitute was presented to the assembly which only changed a few words. While still criticizing the presiding bishop, the substitute softened the language considerably to lines such as: "the current Presiding Bishop used his office to influence the confirmation of the election," and "profound disappointment with the lack of leadership shown by the current Presiding Bishop."[80] This was passed by a voice vote.

The third proposed resolution was entitled, "Financial Intimidation." This one was even more incongruous to the topic at hand than had been the second. It asserted that since the Lambeth Conference of 1998 "financial intimidation" had been used by "the leaders in the Episcopal Church toward Anglican leaders of the Global South."[81]

A fourth proposed resolution was presented to the assembly over the disapproval of the Standing Committee. It came from All Saints of Hilton Head and was read by the Rev. Richard Lindsey. It called on the diocese to "'continue as one body (. . .) fully participating in the Episcopal Church of the United States of America.'"[82] This was the pro-Church party's last ditch effort to stem the tide moving the diocese away from the national Church. The assembly defeated it 229 to 38 (86 percent to 14 percent).[83] Next to R–1, this was the most important vote of the day. The diocese showed overwhelmingly that it no longer wanted to participate fully in the Episcopal Church. What did this mean? If they did not want to "participate" in the Episcopal Church what did they want?

78. [Special Convention].

79. Ibid.

80. *Journal of the Two Hundred and Fourteenth* (. . .) 2003, 165.

81. *Jubilate Deo,* October/November 2003.

82. Malone, E.T., Jr. "At South Carolina Special Convention, Eerie Echoes of Nullification History." Episcopal News Service, The Archives of the Episcopal Church, http://archive.episcopalchurch.org/3577_19626_ENG_HTM.htm.

83. Ibid.

The appeal to foreign primates so far was only vaguely hopeful. There was no substance yet. To the pro-Church party, and perhaps to others, what the convention had said on Oct. 3 sounded suspiciously schismatic. Herbert Drayton, III, a delegate from St. Stephen's of Charleston, well-known as the most "gay-friendly" church of the diocese, arose to address the assembly: "'This is a very painful thing that has happened here today. I sit on the commission on ministry and I have eyes full of tears.'"[84] Salmon coolly replied, "'We are not talking about being against somebody, but opposing a kind of activity that is not normative or moral. I think not to put the truth on the table is not loving anybody.'"[85] The pro-Church minority of the diocese had shown itself to be so small and powerless that the ruling establishment did not even have to show empathy let alone deference to them. The bishop who had tried to please everyone before 2003 no longer needed to do that. There was no question after the General Convention of 2003 that he was closely allied to the conservative, now more accurately called the ultra-conservative, leadership of the diocese.

The pro-Church party in the diocese could only reel in pain as it sensed the diocese's seemingly inexorable move toward schism. Steve Skardon said, "'I think people are very, very concerned. It's tearing every parish apart (. . .). What worries me is these resolutions give the green light for the diocese to pull away from the Episcopal Church, if not sever ties completely. None of us wants to leave the Episcopal Church.'"[86] Andy Black of St. Stephen's, Charleston, said, "'This is nonsense church politics and not a focus on what is really biblical and religious. We are going to continue to be St. Stephen's and loyal members of the Episcopal Church USA, I hope.'"[87] Others decried the breakdown of cohesion in the diocese. The Rev. Richard Lindsey, rector of All Saints, Hilton Head, said, "'The game's not over. What we do today is not the end. General Convention was not the end. This is an issue that cannot be legislated. This diocese if hurting and we need to come together to share the love of Christ and its brokenness.'"[88] The Rev. Jack Nietert, of All Saints, Hampton, added, "'We shouldn't turn our backs on one another when things go wrong. These resolutions are designed to separate us, not bring us together.'"[89]

Salmon and his conservative allies defined the matter differently. To them this was about standing up for the faith as once delivered. It was either right or wrong. There was no middle ground. If it were right, it could not be compromised or negotiated away. In their view, what the Episcopal Church had done was wrong by condoning a sinful sexual behavior. They refused to accept the liberal view that homosexuality was morally neutral. As the Rev. Rick Belser, rector of St. Michael's of Charleston, said, "'I think the discussion is ended. It ended in Minneapolis. We need to do something to speak out

---

84. Ibid.

85. Ibid.

86. Solheim, James. "Dioceses of Ft. Worth, Pittsburgh and South Carolina Repudiate Actions of General Convention." Episcopal News Service, Archive, http://archive.episcopalchurch.org/3577_19562_ENG_HTM.htm.

87. Ibid.

88. Ibid.

89. Ibid.

against [General Convention's actions].'"[90] Harmon went farther, "'This is an extremely serious crisis and we've made it clear we repudiate what happened in Minneapolis (...) but we also know we need emergency intervention by the primates. It's up to them to decide what to do.'"[91] Continuing his call for foreign intervention, he added, "'You and I are a threat to this new movement. If we don't have intervention, we are deeply in trouble.'"[92] He did not elaborate on what the "trouble" would be.

If we can pinpoint a "turning point" in which the Diocese of South Carolina moved clearly to a reliably "anti" attitude toward the Episcopal Church, it would be the special convention of October 3, 2003. Although its regard for the national Church had been declining over many years, the diocese had maintained an identity as an integral part of the Episcopal Church. From the special convention of 2003 onward, this would not be the case. It would increasingly see itself as an outsider diocese with only unhappy, tenuous ties to the national Church. The ultra-conservative viewpoint was well established in the diocese for good. It saw religion as absolute and unchanging truth that must be taken to the world in need of redemption which would occur in the vertical posture of one person and one God. They believed the Episcopal Church had gone wrong by developing horizontal religion and becoming too much a part of the sinful world. They believed there were no absolutes in the Church any more, only relative variables. This is what had happened to homosexuality. The old view that it was inherently sinful and immoral had been replaced in the national Church by the broader societal acceptance of the moral neutrality of homosexuality. Since the ultra-conservatives declared that this new religion, as Salmon called it, was not acceptable, they had two choices, develop some sort of foreign oversight inside the Episcopal Church or leave the Church. Neither one would be simple or easy.

One group in the diocese that decided to leave the Church was All Saints of Pawleys Island, the birthplace of First Promise and the Anglican Mission in America. Soon after General Convention, in August of 2003, the congregation set up a discernment committee to recommend whether the parish should remain in the Episcopal Church and the diocese. In its October meeting, the vestry voted to sever all ties to the diocese and the Episcopal Church.[93] On December 9, the vestry approved changing the corporate charter to remove all references to the diocese and the Episcopal Church.[94] Four days later, Bishop Salmon and Kendall Harmon met for two hours with rector Chuck Murphy and the senior warden who did not reveal any move at separation.[95] Two days after that, on December 15, Salmon received from a member of All Saints, copies of vestry records showing the October and December votes to leave the Church and diocese thus revealing

---

90. Malone, "At South Carolina."
91. Solheim, "Dioceses."
92. Malone, "At South Carolina."
93. Nunley, Jan. "South Carolina Parish, Home to Breakaway Anglican Group, Reduced to Mission Status." Episcopal News Service, December 23, 2003, The Archives of the Episcopal Church, http://www.episcopalarchives.org/cgi-bin/ENS/ENSpress_release.pl?pr_number=032312-2.
94. "26724-All Saints v. Campbell."
95. Nunley, "South Carolina Parish"; "Minutes of the Standing Committee." [December 23, 2003].

the truth to Salmon for the first time.[96] Two days later, on 17 December, Salmon sent a letter to the wardens and vestry members of All Saints telling them they had abandoned their offices and he was reducing the parish to mission status which meant it would be under the bishop's control.[97] The next day, Salmon sent a pastoral letter to the diocese explaining his actions concerning All Saints. The majority of communicants at All Saints refused to accept Salmon's decisions. On December 23, the parish leaders sent out a letter calling a parish-wide meeting on January 8, 2004.[98] On word of the parish meeting, the diocesan Standing Committee called the All Saints vestry to a meeting on January 5, 2004. Gathering separately at noon, the Standing Committee voted five to three to offer to drop the lawsuit against All Saints if the parish vestry would rescind its votes to leave the diocese.[99] It was too little, too late. At the All Saints parish meeting three days later, 507 communicants attended and passed by more than two-thirds majority resolutions to sever all ties to the diocese and the Episcopal Church, to amend its corporate charter to remove all references to the diocese and the Episcopal Church, and to affiliate with the Anglican province of Rwanda through its Anglican Mission in America.[100] On January 15, 2004, the revisions to the parochial charter of incorporation in the Secretary of State's office were officially registered.[101] With that, the matter was over as far as the majority of parishioners of All Saints was concerned. The property issue, however, was still pending. On September 10, 2003, the appeals court had held a hearing, but the sides were still awaiting a decision when the majority of All Saints voted to leave the diocese.

By late December of 2003, the diocesan decision-making leadership (bishop-canon theologian-chancellor-standing committee) were facing the reality of significant schism at home. On the right, they realized that one of the largest parishes was in the process of completely cutting all ties to the diocese. On the left, Salmon reported rumblings too. In December, he received a letter from the Rev. Jim Bills, rector of St. Stephen's of Charleston. Salmon did not disclose the contents, but they may have suggested leaving the diocese in some sense such as transferal to another bishop, presumably one more favorable to the national Church. Salmon talked about Bills's letter with the Standing Committee on 23 December and said: "We may see transferring of two parishes to the jurisdiction of another Bishop."[102] He named St. Stephen's and Holy Cross/Faith Memorial of Pawleys Island. He also mentioned he saw two divided parishes, Grace of Charleston and All Saints of Hilton Head, and implied that they too might leave the diocese.[103] Thus, by the end of the year 2003, schism was very much in the air of the diocese. On one side, one parish had already left the diocese. On the other side, four parishes were possible candidates to leave the diocese. Meanwhile, diocesan leadership and the major-

96. Ibid.
97. "26724–All Saints v. Campbell."
98. Ibid.
99. "Minutes of the Standing Committee." [January 5, 2004].
100. "26724–All Saints v. Campbell."
101. Ibid. In its September 2009 decision on All Saints, the South Carolina Supreme Court ruled that the parish had legally enacted its separation from the diocese and the Episcopal Church.
102. "Minutes of the Standing Committee." [December 23, 2003].
103. Ibid.

ity of its members had turned highly critical, if not hostile, to the national Church and were seeking overseas bishops to intervene in the Episcopal Church to rescue them. The Diocese of South Carolina had not been so close to schism since the Civil War. It had never been so close to disintegration. How much the bishop and his allies understood and appreciated this critically dangerous development remained unclear.

What one can see now is that Bishop Allison's attitude that ideological purity took precedence over institutional development remained in place. By 2003, it was clear that much of the ideologically-driven ruling establishment was willing to risk institutional disintegration in order to preserve the "orthodox" purity of the majority. If this meant repudiating the authority of the national Church and losing numerous parishes of the diocese, then so be it. Having the majority keep the faith once delivered would be worth it all.

Reactions in the Anglican Communion and the Episcopal Church

Reactions in America to the General Convention's affirmation of Robinson were loudest from the protestors, but the Episcopalian dissidents numbered relatively few. By October 3, only four of the 111 dioceses had called "emergency" special conventions to denounce the Church's acts and to appeal to overseas Anglican primates for rescue. On the other side, there were far more voices either praising the acts or calling for forbearance.

While most attention in America focused on the small but loud minority, the same was true of the foreign bishops. Several Anglican primates in countries well-known for laws punishing homosexual acts led the fierce denunciation of the American Church from overseas. Peter Akinola, primate of Nigeria, told the press that Satan had entered the Episcopal Church.[104] Homosexual activity was illegal in Nigeria, punishable by death in the northern part, and by fourteen years' imprisonment elsewhere.[105] Akinola had been an important voice in the Lambeth conference of 1998 that issued the famous statement condemning homosexuality as against the Scriptures. He later said the Episcopal Church "'crossed the Rubicon'" in 2003 by electing Robinson "'inflicting the most devastating wound'" on Anglicanism.[106] Akinola went on to work actively for the replacement of the Episcopal Church as the American branch of the Anglican Communion. In 2007, he made former Episcopal priest Martyn Minns, of Truro, a bishop in the Church of Nigeria and reportedly did so in defiance of the wishes of the Episcopal Presiding Bishop and the Archbishop of Canterbury.[107] The next year, Akinola was one of the principal founders of the Global Anglican Futures Conference (GAFCON) which was to recognize the Anglican Church in North America as the alternative to the Episcopal Church in the Anglican Communion.[108]

104. Religious News Service, August 8, 2003, as quoted in Kirkpatrick, Frank G. *The Episcopal Church in Crisis, How Sex, the Bible, and Authority are Dividing the Faithful*. Westport, CT: Praeger, 2008, 16.

105. "LGBT Rights in Africa," Wikipedia, http://en.wikipedia.org/wiki/LGBT_rights_in_Africa.

106. Beckford, Martin. "Primate of Nigeria Vows to Rescue Anglican Church from Crisis over Sexuality." *The Telegraph*, June 22, 2008, http://www.telegraph.co.uk/news/worldnews/middleeast/israel/2176487/Primate-of-Nigeria.

107. "Peter Akinola," Wikipedia, https://en.wikipedia.org/wiki/Peter_Akinola.

108. Ibid.

Several other Anglican primates in African countries where cultures condemned and punished homosexual acts also severely denounced the Episcopal Church for its reforms favoring homosexuals. Archbishop Bernard Malango, of the Province of Central Africa (Botswana, Malawi, Zambia, Zimbabwe) said the American decisions had "'shattered the Anglican Communion. Deep pain has been inflicted upon us all. We are now experiencing an overwhelming sense of loss of direction of the Anglican Communion.'"[109] "Deep pain inflicted upon us" was something to which homosexuals in his province could relate. In Botswana, homosexual acts were punishable by seven years in prison, and by fourteen in Malawi and Zambia.[110] From Uganda, the words were even harsher. The Anglican primate there, Livingstone Mpalanyi Nkoyoyo, told Ugandans the American Church was "'leading your people astray into satanic ways.'"[111] He promised, "'we will never condone it [homosexuality] anywhere in Christendom.'"[112] Punishment in Uganda for homosexual acts was fourteen years imprisonment for men and seven for women.[113] The Anglican bishop of Egypt, Mouneer Anis, said the American acts "'showed great disrespect to the majority of the members of the Anglican Communion and the church worldwide.'"[114] In Egypt, law inflicted seventeen years imprisonment upon conviction of the crime of homosexual activity.

Even before the General Convention adjourned, the American Anglican Council started preparing a counter action. Soon, David Anderson, the president of AAC, announced a meeting for October 7–9, in Plano, Texas. As talk before, during, and after the meeting proceeded it sounded less as conversation with and more as schism from the national Church. As one participant put it bluntly: "We are appealing for intervention from the Anglican Communion to call upon the Episcopal Church to repent from what it has done, or, failing to repent, to begin a realignment of Anglicanism in North America."[115] That sounded suspiciously like schism.

The ACC-sponsored gathering in October of 2003 was the counter-meeting to the pro-Robinson General Convention. The convergence of the unhappy elements of the Episcopal Church allowed all those who had been long angry, frustrated, and disappointed in the Church to gather behind closed doors for a post-event combination lament, pep rally, revival, and war council. It was arguably the starting place in the far right-wing of the Episcopal Church in their move to split the Church; and it started with a bang.

Advertised under the cryptic title, "A Place to Stand, Declaring, Preparing," it was to gather at Christ Church in Plano, Texas, a well-known highly conservative place, in the diocese of Dallas, whose bishop, James Stanton had led the presentment against

---

109. Solheim, James. "Anglicans, Episcopalians Still Weighing General Convention Decisions." Episcopal News Service, September 11, 2003, The Archives of the Episcopal Church, http://www.episcopalarchives.org/cgi-bin/ENS/ENSpress-Release.pl?pr_number=030911-1.

110. "LGBT Rights in Africa."

111. Solheim, "Anglicans."

112. Ibid.

113. "LGBT Rights in Africa."

114. Solheim, "Anglicans."

115. Figueroa, Andy. October 11, 2003, http://www.phillippians-1-20.us/report3.htm.

Bishop Righter in 1995. As word circulated about the gathering, it became the must-do among the far-right wing of the Church. Seemingly everyone who was anyone in this sub-community lined up to participate. By September 5, the organizers announced 1,400 people had registered and the meeting would be moved from Plano to the Wyndham Anatole Hotel in Dallas. As interest arose, people beyond the conservative bound wanted to attend but they were denied entrance except for journalists. In order to gain entry into the meeting one had to get a badge which could only be obtained by registration of $125 and signing a statement, "A Place to Stand" that read in part, "'All Christians are called to chastity: husbands and wives by exclusive sexual fidelity to each other and single persons by abstinence from sexual intercourse.'"[116] The statement had been written by John Rodgers.[117] The meaning of the pledge was obvious, but one could only wonder how many divorced people signed it. The host, Christ Church rector David H. Roseberry, defended the meeting's exclusivity as "'a family meeting without having to explain our beliefs to the person sitting next to us.'"[118] Not even the Presiding Bishop, Frank Griswold, would be welcomed. Griswold asked David Anderson, ACC president, to allow four men representing the national Church to attend as observers. Anderson turned him down saying there was no room for observers (while there was plenty of room for media).[119]

The conference turned out to be the anti-General Convention of the Episcopal Church. To it came 2,674 pledge signing attendees including 46 current and retired bishops[120], 799 priests and 103 seminarians.[121] Once behind closed doors, they let out all the pent-up anger and frustration that had been building up over several decades while suffering through the evermore hated reforms of the Episcopal Church. This was their moment to vent and they did with unbridled vigor. As anyone would expect, South Carolina was well-represented, and Kendall Harmon was there to regale the crowd. In what one report called "an impassioned address," he blasted the Episcopal Church, but then made a new twist on the theme. He said the mess in the Church was caused at least in part by the new prayer book.[122] It was the new theology of the 1979 prayer book that led the Church astray: "'The full theological measure of its ethos has yet to be completely felt, but we are now at a place of enough distance to begin to reflect with each other

---

116. Blumenthal, Ralph. "Conservative Anglicans Rally to Reorganize Church Power." *The New York Times,* October 8, 2003, http://www.nytimes.com/2003/10/08/us/conservative-anglicans-rally-to-reorganize.

117. Nunley, Jan. "Conservative Group Issues 'Call to Action' against General Convention." Episcopal News Service, October 13, 2003, http://www.episcopalchurch.org/library/article/conservative-group-issues-call-action-against-general-convention. Rodgers, the former dean of Trinity School for Ministry, was one ordained by Bishop Allison and others in 2000 for the Anglican Mission in America.

118. Blumenthal, "Conservative Anglicans."

119. Solheim, James. "No Welcome for Observers at Texas Meeting of Conservatives." October 6, 2003, The Archives of the Episcopal Church, http://www.episcopalarchives.org/cgi-bin/ENS/ENSpress_release.pl?pr_number=031006-0-A.

120. Nunley, "Conservative Group." Twenty-four bishops from the Episcopal Church representing less than 10 percent of the number of bishops.

121. Ibid.

122. Ibid.

about its real impact on our common life.'"[123] The results are "'deeply disconcerting'" he opined then cried: "'We have a theology in practice which moves straight from creation to redemption, a nearly universalistic worldview in which the fall and sin have in essence disappeared!'"[124] Then the author of a graduate thesis on Hell concluded: "'It is a gospel of affirmation rather than the gospel of salvation. We have moved from sinners in the hands of an angry God to clients in the palms of a satisfied therapist.'"[125] The theory that the new prayer book led to the acceptance of homosexuality was certainly an unusual explanation of the Robinson affair; but there would not be any argument from this approving crowd.

Speaker after speaker followed to offer unrestrained, and sometimes equally novel explanations of the fall of the Episcopal Church. One of the most unusual was that of Diane Knippers, president of the Institute for Religion and Democracy. She blamed the problems of the Episcopal Church on its leaders whom, she said, were baby-boomers who went to college in the 1960s and adopted the free-love mentality.[126] General Convention, she said, was "'a stunning display of the prevalent social values of American campuses forty years ago.'"[127] Another rousing orator, Robert Duncan, bishop of Pittsburgh, and leader of the bishops in AAC, called the House of Bishops an "absurdity."[128]

The second day of the meeting had less to do with rousing rhetoric and more to do with practical plans for the future. Bishop Duncan was blunt. He told the assembly he expected Anglican primates to demand the Episcopal Church reverse itself on its decisions favoring homosexuality. If the Church refused, Duncan said he expected the Anglican Communion to split between the "Western" provinces and the "Global South" ones.[129] The latter, he said, would recognize the ACC network as the legitimate presence of Anglicism in America.[130] The day continued with the theme of separation. A panel of four lawyers talked about how parishes should approach property and other legal matters. In a series of "talking points" projected on big screens, attendees were instructed on how to research the histories of the properties, make separate funds, and become familiar with canon laws before proceeding.[131] After numerous other speakers and panels along the same line of thought, the meeting arrived at its high point, a message from the Vatican. Joseph Cardinal Ratzinger, second to Pope John Paul II and future Pope Benedict XVI, wrote the conference to express his support. After reminding the group that Rome had sent St. Augustine to Canterbury, he declared the unity of truth.

Finally, the conference adopted a statement entitled "A Place to Stand: A Call to Action." Right off it repudiated the decisions of General Convention favoring homosexuals. Then, it called the acts of the Church sins and demanded the leaders of the

123. Ibid.
124. Ibid.
125. Ibid.
126. Ibid.
127. Ibid.
128. Ibid.
129. Ibid.
130. Ibid.
131. Ibid.

Episcopal Church repent and reverse the actions of the General Convention. It affirmed the Lambeth Statement of 1998 on sexuality, then appealed to the primates of the Anglican Communion to intervene in the Episcopal Church to discipline the supposedly errant bishops and "guide the realignment of Anglicanism in North America."[132] The only cause the statement listed for foreign intervention was the issue of homosexuality.

The ACC Plano/Dallas conference of October 7–9, 2003, was arguably the effective starting place in the ultra-conservative Episcopalians' movement to break up the Episcopal Church. Although the group supporting this was relatively small, no more than 10 percent of the Episcopal Church, it gained a great deal of attention in the U.S. and overseas. A key difference between the protests following the earlier reforms of race, women's ordination, and new prayer book and the one following homosexuality was the foreign connection. For the first time, the Episcopalian dissidents would have strong and vocal support from conservative foreign bishops, particularly those of middle Africa and southern Asia where anti-homosexuality was the cultural norm. This made the reaction against an openly homosexual bishop and recognition of the blessing of same sex unions in 2003 entirely different and much more serious than the earlier reactions had been. From the Plano/Dallas meeting onward, far right-wing Episcopalians would gradually find enough support at home and overseas to complete their dream of creating an "orthodox" alternative to the supposedly heretical Episcopal Church.

At this point, time was of the essence. Robinson's consecration as bishop had been set for November 2. Ultra-conservatives wanted to do what they could to prevent it or at least to raise a significant opposition to it beforehand to cast a negative shadow across it. Under conservative pressure, the Archbishop of Canterbury, Rowan Williams, had called an extraordinary, some said emergency, session of the primates of the thirty-eight independent provinces of the worldwide Anglican Communion in England, October 14–16. The special convention in South Carolina and the ultra-conservative rally in Plano/Dallas had been timed to precede the Archbishop's meeting in order to influence that conference. Both had issued clear appeals to the foreign primates to intervene in America to stop the pro-homosexual decisions of the Episcopal Church. Exactly how effective they would be remained to be seen.

If the ultra-conservative wing of the Episcopal Church thought that the Archbishop's meeting would prevent Robinson's scheduled consecration, or that the Communion would put enough pressure on the Episcopal Church to make it reverse its pro-homosexual stand, or that the Communion would resolve to intervene in America, they were to be disappointed. The basic problem with any idea of foreign intervention was in the historic nature of the Anglican Communion which was in fact only a friendship association of thirty-eight independent and self-governing churches. Some were national and some international. There was no central government of the Communion, neither executive, legislative, nor judicial authority that could intervene in any one of the provinces. The Communion was bound together, such as it was, by four so-called "Instruments of Communion": the Archbishop of Canterbury, who was only a figurehead outside of England, the periodic primates' meetings, the decennial Lambeth Conferences, and the Anglican Consultative Council. The latter met every two to three years to make non-binding

---

132. "A Place to Stand: Declaring, Preparing." http://www.fwepiscopal.org/news/AACinDallas.html.

advice. Not one of the four Instruments had any right to intervene internally in any one of the independent provinces. The thirty-eight separate churches themselves were structured differently. For instance, many had archbishops, but the Episcopal Church did not. It had a relatively weak executive in a presiding bishop and a virtually all-powerful legislature in a General Convention. Thus, the idea that foreign primates could intervene in the Episcopal Church to change its internal decisions was not tenable. What was possible, though, was to get a majority of the thirty-eight independent churches to shun the Episcopal Church and to declare a replacement in an "orthodox," i.e., anti-homosexual, national church that the conservative majority of the Anglican Communion would recognize as the legitimate Anglican province in the U.S. This, of course, would mean the splitting off of at least the ultra-conservative dioceses of the Episcopal Church as well as dividing the Anglican Communion. In short, the far-right in America would conspire with the conservative primates, mostly African and south Asian, to divide the Anglican Communion and the Episcopal Church. If the idea of foreign intervention were not tenable, the idea of schism was, even if it would destroy the historic structure of the Anglican Communion.

Needless to say, the extraordinary gathering of the heads of the thirty-eight[133] provinces on 15–16 October engendered a great deal of attention in America and the rest of the Anglican world. There were two predominant issues, Robinson's impending consecration, and the Canadian diocese of New Westminster's decision to begin rites for the blessing of same sex unions. Both were parts of the same overall issue, the stance of the Anglican churches on the rights of homosexuals in the church. As one might expect, the thirty-seven present primates had a frank exchange of views in private. At the end of the two-day meeting, the attendees issued a statement that really changed nothing.[134] It criticized but did not condemn the Episcopal Church and the Diocese of New Westminster. On one hand it reaffirmed the 1998 Lambeth Statement that homosexuality was against the Scriptures and on the other hand "acknowledge[d] a legitimate diversity of interpretation."[135] The only substantial part of the statement was the establishment of the Lambeth Commission to explore the inter-provincial relationships of the Communion and to make a report within twelve months.[136] After the meeting, the Archbishop issued a statement admitting the lack of any significant direct action and explaining it away by stating the obvious: "I must make it clear that the Primates' meeting has no legal jurisdiction. It's not a Supreme Court of the Communion."[137] The African primates made

---

133. Thirty-seven attended. The primate of the Philippines was absent.

134. "A Statement by the Primates of the Anglican Communion Meeting in Lambeth Palace." Episcopal News Service, October 16, 2003, http://www.episcopalchurch.org/library/article/statement-primates-anglican-communion-meeting-lambeth-palace.

135. Ibid.

136. Ibid.

137. "Archbishop of Canterbury's Statement at the Final Press Conference of the Primates' Meeting." Anglican Communion News Service, October 17, 2003, https://www.trinitywallstreet.org/blogs/news/archbishop-canterburys-statement-final-press-conference-primates-meeting.

it clear they were not happy and resolved to meet separately later in October.[138] Ultra-conservatives in America also resolved to meet as soon as possible.

Several leading conservatives from America did get a chance to meet privately with Archbishop Williams after the primates' conference. On October 17, the bishops of Pittsburgh, Albany, Central Florida, and Fort Worth, as well as Martyn Minns and David Anderson, talked with Williams.[139] Minns was the rector of Truro Church in Fairfax, Virginia, and Anderson was the head of the American Anglican Council. Minns said that in this meeting Archbishop Williams suggested the creation of what would become known as the Anglican Communion Network. Minns wrote: "'We shared something of our struggles and it was at that conversation the he [Williams] suggested the need for a Network. He called it a Network of Confessing Dioceses and Parishes.'"[140] The claim that the Archbishop of Canterbury himself came up with the idea of the conservative coalition called the Anglican Communion Network spread quickly and widely particularly among the conservatives themselves. Some conservatives implied it meant the stamp of approval for their side from the very top of the Anglican Communion. The problem was, it was not true or was either a misinterpretation or a great exaggeration of what the Archbishop actually said in the private meeting from which no official record was released. After the claim had spread for nearly a year, taking on the patina of fact, the Archbishop's office felt compelled to clear up the misunderstandings. In a statement of September 24, 2004, Lambeth Palace said: "The term 'network" was suggested as offering one appropriate model to provide support for those dissenting from the resolution but intending to remain within ECUSA's structures. The Archbishop felt that this might prove a suitable working concept, but *no proposals as to its potential form, structure or outworking were advanced* [emphasis added]."[141] It went on, "In relation to the discussion of the term 'confessing church' (. . .) the dissent was understood to be on a matter of conscience that, for the dissenter, touched on the integrity of the church itself. No narrower example or more specific comparison, for instance to the church in Germany in the 1930s was intended."[142] John Howe, one of the bishops present in the meeting on the 17th wrote on December 19, 2003, that although the Archbishop encouraged a network, he "'made it clear that he believes any provision for Episcopal oversight must be worked out within ECUSA itself, and that he will not be personally involved.'"[143] Thus, Minns's claim that the Archbishop Williams "suggested" the creation of the Anglican Communion network was contradicted by the Archbishop himself and by one of the other participants in the meeting.

---

138. Harden, Rachel. "Opposition to US Bishop Grows." *Church Times*, as quoted in *Jubilate Deo* (Diocese of South Carolina), October/November 2003, 2.

139. "Chronology of Significant Events." South Carolina Anglican Communion Network, http://www.sc-acn.net.

140. Minns, Martyn. "Is the Anglican Communion Network the Best Way Forward?" As quoted in "What's in a Name?" http://www.rci.rutgers.edu/~lcrew/dojustice/j190.html.

141. "Statement from Lambeth Palace on the 'Network Stories.'" September 24, 2004, as quoted in "What's in a Name?" http://www.rci.rutgers.edu/~lcrew/dojustice/j190.html.

142. Ibid.

143. "What's in a Name?" http://www.rci.rutgers.edu/~lcrew/dojustice/j190.html.

A week after the Archbishop of Canterbury hosted the primates at Lambeth Palace, the board of the American Anglican Council met to plan the future. The board, including Kendall Harmon and IRD president Diane Knippers, met at Truro Church in Fairfax, Virginia, to lay the groundwork for aggressive action. The question was movement to where, or action for what? They claimed they wanted "adequate episcopal oversight," but the reporter from *The New York Times* saw it differently. She wrote, "conservative Episcopalians meeting on Thursday in Fairfax, Va., laid out the groundwork to secede from the Episcopal Church."[144]

Whether they were going to secede was not the stated question at the moment. Of course, in time, a large portion, if not all, of the leadership of AAC did indeed leave the Episcopal Church. At their meeting on October 22–23, 2003, the board planned ways to develop adequate episcopal oversight, that is, to allow parishes and dioceses opposed to the Episcopal Church pro-homosexual reforms to have bishops who refused to accept the validity of the reforms. The directors said the Anglican primates had made provision for such oversight. This was another example of misinterpreting the facts. The primates' October 16 statement actually stated: "we call on the provinces concerned to make adequate provision for episcopal oversight of dissenting minorities within their own area of pastoral care in consultation with the Archbishop of Canterbury on behalf of the Primates."[145] The meaning in the language was perfectly clear. The province would decide on the provision for episcopal oversight. This was not to be up to the dissidents themselves or to the Archbishop or to foreign primates. The initiative would have to come from the constitutional authorities of the Episcopal Church, not from another group such as the AAC. Nevertheless, ACC proceeded as if it were in charge of arranging the oversight. The directors decided to set up a "Network of Confessing Dioceses and Parishes." For this they developed "Guidelines for Congregations Seeking Adequate Episcopal Oversight," and an "Application for Adequate Episcopal Oversight."[146] In addition, they created a "Bishops' Committee on Adequate Episcopal Oversight" to coordinate the various efforts of the parishes and dioceses that wanted to join the Network.

The AAC left murky exactly what this "oversight" scheme meant or how it would operate. The original concept, as enunciated in the primates' October 16 statement was for the oversight to be arranged within the structure of an Anglican province, in this case the Episcopal Church. It did not say that the overseeing bishops had to come from foreign provinces. But, the words that AAC leaders used could be interpreted to mean they intended to be outside the authority of the Episcopal Church, just as the newspaper reporter said. With his usual bluntness, Robert Duncan, the bishop of Pittsburgh, said "'separation has happened and that realignment is a coming reality (. . .). The big question and concern is whether we will be able to be reconfigured in an orderly manner

---

144. Goodstein, Laurie. "With Conservative Episcopalians Making Plans to Separate, Gay Bishop-Elect Stands Firm." *The New York Times*, October 24, 2003, http://www.nytimes.com/2003/10/24/us/with-conservative-episcopalians-making-plans-separate-gay-bishop-elect.

145. "A Statement by the Primates."

146. Virtue, David. "American Anglican Council Prepares for Realignment." Virtueonline, October 23, 2003, http://www.listserv.virtueonline.org/pipermail/virtueonline_listserv.virtueonline.org/2003.

or whether we will slide into chaos.'"[147] Duncan was also quoted as saying, "'We are asking the leaders of the church to rule that those who continue to uphold the historic faith represent the legitimate, bona fide expression of Episcopalianism in the United States.'"[148] Kendall Harmon seemed to be looking ahead too. He said that the Archbishop of Canterbury had told the Americans last week he wanted to avoid a "'wilderness of litigation'" over church property.[149] He continued, "'we're looking at a period of messy realignment. But you've got the head of the Anglican family pleading for responsible leadership and creative solutions.'"[150] He did not explain what that meant. Nor did he or anyone else explain what they meant by the word "realignment" that they used repeatedly. The newspaper reporter interpreted it to mean schism. In retrospect, she was wise.

Bishop Salmon and three other bishops, Jack Iker, of Ft. Worth, James Stanton, of Dallas, and Robert Duncan, of Pittsburgh, traveled to London to meet four Anglican primates and propose the formation of an "orthodox" network, that is, a grouping of Episcopalians who refused to accept the Church actions favoring homosexuals. By the time the American bishops met, someone had drawn up a list of twenty-six points to present to the Global South primates. It lacked a signature, but the handwriting on the top of the page, "Mainstream Mtg. 11/20/03," may have been that of Bishop Duncan[151] The most important items on this list were: Global South would be in communion with the Network; Global South primates would tell the Archbishop of Canterbury that if he did not recognize the Network, they would separate from him; the issue of boundaries would be suspended; issue a Memorandum forming the Network of Confessing Dioceses and Parishes with Bishop Duncan as the Moderator; the Network would refuse communion with the bishops who consecrated Bishop Robinson; and, perhaps most importantly, "We commit to the guerilla warfare of the next year."[152] This list became the working guide from which the later formal Memorandum was derived. Although the list did not explicitly call for schism, it seemed to imply such by suggesting an alliance between Global South and the "orthodox," i.e. ultra-conservative, Episcopalians who were forming an association separate from the organizational structure of the Episcopal Church. The phrase "guerilla warfare" was most revealing.

On November 20, 2003, the four bishops[153] issued a formal "Memorandum of Agreement on Establishing a Network of Confessing Dioceses and Congregations in the Episcopal Church." Unfortunately, it did not clear up what was meant by the scheme of episcopal oversight. The Memorandum had nine items, the first of which declared the alliance had an "apostolic mission to a troubled and fallen church."[154] After declaring

---

147. Ibid.

148. "Episcopal Meeting Tackles Controversy." *Pittsburgh Tribune-Review*, October 7, 2003, http://pittsburghepiscopal.org/property/dots.pdf.

149. Goodstein, "With Conservative."

150. Ibid.

151. House of Bishops, Task Force on Property Disputes. "Memorandum, April 9, 2007." Appendix B, http://pittsburghepiscopal.org/property/dots.pdf.

152. Ibid.

153. Nine bishops were to sign later.

154. "Memorandum of Agreement on Establishing a Network of Confessing Dioceses and Congre-

the Episcopal Church "fallen," the next item said the Network would operate "within the Constitution of ECUSA."[155] One should note the absence of the word "canons." The Network would recognize the constitution but not the canons of the Episcopal Church.[156] The statement went on to name Robert Duncan as "moderator" and to declare that the Network would participate in providing for the episcopal oversight. The document raised more questions than it answered. In the first place, if the Episcopal Church had "fallen" why would any "orthodox" person want to remain in it? In the second place, the Constitution and Canons of the Episcopal Church were the governing documents of the entire Church and they required all diocese to accede to them as a condition of membership in the Church. Dioceses were not allowed to choose one part and not the other. Under the Constitution and Canons, it would not be possible for a part of the Episcopal Church to deny the decisions of the General Convention. In the third place, the primates' statement of October 16 had said the province would arrange the episcopal oversight setup with consultation of the Archbishop and other primates. It was not in the authority of the American Anglican Council or the Anglican Communion Network to declare its right to "participate" in anything of the Anglican Communion.

When the Archbishop of Canterbury learned of all this he immediately rejected every part. He made it clear he would not endorse the Network and would respect only efforts made within the structure of the Episcopal Church. On December 7, 2003, Duncan said he had tried to communicate with the Archbishop several times about the Network matter but had received only silence.[157] A. Hugo Blankingship, Jr., the chancellor of the American Anglican Council, was Duncan's contact with the Archbishop's office. John Rees, the Archbishop's legal adviser, told Blankingship that the Archbishop "won't listen to anything but our staying in ECUSA."[158] He reported to Duncan that there was no chance the Archbishop would recognize the Network at that time.[159] The Network bishops learned they would have to proceed without the support of Archbishop Williams. What Duncan's notes suggested was that the Network's idea of realignment was to replace the Episcopal Church with an "orthodox" church recognized by the Anglican Communion. Indeed, Blankingship said in his email to Duncan of 9 December that the Network's founding Memorandum sounded more like just another protest "than a group ready to become a separate church if necessary."[160]

As soon as Bishop Salmon returned to Charleston from London, he met the diocesan Standing Committee to make a report. He presented the Memorandum to the committee and discussed it with them. He also said the Archbishop of Canterbury had endorsed the establishment of the Network and that he would recognize its status in

---

gations in the Episcopal Church." http://www.americananglican.org/memorandum-of-agreement-on-establishing-a-network-of-confessing.

155. Ibid.

156. The Diocese of South Carolina was to do the same before the schism of 2012. A diocesan convention voted to recognize the constitution but not the canons of the Episcopal Church.

157. House of Bishops, Task Force on Property Disputes, "Memorandum." Appendix C.

158. Ibid.

159. Ibid.

160. Ibid.

the Episcopal Church.[161] At best this was only an assumption of Salmon. In fact, as one has already seen, the Archbishop would reject all of the demands of the November 20 meeting; he never endorsed or recognized the Network. The Rev. Jennie Olbrych made a motion that the committee endorse the Network. It passed unanimously.[162]

Energized by the roaring success of its 7–9 October Plano/Dallas conference, the American Anglican Council pressed ahead its right-wing counter-revolution in new landmark rallies in January of 2004. On January 9–10, it held "Plano East," or, a near replay on the first Plano meeting in October.[163] Once again, the faithful poured out in force as some two thousand conservatives converged on Hylton Memorial Chapel in Woodbridge, Virginia, a megachurch located twenty miles south of Washington D.C. The theme was, as before, to prepare for the coming "realignment" of Anglicanism in America. As to be expected, the tireless Kendall Harmon was front and center. And, this time, one got to hear him expound all morning long on the main day, the 10th. At 9:15 a.m. he gave a talk "Anglican Essentials." At 10:00 he joined an hour and a half panel on "Latest Developments & The Emerging Realignment." With him were other important AAC voices Martyn Minns, Diane Knippers, Hugo Blankingship,[164] and Andrew Pearson.[165]

The ultra-conservative movement reached a landmark in January of 2004 with the formal establishment of its "realignment" organization called the Anglican Communion Network, or, officially the Network of Anglican Communion Dioceses and Parishes. On January 19, over one hundred participants assembled at Christ Church, in Plano, Texas, to enact the Memorandum that the four dissident bishops had composed on November 20 in London. Representatives from twelve dioceses[166] attended along with the Rev. Canon Michael Green, once an assistant to the former Archbishop of Canterbury, George Carey. South Carolina was as well represented as any diocese with at least seven delegates: bishops Salmon and Skilton, Kendall Harmon, the Rev. Steve Wood, the Rev. John Burwell, Lydia Evans, and Clayton Burroughs (of Grace Church, Charleston).[167]

The purpose of the meeting was to provide a stronger organizational unity for the ultra-conservative wing of the Episcopal Church. The form of the unity, however, was

---

161. "Minutes of the Standing Committee." [November 25, 2003].
This author was not able to confirm Salmon's claims the ABC endorsed or recognized the Network.

162. Ibid.

163. "Over 2000 Orthodox Episcopalians to Gather this Week at AAC 'Plano East' Meeting in Virginia." Virtueonline, http://www.virtueonline.org/plano-east-will-draw-2000-orthodox-episcopalians-week.

164. Chancellor of the AAC.

165. Traycik, Auburn Faber. "Plano Plus: Eastern Meeting of Faithful Episcopalians Eclipses Landmark Dallas Gathering." *The Christian Challenge*, January 9, 2004, as quoted in Virtueonline, http://www.virtueonline.org/plano-plus-eastern-meeting-episcopalians-eclipses-dallas. Pearson was "Director of AAC's Affiliates Ministry." Later, he was on the staff of St. Helena's Church of Beaufort, SC under rector Jeffrey Miller, and then of the Cathedral Church of the Advent in Birmingham, AL where he gained the post of dean in 2013.

166. Albany, Central Florida, Dallas, Fort Worth, Pittsburgh, Quincy, Rio Grande, San Joaquin, South Carolina, Springfield, and Western Kansas. Five of the twelve later voted to leave the Episcopal Church while seven remained in the Church.

167. "Minutes of the Standing Committee." [January 27, 2004].

a problem that turned out to be just one of several that almost derailed the group and hinted at future fracture lines among this faction. According to reports, disagreements among the delegates on the first day almost led to the breakup of the meeting.[168] What had brought this coalition together was a negative, that is, opposition to the pro-homosexual reforms of the Episcopal Church. Going beyond that into a positive trajectory was not so easy. The basic problem of the meeting was to define an identity for the new Network. Exactly what was the Network? What was its purpose? How would it function? How would it relate to the Episcopal Church? None of this had been made clear in the Memorandum of November 20 which became the foundation of the Network. Bishop Robert Duncan, the "moderator" of the group told the assembly its purpose was to adopt "'a simple charter (. . .) a structure appropriate to its early life.'"[169] He went on that they should "elect officers, renew relations with the overseas Church, campaign for 'the cause of adequate episcopal oversight' and 'give hope to the orthodox of the Episcopal Church.'"[170] Bishop Salmon, apparently concerned about keeping the tie with the national Church, asked that a copy of the minutes of the meeting be sent to Presiding Bishop Griswold.[171] Still, the assembly almost came apart on trying to define alternate episcopal oversight. The assembly could not seem to come to a consensus on how the episcopal oversight would be constructed or how it would function. Apparently, some delegates feared the ambiguity of the whole oversight issue was only a smokescreen for what the radical fringe of the ultra-conservative coalition really wanted, schism from the Episcopal Church. Finally, a series of speakers delivered theological talks supporting the Network: Robert Munday, Philip Turner, and Kendall Harmon, followed by Canon Michael Green.[172] According to reports, the calls for unity turned the tide and the assembly proceeded to adopt by unanimous vote the charter of the Network.[173] In time, ten dioceses joined the Anglican Communion Network. Five of those later voted to leave the Episcopal Church.[174] The ten dioceses represented roughly the ultra-conservative 10 percent of the Episcopal Church.

The new charter of the Anglican Communion Network, an elaboration of the four bishops' November 20 Memorandum, did nothing to clear up questions about the public purpose of the new organization. As one will see, the Network never achieved any sort of alternate episcopal oversight. The essential reason was that it was impossible under the Constitution and Canons of the Episcopal Church. There was no provision for a church within a church that could disregard the decisions of the governing body, the General Convention. Alternate episcopal oversight was equally impossible under

---

168. "Plano Meeting Boosts Support for Alternative Episcopal Oversight." *The Living Church*, as quoted in *Jubilate Deo* (Diocese of South Carolina), February/March 2004, 14.

169. Ibid.

170. Ibid.

171. Ibid.

172. Ibid.

173. Ibid.

174. "Anglican Communion Network," Wikipedia, http://en.wikipedia.org/wiki/Anglican_Communion_Network. Dioceses joining the ACN: Albany, Central Florida, Pittsburgh, Quincy, Rio Grande, Springfield, Fort Worth, South Carolina, Dallas, and San Joaquin.

existing Episcopal Church law. Dioceses were geographical units, each under its own bishop(s). There was no provision for an Episcopal Church bishop to take jurisdiction over a part of another diocese. The same was true of foreign bishops. There was no legal way for a bishop outside the Episcopal Church to exercise any authority within the Church. Moreover, as one has seen, the Network recognized the constitution but not the canons of the Episcopal Church, another exercise in impossibility. All of this could lead some people to suspect that the real but hidden aim of the Network was not episcopal oversight but the schism of the ultra-conservative dioceses of the Episcopal Church by linking them up with the highly socially conservative Anglican primates overseas. The common bond uniting the American ultra-conservatives and these Third World prelates would be opposition to the liberty and equality of homosexual persons in the church. As of January 2004, it remained to be seen just where this Network was going.

The ultra-conservative counter-revolution against the Episcopal Church in 2003 was led and coordinated largely under the guidance of the American Anglican Council. The Anglican Communion Network, formally established in January of 2004, was largely the construct of the AAC. It is difficult to gauge in detail the full roles of AAC and its parent IRD but one can readily see the powerful influence of the AAC in capitalizing on the ultra-conservative anti-Robinson hysteria of 2003 and unifying and directing this energy into a movement, as the IRD said, to restructure the liberal Episcopal Church. The creation and promotion of the Network for "realignment" in 2003–04 was to be the AAC's great achievement of the day.

The Consecration of Bishop Robinson

Elaborate plans proceeded apace for Gene Robinson's consecration as a bishop of the Episcopal Church.[175] It was set for Sunday, November 2, 2003 in Whittemore Center, the ice skating pavilion at the University of New Hampshire in Durham. As one might imagine, the event drew an enormous amount of attention from the public and the media. Seemingly every known media outlet showed up along with three hundred reporters. Fourteen television trucks spouting UFO-like satellite dishes lined up outside. The whole place swarmed with one hundred police officers. Two police snipers crouched on the roof. Robinson himself wore a bulletproof vest and was accompanied by bodyguards.[176] Outside, loud protesters chanted hateful slurs but they were more than matched by three hundred students from the University of New Hampshire who showed up to drown them out. Showing up too were nearly four thousand people in the audience,[177] two hundred in the choir and forty-eight magnificently attired bishops led by the presiding bishop, Frank Griswold.

Showing up too was the ever-present Kendall Harmon, who with David Bena, the bishop suffragan of Albany, had been sent by the American Anglican Council to stage

---

175. For a detailed description of the events, see Adams, *Going to Heaven*, 169–205.

176. Robinson was not the first bishop to wear a bulletproof vest for consecration. Barbara Harris, the first female bishop, had worn one.

177. Goodstein, Laurie. "Openly Gay Man is Made a Bishop." *The New York Times*, November 3, 2003, http://www.nytimes.com/2003/11/03/us/openly-gay-man-is-made-a-bishop.html.

a publicity-generating counter-event in Durham.[178] Before this event, however, Bena and others were ready to be heard in the proceedings of the consecration. Bena read a formal statement from thirty-eight bishops denouncing the consecration of an openly homosexual man and announcing they, and the majority of bishops of the Anglican Communion, would not recognize Robinson as a bishop.[179]

After the opposition statements, the ceremonies proceeded as the protesters staged a walk-out and headed over to the Durham Evangelical Church to hold a counter-service for four hundred opponents of the consecration. Kendall Harmon was scheduled to preach at this service which he described as "'part of a truthful witness.'"[180] Robinson's consecration he described in his characteristic avoidance of understatement as "'a very, very decisive moment in the history of Christianity.'"[181] Harmon told another reporter he was ashamed to be an Episcopal priest on that day because Robinson and his supporters "'are turning their backs on God.'"[182] Back at Whittemore Center, Robinson's consecration proceeded uninterrupted. Griswold served as chief consecrator assisted by six bishops. At the conclusion, the four thousand people sprang to their feet and let out loud cries of rejoicing. Robinson replied, "'It's not about me; it's about so many other people who find themselves at the margins.'"[183]

The Chapman Memo

The American Anglican Council and its by-product the Anglican Communion Network did not openly advocate schism from the Episcopal Church at this time, but they did call for Episcopalians to reject the validity of the Church's reforms on homosexuality, particularly the consecration of the first openly gay bishop and the acceptance of services for the blessings of same-sex unions. For this they developed the idea of alternate episcopal oversight to link up the dissidents with overseas prelates. This was their stated goal in 2003 and 2004. However, they had no evidence that this idea would ever come to pass. Their claim that the Archbishop of Canterbury originated the notion and was backing it himself turned out to be at the very least a great exaggeration forcing the Archbishop to assure everyone in 2004 he meant any scheme to be within the authority of the Episcopal Church. Suspicions began to grow among pro-Church elements that the AAC/ACN ultra-conservatives were actually scheming to create schism in the Episcopal

---

178. England, Dan and Matthew Davies, "Unexpected Support for Episcopal Church Action." Episcopal News Service, November 1, 2003, http://www.episcopalchurch.org/library/article/unexpected-support-episcopal-church-action.

179. "Bishops Statement of Objection to the Consecration of the Rev. Can. V. Gene Robinson." November 4, 2003, http://www.americananglican.org/bishops-statement-of-objection-to-the-consecration. Of the 38 signatories, 28 were Americans. Of those, 18 were diocesan bishops, 3 assisting or suffragan, and 8 retired. South Carolina Bishop Salmon, Bishop Suffragan Skilton, and retired bishop Allison all signed.

180. Adams, *Going to Heaven*, 197.

181. Ibid.

182. Grossman, Cathy Lynn. "New Hampshire's Robinson Becomes Pioneer Gay Bishop." *USA Today*, November 3, 2003, http://usatoday30.usatoday.com/news/nation/2003-11-02-bobinson_x.htm.

183. Goodstein, "Openly Gay."

Church. The first major verification for this belief came in the Chapman Memo drawn up just weeks after Robinson's consecration.

Presiding Bishop Griswold did not ignore pleas for alternate episcopal oversight. In fact, through the late summer and fall of 2003 and the winter of 2003–04, he and many bishops spent a great deal of time working on proposals for this idea. On October 31, Griswold sent to all Episcopal bishops a confidential letter about oversight and a five-page draft of a plan. He asked the bishops to discuss it among themselves and suggest changes that would be presented at the next House of Bishops meeting, in March of 2004. The draft had been prepared by the Pastoral Development committee of the House of Bishops and the Presiding Bishop's Council of Advice. It began by reiterating the House of Bishop's March 2002 statement called "A Covenant on Episcopal Pastoral Care." This made three points: that the Constitution and Canons of the Episcopal Church were sufficient to deal with the question of oversight, that any oversight would be under the direction of the local bishop, and any plan of oversight would be temporary.[184] To this, the twenty-member Council of Advice added a new "Supplemental Episcopal Pastoral Care" plan that laid out a framework for implementing an oversight arrangement. This would involve consultation of a local parish, the bishop, and perhaps the head of the local province.[185] The point was that all of this would be handled entirely by the diocesan bishops of the Episcopal Church. Griswold stressed this was a draft. He asked for input before the Council of Advice would go over it again and present a final proposal to the House of Bishops for approval next March. Soon after sending the draft to the bishops, Griswold sent it to the Archbishop of Canterbury. The Archbishop told Griswold that the matter of oversight must remain entirely the responsibility of the Episcopal Church and that he would not exercise any "direct intervention."[186]

The Council of Advice met Griswold again on Dec. 2–3, 2003, to go over the "Supplemental" proposal. On December 5, Griswold sent a letter to the Episcopal bishops bringing then up to date about the work on the oversight issue. He stressed again that any plan would be under the diocesan bishops of the Episcopal Church and there would be no foreign intervention of any kind in the Episcopal Church, including from the Archbishop of Canterbury. Griswold's letter was publicized; and immediately the American Anglican Council declared the "Supplemental" plan to be inadequate.[187] Nevertheless, the House of Bishops, meeting on March 23, 2004, adopted a covenant called "Caring for all the Churches: A Response of the House of Bishops of the Episcopal Church to an Expressed Need of the Church." Building on the March 2002 statement and the "Supplemental" proposal of October 2003, the bishops laid out a detailed plan for oversight. In it the local parish would work with its bishop who could appoint an-

184. House of Bishops, Office of Pastoral Development. "Supplemental Episcopal Pastoral Care." http://arc.episcopalchurch.org/pastoraldev/supplemental.html.

185. Ibid.

186. Griswold, (the Most Rev.) Frank. "Presiding Bishop's Letter to Bishops on Supplemental Episcopal Pastoral Care." December 5, 2003, Episcopal News Service, http://episcopalchurch.org/library/article/presiding-bishops-letter-bishops-supplemental-episcopal-pastoral-care.

187. Solheim, James. "Plans for Network of Dissenters Prepares to Take Next Step." Anglican Communion News Service, December 23, 2003, http://www.anglicannews.org/news/2003/12/plans-for-network-of-dissenters-prepares-to-take-next-step.aspx.

other Episcopal Church bishop to provide oversight for the parish. Failing this, the head of the local province could intervene to make a settlement. At any rate, "If an episcopal visitor is to be invited, that bishop shall be a member in good standing in this Church."[188] This final oversight plan made it clear the whole process would remain in the Episcopal Church and any oversight would be another Episcopal bishop. There was to be no foreign intervention of any kind in the Episcopal Church, much to the chagrin of the ultra-conservative "realignment" party.

As soon as Griswold's proposal for oversight was circulated in early December of 2003, the American Anglican Council denounced it and secretly prepared for action. The basic difference was whether the oversight would come from inside or outside the Episcopal Church. The Church insisted it would be inside. The ACC looked beyond the Episcopal Church. The AAC bishops had already been talking with four foreign primates and spreading the unfounded idea that the Archbishop of Canterbury supported them. It was clear the AAC idea of oversight meant foreign intervention. Within weeks of Griswold's December 5 letter, the Chapman Memo appeared.

Geoffrey Chapman was rector of St. Stephen's Episcopal Church in Sewickley, Pennsylvania, in the Diocese of Pittsburgh. He had been an outspoken strong critic of the Episcopal Church's reforms for homosexuals and had been active in AAC. On December 28, 2003, he issued a paper, soon popularly called "the Chapman Memo." Right off, Chapman made it plain he was acting on behalf of the American Anglican Council and its Bishops' Committee on Adequate Episcopal Oversight. He said: "the Strategy Committee" of AAC had worked for months drawing up this plan. He cautioned that one should keep this secret document confidential: "do not pass it on electronically to anyone under any circumstances."[189] There was good reason to keep this secret plan secret. It was explicit; and it uncovered AAC's true intent. First it declared in plain English that its goal was to replace the Episcopal Church: "Our ultimate goal is a realignment of Anglicanism on North American soil (. . .). We believe in the end this should be a 'replacement' jurisdiction."[190] That demolished once and for all the myth that AAC wanted to work only within the structure of the Episcopal Church and showed that any oversight scheme was only a step to separation. As Chapman said: "Bp Griswold's offer of 'Extended Episcopal Care' is unacceptable, fundamentally flawed and disingenuous, and does not meet the needs of our parishes or the intentions of the Primates."[191] The next big point was to keep the property: "We seek to retain ownership of our property as we move into this realignment."[192] Following this, Chapman gave a two-stage process to carry out the "replacement." In the first stage, "parishes would publicly announce that their rela-

---

188. House of Bishops. "Caring for All the Churches: A Response of the House of Bishops of the Episcopal Church to an Expressed Need of the Church." Episcopal News Service, March 23, 2004, http://archive.episcopalchurch.org/3577_32884_ENG_HTM.htm.

189. Nunley, Jan. "Memo Discloses AAC's Strategy for Replacing Episcopal Church." Episcopal News Service, January 14, 2004, http://archive.episcopalchurch.org/3577_26104_ENG_HTM.htm. The Memo was leaked to the press within three weeks.

190. Ibid.

191. Ibid.

192. Ibid.

tionship with their diocesan Bishop is 'severely damaged'"[193] because of the issue of homosexuality. The parishes were to band together in the Anglican Communion Network. In the second stage, predicted for the year 2004, the parishes would move to "negotiated settlements in matters of property, jurisdiction, pastoral succession and communion."[194] If the parishes did not get what they wanted, "disobedience of canon law on a widespread basis may be necessary."[195] To help, "we do have non-geographical oversight available from 'offshore' Bishops, and retired Bishops."[196] Following the two-stage plan, Chapman gave a long list of advice on how to carry it out. He said the "revisionist" bishops were on the defensive now and reticent to move against the "conservatives" who could quickly become the 'victims' in the public mind."[197] This would provide a window of time for the parishes to enact successfully the stages. A point that Chapman emphasized throughout was that parishes must work with the AAC: "Either we hang together or we hang separately!"[198] Finally, he cautioned again to keep all this top secret. At the end, Chapman listed several helpful websites including Kendall Harmon's Titus One Nine and David Virtue's Virtue Online.

Seventeen days later, Alan Cooperman broke the story in *The Washington Post* and suddenly it was everywhere.[199] News outlets around the world carried the story. In England, Stephen Bates of *The Guardian* was blunt under his headline, "US Anglicans Plot to Break Up Church." He wrote, "American Anglican traditionalists are plotting the break-up of their national church and the creation of a new fundamentalist church in the wake of its consecration of the openly gay bishop Gene Robinson."[200] He continued: "In spite of public assurances that they only wish to secure oversight by sympathetic conservative bishops, rebel parishes are being secretly told to prepare for the ultimate goal of breaking up the US Episcopal Church."[201] Bates went on to point out that hardline Evangelicals in England were also maneuvering against their Church leadership. On the same day, the news spread around the world, Jan Nunley of the Episcopal News Service posted a story on the Church website. She had to do little but give excerpts of the Memo that spoke for themselves. As the other reporters, she pointed out: "the organization's [AAC] ultimate goal is to replace the Episcopal Church governed by the General Convention with its own confessionally-based jurisdiction."[202] Nunley went on to say, "The memo appears to contradict recent statements by the AAC that it does not want to break away from the

---

193. Ibid.

194. Ibid.

195. Ibid.

196. Ibid.

197. Ibid.

198. Ibid.

199. Cooperman, Alan. "Plan to Supplant Episcopal Church USA is Revealed." *The Washington Post*, January 14, 2004, http://us-mg205.mail.yahoo.com/neo/launch?partner=sbc&rand=8kjik17aovk.

200. Bates, Stephen. "US Anglicans Plot to Break Up Church." *The Guardian*, January 14, 2014, http://www.theguardian.com/world/2004/jan/15/usa.religion1.

201. Ibid.

202. Nunley, "Memo."

Episcopal Church."[203] To that point, when reporters contacted Chapman he admitted to all and even elaborated on the Memo. Although Chapman had clearly said his Memo was issued on behalf of the AAC, when reporters talked with Bruce Mason, the media director of AAC, Mason did not deny the Memo but he did deny what people said it meant. Mason said that Chapman was "not a policy spokesman and denied that the AAC intends to 'supplant the current structure' of the Episcopal Church."[204] He went on, "'the AAC continues to work within the Episcopal Church."[205] Either Chapman was or was not speaking for the AAC. He said he was. His role and office in AAC were undeniable. This author has seen no record that Chapman ever disclaimed the Memo or disputed what the reporters said about it. The Chapman Memo stood on its own and spoke for itself.

The Chapman Memo was "the smoking gun" in the conspiracy to create schism in the Episcopal Church. It proved that the ultra-conservatives, led by the AAC, were moving to break up the Episcopal Church and to replace it with a very different church of their own liking. It provided the blueprint for parishes and dioceses to follow to accomplish this schism. As it turned out, what the ultra-conservatives meant by "realignment" was not adequate episcopal oversight within the Episcopal Church but replacing the Episcopal Church with one closely tied to the committed opponents of homosexual rights among the Third World primates. Regardless of what the Chapman Memo may have said or meant, one should look at what actually happened. The facts were: the Episcopal Church offered an alternate episcopal oversight plan, the ultra-conservatives refused the plan, no oversight scheme was ever enacted, and five dioceses voted to leave the Episcopal Church aided and supported by several Anglican prelates overseas. Four of the five created a "replacement" church meant to take the place of the Episcopal Church as the legitimate Anglican province in the U.S. The Anglican Communion split, part recognizing the Episcopal Church and part recognizing the "replacement," the Anglican Church in North America. Thus, schism occurred in some way in both the Episcopal Church and the Anglican Communion.

THE DIOCESE OF SOUTH CAROLINA IN THE LATE SALMON YEARS, 2004–2007

The Immediate Backlash against the Episcopal Church

By late 2003, it was clear that the prevailing attitude in the Diocese of South Carolina toward the Episcopal Church was critical-to-hostile. The diocesan leadership's role in the establishment of the Anglican Communion Network in January of 2004 was the outcome of a logical progression of opposition to the Church's reforms, particularly those favoring homosexuals. The officers of the American Anglican Council and its by-product the Anglican Communion Network may have been planning schism against the Church while publicly professing loyalty to it. However, there was no hard evidence

203. Ibid.
204. Ibid.
205. Ibid.

that the South Carolina diocesan leadership plotted schism in 2003–04. Indeed, Bishop Salmon continued to give out mixed signals about loyalty to the Church. While he did not advocate outright schism, he did eagerly participate in the ultra-conservative movements that may have been planning schism. At the same time, he gave no harbor to the schismatics in his own diocese. He continued to press the litigation against All Saints at Pawleys Island on the basis of the Dennis Canon. While Salmon was a vocal critic of the Episcopal Church, he was also a vocal critic of schism, at least in his own diocese. The effect of Salmon's ambivalence about the national Church was that while he may not have advocated schism, the atmosphere of hostility toward the Church that his policies did not counter allowed others to promote opposition to and eventually rejection of the Episcopal Church.

While hostility was the general attitude, there was a minority of communicants in the diocese who wanted to defend the Episcopal Church. By late 2003, at least some of these people had grown alarmed at what they saw as the dangerous trajectory of the diocese toward schism. The voting pattern in the diocesan convention of October 2003 had shown the pro-Church faction to be small, less than 20 percent, and virtually impotent. The power structure of the diocese was overwhelmingly controlled by ideological conservatives by this point. There was no one in the diocesan leadership fighting back for the Episcopal Church. There was no way the small bands of loyalists could change this through the institutional system. The best they could do was try to educate the communicants of the diocese on the state of affairs in the national Church. By 2003, *Jubilate Deo*, the diocesan newspaper, was giving news about the ultra-conservatives in the Episcopal Church as if they were the norm.

In December of 2003, a group of five friends in Charleston met informally to discuss the relationship of the diocese to the national Church in view of the anti-Church resolutions of the recent diocesan convention. They were Barbara Mann, Marcy Walsh, Tom Myers, Dottie Pagliaro, and Lynn Pagliaro. Mann had been on the Church Executive Council from 1997 to 2003, and was chair of the audit committee. She also served as treasurer of Province IV after 1994 as well as member of the standing commission on the structure of the Church (2003–09). The group decided to set up an organization devoted to keeping the Diocese of South Carolina in the Episcopal Church. It was to be called the Episcopal Forum of South Carolina; and its first president was Lynn Pagilaro. This group would become the heart of the resolute Episcopalian loyalist element of the diocese.[206]

The Episcopal Forum was incorporated under South Carolina law as a non-profit corporation. Its by-laws called for twenty-four directors representing the expanse of the diocese. It announced its goal as "to insure that the Episcopal Diocese of SC continues to exist in full participation with ECUSA, its constitutions, canons, and leadership."[207] On February 21, 2004, the Forum sponsored a conference entitled "Seeking Unity in Diversity" in Charleston that was attended by two hundred people.[208] In addition it held

---

206. Mann, Barbara. Interview with author, September 3, 2014.

207. "Meet the Episcopal Forum of SC." *Jubilate Deo* (Diocese of South Carolina), April/May 2004, 7.

208. "Talk at Episcopal Forum Centers on Ways to Avoid Schism." *The Augusta Chronicle* (Augusta, GA), February 23, 2004, http://chronicle.augusta.com/stories/2004/02/23/met_405572.shtnl.

six regional meeting drawing three hundred attendees.[209] The Forum's early officers and directors were: Gayle Fellers, Greg Hayson, Betsy Luke, Barbara Mann, Tom Myers, Dolores Miller, Dottie Pagliaro, Lynn Pagliaro, Jonathan Poston, Jan Van Norte, Warren Redman-Gress, John Sands, Marcy Walsh, and Steve Ward.[210]

By early 2004, there were at least eleven other cases similar to the Forum's where loyalist groups formed in largely conservative dioceses of the Episcopal Church. On 25–27 March 2004, representatives of the twelve groups met at All Saints Church in Atlanta to form Via Media, an umbrella structure for the various loyalist organizations. The pro-Church factions that made up Via Media came from South Carolina, Albany, St. Lawrence Deanery, San Diego, Central Florida, Fort Worth, Pittsburgh, San Joaquin, Southwest Florida, Springfield, Dallas, and Rio Grande. The purpose of Via Media was to serve as a liaison for the twelve local parts that were devoted to counteracting the Anglican Communion Network that the loyalists feared was schismatic.[211]

The diocesan leadership kept a wary eye on the Episcopal Forum. Bishops Salmon and Skilton met with the Forum leadership on January 26, 2004. Apparently, Salmon did not think highly of the Forum. He was reported as saying, "'Their stated purpose is unity, their actual purpose is to support the consecration of Gene Robinson and same sex blessings.'"[212] The next day after the meeting, Salmon reported to the Standing Committee that he had conferred with the Forum and that, although the group was neutral on the recent resolutions of the General Convention, it was "committed to not leaving the Episcopal Church under any circumstances."[213] The committee then shrugged off the Forum.

The Forum's main public competition came from the Anglican Communion Network which was also a diocesan wide association but in opposition. The ACN was created and supported by the power structure of the diocese. There was no way the Forum could compete fairly with ACN across the diocese. Although it eventually counted hundreds of members, the Forum counted no one with any position of authority in the diocesan structure. For instance, no member of the Forum served on the Standing Committee. Frozen out of the power structure of the diocese, the Forum did its best to keep the tie between diocese and Church but in the end, it would be completely powerless to stem the diocesan leadership's drive to schism.

In spite of the Forum's best efforts, the prevailing attitude in the diocese continued to grow more critical of the Episcopal Church. For years, the conservative organization called Scholarly Engagement with Anglican Doctrine (SEAD), based in Charleston, had held a conference every January to bring together conservative clergy and laity. By 2004 it had merged with the Anglican Institute, based on Colorado, to become the Anglican Communion Institute which, despite its name, was not connected to the Anglican

---

209. "Meet the Episcopal Forum."

210. Ibid.

211. Beach, (the Rev.) Foley. "Via Media Groups Join Forces." *The Living Church*, April 2004, 13–14.

212. Zacher, Deborah. "Via Media Groups Appeal to the Center." Episcopal News Service, March 30, 2004, The Archives of the Episcopal Church, http://www.episcopalarchives.org/cgi-bin/ENS/ENSpress_release.pl?pr_number=040330-2a.

213. "Minutes of the Standing Committee." [January 27, 2004].

Communion.[214] On January 8–9, 2004, the ACI sponsored a conference in Charleston called "Future of the Anglican Communion" to call for "disciplinary action against the Episcopal Church, USA, (ECUSA) for its stance on homosexuality and the interpretation of scripture and tradition."[215] A sense of urgency moved through the group of two hundred meeting so soon after the confirmation and consecration of Bishop Gene Robinson. A virtual who's who of dissident Episcopalian voices showed up to decry the Episcopal Church's recent actions such as Peter Walker, Ephraim Radner, Christopher Seitz, Bishop James Stanton of Dallas, and Philip Turner. Also leading the conference was Drexel Gomez, primate of the West Indies. Speakers suggested various punishments for the Episcopal Church. Radner said the Church should be removed from full status in the Anglican Communion to observer.[216] Gomez said that the Third World majority resented the First World's control of the Anglican Communion. The solution to this, and the way to discipline the Episcopal Church, he suggested as promoting the primates' meeting and reducing the power of the First-World-dominated Anglican Consultative Council in the structure of the Anglican Communion. He said, "We must break the stranglehold of this monster called the Anglican Consultative Council."[217] Forum leaders Tom Myers and Lynn Pagliaro attended the conference only to shake their heads. Myers said: "'I don't hear any talk of love here. All that I hear is warlike metaphors and desire for power.'"[218] In time, this annual January conference of Episcopal Church critics would take on the name of "Mere Anglicanism" and rise to hundreds of participants becoming an important rallying point of Episcopalian and Anglican ultra-conservatives and an inspiration to local diocesan communicants opposing the Church.

The Diocese of South Carolina was in the forefront of the formation of the Anglican Communion Network. South Carolina had been one of the dozen founding dioceses at the Plano meeting of January 19, 2004. Upon their return from Dallas to Charleston, the diocesan delegation of seven gave reports to the Standing Committee.[219] In the committee meeting, Craige Borrett reported that a resolution was being prepared and endorsed by many clergy to be presented at the next diocesan convention to have the diocese join the Network.[220] The resolution to join the Network was presented to and adopted by the meeting of the diocesan convention on 5–6 March 2004.[221] In 2005, Bishop Salmon and Kendall Harmon were on the Network's "Steering Committee" with Salmon in charge of liaison with bishops' and Harmon over "Strategic Engagement."[222]

---

214. "North American Conservatives and Global South Anglicans Seek Discipline of ECUSA." Anglican Communion News Service, January 13, 2004, http://www.anglicannews.org/news/2004/01/north-american-conservatives-and-global-south-anglicans-seek-discipline-of-ecusa-aspx.

215. Ibid.

216. Ibid.

217. Ibid.

218. Ibid.

219. "Minutes of the Standing Committee." [January 27, 2004].

220. Ibid.

221. *Journal of the Two Hundred and Fourteenth (. . .)* 2003, 66.

222. Duncan, (the Rt. Rev.) Robert. "Pastoral Letter to the Network from Bp. Duncan." January 25, 2004, http://www.americananglican.org/pastoral-letter-to-the-network-from-bp-duncan/pageprint.

By early 2004, the South Carolina diocesan leadership had fully embraced and incorporated a program of relentless criticism of and hostility to the national Church that would only swell with time. *Jubilate Deo*, the diocesan newspaper, became the major public relations outlet of this program relaying constant criticism of the Church and in time withholding any pro-Episcopal Church opinion, such as news of the Forum. In the February/March 2004 issue, Kendall Harmon contributed an essay, "The Episcopal Church and Corporate Sin," suggesting the Church was guilty of sin because of its adoption of pro-homosexual policies. He also used new judgmental terms into the public discourse. "Reappraisers," he said, were people who were willing to change biblical and traditional views of sexuality, while "reasserters" were those wanted to defend traditional views.[223] This sort of dualism dividing the world into two opposing camps, would be employed by diocesan critics of the Episcopal Church to portray the Church as the alien "other." It would be no wonder then that one witness after another from the independent diocese would take the stand in the circuit court trial in July of 2014 to testify that, though they had been in the Episcopal Church, they really had not been in the Episcopal Church.

Ever more alarmed by the implications of schism in all the diocesan hyperbolic anti-Episcopal talk and actions of early 2004, the Forum tried to counterattack, but to little avail. In the first issue of its newsletter, on March 5, 2004, it raised the rhetorical question, "Is the Network Schismatic?" The answer was not explicitly, but perhaps implicitly by denouncing and rejecting the actions of the Episcopal Church on rights for homosexuals as against the Bible and God.[224] The Forum's calls for reconciliation counted for very little against the powerful words and actions of the whole diocesan power structure, the bishops, Standing Committee, newspaper, and diocesan convention.

By the summer of 2004, the ultra-conservative Anglican Communion Network in South Carolina was organized and ready for action to unite the diocese against the reforms of the Episcopal Church. A steering committee organized with H. Clayton Burrows, as chair.[225] He had been one of the diocese's representatives at the Network's founding meeting in Plano in January of 2004. Other members were: Bill Ervin, Lydia Evans, Ann Harrington, Myron Harrington, Cecil Kirkland, Eric Meace, Jan Pringle, Ned Simmons, Richard Thomasson, and George Wilson.[226] Their website denounced the Episcopal Church as non-scriptural and revisionist.[227] In August and September of 2004, the South Carolina Network sponsored three public "educational workshops," at St. Philip's in Charleston, Church of the Cross in Bluffton, and Church of the Holy Comforter in Sumter.[228] Speakers were Martyn Minns, of Truro Church, Bishop Salmon, Bishop

---

223. Harmon, (the Rev.) Kendall. "The Episcopal Church and Corporate Sin." *Jubilate Deo* (Diocese of South Carolina), February/March 2004, 4.

224. "Episcopal Forum of SC, Diocesan Convention Newsletter." The Episcopal Forum, March 5, 2004, http://www.episcopalforumofsc.org/newsletters/issue%2001efsc-newsletter.pdf.

225. "The South Carolina Anglican Communion Network." http://www.sc-anc.net/pages.asp?pageid=13463.

226. Ibid.

227. Ibid.

228. "A Defining Moment?" *Jubilate Deo* (Diocese of South Carolina), August/September 2004, 2.

Skilton, Kendall Harmon, John Barr, Chuck Owens, Haden McCormick, Peter Rothermel, and Sarah Hey.[229] The stated themes gave a strong hint of the presentations, e.g., Did the General Convention violate the Constitution and Canons of the Episcopal Church? Why can't we just live with our differences? By late 2004, ordinary communicants in South Carolina would have to see their leaders' attitude of relentless hostility toward the Episcopal Church as the accepted official stance of the Diocese of South Carolina.

Meanwhile, national and international movements against the Episcopal Church continued in the wake of the Chapman Memo of December 2003. On March 3, 2004, Alison Barfoot[230] issued her "Draft Proposal for Overseas AEO" [Alternate Episcopal Oversight], better known as the Barfoot Memo. It gave a three-step detailed plan by which Episcopal clergy and congregations could transfer to African bishops by way of the Anglican Communion Network.[231] As the Chapman Memo, the Barfoot plan was clearly a scheme to move people and parishes out of the Episcopal Church.

The *All Saints* Case

Regardless of whatever thoughts Bishop Salmon might have had about the diocese's relationship with the Episcopal Church, he was adamantly opposed to the idea of schism within his own diocese. As one has seen, Salmon was resolved to enforce the Dennis Canon on All Saints of Pawleys Island. After a local court had found that the 1745 deed was effective, the diocese took the case to the state appeals court that held a hearing on September 10, 2003. A minority of the parish formed a separate congregation to remain loyal to the diocese and the Episcopal Church and kept the name All Saints.

On March 8, 2004, the appeals court ruled finding problems with the passage of deed ownership and remanding the case to the circuit court for retrial. On January 20, 2005, the diocesan congregation of All Saints, the minority who remained loyal to the diocese and the Episcopal Church, joined the case and asked the court to recognize them as the legal parish of All Saints and the owner of the parish properties. Bishop Salmon and the diocese participated in this action on the side of the loyalists. The circuit court then consolidated the 2000 and 2005 actions into one case.

The case was handled in the circuit court, Georgetown County, by Judge Thomas W. Cooper, Jr. Early in 2006, the diocese made two offers to All Saints in an attempt to reach an out-of-court settlement. The diocesan Standing Committee first suggested a temporary deal: "a lease agreement for $30,000 per month and upkeep of the property, and legal fees until post-Lambeth, 2008."[232] The diocese made the offer by telephone to Terrell Glenn; All Saints promptly rejected it.[233] On February 27, 2006, the Standing

---

229. Ibid.

230. "Profiles on the Right: Alison Barfoot." http://www.politicalresearch.org/profiles-on-the-right-alison-barfoot. At the time of the Memo, Barfoot was the archbishop of Uganda's assistant for international relations. She had been co-rector of Christ Episcopal Church in Overland KS. Around the time of the Robinson affair, that congregation voted to transfer to Uganda.

231. House of Bishops, Task Force on Property Disputes, "Memorandum." Appendix E.

232. "Minutes of the Standing Committee." [February 27, 2006].

233. Ibid.

Committee decided to make another offer, a permanent deal to sell All Saints the bulk of the property: "'AMiA would assume the 1.2 million debt, pay 2.75 million cash, and pay actual legal fees totaling $400,000, for a total of $4,350,000. The Diocese would retain all property on the west side of the road, keep the name and all the silver.'"[234] The next day, the vestry of All Saints dismissed the offer.[235] Following the collapse of negotiations for a settlement, Judge Cooper held a hearing in his courtroom on March 6, 2006.[236]

On March 13, 2006, Cooper rendered a split decision. On the property, he ruled that the 1745 deed was effectual for the heirs of George Pawley and William Poole and for the inhabitants of Waccamaw. On the second issue, legal rights, Cooper ruled that the Episcopal congregation was entitled to all the rights of All Saints Parish because the Episcopal Church was a hierarchical church. Upon motion of diocesan lawyers, Cooper went on to revoke the majority party's alteration of corporate documents in 2004, eject the dissenting majority from the parish property, and restrain the non-Episcopal majority from acting as the legal parish. Cooper's decision was a victory for the diocese and the Episcopal Church. *Jubilate Deo* reported: "The Diocese is pleased that the congregation and officers who remained loyal to the Diocese and the Episcopal Church were recognized by the court as the true congregation and vestry of All Saints Parish, Waccamaw."[237] At the same time, the diocese was indecisive about what to do on the property issue.[238] The other side appealed Cooper's decision to the South Carolina Supreme Court.

The state Supreme Court held a hearing of the case on March 5, 2009, and rendered a written opinion on September 18, 2009. Concerning the property, the court ruled that All Saints parish was the rightful owner of the property. This was confirmed by the 1903 quit claim deed the diocese had given the parish. Furthermore, the court said the Dennis Canon had no legal effect on the property because the title holder, the parish, had not declared a trust for the diocese or Church as required by law. On the second issue, the legal rights, the court ruled that the parish had legally amended its articles of incorporation under state law in 2004 and therefore the majority party was the legal parish. The state supreme court decision was a complete victory for the majority parish of All Saints.[239] The loyalist minority congregation of All Saints decided to appeal to the United States Supreme Court in early 2010, but found no help from the bishop at the time, Mark Lawrence. They made an out-of-court settlement on March 25, 2010, recognizing the legal rights of the majority group. The diocesan group adopted the name of Christ the King.

Meanwhile, as All Saints won its long court war of independence from the diocese, the parish itself continued to go through a great deal of inner turmoil as matters seemed to spiral out of control in the parish. In 2009, Murphy's Anglican Mission in the Americas was a founding member of the Anglican Church in North America and found a rocky

234. Ibid.
235. Ibid.
236. Ibid.
237. "Diocese of South Carolina Statement on Recent Court Ruling." *Jubilate Deo* (Diocese of South Carolina), April/May 2006.
238. Ibid.
239. "26724–All Saints v. Campbell."

relationship with its archbishop Robert Duncan. The next year, AMiA changed its status in ACNA to "ministry partner": and in 2011 it split from ACNA.[240] In 2011–12, Murphy went through a very public feud with Rwanda that was covered in excruciating detail on Internet sites such as Anglican Ink and Virtue Online.[241] This ended with Murphy and eight other AMiA bishops breaking from the Rwandan church. Afterwards, Murphy affiliated with the Anglican Church of Congo, then changed AMiA into a "Society of Missionary and Apostolic Works" in 2012.[242] By then, AMiA had virtually disintegrated into various factions with only a remnant adhering to Murphy.

All Saints of Pawleys Island went through lurching changes in the decade after its declaration of independence from the diocese. "Under AMiA, All Saints has seen their overarching provincial authority shift back and forth from the Province of Rwanda to ACNA to the Congo to Ghana and then the College of Consulters."[243] Perhaps fatigued with all the instability, All Saints' rector, Rob Grafe, sent the parishioners a letter in July of 2012 suggesting the parish settle down with the ACNA.[244] Apparently he did not tell the AMiA bishop Murphy or the vestry of this first; and, a major split occurred making three warring factions on All Saints' vestry: 1-the pro-Murphy/AMiA side, 2-pro-Grafe/ACNA side; and neutral members who felt "Grafe betrayed them."[245] As one source put it, "a large ruckus church-family fight ensued. Lines were drawn, feelings were hurt, misunderstandings cropped up, accusations flew, and the rumor mill was operating at full tilt."[246] About 20 percent of the parish left All Saints to worship at Grace Anglican Church in Pawleys Island, also in AMiA.[247] Murphy did not remain quiet. On September 8, 2012, he published a blistering letter to ACNA archbishop Duncan.[248] Retired Bishop Allison, one of the bishops who had consecrated Murphy in 2000, felt compelled to go to Murphy's defense in this "dogfight," as did John H. Rodgers.[249] Finally, a congregational vote was taken to decide whether All Saints should stay with Murphy's AMiA or go to ACNA. Necessary to carry was 316. When the vote was tallied, 322 parishioners chose to affiliate with ACNA while 229 wanted to stay with AMiA.[250] This was stunning. After

240. "Chuck Murphy," Wikipedia. https://en.wikipedia.org/wiki/Chuck_Murphy.

241. Conger, George. "Recant or Resign, Rwanda Tells Chuck Murphy," December 5, 2011, http://anglicanink.com/article/recant-or-resign-rwanda-tells-chuck-murphy ; Virtue, David. "Unholy Mess: Clash of Wills, Power & Theological Direction Mark AMiA-ACNA Battle." Virtueonline, September 8, 2012, http://www.virtueonline.org/unholy-mess-clash-wills-power-theological-direction-mark.

242. "Chuck Murphy." Wikipedia.

243. Mueller, Mary Ann. "Pawleys Island, SC: All Saints Votes to Unite with ACNA." Virtueonline, November 7, 2012, http://www.virtueonline.org/pawleys-island-sc-all-saints-votes-unite-acna.

244. Virtue, David. "Pawleys Island, SC: All Saints Rector in Pitched Battle for Job." Virtueonline, August 10, 2012, http://www.virtueonline.org/pawleys-island-sc-all-saints-rector-pitched-battle-his-job.

245. Ibid.

246. Mueller, "Pawleys Island, SC."

247. Ibid.

248. "Pawleys Island, SC (Anglican Dogfight); AMiA's Chuck Murphy Rebuts ACNA's Bob Duncan." Reformed Churchman, September 8, 2012, http://reformationanglicanism.blogspot.com/2012/09/pawleys-island-sc-amias-chuck-murphy.

249. Ibid.

250. Mueller, "Pawleys Island, SC."

thirty years of leading All Saints parish as rector and bishop, Murphy had been voted out by his own church. The senior warden, Martha Lachicotte, resigned along with three other vestry members.[251] In November of 2012, over one hundred Murphy faithful split from All Saints to make their own parish. They chose to set up a new church under Murphy rather than joining AMiA's Grace Anglican Church in Pawleys Island which was led by Murphy's successor at All Saints, Tim Surratt. The new church called itself The Abbey at Pawleys Island. In 2014, Murphy's congregation moved into a permanent home, "The Carriage House," of old Litchfield Plantation.[252] Also in 2014, Grace Anglican Church of Pawleys Island left AMiA and united with Christ the King to become Christ the King-Grace, Waccamaw, under Grace's rector, Tim Surratt.[253] Christ the King had started as the loyalist minority in the All Saints schism of 2004 and had adhered to Bishop Lawrence in the diocesan schism of 2012. The spot in South Carolina called Pawleys Island turned out to be a microcosm of schism with, as of 2014, the Episcopal Church parish of Holy Cross/Faith Memorial, the ACNA parish of All Saints, the independent diocesan church of Christ the King-Grace, and Murphy's AMiA church of the Abbey at Pawleys Island. There were four different "Anglican" churches with four different "Anglican" bishops. In street parlance, Pawleys Island was the "ground zero" of the schismatic movement in South Carolina.

The Backlash against the Episcopal Church, 2004–2006

Meanwhile, in 2004, the American Anglican Council-led Episcopalian ultra-conservatives and their African allies continued expanding their efforts of the "realignment" of American Anglicanism and would continue doing so in 2005, 2006, and 2007. In the spring of 2004, the AAC and its by-product the Anglican Communion Network began gathering various dissident Episcopalian and independent groups to form an "orthodox" Anglican union in America. On 21–22 May 2004, Kendall Harmon participated in a conference called "A Place to Stand in the Midwest" at Christ Church Cranbrook, Bloomfield Hills, Michigan.[254] He joined a panel of speakers including Geoffrey Chapman, author of the Chapman Memo, and David Anderson, president of the American Anglican Council. Harmon returned to his theme of putting blame on the new prayer book blasting the 1979 work with its: "'under-emphasis on God's transcendence, holiness and judgment, combined with a very weak sense of sin, combined with a liturgical practice that makes, for the first time in Anglican history, the confession of sin optional, combined with a strong emphasis on baptism, combined with a baptismal covenant that

---

251. Virtue, David. "Bishop Murphy Establishes 'Mission Pawleys' Parish Following Vote by All Saints to leave AMiA." Virtueonline, December 5, 2012, http://www.virtueonline.org/murphy-establishes-mission-pawleys-following-vote-all-saints.

252. "The Abbey at Pawleys Island." http://www.pawleysabbey.org/murphy/.

253. "Churches: Anglican Groups Will Share Priest and Facilities." *Coastal Observer* (Pawleys Island, SC), February 13, 2014, http://www.coastalobserver.com/articles/2014/021314.html.

254. Gunn, Herb. "Churchmanship vs. Brinksmanship." June 15, 2004, http://www.episcopalchurch.org/library/article/churchmanship-vs-brinksmanship.

is decoupled from its Trinitarian and scriptural mooring.'"[255] Harmon added, "'There has to be a realignment of Anglicanism in North America.'"[256]

A major step in that realignment came in the next few weeks. On June 6, 2004, six men joined to send a letter to the Archbishop of Canterbury: "This letter is a first step in signifying our commitment to make common cause for the gospel of Jesus Christ, and common cause for a missionary and orthodox Anglicanism in North America."[257] They were Robert Duncan, bishop of Pittsburgh and Moderator of the Anglican Communion Network, Chuck Murphy, of the AMiA, David Anderson, of the American Anglican Council, and representatives of the Anglican Province of America, Forward in Faith, and the Reformed Episcopal Church. On June 17, 2004, the group announced itself as the "Common Cause Partners." It was a collection of six independent groups led by Duncan of the ACN and including the AAC, the Anglican Mission in America, Forward in Faith, the Anglican Province in America, and the Reformed Episcopal Church. Anderson said, "'We have maintained since the debacle of General Convention 2003, that realignment in North America is a necessity.'"[258] The Common Cause Partners called a meeting in Atlanta on February 9–11, 2005, that they said was in response to a request of five overseas Anglican primates. Representatives from nine "orthodox" American and Canadian groups drew up a statement that did not explicitly call for the replacement of the Episcopal Church but clearly implied such: "We desire to remain connected with faithful Anglicans worldwide and intend to move forward together to fulfill a compelling picture of a preferable future."[259] In time, this Anglican Communion Network-American Anglican Council-led coalition would evolve into the independent Anglican Church in North America with Robert Duncan, the moderator of ACN becoming the archbishop of the ACNA.

On October 18, 2004, the Lambeth Commission on Communion, set up by the Archbishop of Canterbury, issued the anxiously-awaited Windsor Report, the most important Anglican Communion document of the early 2000s. What the Report said was: to recommend a moratorium on the consecrations of openly homosexual persons and the blessings of same-sex unions, it was inappropriate for a bishop to exercise authority in another diocese without that bishop's permission, to ask those involved in Robinson's consecration to consider withdrawing themselves for functions of the Anglican Communion, to ask for an Anglican Covenant that would require the independent provinces to consult the wider Communion before making major decisions, and to urge those who contributed to disunity to express regret. What the Report did not say was: to make a statement on homosexuality and to discipline or punish the Episcopal Church.[260]

255. Ibid.

256. Ibid.

257. "Anglican Communion Network Announces Commitment of Anglican Groups to Common Cause." June 17, 2004, http://www.sc-anc.net/apps/articles/default.asp?articleid=10161&columnid=1626.

258. Ibid.

259. "Common Cause Partners Stand United (Feb. 2005)." February 11, 2005, http://www.sc-acn.net/apps/articles/default.asp?articleid=10154&columnid=1626.

260. Douglas, Ian and Paul F.M. Zahl. *Understanding the Windsor Report: Two Leaders in the American Church Speak Across the Divide.* New York: Church Publishing, 2005, 162–64.

Around the Communion, the Report engendered mixed reactions from support to cautious regard to outright opposition. Peter Akinola, was particularly offended by the Report and denounced its weakness against the Episcopal Church and its opposition to cross-border interventions.[261]

The ultra-conservatives in South Carolina declared the Windsor Report to be a victory and made a major effort to promote parts of it in the diocese as a denunciation of the Episcopal Church. Apparently, this was led by Kendall Harmon who, even before the Report came out, started campaigning for it. On the day before the Report appeared, David Virtue posted an essay of Harmon's called, "Will Anglican Separation become Anglican Divorce?"[262] In this, Harmon laid out his talking points. He asserted the struggle was not really about homosexuality but about four other big issues: theology, that is, the interpretation of scripture; marriage as the union of one man and one woman; the authority of the church (the Episcopal Church made an "arrogant act of American imperialism"); the superiority of the vertical religion of personal salvation over the horizontal religion of social "affirmation."[263] By this time, Harmon had skillfully framed the differentiation between the diocese and the Episcopal Church as one of religion rather than social policy. By this time, the whole diocesan structure was virtually monopolized by a right-wing clerical/lay union devoted to relentless hostility to the Episcopal Church. The Episcopal Forum functioned to promote unity but not to advance a certain interpretation of issues. The Forum was not set up to debate issues with anyone. Therefore, Harmon's theological interpretation was to continue and to grow in the diocese so that even after the schism the diocesan leadership still insisted that its differences with the Episcopal Church had always been about religion and not about homosexuality.

Immediately after the Windsor Report appeared, Harmon sprang into action. Right away he drew up three resolutions to be approved by the Standing Committee. The first was entitled "Pleading with the House of Bishops to Grasp the Urgency of the Anglican Crisis."[264] It called on the Episcopal bishops to issue "a clear Mind of the House resolution indicating their intention to comply with the specific calls in Section D of the Windsor Report."[265] The second was called "A Plea for Specific Compliance with the Preliminary Calls of the Windsor Report."[266] In this, the diocese would express its regrets that the Episcopal Church affirmed a non-celibate homosexual as a bishop and supported the blessing of same-sex unions and announced its support for the Report's request for moratoria on the consecrations of open homosexuals and the blessings of same-sex unions. The third was entitled "On the Windsor Report call in Regard to Bishops Intervening to Seek to Help those Upholding the Teaching of the Anglican Communion." On this, the diocese would back away from the Report's recommendation against cross-border

---

261. Ibid., 168–69.

262. Harmon, (the Rev.) Kendall. "Will Anglican Separation become Anglican Divorce?" Virtueonline, http://www.virtueonline.org/pipermail/virtueonline_listserv.virtueonline.org/2004-October/007384.html.

263. Ibid.

264. "Minutes of Standing Committee." [December 2, 2004].

265. Ibid.

266. Ibid.

interventions. The resolution said, "The Standing Committee of the Diocese of South Carolina understands the call for a moratorium on these actions to be of lesser concern than those which Windsor Report Section D spends the bulk of its time addressing."[267] It said the diocese would support the moratorium against interventions only until the bishops' meeting of January 2005. Harmon's three resolutions were strong on condemning the Episcopal Church's affirmation of open homosexuals as bishops and the blessing of same-sex unions but weak on opposing foreign bishops' interventions into the United States. Harmon selected the parts of the Windsor Report most critical of the Episcopal Church and promoted those in the diocese. His resolutions also demanded the diocese's two bishops go to the House of Bishops' meeting in January of 2005 to present the resolutions.

Harmon sent his resolutions to the Standing Committee meeting of November 11, 2004 where they were distributed to the committee members. On 2 December, he went in person to the committee to make his case for the resolutions. He told the committee that the diocese should take a leadership position in the Episcopal Church "to see if the Anglican Communion can stay together."[268] The committee made some slight revisions then unanimously adopted Harmon's three resolutions.[269]

By the time of the next diocesan convention meeting, in March of 2005, Harmon's resolutions had changed slightly while enthusiasm for the anti-Episcopal Church parts of the Windsor Report had grown. The convention adopted four resolutions in support of the Report. The first, R–1, was presented by the diocesan Reconciliation Commission.[270] It affirmed the Report's call for moratoria on consecrations of open homosexuals and blessings of same-sex unions but on interventions took the weak position that the diocese would "neither encourage nor initiate cross-boundary interventions."[271] This showed that even the so-called Reconciliation Commission had fallen under the demand to interpret the Windsor Report as opposition to the Episcopal Church. The second, R–3, presented by Harmon, was entitled "Affirmation of the Diocese of South Carolina of its Intention to Live as a Diocesan Member of the Anglican Communion" and called for "submitting to common counsel within the Anglican Communion on matters which impact the larger body."[272] This would end the institutional independence of the Episcopal Church which would have to get permission of the Communion before initiating any important resolution. The third, R–4, also presented by Harmon, was called "A Plea for Specific Compliance with the Preliminary Calls of the Windsor Report." This expressed

267. Ibid.

268. Ibid.

269. Ibid.

270. Bishop Salmon had created this committee the year earlier to promote reconciliation of differing viewpoints in the diocese. Clergy: Dow Sanderson, chair, Ben Smith, Colton Smith, Shay Gaillard, Kent Walley, Jack Nietert, David Williams; laity: Dolores Miller, Bill Martin, Jonathan Poston, Geoff Place, Lonnie Hamilton, Dorothy Carter.

271. *Journal of the Two Hundred and Fifteenth Annual Meeting of the Convention of the Diocese of South Carolina, North Charleston Convention Center, March 4–5, 2005.* Charleston, SC: the diocese, 2005, 66.

272. Ibid., 67.

regret for the Robinson episode and for the blessing of same-sex unions.[273] The fourth, R–5, was presented by the clergy of St. Helena's of Beaufort[274] and was entitled "Diocesan Acknowledgement of Guilt and Repentance."[275] It said, in part,

> The Episcopal Church has erred and strayed from the clear teaching of the Scriptures and has deliberately acted in ways repugnant to the will and teaching of the Church (. . .) by consecrating a practicing homosexual to the episcopate and by allowing for the blessing of same-sex unions against the urgent counsel of the greater Anglican Communion (. . .) the Diocese of South Carolina acknowledge our guilt in the deplorable crisis facing our church (. . .). We have sinned against God and against the Body of Christ and we do hereby repent.[276]

This was the boldest diocesan statement yet against the Episcopal Church. It expressed in the starkest of terms the diocese's opposition to the Church's reforms and made no effort to couch it in theological guise such as Harmon had done. It was clear that the ultra-conservative establishment in South Carolina used the Windsor Report to enhance diocesan hostility to the national Church.

It is interesting to note that Harmon took on a different attitude when it came to foreign bishops intervening in his own diocese. While he was only lukewarm regarding the Windsor Report's call for a moratorium on cross-border interventions, he was not the same when it came to South Carolina. Chuck Murphy had set up the Anglican Mission in America, under the archbishop and primate of Rwanda, and headquartered in Pawleys Island. In March of 2005, Harmon asked the diocesan Standing Committee to take a stand on AMiA church plants within "orthodox dioceses."[277] In response, Dow Sanderson, the chair of the committee, sent a letter to the Rwandan primate to ask that AMiA "not infiltrate dioceses where the leadership is orthodox [e.g. South Carolina]."[278] The diocesan leadership was not consistent in its response to the Windsor Report.

The ultra-conservatives' initial enthusiasm about the Windsor Report's power over the Episcopal Church soon began to flag as the Church more or less refused to accept the terms of the Report. As much as the conservatives may have wished it, there was simply no way the Communion as a whole could interfere in the governance of the Episcopal Church. The Episcopal bishops called a special meeting in Salt Lake City on 12–13 January 2005. Bishop Salmon served as the chief spokesman for the Anglican Communion Network. In the conference, the bishops as a whole expressed regret at the disruption in the Anglican Communion but refused to address the key elements in the Windsor Report putting it off until their regular March meeting. A group of conservative bishops denounced this inaction. Salmon said, "'The primates meeting in February (. . .) the response of the House of Bishops did not rise to the level expected by the

---

273. Ibid., 68.

274. Frank Limehouse, rector, Jeffrey Miller, Mack Avera, Robert Batts. Limehouse became dean of the cathedral church of the Advent in Birmingham AL, and Miller became rector of St. Helena's then, in 2016, rector of St. Philip's of Charleston.

275. Ibid.

276. Ibid.

277. "Minutes of the Standing Committee." [March 28, 2005].

278. Ibid.

Communion.'"[279] The dissident bishops drew up "A Statement of Acceptance of and Submission to the Windsor Report 2004" calling on the Episcopal Church to comply fully with the recommendations of the Report. In all, twenty-nine bishops signed including those from South Carolina: Salmon, Skilton, and Allison. Among the signatures were fifteen diocesan bishops representing perhaps 15 percent of the dioceses of the Episcopal Church.[280]

The next month, February of 2005, thirty-five of the Anglican primates met at the Dromantine Center in Newry, Northern Irleand, and drew up the Dromantine Communiqué requesting the Episcopal Church to voluntarily withdraw from the Anglican Consultative Council until 2008 and to present a response to the Windsor Report at the next Anglican Consultative Council meeting, in June of 2005. In South Carolina, *Jubilate Deo*, the diocesan newspaper edited by Kendall Harmon, printed the lengthy communiqué in its April/May 2005 issue. A few weeks afterwards, the Episcopal House of Bishops met at Camp Allen, Texas, and issued a statement in response to Windsor on March 15, 2005. They expressed regret at the pain their actions caused the Anglican Communion, but held that the polity of the Episcopal Church precluded them from taking any direct action on the Report's requests. Decision would have to be made by the Church's governing body, the General Convention. At the same time, the bishops said they would agree to suspend both consecrations of bishops and the blessings of same-sex unions until the General Convention of 2006.[281]

The Episcopal Church continued to stand its ground. In disregard of the Dromantine Communiqué, the Executive Council sent a full delegation to the next meeting of the Anglican Consultative Council in Nottingham, England, in June of 2005. It also delivered to the Council an official report entitled "To Set Our Hope in Christ: A Response to the Invitation of Windsor Report, Paragraph 135." This was an impressive 130-page compilation of scholarship by seven prominent theologians and one historian explaining in detail how and why the Episcopal Church moved through forty years to its position on same-sex relationships: "'To Set our hope on Christ' is a record of the thoughtful and prayerful deliberations—theological, scriptural and experimental—of Christians committed to seeing the mind of Christ."[282]

The fallout from the Windsor Report continued through 2005, as several bishops' meetings convened to talk about appropriate responses. On 18–21 July, Jon Bruno, the bishop of Los Angeles, hosted a conference of nineteen bishops representing the diversity of opinion in the Church. From the state of South Carolina came both diocesan bishops, Salmon and Dorsey Henderson of Upper South Carolina. At the end of what was described as a full and frank discussion, the bishops issued a short statement saying

---

279. Brust, Cynthia. "ACN Release: Group of Bishops Issue 'A Statement of Acceptance of and Submission to the Windsor Report of 2004.'" http://www.americananglican.org/acn-release-group-of-bishops-issue-a-statement-of-acceptance-of-and-submission.

280. Ibid.

281. "House of Bishops Adopts 'Covenant Statement.'" Anglican News Service, March 16, 2005, http://www.anglicannews.org/news/2005/03/house-of-bishops-adopts-covenant-statement.aspx.

282. "Theologians Offer Response to Windsor Report Request." Episcopal News Service, June 21, 2005, http://archive.episcopalchurch.org/3577_63039_ENG_HTM.htm.

they had talked and would continue to do so in the future. Apparently, nothing more came of the meeting.[283]

The side of opposition to the Episcopal Church actions stepped up its hostility. On April 20, 2005, the Anglican Communion Network Council issued a statement predictably denouncing what it saw as the Church's lack of compliance with the Windsor Report.[284] On 6–8 July 2005, the American Anglican Council, Anglican Communion Network, and numerous American dissident groups met with Drexel Gomez, primate of the West Indies, and Gregory Venables, primate of the Southern Cone, in Nassau, Bahamas, for a secretive meeting that some reports suggested may have been planning a schism in the Anglican Communion.[285] By far the most important ultra-conservative meeting of 2005 was held in Pittsburgh on 11–12 November, and called "Hope and A Future." It drew two thousand and four hundred attendees making it the largest Episcopal dissident assembly at least since "Plano East" in January of 2004. Sponsored by the American Anglican Council's Anglican Communion Network and the Diocese of Pittsburgh under its bishop, and Network moderator, Robert Duncan, the conference included seven Anglican archbishops from Africa, Asia, and the Americas. Notably present was Peter Akinola, primate of Nigeria, and arguably the most important conservative Anglican leader of Africa. He aroused the crowd with: "'This is your (. . .) moment to make up your mind. Many have one leg in [the Episcopal Church] and one leg in the network. If you really want the Global South to partner with you, you must let us know exactly where you stand. Are you Episcopalian or are you network?'"[286] The large crowd leapt to their feet for a loud and sustained ovation. The reporter from the Associated Press judged the conference to be a call for schism: "An international panel of Anglican archbishops called upon a gathering of their conservative American counterparts Friday to split from the rest of the U.S. Episcopal Church."[287]

A twenty-minute video was shown at the conference entitled "Choose This Day."[288] The point of the video was to urge people to make a choice between the Episcopal Church and true religion. Near the end, the narrator said: "It's time to make a choice. Will you hold on to the authority of scripture, or allow God's holy word to be dismantled to fill the trends of our time? (. . .). Will you trust your future to a drifting alien religion, or will you remain faithful to the one true Lord. The choice is yours."[289] Kendall

283. "Meeting of Bishops in Los Angeles Concludes." http://www.americananglican.org/meeting-of-bishops-in-los-angeles-concludes.

284. "Bedford TX: Anglican Communion Network Council Communiqué." Virtueonline, May 15, 2005, http://www.virtueonline.org/portal/modules/news/article.php?storyid=2465.

285. "Nassau Meeting Concludes." *The Living Church*, July 11, 2005, as quoted in Free Republic, July 12, 2005, http://www.freerepublic.com/focus/f-religion/1441356/posts.

286. Levin, Steve. "Anglicans Urge Disgruntled Episcopalians to Join Them." *Pittsburgh Post-Gazette*, November 12, 2005, http://old.post-gazette.com/pg/05316/605308.stm.

287. Mandak, Joe. "Anglican Bishops Urge U.S. Church Split." Associated Press, as quoted in *The Washington Post*, November 11, 2005, http://www.washingtonpost.com/wp-dyn/content/article/2005/11/11/AR2005111100975.html.

288. A transcript of the video was made available at http://www.sarmiento.plus.com/anglican/choosethisday.html.

289. Ibid.

Harmon was one of the featured speakers on the video offering harsh criticism of the Episcopal Church in highly dramatic remarks such as, "This is a battle for the soul of the Western church and it's a battle for the shape of Christianity in the whole world at the beginning of the Twenty-First century," "The reality is that there is a different Gospel that has smuggled its way into the church" and "I mean it was an irrevocable decision to turn back against the teaching of the church."[290] At one point in the recording, a layperson asked Harmon what to do. He gave her a plan that sounded strikingly similar to the Chapman Memo: "Get together as a vestry and articulate your sense of the problem. Start to organize and share with other vestries that are near you, why you think that this is a big deal, and start to build a network of lay people that you can communicate with in other communities around the diocese and actually build a base of communication and activism."[291] Harmon, and the whole video, stopped just short of explicitly calling for schism from the Episcopal Church, but denouncing the Episcopal Church and urging people to make a choice to leave might reasonably be construed as a call for schism.

Attendees were given DVD copies of "Choose This Day" that included another short video entitled "The Decision."[292] It was the story of how two parishes broke away from the Episcopal Church, St. Charles' of Paulsbo, Washington, and St. Stephen's of Oak Harbor, Washington. This too was a barely disguised appeal for schism from the Episcopal Church. At the end of the video, the narrator said, "The people of St. Charles' and St. Stephen's parishes had a choice. They could follow a national church that's turned its back on 2000 years of biblical orthodoxy or they could remain true to God's unchanging holy word. Your church has the same choice."[293] No one could miss the point of the video as no one could miss the point of the convention. The prominence of certain South Carolinians in the meeting added support to the theory that the ultra-conservatives in the diocese of South Carolina might have been advocating schism against the Episcopal Church many years before the break actually occurred in 2012.

As the year 2005 turned into 2006, all eyes turned to the upcoming General Convention in anticipation of how the Episcopal Church would respond to the Windsor Report. The bishops had already announced they would wait until the Convention before taking any action. Conservatives hoped the Convention would bow to the Communion, follow the recommendations in the Report, and back away from the pro-homosexual reforms of the past. That was a tall order. Nevertheless, in the first half of 2006, all conversations in the Church revolved around what responses the Convention should make to the Windsor Report.

The 2006 General Convention met in Columbus, Ohio, from 13 to 21 June.[294] As it turned out, as one might expect, the overriding topic of the day was the Windsor Report, or more precisely, how the Episcopal Church should react to the lengthy presentment

290. Ibid.

291. Ibid.

292. A transcript of the video was made available at http://www.sarmiento.plus.com/anglican/thedecision.html.

293. Ibid.

294. Diocese of South Carolina delegates: clergy, Richard Belser, John Burwell, Mark Goodman, Kendall Harmon; lay, Lydia Evans, Lonnie Hamilton, Robert Kilgo, Wade Logan.

against it drawn up by an august body of representatives of the Anglican Communion. On the evening of 14 June, a public hearing was held in a hotel ballroom. One thousand people crowded into the room with many more waiting outside and listening to audio relay. There was so much interest, and so many speakers (seventy), that the meeting ran on for two and a half hours and would reconvene for the next two evenings. They were there specifically to discuss the proposed resolutions from the Standing Committee on the Episcopal Church and the Anglican Communion. At the June 15 hearing, deputy Kendall Harmon criticized the proposed resolution A161 that urged caution in the selection of bishops whose lifestyles might upset the Anglican Communion. Harmon thought it much too mild: "'The Windsor Report uses clear language. This resolution doesn't take the specific language of Windsor seriously enough. We have been asked to place a moratorium; the timeframe is clear (. . .) yet the language we get is to exercise considerable caution—a fudge. Let's be honest, let's be clear.'"[295] As it turned out, the Convention voted down that particular proposed resolution.

Concerning the recommendations in the Windsor Report, the Convention passed several resolutions, the most important of which was B033, "Exercise Restraint in Consecrating Candidates." It said, "That this Convention therefore call upon Standing Committees and bishops with jurisdiction to exercise restraint by not consenting to the consecration of any candidate to the episcopate whose manner of life presents a challenge to the wider church and will lead to further strains on communion."[296] This "restraint" would be the strongest stand the conservatives would get from the General Convention in response to the Windsor Report. Another resolution, A159, "Affirm Commitment to the Anglican Communion," reaffirmed the Episcopal Church's commitment to the Archbishop of Canterbury and the Anglican Communion. Yet another resolution, A160, "Express Regret for Straining the Bonds of the Church," said the Church regretted the strains its 2003 resolutions had placed on the Communion, apologized to those in the Communion who may have been offended, and asked forgiveness of the same.[297] It is important to note the Convention did not hold its 2003 resolutions to be in error, apologize for them, or repent of any wrongdoing. The conservatives did not miss this point.

Given what the conservatives considered the Convention's inadequate responses to the Windsor Report, Kendall Harmon tried another tactic to outflank the pro-homosexual reforms. He authored a proposed resolution, D069 that said: "Convention acknowledge that the Bible has always been at the center of Anglican belief and life, and declares its belief that Scripture is the Church's supreme authority, and as such ought to be seen as a focus and means of unity."[298] D069 was similar to B001 from the 2003 Convention that had been voted down. The new proposed resolution originated in the House of

295. Davies, Matthew. "From Columbus: Crowded Hearing Spotlights Windsor Report Response." Episcopal News Service, June 14, 2006, http://www.episcopalarchives.org/cgi-bin/ENS/ENSpress_release.pl?pr_number=061406-6-A.

296. "2006-B033." The Acts of Convention 1976-2006, The Archives of the Episcopal Church, http://www.episcopalarchives.org/GC2009/08_wms/2009-C010.pdf.

297. "2006-A160." The Acts of Convention 1976-2012, The Archives of the Episcopal Church, http://www.episcopalarchives.org/cgi-bin/acts/acts_resolution.pl?resolution=2006-A160.

298. "2006-D069." The Acts of Convention 1976-2012, The Archives of the Episcopal Church, http://episcopalarchives.org/cgi-bin/acts/acts_resolution-complete.pl?resolution=2006-D069.

Bishops where the Committee on Prayer Book, Liturgy and Church Music offered to replace it with a substitute: "Convention acknowledge the authority of the triune God, exercised through Scripture."[299] With that wording, the resolution passed both houses of the Convention. Some conservatives saw this too as an unacceptably weak stand since a declaration of the supremacy of scripture would have greatly strengthened their Bible-based attack on the Church's pro-homosexual reforms.

Another lingering issue before the Convention was alternate episcopal oversight, a longstanding demand of ultra-conservatives. On this, the Convention passed Resolution A163, "Affirm Pastoral Care for All Members of the Church," with two main points. It called on bishops to use the Delegated Episcopal Pastoral Oversight plan detailed in the House of Bishops' statement of March 2004, "Caring for all the Churches." The other part opposed cross-diocesan-border interventions such as those from other Anglican provinces.[300]

On the issue of homosexuality, the 2006 General Convention passed two outstanding resolutions. The first, A167, restated the Episcopal Church's apology to gays and lesbians for years of rejection and mistreatment and reiterated the Church's commitment to the full inclusion of homosexual persons into the life of the Church.[301] The other, A095, reaffirmed the Church's support of civil rights for homosexual persons from local to federal governmental levels. On this one, retired South Carolina bishop Allison offered a change in wording but was voted down.[302]

A New Presiding Bishop

Although a great deal of attention in the 2006 General Convention went to the Windsor Report, another major issue gained its own spotlight in the meeting and, in the long run, proved to be more important for the history of the Church, the election of a new presiding bishop for a nine-year term (2006–2015). The Joint Nominating Committee for the Election of the Presiding Bishop presented four nominees which it had already announced publicly in January of 2003: J. Neil Alexander, of Atlanta, Edwin F. Gulick, Jr., of Kentucky, Katharine Jefferts Schori, of Nevada, and Henry N. Parsley, Jr., of Alabama. Three other bishops were then nominated from the floor, their names having been submitted by 1 April.[303] On Sunday, June 18, the House of Bishops met in executive session to elect by majority vote a presiding bishop. Their choice would then have to be confirmed by the House of Deputies.[304]

299. Ibid.

300. "2006–A163." The Acts of Convention 1976–2012, The Archives of the Episcopal Church, http://www.episcopalarchives.org/cgi-bin/acts/acts_resolution-complete.pl?resolution=2006-A163.

301. "2006–A167." The Acts of Convention 1976–2006, The Archives of the Episcopal Church, http://www.episcopalarchives.org/GC2009/08_wms/2009-C010.pdf.

302. "2006–A095." The Acts of Convention 1976–2012, The Archives of the Episcopal Church, http://www.episcopalarchives.org/cgi-bin/acts/acts_resolution-complete.pl?resolution=2006-A095.

303. Francisco Duque-Gomez, bishop of Colombia, Stacy F. Sauls, of Lexington, and Charles E. Jenkins III, of Louisiana.

304. Woerman, Melodie. "From Columbus: General Convention Receives Presiding Bishop Nominees, Welcomes Bishops-Elect." Episcopal News Service, June 17, 2006, http://archive.episcopalchurch.org/3577_76102_ENG-HTM.htm.

Although seven names were placed into nomination for presiding bishops, only two went in with strong showing, Jefferts Schori and Parsley. These represented different viewpoints in the Church, Jefferts Schori coming from a background strongly supporting the reform movements, particularly for gays, and Parsley representing a broader centrist, comprehensive approach. The number needed to elect was 95 of the 188 votes cast. On the first ballot, Jefferts Schori led with 44 votes, Parsley second with 36, and the rest trailing. On the second ballot, Jefferts Schori and Parsley tied at 49 votes. On the third ballot, the five trailing candidates continued sharp declines while Jefferts Schori shot up to 68 votes and Parsley to 63. By now it was clear one of these two would win, either the "liberal" Jefferts Schori, or the "moderate" Parsley. On the fourth ballot, the five also-rans were in near total collapse while Jefferts Schori gained 20 votes to reach 88 and Parsley won 16 more to reach 79. Finally, on the fifth ballot, Jefferts Schori won 95 votes, the minimum for majority, over Parsley's 82. Considering that not even fifteen years earlier the Episcopal Church was roughly one-third liberal, one-third moderate, and one-third conservative, Jefferts Schori's election was a stunning victory for the liberals and validation of the half-century long social reform movement in the Episcopal Church. The result then went to the House of Deputies which voted by orders: lay, 94 yes, 8 no, 7 divided; clerical, 98 yes, 9 no, 4 divided.[305]

Jefferts Schori was the first woman to serve as the presiding bishop of the Episcopal Church and to be a primate of a province of the Anglican Communion. In light of her well-known background of strong advocacy of gay rights, the ultra-conservatives expressed outraged at her election. In fact, it gave a major boost to their lagging "realignment" movement. There were rumors at the time that what finally put Jefferts Schori over the top in the election were cynical last-minute votes from the most conservative bishops. These rumors cannot be verified since the voting was by secret ballot, but it is interesting to note that soon after Jefferts Schori's election, four dioceses voted to leave the Episcopal Church, something they had not done at the last crisis, that of the Robinson affair of 2003.

The ultra-conservatives' outcry against Jefferts Schori's election began immediately. Three dioceses had steadfastly refused to ordain women: Fort Worth, Quincy, and San Joaquin. On the day after the election, Jack Iker, bishop of Fort Worth, read a statement in the House of Bishops, and a deputy read in the House of Deputies, calling on the Archbishop of Canterbury and the primates of the Anglican Communion to provide alternate primatial oversight for the Diocese of Fort Worth. This was a change from the previous calls for oversight that had appealed for bishops to intervene from the outside into the Episcopal Church. What Iker requested was for one of the other thirty-seven primates, or heads, of the Anglican Communion provinces to take authority over the diocese. This, of course, was impossible under the Constitution and Canons of the Episcopal Church. It was also impossible under the oversight provisions of the Archbishop of Canterbury and the Episcopal Church which had repeatedly specified that all arrangements of oversight would be internal to the Episcopal Church. Nevertheless, following Iker, several

---

305. "From Columbus: 26th Presiding Bishop Election Results from the House of Bishops and House of Deputies." Episcopal News Service, June 18, 2006, http://archive.episcopalchurch.org/3577 _76156_ENG_HTM.htm.

other dioceses in the Anglican Communion Network echoed the demand for alternate primatial oversight. The 2006 General Convention had made a double strike of virtually refusing the recommendations of the Windsor Report and electing the most liberal of all the nominees for presiding bishop, who just happened to be a woman. The ten diocesan members of the Anglican Communion Network moved into heightened crisis mode.

Everyone wondered how the Archbishop of Canterbury, Rowan Williams, would react to the news coming from the General Convention. Most of all, the conservatives looked expectantly to the archbishop for support for their condemnation of the Episcopal Church's actions. No one had to wait long. At the conclusion of the Convention, Williams issued a brief statement that said little: "It is not yet clear how far the resolutions passed this week and today represent the adoption by the Episcopal Church of all the proposals set out in the Windsor Report. The wider Communion will therefore need to reflect carefully on the significance of what has been decided before we respond more fully."[306] Just six days after the Convention adjourned, Williams issued a lengthy statement on the work of the General Convention. Not surprisingly, there was something in it for everyone. Williams gave most attention to the structure of the Anglican Communion which he said was a loose confederation held together by generally held bonds as scripture, tradition, and liturgy. He reminded everyone that the Archbishop of Canterbury was only a figurehead: "The idea of an Archbishop of Canterbury resolving any of this by decree is misplaced, however, tempting for many. The Archbishop of Canterbury presides and convenes in the Communion (. . .) he must always act collegially, with the bishops of his own local Church and with the primates and the other instruments of communion."[307] Moreover, he said, "the Communion is an association of local churches, not a single organization with a controlling bureaucracy and a universal system of law."[308] Too, he added, "there has to be a recognition that religious bodies have to deal with the question in their own terms."[309] However, while the Communion was a localized confederation, it also had a corporate nature that should be respected: "it is a question, agonizingly difficult for many, as to what kinds of behavior a Church that seeks to be loyal to the Bible can bless, and what kinds of behavior it must warn against—and so it is a question about how we can make decisions corporately with other Christians, looking together for the mind of Christ as we share the study of the Scriptures."[310] He added, "no member Church can make significant decisions unilaterally and still expect this to make no difference to how it is regarded in the fellowship."[311] Then, Williams promoted the concept of an Anglican Communion covenant: "The idea of a 'covenant'

---

306. "Archbishop of Canterbury's Initial Statement." Anglican Mainstream, http://anglicanmainstream.org/514-2/.

307. Williams, (the Most Rev.) Rowan. "The Challenge and Hope of Being an Anglican Today: A Reflection for the Bishops, Clergy and Faithful of the Anglican Communion." June 27, 2006, http://rowanwilliams.archbishopofcanterbury.org/articles.php/1478/the-challenge-and-hope-of-being-an-anglican-today-a-reflection.

308. Ibid.

309. Ibid.

310. Ibid.

311. Ibid.

between local Churches (. . .) is one method that has been suggested, and it seems to me the best way forward."[312] No doubt, most people were looking for what the archbishop would say about the Convention's response to the Windsor Report. On this, Williams made only one brief remark in his long epistle: "The recent resolutions of the General Convention have not produced a complete response to the challenges of the Windsor Report, but on this specific question there is at the very least an acknowledgement of the gravity of the situation in the extremely hard work that went into shaping the wording of the final formula."[313] On the whole, the archbishop gave only a very mild criticism of the Episcopal Church, but conservatives saw in it two points, rather minor in the letter, that they made into major weapons: the idea of a binding covenant and the rebuke of the Episcopal Church for failure to adhere to the recommendations of the Windsor Report. Conservatives, particularly the ultra-conservatives, interpreted the letter as their victory, under the banner of the Archbishop of Canterbury, and over the Episcopal Church. They turned to pressing two initiatives in the Communion, a covenant document and alternative primatial oversight.

South Carolina was one of the dioceses reacting strongly and immediately to the Convention. At its conclusion, on June 21, bishops Salmon and James Stanton, of Dallas, drew up a statement condemning the Convention. It was signed by 22 other bishops, 14 active and 8 retired and publicized. Salmon, William Skilton, and FitzSimons Allison signed for South Carolina. The statement set the tone that South Carolina would follow from then onward. It denounced the Convention's response to the Windsor Report: "The responses which the Convention has given to the clear and simple requests of the Lambeth Commission (. . .) are clearly and simply inadequate."[314] It continued, "We therefore disassociate ourselves from those acts of this Convention that do not fully comply with the Windsor Report."[315] Then it made an ominous assertion: "We continue as The Episcopal Church in this country."[316]

Shortly thereafter, bishops Salmon and Skilton issued a pastoral letter to the diocese.[317] They blasted the General Convention in no uncertain terms for choosing Jefferts Schori and giving inadequate response to the Windsor Report. On the election, they said, "We elected as Presiding Bishop the person of all the seven candidates who is in deepest disagreement with the theology of the Anglican Communion."[318] They continued, "and who with her whole diocese moved ahead to allow same sex blessings in October 2003 on the eve of the Primates meeting later that same week."[319] On the Windsor Report,

---

312. Ibid.

313. Ibid.

314. "To the Faithful In Christ Jesus Throughout the World." June 21, 2006, http://www.americananglican.org/bishops-statement-general-convention-actions-inadequate.

315. Ibid.

316. Ibid.

317. Salmon, (the Rt. Rev.) Edward L., Jr. and (the Rt. Rev.) William J. Skilton. "A Pastoral Letter to the Diocese of South Carolina in Response to the 2006 General Convention." *Jubilate Deo* (Diocese of South Carolina), August/September 2006, 1.

318. Ibid.

319. Ibid.

the bishops said the Convention had failed to embrace the essential recommendations of the Report. Perhaps with the case of All Saints of Pawleys Island in mind, the bishops went on to appeal to the diocese to remain united and not act separately as individuals or parishes. They also announced the Standing Committee would take up the matter of oversight on June 28 and the diocesan clergy would convene on 5 July.

The Standing Committee did meet in Charleston on the 28th to take up the idea of alternate primatial oversight as Iker had presented it to the House of Bishops on June 19. "The appeal for alternative Primatial Oversight was discussed thoroughly. Robert Kilgo moved that we proceed with a letter to the Archbishop of Canterbury, copied to the Primates and the Panel of Reference. Steve Wood seconded, and the motion carried with one abstention."[320] Again, as with Iker, it was unclear exactly what the Standing Committee thought they were going to accomplish since it was already well known that both the Archbishop and the Episcopal Church had made it entirely clear that any oversight arrangement would have to be internal to the Episcopal Church. Indeed, the archbishop had just said in his letter to 27 June that he had no authority to intervene in the provinces of the Anglican Communion. If there was no chance episcopal oversight could be established from outside the Church, there was certainly no chance the Episcopal Church, or the Archbishop, would agree to have the head of a foreign province exercise jurisdiction in the United States. Besides, even if the Archbishop changed his mind and supported alternative primatial oversight, he would have no way to enforce it since he had no authority over the self-governing Episcopal Church. Nevertheless, the diocesan Standing Committee presented its proposed resolution on alternative oversight to the next diocesan convention, on 9–10 November 2006. They offered it as R–1, "Alternative Primatial Relationship." In this, the diocese would affirm the committee's appeal to the Archbishop of Canterbury for some kind of alternative primatial relationship although it gave no details of what it expected in the relationship.[321] The delegates dutifully passed it by voice vote with only a small dissent.[322]

The Standing Committee drew up a statement for the diocese that it circulated, and printed in the next issue of *Jubilate Deo*. The first half of it concerned the archbishop's letter of 27 June. It interpreted his remarks as condemning the Episcopal Church for its reforms for homosexuals and its lack of response to the Windsor Report. Likewise, it hailed the archbishop's call for an Anglican Communion covenant. Because of these factors, the statement went on: "the status quo is now impossible" then concluded: "we do hereby request of Archbishop Williams that he, in consultation with the Primates of the Communion and the Panel of Reference, speedily provide alternative Primatial

---

320. "Minutes of Standing Committee." [June 28, 2006].

321. *Journal of the Two Hundred and Sixteenth Annual Meeting of the Convention of the Diocese of South Carolina, North Charleston Convention Center, November 9–10, 2006*. Charleston, SC: the diocese, 2006, 64.

322. The approval of APR was not unanimous. St. Stephen's of Charleston passed a resolution on 26 December 2006 disassociating itself from the diocesan request for APR and reaffirming its commitment to the Episcopal Church. See: "St. Stephens Church Charleston Resolves to Support the Episcopal Church." eNewsletter, Episcopal Forum of SC, January 13, 2007, http://www.mynewsletterbuilder.com/tools/view_newsletter.php?newsletter_id=1409588636.

oversight for the Diocese of South Carolina."[323] Other dioceses that asked for some kind of alternative oversight were Pittsburgh, San Joaquin, Central Florida, Springfield, Dallas, and Quincy.[324] They represented about seven percent of the Episcopal Church.

The General Convention of 2006 dealt a major blow to the ultra-conservatives' hope that the Windsor Report would force the Episcopal Church to backtrack on its reforms favoring homosexuals, particularly on ordinations and same-sex blessings. However, they were not through with their efforts to achieve the same goal. By late summer of 2006 the dissidents united in the Anglican Communion Network turned to two other strategies to getting the Episcopal Church to retreat on its social policies. One was the Anglican covenant idea. Presumably a written covenant would function as a sort of bond for the Communion and provide a measure of authority over the individual churches. Perhaps the Communion as a whole could use the covenant to put enough pressure on the Episcopal Church to change its liberal ways if it wanted to stay in the Anglican Communion. The problem with this idea was time. It would take years to agree on the wording of a covenant and to get the member provinces to approve it.

Failing to get the Episcopal Church to agree to foreign oversight, the Anglican Communion Network bishops decided in the aftermath of the 2006 General Convention to appeal directly to the Archbishop of Canterbury although the Archbishop had made it clear in the past that any plan would have to be handled by the Episcopal Church. As we have seen, one bishop, Jack Iker of Ft. Worth, had even called for alternative oversight during the Convention itself and on the floor of the House of Bishops. Several other bishops had followed in quick succession including those from South Carolina. A few weeks after the Convention, the Archbishop responded to the pleas coming his way and called a meeting in New York. He sent as his representative, the secretary general of the Anglican Communion, Kenneth Kearon, and invited the presiding bishop, Frank Griswold, the presiding bishop-elect, Katharine Jefferts Schori, along with Jack Iker, bishop of Ft. Worth, and Robert Duncan, bishop of Pittsburgh. He asked Peter Lee, bishop of Virginia, and John Lipscomb, bishop of Southwest Florida, to set as co-chairs of the meeting. On Iker's and Duncan's invitation, Edward Salmon, of South Carolina, and James Stanton, of Dallas, also attended the gathering. The meeting, 11–13 September, 2006, turned out to be a complete failure: "[we] were unable to come to common agreement on the way forward. We could not come to consensus on a common plan to move forward to meet the needs of the dioceses that issued the appeal for Alternate Primatial Oversight."[325] No doubt the sticking point remained whether the oversight would come from within or without the Episcopal Church. A few days later, a collection of conserva-

---

323. "Statement of the Standing Committee of the Diocese of South Carolina." *Jubilate Deo* (Diocese of South Carolina), August/September 2006, 1.

324. On 27 October 2006, James Stanton, bishop of Dallas, issued a statement that his diocese was not seeking, and had never asked for, alternative primatial oversight. His diocesan convention had recently rejected a proposal to remove all references to the Episcopal Church. This meant that six dioceses sought some kind of alternative oversight. Schjonberg, Mary Frances. "Dallas Bishop Clarifies Request for 'Alternative Primatial Oversight.'" Episcopal News Service, October 27, 2006, http://www.episcopalarchives.org/cgi-bin/ENS/ENSpress_release.pl?pr_number=102706-3-A.

325. "New York Bishops Summit Statement." September 13, 2006, http://www.americananglican.org/new-york-bishops-summit-statement.

tive bishops met at Camp Allen, Texas, and issued a statement that included another call for "alternative primatial relationship."[326] Bishop Salmon was one of the twenty-one bishops signing the letter.

The group that had met in New York in September met there again on 27 November to draw up a plan for oversight. Once again, Kearon represented the Archbishop of Canterbury, but several others failed to attend this meeting including bishops Salmon, Iker, Duncan, and Stanton, the core of the dissenting bishops. The attending group issued a statement called "A Response to 'An Appeal to the Archbishop of Canterbury.'" It outlined a plan to supplement the House of Bishop's Delegated Episcopal Pastoral Oversight (DEPO) scheme of March 2004 calling for a Primatial Vicar appointed by the presiding bishop, in consultation with the Archbishop of Canterbury, to be the presiding bishop's designated pastor in the petitioning dioceses. The Primatial Vicar would be accountable to the presiding bishop and would report to an Advisory Panel of four persons, one appointed by the Archbishop of Canterbury, one by the presiding bishop, a bishop selected by the petitioning dioceses, and the president of the House of Deputies. Both the Primatial Vicar and the Advisory Panel would be subject to the constitution and canons of the Episcopal Church. Finally, the plan was to last for three years.[327]

As the House of Bishops DEPO plan of March 2004, the new Primatial Vicar offer of November 2006 was immediately dismissed by the ultra-conservatives it was supposed to appease. As to be expected, the American Anglican Council blasted the offer, threw in its author for good measure, and declared it dead. Three days after the appearance of the offer, the AAC issued a statement:

> The proposal does not take into account the heart of the issue and problem which is that Katharine Jefferts Schori has adopted a form of faith, theology and Christology that is so seriously out of step with historic Anglicanism and Christianity that it calls into question her capacity to give appropriate leadership on this matter. It keeps all the power in her hands. The proposal is to be in consultation with not the consent of the Archbishop of Canterbury. Thus she makes all the decisions. It is a non-starter.[328]

Bishop Duncan, head of the Anglican Communion Network, likewise rejected the offer: "'what is proposed is neither primatial, nor oversight, nor is it an alternative to the spiritual authority of one who, by both teaching and action, has expressly rejected the Windsor Report and its recommendations. This is obviously not what we asked for.'"[329] Bishop Iker told his diocese of Ft. Worth: "'I find it unacceptable and unworkable in its present form.'"[330] Perhaps speaking for the whole group of ACN bishops, Iker said in the first place he had appealed to the Archbishop of Canterbury, not the presiding bishop,

---

326. "A Letter to the House of Bishops of the Episcopal Church." September 22, 2006, http://www.americananglican.org/episcopal-bishops-meeting-in-texas-send-letter-to-house-of-bishops.

327. "A Response to 'An Appeal to the Archbishop of Canterbury.'" November 27, 2006, http://www.americananglican.org/presiding-bishop-other-bishops-proposal-responding-to-appeal-to-canterbury.

328. "Pittsburgh National Church 'Response' Falls Short." Virtueonline, November 30, 2006, http://new.virtueonline.org/pittsburgh-national-church-response-falls-short.

329. Ibid.

330. Ibid.

and had asked for an alternate primate, that is, one outside the Episcopal Church: "'The new proposal is deficient in that it seeks to reinforce the PB's authority over us rather than provide an acceptable alternative. We cannot accept a Primatial Vicar appointed by her and accountable to her.'"[331] Yet again, the sticking point was whether the oversight would come from within or without the Episcopal Church. Thus, the Episcopal Church's two offers of alternative oversight, the House of Bishop's DEPO plan of March 2004 and the presiding bishop's Primatial Vicar offer of November 2006, died as they were dismissed on the spot by the ultra-conservatives who continued to insist on the impossible demand of a foreign Anglican primate providing oversight in the Episcopal Church.

It is possible that the ACN bishops rejected the presiding bishop's Primatial Vicar plan because they expected something better coming from the February 2007 meeting of the primates in Dar es Salaam. If so, they were not to be disappointed. The primates' Dar es Salaam Communiqué of 19 February 2007, presented a scheme significantly different that the presiding bishop's, one much more to the ultra-conservatives liking. It would set up a Pastoral Council of five members, two appointed by the Anglican primates, two by the presiding bishop, and a chair appointed by the Archbishop of Canterbury. Then, the petitioning bishops would choose a Primatial Vicar who would be responsible to the Pastoral Council. The presiding bishop and the Pastoral Council would delegate powers and duties to the Primatial Vicar. In short, authority in the petitioning dioceses would move from the Episcopal Church to a majority non-Episcopal Church Pastoral Council. The dissident bishops would choose their own Primatial Vicar who would answer to the Council, not to the presiding bishop. This sort of foreign intervention scheme was just what the ACN bishops had had in mind all along.[332]

If the DEPO and Primatial Vicar plans were dead on arrival at the ultra-conservative side, the Dar es Salaam proposal was just as dead on arrival at the Episcopal Church side. A month after the primates met, the Episcopal Church House of Bishops assembled at Camp Allen, Texas, and flatly rejected the primates' whole proposal. The bishops issued a lengthy statement explaining in no uncertain terms their reasons for dismissing the plan: "We believe that to participate in the Primates' Pastoral scheme would be injurious to The Episcopal Church for many reasons."[333] The bishops did not just disagree with the plan, they declared it would actually injure the institutional structure of the Episcopal Church. They went on to give a long list of reasons, the first of which was "it violates our church law in that it would call for a delegation of primatial authority not permissible under our Canons and a compromise of our authority as a Church not permissible under our Constitution."[334] Once again, it was the same old sticking point. The Episcopal Church would not accept an oversight plan that allowed foreign bishops to exercise authority within the Church.

---

331. Ibid.

332. "Primates Meeting Communiqué." Episcopal News Service, February 19, 2007, http://archive.episcopalchurch.org/3577_82571_ENG_HTM.htm.

333. "Bishops' 'Mind of the House' Resolutions." Episcopal News Service, March 20, 2007, www.episcopalchurch.org/library/article/bishops-mind-house-resolutions.

334. Ibid.

The ultra-conservatives lost no time in denouncing the House of Bishops' stand against the primates. The American Anglican Council published a statement on the next day, March 21: "The AAC is strongly opposed to the three 'Mind of the House' resolutions adopted yesterday that expressly reject the pastoral scheme outlined by the primates' recent Dar es Salaam Communiqué."[335] As for the Episcopal Church, David Anderson, president of AAC said: "The church's desire for complete power and autonomy goes hand in hand with its rebellion against Scriptural authority."[336] The AAC went on to ask for intervention from the Communion in defiance of the Episcopal Church: "The AAC urges the Archbishop of Canterbury to proceed along with the primates in settling up the pastoral council, filling any defaulted positions. If they do not move forward with the plan, the situation in the U.S. church will remain intolerable for those Episcopalians who desire to remain faithful to the biblical Anglican faith."[337]

By the spring of 2007, all three plans of oversight had failed to be accepted by one side or the other, the DEPO, the Primatial Vicar, and the Dar es Salaam proposal. The entire official structure of the Episcopal Church refused the Dar es Salaam scheme. On June 14, 2007, the Executive Council rejected the plan outright for the same reasons the House of Bishops had given.[338] On 20–25 September 2007, the House of Bishops met again, this time in New Orleans. The Archbishop of Canterbury, Rowan Williams, also attended perhaps pressed by the urgency of the moment. While the primates in Dar es Salaam had offered their oversight scheme they had also given the Episcopal Church a deadline of 30 September to assure the Communion it would oppose both the consecrations of open homosexuals and the blessings of same-sex unions. In their sessions, the bishops reiterated resolution B033 of the 2006 Convention that said dioceses would use "restraint" in approving open homosexuals as bishops and assurance that the Church as a whole did not have a blessing of same-sex unions. Most bishops felt this should satisfy the Dar es Salaam requests, but many conservatives said it did not go far enough. At the same time, the presiding bishop used the meeting to declare a renewed initiative on oversight. Going back to the original DEPO plan of March 2004, Jefferts Schori announced that eight bishops from across the theological spectrum had agreed to serve as episcopal visitors to diocese that sought alternative oversight.[339]

---

335. "AAC Statement on the Episcopal House of Bishops' March 2007 Meeting." American Anglican Council, March 21, 2007, http://www.americananglican.org/aac-statement-on-the-house-of-bishops-march-07-meeting.

336. Ibid.

337. Ibid.

338. Schjonberg, Mary Frances "Executive Council Declines to Participate in Primates' 'Pastoral Scheme.'" Episcopal News Service, June 26, 2007, as quoted in Anglican Communion News Service, http://www.anglicannews.org/news/2007/06/executive-council-declines-to-participate-in-primates-pastoral-scheme.aspx.

339. Williams, Bob. "Eight Bishops Agree to Serve as 'Episcopal Visitors.'" Episcopal News Service, September 20, 2007, http://archive.episcopalchurch.org/79901_90174_ENG_HTM.htm. Frank Brookhart, Montana; Dorsey Henderson, of Upper South Carolina; John Howe, of Central Florida; Gary Lillibridge, of West Texas; Michael Smith, of North Dakota; James Stanton, of Dallas; Geralyn Wolf, of Rhode Island; and Clarence Coleridge, retired of Connecticut.

As one might imagine, the ultra-conservatives were disappointed at the House of Bishops' response to the Dar es Salaam requests and to Jefferts Schori's oversight efforts. Bishop Salmon sent a report back to the diocese saying he had addressed the House in dissent to their statement. He gave several reasons for his opposition, most importantly that the presiding bishop's oversight initiative was not acceptable because "it did not provide alternative oversight that met the needs of those who asked for it."[340] He also said the bishops' statement in response to the requests of the Dar es Salaam Communiqué was not adequate.

In the end, nothing came of the dissident Episcopalians' appeal for alternate oversight. As South Carolina, none of the other ACN dioceses liked Jefferts Schori's September 2007 offer of episcopal visitors. By late 2007, all of the various oversight proposals since 2004 had been batted down by one side or the other. The opposing forces would not budge from their positions of whether the oversight arrangement should be from within or from without of the Episcopal Church. The Church's response was the same as it had been throughout the 1980s and 1990s on the old idea of a church-within-a-church for the irreconcilables. Any arrangement in the Episcopal Church would have to conform to the constitution and canons of the Church. This was non-negotiable on the Church side. There was no way the Church could compromise on this point. In opposition, the ultra-conservatives absolutely refused any plan where authority remained in the Episcopal Church. They consistently demanded foreign intervention for their dioceses. They continued to demand this even after the Archbishop of Canterbury made it plain he could not and would not interfere in the Episcopal Church and the Church made its position very clear. This raised the question of sincerity on the ultra-conservatives' part. Did they know their demand was impossible? If so, what was their motivation in making it? Why did they immediately reject each Church plan without offering a compromise settlement? Although the present evidence cannot answer these questions, one can see what happened soon after the ultra-conservatives rejected Jefferts Schori's offer of September 2007. This turned out to be the last of the alternate oversight issue. Before the end of the year, one ultra-conservative diocese voted to separate from the Episcopal Church and three more followed in short order. Whether the ultra-conservatives' alternate oversight demand was sincere or only a ruse to prepare for schism remained to be seen. As for South Carolina, nothing came of the alternate oversight idea in the short run as the diocese became preoccupied with the selection, installation, and settlement of a new bishop.

As the months of 2006 and 2007 moved along and the South Carolina diocesan leadership became ever more hostile to the national Church, the pro-Church Episcopal Forum of South Carolina stepped up its activities to promote unity with the Church. The Forum had to do this on its own since it was excluded from the diocesan power structure. *Jubilate Deo* would soon stop carrying any information about the Forum. The Forum did what it could to defend the ties to the Episcopal Church through conferences, meetings, luncheons, press releases, newsletters, and a website where hundreds of members enrolled in the Forum. The leaders of the Forum were under no illusions about their situation in the diocese. They knew the odds were against them, yet they worked on.

---

340. Salmon, (the Rt. Rev. Edward L., Jr. "A Report on the New Orleans House of Bishops." [September 25, 2007?], http://americananglican.org/bishop-salmon-re-hob-meeting.

Their survey of diocesan clergy in 2006 found that only 31 percent of the clergy believed the Episcopal Church should not break up over the issue of homosexuality and only 8 percent said they would stay with the Episcopal Church after a schism.[341]

The diocesan power structure, now relentlessly critical of the national Church, more or less ignored the Forum. They went about diocesan business almost as if the Forum did not exist. The Forum Board must have felt increasingly frustrated at their exclusion in the diocese and their continuing failure to exert any influence on the apparently inexorable trajectory of the diocese away from the national Church. Since nothing seemed to work in the diocese after months of trying, the Forum Board resolved to appeal to the national Church for help. In June of 2007, Lynn Pagliaro, the president of the Forum, sent a letter to the presiding bishop, the president of the House of Deputies, and the chancellor of the Episcopal Church pointing out the situation of the local Church loyalists: "TEC has been weakened in the Diocese of SC by the systematic exclusion of clergy and lay leaders who support TEC, from the leadership of congregations and diocese. We are convinced that the situation is now critical and deserves your immediate intervention."[342] He continued, "Clergy in this diocese have a bias and have encouraged disinformation about TEC (. . .) Episcopalians, now affiliated with EFSC, have experienced isolation and alienation in their parishes and in the Diocese."[343] Then, Pagliaro asked for intervention: "We urge you to consider options for intervention by TEC into the leadership of this Diocese (. . .). We encourage you to consider the possibility of appointing an interim bishop."[344] It should be recalled that Bishop Salmon had passed the mandatory age of retirement, and at this time no bishop had been affirmed to replace him. Apparently, Pagliaro got no positive response to his letter. The presiding bishop did not intervene.[345] In fact, soon afterwards, and on his second try, Salmon's replacement, Mark Lawrence, received the necessary consents for approval as the new bishop of South Carolina.

The Search for a New Bishop

The Constitution of the Episcopal Church required that a bishop must give up his or her office upon reaching the age of seventy-two. Article II, Section 9 of the Constitution

---

341. "Majority of SC Clergy Surveyed would Leave ECUSA." eNewsletter, Episcopal Forum of SC, August 21, 2006, http://mynewsletterbuilder.com/tools/view_newsletter.php?newsletter_is=1409576927.

342. Pagliaro, Lynn A. "The State of Leadership in The Episcopal Diocese of SC–June 2007." eNewsletter, Episcopal Forum of SC, June 20, 2007, http://www.mynewsletterbuilder.com/tools/view_newsletter.php?newsletter_id=1409605490#article_2.

343. Ibid.

344. Ibid.

345. Apparently unknown to the Forum and the public, the presiding bishop had already agreed to leave Salmon as the effective bishop. On September 12, 2005, the committee received word that the presiding bishop would extend Salmon's term by three months, to April 30, 2006, and then recognize the standing committee as the ecclesiastical authority of the diocese. The committee added that Salmon would remain "Bishop in Residence" through the consecration of his successor and that Salmon would have voice and vote in the General Convention of 2006. "Minutes of Standing Committee." [September 12, 2005].

read simply: "Upon attaining the age of seventy-two years a Bishop shall resign from all jurisdiction." For Bishop Salmon, this would be on January 30, 2006. The rules for choosing a new bishop in the Episcopal Church were similarly straightforward: candidate at least thirty years of age, consents by a majority of the diocesan standing committees and a majority of diocesan bishops. In case of a diocesan election in less than 120 days before a General Convention, the House of Deputies would substitute for the standing committees. Finally, at least three bishops were required to participate in a new bishop's consecration. The Church rules were short, simple, and clear; and usually the selection of a new bishop was a routine formality. Rarely did any problem arise in a diocese's selection. But this was not an ordinary time. The highly-charged atmosphere in South Carolina guaranteed this transition would also be highly charged. As one will see, it would be almost four years between the time Bishop Salmon first informed the standing committee of his upcoming retirement and the consecration of his replacement in the Diocese of South Carolina. The issue would all but consume the diocese in 2006 and 2007. The question at hand was whether this transitional moment would strengthen or loosen the already tenuous bond between diocese and national Church.

The movement to put in place a new bishop began on April 6, 2004, when Bishop Salmon met the diocesan standing committee and "discussed possible approaches to the election of a new bishop in late 2005."[346] The next month, he returned to the committee and announced that the 2005–06 Standing Committee would preside over the election of the new bishop, but the current Standing Committee would "set the parameters."[347] The committee adopted a structure for a Nominating Committee of twelve members: three chosen by Bishop Salmon, three by the Standing Committee, three by the Diocesan Council, and three by the Diocesan Convention. This would guarantee the diocesan ruling establishment would control the selection process as the ordinary people of the diocese would be given choice of only a quarter of the seats through their delegates in the diocesan convention. Also, and very importantly, the committee resolved that no nomination from the floor be accepted "to insure that the Nominating Committee has adequate time for background checks, etc."[348] The apparatus to choose a new bishop that Bishop Salmon and the Standing Committee set up in May of 2004 sealed off even the remote possibility of a challenge to the diocesan ruling clique's control over selection of a new bishop. They would control the majority of the nominating committee, through that the choice of the candidates, and through that the choice of the new bishop. This reality was a reflection of the centralized power structure that had emerged in the diocese by at least the year 2003.

Having set up the form for choosing a new bishop, several months later, Bishop Salmon invited to the Standing Committee meeting the Rt. Rev. Clayton Matthews, the Episcopal Church's bishop for the Office of Pastoral Development, the officer who advised dioceses on the selections of new bishops. He attended the Standing Committee session on November 11, 2004, and suggested a time line of activity for the year 2005: January-February, compile profile, draw up questionnaire for diocese, compile questions for focus groups; March, focus groups and retreat; April, printing of profile; May, mail

346. "Minutes of the Standing Committee." [April 6, 2004].
347. Ibid. [May 13, 2004].
348. Ibid.

profile and nominating forms; June-August, screening nominations; September-October, visiting nominees; October, ending petition; November, walk about of nominees; 10 December, election.[349]

By December of 2004, the Standing Committee was ready to begin implementing the agreed-upon plan. At the committee's meeting that month a question arose of whether to use a consultant for the search. Bishop Salmon advised against it. The Standing Committee decided it would not use one from the Episcopal Church but would ask the officers in the dioceses of Rio Grande and San Diego about their experiences using consultants. The committee agreed to prepare for a retreat, compile parochial reports, draft a vision statement and a profile, and draw up questions for focus groups. It also set as the walk-about date, December 3, and the election as December 10, 2005.[350]

The issue of choosing a new bishop for South Carolina raised the question of the diocese's bishop suffragan, William Skilton. Historically, bishops suffragan had been given priority to be the new diocesan bishop although this was not automatic, such as for a bishop coadjutor. It was a common practice in the Episcopal Church to give at least prime consideration to elevating the suffragan. Often bishops suffragan were elected as diocesan bishops in other dioceses. Skilton had been bishop suffragan of the Diocese of South Carolina since March 2, 1996. Through the years, he had made a record for himself as a consistent ally of Bishop Salmon and as a well-regarded and vocal advocate of conservative causes. However, apparently from the start, Bishop Salmon and the Standing Committee resolved not to choose Skilton as a candidate to be diocesan bishop and, indeed, to nudge him into retirement at the age of sixty-six. The evidence of what happened in this matter was sketchy, but records showed that the Standing Committee met at Camp St. Christopher on the afternoon of March 28, 2005. The chair, Dow Sanderson, presented a letter to be sent to Bishop Skilton. The committee approved the letter with minor changes; Sanderson said he would deliver it to Skilton on March 30.[351] The record did not disclose the content of the letter. That evening, the Standing Committee held a joint session with the new Search Committee. The minutes of that meeting showed no mention of Skilton, only of Bishop Salmon serving temporarily until a new bishop could be installed. On May 12, 2005, Bishop Salmon met the Standing Committee and discussed with them Skilton's retirement.[352] Thus, the records showed that the bishop and Standing Committee were preparing for Skilton's retirement before any candidates for bishop were selected or the presiding bishop had agreed to allow Salmon to serve as temporary bishop after his retirement. At the same time, there was no word about continuing the office of bishop suffragan in the diocese.

Following Bishop Salmon's discussion of Skilton's retirement with the Standing Committee on May 12, 2005, there was a blank in the records concerning this for the next year and a half. By late 2006, however, Skilton had worked out a deal with the Standing Committee to finalize his retirement. The diocese would provide him a payment of approximately $20,000 a year and he would announce his retirement date as December

---

349. Ibid. [November 11, 2004].
350. Ibid. [December 2, 2004].
351. Ibid. [March 28, 2005].
352. Ibid. [May 12, 2005].

31, 2006. In the April/May 2007 issue of *Jubilate Deo*, the chair of the Standing Committee, Haden McCormick, thanked Skilton for his "sensitivity and cooperation over these past weeks as we discussed and designed his retirement." McCormick then added: "After Bill had made his decision to step down, he agreed to absent himself from the Diocesan office and curtail his normal activities during this time of transition." Publicly, Skilton was gracious about what had happened to him posting a kind letter on January 25, 2007: "This decision, freely made by me is at the request of the Standing Committee of the Diocese and with the concurrence of the bishop-elect Mark Lawrence."[353] He added, "I believe my departure will enable Father Lawrence to create a diocesan staff that will more effectively respond to his developing vision and gifts that he brings to the Diocese."[354] Skilton's words were generous; however, his retirement had actually been determined before Mark Lawrence was nominated to be bishop. It is interesting to note that after he became bishop, Lawrence did not resurrect the office of bishop suffragan but did create a new position of Canon to the Ordinary as an assistant to the bishop.

By March of 2005, the new Bishop's Search Committee was in place having been set up by the plan Bishop Salmon and the Standing Committee had devised in May of 2004. The chair was the Rev. Greg Kronz, of St. Luke's of Hilton Head where he had been since 1992. He was originally from Pittsburgh, had graduated from Trinity Episcopal School for Ministry, and had served St. Stephen's in Wilkinsburg, Pennsylvania, Diocese of Pittsburgh, from 1985 to 1986.[355] It just so happened that Mark Lawrence was in the same diocese (1984–97) and had graduated from the same seminary. In his deposition for the circuit court trial of 2013, Lawrence said "I knew Greg Kronz from—he was an associate of a rector of St. Stephen's Wiklinsburg when I was rector of St. Stephen's McKeesport."[356] Kronz also happened to be on the Standing Committee, one of the three from the committee placed on the search committee. The two other members of the search committee from the Standing Committee were Frances Fuchs, of St. John's on Johns Island and the Rev. Frank Limehouse, who soon resigned to be replaced by the Rev. Jeffrey Miller, of St. Helena's in Beaufort. In addition to Kronz, there was another connection to Mark Lawrence and the Diocese of Pittsburgh, the Rev. Jim Simons. Dow Sanderson, chair of the standing committee in 2005, later testified: "We asked for and received an adviser, a chaplain from The Episcopal Church. He was from the Diocese of Pittsburgh, the Reverend Jim Simons."[357] Simons was graduated from Trinity Episcopal School for Ministry in 1985. And served as rector of St. Michael's of the Valley, in Ligonier, some forty miles from Lawrence's parish in McKeesport.[358]

---

353. Skilton, (the Rt. Rev.) William J. "A Letter from Bishop Skilton." [January 25, 2007] *Jubilate Deo* (Diocese of South Carolina), April/May 2007, 2.

354. Ibid.

355. Chalfant-Walker, (the Rev.) Nancy. E-mail message to author, February 21, 2016.

356. "Deposition Transcript—Mark J. Lawrence." South Carolina, Court of Common Pleas, Dorchester County, Case No. 2013-CP-18-00013, Exhibit D-24, July 23, 2014, 24.

357. "Deposition of Marshall Dow Sanderson," State of South Carolina, Court of Common Pleas, County of Dorchester, Case No. 2013-CP-18-00013, June 2, 2014, 44.

358. Simons, (the Rev.) Jim. "About Me." Three Rivers Episcopal, http://www.blogger.com/profile/06889838893337097340.

Among the other nine members of the Bishop's Search Committee were five clergymen, making seven clergy among the twelve members of the committee: Craige Borrett, of Christ/St. Paul's of Younge's Island, Paul Fuener, of Prince George, Georgetown, Anthony Kowbeidu, of St. Andrew's of Mt. Pleasant, John Scott, of Epiphany of Eutawville, and David Thurlow, of St. Matthias of Summerton. The lay members of the committee, in addition to Fuchs, were: John Bowden, of St. Paul's of Orangeburg, Lydia Evans, of St. Philip's of Charleston, Martha Flowers, of St. Bartholomew's of Hartsville, and Dr. Keith Lackey, of Holy Communion of Charleston.

Several observations about the Search Committee should be made. The most important point was that the committee very much represented the establishment of the diocese. Indeed, three-quarters of the members had been appointed by that ruling establishment. There was no one on the committee from the Episcopal Forum or from what were well-known to be moderate or pro-Episcopal Church congregations, even from one of the largest parishes in the diocese, Grace Church of Charleston. In the second place, this was a panel controlled by the clergy who held a seven-to-five majority over the laity. All of the clergy were well-known for their conservative viewpoints. Every one of them would go on to support Bishop Lawrence in the schism of 2012 (except Limehouse who was in Alabama) and would leave the Episcopal Church with him. In the third place, four of the five lay members of the committee came from churches which would follow Lawrence out of the Episcopal Church. The only one that did not come from a secessionist parish, Keith Lackey of Holy Communion, later left the Episcopal Church for the Roman Catholic Ordinariate. In short, the committee to select the next bishop of South Carolina clearly reflected the ultra-conservative viewpoint manifested so clearly in the Anglican Communion Network.

The first official meeting of the new Search Committee was on the evening of Monday, March 28, 2005, at Camp Saint Christopher where the committee met jointly with the diocesan Standing Committee. The first topic of discussion was a timeframe for the election of a new bishop. A complicating factor in setting up a schedule was that the House of Bishops, meeting in Camp Allen, Texas, just a few days earlier had resolved not to approve any new bishops in the Episcopal Church until the next General Convention, June 13, 2006. That meant South Carolina could elect a new bishop but could not get him or her confirmed by the Church before June of 2006. This left the Search Committee with two options, election before the Convention and consent by the bishops and deputies during the Convention, or election after the Convention and consent by the bishops and standing committees. The Episcopal Church Constitution and Canons of 2003, in effect in 2005, said the diocese's choice of a bishop required "the consent of a majority of the Standing Committees of all the Dioceses, and the consent of a majority of the Bishops of this Church exercising jurisdiction. But if the election shall have taken place within three months next before the meeting of the General Convention, the consent of the House of Deputies shall be required in place of that of a majority of the Standing Committees."[359]

First of all, the two committees decided to cancel the regular annual diocesan convention meeting in March of 2006. Then they resolved to keep their choice of a bishop

---

359. *Constitution and Canons, The Episcopal Church.* [2003].

from going to the General Convention and, strangely enough, backed it up with misinformation: "We do not want the election tied to General Convention, which requires a simple majority. Otherwise, two-thirds of the Bishops and Standing Committees must consent."[360] It was not true that two-thirds of bishops and standing committees had to consent; the Constitution and Canons of 2003 clearly stated a simple majority. The appearance of the misinformation remained a puzzle. Besides, why did the committees think it would be easier to get two-thirds approval than a simple majority? Perhaps they assumed that if they chose a controversial candidate, there would be too much opposition to him on the floor of the Convention, too much risk of rejection. The joint committees did not explain their reasoning, but they made it entirely clear they were adamantly opposed to allowing the decision to go to the General Convention of 2006. By contrast, it is interesting to note that the Diocese of New Hampshire felt no hesitancy in electing Gene Robinson in 2003 knowing it would go to a vote in the General Convention of that year; and Robinson had been arguably the most controversial candidate in the history of the Episcopal Church. Although New Hampshire had not backed away from controversy, South Carolina now resolved to do so. To emphasize the point, Dow Sanderson, chair of the standing committee put a notice in *Jubilate Deo* stating: "Bishop Matthew's statement as reported that we would time our election to have the consents coincide with General Convention is without any basis in fact whatsoever."[361] Thus, one item appeared inalterably settled by the Search Committee, the election of the new bishop would be held after June of 2006. If fear of the General Convention's rejection of their choice did indeed drive the Search Committee to delay the election until after the Convention, this did not bode well for the future.

The Standing Committee and the Search Committee decided to spend six months preparing for the nomination process. The general idea in this period was to make a self-examination of the diocese and to reflect on what qualities the diocese might desire in a new bishop. In April and May of 2005, meetings were held in every deanery to collect information to put in the diocesan "Profile" and to compose questions to be put to the candidates. The Profile was to be a report on the state of the diocese, its structure, people, and programs. In addition, in June, questionnaires were given to all the clergy to gather information to be put into the composite. In July and August, the search committee met to finish the compilation of the Profile that was sent to the printer on 1 September. On 15 September, the committee sent out the Profile and nomination forms to all the clergy of the diocese, all bishops, and all standing committees of the Episcopal Church. The Search Committee then received nominations until 24 October 2005.[362]

At the close of nominations, the Search Committee met on 25 October to review the possible candidates. They resolved to start a screening process to review the nominees

---

360. "Minutes of Joint Meeting, Standing and Search Committees, March 28, 2005." Diocese of South Carolina.

361. Sanderson, (the Rev.) Dow. "Standing Committee Chairman's Brief Statement on the South Carolina Episcopal Election." *Jubilate Deo* (Diocese of South Carolina), April/May 2005.

362. "Search Committee Update." *Jubilate Deo* (Diocese of South Carolina), October/November 2005; "Bishop of SC Search Committee Timeline." *Jubilate Deo* (Diocese of South Carolina), February/March 2006.

and cull out the least appropriate ones. As preparation for this, they sent out a questionnaire to all potential candidates. This first winnowing-out period was to last for three months until the committee would meet again in January of 2006.[363]

The screening process went on for months, well into the year 2006. In January, the Search Committee, with the advice of its chaplain, the Rev. Jim Simons from the Diocese of Pittsburgh, "was able to considerably narrow the list of nominees."[364] The next month, the committee met again to draw up a list of questions for the remaining nominees.[365] At that time, they expected to conduct their interviews in March and arrive at their final list of candidates in June, but not to announce the names until after the General Convention.

On May 3, 2006, the Standing Committee met to finalize plans for the last phase of the search. Kronz told the committee that the Search Committee had scheduled its in-person interviews for June 5–7 at Camp St. Christopher. The committee expected to send the names of the finalists to the Standing Committee on July 6 and to hold a "walkabout" at St. Philip's of Charleston, on 9 September so the clergy and delegates could get to know the finalists for bishop. The Standing Committee also considered two petition candidates, the Rev. Charles Walton[366] and the Rev. Mark Goodman. Goodman was asked for an interview on May 22 but was not included among the finalists.[367]

As May arrived in 2006, and after seven months of looking for a new bishop, the Search Committee was apparently disappointed at the final crop of candidates. At some point around this time, the Search Committee appealed to the retired bishop of Pittsburgh, Alden Hathaway, to ask the Very Rev. Mark Lawrence if he would allow his name to be put into nomination. Lawrence was rector of St. Paul's Episcopal Church, in Bakersfield, California. Hathaway, then living in Tallahassee, Florida, had been Lawrence's bishop in the Diocese of Pittsburgh. Apparently up until May of 2006, Lawrence had had no contact with the Search Committee. However, there were ties between Lawrence and the committee. Likewise, Hathaway had many contacts in South Carolina. Indeed, in 2007, he joined the staff of St. Helena's Church, in Beaufort, where Jeff Miller was rector. As bishop of Pittsburgh, Hathaway had confirmed and ordained Miller.[368] On the morning of May 3, Hathaway telephoned Lawrence in Bakersfield and asked if Lawrence would allow his name to be put up for nomination as bishop of South Carolina. "He [Hathaway] said that he had been asked by the search committee of South Carolina if I

---

363. "News from the Search Committee." *Jubilate Deo* (Diocese of South Carolina), December 2005/January 2006.

364. "News from the Bishop's Search Committee." *Jubilate Deo* (Diocese of South Carolina), April/May 2006.

365. Ibid.

366. Charles Walton retired soon thereafter, remained with Lawrence in the schism, and continued serving missions. Goodman, rector of Trinity in Myrtle Beach, came in second in 2007 for bishop of Oklahoma, then was chosen as dean of St. John's Cathedral, in Albuquerque where he remained as of 2016.

367. "Minutes of the Standing Committee." [May 3, 2006].

368. "St. Helena's, Meet the Clergy." http://www.sthelenas1712.org/about/meet-the-clergy.

would allow my name to be put in for the search for bishop."[369] Lawrence later said as the word "yes" slipped from his mouth, he wanted to silence it in mid-air.[370]

To Lawrence, Hathaway's call on May 3 was no accident. It was nothing less than the hand of God. He later recounted that it was the last of three signs that God had given him in early 2006. The first came in March when Lawrence was hosting a healing ministry conference at St. Paul's. In the midst of a service, a visiting priest began speaking in tongues: "At first, it rang with an African cadence, and he could see himself soaring over the great savannahs. The sound transformed, sounding more Celtic, and Lawrence soared over Irish hillsides. Then a Negro spiritual led him to the deep South, until he again heard recognizable words in English."[371] At that point, three times an inner voice spoke to him: "'The journey begins. Pack your things. Give your children your blessing. You've been in one place long enough.'"[372] Afterwards, a shaken Lawrence went over to his wife, Allison, "eyes wide, and damp with emotion."[373] Allison later recalled, "'I looked at his face and thought, 'Oh, my gosh.'"[374] For weeks thereafter, Lawrence said he "had a clear sense from the Lord that He was calling me into something that would require me to leave my parish."[375]

The second sign Lawrence identified as an unexpected phone call from a friend of thirty years who lived in Ohio. The friend told Lawrence, "'I was praying for you today and felt that the Lord will be using you to 'prepare the faithful for the battle ahead, both inwardly and outwardly.'"[376] The friend said he had a profound sense God was saying He was about to move Lawrence from Bakersfield.[377] Then came the third sign. Three days after his Ohio friend's call, Hathaway telephoned, on May 3, to ask for Lawrence's nomination. Lawrence said, "When the bishop called, I knew in my heart that I was meant to stand for this election."[378] It seemed clear that Lawrence understood what he saw as three signs from God, of early 2006, as his divinely-ordained destiny to become the next bishop of South Carolina.

It is important to note that the mysterious origin of the last-minute initiative for Lawrence's nomination came from the Search Committee itself. According to Lawrence's later deposition testimony, some member or members of the committee asked Hathaway to contact Lawrence to see if he would be agreeable to his nomination. As there was little time left for the completion of the search, time was of the essence. Shortly

369. "Deposition Transcript—Mark J. Lawrence," 22.

370. Hawes, Jennifer Berry. "The Rt. Rev. Mark Lawrence Feels Hand of God Down Journey through Episcopal Church Schism." *The Post and Courier* (Charleston, SC), September 15, 2013. www.postandcourier.com/features/faith_and_values/the-rt-rev-mark-lawrence-bishop-feels-hand-of-god/article_db9e2ff4-a623-55f8-8501-a0d74657f126.html.

371. Ibid.

372. Ibid.

373. Ibid.

374. Ibid.

375. "ACN: An Interview with Mark Lawrence." September 26, 2006, http:///www.virtueonline.org/portal/modules/news/article.php?storyid=476088&com+id=5395&com_rootid=5395.

376. Ibid.

377. Hawes, "Rt. Rev."

378. "ACN: An Interview."

after Hathaway's call, Lawrence got another call from either Kronz or Miller explaining the papers that the applicants needed to complete; and Lawrence finished and returned them quickly. Then, he promptly received a call that three Search Committee members were traveling to California to meet with him: Craige Borrett, Lydia Evans, and Frances Fuchs. Soon after the visit, he received another call, an invitation from the Search Committee to go to South Carolina for an on-site interview. As a sign of the committee's urgent interest, it was only a month from the time Hathaway called Lawrence and his appearance in South Carolina for an interview as one of four finalists. The Search Committee met with each of the last four nominees, one at a time, from 5 to 7 June 2006, at Camp St. Christopher. It had been a hectic month leading up to this.

Lawrence's trip to South Carolina in early June was his first to the state except for brief traveling stops. The three other finalists who had been invited to meet the search committee at the Camp were: Ellis English Brust, Stephen D. Wood, and Marcus B. Robertson. Brust[379] was the chief operating officer of the American Anglican Council, headquartered in Atlanta. Wood[380] was rector of St. Andrew's parish in Mt. Pleasant. Robertson was rector of Christ Church, Savannah.[381] On this occasion, Lawrence met the entire Search Committee for discussions, conducted a Eucharist and preached a sermon, then returned home to California.

Soon thereafter, Lawrence received a phone call from Kronz telling him he was a finalist and inviting him to meet the diocesan Standing Committee in Charleston, at St. Philip's Church, on July 6, 2006. The committee interviewed the four finalists sent up by the Search Committee: Lawrence, Brust, Wood, and the Rev. John Burwell, rector of Holy Cross Church on Sullivan's Island. Since the Search Committee interviews of a month earlier at the Camp, Robertson had been dropped from consideration and Burwell added. The committee called in the candidates one at a time for discussions. Following the interviews, the Standing Committee voted on the final list for election. The committee approved three: Lawrence, Brust, and Wood, but voted down the fourth, Burwell.[382] On July 27, the Standing Committee announced the names of the three final-

---

379. "Ellis Brust." Linkedin.com, http://www.linkedin.com/in/ellisbrust. Brust had served several churches in Texas from 1984 to 1999. He was Canon to the Ordinary in the Diocese of Florida from 1999 to 2003. From 2003 to December of 2006 he was Chief Operating Officer of the American Anglican Council. From December 2006 to October of 2009 he was President & CEO of Anglican Mission in the Americas, at Pawleys Island, SC. Later, he was pastor of Epiphany Anglican Church in Mission Viejo, CA, and, as of 2016, rector of Anglican Church of the Apostles, Kansas City, Missouri.

380. Wood, originally from Cleveland, Ohio, was educated at Virginia Theological Seminary, and ordained in 1991. In the 1990s he served churches in Ohio. In 2000, he became rector of St. Andrew's of Mt. Pleasant, an evangelical church that grew to over 2,000 members and expressed a markedly conservative theological and social outlook. In 2010, St. Andrew's left the Episcopal diocese of SC with the local property. St. Andrew's joined the Anglican Church in North America. In 2012, Wood was made the bishop of the ACNA Diocese of the Carolinas.

381. All four finalists later left the Episcopal Church. Brust left a few weeks after the election, for the Anglican Mission in America, Wood with St. Andrew's departure from the diocese of SC in 2010, and Robertson as Christ Church, Savannah, voted to leave the Episcopal Church in 2007. In 2011, the Georgia supreme court returned the Christ Church property to the Episcopal diocese of Georgia and Robertson led the Anglican congregation to other quarters.

382. "Minutes of the Standing Committee." [July 6, 2006].

ists.[383] In two dizzying months, Lawrence had gone from being oblivious of the search to being one of the finalists for election as bishop of the diocese of South Carolina.

Although the Standing Committee had settled on a slate of three names, apparently not everyone was satisfied with the choices. A group of clergy gathered to make a last-ditch appeal to get the Rev. Dow Sanderson, chair of the Standing Committee, to be a candidate even though he had made it clear he was not interested. At the Standing Committee meeting of August 28, the Reverends Mike Malone, Mike Lumpkin, and David Thurlow presented a petition trying to draft Sanderson. It had been signed by twenty-four clergy delegates and seven lay delegates.[384] With the presenters and Sanderson out of the room, the committee unanimously denied the request, leaving only the three finalists. They then discussed plans for the candidates' "walkabout."[385]

The walkabouts occurred as scheduled on 9 September at St. Philip's of Charleston. There, the convention delegates and clergy got their first chance, and last before the election a few days later, to greet and meet the three finalists: Lawrence, Brust, and Wood. Each had filled out lengthy answers to questions posed for them all. It was interesting to note that the only people of the diocese who got to speak with the candidates were the search and standing committees, the clergy, and the delegates to the convention. After the event, Lawrence returned home to California, for the third time in three months.

How did Lawrence feel about the situation at this point? He was posed this in his deposition of June 3, 2014. Lawyer Thomas Tisdale asked Lawrence if he had considered whether or not he would accept the call to be the bishop. Lawrence responded that he accepted it all as the will of God:

> I don't think one allows a process of this magnitude to go forward without allowing the fact that if it happens it's only God that's made the call, especially someone in my situation. And I was only in the process because I thought that God had placed me in the process, not because I felt that God had called me to be the bishop of South Carolina. And so I did that as an act of faith.[386]

As if to emphasize the point, Lawrence related a dream he had the night before the bishop's election on September 16:

> I had a dream the night before the election. And in the dream it was a kind of Narnia type environment. (. . .) Narnia, as in C.S. Lewis's The Lion, the Witch and the Wardrobe and other such novels by him (. . .) And in the dream a queen stood up and said that I, Mark, had a monumental task calling me forward when I was too afraid to go alone. Something to that effect. That may not be verbatim, but that's pretty close (. . .) Told me that there was more in this than just me. There's a divinity that shapes our ends, as Hamlet put it in Shakespeare.[387]

---

383. Schjonberg, Mary Frances. "San Joaquin Priest Elected Episcopal Bishop of South Carolina." Episcopal News Service, September 16, 2006, http://archive.episcopalchurch.org/3577_77855_ENG_HTM.htm.

384. Ibid.

385. "Minutes of the Standing Committee." [August 28, 2006].

386. "Deposition Transcript—Mark J. Lawrence," 58.

387. Ibid., 59. Lawrence also recounted the dream in a phone call the day after his election as bishop. See: *Jubilate Deo* (Diocese of South Carolina), October/November 2006.

The Election of a New Bishop

Finally, after more than a year and a half of preparations, the special convention to elect a new bishop convened at St. Philip's of Charleston on Saturday, September 16, 2006. Virtually the entire diocese was represented at this exciting event. Present were 106 clergy and 223 lay delegates representing 71 local churches. Dow Sanderson, chair of the Standing Committee, placed the names of the three finalists into nomination. Since there could be no nomination from the floor, a vote was called. The election was by simple majority. Of the 106 clergy, 54 were necessary. Parishes were given one vote each and missions one-half vote each. For the local churches, 28 votes were necessary for a majority. When the results were announced, 72 clergy and 42 and 1/2 churches voted for Lawrence, a landslide on the first ballot.[388] Dow Sanderson then telephoned Lawrence and informed him he had been elected on the first ballot. Lawrence accepted the decision. When asked later what his response was, he said: "awe and dread."[389] The diocese triumphantly announced to the world that it had elected a new bishop.

Unfortunately for readers today, little can be documented about the eighteen months of work of the Bishop's Search Committee. If the committee records existed, they have not been made available to the public, or at least this author was not able to locate them. They were not entered as evidence in the circuit court trial of July 2014. However, in the trial, Greg Kronz, the committee chair, testified on the stand that between thirty and fifty nominations came into the committee in September and October of 2005.[390] In the weeks after 25 October, Kronz said, the committee arrived at ten to twelve names and decided to visit those in order to end with three finalists.[391] Other than the sketchy facts presented in the preceding paragraphs, the work of the Search Committee remained secret.

The matter of the Search Committee of 2005–2006 leaves us with more questions than answers. In the first place, all of the members of the committee came from parishes known to be sympathetic to the controversial diocesan positions *vis à vis* the Episcopal Church. In the second place, the search process was entirely controlled by the diocesan power structure. All candidates would have to be approved by the search and standing committees. The ordinary communicants of the diocese would have no power in the selection process. In the third place, the search committee eliminated as many as forty-seven names from consideration. Who were they? Why were they dropped from consideration? How did the committee decide to invite Lawrence to apply? Who on the committee promoted him? In the next place, why did the two committees resolve to avoid the General Convention? They said at the start they would not allow the Convention to vote on approving their choice. They still had to get a majority of bishops and standing committees to give consent to their choice. What was the reason for not having

---

388. *Journal of the Two Hundred and Sixteenth (. . .)* 2006, 149.

389. Ibid., 56.

390. "Transcript of Record," State of South Carolina, County of Dorchester, Court of Common Pleas, Case No. 2013-CP-18-00013, July 8–25, 2014. July 23, 2014, Vol. XII, 2290.

391. Ibid.

the House of Deputies vote on their bishop-elect? Moreover, why was Lawrence elected in a landslide on the first ballot? He was little-known in the diocese before then.

Another question has persisted for a long time of whether the Search Committee actively sought a bishop who would take the diocese out of the Episcopal Church, and do so with the property in hand. If so, did the committee choose each of the three finalists with the understanding that, if elected, he would lead the diocese out of the Church? Thus, was Mark Lawrence chosen to be bishop on an agreement with the committee that he would make a schism from the Episcopal Church? These are, of course, enormously important questions in the history of the schism in South Carolina because if found to be true, they would prove the existence of a conspiracy to create a schism as early as 2005, seven years before the actual schism. However, they are impossible to answer definitively today considering the absence of the Search Committee's official records. Nevertheless, we have a few hints that need to be mentioned.

The most important piece of documented evidence of a conspiracy was an affidavit of the Rev. Thomas M. Rickenbaker made on December 18, 2013. Rickenbaker was rector of St. Paul's Episcopal Church, in Edenton, North Carolina, when he was contacted in late 2005 by the search committee inquiring whether be might be interested in being a nominee for the office of bishop of South Carolina. He answered in the affirmative and submitted the required forms and questionnaires. Six to eight weeks later, Kronz contacted Rickenbaker and asked to visit him in Edenton. Rickenbaker agreed; and about a month later, perhaps December of 2005 or January of 2006, Kronz and Paul Fuener, another search committee member, arrived for an interview. In Rickenbaker's words:

> The first question posed to me was, "What can you do to help us leave The Episcopal Church and take our property with us? I said I was not interested in that course of action in any way, shape, or form; and that I was greatly disappointed that the question was even being asked. I asked them why such a question was even asked. Father Fuener responded by saying that, "We are looking for a bishop who will or is willing to lead us out of the Episcopal Church and take our property with us." The two committee representatives came to the two Sunday services that next day at St. Paul's and then left. A few weeks later, I was informed by Father Kronz that I had been eliminated from the selection process.[392]

Rickenbaker did not appear in person during the circuit court trial in July of 2014, but did provide a statement to the Church's lawyers that was read aloud in the court on July 22. In it, he reiterated the information in his affidavit and added a few details. He said he shared the news of the incident with several people including his bishop, the Rt. Rev. Clifton Daniel, III.[393]

Kronz and Fuener both publicly denied the accusation. The day after Rickenbaker's deposition was read in court, Kronz took the stand to refute it. He was asked directly by the diocesan lawyer, Henrietta Golding, "Did you or Mr. Fuener—or Father Fuener excuse me, ever inquire as to whether or not Reverend Rickenbaker was inclined to leave a diocese or take a diocese away from the national Church?" Kronz answered,

---

392. "Affidavit of Thomas M. Rickenbaker." December 18, 2013, State of South Carolina, County of Dorchester, In the Court of Common Pleas for the First Judicial Circuit, Case No. 2013-CP-18-00013.

393. "Transcript of Record," July 22, 2014, Vol. XI, 2026.

"No."³⁹⁴ Fuener had already made his response. At the time of the affidavit, in December of 2013, he said: "'I am confident that his [Rickenbaker's] recollection of our interview is seriously in error, if not worse.'"³⁹⁵ Neither side produced any hard evidence supporting their position.

Another moment in court gave support to a conspiracy theory. On July 15, the Rev. Dow Sanderson took the stand in the circuit court trial to testify that Jeff Miller told him in August of 2009 that the diocese had elected Lawrence to take them out of the Episcopal Church. Miller had been on the Search Committee.³⁹⁶

Even though the existing evidence of a conspiracy between the search committee and Lawrence in 2006 was rather thin, it did disclose the fact that, in 2005 and 2006, the search committee set up very definite and limited criteria for the selection of the new bishop which would all but guarantee the new bishop would be a strong ultra-conservative. Many of the questions in the questionnaire given to Lawrence dealt with the highly contentious issues of homosexuality, the relationship with an Anglican primate outside of the Episcopal Church, and schism from the Episcopal Church. Obviously, his answers satisfied the search committee very well.

Mark Lawrence instantly and abundantly fulfilled all the requirements for a new bishop long set up by a diocesan power structure that had grown thoroughly hostile to the Episcopal Church. They proceeded right away with numerous joyous plans for Lawrence's consecration in the near future and to celebrate a smooth transition from the old bishop, Salmon, to the new. The problem was that, under the Constitution and Canons of the Episcopal Church, Lawrence could not be consecrated as the new bishop until and unless the diocese received consents from a majority of Episcopal Church diocesan bishops and standing committees within 120 days after notification. What the South Carolina power structure did not quite appreciate was that over many years they had moved from the mainstream of the Episcopal Church to the far-right edge so that their idea of a good bishop was far removed from that of most Episcopalians. While South Carolinians may have been overjoyed at Lawrence's election, there were many Church people across America who were anything but thrilled. Some were downright appalled and resolved to do their best to keep the Church from accepting Lawrence as a bishop. As the consent forms went out to all of the 111 dioceses of the Episcopal Church, there very much remained an open question of whether the majority of those dioceses would agree that Mark Lawrence should be entrusted with the office of bishop in the Episcopal Church. As it would turn out, electing Lawrence a bishop would prove to be much easier than making him one.

Although the people of South Carolina did not know Lawrence personally, they, and many other people in the Episcopal Church knew his words and actions well. He had made quite a name for himself as the minority spokesman in the House of Deputies

394. Ibid, July 23, 2014, Vol. XII, 2292.

395. Hawes, Jennifer Berry. "Judge Impedes Episcopalians' Efforts to Portray Conspiracy to Leave Church and Take Assets." *The Post and Courier* (Charleston, SC), December 29, 2013, http://www.postandcourier.com/features/faith_and_values/judge-impedes-episcopalisns-efforts-to-portray-conspiracy-to-leave-church/article_effc4787-a0e5-52ef-bd6c-508c3fb37a25.html.

396. "Transcript of Record," July 15, 2014, Vol. VI, 1313.

during the futile resistance to the consent for Gene Robinson in the General Convention of 2003. Too, as a dean, he had become quite a voice in his home diocese, San Joaquin. In the wake of the Robinson affair, San Joaquin turned evermore hostile to the Episcopal Church and began openly to discuss "disassociation," that is, withdrawal of the diocese from the Episcopal Church and adherence to a foreign primate in the Anglican Communion.

In the midst of all the excited talk in San Joaquin about leaving the Episcopal Church, Lawrence published two essays that could only be described as highly supportive of the idea. The first appeared either in late 2005 or January of 2006.[397] In "A Prognosis for This Body Episcopal," Lawrence made two main points: the Episcopal Church in its present state is heading to failure and death, and to save itself, the Church must surrender its autonomy and adhere to the will of the majority of the Anglican Communion. On the first point, Lawrence said, "The Episcopal Church in the United States of America (ECUSA) is dying-a comatose patient on life-support."[398] What caused this terminal illness, Lawrence suggested, was too much democracy, too much nationalism, and too much provincialism: "the ethos of democracy rather than Anglicanism," and "its fatal allegiance to provincialism" with "strident nationalism."[399] Moreover, given its nature, the Anglican Communion could not prevent the Episcopal Church from its self-inflicted disease: "The actions of ECUSA in the consecration of Gene Robinson in 2003, and the same-sex blessings in the Diocese of New Westminster in Canada, have revealed the Achilles heel of the Anglican Communion. While claiming to be a worldwide communion within the one, holy, catholic, and apostolic Church, it is actually only a loose confederation of provinces each unduly autonomous, with profoundly different forms of governance, ethos, and doctrinal commitments."[400] *Unduly autonomous.* The only solution to this "desperate" situation, in Lawrence's view, was for the Episcopal Church to give up its independence to the Anglican Communion: "Our very survival, let alone our growth, necessitates the surrender of our autonomy to the governance of the larger church-that is, the Anglican Communion."[401] He added, "It will mean that ECUSA's polity, as well as the other autonomously governed provinces, will be supplanted by a new emerging form of Anglican governance sufficient for the age of globalism."[402] Since Lawrence had already pointed out that the Anglican Communion was a loose confederation of autonomous churches, he proposed two enormous changes: a radical reform of the Communion to create an authoritarian rule over the individual provinces, and the Episcopal Church's surrender of its independence to this international authority. It was difficult to imagine that, given the constitution and canons of the Episcopal Church, either one of those was within the realm of possibility. Nevertheless, *The Living Church*

397. On Jan. 30, 2006, David Virtue posted it on his website Virtueonline.org.

398. Lawrence, (the Very Rev.) Mark. "A Prognosis for This Body Episcopal." Virtueonline, January 30, 2006, http://www.virtueonline.org/portal/modules/news/article.php?storyid=3542&com_id=31940&com_rootid=3194.

399. Ibid.

400. Ibid.

401. Ibid.

402. Ibid.

printed a shortened version of Lawrence's essay on the dying church, June 11, 2006. Lawrence first published his "Prognosis" essay at least four months before he became a candidate for bishop.

Lawrence published a second popular essay "Remaining Anglican: In Defense of Dissociation" after he became a finalist for bishop. He posted it on St. Paul's Church website on 23 July 2006, between the time of his interview with the standing committee and the walkabout at St. Philip's.[403] The title gave one a good idea of the content. Lawrence began by saying the San Joaquin diocesan standing committee had asked for alternative primatial oversight "and began steps to dissociate from The Episcopal Church."[404] He implied the two were part of the same package. He went on to explain in several paragraphs why leaving the Episcopal Church was good for the diocese and, curiously enough, for the Episcopal Church. Without using the word, he called the Episcopal Church heretical: "TEC has cast aside scriptural faithfulness (. . .). Even more disturbing is our grave disregard of fundamental Christian doctrines such as the nature of God, the uniqueness of Christ, the integrity and unity of the Spirit's work, and the need of humankind for the redemptive work of the cross—for instance, assuming our sexual proclivities, given by nurture or nature, are, by that fact, necessarily God-given."[405] He added, "The Episcopal Church, in its obsession to be what it has termed inclusive, has excluded the absolute priority of Holy Scripture and the historic continuity of the catholic faith."[406] As for schism doing good for the Episcopal Church, Lawrence opined, "perhaps our Standing Committee's action of dissociation, along with eight other dioceses at present, will demonstrate the seriousness of TEC's dysfunction. I love this Church enough to practice what those in the counseling professions call tough-love."[407] In short, Lawrence clearly implied that schism was better than heresy.

It is interesting to compare Lawrence's two early essays, the first written before he was a nominee, the second after he was a finalist. The audience of his first essay, "Prognosis" was his home diocese of San Joaquin. It first focused on salvation for the Episcopal Church by submission to a unified authority in the Anglican Communion. The audience for his second essay "Dissociation" was no doubt the Diocese of South Carolina. It was a much harsher denunciation of the Episcopal Church as having abandoned traditional faith. It called for dioceses to "dissociate" from the Church as a way to save themselves and the Church. Without using the word schism, the call for schism seemed unmistakable. If a diocese disassociated from the Episcopal Church, it would be leaving the Episcopal Church. Lawrence's words in his two essays spoke for themselves.

In the prepared answers for the clergy and delegates in his walkabout at St. Philip's on 9 September, Lawrence repeated his essay of 23 July defending diocesan "dissociation" from the Episcopal Church almost in its entirety. His views could hardly have been any clearer in his two public essays before his election in 2006. They were certainly plain

403. Lawrence, (the Very Rev.) Mark. "Remaining Anglican: In Defense of Dissociation." July 23, 2006, http://www.deimel.org/church_resources/ml_archive2.htm.

404. Ibid.

405. Ibid.

406. Ibid.

407. Ibid.

to the Episcopal Forum and to half of the Episcopal Church both of which recoiled in dread and fear if not shocked disbelief that the essays' author seriously wanted to be a bishop in a church he had condemned and asserted needed breaking up. Returning to the question of whether there was an agreement between the diocesan power structure and Lawrence that they would hire him to lead the diocese out of the Episcopal Church, there did not need to be any such written or unwritten understanding. All the power structure needed to do was read his two essays "Prognosis" and "Dissociation." Nothing more needed to be said, or even understood. No doubt, they saw Lawrence as their man of the hour; and they validated that in a big landslide election on the first ballot.

The conversations between Lawrence and the Search Committee in his interview on 5–7 June and the Standing Committee in the interview on 6 July were secret. However, there were some bits and pieces of Lawrence's remarks during the nomination process that provided further insight into his presentations and to the two committees. Apparently, the Search Committee gave nominees a questionnaire to fill out with responses ranging from 1-strongly agree, 2-agree, 3-unsure, 4-disagree, to 5-strongly disagree.[408] Some of the questions dealt with homosexuality. One, "There should be room in the Episcopal Church for priests and bishops who accept homosexual conduct as a valid, non-sinful choice;" Lawrence marked "Disagree."[409] Another, "There should be room in the Episcopal Church for priests and bishops who consider homosexual contact a sin;" Lawrence responded "Strongly disagree."[410] Then another, "The church should not divide over this [homosexuality];" Lawrence wrote "Strongly disagree."[411] Having given a clear attitude to homosexuality, Lawrence moved on to a string of questions about schism. In one, "If the Diocese of South Carolina does not become separate in some formal way from ECUSA, I intend to resign my orders as an Episcopal priest;" Lawrence responded, "Unsure."[412] Next came what may have been the most important question on the list: "If the Diocese of South Carolina separates in some formal way from ECUSA, I intend to transfer from this diocese to an ECUSA diocese;" Lawrence wrote "Strongly disagree."[413] By this, he made it clear he would stay with the diocese after a schism. The bishop staying with the diocese would have been reassuring to anyone seeking schism. On a time frame, one question read: "The solution to our problem in ECUSA is time; we should wait and let the fuss die down;" Lawrence answered, "Strongly disagree."[414] On the role in the Church, one question said: "The solution to our problem in ECUSA is for the conservatives to go along and get along (not that big an issue);" on this Lawrence put, "Strongly disagree."[415] Another question was: "As a priest, I should not follow my bishop's direction

---

408. Deimel, Lionel E. "No Consents, A Crucial Test for the Episcopal Church." October 16, 2006, http://www.deimel/org/church_resources/no_consents.htm.

409. Ibid.

410. Ibid.

411. Ibid.

412. Ibid.

413. Ibid.

414. Ibid.

415. Ibid.

when it conflicts with Scripture, traditionally interpreted by the Anglican Church;" Lawrence responded, "Strongly agree."[416]

The questionnaire revealed much about the Search Committee and the nominee. The committee appeared to be greatly interested in finding a candidate with a highly negative view of homosexuality and positive attitude to schism. Lawrence's answers could have been interpreted easily as condemning equal rights for homosexuals in the Church and supporting the idea of schism from the Church. Again, as with Lawrence's two essays, there did not need to be a written or verbal agreement between the committees and Lawrence because his views on the relationship between a diocese and the Episcopal Church were well known and obviously ultimately very satisfying to the two committees.

Lawrence's clearly stated ideas advocating the "dissociation" of dioceses from the Episcopal Church may have warmed the hearts of the South Carolina diocesan ruling establishment but they sent chills down the spines of those who wanted to keep the Diocese of South Carolina in the Episcopal Church. The Episcopal Forum was most upset even before the election. On 5 September, the group published an open letter in the Charleston *Post and Courier* imploring the Episcopalians of South Carolina to remain faithful to the Church. It pointed out that the diocese had joined a small minority of dioceses in the Anglican Communion Network "that threatens to lead us out of The Episcopal Church."[417] It continued, "Published statements by our diocesan leaders and the three nominees have raised concerns that our new bishop may lead us even further away from union with The Episcopal Church. We pray that in this election the Holy Spirit will unify our diocese and lead it in a ministry of hope and reconciliation."[418] As usual, there was no evidence that the Forum had any effect on the power structure of the diocese.

The Failure to Gain Consents

Once Lawrence was elected by the diocesan convention, the focus of the matter then turned to the consents from the bishops and standing committees of the Episcopal Church. Church rules said that 120 days would be allotted to receive the consents once the announcement was sent out. The Diocese of South Carolina sent out the appeal for consents on November 9, 2006. The deadline for returns was set at March 9, 2007. In order to be qualified for consecration, Lawrence would have to receive a simple majority of consents from the diocesan bishops and from the diocesan standing committees of the 111 dioceses. A majority would be fifty-six bishops and fifty-six standing committees.

Even before the announcement went out, alarmed pro-Church forces began campaigning for the bishops and standing committees across the country to reject Lawrence. Campaigns of this sort were certainly neither new nor infrequent in the Episcopal

---

416. Ibid.

417. "Open Letter to Episcopalians in the Diocese of South Carolina." Episcopal Forum of SC, September 6, 2006, http://www.mynewsletterbuilder.com/tools/view_newsletter.php?newsletter_id=1409577888.

418. Ibid.

Church. Easily the most famous of these was the fierce and highly public conservative-led battle to prevent Gene Robinson's confirmation in the General Convention of 2003. As one has seen, Kendall Harmon had been quite active in the movement to prevent the consents for Barbara Harris in 1988. Years earlier there had been another right-wing push to stop the confirmation of John Spong. Harris, Spong, and Robinson had been approved, but there were cases where candidates failed to gain confirmation. In 1875, James DeKoven was rejected for bishop of Illinois, for his Anglo-Catholic views. In 1934, John Torok was turned down by the General Convention.[419] Critics of Lawrence began to rally in hopes of giving the same fate to the new candidate of South Carolina.

The first public offensive in the campaign to stop Lawrence came from Lionel E. Deimel and the group known as Via Media USA. Deimel was a blogger and part of the Progressive Episcopalians of Pittsburgh, a pro-Church faction in the diocese of Pittsburgh which was then, much like South Carolina, in a struggle against the Episcopal Church. The bishop of Pittsburgh, Robert Duncan was head of the Anglican Communion Network, and arguably the leader of the "realignment" movement. On 16 October 2006, Deimel posted a long essay on his blog outlining the details of the case for rejecting Lawrence. On reviewing Lawrence's writings and answers to the questionnaire for nominees, Deimel wrote: "Mark Lawrence is schismatic (believes the church should be divided over views on homosexuality) (. . .) he is prepared to act against both the vows he has already taken and those he would take should he be consecrated a bishop in The Episcopal Church."[420] He continued, "If Lawrence is to be consecrated a bishop in this church, he will be asked to "guard the faith, unity, and discipline of the [Episcopal] Church (. . .) How can he possibly take such a vow unless he renounces the statements he has made about The Episcopal Church?"[421] Deimel concluded: "The consent process does the church a disservice if it cannot prevent consecration of one such as Mark Lawrence. The unity and integrity of The Episcopal Church are at stake, and its resolve is being tested. I pray that we find the courage to do what is right for our church when consent to the consecration of Mark Lawrence is considered."[422]

The day after Deimel's essay appeared, Via Media, the multi-diocesan party to promote unity in the Episcopal Church, to which the Episcopal Forum was related, sent Deimel's article and a letter to every diocesan bishop and another to every standing committee in the Episcopal Church encouraging rejection of Lawrence. Christopher Wilkins, the facilitator of Via Media wrote: "Fr. Lawrence's episcopacy would represent a threat to the unity of our church and to the cohesion of the Diocese of South Carolina (. . .) Fr. Lawrence has endorsed separating the Diocese of South Carolina from the Episcopal Church, and has advocated that the authority of the General Convention be surrendered to the primates of the Anglican Communion."[423]

---

419. In 2009, Kevin Forrester was elected in Northern Michigan, only to fail to get a majority of consents whereupon the presiding bishop declared his election null and void requiring the diocese to elect a new candidate.

420. Deimel, "No Consents."

421. Ibid.

422. Ibid.

423. Ibid.

A few days after Via Media sent out its appeal to every one of the 111 dioceses, the Episcopal Forum sent its own message to every diocesan bishop and standing committee in the Episcopal Church. Although it stopped just short of demanding the rejection of Lawrence, it strongly discouraged giving consent. First, the Forum leaders aired their frustration in influencing diocesan matters: "In our diocesan election process only candidates who had declared themselves ready to sever their ties to The Episcopal Church were on the ballot. Although several more moderate candidates were proposed by both nomination and petition, they were excluded from the election (…) his [Lawrence's] election is being touted in the diocese as a mandate for separation from The Episcopal Church."[424] They continued, "There is a climate of intolerance in this diocese (…) many of us feel spiritually harassed."[425] Finally, the Forum leaders more than suggested rejection: "We question whether a person who repudiates our national Church and is working to replace The Episcopal Church with another organized church structure should be considered qualified to be a bishop in this or any other diocese."[426] Thus, by the time the official call for consents from the 111 dioceses went out on November 9, every diocesan bishop and standing committee in the Episcopal Church had received three appeals for rejection of Lawrence's consecration, from Deimel, Via Media, and the Episcopal Forum of South Carolina.

Mark Lawrence, the one-time champion wrestler, was not a person to be easily thrown and pinned down on the floor. He came back fighting. At some time, perhaps in the few weeks after his election, Lawrence had been sent a list of eight questions from the bishops of Province IV, the southeastern U.S.[427] A few days after Deimel, Via Media, and the Forum had sent out their anti-Lawrence appeals to the bishops and standing committees, Lawrence sent his own counter-letter, on 6 November, to all the bishops and standing committees. He denounced Deimel, not by name, and the Via Media, by name: "a misleading article and letter written by a group which presents itself, wrongly enough, under the noble and historic phrase, *Via Media*."[428] He then gave the eight questions and answers the Province IV bishops had asked him. Number One: "In what ways will you work to keep the Diocese of South Carolina in the Episcopal Church?" Lawrence talked all around the question and did not answer it directly ending with: "I shall commit myself to work at least as hard at keeping the Diocese of South Carolina in The Episcopal Church, as my sister and brother bishops work at keeping The Episcopal Church in covenanted relationship with the worldwide Anglican Communion." What was that supposed to mean? There was no covenant in the Anglican Communion. Number Two, "What would be your response if the convention of the Diocese of South Carolina voted to leave The Episcopal Church?" Lawrence's response was to refuse to answer the question. Number

---

424. "Message Sent to Every Diocesan Bishop and Standing Committee." eNewsletter, Episcopal Forum of SC, October 31, 2006, http://mynewsletterbuilder.com/tools/view_newsletter.php?newsletter_id=1409582337.

425. Ibid.

426. Ibid.

427. "Deposition Transcript—Mark J. Lawrence," 61–65.

428. Lawrence, (the Very Rev.) Mark. To the bishops and standing committees. November 6, 2006, http://www.sarmiento.plus.com/anglican/marklawrenceanswers.html.

Three, "Will the Presiding Bishop be welcome to preside at your consecration?" No. Number Four, "Do you intend to participate fully in attending meetings of the House of Bishops, including Eucharist?" Lawrence gave a conditional answer; he would as long as it was not injurious to his spiritual health. He did not explain what would be "injurious." Number Five, "What is your response to the request of the Standing Committee of the Diocese of South Carolina seeking 'alternative primatial oversight'?" For this Lawrence repeated the answer he gave in the walkabout of 9 September which itself was taken from his June essay tellingly entitled "Remaining Anglican: In Defense of Dissociation." Not surprisingly, Lawrence omitted the title of the essay in this answer. Number Six, "Do you recognize Katharine Jefferts Schori as Presiding Bishop of The Episcopal Church and as your Primate?" In another conditional answer, Lawrence said he recognized her as legitimately elected, but because of her stand on homosexuality she had compromised her ability to function in primatial authority. Number Seven, "Will you uphold the Doctrine, Discipline and Worship of the Episcopal Church as now constituted?" Lawrence said he would as he understood it to be loyalty to the Anglican Communion. Number Eight, "Some further thoughts regarding our present predicament in The Episcopal Church." Lawrence said: "neither the Standing Committee of South Carolina not I have made any plans to leave TEC."[429] This was literally true, but one could argue that South Carolina, in the Anglican Communion Network with its demand for alternative oversight, was consciously moving toward schism. The ACN dioceses demanded foreign oversight, which both the Episcopal Church and the Archbishop of Canterbury had clearly rejected. In that case, the only logical way a diocese could reach foreign oversight was to leave the Episcopal Church for another Anglican province.

The tone and content of Lawrence's answers to the questions from the bishops of Province IV were different from those in his answers to the questions from the Search Committee. To be sure the audiences were not the same. The search and standing committees no doubt sought a bishop who would continue the diocese's well-established adversarial relationship with the Episcopal Church while the Episcopal bishops would naturally want a bishop loyal to the national Church. By way of comparison one can look at similar questions from the Search Committee's questionnaire and the Province IV questions. In the first, the committee asked, "If the Diocese of South Carolina separates in some formal way from ECUSA, I intend to transfer from this diocese to an ECUSA diocese."[430] Lawrence responded, "strongly disagree."[431] Thus, Lawrence stated unequivocally that he would remain with the diocese of South Carolina if it left the Episcopal Church. This, of course, would mean that he too would leave the Episcopal Church since he could not remain an Episcopal bishop of a non-Episcopal diocese. In the other set of questions, the bishops asked the same question in other words, "What would be your response if the convention of the Diocese of South Carolina voted to leave The Episcopal Church?"[432] Lawrence responded, "I don't think that speculative questions of this nature as to what a person will do in some imagined future are either reasonable or helpful.

429. Ibid.
430. Deimel, "No Consents."
431. Ibid.
432. Lawrence, To the bishops and standing committees.

I mean no disrespect by this, but I will say in all fairness, I can think up many such questions of an imagined future crisis that could send any of us into a conundrum of canonical contradictions."[433] In effect, Lawrence refused to answer the question that he had had no hesitancy about answering boldly in the Search Committee questionnaire. One can only imagine that if Lawrence had given the bishops the same response he had given the search committee to the same question, he would have seriously diminished his chances of getting the necessary consents.

Lawrence sent his letter and answers to the eight questions to all the bishops and standing committees of the Episcopal Church. He did not send any of the material he had submitted to the Search Committee and Standing Committee in the search process, only answers he had given to bishops outside of South Carolina. If one looks at his responses to the questions from Province IV, one can see a pattern of avoiding direct answers. When Lawrence did answer a question, he couched his response in conditional terms. He did not promise directly to stay in the Episcopal Church or to keep the diocese of South Carolina in the Episcopal Church. Soon thereafter, Lionel Deimel published on his blog, "The Annotated Mark Lawrence," a point-by-point minutely detailed critique of Lawrence's letter and answers. It was a piercing review that was freely available for everyone to read on the Internet.[434] Thus, it remained to be seen in November of 2006 whether Lawrence would win over a majority of the bishops and standing committees in a church where so many people questioned his loyalty.

Apparently, the diocesan leadership assumed Lawrence's consents were simply *pro forma* and would produce a comfortable majority within a few weeks. They confidently set Lawrence's consecration date at 24 February 2007. It was to be held in the Summerall Chapel of the Citadel military college in Charleston. In the week before that, there were to be several celebratory events marking the transition from one bishop to another. On 16 February, there was to be a festival coral Evensong at St. Michael's of Charleston followed by a gala dinner in honor of Bishop Salmon in the historic Hibernian Hall of Charleston. On 18 February, there was be a Solemn Mass of Thanksgiving at the Church of the Holy Communion in Charleston. The Rev. Jennie Olbrych chaired the episcopal transition planning committee.[435]

The diocesan plans for an early consecration proved to be far too optimistic. Two months after the diocese had sent out the notice of consent, on 9 November, to all of the Church dioceses, there were signs that Lawrence's approval was in serious trouble. Neither the bishops nor the standing committees had given a majority consent. In fact, numerous dioceses had announced their opposition. The standing committee of the Diocese of Kansas perhaps spoke for these dioceses in its blunt rejection:

> Lawrence refuses to commit to keeping his diocese within the Episcopal Church (. . .). A vow to conform to the doctrine and guard the faith and unity of the Episcopal Church cannot be conditioned by a candidate for bishop on doing so only if the Episcopal Church conforms to his beliefs (. . .). A bishop of the

---

433. Ibid.

434. Deimel, Lionel E. "The Annotated Mark Lawrence." December 16, 2006, http://www.deimel.org/commentary/annot_ml.htm.

435. "Hail and Farewell." *Jubilate Deo* (Diocese of South Carolina), December 2006/January 2007.

> Episcopal Church cannot precondition his or her acceptance of the authority of the Presiding Bishop on whether the Presiding Bishop conforms to certain beliefs of that bishop (. . .) we must withhold our consent (. . .) we are not satisfied that he will 'conform to the doctrine, discipline and worship of the Episcopal Church' and 'guard the faith, unity and discipline of the Church.'[436]

In its rejection, the standing committee of the Diocese of Bethlehem said,

> Lawrence's own words suggest rather that he would work with those who would expel the Episcopal Church from the Anglican Communion. We do not see how Father Lawrence can claim to promise to uphold the doctrine, discipline and worship of the Episcopal Church. He would see himself as a bishop of the Anglican Communion and not of the Episcopal Church. However, we are in the Anglican Communion by virtue of our being a part of the Episcopal Church.[437]

In the Diocese of Newark, the Rev. Elizabeth Kaeton, head of the diocesan standing committee later wrote that her committee rejected Lawrence because of "'The deep concern and, indeed, conviction (not fear) that Mark Lawrence, as bishop, would lead the Diocese of So. Carolina away from the Episcopal Church, was seen as sufficient impediment on account of which he ought not be ordained to that Holy Order.'"[438]

After two months' time and with the consents of a majority of bishops and standing committees nowhere in sight, the diocesan Standing Committee decided to postpone the plans they had made for the consecration until after Easter. At home in Bakersfield, Lawrence, perhaps sensing impending defeat, began the blame game in a long and prickly letter to his parish on 12 January 2007. He accused some in the Church of being hypocritical when it came to him: "I do suspect, however, that some have changed their position regarding this matter [consents] as it applies to me—holding one position when it applied to a bishop-elect who held their position on issues, and quite another now."[439] Was he implying a double standard, that some would defend one controversial candidate, Gene Robinson, yet reject another, himself? He continued, "Frankly, I find it ironic that those of my generation who were so quick to trumpet the need for nonconformity when they were opposed to the 'establishment' are most ungracious towards those whom they think do not conform now that they are holding the reigns [sic] of power."[440] And, he added, "It gets harder not to come to the sad conclusion that inclusivity in this 'faith community' is becoming more narrowly defined by an exclusivistic agenda."[441] Specifically, Lawrence put blame on Via Media which he called "an advocacy group (. . .) misrepresented several of my written statements and attributed intentions

---

436. "The Episcopal Church Stays Its Course." eNewsletter, Episcopal Forum of SC, January 13, 2007, http://www.mynewsletterbuilder.com/tools/view_mynewsletter.php?newsletter_id=1409588636.

437. Ibid.

438. Medina, Louis. "God's Plan, Episcopal Pastor Extends Pursuit of Bishophood." *Bakersfield Californian*, June 5, 2007, as quoted in Virtueonline, July 6, 2007, http://www.virtueonline.com/portal/modules/news/article.php?storyid=6124&com_id=71049&com_rootid=7103.

439. Lawrence, (the Very Rev.) Mark. "Dear Friends at St. Paul's." January 12, 2007, http://www.virtueonline.org/portal/modules/news/article.php?storyid=5324&com_id=61743&com_rootid6174.

440. Ibid.

441. Ibid.

to me that I did not have. Once this group's mailing muddied the water it has been difficult to settle the pond."[442] Interesting enough, Lawrence did not mention the Episcopal Forum which had also contacted all the dioceses to discourage consents.

As the weeks moved along, it looked more and more as if Lawrence would not receive the consents he needed. In February of 2007, with only a few weeks to go, the Standing Committee announced it was shy of a majority of both bishops and standing committees. According to some reports, Lawrence's advocates within and without the diocese carried on an active campaign with bishops and standing committees to reach the consents. One source said, "Furious lobbying has occurred since the Diocese of South Carolina reported last month [February] that 'yes' votes for consecration had topped out at 46, 10 short of the required 56 needed for a simple majority."[443] Another source said the conservative website "Stand Firm" waged a lobbying campaign.[444] The Rev. Haden McCormick, head of the Standing Committee, later recognized "the many clergy and lay people throughout the world that have worked tirelessly on Fr. Mark's behalf making phone calls and communicating through the electronic media in an effort to secure a majority of consents."[445] Another source reported: "South Carolinians waged a grass-roots campaign that persuaded some committees to change their votes."[446] At some point before 1 March, the presiding bishop added three days to the deadline for consents from the 120 days ending on Friday, March 9, 2007 to 123 days ending on Monday, March 12.

As March arrived, with only twelve days to go, events began to move quickly. On 1 March, the presiding bishop called Haden McCormick to deliver the news that a majority of diocesan bishops had granted their consents.[447] Two days later, McCormick announced that only 46 standing committees had given consents, 10 short of a majority.[448] That meant 65 had not done so. It is interesting to note the dioceses that had, and had not, given consents as of 3 March. Lawrence's strongest support came, not surprisingly,

---

442. Ibid.

443. Levin, Steve. "Episcopal Nominee at Center of Storm." *Pittsburgh Post-Gazette*, March 10, 2007, as quoted in Virtueonline, March 12, 2007, http://www.virtueonline.org/portal/modules/news/article.php?storyid=5662&com_id=66601&com_rootid6660.

444. Deimel, Lionel E. "Deimel on Lawrence's Failed Bid: 'Most Episcopalians Relieved.'" March 15, 2007, http://deimel.org/commentary/mistmt.htm.

445. McCormick, (the Rev.) J. Haden. "Election of Mark Lawrence to be Bishop of the Diocese of South Carolina Ruled Null & Void." March 15, 2007, as quoted in eNewsletter, Episcopal Forum of SC, http://mynewsletterbuilder.com/tools/view_newsletter_id=1409595388.

446. Parker, Adam. "Ex-candidate for Bishop Asks Members to Choose." *The Post and Courier* (Charleston, SC), March 17, 2007, as quoted in Virtueonline, March 17, 2007, http://www.virtueonline.org/portal/modules/news/article.php?storyid=5696&com_id=66935&com_rootid=6693. See also: "Mark Lawrence Plays the Victim." Episcopal Café, March 17, 2007, www.episcopalcafe.com/mark_lawrence_plays_the_victim.

447. "Diocese of South Carolina: Very Rev. Mark Lawrence Receives Necessary Consents." Virtueonline, March 3, 2007, http://www.virtueonline.org/portal/modules/news/article.php?storyid=5625&com_id=66119&com_rootid=6611.

448. "The Rev. J. Haden McCormick Gives Update on Consent Progress." eNewsletter, Episcopal Forum of SC, March 5, 2007, http://www.mynewsletterbuilder.com/tools/view_nesletter.php?newsletter_id=1409594081.

from Province IV, the southeastern U.S. There, 13 of the 20 diocesan standing committees had consented. His next strongest support was in the southwest, Louisiana to New Mexico, 7 out of 12. His weakest response was from Province I, New York and New England where only 1 of the 7 dioceses had agreed. He was not popular too in his home province, VIII, with just 4 of the 17 dioceses giving consent. The Latin American countries in Province IX were also slow to arrive, with only 3 of 11 giving consent.[449] The worry among the diocesan leaders could not be disguised. Kendall Harmon said, "'This is very big. For the first time in at least 60 years, a bishop is in real danger of not getting consent.'"[450]

If "furious lobbying" was going on, as one account said, perhaps the biggest lobbyist of them all turned out to be Mark Lawrence who made a bold eleventh-hour effort to sway votes. He sent a letter on 7 March addressed to the Episcopal Church standing committees. Absent was combativeness, couching of ideas, convoluted verbosity, and obfuscation. This Lawrence was short, direct, and conciliatory, as in: "Standing Committees, which are earnestly seeking to make a godly discernment."[451] This time, instead of blaming the problem on this or that against him, he cogently identified the overriding question as doubt of his loyalty to the Episcopal Church. To address this, he went straight to the point: "I will make the vows of conformity as written in the BCP and the Constitution and Canons (III.11.8). I will heartily make the vows conforming 'to the doctrine, discipline, and worship' of the Episcopal Church, as well as the trustworthiness of the Holy Scripture. So to put it as clearly as I can, my intention is to remain in The Episcopal Church."[452] Yet, if one read the words carefully, one could see that these statements were not unconditional. *I will make the vows.* Making a vow was not the same as keeping a vow. *My intention is to remain.* Intention to remain is not the same as inflexible resolution to remain. It is only an attitude that may change. Thus, it remained to be seen whether this letter would assuage enough fears of disloyalty to bring in the few more consents Lawrence needed to gain a majority.

Judging by the flurry of activity soon thereafter, Lawrence's last-minute letter may indeed have been the turning point. Within two days after the letter appeared, six standing committees sent in their consents, leaving only four short of a majority.[453] One report said that five standing committees changed their "no" votes to "yes": South Virginia, Georgia, Virginia, East Tennessee, and Kentucky.[454] Five other standing committees finally decided their votes would be "yes": Virgin Islands, Ohio, Eau Claire, Central Ecuador, and Honduras. Five days later, on the deadline of Monday, 12 March, it appeared

449. Ibid.

450. Parker, Adam. "Clock is Ticking for S.C. Diocese Bishop-Elect 10 Votes Shy of Needed Majority." *The Post and Courier* (Charleston, SC), as quoted in Virtueonline, March 6, 2007, http://www.virtueonline.org/charleston-sc-clock-ticking-sc-diocese-bishop-elect-10-voted-shy.

451. Lawrence, (the Very Rev.) Mark. "Dear Standing Committees of the Episcopal Church." March 7, 2007, as quoted in eNewsletter, Episcopal Forum of SC, March 7, 2007, http://mynewsletterbuilder.com/tools/view_newsletter.php?newsletter_id=1409594504.

452. Ibid.

453. Levin, "Episcopal Nominee."

454. "South Carolina: Consents at 55, 56 Needed." Virtueonline, March 12, 2007, http://www.virtueonline.org/portal/modules/news/article.php?storyid=5663&com_id=66588&com_rootid=6658.

that a total of fifty-six had arrived, the bare majority necessary. Then, just as the diocesan establishment began to breathe a tentative sigh of relief, the presiding bishop called, on 15 March, to inform McCormick that she had ruled null and void the election of Mark Lawrence to be the next bishop of South Carolina. The problem, she said, was that several committees had made non-canonical, and therefore invalid, electronic submissions and there were not enough properly filed consents to make a majority. The Constitution and Canons of the Episcopal Church clearly directed that a majority of a standing committee must write their signatures on a specified form of consent: "Evidence of the consent of each Standing Committee shall be a testimonial in the following words, signed by a majority of all the members of the Committee: We being a majority (. . .)."[455] Electronic forms were unacceptable because they lacked the signatures as required by the canon. Once its election had been declared null and void, the canons required a diocese to proceed to hold a new election for bishop and the process of consents to begin all over again.

One of the widely-held beliefs in the Diocese of South Carolina before, during, and after the schism was that the Episcopal Church had been unfair to Lawrence, or had treated him badly. Numerous pro-Lawrence witnesses took the stand in the circuit court trial of 2014 to echo the victimization theme. In particular, many people blamed Lawrence's treatment on the visible head of the Episcopal Church, the presiding bishop, Jefferts Schori. It appeared to some people in South Carolina, who suspected her motives, that perhaps she used a petty technicality to block Lawrence from becoming a bishop. Nevertheless, it was obviously true that she had bent the rules in Lawrence's favor by adding three days to the 120 given in the canons. If she had strictly adhered to the 120, she could easily have overruled the election because on that day, 9 March, Lawrence was several votes short of approval even counting the electronic submissions. Jefferts Schori told a reporter, "'I am distressed by the recent failed election in the Diocese of South Carolina. The Rev. Mark Lawrence and his family continue in my prayers, especially at a time that is undoubtedly filled with grief and uncertainty. I grieve as well for the people for the diocese as they seek to continue their transition into a new chapter of leadership.'"[456]

Both Haden McCormick and Bishop Salmon called Lawrence with the news from the presiding bishop. Lawrence testified later that he considered withdrawing from consideration.[457] Apparently, there was a good deal of discussion among the three men about what to do next until everyone agreed to place Lawrence again as the candidate for election. As Lawrence described it later: "They called to talk about where we go from here. And so there's conversations about what to do, what not to do (. . .) And it's a little bit of a circuitous path, but eventually they decide to hold another election and to have me be a part of it."[458]

The reaction in South Carolina to the news of Lawrence's failure to win confirmation ran from relief among the pro-Church minority and their friends to disbelief, shock,

---

455. *Constitution and Canons, The Episcopal Church.* New York: the church, 2006. http:www.episcopalarchives.org/e-archives/canons/CandC_FINAL_11.29.2006.pdf.

456. Medina, "God's Plan."

457. "Deposition Transcript—Mark J. Lawrence," 72.

458. Ibid., 73.

disappointment, anger, resentment, and defiance among the anti-Church majority and their allies elsewhere. The tone for the latter group was set by McCormick in his very first announcement of the news. He said, "Fr. Lawrence has modeled exemplary patience and calmness by enduring a level of scrutiny and persecution that is without precedent in The Episcopal Church (TEC)."[459] *Persecution.* This set the theory that Lawrence had failed not from any fault of his own but from hostile exterior forces. Kendall Harmon continued this theme. He said the Episcopal Church had a double standard when it came to conservatives. It was willing to bend far to approve a controversial liberal (Robinson), but not willing to bend for a controversial conservative. Harmon said: "'It speaks volumes that a double standard is used for conservatives, and it is further evidence that conservatives are not leaving, they're being driven out of the Episcopal Church.'"[460] He did not explain how they were being "driven out." The analogy of Lawrence to Robinson was a false one since there was never any question of Robinson's loyalty to the Episcopal Church.

Retired bishop Allison, then well-known for his defiance of Church rules, suggested going farther than just complaining about matters. He said the diocese should proceed and consecrate Lawrence anyway regardless of the Episcopal Church Constitution and Canons: "'I respect him [Lawrence] for doing the canonical thing, but I think he should go ahead and be consecrated anyway.'"[461] He said the Episcopal Church was walking away from the Christian faith; and he threw in its leaders for good measure: "'Schori and David Booth Beers are so embarrassing to The Episcopal Church and worldwide Anglican Communion.'"[462] As for those who withheld consent: "'those who did not give consent elevate the canons above the Christian Faith.'"[463] The obvious problem with consecrating Lawrence anyway was that he would not have been a bishop in the Episcopal Church and therefore in the Anglican Communion.

Apparently, no one was more vocal about Lawrence's rejection than Lawrence himself. When contacted by reporters for his reactions, the scrappy former wrestler shot back against his opponents: "'It's astonishing the way people have flung mud. It's ludicrous what is being portrayed here;'"[464] and, "'People went berserk, people went apoplectic.'"[465] He added, "'They took my structural reflections as a lack of loyalty to the Episcopal Church. That's just nonsense.'"[466] Continuing in a best-defense-is-a-good-offense mode, he said, "'What's happened is that a radicalized group with a political agenda has been exercising its influence on the Episcopal Church over the last 30 years or so, accusing

459. McCormick, "Election."

460. Cooperman, Alan. "Episcopal Church Rejects S.C. Bishop." *The Washington Post*, March 17, 2007, as quoted in Virtueonline, March 17, 2007, http://www.virtueonline.org/portal/modules/news/article.php?storyid=5692&com_id=6691&com_rootid=6691.

461. Kwon, Lillian. "Bishop: Episcopal Church Walking Away from the Christian Faith." *The Christian Post*, March 27, 2007, as quoted in Virtueonline, March 23, 2007, http://www.cirtueonline.org/portal/modules/news/article.php?storyid=5734&com_id=67286&com_rootid=6728.

462. Ibid.

463. Ibid.

464. Parker, "Ex-candidate."

465. Ibid.

466. Ibid.

the orthodox and middle-of-the-road Episcopalians of homophobia and bigotry when certain theological concerns arise."[467] Lawrence told another reporter, "A curtain has been drawn back on the stage of the Episcopal Church, and everyone can now look into what I would call the theater of the absurd."[468] At the same time, the theme of victimization reappeared. A hometown reporter wrote, "Lawrence said there was the grueling questioning by the bishops and standing committees of the 111 dioceses in the Episcopal Church who voted to consent or not to the South Carolina election. Lawrence has called the process 'abuse' and 'harassment.'"[469] The reader was left wondering how and when Lawrence had suffered "grueling questioning," "abuse," and "harassment." As for the future, Lawrence indicated he believed his election was divinely inspired and he should continue to pursue it. He said, "'My position is that it would be wrong for me to remove myself from a process that is a continuation of what began in September. (The South Carolina Diocese) believe the Holy Spirit spoke when I was elected.'"[470] He added, "You cannot walk this path of God's leading without being blessed by it, even if it includes controversy, misrepresentation, rejection. The pathway of suffering is the main road in the Kingdom of God because our Lord walked that way.'"[471] Apparently, since Lawrence believed his election was the work of the Holy Spirit and his defeat was the work of misguided opponents, he saw no need to change his views. The greatest concern causing dioceses to withhold consents had been about Lawrence's loyalty to the Episcopal Church. Apparently not bothered by any such concern, Lawrence told a reporter that, "he wants to find a way to establish a single international church, but one that allows for constituents to preserve a degree of autonomy."[472] In a letter of 22 August to his parish, St. Paul's, Lawrence said, "'I also hold strong convictions on remaining in covenanted fellowship with the worldwide Anglican Communion, rather than following, as some have suggested, the pathway of an overly autonomous provincial or national church.'"[473]

The Success in Gaining Consents

Soon after receiving the news of Lawrence's rejection, on March 15, the diocesan leadership, and Lawrence, resolved that the diocese would hold a new election and seek consents instead of going all the way back to restart the whole search process. Since he had actually been approved by a majority of dioceses on the first try, there was no reason to think he would not gain the requisite consents a second time. But first they had to go through the formalities. On April 17, 2007, the diocesan Standing Committee unanimously passed a resolution to reconvene the meeting of the diocesan convention.

467. Ibid.
468. Cooperman, "Episcopal Church."
469. Medina, "God's Plan."
470. Ibid.
471. Ibid.
472. Cooperman, "Episcopal Church."
473. Schjonberg, Mary Frances. "Episcopal Forum Tells Bishops, Standing Committees of the Concern about Lawrence." Episcopal News Service, September 18, 2007, http://www.spiscopalchurch.org/es/node/191863.

In its last session, on 10 November 2006, the convention had recessed and not adjourned leaving open the possibility that it could be re-convened at any time. On the same day as the Standing Committee resolution, Bishop Salmon sent a letter to all of the clergy of the diocese informing them of the details of the plans for Lawrence's re-election. The convention would resume, he said, on 9 June, and vote on Rule 22 which, if passed by a two-thirds majority would allow the diocese to resume the election process instead of having to start all over with the entire search procedure. The convention would then call for a new election convention in which Lawrence would be voted on again and, if elected, be submitted for the necessary consents.[474]

The 216th meeting of the convention of the Diocese of South Carolina re-convened at St. James Church, on James Island, Charleston, on Saturday, June 9, 2007. The turn-out for the meeting was a big majority but not as many as for Lawrence's election: 87 clergy and 183 lay delegates representing 62 parishes and missions.[475] It was clear that the diocesan leadership wanted to finish quickly so that Lawrence could be reelected and complete the consent process as soon as possible. To do this they had to suspend the rules so that they could call a new election right away instead of having to start the search all over again. The vote to suspend was 82 to 5 in the clergy and 51 to 3 of the local churches in the lay order.[476] The delegates from Grace Church of Charleston, Ted Halkward and Steve Skardon, tried to stop the steamroller but they were drowned out by the likes of Lydia Evans, Kendall Harmon, Anthony Kowbeidu, and Lonnie Hamilton.[477] It was announced that the special convention to elect a bishop would be held on 4 August 2007, at St. James. The diocesan leaders did set up a process by which other names could be submitted by petition with a deadline of July 11. Not surprisingly, no one offered a petition for another candidate. Lawrence's was to be the only name on the ballot of the special convention.

It was clear to everyone that the pro-Church party in South Carolina had been relegated to near-invisibility to the diocesan leadership. Only three churches had voted against the process to push through Lawrence's reelection. The Episcopal Forum became evermore frustrated and critical of the diocesan leaders. Since they had been completely stymied in their efforts to reopen the search, the Forum leaders decided to appeal directly to the national Church. Lynn Pagliardo, president of the Forum, sent a letter to Jefferts Schori, the presiding bishop, and Bonnie Anderson, the president of the House of Deputies in June of 2007. The major concern of the Forum was that the selection process for a new bishop was being controlled by those who "advocated separation unless TEC rescinded certain actions."[478] Pagliardo asked Jefferts Schori to appoint an interim

---

474. Salmon, (the Rt. Rev.) Edward L., Jr. Letter to the clergy. April 17, 2007, as quoted in Episcopal Café, http://www.episcopalcafe.com/lead/dioceses/reelecting_mark_lawrence.html.

475. *Journal of the Two Hundred and Seventeenth Annual Meeting of the Convention, January 25, 2008, St. Paul's Episcopal Church, Summerville.* Charleston, SC: the diocese, 2008, Appendix IX, 145.

476. Ibid.

477. Ibid.

478. Pagliardo, Lynn A. Letter to Katharine Jefferts Schori and Bonnie Anderson, June 2007, http://mynewsletterbuilder.com/tools/view_newsletter.php?newsletter_id=1409605490.

bishop[479] who would respect both the conservative views and the Episcopal Church.[480] As it turned out, the presiding bishop did not appoint an interim bishop and did not interfere with the process going on in South Carolina.

Although the national Church did not get involved in the politics of South Carolina, the Church's Executive Committee did make an important statement on June 15, 2007, which was directed to San Joaquin, Pittsburgh and the other dioceses that were leaning toward leaving the Episcopal Church. This resolution reminded everyone that all diocesan constitutions must give accession to the Constitution and Canons of the Episcopal Church (Article V, Section 1). Therefore, "Any amendment to a diocesan constitution that purports in any way to limit, or lessen an unqualified accession to the constitution of The Episcopal Church is null and void."[481] The dioceses in question responded that the Council had no authority to govern the Church.

The second election of Lawrence was a quick formality since his was the only name under consideration. As in the first case, no nomination would be allowed from the floor. Thus, the special convention that met at St. James Church on James Island on 4 August 2007, generated much less interest that had the first election. A total of 57 parishes and missions were represented, 14 fewer than the first election, 82 clergy instead of 106, and 201 lay delegates rather than 223. Lawrence was promptly reelected with very little dissent. Among the clergy, 78 voted for Lawrence, 2 voted no, and 2 abstained; in the parishes, 43 voted for Lawrence, 3 no, and 1 abstained; for the missions, 7 polled for Lawrence, and 1 abstained. The crowd arose for a standing ovation after which the meeting adjourned.[482]

On 31 August, the Standing Committee sent out the consent forms along with an explanatory letter of the measures the diocese had taken to reelect Lawrence. The 120-day deadline would be 28 December. As before, the Episcopal Forum sent out a letter, on 15 September, to all bishops and standing committees discouraging them from consenting to Lawrence's election but stopping short of an outright appeal for rejection. It concluded: "We question whether a person who has repudiated the polity of our national Church should be considered qualified to be a bishop in The Episcopal Church. Please give our concerns your prayerful attention as you consider your consent to this election."[483]

Very little existed in the public record about the second consent process. In the middle of the process, on September 18, the South Carolina Standing Committee passed a resolution inviting presiding bishop Jefferts Schori to visit the diocese in February of 2008. What connection this had to the consents, or to the refusal to allow her to

479. Since he had retired, Salmon was acting bishop.

480. Ibid.

481. Schjonberg, Mary Frances "Executive Council Resolution on Constitutions Generates Mixed Reactions." Episcopal News Service, June 19, 2007, as quoted in eNewsletter, Episcopal Forum of SC, June 20, 2007, http://www.mynewsletterbuilder.com/tools/view_newsletter.php?newsletter_id=14096054490#article_3.

482. *Journal of the Two Hundred and Seventeenth (. . .)* 2008, Appendix X, 147.

483. "Text of EFSC Letters to Diocesan Bishops and Members of Diocesan Standing Committees." Episcopal Forum of SC, September 14, 2007, http://mynewsletterbuilder.com/tools/view_newsletter.php?newsletter_id=1409617792.

be the chief consecrator for Lawrence, one can only imagine. How much lobbying was done this time, one can only guess. We do know that the properly constructed consents came in rather quickly. Just past the half-way mark of the 120 period for consents, the presiding bishop announced, on 29 October, that the majority of bishops and standing committees had given their consents to Lawrence's election as the next bishop of South Carolina. At long last, the matter was over after almost four years of preparation. South Carolina would have a new bishop to replace the past-retirement Bishop Salmon. Only time would tell whether the new bishop's stated "intention" to remain in the Episcopal Church would hold long term, or whether the Forum, the Via Media, and Deimel had been right all along to oppose his consecration.

Bishop Salmon ended his official role in the Diocese of South Carolina on 26 January 2008, but remained active in the Episcopal Church. After the end of his episcopacy, he served parishes in Maryland and continued sitting on numerous boards of conservative institutions as Nashotah House, where he was chair, the *Anglican Digest*, and the Anglican Communion Institute. From November 2008 to May 2009, he was acting dean of Nashotah House.[484] On 27 June 2011, the board of Nashotah elected Salmon dean and president of the institution, a position he held until 30 January 2015, when the next president, Steven Peay replaced him. Salmon consciously endeavored to improve the relations that had grown badly strained between the highly traditional Anglo-Catholic seminary and the Episcopal Church. In February of 2014, he invited the presiding bishop, Jefferts Schori, to visit and preach at the House. Her appearance in April caused a storm of protest and calls for his resignation, particularly from the parties that had left the Episcopal Church. He was involved in another controversy when complaints from the dioceses of Quincy and Fort Worth were made about Salmon having filed amici briefs in court on the side of those two breakaway dioceses. He was one of nine bishops who signed an Episcopal Church agreement, in March of 2013, expressing regret and promising to stop supporting the secessionist dioceses in court.[485] In Church politics, Salmon remained a conservative participating with the "Communion Partners" to protest the Church's 2012 decision to offer the blessings of same-sex unions and the Church's 2015 resolution to change the canons to allow same-sex marriage. In 2015, he attended the General Convention but not as part of the South Carolina delegation. Salmon refused to support the schism in South Carolina and the work of the breakaway diocese afterwards. Soon after he died on June 9, 2016, at the age of eighty-three, the two parts of the old diocese both claimed him as their own and held separate memorial services, in their respective cathedrals only a few blocks apart in Charleston.

In January of 2008, at long last, Bishop Salmon could make plans to hand over the leadership of the diocese to his successor after almost eighteen years as bishop. In assessing his tenure from 1990 to 2008, one can see remarkable growth in the diocese: baptized membership up 30 percent from 24,221 to 31,559; communicant numbers up

---

484. "Bishop Edward L. Salmon, Jr." Nashotah House, http://www.nashotah.edu/about/393/.

485. "Conciliation Meeting Outcome Announced." Episcopal Church, March 8, 2013, http://www.episcopalchurch.org/notice/conciliation-meeting-outcome-announced ; "Nine Episcopal Bishops Agree to Sanctions for Supporting Breakaway Congregations." *Journal Sentinel* (Milwaukee), March 23, 2013, http://www.jsonline.com/news/religion/nine-episcopal-bishops-agree-to-sanctions-for-supporting.

50 percent from 18,418 to 27,670; and budget income up 60 percent from $1,856,338 to $2,995,289.[486] And, this was in spite of the fact that All Saints of Pawleys Island, one of the largest parishes in the diocese, had left the Episcopal Church in Salmon's term.

The broader question of what difference Salmon made in the diocese was not so easy to quantify. He was quite a contrast to his two predecessors, Temple who was a mainstream, loyal Episcopalian committed to institutional growth and integrity, and Allison who was a doctrinaire theologian committed to ideological purity. Salmon was neither. He can perhaps best be summarized as a pragmatic and conservative Churchman. Since the diocese was already quite conservative when he arrived and continued to move to the right, perhaps he too became more conservative as time went by in order to accommodate the majority of his own diocese. Yet, at the same time, he never advocated schism from the Episcopal Church. This left him in a rather strange position of actively supporting the ultra-conservatives while struggling against schism. As one has seen, he was almost always among the protesting bishops in the wake of one or another controversial action of the Episcopal Church. Too, he was an original bishop of the Anglican Communion Network and pressed the idea of alternative primatial arrangement. Yet, there is no evidence that he saw any of this as being ultimately schismatic. Perhaps he saw all of this protest activity as leverage to influence the Episcopal Church to move back to a more conservative position rather than as a pathway to separation from the Church. He did not support his fellow bishops in their movements toward separation, Schofield, Duncan, Iker, and Ackerman. Moreover, he acted to prevent All Saints parish in his own diocese from leaving the Episcopal Church and from taking the property which under the Dennis Canon belonged to the diocese and the Episcopal Church. He carried out years of litigation against All Saints to preserve the diocesan/Church trust interest in the property. The fact that the effort eventually failed had nothing to do with his role in it.

Regardless of Salmon's intentions, the reality was that he left a diocese that was by far larger and wealthier than ever before and at the same much more conservative than ever before, in fact teetering on the extreme right edge of the Episcopal Church. One could only describe the attitude of the Diocese of South Carolina toward the Episcopal Church at the end of his tenure as adversarial. By 2008, the ancient bonds of affection were severely strained, not quite broken but very near the breaking point. Moreover, he apparently played an important role in choosing as his successor a man whom many people in the Church regarded as an advocate of schism from to the Episcopal Church. Over the many years, Salmon had tried to play a balancing act of loyalty to the Episcopal Church and active support for the elements opposing the Church. In the long run, this proved to be an impossibility. Events overtook him, and, in the end Salmon left the future of the diocese in the hands of people who did not share his sense of diocesan loyalty to the Episcopal Church.

---

486. *Journal of the Two Hundred and First (. . .)* 1991, 247, 126–27; *Journal of the Two Hundred and Seventeenth (. . .)* 2008, 91, 149.

FOUR DIOCESES DECLARE SEPARATION FROM THE EPISCOPAL CHURCH

In spite of the Church's offers of alternate episcopal oversight and in spite of the Anglican Communion Network's publicly stated goal of remaining in the Episcopal Church, in 2007 and 2008, four dioceses voted to leave the Episcopal Church: San Joaquin, Pittsburgh, Quincy, and Fort Worth. South Carolina became the fifth in 2012. The question of the moment is: Why did the fourth reform movement of equality for homosexuals produce diocesan schisms while the first three reform movements of civil rights, women's ordination, and new prayer book had not? All of the earlier ones did cause some Episcopalians to abandon the Church, but only as individuals and parishes. No diocese resolved to leave the Episcopal Church until the fourth movement on homosexuality happened. What was the difference between the fourth reform and the first three? The solution to this problem lies in several factors. In the first place, the issue of homosexuality was different than the earlier three because it operated on two levels, morality and church polity, and interacted differently with separate factions of the Episcopal Church. Conservatives sincerely believed that homosexual behavior was sinful because of the half-dozen references in the Bible that they said condemned homosexual acts. If it were sin, it could not be condoned by the Church in any way such as conferring Holy Orders on practicing homosexuals. Liberals said that homosexuality was morally neutral and the Bible verses referring to homosexuality did not necessarily condemn homosexual acts. To them, it was an issue of human rights. In the end, when the Episcopal Church gave de facto approval of the liberal view, the ultra-conservatives refused to accept the Church's actions. They did not just disapprove, they rejected the validity of the Church's decisions. In the second place, well-funded, well-organized, right-wing activist organizations went to war against the Episcopal Church in its decisions favoring homosexuals. Although dissident Episcopalian organizations had existed through the decades since the 1960s, they did not compare in strength and importance to those of the 1990s, particularly the IRD's off-shoot, the American Anglican Council. It provided the funding, leadership, organization, and facility that cultivated resentment against the Church into something more. In the third place, the issue of homosexuality had a foreign tie that the earlier three did not have. In the 1990s, Third World Anglican primates, particularly in equatorial Africa, began maneuvering in the Anglican Communion to block the approval of rights for homosexuals. They gained a landmark success in the Lambeth Conference of 1998 by getting in its statement on sexuality a condemnation of homosexuality. From then on, the ultra-conservatives in America could count on the support of some powerful allies overseas. As with the organizations, significant foreign support had not occurred in any of the earlier three reform movements. Another factor should be considered too, technology. The computer revolution produced the Internet in 1995. After that, activist elements for any cause found it much easier to spread information, arouse the public, and organize and direct focused interest movements. Again, that was something that had not existed during the first three reforms. Yet another factor that might be considered was the cumulative effect of all the post-Second World War reforms. By the 1990s, Episcopalian conservatives suffered from battle fatigue, or exhaustion. A fourth reform, which just happened to be the most long-lasting (1976–2003), contentious and wearing of all, was too much to bear. The most disgruntled anti-reform pockets of the Church simply quit. It is interesting to note that three of the four dioceses that voted to leave in 2007–08 had also refused to accept one of the three earlier reforms, women's ordination. Yet another theory held the schisms to be backlash of the white, male privileged elite who felt besieged and mortally threatened by the Episcopal Church's social reforms promoting blacks, women, and homosexuals. In a thoughtful essay, Ian Douglas wrote, "The radical transition afoot in the Anglican Communion is terrifying for it means that Anglicans in the West—especially heterosexual, white, male clerics—will no longer have the power and control that they have enjoyed for so long."[487]

What happened in the Episcopal Church between the 1950s and the early 2000s, went much deeper than just favoring or opposing reforms. In a sense, it was a war for the soul of the Episcopal Church. This resulted from a difference in the philosophy of the nature and purpose of religion. The opponents in all four reform movements were committed evangelicals and Anglo-Catholics. By the time the fourth reform movement reached its height in the 1990s and early 2000s, the most partisan elements among the evangelicals and Anglo-Catholics had given up hope that the Episcopal Church would ever return to what they commonly called "orthodoxy." Some of them decided they had to leave the Church that they believed had abandoned the essentials of Christianity, hence the five schisms.

As we have seen, in the 1980s and early 1990s, the Episcopal Church was divided roughly into thirds on the homosexuality issue. One-third opposed recognizing homosexual acts as morally neutral and therefore opposed to granting equal rights in the Church to homosexuals. Among that third, about a third were ultra-conservatives. They accounted for vaguely 10 percent of the Episcopal Church, or a dozen dioceses out of 111. They did not just oppose rights for homosexuals, they refused to accept the validity of the Church's reforms for homosexual persons. They were the irreconcilables; and they appealed to foreign powers in the Anglican Communion to rescue them from the heretical Episcopal Church in what they liked to call the Anglican "realignment" of North America. This began in earnest just after Gene Robinson's confirmation in 2003 as the ultra-conservatives rallied, sent four bishops to Canterbury and set up the Anglican Communion Network. The ultra-conservative cause found new urgency with the election of Katharine Jefferts Schori as presiding bishop in 2006. The ACN dioceses demanded alternative primatial oversight, that is, transferal of their dioceses to a foreign Anglican primate. This was impossible under the Constitution and Canons of the Episcopal Church; and the Archbishop of Canterbury reminded everyone that he could not interfere in a province of the Anglican Communion. The Episcopal Church offered three plans for alternate oversight: the Delegated Episcopal Pastoral Oversight offer of March, 2004; the Primatial Vicar scheme of November, 2006; and the Episcopal Visitors arrangement of September, 2007. The ultra-conservatives flatly rejected all of these plans as they demanded foreign oversight. The various movements in the Anglican Communion

---

487. Douglas, Ian T. "'The Exigency of Times and Occasions' Power and Identity in the Anglican Communion Today." In *Beyond Colonial Anglicanism: The Anglican Communion in the Twenty-First Century*, edited by Ian T. Douglas and Kwok Pui-Ian, 25–46. New York: Church Publishing, 2001.

against the Episcopal Church reforms, as the Windsor Report, had little to no effect on the situation of the ultra-conservatives in the Church. Of the ten dioceses in the Anglican Communion Network, in time, five voted to declare their independence from the Episcopal Church and affiliate with foreign primates in the Anglican Communion. They were the five dioceses that made schism against the Episcopal Church between 2007 and 2012: San Joaquin, Pittsburgh, Fort Worth, Quincy, and South Carolina.

San Joaquin

The first diocese to vote to leave the Episcopal Church was San Joaquin, Mark Lawrence's home diocese. From 1997 to 2007, he was rector of St. Paul's of Bakersfield and a dean under Bishop John-David Schofield (bishop since 1988). He had been long well-established in the diocese when he was elected bishop of South Carolina. San Joaquin, geographically the San Joaquin valley of California, including cities as Bakersfield, Fresno, Modesto, Merced, Porterville, and Stockton, was a relatively small diocese at around seven thousand members in forty-eight local churches. However, it had an outsized importance as one of the most conservative dioceses in the Episcopal Church, one of only three of 111 dioceses that refused to ordain women to the priesthood. Bishop Schofield's leadership might be summed up in an observation of a witness to Schofield's public presentation on the eve of his election: "When Bishop Schofield entered our room, his first words were, 'I want you to know three things: I am against abortion, I am against the ordination of women, and I am against the ordination of homosexuals.'"[488] Upon becoming bishop in 1988, Schofield moved into the most conservative section of the Episcopal Church. For instance, he was one of the ten bishops to deliver the Presentment against Righter in 1996.

Plans for leaving the Episcopal Church were well underway at least by 2005. On 7 March of that year, Bishop Schofield met the clergy of the diocese for a discussion of future plans. According to one of the clergymen present: "Bp. Schofield indicated that the separation might happen as soon as in a few months or at least by General Convention 2006. He assured us that the switching sides (understood as the [Anglican Communion] Network taking the place of the Episcopal Church) would happen by next year."[489] He continued, "He told us that the decision needs to be made (i.e. we need to make the decision to leave behind the Episcopal Church and align ourselves with the Anglican Communion) because the split is already here."[490] Then, the bishop told the clergy that they and their churches would have to choose whether they would stay with the diocese.[491] It should be recalled that the Very Rev. Mark Lawrence was the dean of the Bakersfeild deanery.

---

488. Jennings, Richard. "Have Some Madera." In *Hurt, Joy, and the Grace of God: A Resurrection Story of the Episcopal Diocese of San Joaquin, California*, edited by Jane Onstad Lamb, 43–54. New York: Applecart Books, 2012.

489. Matters, (the Rev.) Richard. "Notes from a Verbal Report Given by the Rt. Rev. John-David Schofield to the Clergy of the Diocese of San Joaquin on March 7, 2005." http://www.viamediausa.org.

490. Ibid.

491. Ibid.

The next year, the diocese began its action to break from the Episcopal Church. On April 8, 2006, Schofield and the diocesan council petitioned "the Orthodox Primates of the Anglican Communion, the Archbishop of Canterbury and the Anglican Consultative Council to recognize the Diocese of San Joaquin 'as a constituent member of the Anglican Communion (. . .) without relying on subsidiary recognition from or through ECUSA.'"[492] The diocesan standing committee affirmed this action on 24 June 2006.[493] While the majority of the diocese moved along, a minority of clergy and communicants organized to remain faithful to the Episcopal Church. By 2004, a group called Remain Episcopal had formed in the diocese. It eventually established a chapter in Bakersfield.[494]

With the diocesan leadership on board, Schofield prepared for the first vote on realignment. In the fall of 2006, he sent a letter to the diocese ahead of the annual meeting of the convention: "We have a commitment from the Southern Cone (Archbishop Greg Venables) that the bishops of his dioceses are open to our joining their Province (. . .) The Diocese could be in the vanguard of a new 39th Anglican Province in North America. At present, there are seven or more dioceses lined up behind us waiting to follow our leadership example."[495] On seeing this, the new presiding bishop sent Schofield a stern warning: "I have seen reports of your letter (. . .) which apparently urges delegates to your upcoming Diocesan Convention to take action to leave the Episcopal Church (. . .) such action would likely be seen as a violation of your ordination vows (. . .) I must strongly urge you to reconsider the consequences."[496] On 2 December 2006, the diocesan convention overwhelmingly passed resolutions removing all references to the Episcopal Church. Schofield said, "'This amending process is the first step in the removal from our constitution of any reference to the Episcopal Church because, in our opinion, they have decided to walk apart from the Anglican Communion.'"[497] To become official, the changes would have to be passed a second time, at the next diocesan convention.

At the time of the San Joaquin diocesan vote to secede from the Episcopal Church, Mark Lawrence, a dean of the Diocese of San Joaquin, had already been elected in South Carolina, the forms for consent had been sent, and everyone was awaiting his confirmation by the dioceses. Lawrence's first election occurred before San Joaquin's first vote, in 2006, to secede. The next year, in August of 2007, when he was reelected, there was no record that anyone asked him about his vote in the San Joaquin secessionist convention

---

492. Schofield, (the Rt. Rev.) John-David. "A Pastoral Letter to the Diocese of San Joaquin." July 12, 2006, http://www.americananglican.org/a-pastoral-letter-to-the-diocese-of-san-joaquin.

493. Ibid.

494. Vivian, Tim. "Growing with Grace." In *Hurt, Joy, and the Grace of God: A Resurrection Story of the Episcopal Diocese of San Joaquin, California*, edited by Jan Onstad Lamb, 143–47. New York: Applecart Books, 2012.

495. Schofield, (the Rt. Rev.) John-David. "A Message from your Bishop about the 47th Annual Convention." As quoted in eNewsletter, Episcopal Forum of SC, November 21, 2006, http://www.mynewsletterbuilder.com/tools/view_newsletter.php?newsletter_id=1409584140.

496. "The Presiding Bishop of ECUSA Made Public a Letter that she sent to the Bishop of San Joaquin." eNewsletter, Episcopal Forum of SC, November 21, 2006, http://www.mynewsletterbuilder.com/tools/view_newsletter.php?newsletter_id=1409584140.

497. Goodstein, Laurie and Carolyn Marshall, "Episcopal Diocese Votes to Secede from Church." *The New York Times*, December 3, 2006, http://www.nytimes.com/2006/12/03/us/03episcopal.html.

of December of 2006. However, he expressed his attitude on the topic clearly in the two essays he published supporting "dissociation." Later, after San Joaquin's second, and final, vote in December of 2007, in which he did not participate, Lawrence was asked what his vote would have been. He refused to answer. Thus, when Lawrence became the bishop of South Carolina he left a diocese, in the leadership of which he was involved, that had spent several years moving to separate itself from the Episcopal Church. On 8 December 2007, the San Joaquin diocesan convention voted 70 to 12 in the clergy and 103 to 10 in the laity to remove all references to the Episcopal Church.[498] The Diocese of San Joaquin voted to join the province of the Southern Cone. Schofield enforced this in January of 2008 when he demanded the resignation of six of the eight members of the standing committee because they had not publicly confirmed their adherence to the Southern Cone.[499] Mark Lawrence apparently transferred his canonical residence to South Carolina just weeks before the San Joaquin vote to leave the Episcopal Church.

The Episcopal Church took action immediately. On 11 January 2008, Presiding Bishop Jefferts Schori issued an official inhibition to Schofield restricting him from exercising the office of bishop. On March 1, 2008, Schofield resigned from the House of Bishops. On March 12, he was deposed from the office of bishop by action of the House of Bishops. On March 29, a special convention of the Episcopal Church diocese met to reorganize the diocese of San Joaquin after the exodus of the majority and elected Jerry Lamb as bishop provisional. The Episcopal Church's Executive Council allocated $700,000 in aid to the diocese. Bishop Lamb went on to depose the sixty-one clergy who had remained with Schofield to affiliate with Southern Cone.[500] Lamb was followed as provisional bishop by Chester Lovelle Talton, 2011–2014, and David Rice, 2014–. The secessionist group took the name the Anglican Diocese of San Joaquin. Schofield was succeeded as bishop by Eric Menees in 2011. In 2009, this diocese transferred from Southern Cone to the newly formed Anglican Church in North America.

Of all the five dioceses that voted to leave the Episcopal Church, the litigation around that of San Joaquin has been the most favorable to the Episcopal Church. Episcopal Bishop Lamb brought suit against Anglican Bishop Scofield in the Superior Court of California, County of Fresno, Judge Adolfo Corona. The judge held a hearing on 5 May 2009, and issued an Order on 21 July 2009, finding all in favor of the Episcopal Church side.[501] Corona said, "It is beyond dispute that the Episcopal Church is a hierarchical church."[502] He pointed out that the diocesan accession to the constitution and canons of the Episcopal Church was binding and that the diocese had no right to counteract

---

498. McCaughan, Pat. "San Joaquin Votes to Leave Episcopal Church, realign with Southern Cone." Episcopal News Service, December 8, 2007, http://archive.episcopalchurch.org/79425_92524_HTM.htm.

499. "Schofield Fires Most of San Joaquin Standing Committee." Episcopal Café, January 20, 2008, http://www.episcopalcafe.com/schofield_fires_most_of_san_joaquin_standing_committee.

500. "Episcopal Diocese of San Joaquin," Wikipedia, http://en.wikipedia.org/wiki/Episcopal_Diocese_of-San_Joaquin.

501. "Order on Plaintiffs' Motion for Summary Adjudication." Superior Court of California, County of Fresno, No. 08 CECG 01425, July 21, 2009, http://episcopaldiocesefortworth.org/assets/20090721-Legal-San-Joaquin-Order-Motion-Summary-Adjudication.pdf.

502. Ibid., 5.

that. A diocese could not on its own leave the Church. Lamb was the only legal bishop of the diocese; and the Episcopal diocese was entitled to the legal rights and assets of the diocese.

Schofield appealed this decision to the Fifth Court of Appeals in Fresno. On 11 November 2010, that court overturned Judge Corona's 21 July 2009 Order directing that the dispute must be judged under neutral principles where the court would decide the property issues under the appropriate laws with the two sides being treated equally. The case was remanded to the Superior Court. The Episcopal diocese went to the Superior Court, Fresno County, and asked for a summary judgment to bypass another trial. On March 7, 2013, Judge Jeffrey Y. Hamilton, Jr. held a hearing, and denied the request on 25 April 2013. The trial was held 6–13 January 2014 in the Superior Court of California, Fresno County, with Judge Donald S. Black presiding. The highlight of this trial was a videotaped deposition of Schofield, who had died in October of 2013. Judge Black issued his "Tentative and Proposed Statement of Decision," on May 5, 2014.[503] This was the strongest defense of the Episcopal Church side in all the post-schism litigation in the United States. Black wrote:

> Diocesan bishops are at all times subject to and bound by the Church's Constitution, Canons and Book of Common Prayer. None of these documents authorizes a diocesan Bishop to waive, to declare null and void, or modify or amend any of the Church's Constitution and Canons. In fact, both Article 8 of the Church's Constitution and the ordination service in the Book of Common Prayer obligate every member of the clergy, as a condition of ordination, to subscribe to the written "declaration of conformity."[504]

Moreover, Black rejected the idea a diocese could leave the Church: "Because a diocese is a geographical construct of the Church, it makes no sense that a diocese can 'leave' the Church."[505] In the end, Black ruled that the property belonged to the Episcopal diocese. In April of 2015, the Anglican diocese appealed Black's decision to the California Fifth Court of Appeals in Fresno. The Episcopal diocese went back to Judge Black and asked him to enforce his decision on returning the property. Black denied the motion on 16 April 2015, leaving the Anglican diocese in occupation of the properties for the moment. The appeals court heard presentations on March 9, 2016, and issued a unanimous opinion on April 5, 2016, upholding the lower court's judgment that found all in favor of the Episcopal diocese.[506] On April 20, 2016, the Anglican diocese petitioned the appeals court for a rehearing. On 4 May, the court denied the petition. On May 13, 2016, the Anglican diocese petitioned the California Supreme Court for review of Judge Black's decision of May 5, 2014. On July 13, 2016, that court denied the review thus ending eight years of litigation. Black's decision stood as the final word. Bishop Menees of the

---

503. "Tentative and Proposed Statement of Decision." Superior Court of California, County of Fresno, Case N. 08 CECG 01425, May 5, 2014, https://b89fb00bc7de3e5ff5b5-4bbf770es9398b05660cd4f2df22548.ssl.cf2.rackcdn.com/TentativeDecision.pdf.

504. Ibid., 5

505. Ibid., 26.

506. "Opinion," Court of Appeal of the State of California, Fifth Appellate District, F070264, April 5, 2016.

Anglican diocese acknowledged the legal defeat and announced the imminent return of the properties in question to the Episcopal diocese.

Meanwhile there were separate cases of litigation of local properties in the diocese as several local churches were ordered back to the Episcopal diocese. In the scope of this book, the most important of these was Mark Lawrence's old parish of St. Paul's of Bakersfield. In February of 2013, the Superior Court of Kern County, Judge Sidney P. Chapin, ruled that St. Paul's and St. Michael's churches belonged to the Episcopal diocese and ordered the Anglican occupants to vacate.[507] Anglican bishop Menees decided not to appeal on account of expense.[508] Two house churches in Bakersfield, Grace and St. Brigid's, combined to make a home in St. Paul's holding a festival Eucharist on 28 July for over two hundred people. The theme of the day was inclusion.[509] The Anglican congregation moved out of St. Paul's facilities, took the name of Trinity Anglican Church, and began meeting at St. John's Lutheran Church on Buena Vista Road in Bakersfield. On December 3, 2014, Mark Lawrence ordained his son Joseph there. The parish church of St. Paul's, that Mark Lawrence had served for ten years, returned to the Episcopal Church after five years away.

Pittsburgh

The second diocese to vote to leave the Episcopal Church was Pittsburgh which, as San Joaquin, also had strong ties to Mark Lawrence. Lawrence had been rector of St. Stephen's, McKeesport, in the Diocese of Pittsburgh, from 1983 to 1997. It should be recalled that Greg Kronz, the chair of the South Carolina Bishop's Search Committee, had also served in Pittsburgh when Lawrence was there. Too, it was Kronz's search committee that asked Alden Hathaway, bishop of Pittsburgh 1981–1997, to contact Mark Lawrence in May of 2006 soliciting his application to be bishop of South Carolina.

One should recall too that it was the Diocese of Pittsburgh that conservative leaders, as the future bishop, Fitz Allison, had chosen for the location of their new evangelical seminary, in 1976, that settled in Ambridge. Trinity Episcopal School for Ministry rapidly became the most important center in the country for the training of distinctively conservative evangelical clergy, many of whom wound up in South Carolina. Mark Lawrence was an early graduate. After Hathaway became bishop in 1981, the diocese of Pittsburgh followed a path strikingly similar to that of Allison's South Carolina, taking an increasingly critical attitude towards the Episcopal Church, particularly on the issue of homosexuality. In this, the young priest Mark Lawrence played a small, but not insignificant part in the Diocese of Pittsburgh.

---

507. Cox, John. "Episcopal Church Regains Control of Two Buildings; Some Anglicans Must Move." *Bakersfield Californian*, May 12, 2013, http://www.bakersfieldcalifornian.com/local/x1891153851/Episcopal-Church-regains-control-of-two-buildings.

508. Ibid.

509. McCaughan, Pat. "Inclusion, Diversity Mark Homecomings for San Joaquin Churches." Episcopal News Service, August 13, 2013, http://episcopaldigitalnetwork.com/ens/2013/08/13/inclusion-diversity-mark-homecoming-for-san-joaquin-churches.

The evangelical and conservative Bishop Hathaway led the Diocese of Pittsburgh in an increasingly hostile posture *vis à vis* the Episcopal Church, but it was his successor, Robert Duncan, who effectuated the schism in Pittsburgh. Hathaway appointed Duncan canon to the ordinary, that is, assistant to the bishop, in 1992. In the process to choose a bishop to replace Hathaway, Duncan was not named a candidate by the nominating committee, but was nominated from the floor in the 2 December 1995 convention and elected bishop coadjutor on the third ballot carrying 61 of 102 votes among the clergy and 100 of 169 among the lay delegates.[510] He became the sole bishop of Pittsburgh on 13 September 1997. Within the next few years, the Diocese of Pittsburgh would count about twenty thousand baptized members in seventy-four local churches.

As we have seen in the previous pages, Duncan was from the start one of the most important, if not the most important, of the Episcopal bishops promoting what is known as the "Anglican realignment" in North America, the movement that incubated the schisms. After the American Anglican Council formed in 1996, Duncan became actively involved in it and head of its bishop's committee. He was the predominant bishop in the opposition to Gene Robinson in 2003. He presented the protest statement against Robinson's affirmation in the House of Bishops and led a walkout at that time. After the Robinson vote, Duncan spearheaded the movement to secure foreign primatial oversight going, with several other bishops, to the Archbishop of Canterbury and helping draw up the papers that led to the formation of the Anglican Communion Network, with himself as the head, or, "Moderator." At the same time, his associate, Geoffrey Chapman, a priest in Duncan's diocese, issued the so-called Chapman Memo, the blueprint for schism from the Episcopal Church. Duncan officially denied he wanted a schism; however, he refused every Episcopal Church offer of oversight, continued making the impossible demand of foreign oversight, built up ties with foreign bishops some of whom had cut off communion with the Episcopal Church after Robinson, and hosted the big Hope and a Future conference in Pittsburgh in November 2005 that made clear the cause of schism.

By 2002, Bishop Duncan and the majority of the diocese were in the process of differentiating the diocese from the national Church. In March of that year, the convention of the Diocese of South Carolina passed a resolution condemning the Church for its supposed move toward the neutralization of language for the Trinity and acts favoring homosexuals as well as enforcing the right of women to be ordained in the Episcopal dioceses. The resolution said South Carolina would nullify the acts of General Convention it considered to be contrary to "the Faith once delivered." The diocesan leadership in Pittsburgh resolved to follow this and, in the summer of 2002, began circulating "Resolution One" that was virtually the same as that of South Carolina. Duncan called it a "fire wall" to protect the "orthodox" against the errors of the national Church. It sailed through with large majorities among the clergy and laity at the diocesan convention on November 2, 2002.[511] A group formed to oppose the action. First called Those Opposed to Resolution One, it evolved into Progressive Episcopalians of Pittsburgh. By 2004,

---

510. Bonner, Jeremy. "Called Out of Darkness Into Marvelous Light, A History of the Episcopal Diocese of Pittsburgh, 1750–2006" 377. Published, Eugene, OR: Wipf and Stock, 2009.

511. "'Firewall' Resolution Passes in Pittsburgh." Episcopal News Service, November 5, 2002, http://episcopalarchives.org/cgi-bin/ENS/ENSpress_release.pl?pr_number=2002-255.

PEP took the lead in established a network of Church loyalists in conservative dioceses, called Via Media. The Episcopal Forum of South Carolina was part of this.

By the start of 2003, the eve of the Robinson affair, Pittsburgh, as South Carolina, was well established in its posture of hostility to the national Church, particularly on the issue of homosexuality. At the start of the year, the two dioceses were strikingly similar, but by the end of the year this was to change. The major factor in the different tracks of the two was property. In South Carolina, the diocese faced an impending major defection, All Saints of Pawleys Island. Bishop Salmon was resolved to apply the Dennis Canon to keep All Saints from leaving the diocese with the property in hand. While South Carolina railed out against the national Church it also promoted the Church's policy on property. Not so in Pittsburgh. Following the Robinson vote in 2003, Duncan called a special diocesan convention on 27 September. The meeting passed several controversial resolutions, the most important of which declared that all local parish property belonged to the parishes and not to the diocese or the Episcopal Church, a direct rejection of the Dennis Canon. When the South Carolina special convention met a few days later, there was no proposal on property so as not to encourage the teetering All Saints to bolt the diocese with the property. This is where the two dioceses parted. Pittsburgh voted to revoke the Dennis Canon. South Carolina's own vote to remove the Dennis Canon came six years later, after the diocese had exhausted litigation trying to enforce it against All Saints in state courts.

While most communicants in Pittsburgh supported Duncan, there remained a sizeable and resolute minority opposing his schismatic moves. A large and important parish on the pro-Church side, Calvary Church of Pittsburgh, decided to take legal action immediately against the resolutions passed in the special convention.[512] On 24 October 2003, Calvary filed a suit in the Court of Common Pleas of Allegheny County Pennsylvania to prevent the officers of the diocese from transferring any property in violation of the constitution and canons of the Episcopal Church. St. Stephen's of Wilkinsburg soon joined the suit. Duncan continued undeterred. The diocesan convention of 7 November 2003 passed a resolution declaring local sovereignty over the national Church, a virtual declaration of independence. This was reaffirmed by another vote in the next annual convention of November 2004. Calvary Church's court case came to a settlement on 14 October 2005, just before the diocesan convention, in a "Stipulation" agreement between Calvary and Duncan approved by Judge Joseph James. It said: "Property (. . .) held or administered by the Episcopal Diocese of Pittsburgh of the Episcopal Church (. . .) shall continue to be so held or administered by the Diocese regardless of whether some or even a majority of the parishes in the Diocese might decide not to remain in the Episcopal Church."[513] It went on to revoke specifically Resolution 6, on property, passed by the special convention of 27 September 2003, and to set up a structure for mediation for parishes wishing to leave the Episcopal Church. This "Stipulation" of 14 October 2005

---

512. See especially, a first-hand narrative of Calvary's case by the church's rector, (the Rev. Dr.) Harold T. Lewis, *The Recent Unpleasantness: Calvary Church's Role in the Preservation of the Episcopal Church in the Diocese of Pittsburgh.* Eugene, OR: Wipf and Stock, 2015.

513. "Stipulation by Counsel." In the Court of Common Pleas of Allegheny County, Pennsylvania, Civil Division, No. GD-03–020941, October 14, 2005.

was to be the crucial point in the history of Pittsburgh's schism because, as subsequent judicial decisions showed, it settled once and for all the legal issues of property, and did so in the interest of the Episcopal Church diocese.

Once again, the "Stipulation," as Calvary's initial lawsuit, apparently had no effect on Duncan's actions against the national Church. On 29 December 2006, he registered with the Commonwealth of Pennsylvania a new corporation under the name of "Episcopal Diocese of Pittsburgh" without mentioning the General Convention.[514] The pro-Church parties, as the Progressive Episcopalians of Pittsburgh, took action too. "In early 2007 members interested in staying in the Episcopal Church had begun meeting in Maryland with the Province III officers and representatives of the presiding bishop. PEP organized the meetings."[515] "Independently, the legal team of Calvary joined with some members of this group to file a presentment in 2007 against Bishop Duncan for abandoning the Communion."[516]

According to Duncan, the final factor in his decision to leave the Episcopal Church came in March of 2007 when the House of Bishops, meeting in Camp Allen, Texas, completely and adamantly rejected the Dar es Salaam proposal of a month earlier to give foreign bishops the right to intervene in the Episcopal Church. The Anglican Communion Network bishops demanded foreign oversight, but the Episcopal Church steadfastly refused that and offered only schemes within the Church. Duncan said he returned from Camp Allen to Pittsburgh and told the diocesan leaders he could no longer stay in the Episcopal Church.[517] At the next convention, on 2 November 2007, the diocese passed resolutions removing accession to the constitution and canons of the Episcopal Church, 109–24 among the clergy and 118–58 among the laity.[518] Meanwhile, the Episcopal Church Title IV Review Committee had been considering the materials the loyal Episcopalians of Pittsburgh had presented against Duncan. On 15 December 2007, the Committee certified to the presiding bishop that Duncan had abandoned the Church by open renunciation of its Doctrine, Discipline, and Worship.[519] The three senior bishops of the Church had the right to place an "inhibition" on Duncan suspending him for all official duties but chose not to do so.[520] On 15 January 2008, Jefferts Schori, the presiding bishop, informed Duncan of the certification and asked him for confirmation, within two months, of his loyalty to the Episcopal Church. Duncan sent a letter back to Jefferts Schori on 14 March 2008 denying all of the charges against him.

514. "Anglican Diocese of Pittsburgh," Wikipedia, http://en.wikipedia.org/wiki/Anglican_Diocese_of_Pittsburgh.

515. Gundersen, Joan R. "A History of the Episcopal Church in the Diocese of Pittsburgh." March 12, 2013, http://www.episcopalpgh.org/archives/resources/history/.

516. Ibid.

517. Rodgers, Ann. "Bishop Robert Duncan is Trading Sacred Places." *Pittsburgh Post-Gazette*, June 21, 2009, http://www.post-gazette.com/local/region/2009/06/20/Bishop-Robert-Duncan-is-trading-sacred-places.

518. "Episcopal Diocese of Pittsburgh," Wikipedia, http://en.wikipedia.org/wiki/Episcopal_Diocese_of_Pittsburgh.

519. House of Bishops, Task Force on Property Disputes, "Memorandum, September 5, 2008." http://standfirminfaith.com/media/Duncan_Task_Force_Memo_9.5.08.pdf.

520. The first diocesan vote, in 2007, to disaffiliate would become official only by a second vote, in 2008.

The Episcopal Church Task Force on Property Disputes examined a great deal of information on Duncan's actions in Pittsburgh. On September 5, 2008, it presented a report to the House of Bishops concluding: "Bishop Duncan has very carefully planned and executed a strategy to remove the Episcopal Diocese of Pittsburgh, as well as its assets and the assets of its parishes sympathetic to his viewpoints, from TEC. At this point, there is no doubt that Bishop Duncan has left The Episcopal Church."[521] On 18 September 2008, the House of Bishops voted to depose Duncan, 88 in favor, 34 against, and 4 abstaining.[522] Jefferts Schori followed up and issued a formal deposition, or removal of ordination and office, of Duncan effective on 20 September 2008. "The Standing Committee [of Pittsburgh] then hired Duncan as a consultant and continued plans for the October 3–4, 2008 convention."[523] On 4 October 2008, the diocesan convention voted a second and final time to remove accession to the constitution and canons of the Episcopal Church. The vote: clergy, 121 yes, 33 no, 5 abstain; laity, 110 yes, 69 no, and 3 abstain.[524] The convention also voted to join the Anglican province of the Southern Cone, based in Buenos Aires, Argentina. On 7 November 2008, Duncan was again elected bishop of the "realigned" diocese that took the name of the Anglican Diocese of Pittsburgh In October of 2009.

The Episcopal Diocese of Pittsburgh immediately reorganized with some help from the national Church. Within four days of the diocesan vote on "realignment," the Standing Committee was reformed around one remaining member, the Rev. James Simons, and many diocesan offices were filled. A special convention met 11–12 December 2008 with twenty-seven congregations represented and reorganized the Church diocese. Robert Johnson served as the first assisting Bishop, replaced in 2009 by provisional bishop Kenneth Price. In 2012, Dorsey McConnell became the new diocesan bishop.[525]

The Anglican side lost no time in organizing too. On 1 December 2008, the Anglican Communion Network, which had been set up in January of 2004 with Duncan as "Moderator," and allied groups met in Wheaton, Illinois, to create a new entity to call itself the Anglican Church in North America. It brought together the four secessionist groups from the Episcopal Church and many independent bodies[526] to form a constitution and canons and to declare itself a(n) [Anglican] "province."[527] On 21 June 2009, Duncan was elected as the first archbishop of the ACNA and was consecrated shortly

---

521. Ibid.

522. "Duncan Deposed." Episcopal Café, September 18, 2008, http://www.episcopalcafe.com/lead/bishops/duncan_deposed.html.

523. Gundersen, "History."

524. Mandak, Joe. "Pittsburgh Diocese Votes to Split from Episcopal Church." Associated Press, in *USAToday*, October 6, 2008, http://usatoday30.usatoday.com/news/religion/2008-10-06-episcopal-divided_n.htm.

525. Gundersen, "History."

526. American Anglican Council, Anglican Coalition in Canada, Anglican Communion Network, Anglican Mission in the Americas, Anglican Network in Canada, Convocation of Anglicans in North America, Forward in Faith, North America, Missionary Convocation of Kenya, Missionary Convocation of the Southern Cone, Missionary Convocation of Uganda, Reformed Episcopal Church.

527. It sometimes called itself a province in formation or a province in transition. It has not been recognized as a province of the Anglican Communion.

thereafter by several Anglican primates who had been the core of the formation of the Global Anglican Futures Conference (GAFCON) in July of 2008. GAFCON recognized ACNA as the legitimate Anglican province in North America and made Duncan a member of its primates' council. In 2014, Duncan retired as archbishop to be followed by Foley Beach. In January of 2016, Beach attended, but did not vote, in the Anglican primates' gathering in Canterbury. In their communiqué at the meeting, the primates referred any application of ACNA for membership in the Anglican Communion to the Anglican Consultative Council and advised the ACC against admitting ACNA to the Communion. After that, there would be little chance ACNA would ever be a province of the Anglican Communion. On 7 November 2015, Duncan announced his retirement as bishop of the Anglican Diocese of Pittsburgh effective June 30, 2016. On April 23, 2016, a diocesan convention elected the Rev. James Hobby, rector of an Anglican church in Thomasville, Georgia, bishop over the leading local candidate the Rev. Jonathan Millard.[528] Before the vote, Duncan warned the assembly that the ACNA College of Bishops probably would not confirm the choice of Millard since he was divorced. Under ACNA rules, the College of Bishops must confirm a diocesan election of a bishop by a two-thirds vote. Millard led the voting on the first two ballots; Hobby won on the fifth ballot.

The litigation between the Episcopal and Anglican dioceses of Pittsburgh moved along and ended relatively quickly. In January of 2009, the Anglican diocese made a motion in the Court of Common Pleas essentially claiming the property. By then the Episcopal diocese and the Episcopal Church had joined Calvary Church in its legal action to get the "Stipulation" of 2005 enforced. On 6 October 2009, Judge Joseph James of the Court of Common Pleas, Allegheny County, ruled that the October 14, 2005, "Stipulation," which he had overseen, had clearly required that all property remain with the Episcopal Church diocese.[529] On January 29, 2010, Judge James issued his final order directing the Anglican side to turn over all of the assets of the old diocese to the Episcopal diocese.[530] The Anglicans appealed James's decision to the state appeals court, called the Commonwealth Court of Appeals, on 9 November 2010; and on 2 February 2011, the Court completely affirmed James's decision.[531] In March, it rejected the Anglicans' request for a rehearing. That same month, the Anglican diocese appealed to the Pennsylvania Supreme Court. On October 17, 2011, that Court denied the appeal thereby ending the litigation in state courts and leaving Judge James's 2009 decision as the law. The Anglican diocese decided not to appeal to the United States Supreme Court. The key to it all had been the "Stipulation" of October 14, 2005, in which Duncan had agreed that the Episcopal Diocese would own the property. Unfortunately for him, the Episcopal diocese he had in mind was not the same one the courts recognized.

Not all of the local parishes turned over their properties to the Episcopal diocese and vacated. Indeed, the court actions did not settle the question of the fifteen ACNA

---

528. "Holy Spirit Stirring in ACNA Pittsburgh Diocese?" Episcopal Café, April 25, 2016, http://episcopalcafe.com/holy-spitit-stirring-in-acna-pittsburgh-diocese/.

529. Lewis, *Recent Unpleasantness*, 95.

530. Gundersen, "History."

531. Lewis, *Recent Unpleasantness*, 96.

parishes that held sole title to the properties. These may still wind up in court.⁵³² Some ACNA congregations did vacate the properties the courts had awarded to the Episcopal diocese, but seven refused to do so and continued to occupy the premises.⁵³³ Some other parishes returned to the Episcopal Church. Trinity Cathedral in Pittsburgh, which had allowed use by both parties, became the Episcopal cathedral only in 2011. Other churches returned to the Episcopal diocese: St. John's of Donora, Church of the Atonement of Carnegie, St. Michael's of Wayne Township, Church of the Good Shepherd of Hazelwood, and Church of the Advent of Brookline.⁵³⁴ In 2015, the Episcopal Diocese of Pittsburgh listed 34 local churches with 8,688 members.⁵³⁵ The Anglican Diocese of Pittsburgh reported in its annual journal of 2014 around 40 local churches in Pennsylvania (and several outside the state) with a total membership of 7,937.⁵³⁶ In their 2015 journal, they reported 6,929 members, of which 5,765 were in the churches within the territory of the old diocese of Pittsburgh.⁵³⁷

Quincy

The Diocese of Quincy was created in 1877 in the western region of the state of Illinois. With just 2,200 members in 2008, it was one of the smallest dioceses of the Episcopal Church. Originally based in Quincy, the cathedral seat was relocated to St. Paul's of Peoria in 1963. Known for its Anglo Catholic tradition, the diocese was one of only three in the Episcopal Church that had not ordained a woman to the priesthood by 2008 although it had two female deacons before the schism.⁵³⁸ In 1994, Keith Lyon Ackerman became the bishop of Quincy. A native of McKeesport, Pennsylvania, he had been rector of St. Mary's of Charleroi, Diocese of Pittsburgh, from 1976 to 1989, during which time he befriended Mark Lawrence, rector in nearby McKeesport from 1983 to 1997. Known for his devotion to Anglo Catholicism, Ackerman was at one time president of Forward in Faith, "known for its opposition to the ordination of women as well as to liberal Anglican views on homosexuality,"⁵³⁹ as well as superior-general of the Confraternity of the Blessed Sacrament. He was also a member of the Society of King Charles the Martyr, the Guild of All Souls, the Society of Mary, and the Society of Our Lady of Walsingham.⁵⁴⁰ Under Ackerman's guidance, Quincy actively participated in the movement of ultra-

---

532. Gundersen, Joan R. Email message to author, September 22, 2016.

533. Ibid.

534. Ibid.

535. Ibid.

536. *Convention Journal, One Hundred Forty-Ninth Annual Convention of the Anglican Diocese of Pittsburgh, November 7 & 8, A.D. 2014*. Pittsburgh: the diocese, [2015?], 122. The membership figures include several congregations outside of Pennsylvania.

537. Gundersen, email to author.

538. "Episcopal Diocese of Quincy," Wikipedia, http://en.wikipedia.org/wiki/Episcopal_Diocese_of_Quincy.

539. "Keith Ackerman," Wikipedia, http://en.wikipedia.org/wiki/Keith_Ackerman.

540. "Diocese of Quincy (ACNA)," Wikipedia, http://en.wikipedia.org/wiki/Diocese_of_Quincy_(ACNA).

conservative dioceses that rejected Gene Robinson's affirmation as bishop and set up the Anglican Communion Network pressuring for alternate primatial oversight and the creation of a replacement church in America.

The schism in Quincy was several years in the making. In the aftermath of the Robinson matter, Quincy joined the Anglican Communion Network, but that did not result in the alternate oversight the ultra-conservatives sought. The election of a woman, Katharine Jefferts Schori, as presiding bishop in 2006, spurred a renewed demand for alternate oversight, particularly among the traditionally Anglo Catholic dioceses, as Quincy. The Diocese of Quincy called an urgent special convention, on 16 September 2006. The majority of the diocese declared they were unwilling to accept the leadership of the new presiding bishop and passed resolutions asking for oversight from another Anglican primate, condemning the Church's actions favoring homosexuals, and withdrawing from the local province and the General Convention of the Episcopal Church.[541] Two years later, Ackerman resigned as diocesan bishop effective November 1, 2008. On 7 November 2008, the annual meeting of the Synod (diocese) voted to revoke the diocese's accession to the Constitution and Canons of the Episcopal Church, to withdraw from the Episcopal Church, and to join the Anglican Province of the Southern Cone. Of the 22 local churches, 18 followed the schism with about 1,400 of the original 2,200 members. Four congregations resolved to remain with the Episcopal Church, the largest being the cathedral of St. Paul in Peoria. Episcopalian minorities formed in 4 of the departing churches, and another church was formed bring to 9 the total of local congregations remaining with the Episcopal Church.[542]

The Episcopalians set up a Committee to Reorganize the Diocese of Quincy on 13 December 2008. Keith Whitmore, assistant bishop of Atlanta served as temporary consulting bishop. On 4 April 2009, a special convention met at St. Paul's of Peoria to elect John Clark Buchanan, retired bishop of West Missouri, as the provisional bishop. On 1 September 2013, the Episcopal Diocese of Quincy merged into the Diocese of Chicago to become a deanery.

In July of 2009, Ackerman wrote to presiding bishop Jefferts Schori that he would serve as a bishop in the Diocese of Bolivia, in the Province of the Southern Cone. On 7 October 2009 Jefferts Schori sent a letter to Ackerman: "'As you know, there is no provision for transferring a bishop to another province. I am therefore releasing you from the obligations of ordained ministry in this Church.'"[543] That same day, the presiding bishop issued an official "Renunciation of Ordained Ministry and Declaration of Removal and Release," in which she declared that Ackerman was "removed from the Ordained Minis-

---

541. Schjonberg, Mary Frances. "Episcopal Diocese of Quincy Seeks Alternative Oversight." Episcopal News Service, September 19, 2006, http://archive.episcopalchurch.org/3577_77919_ENG_HTM.htm.

542. "Chicago, Quincy Choose Unity." *The Living Church*, June 8, 2013, http://livingchurch.org/chicago-quincy-choose-unity. As of 2013, the Episcopal congregations in the Diocese of Quincy were: All Saints of Moline, St. John's of Kewannee, Grace of Galesburg, St. Paul's of Peoria, St. James of Lewistown, St. George's of Macomb, St. Paul's of Warsaw, St. James of Griggsville, and Bread of Life Fellowship of Peoria.

543. "Quincy: Presiding Bishop Accepts Keith Ackerman's Renunciation." Episcopal News Service, October 16, 2009, http://archive.episcopalchurch.org/81803_115631_ENG_HTM.htm.

try of this Church (. . .) and is deprived of the right to exercise the gifts and spiritual authority as a Minister of God's Word and Sacraments conferred on him in Ordination."[544] Unlike Schofield and Duncan before him, Ackerman was not deposed by the House of Bishops. The presiding bishop interpreted his statement of July as his voluntary and written renunciation of ministry. Since neither Schofield nor Duncan had renounced their ministries, their cases had to be decided by vote of the House of Bishops.

Litigation between the secessionist diocese and the Episcopal Church began almost immediately after the schism of November 2008. Legal actions concerning Quincy took place in five main stages over the next six years. In the first part, in January of 2009, attorneys for the national Church asked bankers of the National City Bank for a freeze on the diocesan funds of $3,579,778.[545] The bankers agreed. A few weeks thereafter, on 30 March 2009, the majority group, Diocese of Quincy (hereafter DOQ), filed suit in the local circuit court seeking recognition of ownership of the assets. The Episcopal Church side (hereafter TEC) filed a counter claim and motion for judgment in its favor on 3 March 2010. Judge Thomas Ortbal, of the Eighth Judicial Circuit Court, Adams County, Illinois, took up the case, received voluminous written material, and held a hearing on 14 November 2011. In the meantime, three retired Episcopal bishops submitted an affidavit to Judge Ortbal's court. Former South Carolina bishop Edward Salmon was one of the three.[546] They "asserted opinions regarding the polity of the church adverse to the interests and legal positions of the Episcopal Church."[547] On 16 December 2011, Ortbal issued his "Opinion and Order" on the case denying TEC's motion for a summary judgment. He rejected TEC's argument that the Church was shown to be conclusively hierarchical and the court should defer to it. He directed a proceeding under "neutral principles" where the two sides would be regarded neutrally under local property laws.[548] The first stage of litigation ended by favoring the secessionist side.

The second stage of litigation was a trial and judgment in 2013. Formal trial began in Ortbal's courtroom in Quincy, in April. It proceeded on April 9–10, 22–26, 29–30, May 1–2, and ended with closing arguments on June 25. This was the first full, formal trial concerning the right of a diocese to secede from the Episcopal Church with eleven witnesses and about 15,000 pages of evidence. Court trials in San Joaquin and South Carolina would come the next year. This trial was the model that the lawyers used for the South Carolina trial that occurred in July of 2014. One of the lawyers for DOQ was Alan Runyan who was the lead lawyer for the South Carolina secessionist side. After considering a great deal of material, Judge Ortbal issued his written decision on 6 September

---

544. "Renunciation of Ordained Ministry and Declaration of Removal and Release." October 7, 2009, http://www.episcopalchurch.org/files/attached-files/ackerman_letter.pdf.

545. "Opinion," Appellate Court of Illinois, Fourth District, Appeal from Circuit Court of Adams County, No. 09MR31, July 24, 2014, 2.

546. Bruce MacPherson, formerly of Western Louisiana, and Peter Beckwith, formerly of Springfield, were the other two.

547. "Accord." As quoted in "Fort Worth, Quincy: Conciliation Meeting Outcome Announced." Episcopal Church, Office of Public Affairs, March 8, 2013. http://episcopaldigitalnetwork.com/ens/2013/03/08/conciliation-meeting-outcome-announced.

548. "Opinion and Order." Circuit Court of the Eighth Judicial Circuit, Adams County, Illinois, Case N. 09-MR-31, December 16, 2011.

2013. In it, he rigidly adhered to a strict constructionist approach to the questions at hand. Among his main points were: the Episcopal Church's Constitution and Canons did not explicitly create a clear hierarchy, the General Convention had no explicit right to exercise authority over the dioceses, and there was no explicit provision to keep a diocese from leaving the Church. He dismissed the power of the Dennis Canon to create an explicit trust in property. He claimed that TEC's claims could not be substantiated because they were not explicitly spelled out. Following neutral principles and regarding the two sides equally, he said he had no choice but to find all in favor of DOQ. This was a sweeping, stunning, and explicit legal victory for the secessionist diocese and for the right of dioceses to leave the Episcopal Church with the legal rights and property in hand.

A few days later, on September 20, TEC filed a motion for a stay of Ortbal's judgment pending an appeal. This would keep the bank deposits frozen. On 9 October 2013, Judge Ortbal issued his "Final Order and Judgment" directing that all assets were owned by DOQ and that the National City Bank must release the first one million dollars while holding the rest pending TEC's appeal.[549] Objecting to the million dollars being released to DOQ, TEC went immediately to the Illinois Fourth District Court of Appeals, in Springfield, and got an emergency stay once again freezing all the bank funds pending the appeal. Friends of DOQ put out a call for contributions for the legal expenses to be made to a fund managed by the American Anglican Council.[550]

This led to the third step in litigation, the appeal. TEC filed an appeal of Judge Ortbal's decision with the Illinois Court of Appeals, Fourth District, in Springfield, on October 15, 2013. At the same time, TEC went to the Tenth Judicial Circuit Court, in Peoria, asking for a judgment to return local properties to TEC, particularly St. George's of Macomb, Grace of Galesburg, Trinity of Rock Island and Christ Church of Moline.[551] The Fourth District Appeals Court ruled on July 24, 2014, giving complete affirmation to Judge Ortbal's decision of 6 September 2013. The appeals judges agreed that it could not be demonstrated conclusively that the Episcopal Church was hierarchical and that following neutral principles, the court would have to side with the duly incorporated DOQ. This was another resounding victory for DOQ and for the secessionist cause. Two major, and sweeping, decisions in a row all but wrapped up the litigation in Illinois. However, there was still the state supreme court.

The fourth stage of litigation was TEC's appeal to the Illinois Supreme Court. Having failed in the circuit and appeals courts, TEC made a formal petition to the state supreme court, but on 26 November 2014, that court denied the request leaving the appeals court as the final word, with disposition set as December 31, 2014.[552] The high-

---

549. "Final Order and Judgment." Circuit Court of the Eighth Judicial Circuit of the State of Illinois, Adams County, No. 09-MR-31, October 9, 2013.

550. Haley, Allan S. "Quincy Funds Frozen Again; Defense Funds Need Help." October 29, 2013, http://accurmudgeon.blogspot.com/2013/10/quincy-funds-frozen-again-defense-fund.html.

551. "Episcopal Diocese of Chicago and the Episcopal Church File Suit in Peoria." Episcopal Diocese of Chicago, November 6, 2013, http://www.episcopalchicago.org/our-stories/2013/11/06/diocese-and-episcopal-church-file-suit-peoria.

552. "Order." Circuit Court of the Eighth Judicial Circuit of the State of Illinois, Adams County, No. 09-MR-31, October [9], 2013.

est state court's refusal to take the Church case seemed to mean the end of the course of litigation in the state courts of Illinois. But this turned out to be not quite the case.

In fact, there was yet another, a fifth stage in the litigation of Quincy. On 30 December 2014, TEC attorneys sent a letter to the National City Bank claiming that $774,599 of the diocesan funds belonged to TEC and should remain frozen.[553] To counter this, DOQ entered a motion for judgment with the Eighth Circuit Court, in Quincy, to enforce Judge Ortbal's and the Appeals Court's rulings. Judge Mark Drummond held a hearing on February 17 and issued a written "Order" on February 20, 2015, in which he sternly reprimanded the TEC lawyers. He ordered them in no uncertain terms to "cease and desist" in any and all attempts to modify the judgments in the two earlier decisions, Ortbal's and the Appeals Court. To press his point, Drummond ordered TEC to pay DOQ's legal fees after December 30, 2014, the date TEC contacted the bank.[554] Drummond issued his final order in this case on 20 February 2015. The Church side appealed it to the Fourth District Appellate Court of Illinois. On May 13, 2016, this court issued its decision entirely affirming Drummond's order.[555]

Retired Episcopal bishops Salmon, Beckwith, and MacPherson's affidavit to Judge Ortbal's circuit court on 6 October 2011, supporting the anti-Episcopal Church side created a backlash in the Quincy Episcopal diocese. As one will see, in the litigation concerning Fort Worth, three active and four retired bishops also submitted a brief in aid of the schismatic diocese and against the Episcopal Church. Likewise, there was a reaction among the Episcopal Church party there. In Quincy, the Episcopal diocesan Standing Committee made a complaint to the national Church against the three retired bishops following Canon IV.10 of the Constitution and Canons of the Episcopal Church and were joined by the Standing Committee of the Episcopal Church diocese of Fort Worth. For Quincy, the complainants were clergy: James Clement, Robert Dedmon, and John Blossom, and laity: Tobyn Leigh, Christine Barrow, and Janna Haworth.[556] Following the canon, Church officials convened a private conciliation meeting for the contending parties in Richmond, Virginia, on 8–9 January 2013. As a result, an "Accord," was drawn up which the parties on the two sides signed. Item Four of the Accord stated that the bishops in question expressed regret for any harm they may have done in litigation; and Item Five said the bishops agreed not to file any more court papers against the Episcopal Church, at least for the time being.[557] It was interesting to note that South Carolina retired bishop Salmon was the only bishop who had taken part in the legal actions against the Episcopal Church in both Quincy and Fort Worth and thus was the only bishop reprimanded in both cases. Although the reconciliation meeting was secret, the Accord itself was released to the public on March 8, 2013.

---

553. Ibid.

554. Ibid.

555. "The Diocese of Quincy v. The Episcopal Church." In the Appellate Court of Illinois Fourth District, May 13, 2016, http://www.illinoiscourts.gov/Opinions/AppellateCourt/2016/4thDistrict/4150193.pdf.

556. "Accord."

557. Ibid.

The six years of litigation between the Diocese of Quincy and the Episcopal Church ended in 2015 with a complete and total victory for the independent diocese. By applying a strict interpretation approach, both the circuit court and appeals court judges ruled that the Constitution and Canons of the Episcopal Church did not create a hierarchical church, that dioceses may function independently under state corporate laws, that the Dennis Canon did not create an explicit trust for the Church, and that neutral principles can be applied to settle the issues. Following these guidelines, the judges found the entire settlement to be favorable to the local diocese. It was all the ultra-conservatives could have wished for.

Since Illinois was the first state to settle the issue of the Church-diocesan relationship in court, advocates of local rights were quick to declare the Illinois decisions to be the precedent for the whole nation. Pennsylvania had been settled early on and was not contested in a court trial. The San Joaquin, Fort Worth, and South Carolina cases were still working their ways through the systems when the Illinois courts handed down their final judgments in 2014 and 2015. However, Illinois turned out to be not the precedent for the country that the anti-Episcopal Church party hoped for. In San Joaquin, the appeals court decision in April of 2016 stated clearly that the Illinois court decisions concerning the Church-diocesan tie had no bearing on California courts since the cases and state laws were not identical. In fact, the San Joaquin court decisions turned out to be the exact opposite of the Illinois ones. The difference was that Illinois judges insisted on a narrow interpretation of the law while California judges followed a much broader approach. Thus, although they followed the same neutral principles guideline, two state court systems arrived at seemingly contradictory judgments on the same issue, the relationship between the Episcopal Church and its dioceses. Illinois judges declared neutral principles compelled them to rule entirely for the breakaway diocese while the California judges said neutral principles led them to side unequivocally with the national Church.

Fort Worth

The fourth diocese in which the majority voted to leave the Episcopal Church was Fort Worth, in Texas. The Diocese of Fort Worth, covering the twenty-four counties around the city of Fort Worth, was created in 1983 from the Diocese of Dallas. Both dioceses had a tradition of Anglo Catholicism. Before the schism, the Diocese of Fort Worth counted 55 local churches with about 19,000 members. The Rt. Rev. Jack Iker became Bishop Coadjutor in 1993 and Diocesan Bishop in 1995. As bishops Schofield of San Joaquin and Ackerman of Quincy, Iker was known for his devotion to conservative Anglo Catholicism. These three bishops were to remain the only three diocesan bishops to refuse to ordain women to the priesthood. And, as the others, Iker was actively involved in the highly conservative associations such as Forward in Faith and the American Anglican Council.[558] He, too, was the predominant power in his diocese. Writing soon after the schism, one reporter said, "He runs his diocese with an iron hand and has packed it

---

558. "Biographical Sketch of the Rt. Rev. Jack Leo Iker." http://www.fwepiscopal.org/bishop/biography.html.

full of traditionalists who think like he does; some of his congregations are so uniformly conservative, in fact, that his opponents refer to them as 'Ikerpalians.'"[559]

As San Joaquin, Pittsburgh, and Quincy, Fort Worth played an integral part in the so-called "Anglican Realignment" movement that gained force in the Episcopal Church after the affirmation of Gene Robinson as a bishop in 2003. As one has seen, Bishop Iker arose in the House of Bishops on the day after Jefferts Schori was elected presiding bishop to appeal to the Archbishop of Canterbury for alternate primatial oversight for his diocese. It did not happen because there was no provision for such an arrangement in the Episcopal Church Constitution and Canons and the Archbishop had no authority to intervene in an independent province of the Anglican Communion. As one has seen too, the ultra-conservatives spurned all the offers of the Episcopal Church to provide alternate oversight within the structure of the Church. They demanded oversight from a foreign primate, something the Episcopal Church would not and could not allow. Meanwhile, a pro-Episcopal Church group formed called Via Media Fort Worth.

As San Joaquin, Pittsburgh, and Quincy before it, the diocese of Fort Worth began preparing to declare its own alternative primatial oversight. In the fall of 2007, the proposed resolutions for the upcoming diocesan convention circulated. They called for the first of two passages to change the diocesan constitution and canons to remove affiliation from the Episcopal Church. A few days before the convention, presiding bishop Jefferts Schori sent a letter to Iker warning him that if he proceeded with the resolutions, she would be compelled to consider whether he had abandoned the communion of the Episcopal Church.[560] To this, Iker immediately dispatched a fiery reply to the presiding bishop railing against her "attempt to interfere in the internal life of this diocese" sprinkling his remarks with words such as "threatening," "misuse," "intimidate," "manipulate," "aggressive," "dictatorial," and "threats."[561] Jefferts Schori sent Iker another letter on 9 January 2008, after the diocesan convention had passed the first round of resolutions to leave the Episcopal Church. Once again, she warned Iker that encouragement of the diocesan convention to pursue such resolutions would be a violation of his ordination vows.[562] Apparently, Iker did not respond to the presiding bishop but he did issue a statement to the diocese complaining about her "threats of dire consequences if we don't comply with the party line."[563]

Jefferts Schori's warnings of "dire consequences" had no effect on the movement in Fort Worth to leave the Episcopal Church. Meanwhile, Church loyalists began to organize to keep ties with the national Church. On January 15, 2008, Sam Hulsey, the retired bishop of Northwest Texas (1980–1997), hosted a meeting in his Ft. Worth home for the

559. Gwynne, S.C. "Bishop Takes Castle." *Texas Monthly*, February 2010, 4, http://www.texasmonthly.com/story/bishop-takes-castle.

560. Jefferts Schori, (the Most Rev.) Katharine. Letter to (the Rt. Rev.) Jack Iker, November 8, 2007, http://www.fwepiscopal.org/bishop/bishoppbreply.html.

561. Iker, (the Rt. Rev.) Jack. Letter to (the Most Rev.) Katharine Jefferts Schori, November 12, 2007, http://www.fwepiscopal.org/bishops/bishoppbreply.html.

562. Jefferts Schori, (the Most Rev.) Katharine. Letter to (the Rt. Rev.) Jack Iker, January 9, 2008, http://www.standfirminfaith.com/media/schori010908.pdf.

563. Iker, (the Rt. Rev.) Jack. "A Message from Bishop Iker." January 18, 2008, http://www.fwepiscopal.org/bishop/message010908.html.

clergy of the diocese who wanted to remain in the Episcopal Church.[564] Another group of diocesan clergy, apparently with the blessing of Iker, went to the Roman Catholic bishop of Ft. Worth in the summer of 2008 to discuss ways in which the diocese could unite with the Roman Catholic Church. Nothing came of these talks.[565] Preparations moved ahead for the second, and last, passage of resolutions removing the diocese from the Episcopal Church. The resolutions passed in the diocesan convention meeting of 14–15 November 2008 at St. Vincent's Cathedral in Bedford. The vote was 72–19 in the clergy and 102–25 in the laity.[566] As the three earlier secessionist dioceses, the convention voted to align with the Anglican Province of the Southern Cone.

The Episcopal Church acted immediately. In fact, the Title IV Review Committee started reviewing the Iker case on August 26, 2008. Five days after the convention vote, that Committee met and found by majority vote that the Rt. Rev. Jack Iker had abandoned the communion of the Episcopal Church. The next day, November 21, 2008, Jefferts Schori officially inhibited Iker from exercising the office of bishop. Three days later, Iker issued a public statement in which he and the Standing Committee rejected the presiding bishop's authority and announced they had left the Episcopal Church for another province.[567] On December 5, 2008, the presiding bishop issued an official "Renunciation of Ordained Ministry and Declaration of Removal and Release," accepting Iker's renunciation of the ordained ministry in the Episcopal Church and removing him from the rights of office in the Church.[568] In a subsequent letter to the House of Bishops, Jefferts Schori explained why she handled the Iker case differently than those of Schofield and Duncan. Schofield and Duncan had been removed by deposition of the House of Bishops but Iker was removed by action of the presiding bishop. She said it was mostly a matter of timing. The Bishops met shortly after the Schofield and Duncan cases arose. With Iker, however, it would be months before the Bishops would meet and in the interim the Episcopalians in Fort Worth would be unable to fill the vacant diocesan offices. Thus, she said she moved quickly in order to facilitate the continuity of the Diocese of Fort Worth.[569]

The Episcopal Church's reorganization of its diocese did indeed move quickly. Soon after removing Iker, Jefferts Schori declared the diocesan Standing Committee vacant and called a special convention that was held at Trinity Church, in Fort Worth, on February 7, 2009. Twenty-three clergy attended as well as 62 lay delegates from 31 of the 55

564. Ibid.

565. "Fort Worth Requests Union with Roman Catholic Church." Episcopal Café, August 11, 2008, http://episcopalcafe.com/fort_worth_requests_union_with_roman_catholic_church.

566. "Episcopal Diocese of Fort Worth (ACNA)," Wikipedia, http://en.wikipedia.org/wiki/Episcopal_Diocese_of_Fort_Worth_(ACNA).

567. "Responses to Attempted Inhibition of the Bishop." November 24, 2008, http://www.fwepiscopal.org/downloads/reFortWorthBishopinhibition.pdf.

568. "Renunciation of Ordained Ministry and Declaration of Removal and Release," December 5, 2008. http://www.episcopalchurch.org/files/attached-files/12-5-08_jack_iker.pdf.

569. Jefferts Schori, (the Most Rev.) Katharine. "Presiding Bishop Katharine Jefferts Schori's Letter to the Episcopal Church's House of Bishops." n.d. http://archivesepiscopalchurch.org/documents/ELO_120508_KJSHPBletter.pdf.

congregations.[570] Jefferts Schori presided over the meeting that chose the Rt. Rev. Edwin "Ted" Gulick, Jr. as bishop provisional and filled the vacant offices. In time, Wallis Ohl, Rayford B. High, Jr., and J. Scott Mayer also served as bishops provisional. As of 2016, the Episcopal Church diocese listed seventeen local churches and thirty-six mission stations and about eight thousand members. The Anglican diocese listed about forty local churches within the old diocesan boundary and a dozen beyond. Both dioceses continued using the name and insignia of the Episcopal Diocese of Fort Worth. In 2009, the secessionist Episcopal Diocese of Fort Worth was a founding member of the Anglican Church in North America with Jack Iker continuing as its bishop.

Litigation between the two dioceses began soon after the schism. Two months after the Episcopal Church diocese was reorganized, it went to court, on April 14, 2009, in the Texas state 141st District Court, Tarrant County, Fort Worth, seeking to recover the property and assets of the old diocese which were being held by the secessionist party.[571] The other three cases of diocesan litigation, San Joaquin, Pittsburgh, and Quincy, had all proceeded entirely in state courts. Fort Worth became the first case to be entered into both state and federal courts. After the schism, Iker and his diocese continued using the official names and insignia (shield) of the old diocese. In July of 2010, the Church side registered the names and insignia of the old diocese for the Episcopal Church diocese in the United States Patent Office. A few weeks later, the Church diocese entered a lawsuit against Iker in the United States District Court in the Northern District of Texas, Fort Worth Division, Judge Terry R. Means, on 21 September 2010, charging Iker to be in violation of the Lanham Act by action of trademark infringement.[572] On December 13, 2010, the Church lawyers presented to the court a sixty-one-page brief arguing their case. On January 6, 2011, the U.S. court responded by ordering a stay in the proceedings until the state court resolved the lawsuit there. Both dioceses continued using identical names and insignia.

Meanwhile the state 141st District Court proceeded with the suit the Church lawyers had entered on 14 April 2009. Judge John P. Chupp issued a summary judgment on January 21, 2011, and an amended order on February 8, 2011, in which he ruled all in favor of the Church diocese. He declared: "The Episcopal Church (. . .) is a hierarchical church as a matter of law."[573] He went on that the party remaining loyal to the Episcopal Church was the rightful party and that the efforts of the majority faction to amend the corporate documents were illegal. Finally, he ordered the defendants to turn over all

---

570. *Journal of the Twenty-Seventh Annual Convention of the Episcopal Diocese of Fort Worth, November 13-14, 2009 & Special Meeting of the Convention, February 7, 2009.* Fort Worth: the diocese, 2010, 5–13.

571. "Judge Grants Episcopal Parties' Motions for Summary Judgment, Orders Surrender of Diocesan Property." January 21, 2011, http://episcopaldiocesefortworth.org/judge-grants-episcopal-parties-motions-for-summary-judgment.

572. "Episcopal Diocese of Fort Worth v. the Rt. Rev. Jack Leo Iker." United States District Court, Northern District of Texas, Fort Worth Division, September 21, 2010, http://www.ndtextblog.com/wo-content/uploads/2010/17715275545.pdf.

573. "The Episcopal Church v. Franklin Salazar." District Court of Tarrant County, Texas 141st District Court, February 8, 2011, 1.

property and assets of the old diocese to the loyalist diocese. This was a complete victory for the Church side.

Iker planned an appeal of Chupp's decision to the Texas Second Court of Appeals, in Fort Worth. However, he quickly decided to appeal directly to the Texas Supreme Court after the state Third Court of Appeals, in Austin, ruled in favor of the Episcopal Church in the case of the Church of the Good Shepherd in San Angelo, in the Diocese of Northwest Texas.[574] Three judges of the appeals court ruled unanimously on March 16, 2011, to uphold the lower court ruling in favor of the Episcopal Church party in the parish.[575] The majority of parishioners had voted in 2006 to leave the diocese for the province of Uganda. Upon this ruling, Iker decided to bypass the state appeals court and go directly to the state supreme court which, on August 31, 2012, agreed to accept the appeal. It set oral arguments for 16 October 2012.

Retired Bishop Edward Salmon decided to intervene in the litigation in Fort Worth as he had in Quincy where, in 2011, he had filed an affidavit in support of the anti-Episcopal Church side. On 23 April 2012, Salmon submitted an amicus brief with the Texas Supreme Court supporting Iker's side. Complainants in Fort Worth filed an official complaint with the Episcopal Church under Canon IV against Salmon and the other six bishops endorsing the brief.[576] As one has seen, the complaints from the Quincy and Fort Worth Episcopalians led to a conciliation meeting on January 8–9, 2013, and a settlement in a written Accord on 8 March 2013.

The Supreme Court of Texas was composed of nine justices, all elected statewide to six-year terms. Texas is one of only seven states in the U.S. to elect justices on partisan ballots.[577] Since around the year 2000, all justices on the court have been Republicans. Given the conservative Republican nature of Texas politics over the past two decades, one could reasonably expect the popularly elected supreme court to favor conservative opinions.

It should not be surprising then that the Texas supreme court took a conservative and strict construction approach to Chupp's decision. On 30 August 2013, five of the nine justices joined in an opinion reversing and remanding Chupp's order of 8 February 2011. The decision was written by Justice Phil Johnson who was joined by Chief Justice Nathan L. Hecht, Justice Paul W. Green, Justice Eva Guzman, and former Chief Justice Wallace B. Jefferson.[578] While the decision pointed out three structural tiers of the Episcopal Church, General Convention-diocese-parish, it proceeded to treat the diocese as an independent unit. The decision failed to point out that the diocese owed its existence

---

574. Walker, Patrick M. "Texas Supreme Court Agrees to Hear Fort Worth Episcopal Dispute." *Star-Telegram* (Ft. Worth, TX), September 5, 2012, http://www.star-telegram.com/2012/09/04/4230156/texas-supreme-court-agrees-to.html.

575. On August 31, 2013, the Texas Supreme Court reversed the appeals court ruling.

576. Complainants: Clergy—Bishop Wallis Ohl, Susan Slaughter, William Standord, David Madison; Laity—Martha Fagley, Elinor Normand, Margaret Mieuli. Respondents: Edward Salmon, Maurice Benitez (retired, Texas), John Howe (retired, Central Florida), Paul Lambert (suffragan, Dallas), William Love (Albany), Daniel Martins (Springfield), James Stanton (Dallas).

577. "Supreme Court of Texas," Wikipedia, http://en.wikipedia.org/wiki/Supreme_Court_of_Texas.

578. "The Episcopal Diocese of Fort Worth v. The Episcopal Church." In the Supreme Court of Texas, August 30, 2013.

to its accession to the Constitution and Canons of the Episcopal Church. In a moment of highly strict interpretation, the justices said the Dennis Canon could not prevail under Texas law because it did not contain specific terms making it irrevocable. In other words, a diocese could give accession to the Constitution and Canons of the Episcopal Church and then revoke its adherence to any canon unless the canon expressly forbade such. In the end, the judges remanded the case to the District Court to be reheard under neutral principles and gave clear direction that the lower court should favor the Iker side: "The corporation was incorporated pursuant to Texas corporation law and that law dictates how the corporation can be operated."[579] Thus, the state high court overturned Chupp's decision, remanded, and directed him to follow a narrow interpretation of law favoring local rights. It did not issue a new opinion.

The court had a five to four split. The four dissenters, Justice Don R. Willett, Justice Debra Lehrmann, Justice Jeffrey S. Boyd, and Justice John P. Devine, submitted a minority opinion written by Willett.[580] They held that the case should not have been accepted by the high court in the first place because direct appeal from a lower was allowed only on questions of the constitutionality of a statute. There was no question of constitutionality involved in this case. If the court had refused to take the case, Chupp's order would have remained standing pending a possible appeal to the state court of appeals. The Texas supreme court's decision was a stunning success for the secessionist diocese and set-back for the Church side as it all but gave the settlement to Iker who announced "'a final victory is only a matter of time.'"[581]

The Episcopal Church side tried to get the state supreme court to reconsider the case. On October 18, 2013, Church lawyers filed a motion for a rehearing. On 6 December, the Iker side lawyers submitted their brief against it. On 21 March 2014, the state high court denied the Church's motion for a rehearing.

After the denial for a rehearing, Church lawyers could proceed with an appeal to the United States Supreme Court. No diocesan case had reached the U.S. Supreme Court although numerous cases of parishes leaving the Episcopal Church and claiming the property had gone to the Court only to be rebuffed. For years, the high court's refusal to hear these appeals had let stand the lower courts' decisions favoring the Church and its dioceses. The Court had yet to take a case concerning the relationship of Episcopal Church and diocese involving the critical issues of the First Amendment, rights of hierarchy, and boundaries between the deference and neutral principles. A decision by the U.S. Supreme Court would not only settle the issue of the legal relationship between Church and diocese, but could also resolve some of the perplexing problems of the interface between the constitution and religion. These would all be points of obvious national importance.

Meanwhile, Church lawyers asked the Texas Supreme Court to issue a stay of its mandate pending the Church's appeal to the U.S. Supreme Court. On 25 and 31 March

579. Ibid.

580. Ibid. [dissenting opinion].

581. Miller, Bill. "Texas Supreme Court Overturns Lower Court Decision in Dispute Between Episcopal Groups." *Star-Telegram* (Ft. Worth, TX), August 30, 2013, http://www.star-telegram.com/2013/08/30/5122692/texas-supreme-court-overturns.html.

2014, they filed briefs with the state high court asking for a stay. On 17 April, the court denied the request. The case would be remanded right away to the District Court. On 13 June, Judge Chupp issued a "Docket Control Order" giving a court schedule with a projected date of final hearing on December 17, 2014.[582]

On June 19, 2014, the Episcopal Church appealed to the United States Supreme Court by filing a petition for a writ of certiorari.[583] The Church, the Church's diocese of Fort Worth, and the Diocese of Northwest Texas joined in the petition of 191 pages. Basically, the case rested on two major points: 1-whether a trust can be enforced by the governing documents of a church or is subject only to local laws, that is, should precedent rest in the Episcopal Church Constitution and Canons or in local property laws, and 2-the boundaries of neutral principles and deference in church property cases, that is, how far may courts go in property issues of hierarchical churches?[584]

The independent diocese immediately scoffed at the Church's appeal to the U.S. Supreme Court. The next day, June 20, the diocese issued a press release saying there was little chance the Court would take the case because: 1-there was no final judgment, 2-the issues were Texas laws, not matters of the U.S. Constitution, and 3-neutral principles prevailed in the nation.[585] The diocesan leaders were so sure the appeal would be denied right off that they waived their right to submit a response. The strength of the diocese's position was that there had not been a final state court decision and that the Texas Supreme Court had not made a written judgment in the case. They had remanded the case to the lower court with direction for new proceedings. It was true that the high court would most likely be reluctant to take an appeal of a case that had not been settled in lower courts.

As it turned out, the Iker diocese's assessment about the Supreme Court was both right and wrong. Owing to the importance of the issues, numerous other churches and institutions rushed to file "amici curiae" (friends of the court) briefs with the Supreme Court in support of the Episcopal Church's appeal. They were primarily concerned with the matters of the First Amendment, requiring the state to refrain from interfering in a religious institution, and the rights of hierarchical churches. On 21 July 2014, an amicus brief was filed by: the Episcopal Church in South Carolina, the Presbyterian Church (U.S.A.), Grace Presbytery, Presbytery of the New Covenant, and the United Methodist Church.[586] On the same day another was filed by the conferences of the United Method-

---

582. "Docket Control Order." In the District Court of Tarrant County, Texas, 141st District Court, June 13, 2014, http://www.episcopaldioceseoffortworth.org/assets/20140614-legal-141–252083-11-docket-control-order-judge-chupp.pdf.

583. "Petition for a Writ of Certiorari," The Episcopal Church v. The Episcopal Diocese of Fort Worth, in the Supreme Court of the United States, June 19, 2014, http://episcopaldioceseoffortworth.org/assets/20140619-legal-us-supreme-court-No-PetititonForAWritofCertorari.pdf.

584. "Episcopal Parties File Petition for Review by U.S. Supreme Court." Episcopal Diocese of Fort Worth, as quoted in Episcopal News Service, June 19, 2014, http://episcopaldigitalnetwork.com/ens/2014/06/20/episcopal-parties-file-petition-for-review-by-u-s-supreme-court.

585. "Diocese will Waive Response to TEC's U.S. Supreme Court Appeal." June 20, 2014, http://fwepiscopal.org/news/supremecourt.html.

586. "Brief for the Episcopal Church in South Carolina." In the Supreme Court of the United States, July 21, 2014, http://www.episcopalchurchsc.org/uploads/1/2/9/8/12989303/amicus_brief_tecsc_2014-07-21.pdf.

ist Church in Texas. On 28 July, the Greek Orthodox Archdiocese of America submitted an amicus brief supporting the Church's appeal.[587] Subsequently, the African Methodist Episcopal Church joined by filing an amicus for the Church.[588] Also filing for the Church was the Rutherford Institute, of Charlottesville, Virginia, a prominent association for the promotion of civil liberties in the U.S.[589] Thus, the Church's appeal was not a trivial matter to be rejected offhand by the Court. On July 28, the Court requested a response from the independent diocese with a deadline of 27 August, later extended to 26 September. The Iker diocese filed a response with the Court on 26 September basically arguing in favor of neutral principles. On 14 October, the Church side submitted a reply. The next day, the clerks of the Court sent the materials to the justices to be considered in their conference of 31 October. On November 3, the Court announced that the justices had denied "cert," that is, had refused to take the Church's appeal.[590] The justices gave no explanation for their rejection of the case. This meant the case would have to be settled in the state court of Texas.

Meanwhile, Judge Chupp, in the 141st District Court followed the docket schedule he had issued on June 13, 2014, but gave extensions. On December 1, 2014, the two sides submitted to him their motions for summary judgments, and subsequently their responses. On February 20, 2015, Chupp held a hearing of an hour and a half to listen to oral arguments then accepted the written orders, or requests, from the two sides. Shortly thereafter, on 2 March, Chupp issued his decision in a terse four sentence page giving all to the independent diocesan side. He gave no reason or explanation. Chupp issued his "Final Judgment" on the case on July 24, 2015. In a short, three and a half pages, he listed nine points, or statements of decision. He said, following neutral principles, the independent diocese held all the rights and assets of the old diocese. As in the preliminary judgment of 2 March, Chupp gave not a word of explanation for any of his nine points of decision.[591] This was in contrast to his earlier rulings, on 21 January and 8 February 2011, in which he had offered explanations and reasons for his decisions favoring the Church side.

Judge Chupp noted in the last sentence of his Final Judgment that this decision could be appealed. The Church side did enter the matter with the Texas Second Court of Appeals, in Fort Worth. On 18 August, Chupp signed an order suspending the enforcement of his Final Judgment pending the appeals court action. On December 3, 2015, the Church side submitted two briefs, one from the local Church diocese and the other

---

587. "Brief of the Greek Orthodox Archdiocese." In the Supreme Court of the United States, July 28, 2014, http://www.episcopalchurchsc.org/uploads/1/2/9/8/12989303/_greek_orthodox_church_amicus_brief_13-1520_final.pdf.

588. "Ryan A. Shores to Supreme Court of the United States." August 27, 2014.

589. "Brief of the Rutherford Institute." In the Supreme Court of the United States, August 27, 2014, http://sblog.s3.amazonaws.com/wp-content/uploads/2014/09/13-1520-amicus-rutherford.pdf.

590. "The Episcopal Church v. The Episcopal Diocese of Fort Worth." Scotusblog, November 3, 2014, http://www.scotusblog.com/case-files/cases/the-episcopal-church-v-the-episcopal-doiocese-of-fort-worth.

591. "Final Judgment." The Episcopal Church v. Franklin Salazar, In the District Court, Tarrant County, Texas, 141st Judicial District, July 24, 2015.

from the Episcopal Church.[592] On March 4, 2016, the independent diocese entered its response briefs to the two from the Church side.[593]

The Second Court of Appeals, in Fort Worth, was composed of seven justices. Three were assigned to this case: Anne Gardner, presiding, Lee Gabriel, and Bonnie Sudderth. They held a hearing of oral arguments, lasting 39 minutes, on April 19, 2016 at 1:30 p.m.[594] Daniel L. Tobey, attorney for the Church diocese argued that the Episcopal Church was hierarchical, that the diocese made an irrevocable contract by giving accession to the Church's Constitution and Canons, and that the trial court erred in its application of neutral principles. Scott A. Brister, lawyer for the independent diocese, countered that the court had indeed properly followed neutral principles, and that Texas law governed all matters of property ownership. One or more of the judges interrupted Brister twice, once to wonder if the lawyer was getting into ecclesiastical issues, and the other to remark that the Texas Supreme Court had not rendered a judgment. In his rebuttal, Tobey asserted that only the Church could decide on the true diocese, not the courts. As it had been for so many years, the basic issue before the court remained the same, whether sovereignty rested in the national Church or in the local diocese.

Thus, by the time of the schism in South Carolina, in 2012, four dioceses had already experienced division and litigation, San Joaquin, Pittsburgh, Quincy, and Fort Worth. The majorities in these had voted to remove the dioceses from the Episcopal Church and to join, first another Anglican province, Southern Cone, then the new Anglican Church in North America. Robert Duncan, the bishop of Pittsburgh who had led the schism of that diocese, became the first archbishop of the new church. In all four cases, minorities reorganized the Episcopal Church dioceses with the help of the national Church. In all four cases, too, the Church went to court to enforce its claim of sovereignty over the dioceses.

The basic issue in all of the litigation between the Episcopal Church and the secessionist dioceses was sovereignty. The Church claimed that it was an hierarchical institution with authority in a central body called the General Convention. Dioceses existed only in context of the larger body. The secessionists insisted that sovereignty rested in the local dioceses that were independent and self-governing. That fact, they held, gave the diocese control of the legal rights and properties. The Church argued that civic courts could not interfere in a hierarchical church because such was forbidden in the First Amendment of the United States Constitution. The secessionists demanded that courts

592. "Brief of Appellants The Local Episcopal Parties and Congregations." Court of Appeals for the Second District of Texas, Fort Worth, Texas, December 3, 2015, http://episcopaldioceseoffortworth.org/assets/12-3-15-Brief-of-Appellants-The-Local-Episcopal-Parties-and-Congregations.pdf ; "Brief of Appellant The Episcopal Church and The Most Rev. Katharine Jefferts Schori." Court of Appeals for the Second District of Texas, Fort Worth, Texas, December 3, 2015, http://episcopaldioceseoffortworth.org/assets/12-3-15-Brief-of-Appellant-The-Episcopal-Church-and-The-Most-Rev.-Katharine-Jefferts-Schori-12032015.pdf.

593. "Appellees' Response Brief to Local Episcopal Parties" In the [Texas] Second Court of Appeals, March 4, 2016, http://www.fwepiscopal.org/downloads/Appellees-ResponsetoLocalParties-030416.pdf ; "Appellees' Response Brief to the Episcopal Church." In the [Texas] Second Court of Appeals, March 4, 2016, http://www.fwepiscopal.org/downloads/AppelleesResponsetoTEC-appeal-030146.pdf.

594. Texas, Second Court of Appeals. Audio recording, April 19, 2016, http://episcopaldioceseoffortworth.org/court-of-appeals-hears-arguments/.

follow only neutral principles, treating the two sides equally, and following only local property laws.

Local state courts took up the Church lawsuits, but in no instance did a state supreme court hand down a decision settling the issues at hand. In three states, Pennsylvania, Illinois, and California, the supreme courts either rejected the cases or remanded them to the lower courts. By the time of the South Carolina crisis of 2012, no state supreme court had rendered a judgment that might have influenced the course of litigation around the country. The decisions of the lower state courts varied greatly. In Pennsylvania and California, they ruled entirely in favor of the Church. The opposite was in Quincy where the courts ruled consistently on the side of the secessionist diocese. The strangest experience of all was in Texas where the same judge in the same court issued diametrically opposed decisions, one entirely in favor of the Church and the next completely on the side of the secessionists. Along the way, the various state courts gave the country a jumble of contradictory opinions. Instead of clarifying settlements of the issues, the courts only added to the chaos. The one court that could have resolved all the issues, the United States Supreme Court, refused to take up the matter. This was probably not because they did not want to tackle the difficult issues involved but because the lower courts had not rendered a final judgment on which they could rule. At any rate, the failure of the highest court in the nation to settle the differences only left the confusion in the country to brew indefinitely.

The conflicting opinions from the courts derived from the approaches to the law the judges took. Strict constructionists looked for literal interpretations. Unfortunately for the Church side, the Episcopal Church Constitution and Canons too often lacked literal guidance. There was no provision explicitly forbidding dioceses from seceding. There was no supremacy clause giving the General Convention direct power over the dioceses. Strict construction worked to the advantage of the secessionists. The most extreme example of this came in the Texas Supreme Court which ruled that the Dennis Canon could not be enforced in Texas because it did not contain a provision to prevent it from being revoked. Loose construction worked to the advantage of the Church side, as in California. In this, judges read implied or generally meant provisions into their judgments. Something could be true without being literally true. In California, judges followed neutral principles and still found the Church to be hierarchical.

The first secession of the majority of a diocese began by 2006, six years before South Carolina made its schism. This gave the diocesan leaders in South Carolina plenty of time to study the successes and failures of the first four examples. This would be especially true in the confusing myriad of court actions here and there.

The Robinson affair of 2003 galvanized the anti-homosexual-rights ultra-conservative Episcopalians to organize a movement to break up the Episcopal Church. The ultras refused to accept the validity of the Church's reforms for homosexuals. They demanded alternative primatial oversight. By that they meant the authority of a foreign Anglican primate over their dioceses. This was something the Episcopal Church could not and would not accept. The ultras appealed to the Archbishop of Canterbury who would not and could not interfere in an independent province of the Anglican Communion. The dozen ultra-conservative dioceses organized a union for their cause called the Anglican

Communion Network. The election of a woman, and a pro-homosexual-rights one at that, as presiding bishop, was more than the most disaffected dioceses could take. The three dioceses that had steadfastly refused to ordain women to the priesthood plus Pittsburgh, whose bishop was head of the Anglican Communion Network, all resolved to find their own alternative primatial oversight. In 2006, 2007, and 2008, the majorities in San Joaquin, Pittsburgh, Quincy, and Fort Worth all voted to break away from the Episcopal Church and join a foreign Anglican province, the Southern Cone. The Episcopal Church claimed they had no right to take with them the legal rights and properties of the old dioceses and went to court to stop them. However, years of expensive litigation rendered the Church only mixed success. State courts from one side of the country to the other handed out only a buffet of wildly varying opinions. There was no judicial consensus at all, far from it. Federal courts avoided the issues altogether, even when the Church called on them.

It was in an atmosphere of volatility, confusion, factional contention, and conflict in the Episcopal Church that the Diocese of South Carolina prepared to install its controversial new bishop, Mark Lawrence, in January of 2008, only a few weeks after his home diocese, San Joaquin, had voted to leave the Episcopal Church. South Carolina was one of the dozen ultra-conservative dioceses, but also one of the majority of them that had remained, however tenuously, in the Church. Whether South Carolina would remain or follow the four hardliners out was very much the question at hand as the year 2008 began.

3

The Diocese of South Carolina in the Early Lawrence Years, 2008–2009

THE LIFE OF MARK JOSEPH LAWRENCE TO 2008

Bakersfield

WHO WAS THIS MARK Lawrence, this little-known fifty-seven-year-old priest who had provoked so much contentious emotional response from all sides in his 2006–2007 candidacy for bishop of South Carolina? At first glance, this native of cross-continental Bakersfield, California, seemed about as far removed from the Carolina Low Country as one could imagine. Bakersfield is where one should begin.

Most travelers heading to California in the early twentieth century moved westward along old U.S. Route Sixty-Six or later along Interstate Highway Forty and entered the state at Needles, the little town squeezed between the narrow green ribbon of the Colorado River valley to the east and the vast arid wilderness to the west. No doubt many an exhausted journeyman collapsed into town and rejoiced thanking God that they had made it at long last into the Promised Land, the golden state of California. Celebration would be premature however. Little did they know that just beyond Needles lay one of Mother Nature's cruelest jokes, that incredibly daunting expanse called the Mojave Desert, two hundred miles of virtually uninhabited, barren, waterless, nearly lifeless wilderness where for most of the year the searing sun sent temperatures daily over one hundred degrees and hot winds blew relentlessly across this other-worldly terrain. But only after traversing this hell of California could one hope to reach the heaven of California. It was the final and greatest test of endurance for many a bone-weary traveler and his worn-out vehicle, but alas, one that could not be avoided.

Going westward down Route Sixty-Six or Interstate Forty some one hundred and fifty miles across this no-man's land, the traveler reached the small city of Barstow, the transportation hub near the western edge of the Mojave Desert. Taking a westward path, one moved some fifty miles on California Highway Fifty-Eight to reach the Tehachapi Mountains and then soon crossed over the crest at around four thousand feet. On descending the western slopes, the traveler would be startled to see unfolding below him a breath-taking, almost magical scene, a magnificent lush green valley as far as the eye could see. It was the San Joaquin Valley, the southern part of the great Central Valley of California. To countless pilgrims who had risked everything to get to California, this was the end of the one-way road. They had arrived in the land of milk and honey. The first city they reached in this far-distant heaven was Bakersfield.

Mark Lawrence's father's people were among the thousands of migrating Okies and Arkies of the 1930s. His father was Leo Douglas Lawrence, the second son of Perry and Myrtle Lawrence of Waldron, Arkansas, born on May 22, 1919.[1] Waldron was a small town in Scott County, a sparsely populated rural county with a high poverty rate lying just south of Fort Smith on the Oklahoma state line. When Leo was two years old, his father Perry was killed "struck by lightning that rolled like a fireball into his Arkansas barn."[2] The widow Myrtle then eked out a living for herself and her two young sons by teaching in country schools. When the depth of the Great Depression hit in 1933, the extended Lawrence family, having lost their farm and store, decided to give up on dismal Arkansas and join the trek to golden California and Myrtle agreed to join in. She gathered her two teenage boys, packed up everything and joined her family in the parade of desperate country people slowly and fitfully making their way along the crowded great mother road toward the setting sun and the fantasy land beyond the western horizon.

For many an Okie and Arkie, California was a dream realized but it was far from perfect. Some exhausted migrants were denied admission to the state, coldly turned back at the Colorado River. Those who did get in all encountered a certain amount of hateful social discrimination. Well-established residents sneered at the rough hillbillies-come-to-town while working people bitterly resented the competition for precious jobs made scarce by the Depression even in golden California. Violence against the newcomers was not rare. Fourteen-year-old Leo, a feisty adolescent, did not take the slights lightly. "His hair sheared in the shape of a bowl earned him and those like him, the shunning name, Okie. So he grew up fiercely independent," according to his son Mark.[3] Myrtle Lawrence settled her family in Bakersfield where Leo graduated from the Kern County Union High School in 1937.[4] The Census of 1940 showed the Lawrences living at 824 Ninth Street, Bakersfield: Myrtle, age forty-five, Leo, age twenty, Louis, age twenty-three, and Louis's wife, Daphne, age eighteen.[5] In the Second World War, Leo, then in his early twenties, served in both the Naval Air Corps and the U.S. Army. After the war, he went to work for the U.S. Postal Service in Bakersfield where for the next thirty-three years he served in numerous capacities as Employee Union Leadership, Supervisor, Civil Service

---

1. Tatum, Mildred. "Leo D. Lawrence." Miscellaneous Scott County Obituaries, Surname "L." http://www.argenweb.ne/scott/ctdobl.htm.

2. "Answers to Prepared Walkabout Questions for the Episcopal Nominees (II): Mark Lawrence," September 9, 2006, http://www.episcopalforumofsc.org/Overview%20Documents/Answers_to_prepared_Walkabout_Questions.pdf.

3. Ibid. 2.

4. Tatum, 1.

5. "Leo Lawrence in the 1940 Census." http://www.ancestry.com/1940-census/usa/california/Leo-Lawrence_2d16mr.

Examiner, RFD Carrier, and Credit Union Management.[6] He earned a reputation for "constancy, practicality, and dependability."[7] In thirty-three years he missed only six days of work.[8] He was also a busy and active man outside of his regular job. He served as a reserve deputy sheriff for eight years, cashier for the Kern County Agricultural Fair for eleven years, licensed real estate agent for thirty years, and income tax preparer for forty-seven years. Yet he still found time to remain active in the American Legion and other veteran organizations as well as numerous retired federal employees' associations.

What Mark Lawrence perhaps inherited from his remarkable father was self-reliance and individualism. He once testified that he believed he inherited his father's strong ethic of hard work.[9] At another time he recalled "He [my father] made it out to California selling soap on the back of a flatbed truck. We came up—he came up through the school of hard knocks with a deprivation mentality, having grown up during the Dust Bowl days. He—I think that was inculcated in me."[10] For Leo Lawrence, life was a battle against the odds, but if one worked hard enough, if one fought hard enough against life's road blocks, one could break through them to prevail very well. This victory, however, could only come from within, from relentless hard work and the resolve of the inner self. The arduous trek to California, the hostile reception in the golden state, the joblessness of the Depression, the war against the evil threat of fascism, all were obstacles that Leo had had to face to reach the good life he enjoyed after marriage. He spent the rest of his life working hard to ensure a future that he had already gained as if everything could slip away from his hands at once and he would be returned to the hard-scrabble poverty of his childhood. His story was repeated countless times in the lives of poor boys and girls who came out of the Great Depression and the Second World War. However, it was these people whom we now commonly call America's "Greatest Generation," and for good reason.

Mark Lawrence's mother was Bertha Ann Coombs Lawrence, a fourth-generation Californian, descendant of the Renfro, Dwight, and Coombs families of small farmers at Rosedale, now in the western part of Bakersfield.[11] She was born in Bakersfield on February 24, 1920, to William McKinley Coombs and Adelia Dwight Coombs. Bertha's mother died soon after childbirth; and Bertha was reared by her father's sister and her husband. She graduated from East Bakersfield High School in 1944 and soon went to work at the post office where she met Leo Lawrence. The two married on August 4, 1946, and had three children: E. Porter, Pamela, and Mark. For two decades, she was employed at Lane's and Crites' Jewelers in East Bakersfield. Leo and Bertha were married for fifty-seven years. Leo died in 2003, Bertha in 2012.

If Mark Lawrence learned from his father self-reliance and an ethic of hard work, he had in his mother a different model, one who put profound faith in The Other, God.

6. Tatum, 1.
7. Ibid.
8. Ibid.
9. "Answers to Prepared," 2.
10. "Deposition Transcript—Mark J. Lawrence," 57.
11. "Bertha Ann Coombs Lawrence (1926–2012)." http://www.legacy.com/obituaries/Bakersfield/obituary-print.aspx?n=bertha-ann-coombs-lawrence&

Leo was never one much for church. In fact, he consented to be baptized only eleven days before he died on July 25, 2003.[12] For Bertha, however, faith was always the bedrock foundation of her life. Mark called his mother "Mrs. Methodist."[13] She was for many years a devout and devoted member of Trinity United Methodist Church in East Bakersfield serving on various levels of the United Methodist Women. She was a delegate to the district and national conventions of the UMW; and was given the Bishop's Award in 1996.[14] What Mark saw in his mother was a person who put deep and abiding faith in an omnipotent God to guide her life.

The lessons from each of his parents were not necessarily compatible; indeed, they may have been contradictory. Could his father's self-reliance and his mother's humble faith in the guiding hand of an all-powerful greater force be easily combined? How is one to live his life, through hard-fought self-made victories over obstacles, or by quiet surrender to the Divine Will?

In the long run, his mother apparently had the greater influence on Mark Lawrence. If Leo were important in Mark's character development, Bertha was perhaps even more so. She was in many ways the rock and beacon of his life. This author found no epitaph from Mark Lawrence after his father died. However, following his mother's death in 2012, Lawrence wrote two poignant memoirs reflecting how deeply she had affected his life: a letter "Bertha Ann Coombs Lawrence" of January 8, 2013 that he posted on the Diocese of South Carolina website and on *The Living Church* website,[15] and "A Christmas Message from Bishop Lawrence" that he placed on the Diocese of South Carolina website, December 23, 2013.[16] These can only be seen as heartfelt outpourings of love from an adoring and grateful son. Yet, this mother's son was also the offspring of the pugnacious Leo Lawrence.

Mark Lawrence was born on March 19, 1950, in Mercy Hospital, Bakersfield, so severely premature the doctors feared he would not live.[17] He was so small that he went home from the hospital in a shoebox. At six weeks, he nearly died from a blockage of the esophagus. Undersized for his age, growing up for the little boy Mark was a struggle to catch up with the other boys in physical development. But from his father he learned not to give up and to fight resolutely against the odds to victory. In the course of his gradual development he fell in love with the great outdoors where he could improve his strength and physical capacity hiking, camping, canoeing, and fishing in the magnificent mountains that lay in sight of Bakersfield. He found too that the sport of wrestling suited his small, but muscular and tough, teenage frame that was not made for football or basketball. In school, he excelled as a wrestler, even going undefeated one year. His

12. Tatum, 2.

13. Lawrence, (the Rt. Rev.) Mark. "Bertha Ann Coombs Lawrence." Diocese of South Carolina, January 8, 2013, http://us1.campaign-archive2.com/?u=4961327fa871e140b6aecfe0e&id=d8444c6cfc&e=37dd4515d.

14. "Bertha Ann Coombs."

15. Lawrence, "Bertha Ann Coombs."

16. Lawrence, (the Rt. Rev.) Mark. "A Christmas Message from Bishop Lawrence." December 23, 2013, http://your-cathedral.org/a-christmas-message-from-bishop-lawrence.

17. Hawes. "The Rt. Rev. Mark Lawrence."

older brother Porter, however, did not do so well in his struggles against life. He got into drugs, landed a couple of years in prison, flamed out and died too soon.[18] If older brother Porter failed to internalize the models of his father and mother, Mark would not make that mistake. He would not go down Porter's road to self-destruction. He would learn well from his parents.

Finding Religion

It took Mark Lawrence a long time to find himself, to find direction and meaning in life. His mother had him christened in the Methodist church. He grew up a nominal Methodist but only showed alternating mild interest, indifference, and hostility to church. Many years later, Lawrence testified, "I grew up in the Methodist church. I left it sometime roughly in junior high. I occasionally would go with my mother, somebody else during my high school years. But it was poor attendance at best, during those years. Drifted into agnosticism."[19] It would be a long time before Mark would come to have the deep level of faith that he always saw in his mother, but in the long run he did follow his mother's example.

As Mark Lawrence has said, his long religious journey has been a tortured, sometimes tormented, even traumatic experience lurching between emotional lows and highs.[20] As a teenager he shunned religion preferring popular culture and the outdoors. He was graduated from high school in 1968 with little thought of what to do in life. He then attended Bakersfield College, the local community college for two years. After finishing there, he transferred to California State University Sacramento. "He left for college an agnostic, at best."[21] In the autumn of 1970, while a student at Sacramento State, Lawrence was involved in an automobile accident and dropped out of college.[22] "And the day I arrived back in my hometown a friend called and said he had a place up in the mountains, why don't I come up and join him (. . .). So I went up and wrote and chopped wood, did various things for a season."[23] By the winter of 1970–71, Lawrence was back home in Bakersfield taking a few courses at the junior college. In 1971, he returned to Sacramento State for a semester. Years later, Lawrence recalled "[I] Was converted that semester, reading the works of Saint Augustine, John Calvin and Soren Kierkegaard; primarily Soren Kierkegaard, who mapped out the despair of the human condition without God. And I took a leap of faith into the void, only to find a Father and his Son on the far side."[24] He read Kierkegaard's *Fear and Trembling*, a powerful book that forced him to contemplate the meaning of life and one's relationship with the divine. He began to wrestle mightily with the great questions of life as he had wrestled

18. Lawrence, "Christmas Message.".
19. "Deposition Transcript—Mark J. Lawrence," 14.
20. Hawes, "The Rt. Rev. Mark Lawrence," 2.
21. Ibid.
22. "Deposition Transcript—Mark J. Lawrence," 10.
23. Ibid.
24. Ibid., 11.

hard in school for sport. One day, in 1971, he fell to his knees and prayed for guidance from God.[25] Four days later, he saw a sign for a revival and went inside The Apostolic Church of the Holy Ghost of Jesus Christ Our Lord, Ebenezer, a predominantly African American Pentecostal church at Sacramento.[26] He was about to have the formative religious experience of his lifetime.

This was a highly charged pentecostal church that offered the out-of-the-mainstream ecstatically emotional experience called baptism by the Holy Ghost, a practice that had become popular with the newly booming pentecostal and charismatic communities that had recently popped up on the fringes of traditional religion. As two hundred people sang, shouted, and swayed, Mark reluctantly got in a line of people waiting to be touched by a woman whose slightest glance on the forehead sent them dancing wildly and fainting. She said she was offering people baptism by the Holy Ghost. When the woman touched Mark, he fell helplessly to the floor as if his body were completely consumed by another force. "'I felt the Lord tell me, 'You won't be able to get up and stand until you're ready to stand up for Jesus.'"[27] Struggling to his feet he then put on a white robe and was immersed in a pool of water three times as the congregation sang an old spiritual. He came out of the water feeling as a new man, more cleansed and purified than ever. He believed he had been baptized by the Holy Ghost in the touch of the woman and by water in the immersion. His life was profoundly changed forever.[28] At the age of twenty-one, Mark Lawrence had found God and himself. Forever after he would believe that, now filled with the Holy Ghost, his life had been taken over by God and he would live guided by the great Divine Will.[29] Lawrence later recalled, "It was such a profound upheaval for me in terms of world view, understanding of life, purpose, meaning, that after that semester was over I dropped out, came back down to my hometown, got a job, helped start a Christian coffeehouse in the downtown section of the city."[30] Bertha Lawrence's son had found the faith that he would follow for the rest of his life.

Soon thereafter, in 1972, Mark Lawrence transferred to Southern California College, now Vanguard University, an Assemblies of God school in Costa Mesa California, fifty miles south of Los Angeles. It calls itself "an institution of the Pentecostal tradition which was birthed out of the Azusa Street Revival in Los Angeles, California, at the turn of the century."[31] The Azusa Street Revival was the origin of the vast Pentecostal move-

---

25. Martinez, Leonel. "St. Paul's New Rector Facing Tough Challenge." *Bakersfield Californian*, September 20, 1997, F 2.

26. Ibid.

27. Ibid.

28. Ibid., 3.

29. Lawrence has continued this emphasis on the Holy Spirit throughout his life. For instance, in February of 2014 he spoke to a men's conference on "The Work of the Holy Spirit in the Believer's Life." The advertisement for the conference said that when he spoke to a similar group on 2009 "Many returned to their parishes not only filled with the Holy Spirit, but filled with a burning passion for discipleship that spreads throughout their churches." See: Christian Men's Conference, February 21–23, 2014." Diocese of South Carolina. www.diosc.com/sys/index.php?option=com_content&view=article&id=93&Itemid=114.

30. "Deposition Transcript—Mark J. Lawrence," 11–12.

31. "Vanguard University. Our History." http://www.vanguard.edu/about/our-history/.

ment that swept the country in the twentieth century. Lawrence enrolled on a wrestling scholarship.[32] It was at this college that Mark met a fellow student, Allison Kathleen Taylor. A month after they began dating in 1973, he proposed marriage and she accepted.[33] After attending Southern California College for two semesters, and with still a year to go before graduation, Lawrence transferred back to Sacramento State. He recalled later, "We ran out of money after about a month. We moved back to my hometown."[34]

Back in Bakersfield the newly married couple bought a house as Mark took a job "driving a cotton picker, then got hired by the Santa Fe Railroad" as an electrician.[35] He enrolled at California State University, Bakersfield, the fourth college he attended. While working full-time on the railroad, he took the courses necessary to finish the degree of Bachelor of Arts in English Literature in 1976. At the age of twenty-six, it had taken eight years for him to complete the bachelor's degree. The Lawrences attended an Assemblies of God church, but found it "needlessly chaotic."[36] As a change, they decided to visit Saint Paul's Episcopal Church, a venerable institution in the heart of Bakersfield, and were impressed by the beauty of the liturgy and overawed by the Eucharist. In another way, communion at the altar rail filled him with the Holy Ghost reminiscent of the woman's touch back at the Apostolic Church. The couple felt as if they had found a new home and happily threw themselves into church activities.

At this point, Mark Lawrence's religion would have been a combination of three sources: the Methodism of his youth; the emotional, or heart-driven, charismatic Pentecostalism he had experienced at the Apostolic Church; and the rational, or mind-driven, Episcopalianism he had come to know at St. Paul's. As an adult, Lawrence embraced two varying strands of Christianity. One part was an emotional, charismatic Pentecostalism that characteristically drew much from Biblical fundamentalist roots, assumed a rigidly God-given social order, and practiced a stridently vertical religion. The other was the stoical orderly and rational ritualism of the Prayer Book. Anglicanism is often referred to as a three-legged stool: Scripture, tradition, and reason. Lawrence's religious substance always rested heavily on the first leg, his understanding of the Bible, even while his form also rested on the other legs of human order and reason. Even after the schism, Lawrence insisted that Scripture was the only source of authority. As an Episcopalian, then, Lawrence clung to a far-evangelical view that was rapidly diminishing in size and influence in a Church that had already turned its focus to social reform when he joined it in the 1970s.

All of this was of little concern to Mark Lawrence at this point. He had important life decisions to make. Now graduated from college and in his mid-twenties he was facing the problem of what to do with his life. Working on the railroad was not the answer. But what was? It was time to get serious and plan to provide for his little, and growing, family. As time went by, he began to contemplate a calling to the ordained ministry of

---

32. "Deposition Transcript—Mark J. Lawrence," 12.
33. Hawes, "The Rt. Rev. Mark Lawrence," 3.
34. "Deposition Transcript—Mark J. Lawrence," 13.
35. Ibid.
36. Hawes, "The Rt. Rev. Mark Lawrence," 3.

the Episcopal Church. At a conference of the Episcopal Charismatic Fellowship[37], he met the Rev. Todd Ewald, the president of the conference.[38] Ewald asked Mark if he felt God were calling him to be a priest. He said he saw the word "priest" hang in the air and responded "Yes!" Mark felt guided by the Holy Ghost to enter the ordained ministry. After a discernment process and supported by his home parish of St. Paul's, Bakersfield, and the San Joaquin diocesan structure, in the fall of 1977 he moved his little family across the country to the new Trinity Episcopal School for Ministry in suburban Pittsburgh, Pennsylvania, the Diocese of Pittsburgh, where he finished his divinity degree in 1980.[39]

Ministry, 1980–2007

Returning to California, Lawrence was ordained a deacon by Bishop Victor Rivera of San Joaquin, on August 2, 1980, at the age of thirty.[40] He first served Holy Family Episcopal Church, in Fresno, and as a chaplain at California State University, Fresno. Later Lawrence recalled that after a year, "Bishop Rivera sent me down to St. Mark's, Shafter, to mop up the blood (. . .). There had been a difficult relationship between the previous vicar and the congregation, and he thought it had been devastated. My job was to go down and straighten things out."[41] Lawrence was ordained a priest on July 18, 1981, by Bishop Rivera, in St. Paul's Episcopal Church, Visalia, California. He remained at St. Mark's, of Shafter, for the next three years. By 1984, Lawrence said he felt God calling him to return to the Diocese of Pittsburgh, a place he had come to know and care for while a student at Trinity. Thus was to begin a thirteen year residency in McKeesport, Pennsylvania. And, once again his life would be profoundly changed in ways he could not have foreseen.

---

37. The charismatic movement in the Episcopal Church began around 1960 and featured baptism by the Holy Ghost and speaking in tongues. The Episcopal Charismatic Fellowship was founded in Dallas TX in February of 1973 at a conference attended by 300 clergy. In time, the name was changed to Episcopal Renewal Ministries.

38. Hawes, "The Rt. Rev. Mark Lawrence," 3.

When the Rev. Todd W. Ewald was rector of Holy Innocents Episcopal Church in Corte Madera (Marin County), California in 1963 he held sessions of speaking in tongues following the regular prayer services on Thursdays. *Milwaukee Journal*, 11 May 1963, p. 4.

Ewald served Holy Innocents for some thirty years and maintained an uneasy relationship with the controversial diocesan bishop, James Pike. After he retired, his wife was diagnosed with cancer. The couple was childless. The Ewalds committed suicide in their home leaving the church, diocese, and town in shock.

39. By the time Lawrence finished his degree, Trinity had settled in its permanent home of Ambridge, Pennsylvania.

40. "Certificate of Abandonment of the Episcopal Church and Statement of the Acts or Declarations which Show Such Abandonment." September 18, 2012. State of South Carolina, Court of Common Pleas, County of Dorchester, Case No. 2013-CP-18-00013, Exhibit D-22, July 8, 2014.

41. "Deposition Transcript—Mark J. Lawrence," 17.

McKeesport, Pennsylvania

McKeesport, Pennsylvania was a world away from Bakersfield, California, in more ways than one. It was founded in 1795 at the confluence of the Monongahela and Youghiogheny rivers, a few miles upstream from the present-day Pittsburgh. The Monongahela valley of southwestern Pennsylvania, rich in minerals, boomed as a steel making region in the late nineteenth and early twentieth centuries. McKeesport became the home of the National Tube Works, a major maker of iron pipes that hired 10,000 workers. Prosperity, and population, peaked in the 1940s when steel mills and other factories began to close after the Second World War. From a high of 55,355 people in 1940, McKeesport began a steady decline. In 1960, the population was down to 45,000, then 31,000 in 1980, and 24,000 in 2000.[42] National Tube closed in the 1980s. Mark Lawrence arrived in a city that had lost half its population in forty years and had lost even more in morale. Unemployment was sky-high with no relief in sight. *Time* magazine called it "'the center of industrial devastation and white poverty.'"[43]

Saint Stephen's Episcopal Church in McKeesport stands near the middle of town at the corner of Walnut and Eighth avenues. An original wooden church was constructed in 1872 for services but by 1886 it had been moved to the back of the property and the cornerstone of an impressive new stone building was laid that year. It was the first stone building in McKeesport and cost the considerable sum of $15,000 reflecting the town's growing prosperity.[44] Since then it has stood proudly raising aloft its grand tower as one of the venerable old buildings of the city.

Handsome building or not, the parish and its rust belt city seemed locked in a hopeless downward spiral. Indeed, years later Lawrence called St. Stephen's "a ghetto parish."[45] It was into this that Leo Lawrence's son volunteered to move in 1984 at the age of thirty-four taking his wife and three small children to a job paying a relatively low salary.[46] Young, enthusiastic, energetic and, as he would say, full of the Holy Ghost, Lawrence arrived full steam ahead and ready to tackle every challenge at hand, no matter how formidable. He knew that he would need every bit of his father's drive and resolve as well as his mother's faith.

When he arrived, Lawrence found a parish listing 413 baptized members and 365 communicants.[47] Average Sunday attendance stood at 150.[48] The spirit of the place was definitely not upbeat. It was clear that it had seen better days. Undaunted, the young new rector declared: "'If Christians do the sometimes unglamorous but faithful work, in

---

42. "McKeesport, Pennsylvania." Wikipedia, http://en.wikipedia.org/wiki/McKeesport_Pennsylvania.

43. Hawes, "The Rt. Rev. Mark Lawrence," 4.

44. "History." St. Stephen's Episcopal Church, McKeesport PA, http://ststephensmckeesport.com/our-history/.

45. "Deposition Transcript—Mark J. Lawrence," 93.

46. He once told a newspaper reporter that he and his family started out in McKeesport "under the poverty level." Hawes, "The Rt. Rev. Mark Lawrence," 5.

47. *Journal of the One Hundred Twentieth Annual Convention of the Diocese of Pittsburgh*, 1985. Pittsburgh: the diocese, 1985.

48. Waits, Fentress. "Parish Profile." *Trinity, Episcopal Diocese of Pittsburgh*, Vol. 18, No. 5 (February 1997) 6.

most cases the church will grow, even in places where many people think it will not.'"[49] Against the odds of a declining town, Lawrence set to work to build up the flagging parish. In his thirteen-year tenure, 1984–1997, average Sunday attendance arose to 230, the communicant number to 448 while the Sunday School ballooned.[50] He became well-known as an effective teacher and preacher. A parish profile in 1997 said that, on Tuesday nights, thirty people regularly gathered for Bible study. Another group met on Tuesday mornings. A women's fellowship group flourished. A club called the Crafters met once a week for fund-raising projects to raise money for outreach. Local chapters of the Order of St. Luke and the Brotherhood of Saint Andrew carried out work in the community. Another group helped at a food pantry and cooked for a soup kitchen. Still another called the Caregivers, kept track of parishioners who needed various forms of help. With the aid of a part-time youth minister, the parish developed a strong program for young people. Occasionally, the parish held joint services with an African American and a Lutheran church.[51] It was abundantly clear that Lawrence brought new life to a declining parish. He turned it around.

While working to build the parish, and after a few years' time, Lawrence slowly began to rise in the diocesan structure. He became chair of the Board of Examining Chaplains; member of the Commission on Ministry; member of the board of Calvary Camp; chair of a diocesan committee; member of the Cathedral Chapter; member of the Diocesan Budget Review; member of the Bishop's Advisory Group; and leader of Cursillo.[52] He topped this off by gaining election to the diocesan Standing Committee in 1995. It was abundantly clear too that he was held in esteem by his fellow clergy, many of whom were older and more experienced than he.

By all accounts, the parish held its young and energetic rector in high regard. In 1994 more than 150 people gathered to surprise the Lawrences with a dinner at the Youghiogheny Country Club celebrating his ten years of service. "Gifts included a weekend for Father Lawrence and his wife at Nemecolin Woods Resort, a check, and a photographic remembrance of the evening signed by all who attended."[53]

The Diocese of Pittsburgh and the Episcopal Church

While Lawrence was busy working to build up his local parish in McKeesport, the larger Episcopal Church beyond was beginning to test the limits of the tenuous bonds holding together this broad and varied old religious institution. If the movement of the national Church after 1960 could be called a revolution, what developed in the Diocese of Pittsburgh at the same time could be called a counter-revolution. The traditionalist minority struggled against the tide to keep the emphasis on the vertical. As time went by, and the

---

49. Ibid.
50. Ibid.
51. Ibid.
52. Ibid., Vol. 18, No. 2 (October 1994) 17.
53. Ibid., Vol. 16, No. 3 (November 1994) 14.

Episcopal Church continued to expand its social gospel, the traditionalists grew alarmed, moved closer together, and retrenched to reassert the vertical meaning of religion.

Nowhere in the country did this retrenchment become more pronounced than in the Diocese of Pittsburgh. And, there the very core of this movement could be found in the Trinity Episcopal School for Ministry, located in Ambridge, a town on the Ohio River a dozen miles northwest of Pittsburgh. In time, Trinity became a magnet for various conservative Episcopalian elements, most notably after the rise of the homosexuality issue in the Episcopal Church in the early 1990s. The Diocese of Pittsburgh took a rightward turn in 1981 when Alden Hathaway became bishop. In a real sense, then, by the 1980s the Diocese of Pittsburgh had become the incubator of the national movement of the Episcopal counter-revolution, and Trinity was its wellspring. Mark Lawrence happened to be an active part of this diocese in the 1970s, 1980s, and 1990s at the very time the counter-revolution was coalescing and rising there.

The unease that traditionalists in Pittsburgh and in numerous other dioceses around the Episcopal Church felt in the 1970s and 1980s changed into something much stronger in 1989, 1990, and 1991. In those years, Bishop Spong and Assistant Bishop Righter, of the Diocese of Newark, ordained to the priesthood two open and partnered homosexual men. Conservatives around the country were outraged and focused their ire on the national Church. Lawrence was one of these. He arose in the Pittsburgh diocesan convention in November of 1991 to present the Werner-Simons resolution.[54] It allowed parishes to divert money heretofore sent to the national church headquarters in New York to other ministries. Moreover, "Lawrence took the opportunity to criticize the House of Bishops for failing to censure those statements of some of its more colorful members that impaired the unity of the Church."[55] The resolution passed overwhelmingly, 133 to 77.[56] The Rev. Mark Lawrence had taken the first small step on what would become a long, twenty-one-year journey of criticism of, and struggle with, the national Episcopal Church. Lawrence's first (1991) and last (2012) public criticisms of the Episcopal Church came from the same issue, homosexuality.

Life Ties

Among the prominent faculty of Trinity who were also priests of the Episcopal Diocese of Pittsburgh when Lawrence arrived there in 1984 were: William D. Henning, Jr., John Hewitt Rodgers, Jr., Peter Hugh Davids, Stephen Noll, Leslie Parke Fairfield, and Robert F. Madden. Rodgers was dean and president of Trinity from 1978 to 1990. In the year 2000, he was one of two bishops consecrated by retired bishop of South Carolina, Allison, and four other bishops in a controversial service in Singapore. He was one of the founders and first bishops of the Anglican Mission in the Americas, a group that broke away from the Episcopal Church.[57] Davids, whose undergraduate education was

---

54. Originally presented by the Rev. George Werner, the dean of the cathedral, and the Rev. James Simons.

55. Bonner, "Called out," 374.

56. Ibid.

57. "Who's Who in the Anglican Mission in America." http://communityoffacts.tripod.com/id8.html.

at Wheaton College, went on the become professor at Houston Baptist University. Noll became a prominent writer and speaker advocating for the Global South movement which combined conservative parts of the Anglican Communion to challenge the traditional structure based in the Global North. He served as First Vice Chancellor of Uganda Christian University beginning in 2000 and "guided the University to receive a Government Charter in 2004, the first of its kind in Uganda."[58] He was a visible supporter of the majority movement to separate the Diocese of Pittsburgh from the Episcopal Church in 2008. Yet another priest who arrived at Trinity, in 1995, during Lawrence's tenure in McKeesport was Peter C. Moore who became the fourth dean, the president, and the first chair of the board of trustees of the school. He later moved to Charleston, South Carolina, to join the staff of Saint Michael's Church as Associate for Transformational Discipleship and to become a prominent defender of Lawrence in the crisis of 2012. Thus, of the six clerical faculty listed above, only one, Davids, remained on the clergy roll of the Episcopal Diocese of Pittsburgh in 2013.[59]

Lawrence also formed bonds with numerous clergy of the Diocese of Pittsburgh during his years there, a network of ties that was to prove crucial in his life thereafter. Among the most important of these fellow travelers in Pittsburgh were: Alden Hathaway, Robert Duncan, Keith Ackerman, Geoffrey Chapman, Gregory Kronz, and Paul Fuener. As we have already seen, Hathaway, as bishop of the Diocese of Pittsburgh from 1981 to 1997 left a distinctly traditionalist stamp on the diocese. After his retirement, he joined the staff of St. John's Episcopal Church, the downtown church, in Tallahassee, Florida. In 2007 he moved to Beaufort, South Carolina, to join the staff of the traditionalist parish of St. Helena's Episcopal Church as "Bishop in Residence."[60] As for Duncan, we have already seen how he led the majority of the old Diocese of Pittsburgh out of the Episcopal Church and became the Archbishop of the Anglican Church in North America. We have seen how Bishop Ackerman led the majority of Quincy out of the Episcopal Church. Although he was distinctly Anglo-Catholic, he maintained close relations with evangelical Lawrence. In regard to Chapman, we have seen that he was the author of the landmark Chapman Memo, the document widely regarded as the "smoking gun" fired by the anti-Episcopal party that sought to break up, and replace, the Episcopal Church.

Gregory Kronz and Paul Fuener old cohorts from the Diocese of Pittsburgh days, were chair and member of the search committee that nominated Lawrence for the office of bishop of South Carolina, 2005–07. Kronz, a native of Pittsburgh and graduate of Trinity, served as assistant at St. Stephen's of Wilkinsburg while Lawrence was at McKeesport. Wilkinsburg is a Pittsburgh suburban town a few miles north of McKeesport. In 1992, Kronz became rector of the traditionalist parish of St. Luke's on Hilton Head, Diocese of South Carolina. Beginning in 2005 he served as chair of the bishop's search committee that nominated Lawrence as one of the three final candidates. Kronz remained a stalwart defender of his choice through the crisis and schism. Fuener was graduated from Trinity School in 1996 and became assistant to Geoffrey Chapman at St.

---

58. "Uganda Christian University," Wikipedia, http://en.wikipedia.org/wiki/Uganda_Christian_University.

59. "Clergy of the Diocese." Episcopal Diocese of Pittsburgh, http://www.episcopalpgh.org.

60. "Alden Hathaway," Wikipedia, http://en.wikipedia.org/wiki/Alden_Hathaway.

Stephen's of Sewickley, Pennsylvania, where he remained until 2000. That year, he moved to Georgetown, South Carolina, to become rector of Prince George Winyah parish. In the Diocese of South Carolina, he served in numerous capacities including membership on the bishop's search committee. For some time, he served as chair of the Diocese of South Carolina's standing committee, a body that we will see remained strongly tied to Lawrence through the schism.

For many years, even before Lawrence's day, there have been innumerable links between the Diocese of Pittsburgh and the Diocese of South Carolina, connections that have increased over time. As we have seen, some of the clergy in South Carolina moved there from Pittsburgh, and many more were educated at Trinity School before taking posts in South Carolina. For several years, Trinity held "Trinity Jan Term South" at All Saints, Pawleys Island, South Carolina featuring teachers as Hathaway, Whitacre, and Fairfield in a short term of courses.[61] Beyond education, there have been other ties such as South Carolina's bishop Salmon serving as a consultant to the Pittsburgh search committee in 1995 making nominations for a bishop coadjutor.[62] He spent the day of February 18 advising the committee.

Back to Bakersfield

In 1997, the search committee for a new rector of St. Paul's parish in Bakersfield contacted Lawrence. Upon conversations with the committee, this native of Bakersfield said he felt the call of God to return to his hometown, his home parish, and his home diocese of San Joaquin. Perhaps he felt he had accomplished all he could in his thirteen-year tenure in McKeesport. Nevertheless, it must not have been an easy decision to uproot his family of wife and five children and move them two thousand miles across the continent. The parishioners at St. Stephen's hated to see him go. Years later, after the majority of the Diocese of Pittsburgh split away from the Episcopal Church, St. Stephen's was torn between following Bishop Duncan and staying in the Episcopal Church. The faithful people of St. Stephen's, certainly no strangers to adversity, agonized over this dilemma for some time before the parish finally settled on remaining in the Episcopal Church. Nevertheless, everyone seemed to agree on nothing but gratitude that Mark Lawrence had sojourned among them. Indeed, a delegation from McKeesport traveled to Charleston to attend Lawrence's consecration as bishop in January of 2008. He is fondly remembered to this day in St. Stephen's Episcopal Church of McKeesport.

Once again, the exchange of McKeesport to Bakersfield would be night-and-day. Bakersfield remained a booming, prosperous city in a booming and prosperous region and state with no upward end in sight. The dismal struggles of the depressed rust belt Mon valley of Pennsylvania would be traded for the sunny optimism of the lush San Joaquin Valley. In the prime of life, at the age of forty-seven, and with five children to support, Lawrence returned to his hometown of Bakersfield, no doubt to enjoy for himself and his family a new level of income, prosperity and comfort.

61. *Trinity*, Vol. 16, No. 3 (November 1994) 13.
62. Ibid., Vol. 16, No. 6 (March 1995) 1.

At more than 500 communicants, St. Paul's was the fourth largest church in the diocese. It was also the first, and most prominent, of the three Episcopal churches in Bakersfield offering a lovely and imposing Spanish colonial church edifice with a prominent square bell tower and large, impressive plant near the center of the city, only a few blocks west of the downtown. Reflecting the surrounding prosperity, the parish had recently accomplished great things. In 1982, it paid off its mortgage and became debt free for the first time since the 1952 earthquake had destroyed the previous church building.[63] In 1983, the parish purchased a neighboring lot for $75,000 to use as a parking lot.[64] In 1985, St. Paul's was recognized as the largest contributor to outreach of any parish in the diocese.[65] Then, in 1994, the parish began an optimistic capital campaign that was to reach the astounding goal of $671,000.[66] As part of this, a great new organ was dedicated a year before Lawrence arrived.

As in McKeesport, Lawrence arrived at St. Paul's ready to throw himself into long and hard work for his parish. And, as before, all accounts hailed the results. Lawrence once again was a popular and effective leader who energized the parish into new growth and liveliness. Much as he had done at St. Stephens, Lawrence organized internal groups to care for and minister to various needs of the parishioners, visiting the shut-ins and those hospitalized, greeting newcomers, contacting lapsed members, creating small fellowship groups, training group leaders, and developing a youth ministry.[67] Also, the parish set up a new endowment fund that grew to $185,000 by 2004.[68] A garden and columbarium were completed in 2004.[69] As always, Lawrence was well-known for his teaching and preaching that pleased the old and attracted newcomers. Numbers rose, to 800 communicants by the time Lawrence left St Paul's. Giving testament to his popularity, sixty-five parishioners of St. Paul's traveled across the country to Charleston for the consecration of their onetime rector as the new bishop of South Carolina in January of 2008.[70] Several of them participated in the service.

Lawrence and the Episcopal Church Issues of Homosexuality

While building up St. Paul's internally, Lawrence was also watching the growing storm in the national Episcopal Church around the issue of homosexuality. The most conservative dioceses, as San Joaquin, grew alarmed at the prospect of an openly homosexual person becoming a bishop of the Church. Just such a prospect was looming large on the national stage as 2003 arrived. In New Hampshire, the diocesan convention elected the

63. "The San Joaquin Anglican," July 2013, 14. http://www.dioceseofsanjoaquin.net.
64. Ibid.
65. Ibid.
66. Ibid.
67. Ibid., 15.
68. Ibid.
69. Ibid.
70. Pryor, John. "Mark Lawrence, 14th Bishop of South Carolina." *Bakersfield Californian*, January 26, 2008, http://www.bakersfieldcalifornian.com/local/x1699487548/Mark-Lawrence-14th-Bishop-of-South-Carolina.

Rev. Gene Robinson as a bishop in the spring of that year, an action that would have to be voted on by the General Convention of the Church in the summer of 2003. As a member of the Committee on Consecration of Bishops at the Convention, Lawrence led a minority group of three, with Anthony J. Clark and John E. Masters,[71] to draw up a dissenting report that requested the rejection of Robinson and spoke on the floor appealing to the deputies to vote against the majority report which favored Robinson. Although Robinson was approved by large majorities in the Convention, Lawrence had won for himself a certain notoriety, an attention and respect from other distressed conservatives, most notably those from South Carolina, who agreed with him. Although he lost the battle, in his own narrow way he had not lost the war. He would return to fight another day.

Church politics on the national scene grew ever more contentious. If the conservatives were reeling from the Robinson brawl of 2003, there was more to come in 2006 as the majority of the general convention that year elected the first woman presiding bishop of the Episcopal Church. And this was not just any woman, it was an outspoken woman who had already gained a name for herself as an advocate for rights for homosexual persons. Her election was Robinson times two. At the same moment, the convention that elected Jefferts Schori gave only tepid response to the Windsor Report. This was a disappointment to the conservatives who had been banking on the Report to end the practice of the ordination of homosexual persons in the Episcopal Church. For many conservatives, it was all too much. They immediately circled the wagons to demand "alternative primatial oversight" from a primate other than Jefferts Schori.

Separatism boiled up in Lawrence's diocese, San Joaquin. Finally, on December 8, 2007, the diocesan convention voted, for the second and last time, to leave the Episcopal Church for the Anglican Province of the Southern Cone. This was the first vote of a diocese to secede from the Episcopal Church in this period. Lawrence, who had recently, at long last, gained the requisite assents to become the legal bishop of South Carolina, missed the convention. He was on sabbatical leave in North Carolina at the time. His parish, St. Paul's, enthusiastically supported leaving the Episcopal Church. When asked later whether he would have voted with the majority to leave the Church, he said: "'I do not know because, in reality, I haven't had to face that situation. No one knows what they'd do in that set of circumstances.'"[72] This was remarkable considering that he had shown no such hesitancy or uncertainty about his opinions in his earlier public declarations such as "A Prognosis for the Body Episcopal" and "Remaining Anglican: In Defense of Dissociation." It was remarkable too because Lawrence told a reporter "'The Diocese of San Joaquin made their vote out of the integrity of their specific situation.'"[73] Even as an Episcopal bishop, Lawrence attended services at St. Paul's, then not an Episcopal church, including his son's ordination service.

The majority of the members of Lawrence's parish, St. Paul's, supported the diocesan move to leave the Episcopal Church. The parish changed its name to St. Paul's Anglican Church. The Episcopal diocese of San Joaquin, however, took legal action to

71. Clark was Dean of St. Luke's Cathedral, Orlando, Diocese of Central Florida and a leader of the "Communion Partners Rectors" group; Masters, a lawyer, was Chancellor of the Diocese of Wyoming.

72. Medina, Louis. "Local Leader has Vision for Future." *Bakersfield Californian*, December 21, 2007.

73. Ibid.

regain the property. As a result, and after occupying the church campus for over five years, the Anglican congregation surrendered it to the Episcopal bishop in 2013 and moved out to establish Trinity Anglican Church. The Episcopalians returned in July of 2013 and rejoiced in a festival celebration of homecoming to Bishop Lawrence's home church, St. Paul's Episcopal Church, Bakersfield.

BUILDING BONDS, 2008

The Ordination and Consecration of Bishop Lawrence

Mark Lawrence was ordained, consecrated, and installed as the XIV bishop of the Diocese of South Carolina on Saturday, January 26, 2008, at the Cathedral Church of St. Luke and Saint Paul in downtown Charleston.[74] There had been an arduous, nearly two-year struggle to reach this point. Lawrence had been elected, denied consent, re-elected and finally narrowly given consent amid many anguished partisan objections, reservations, and questions among people in South Carolina and beyond. Here was a time to bring together the differing parties for reconciliation, unity, and peace, a time Lawrence could show that he would be the bishop for all communicants and that his diocese would be comprehensive for all people. His consecration moment offered a golden opportunity to unify a weary and fractured diocese.

The consecration service occurred on the morning of the 26th, but the string of gala festivities actually covered two days, the 25th and the 26th.[75] As Lawrence described it in his diary, on Friday the 25th he enjoyed a throng at a grand dinner in the elegant downtown hotel, the Francis Marion, a stone's throw from the cathedral: "7:00 reception and dinner at the Francis Marion. Bishops, diocesan leaders, civic dignitaries, friends and family from north, south and west as well as Bishops from Canada, Nigeria, Dar es Salaam, England, Dominican Republic. Elegant and delicious dining-wonderful to be with family, long-time friends, recent friends and new friends in South Carolina. To bed around 11:30 p.m."[76]

The Presiding Bishop had been pointedly not invited to the consecration even though she had been commonly welcomed as the presiding officer at bishops' consecrations throughout the Episcopal Church. In fact, *The Book of Common Prayer* clearly encourages, but does not require it: "When a bishop is to be ordained, the Presiding Bishop of the Church, or a bishop appointed by the Presiding Bishop, presides and serves as chief consecrator."[77] In South Carolina, the planners of this event wanted this particular presiding bishop nowhere around, an action that spoke volumes about where feelings

---

74. *The Book of Common Prayer*, 511, requires that, if possible, the consecration be held on a Sunday or a holy day. 26 January 2008 was the feast of Sts. Timothy and Titus.

75. Three days if one counts the full (50–60) house of people still filling the episcopal residence at 50 Smith Street on 27 January. *Journal of the Two Hundred and Eighteenth Annual Meeting of the Convention of the Diocese of South Carolina, Christ Episcopal Church, Mt. Pleasant, SC, March 12, 13, 2009*, Charleston, SC: the diocese, 2009, Bishop's Diary," 37.

76. Ibid.

77. *The Book of Common Prayer*, 511.

stood between the Diocese of South Carolina and the national Church. Indeed, Mark Lawrence made it clear even before he received the consents to his election, that he did not want Jefferts Schori at his consecration. During the consent process, the bishops of the Fourth Province sent Lawerence a questionnaire containing a question of whether Lawrence would have the presiding bishop as the chief consecrator. He later testified, "I said I thought—that that would be profoundly unhelpful for the Diocese of South Carolina in its unity."[78] Tactfully, Jefferts Schori did not press her prerogative. Instead, she agreed to appoint as the chief consecrator the Rt. Rev. Clifton Daniel, bishop of East Carolina, and head of the bishops' conference of the IV Province (Southeast) of the Episcopal Church. David Booth Beers was also there as chancellor of the presiding bishop to see that all legal matters were handled properly. He asked Lawrence whether he was ready to sign the oath of conformity; Lawrence replied affirmatively.[79]

"The Ordination of a Bishop" is a liturgical service given in the Episcopal Church's *Book of Common Prayer*, pages 512–24. It has two main parts, ordination and consecration. All persons aspiring to the office of bishop in the Episcopal Church must submit to this required Prayer Book service. The first part of the liturgy is called "The Presentation." The very first words that the new bishop utters alone in the service is to promise to recognize the Scriptures and to support the Episcopal Church. Thus, in his first words in the consecration service, Lawrence said: "I, Mark Joseph Lawrence, (. . .) do solemnly engage to conform to the doctrine, discipline, and worship of The Episcopal Church."[80] It is a simple statement, concise and precise. It has no condition or qualifier. *Discipline*. Lawrence promised to conform to the discipline of the Episcopal Church. However much he might come to wish it otherwise later, Mark Lawrence was now under the authority of the Constitution and Canons of the Episcopal Church. He had given his solemn oath before God and the world.

In spite of cold and gray weather threatening rain, the 11:00 a.m. consecration service was a huge and joyous event. The cathedral, seating 1100, was filled to overflowing. There were so many bishops, and the procession was so long, that it took thirty minutes for the six large groups of entrants to progress up the aisle.[81] Even though mainstream Daniel was the chief consecrator, it was the dozens of conservative bishops who dominated the day. Co-consecrators were names such as Salmon, Allison, and Ackerman, now bishop of Quincy. There were even numerous bishops from foreign countries as Britain, Canada, Nigeria, and the Dominican Republic. The preacher of the day was Lawrence's old bishop from the McKeesport days, Alden Hathaway, whose opening line set the tone of his uneasy discourse: "It is the worst of times. It is the best of times,"[82]

---

78. "Deposition Transcript—Mark J. Lawrence," 64.

79. Tisdale, Thomas S. Interview with author, September 5, 2014.

80. *The Book of Common Prayer*, 513.

81. Belser, (the Rev.) Rick. "The Holy Spirit Prevails." *Jubilate Deo* (Diocese of South Carolina), February/March 2008, 8.

82. "Bishop Alden Hathaway's Sermon at Mark Lawrence's Consecration." http://www.kendallharmonnet.t19/index.php/t19/article/9616/. Charles Dickens's opening paragraph of *A Tale of Two Cities* starts: "It was the best of times, it was the worst of times, it was the age of wisdom, it was the age of foolishness (. . .) we were all going direct to Heaven, we were all going direct the other way."

a play of Charles Dickens's immortal first lines of his great classic *A Tale of Two Cities*. It did not take much imagination for the listeners to predict what the preacher would describe as the worst and the best. As the worst, he predictably denounced the Episcopal Church (the Church to which Lawrence had just vowed conformity): "neounitarian, pluralist, revisionist."[83] As the best he hailed, unsurprisingly, the traditionalists such as Lawrence who would defend the true faith. Unknown to the preacher, events would show that this sermon of repelling dualities actually set the scenario exactly for what was to come in Lawrence's episcopacy, a struggle to the breaking point between Hathaway's envisioned Manichaean opposites, "the worst" and "the best."

Lawrence described the consecration service as "Noble, dignified, celebratory, worshipful, joyful (. . .). God's spirit shook and jolted me."[84] He wrote in his diary that he finally returned home at 3:30 p.m. to find a house full of friends from Bakersfield, McKeesport, and elsewhere in the dioceses of San Joaquin and Pittsburgh. The festivities resumed shortly thereafter as Trinity School for Ministry people assembled a few blocks away at the Maritime Center. Trinity students, alumni, faculty, administrators, trustees gathered to celebrate with revelry the first elevation of a Trinity graduate to the office of bishop of the Episcopal Church. These were the people closest to Lawrence's heart; and it was with them that the one-time wrestler finally collapsed to the mat to savor his hard-won victory. He later wrote: "Good food, good fellowship, enjoyable time-program was inspiring-Bishops John Rogers, Bill Frey, Alden Hathaway (. . .) to bed by 11:30 p.m."[85]

Indeed, this heady two-day festival may well have been the last great revelry of the Episcopalian traditionalists.[86] Only a few weeks earlier, San Joaquin had voted to leave the Episcopal Church for the Southern Cone and real trouble brewed in Pittsburgh. In short order, cracks, then fissures, and then breaks would form to tear apart so much of the far-right wing of the Episcopal Church. The hard-won consecration of traditionalist leader Lawrence was the swan song of a troubled band that had grown bitterly discontented with their national Church. None of that mattered much, however, on January 25 and 26, 2008, as the counter-revolutionary Episcopalians and Anglicans basked in the glow of their small but significant victory that had followed on the heels of one troubling defeat after another. At this time and this place, at least, vertical religion had banished the horizontal. Lawrence and his friends had won a small but not insignificant battle in a great war they were losing.

Lawrence's consecration had been an opportunity to heal, reconcile, and unify an already badly fractured diocese and a time to demonstrate his commitment to the Episcopal Church. Instead, the event turned into the opposite. The exclusion of the presiding bishop had been only the start. Many bishops attended from southeastern dioceses but they along with chief consecrator Daniel were downplayed. Hathaway's sermon set the

83. Ibid.

84. *Journal of the Two Hundred and Eighteenth (. . .)* 2009, 37.

85. Ibid.

86. In fact, some of these traditionalists celebrating in Charleston were not Episcopalians. Certainly, many people who had come from San Joaquin were no longer members of the Episcopal Church as the majority of the diocese had just voted to leave the Church for the Southern Cone. St. Paul's of Bakersfield, well represented at the consecration, voted with the majority of the diocese.

tone for the whole event, a hostile differentiation between the traditionalists and their church. Throughout the two days, Lawrence surrounded himself with fellow traditionalists rather than moderates and liberals, even those in his own diocese. Lawrence's consecration events foreshadowed a troubling and troubled partisan episcopacy.

The Presiding Bishop's Visit to Charleston, February 24–25, 2008

Before his consecration, when Bishop-elect Lawrence made it plain to Presiding Bishop Jefferts Schori that he did not want her present at the ceremonies, the standing committee extended to her an invitation to visit the diocese.[87] In his deposition for the circuit court trial made on June 3, 2014, Lawrence testified that the presiding bishop herself created the situation leading to her visit:

> I believe a parish [Holy Cross/Faith Memorial, Pawleys Island ?] had invited her to be—to come to the parish. The parish does not have authority to invite the presiding bishop to come. But the presiding bishop said she was inclined to accept the invitation. It was during a consent process which was already controversial because it was the second consent process.
>
> The presiding bishop, in a very pastorally unhelpful way, said she wanted to come. That raised the stakes for things, and the standing committee was put in the squeeze. This is my recollection and understanding from someone told from a distance.[88]

He concluded: "So with an inappropriate pastoral sensitivity, she makes statements to come. So the standing committee invites her."[89]

Jefferts Schori accepted and a date was set for Sunday, February 24 and Monday, February 25, 2008. At the standing committee meeting of February 12, 2008, Bishop Lawrence distributed a schedule for the visit. The Rev. Haden McCormick, chair of the committee and head of the visitation committee gave the purpose of the presiding bishop's visit as "an opportunity for members of the Diocese of South Carolina to show hospitality, to bear witness to Jesus Christ, and to maintain differentiation between our identity as a diocese and The Episcopal Church."[90] *Maintain differentiation.* There was nothing about listening to her let alone seeking any peace or reconciliation between the diocese and the Church. Jefferts Schori had been invited only to listen to the leaders of South Carolina who were going to show her how and why the diocese was distancing itself from the Church. This was something apparently she did not know in advance. One might wonder just what the leaders meant by differentiation, where they saw this going, and why it was important to them to go there. The schedule called for her to arrive in Charleston at noon on the 24th, visit St. Philip's Church in Charleston for evensong at 3:30 p.m. and have a reception following in the parish hall. The next morning, she was to meet the clergy of the diocese at St. Andrew's Church in Mount Pleasant for a long

---

87. "Deposition Transcript—Mark J. Lawrence," 83.
88. Ibid.
89. Ibid., 84.
90. "Minutes of the Standing Committee." [February 12, 2008].

question and answer session. And finally, she was to visit the Bishop Gadsden retirement community, on James Island, that day at 5:30 p.m.

The presiding bishop's reception in Charleston was outwardly polite but inwardly strained and tense. The traditionalist leaders of the Diocese of South Carolina, now emboldened by their success at having put Lawrence on the bishop's throne and their heady festival consecration, were in no mood to flatter a woman many of whom considered to be their *bête noire*, the very leader of the errant liberal faction of the Episcopal Church. They limited her church visits to St. Philip's, one of the most conservative parishes in Charleston, and to St. Andrew's of suburban Mount Pleasant, arguably the most conservative church in the diocese, and one that would soon bolt the diocese and the Episcopal Church. At St. Philip's and St. Andrew's, the presiding bishop was not invited to officiate at a service. At evensong in St. Philip's, "she was deliberately excluded from the liturgy except for processing beside Bishop Lawrence and offering a brief prayer."[91] At the following reception, however, the people-in-the-pew Episcopalians who had come to see her could not be restrained. They broke out into loud and sustained applause in a standing ovation.[92] A reception line formed with the two bishops standing together, Lawrence made a short remark and Jefferts Schori a "very brief greeting"[93] whereupon a parish spokesman announced that the assembly had to clear out of the room to make way for a Lenten study group that had been scheduled to use the room. Lawrence led the party to the bishop's residence at 50 Smith Street for a dinner that included several clergy, the presiding bishop, her husband, her canon, and her public relations person.[94]

If Jefferts Schori thought her public reception was strained on Sunday, she was in for much more of such on Monday morning when she was to meet the clergy of the diocese for two hours supposed give-and-take in a question-and-answer session. Lawrence later testified that the purpose of the meeting was "to see if we could bring greater clarity and greater charity towards one another."[95] Once behind closed doors, and even with the video cameras rolling, the traditionalist priests of South Carolina poured out their true feelings to her face. As it was closed to the public, we do not have a complete transcript of the session, but we do have a set of twelve videos totaling about ninety minutes, or half of the entire session.[96] Unfortunately, long excerpts were edited out of the video record. Apparently, most of these intentional gaps dealt with the presiding bishop's responses so that we cannot know today the totality of her presentation to the clergy.

What we do know of the session is arresting. Jefferts Schori was seated alone in front under the spot lights, facing the clerical congregation that must have numbered a hundred. Speakers addressed her, backs to audience, either from the side or from a central lectern with a microphone. What was supposed to be an informal give-and-take

---

91. "PB Katharine Jefferts Schori's Peculiar Visit." eNewsletter, Episcopal Forum of SC, February 29, 2008, http://mynewsletterbuilder.com/tools/view_newsletter.php?newsletter_id=1409649931.

92. Ibid.

93. Ibid.

94. "Deposition Transcript—Mark J. Lawrence," 85.

95. Ibid., 86.

96. "Clarity Ensued." Video recording, *The Living Church*, http://www.livingchurch.org/clarity-ensued.

mutual exchange turned mostly into one-way mini-sermons and speeches delivered to the cornered presiding bishop as she remained seated alone a few feet away.

The planned performance started with the lead man, Lawrence, delivering a ten-minute dramatic oration to Jefferts Schori that wasted no time getting to the point: the Episcopal Church had gone off the rails. In his pentecostalist preacher's tone and cadence, the newly-minted Right Reverend Bishop of South Carolina lectured the Most Reverend Primate of the Episcopal Church on the "brokenness within our Communion," on the causes of the "differentiation" between the diocese and the national church, and the "troubling" trajectory of the Episcopal Church.[97] He was just warming up. He went on to confront her point-blank to demand that she stop: 1-the "spin" that only a "small group" of people were leaving the Episcopal Church; 2-the "disparity of talk" that the Holy Spirit was doing things contrary to the Scriptures, things that the Episcopal Church had incorporated into its errant polity that were contrary to the Scriptures; and 3-the "deprecation" of the fundamental doctrine of the church that Christ alone is the source of man's salvation into the "uncatholic religion" of "no real meaning" of sin and grace.[98] It was full frontal attack of vertical against horizontal religion. Lawrence's spirited and strong presentation set the stage for the remainder of the session. His aggressive words became the team's talking points. Jefferts Schori was in for two hours of one traditionalist clergyman after another alternating in lectures, sermons, demands, and accusations. There was not one word of agreement with or support for her. Meanwhile, it was interesting to note who did not go to the podium: a woman, a moderate, a liberal, or another bishop. It was clear the militant traditionalists were organized, prepared, and unrestrained.

One has only to watch the available videos to see the presiding bishop's remarkably cool, calm, almost serene demeanor throughout this tortuously long meeting. Indeed, throughout it all she showed only one slight ripple of emotion as we will see later on. When it came her turn to give her opening remarks, she called for a moment of quiet reflection and talked about the need for, and the meaning of the word "conversation," the communication of an intimate community.[99] She went on to offer her horizontal religious view that we "encounter the image of God in our neighbors."[100] Lawrence, however, would have none of it. She was on his turf. Interrupting her, he shot back that Christ alone was the Messiah, the sacrifice of God for man's salvation. He demanded that the Episcopal Church get back to "the redeeming Grace of Jesus Christ."[101] He insisted that the ultimate issue was between the religion of general revelation (horizontal), that Jefferts Schori supposedly espoused, and the religion of God's redemption through Christ's sacrifice (vertical) which he advocated. Vertical would surrender no ground to horizontal on this day at this place. It was clear by this point that Jefferts Schori's meaning of conversation had fallen on deaf ears.

97. Ibid., Part 1, Part 2.
98. Ibid.
99. Ibid., Part 3.
100. Ibid.
101. Ibid.

There was much more to come. Lawrence proceeded to open the Bible to preach to the presiding bishop from Colossians, "Christ is the image of God."[102] Jesus Christ is not a way, Lawrence insisted, implying that Jefferts Schori denied the uniqueness of Christ, He is the way, the one and only gift of God for man's salvation.[103] The Episcopal Church, he said, was lowering Him down to make Him less than He is. Then a breathtaking shot: "*Time* magazine may misquote us," Lawrence accusingly proclaimed Jefferts Schori, but it would "be helpful for you to say they took it out of context."[104] A hush fell over the room. It was truly astonishing to see a newly minted diocesan bishop demand that the presiding bishop of the Episcopal Church recant her own words. Cool and calm as ever, Jefferts Schori refused to be ruffled. She deliberately ignored this jab and stood to proclaim calmly that she too believed that Jesus Christ died for all the world. She continued that God works in ways that we humans cannot know or comprehend and added that she did not believe that God had abrogated the Covenant with the Jews. Lawrence retorted that salvation of man is "fulfilled in Christ. That is what I want to hear [from you]."[105] *What I want to hear.* It was another breathtaking moment. Once again, Jefferts Schori, outwardly perfectly composed as ever, ignored this astonishingly impertinent challenge.

The tension in the room moved on to a new level when Kendall Harmon took the podium for the second round of questions. After raising the red flag that he meant no disrespect to the presiding bishop, he proceeded to question her character on three counts. Whereas Lawrence had been more theological, Harmon turned to be more personal. First, he said she had given an interview to a Burlington, Vermont, newspaper in which she stated that "a handful of our church leaders would like us never to ordain a gay or lesbian person."[106] "False," "Untrue," "offensive,"[107] protested Harmon adding without any apparent irony that this diocese had never discriminated against gay and lesbian persons. (This was remarkable coming from the Harmon who had been fighting a war concerning homosexuality for at least eighteen years. Besides, one could only wonder, who were the gay and lesbian priests in South Carolina and why would they be supporting a movement fighting against rights for people like themselves?) On the second point, Harmon insisted that Jefferts Schori had said that only a tiny minority, maybe one percent of Episcopalians were discontent with the Church. "That is not true," Harmon asserted.[108] It is a "profound distortion."[109] The numbers, he insisted, were much greater than that. On the third point, Harmon ridiculed the Episcopal Church's claim of reconciliation and inclusion insisting that many "of us" had experienced just the opposite from the Church.[110] He went on to try to shame her by bringing up a case of an eighty-five-year-old retired bishop, where Harmon insisted she had failed miserably and

102. Ibid., Part 4.
103. Ibid.
104. Ibid.
105. Ibid.
106. Ibid., Part 5.
107. Ibid
108. Ibid.
109. Ibid.
110. Ibid.

cruelly in her pastoral responsibilities. He added that there were lots of examples where the Episcopal Church had failed and that a great many Episcopalians were unhappy with their church. You are painting a "misleading picture," he shot at the Presiding Bishop as he insisted that Church decisions had not come from an overwhelming majority.[111] Jefferts Schori, perhaps a little taken aback by Harmon's unmistakable insinuations against her personal character, could only respond, somewhat defensively, that the Episcopal Church had done "good and creative" work on the issue of homosexuality.[112] Unfortunately, the heavily edited video omitted Jefferts Schori's full response to Harmon's astounding remarks.

The following speakers were less accusatory, but they too brought a long list of complaints and accusations against the presiding bishop and the Episcopal Church. The third act was John Barr who insisted that Jefferts Schori tell how she would teach the Scriptures.[113] She responded that the "Bible is the root of what propels us in the world"[114] and that we Anglicans follow tradition, the mind, and Scripture, but not Scripture alone. The fourth act, Dow Sanderson arose to defend the diocese's request for alternate primatial oversight.[115] When another speaker insisted that the Prayer Book was unambiguous, that it was absolutely certain, Jefferts Schori explained the obvious, that the Prayer Book had grown and changed as our understanding of theology had grown and developed over time. One speaker arose to dispute the presiding bishop's description of Anglicans and the Scriptures and quipped that he was glad there was one orthodox bishop here, meaning Lawrence. That was a step too far. Still perfectly composed and calm, if a bit weary, the presiding bishop arose from her seat, faced the hushed audience and said quietly, "I am offended with the assumption there is only one orthodox bishop around here."[116] The previous speaker apologized. It was downhill the rest of the way. The remainder of the questions dealt with the authority of Scriptures and the polity of the Episcopal Church, by now old issues.

The presiding bishop did her best to explain to the unhearing crowd the Pauline "broad" theory of the Body while calling for acceptance of diversity, comprehensiveness, and adaptation to changing conditions. Long before the end, however, it was abundantly clear to everyone what this meeting was all about. One participant observed "Ms. Jefferts-Schori gestured dramatically to express her bewilderment over the communication gap (. . .) and concluded by saying 'I am struck by our inability to communicate.'"[117] She was right. There had been no communication as she had first defined the word. There were two sets of people talking at, and beyond, each other, the presiding bishop

111. Ibid., Part 6.

112. Ibid.

113. Ibid.

114. Ibid., Part 8.

115. Of the four opening acts of this drama, only one, Dow Sanderson, was to remain with the Episcopal Church in the schism. As rector of Holy Communion, he was the most prominent of the Anglo-Catholics in the diocese.

116. Ibid., Part 11.

117. Wood, (the Rev.) Steve. "Conclusion of the Clergy Day." As quoted in "PB Katharine Jefferts Schori's Peculiar Visit," eNewsletter, Episcopal Forum of SC, February 29, 2008, http://mynewsletterbuilder.com/tools/view_newsletter.php?newsletter_id=1409649931.

and the clerical leadership of the diocese. The gulf between the two sets was so wide, the theologies so different, that it was impossible for them to communicate on any amicable level, at least in that setting. In a very real sense, if not a technical one, the schism of the Diocese of South Carolina and the Episcopal Church had already occurred in South Carolina.

The presiding bishop was also shown various diocesan ministries including St. John's Chapel in Charleston, Holy Cross on Sullivan's Island, and Christ-St. Paul's at Yonges Island.[118] Her last event was a visit to the upscale retirement community called Bishop Gadsden, on James Island, in Charleston, where some of the residents were proud descendants of famous old South of Broad Episcopalian families that could trace their ancestry back long before the origin of the diocese. She and Lawrence arrived at Bishop Gadsden at 5:30 p.m. to tour the facility and greet the aged residents who joyfully swarmed the Presiding Bishop with "loud and sustained applause."[119] Considering her experience earlier in the day, that must have been heartwarming to her along with the remarks of Bill Trawick, the president of Bishop Gadsden who assured her "you have many friends here at Bishop Gadsden and throughout the Diocese (. . .) We are grateful for your thoughtful and gracious leadership of our Church."[120] Sorely needed comforting words indeed.

Jefferts Schori may have had "many friends" at Bishop Gadsden but she obviously did not among the clerical structure of the Diocese of South Carolina. Bishop Lawrence boasted triumphantly to the standing committee that the goals of hospitality, witness, and differentiation had been met. No one could have any doubt about the second and third. Lawrence added "While Monday morning's meeting with the diocesan clergy was intense, differentiation was established, providing 'clarity in charity.'"[121] No one could doubt the clarity, but the charity was up for debate. At any rate, it was clear that the diocesan leaders had scored a soaring victory over the hapless presiding bishop, at least in the eyes of most of the diocesan clergy. Differentiation had been met loudly and clearly. It was a thorough triumph of fundamentalist dualism, good against evil, "us" against "them."

The next issue of Harmon's edited diocesan newsletter, *Jubilate Deo*, carried several articles for public consumption about the visit. The lead article, entitled "Hospitality, Witness, and Differentiation" (note the operative words, "witness" and "differentiation") was a compilation of lengthy excerpts from Lawrence's remarks at the clergy session but not a word from the presiding bishop. Lawrence wrote in his diary that he had had a three-hour "prolonged, in depth meeting with Dr. Kendall Harmon" just before he wrote his article for *Jubilate Deo*.[122] Harmon, who had so personally confronted Jefferts Schori at the clergy session, contributed an article apparently meant to castigate the presiding bishop, but it actually inadvertently revealed that Lawrence, Harmon, Barr, and Sander-

---

118. Harmon, (the Rev.) Kendall. "The Presiding Bishop Katharine Jefferts Schori Visits the Diocese." *Jubilate Deo* (Diocese of South Carolina), April/May 2008, 1.

119. Ibid.

120. Ibid.

121. "Minutes of the Standing Committee." [February 26, 2008].

122. *Journal of the Two Hundred and Eighteenh (. . .)* 2009, 41.

son had staged a pre-planned barrage of questions and remarks in what Harmon called a "focus on four topics."[123] In yet another article, Al Zadig, of St. Michael's of Charleston, said that the presiding bishop showed a "vacuum of any coherent theology."[124] He added, "I felt as if the head of the Unitarian Church were at the microphone and not the Presiding Bishop of the Episcopal Church."[125] Actually, Zadig may have had the most astute observation of all: "we are not two churches under one roof but two very different religions."[126] This issue of *Jubilate Deo* offered not one quote from the presiding bishop, let alone a word of praise.

What is one to make of this strange interlude of the presiding bishop's only visit to Lawrence's diocese? Why have this hidden charade? Why the questions and answers with the clergy? What did either side have to gain? Surely each side knew in advance they would change no mind. Or did they? On the presiding bishop's side, she certainly had great concern about the ominous secession movement that was rising under her watch. One diocese had just voted to leave the Episcopal Church and several others were making threatening sounds. Perhaps this was her last-ditch effort to sway South Carolina. Or, perhaps it was an attempt to persuade some of the wavering clergy of South Carolina to remain with the Episcopal Church whatever happened.

The same thing may be true on the other side in reverse. It may have been a dress rehearsal for secession. Or, it may have been a conveniently staged performance by the counter-revolutionary leadership clique around the bishop to convince undecided clergy to stick with Lawrence in the stormy days they expected ahead. Lawrence testified later that he saw the visit as a bonding experience for himself and his clergy: "It seemed to make people feel confident in their new bishop who had only been a bishop for less than a month."[127] As we will see, the clergy of the Diocese of South Carolina were still ambivalent about their relationship with the Episcopal Church. A year later they would vote down a resolution to suspend the general convention. This would show that even a year into the Lawrence episcopacy, there was still positive attachment to the Church among the majority of the priests of the diocese.

It is important to note that the presiding bishop's visit had been controlled and regulated by the diocesan power structure. They set it up primarily for her to hear their grievances, something she endured under the hostile bright lights for hours. They allowed her no occasion to lead a public service, let alone celebrate a Eucharist. They gave no opportunity for the general laity to have free access to her. The two events in which she did meet the public, the receptions at St. Philip's and Bishop Gadsden were confined in various ways. But even in those two events, swarms of lay people freely displayed an overwhelming affection and support for their presiding bishop. That was something the handlers could not control.

---

123. Harmon, "The Presiding Bishop."

124. Zadig, (the Rev.) Alfred T.K. "Point of View, A Visit from the Presiding Bishop." *Jubilate Deo* (Diocese of South Carolina), April/May 2008, 7.

125. Ibid.

126. Ibid.

127. "Deposition Transcript—Mark J. Lawrence," 86.

Building Bonds before Lambeth 2008

Lawrence had been consecrated bishop just in time to prepare to attend the once-a-decade Lambeth Conference, the meeting of the bishops of all the Anglican Communion provinces hosted in England by the Archbishop of Canterbury, the figurehead of the Communion. In 2008, it was to be held in July and August. The first year of Lawrence's episcopacy may be divided into three periods: before Lambeth, January–June 2008; Lambeth, June–August 2008; and, the aftermath of Lambeth, August 2008–February 2009.

Exhilarated by his consecration, new surroundings, new challenges, and successful management of the presiding bishop's visit, Lawrence threw himself into his new role as diocesan bishop with all of his customary zeal and hard work. His standoff with the national Church could be minimized for the moment considering that it would be a year and a half before the next general convention of the Episcopal Church. This allowed a breathing space for the outsider to focus on his immediate goal on coming into office of building strong bonds. Thus, he set about to construct close ties between himself and the elements important to his particular viewpoint: the leadership structure of the diocese, the clergy and communicants of the diocese, the counter-revolutionary Episcopal and Anglican network beyond in America, and the conservative Anglicans overseas. As he told an interviewer, "I'm personally committed to network with people as best I can and not find myself at odds with people that are theologically on the same page as I am."[128] He immediately went to work on a year-long break-neck round of building bonds with all of these parties.

Lawrence's first meeting of the House of Bishops of the Episcopal Church came March 7–12, 2008, when the prelates gathered at Camp Allen Texas. Looking back, it is ironic that the mentor bishop assigned to tutor, or guide, Lawrence was none other than Charles vonRosenberg, of East Tennessee.[129] Under this program, Lawrence talked with vonRosenberg on the telephone at least once a month for the next three years.[130] Lawrence noted little about the March House of Bishops meeting in his diary except that he met with the "Windsor Bishops."[131] This would have been the conservative bishops who were promoting the Windsor Report. Once again, Lawrence strengthened his ties with like-minded prelates.

One important piece of business at the bishops' meeting that Lawrence did not mention in his diary was the matter of John-David Schofield, Lawrence's old bishop, mentor, sponsor, good friend, and ally in San Joaquin. Following on the majority vote of the San Joaquin diocesan convention to sever all ties with the Episcopal Church on December 8, 2007, Presiding Bishop Jefferts Schori issued an official inhibition to Schofield on January 11, 2008, that removed his rights to exercise authority as an Episcopal

---

128. "AAC Interviews Bishop Mark Lawrence." American Anglican Council, April 11, 2008, http://www.americananglican.org/aac-interview-bishop-mark-lawrence.

129. The same vonRosenberg who replaced Lawrence as the bishop of the Episcopal Church in South Carolina.

130. vonRosenberg, (the Rt. Rev.) Charles. Telephone conversation with author, June 7, 2016. vonRosenberg did not divulge the contents of his conversations with Lawrence.

131. *Journal of the Two Hundred and Eighteenth (. . .)* 2009, 42.

bishop. On March 12, the bishops formally voted to depose Schofield as an Episcopal bishop. One might imagine that Lawrence spoke passionately in defense of his old friend before the vote. When the question of proper procedure was raised, the presiding bishop, the parliamentarian, and the chancellor issued assurances that all actions had followed the Constitution and Canons of the Episcopal Church. It was on this point that Lawrence loudly disagreed. Returning home, Lawrence reported the incident to the diocesan standing committee that agreed to file a protest with the House of Bishops.[132]

Upset about Schofield's deposition, Lawrence returned to Charleston ready to strike back. Once Easter was over, he moved. On March 26, he had a long telephone conversation with close friend and ally Robert Duncan, bishop of Pittsburgh followed by a three-hour meeting with the standing committee and a talk with Wade Logan, the chancellor.[133] The next day, he worked on a letter to the presiding bishop protesting the deposition. The two-page letter, signed by Lawrence and John Burwell, head of the standing committee, was dated March 27. It argued that the deposition was non-canonical since it was passed by a majority of present bishops and not by a majority of all Episcopal Church bishops, present and non-present. Fewer than half of all bishops in the Episcopal Church had attended the meeting, therefore many fewer than half of all bishops had voted to depose Schofield. The letter to the presiding bishop concluded: "we must respectfully refuse to recognize the depositions, and we will not recognize any new bishop who may be elected to replace Bishop Schofield, unless and until the canons are followed."[134] On March 28, Lawrence followed up in phone calls with the presiding bishop's office and Kendall Harmon.[135]

It is interesting to note that Lawrence did not argue whether Schofield had been guilty of the charge of abandonment of communion. He said nothing about the specific acts that Schofield had done that led up to the deposition. Instead, Lawrence argued on the grounds of procedure. He said it violated church polity as given in the Constitution and Canons of the Episcopal Church. The rules, he argued, had been misinterpreted and misapplied, and therefore, the deposition was invalid. As we will see, this argument on church polity would become one of the three main broad charges Lawrence would develop in his opposition to the Episcopal Church in years to come, theology, polity, and morality. His first clear statement on this came in the matter of Schofield, just two months after Lawrence had been consecrated bishop.

Lawrence's letter of March 27 was highly significant historically because it set the basic template of his relationship with the Episcopal Church thereafter. Only two months into his episcopacy, this was, in fact, his first official confrontation as a bishop with the authority of the national Church. In the first place, it was drawn up by Lawrence and the standing committee alone. One might reasonably assume that Lawrence proposed the idea, if not the final wording, to be approved by the committee. In the second place, it

---

132. "Minutes of the Standing Committee." [March 26, 2008].

133. *Journal of the Two Hundred and Eighteenth* (. . .) 2009, 44.

134. "Diocese of South Carolina Protests Presiding Bishop's Failure to Follow the Canons." Virtueonline, March 29, 2008, http://www.virtueonline.org. The letter actually protested the depositions of two bishops: Schofield and William Cox.

135. *Journal of the Two Hundred and Eighteenth* (. . .) 2009, 44.

presumed to reject the national Church leadership's interpretation of the Constitution and Canons. Thirdly, it made its own interpretation of the Constitution and Canons which it insisted was the only accurate one. In the fourth place, it rejected an official action of the constituted authorities of the Episcopal Church in favor of its own local decision. Nullification, local rights, and local sovereignty were the themes that appeared in this letter. As we will see, they were to recur, time and again, in the next five years.

Amid a hectic round of non-stop internal diocesan duties and frequent car travel in the Low Country that would have worn out a less hardy person, Lawrence found time to journey outside the diocese to meetings important to his program of building bonds. Counting the House of Bishops meeting in March, Lawrence made six out-of-state trips in his first six months in office, four for conservative conferences and two for Episcopal Church business. On April 24, he flew to O'Hare airport in Chicago to meet other conservative Anglican Network bishops and returned home the same day. May 14–16, he went to Pittsburgh to attend the Trinity School for Ministry Board of Trustees meeting in Ambridge and to attend graduation. A few days later, on May 21, he flew to Milwaukee to attend graduation at Nashotah House, receive an honorary Doctor of Divinity degree and to meet with Robert Duncan and numerous others in the conservative American Anglican Council. Soon thereafter, June 3–4, he attended the Province IV bishops' meeting at Kanuga, North Carolina, where the conversations centered on the upcoming gathering at Lambeth. Then, on June 23, he left for Jerusalem to attend the five-day meeting of GAFCON, the Global Anglican Future Conference.[136]

GAFCON I was by far the most important conference Lawrence attended before Lambeth. Called and led by equatorial African primates and traditionalist bishops of the U.S., Australia, Canada, and England, this pre-Lambeth conference drew 1,148 attendees, all committed to the "orthodox" or traditionalist interpretation of Anglicanism to which Lawrence had always ascribed. Lawrence was one of 291 bishops there. The conference created the network called the Fellowship of Confessing Anglicans and declared that recognition of the Archbishop of Canterbury was not necessary for Anglican identity. Although the group boldly denied it, this created a rival to the Lambeth conference and to the traditional structure of the Anglican Communion. It was an attempt to shift power in the Communion from the Global North, especially England and America, to the Global South. This was part of larger ongoing Anglican Realignment movement.

The conference issued a formal statement called the Jerusalem Declaration on June 29, 2008.[137] It became a major landmark of the Realignment movement, to be noted often by conservative leaders, as Lawrence, for years thereafter. It was a list of fourteen points, most dealing with traditional statements of Anglican identity such as the Thirty Nine Articles. One, however, plainly struck against rights for homosexuals: "the unchangeable standard of Christian marriage between one man and one woman as the proper place for sexual intimacy."[138] Another directly repudiated the legitimacy of the Episcopal Church and the Anglican Church of Canada by clear implication if not

---

136. Ibid., 46–52.

137. "Global Anglican Future Conference," Wikipedia, http://en.wikipedia.org/wiki/Global_Anglican_Future_Conference.

138. "Jerusalem Declaration." http://gafcon.org/resources/the-complete-jerusalem-statement.

by name: "We reject the authority of those churches and leaders who have denied the orthodox faith in word or deed."[139]

Actually, the Jerusalem Declaration was only one part of a longer "Statement on the Global Anglican Future" issued by the conference. It predictably condemned the (pro-homosexual) "false gospel" that diminished the Scriptures, denied the uniqueness of Christ, "promotes a variety of sexual preferences and immoral behavior as a universal human right"[140] and approved the blessing of same-sex unions (two of the four points dealt with homosexuality). Moreover, the statement continued that GAFCON was "out of communion" with churches, e.g., Episcopal, of the false gospel. It also called on confessing Anglicans to leave the errant churches, e.g., Episcopal, and realign with the Global South Anglicans.[141] Throughout it all, however, it was clear that amid all the high flown theological rhetoric, the driving concern of the conference was the issue of homosexuality. It was a counter-offensive against the "liberal" actions on sexuality developing in the North yet threatening the growth and integrity of Anglicanism in the far more traditional cultures of the Global South.

What role did the bishop of South Carolina play in GAFCON and its statements? His published bishop's diary tells us little of his actions during the conference except that he spent sessions working on the declarations and met often with his like-minded friendly bishops. His immediate attitude, however, was very favorable to the meeting. Shortly afterwards, he gave an interview to Steve Waring of *The Living Church* and enthusiastically declared that GAFCON was the heir-apparent to assume leadership of the worldwide Anglican Communion. Criticizing the existing Instruments of Communion that tie together the loose Anglican Communion as inadequate, Lawrence said, "'I witnessed a new birth last month (. . .). The Global South has come to its place of maturity.'"[142] He told the standing committee back in Charleston that the final GAFCON statement was "by and large, a good document."[143]

Lawrence gave warm support to GAFCON and its Jerusalem Declaration then and in the months to come. It was astonishing to see a man who only six months earlier had sworn a sacred oath to support the institution that entrusted him with a high office of authority now praising a movement that condemned the very institution that had awarded him his office. GAFCON rejected the authority of the Episcopal Church, broke communion with it, called on its members to abandon it, and encouraged Global South primatial expansion over the United States.

Lambeth 2008

The 2008 Lambeth conference met in Canterbury from July 16 to August 4 under the leadership of the Archbishop of Canterbury, Rowan Williams. Invitations were sent to

139. Ibid.
140. Ibid.
141. Ibid.
142. "Bishop Lawrence: GAFCON is Heir Apparent." *The Living Church*, August 3, 2008, as quoted in Anglican Church League, August 4, 2008, http://acl.asn.au/gafcon-heir-apparent/.
143. "Minutes of the Standing Committee." [July 1, 2008].

880 bishops around the world; about 650 attended. Some notables that pointedly boycotted the meeting were the primates prominent in GAFCON: Nigeria, Uganda, Rwanda, Kenya. To defuse the crisis that could potentially rend the Communion, Rowan ruled out reopening the Lambeth 1998 controversial Resolution 1.10 on homosexuality. Therefore, Lambeth 2008 was a relatively mild and non-controversial meeting.[144]

Lawrence arrived in London on July 7. He spent the next few days sightseeing in southwest England and Wales. From July 11 to 16, he remained in Exeter where he joined a group of other bishops to speak on their diocesan lives and to continue touring the area. On the 16th, he joined the hundreds of other Anglican bishops at the opening of the Lambeth Conference in Canterbury where he remained until August 4. Lawrence's diary shows a dizzying round of church services, group sessions, study groups, meals, meetings, and touring all with little or no controversy. He met often with other like-minded bishops, informally and formally, and when given the chance, most often chose to attend sessions on human sexuality.[145] Indeed, in his report of July 22 printed in *Jubilate Deo* he devoted the majority of the space to a critique of a session on human sexuality that he dismissed as far too superficial and as a pro-gay set-up.[146] Nevertheless, he continued to attend daily sessions on sexuality. No doubt the most valuable part of the conference for Lawrence was his interactions with other conservative bishops from around the world. In one notable session, on July 22, he met with one hundred bishops from the Global South, Common Cause, and Communion Partners to discuss and promote the proposed Anglican Covenant, a favorite project of the conservatives.[147] Returning home, he told the standing committee that the "unintended consequence of Lambeth has been the nullification of the final instrument of unity."[148] He went on that the connections he had made with other Anglicans had the "advantage of building broader structural relationships in order to provide differentiation between our diocese and TEC."[149] Subsequent events suggested that Lawrence's experience in Jerusalem may have been a turning point for him. After this, he seemed to show increasing confidence that the Anglican Realignment movement provided a viable choice for the future of the diocese. Perhaps the diocese could remain sufficiently "Anglican" by bonding with the conservative majority in the Anglican Communion which now had unifying structure in GAFCON and Global South. If so, the diocese would not need to remain in the Episcopal Church to be truly a part of the Anglican world.

---

144. "Lambeth Conferences," Wikipedia, https://en.wikipedia.org/wiki/Lambeth_Conferences.
145. *Journal of the Two Hundred and Eighteenth (. . .)* 2009, 55–56.
146. "Lambeth Notes." *Jubilate Deo* (Diocese of South Carolina), August/September 2008, 1–2.
147. Ibid.
148. "Minutes of the Standing Committee." [September 4, 2008]. Lawrence's meaning was unclear. The "final instrument of unity" was presumably the Anglican Consultative Council which, in fact, continued functioning as before.
149. Ibid.

Building Bonds after Lambeth 2008

Bishop Lawrence returned to Charleston on August 5, 2008. After a couple of weeks of vacation to visit family in California, he resumed his usual busy schedule and purpose of building bonds. One way of strengthening ties internally was by holding meetings with the diocesan clergy. He held a three-hour session on September 11, at St. Paul's, Summerville, to inform the gathering of one hundred priests of his experiences at GAFCON and Lambeth. He wrote in his diary: "Many difficult issues discussed and deliberated upon."[150] He did not elaborate. Joy Hunter, however, writing in *Jubilate Deo* did elaborate in describing the clergy conference. According to her article, Lawrence continued his harsh criticism of the Episcopal Church's 2003 decision to affirm an openly homosexual bishop relaying tales of woe from Global South bishops he had met who described local negative reactions to this.[151] He went on to introduce a major theme that he would continually expand through his episcopacy, that the diocese consider itself part of the worldwide Anglican Communion more than a part of the Episcopal Church. He said, "'I'm concerned that we not merely fight the battles of the past but prepare for the emerging Anglicanism of the future.'"[152] The "emerging Anglicanism" of the future would presumably be the strongly conservative Global South organization, GAFCON. Discussion at the meeting turned to the question of whether the diocese would remain in the Episcopal Church. Lawrence played coy telling the assembly that the diocese could stay intact and in the Episcopal Church but that certain developments in the Church, namely in the upcoming 2009 General Convention might make that challenging. One should not forget that only a few months earlier, Lawrence had made a solemn oath of loyalty to the Episcopal Church.

Another issue eating away at Lawrence's tenuous attachment to the Episcopal Church was the situation with his close friend and mentor from the early days in the Diocese of Pittsburgh and constant ally in various conservative movements, Robert Duncan, the bishop of Pittsburgh. On January 15, 2008, Duncan was found to have abandoned the communion of the Episcopal Church by the Title IV Review Committee of the Church. The evidence was overwhelming to the committee. The Presiding Bishop then asked Duncan for a letter of reaffirmation of his vows to conform to the Episcopal Church. Duncan refused and responded on March 14 by denying all of the charges against him. The matter was then to be taken up at the next meeting of the House of Bishops scheduled for September in Salt Lake City.[153]

Lawrence flew to Salt Lake City on September 15 for a four-day meeting of the House of Bishops already preparing himself for the coming confrontation. On arrival, he immediately began a three-day round of huddles with conservative colleagues to talk about the Duncan issue.[154] Lawrence prepared a case to present to the House before

---

150. *Journal of the Two Hundred and Eighteenth* (. . .) 2009, 59.

151. Hunter, Joy. "Clergy Gather with Bishop." *Jubilate Deo* (Diocese of South Carolina), October/November 2008, 1.

152. Ibid.

153. "Robert Duncan (bishop)," Wikipedia, http://en.wikipedia.org/wiki/Robert_Duncan_(bishop).

154. *Journal of the Two Hundred and Eighteenth* (. . .) 2009, 60.

the vote: "September 18 (. . .). Prepare my challenge argument in not consenting to the deposition to be spoken during the Committee of the Whole during our morning proceedings."[155] Sure enough, Lawrence did speak to the house challenging the interpretation of what constituted a vote of the majority of bishops. He said it should be all bishops of the Episcopal Church, not just the ones present. This was the same argument he had made in the case of Schofield back in March. Moreover, as in the case of Schofield, Lawrence argued only on the issue of procedure, on the polity of the Church. As with Schofield, he said nothing about the actual charges against Duncan on abandonment of communion, the very issue on which the vote was to be taken. Lawrence's procedural objection was overruled by a lopsided voice vote of the assembly. The bishops then proceeded to vote: 88 to depose Duncan, 35 not to depose, and 4 abstentions. Lawrence wrote: "Somber day for the HOB. I am saddened (. . .) but not depressed."[156]

Lawrence the competitive wrestler was not through with this issue. Far from it. The next day the House adjourned and Lawrence returned to Charleston, "Glad to be back."[157] A few days later, Lawrence contributed a lengthy essay, long on assertions and short on evidence, to the stridently "orthodox" website, Virtue Online, reiterating themes he had already established and would continue to develop: the present crisis in the Episcopal Church is the result of the Church's willful drifting from traditional religion, the Episcopal Church leadership is deliberately misinterpreting the Canons and Constitution of the Episcopal Church, and the liberal leadership of the Church is persecuting the conservative minority.[158] With new momentum, Lawrence continued his busy schedule of going around the diocese talking up his thoughts with clergy and vestries. By late October, he was putting his thoughts into guidance for the standing committee and talking with its members.[159] On November 6, the committee met and unanimously passed two resolutions, that one might reasonably assume came from Lawrence, on GAFCON and Duncan: "subscribe to as a standard of faith the Jerusalem Declaration as set forth at the GAFCON conference," and "does not recognize the non-canonical deposition of (. . .) Duncan."[160] One can only wonder if the standing committee fully appreciated the positions they were taking on these two issues. By affirming the Jerusalem Statement, they were renouncing their own Church (*"We reject the authority of those churches and leaders who have denied the orthodox faith."*).

As Lawrence continued his busy schedule, he also continued his out-of-state travels. On September 30, he flew to Pittsburgh to spend several days devoted to the Trinity School at Ambridge and to attend its Board of Trustees meeting.[161] From October 6 to

155. Ibid.

156. Ibid.

157. Ibid.

158. Lawrence, (the Rt. Rev.) Mark. "South Carolina: Increased Challenges for Diocese in Wake of HOB Actions, Says Bp." Virtueonline, http://www.virtueonline.org/portal/modules/news/print.php?storyid=9107.

159. *Journal of the Two Hundred and Eighteenth* (. . .) 2009, 65.

160. "Standing Committee Passes Unanimous Resolutions." *Jubilate Deo* (Diocese of South Carolina), December 2008/January 2009, 1.

161. *Journal of the Two Hundred and Eighteenth* (. . .) 2009, 61.

8, he was in Sewanee, Tennessee, to receive an honorary doctorate from the University of the South and to attend the Board of Trustees meeting.[162] From December 3 to 5, he attended the Province IV bishops' conference in Live Oak, Florida.[163] On December 8, Lawrence left for a two day convention of the Anglican Communion Network and to confer with its bishops.[164] From February 16 to 18, 2009, he was in Belleville, Illinois, to lead a retreat for his good friend and conservative ally, Peter Beckwith, of the Diocese of Springfield.[165]

While it was clear to Lawrence on his travels around the diocese that he had the enthusiastic support of a great many people in the diocese, there were still important pockets that doubted the bishop's attachment to the Episcopal Church. The Episcopal Forum had been the center of the opposition to Lawrence's selection as bishop. Perhaps to assuage their fears, Lawrence agreed to meet with the group on November 6. He spent three hours with eighty people of the Forum at the Harbour Club having lunch, giving a talk, and speaking with individual members in "Vigorous exchange at times."[166] It was generous of the bishop to share his time with the Forum, but one can be certain that no mind was changed. The summary of comments the Forum later posted on its website mainly showed a frustration with an inability to truly communicate, in much the same way the presiding bishop had complained on February 25.[167] Nevertheless, the Forum somewhat optimistically proclaimed in its December newsletter: "Diocese of SC Plans to Remain in TEC."

One fear that was expressed by attendees at the Forum conference was that Lawrence would take the diocese out of the Episcopal Church as soon as a viable alternative organization developed. The formation of a conservative shadow church came soon thereafter, when on December 3, a collection of friendly conservative leaders met in Wheaton, Illinois, to form what they would soon call the Anglican Church in North America.[168] It was meant to be an "orthodox" replacement for the Episcopal Church to be recognized and supported by the Global South rather than Canterbury. With wide differences among them, the dozen socially counter-revolutionary groups that formed this coalition had one common tie: opposition to the Episcopal Church. One of the original constituent entities forming this new church was the Anglican Communion Network in which South Carolina had played a prominent part.

---

162. Ibid., 62. In 2012 there was not one student in the School of Theology from the Diocese of South Carolina. Lawrence favored Trinity School for Ministry and Nashotah House. He served on the boards of trustees of both.

163. Ibid., 67.

164. Ibid., 68.

165. *Journal of the Two Hundred and Nineteenth Annual Meeting of the Convention of the Diocese of South Carolina, St. Paul's Episcopal Church, Summerville, SC, March 26th and October 15, 2010.* Charleston, SC: the diocese, 2010, "Bishop's Journal, 2009," 38.

166. *Journal of the Two Hundred and Eighteenth (. . .) 2009,* 65.

167. "Report on the 11/6/08 Episcopal Forum with Bishop Lawrence." Episcopal Forum of SC, http://www.episcopalforumofsc.org/forumreports.html.

168. Goodstein, Laurie. "Episcopal Split as Conservatives form New Group." *The New York Times,* December 3, 2008, http://www.nytimes.com/2008/12/04/us/04episcopal.html?pagewanted=all&_r=0.

Thus, as Bishop Lawrence finished his first year and approached the first annual diocesan convention over which he would preside, the state of the Diocese of South Carolina could be described as uneasy at best and tumultuous at worst. Strains and tensions had grown noticeably stronger in the year. The prominence and power of the conservatives, having placed Lawrence on the bishop's throne, was rising while the confusion and unease among the suspicious moderate and liberal communicants did not abate. Lawrence himself spent the year working tirelessly mostly traveling about the diocese influencing as many clergy and laity as possible and traveling afar building alliances with domestic and foreign conservative elements. He started the year vowing to adhere to the Episcopal Church then spent the rest of the year denouncing its trajectory and quarreling with its policies and procedures.

One large concept, certainly not new to Lawrence, but one he increasingly promoted, was the idea that South Carolinians should think of themselves as "Anglicans" first and members of a worldwide religion rather than a national one. Of all places, it was important to do this in South Carolina where the Episcopal Church was long the established religion of high society. South of Broad in Charleston, practically everybody who was anybody in the old clans was an Episcopalian. The ancient exclusive social clubs of Charleston and its vicinity, as the South Carolina Society and the Saint Cecelia Society, were all but monopolized by hereditary Episcopalian families. Perhaps nowhere in the country was church tied to society as much as it was in the historic Holy City. It would not be an easy task to convince these people that they should stop thinking of themselves as members of the Episcopal Church after more than two centuries of proudly ingrained identity.

If differentiation from the Episcopal Church were the policy, the enactment of it followed. Lawrence's argument against the depositions of Schofield and Duncan on procedural lines was not a convincing one, at least among the national Church leaders. The Episcopal Church's presiding bishop, chancellor, and parliamentarian all shrugged it off. The body of bishops refused to buy it. Knowing that it did not matter to the national leadership, Lawrence may well have made the arguments really for home consumption for it was back in South Carolina that he used the issue of procedure to energize the standing committee to send letters of protest to the presiding bishop and to nullify the national church decisions. The effect in South Carolina was to generate even greater animosity from the diocesan leadership to the Episcopal Church. In complaining bitterly about the depositions of his dear friends Schofield and Duncan, Lawrence established the working pattern that he would repeat in his episcopacy.

Thus, in his first year as bishop, Lawrence demonstrated almost continuous criticism of the Episcopal Church. He refused to have the presiding bishop attend his consecration which was virtually a counter-revolutionary festival. When Jefferts Schori did visit, she was forced to listen for hours to non-stop complaints against her and the Episcopal Church. Lawrence traveled out of state a dozen times, often on non-Episcopal Church business to meet with other traditionalist bishops. Even at Lambeth, he sought out his philosophical friends. He loudly and strongly protested the official Episcopal Church depositions of his allies Schofield and Duncan. He campaigned to have communicants think of themselves only as "Anglicans" connected to a global church. And, most seriously he warmly supported GAFCON's Jerusalem Declaration that repudiated the authority of the Episcopal Church. While Lawrence had kept his word of not intending to leave the Episcopal Church, he built in his first year a clear and rising criticism of the national Church as he built bonds within and without the diocese. His second year would show whether these bonds and this critical Episcopalian attitude would rise or fall.

TESTING BONDS, 2009

The Background of the General Convention of 2009

The second year of Lawrence's episcopacy was dominated by the General Convention of the Episcopal Church, the triennial meeting of the Church to be held in July of 2009, in Anaheim, California. In South Carolina, the Convention cast a big shadow, both in the first half of the year and the second. In many ways, Lawrence and the diocese spent the first half of the 2009 preparing for it. And, the very first event in Lawrence's second year as bishop was the most important, the annual diocesan convention in March.

The two hundred and eighteenth annual meeting of the diocese was held at Christ Church of Mount Pleasant, March 12–13, 2009. It was the first convention in which Lawrence presided as the diocesan bishop. He had spoken at the 2008 convention, but Bishop Salmon had presided. Now, Lawrence, the lone bishop with authority, was ready to use his diocesan convention as a grand stage on which he could act out the themes he had already well-established in his first year: hostility to the Episcopal Church, rejection of its authority over the diocese, and promotion of Anglican identity over Episcopal. He wasted no time getting to it. He described a virtual state of war between the diocese, which he believed was holding the true religion, and the mother Church that had abandoned the traditional faith. His most telling line summed it up: "Either Episcopalianism will repent of its unscriptural autonomy or it will spread its splintering tentacles of the last forty years throughout the Anglican Communion."[169] Lawrence revealed what he saw as the fundamental issue at stake: the whole trajectory of the Episcopal Church in the last forty years. These were the decades in which the Church had developed horizontal religion promoting civil rights, women's ordination, prayer book reform, and equality for homosexual persons. Apparently, Lawrence's war was to defeat and stop this errant social gospel religion and reestablish the supremacy of the once-reigning vertical religion, the one that he believed held all the truths of God, the faith once delivered. As he said, he had resolved that no less than the entire future of the Anglican Communion rested on this.

Under his overall theme, Lawrence returned to his by now familiar three complaints against the Episcopal Church: "compromise toward the Uniqueness of Christ, certain non-Canonical actions of the Presiding Bishop and the HOB; as well as the controversies regarding Human Sexuality."[170] These three complaints remained consistent through the

---

169. *The Journal of the Two Hundred and Eighteenth* (. . .) 2009, 35.

170. Ibid. Lawrence continued his theme of complaint against the Episcopal Church on the three points of polity, theology, and sexuality throughout his episcopacy.

schism; and he would reiterate them many times to come in the next few years. The differentiation between the diocese and the national Church was so pronounced, he said, that the constitutional provision "'The Church in the Diocese of South Carolina accedes to and adopts the Constitution and Canons of the Protestant Episcopal Church,'" may need to be reinterpreted.[171] This was the first time in which Lawrence publicly suggested that the Diocese of South Carolina might not continue in the Episcopal Church. Revoking the clause of accession would mean secession from the Church.

In his address, Lawrence also emphasized another theme by now standard in his rhetoric, that South Carolinians should think of themselves as world-wide Anglicans rather than Episcopalians. He proclaimed a new motto: "Making Biblical Anglicans for a Global Age."[172] The operative words here were "Biblical," "Anglicans," and "Global." Biblical meant that they would follow the Scriptures in all things, while presumably the heretical Episcopal Church did not. The word Anglican connoted identity beyond the Episcopal Church. Global implied links with Anglican provinces overseas, particularly in the distinctly socially conservative Global South. He went on to talk at length about ways and means to strengthen ties with conservative Anglicans overseas. He announced the creation of an Anglican Communion Development Committee, to be headed by Kendall Harmon.[173] Thus, in his first bishop's address to an annual diocesan convention, Lawrence clearly set the themes the diocese would follow.

Beyond the bishop's stage-setting debut address, there was other important business at the convention. As an effective way of protesting against the Episcopal Church, Craige Borrett and Kendall Harmon introduced Resolution R-3 to the assembly. It called for the suspension of the General Convention.[174] This would mean presumably that South Carolina would boycott the General Convention meeting that was scheduled for July 2009. Such an act would at least alert the national Church of South Carolina's discontent. The resolution was openly discussed and a vote was taken. It was defeated in the Clergy Order.[175] This was a highly significant moment for South Carolina because it showed that the majority of the clergy of the diocese were not yet willing to go as far as the diocesan leadership in striking out at the Episcopal Church. Apparently, Harmon and the other conservative leaders had not counted their votes ahead of time. Lawrence's role in this was not mentioned in the record, but it was hard to imagine that he had nothing to do with it. He communicated with Harmon often and regularly as shown in his diary. If the conservative leaders were embarrassed by their defeat, it did not show in the record either, but it was interesting to note that hereafter no resolution they proposed encountered defeat.

Although R-3 was defeated, Harmon and Borrett also proposed two other resolutions that passed, R-2 affirming the Uniqueness of Christ and R-4 that withheld consent for an episcopal election in Northern Michigan.[176] R-2 no doubt was meant to strike

---

171. Ibid.

172. Ibid., 31. This phrase was to become a sort of motto used from then on.

173. Ibid., 34.

174. *Journal of the Two Hundred and Eighteenth* (. . .) 2009, 28.

175. Ibid.

176. Ibid.

against the presiding bishop whom conservatives accused of denying that Christ was the only way for the salvation. Another resolution also passed, R–1, supporting the Anglican Covenant, a move that conservatives promoted in the belief that under the Covenant terms the Episcopal Church would be forced to accede to the will of the conservative majority of Anglican provinces. It had been proposed by Lawrence and the standing committee.[177]

The defeat of R–3 did not assuage the fears of the pro-Episcopal side. The increasingly ominous soundings of the diocese were clear to the leaders of the Episcopal Forum who called a conference entitled "What Happens to the Episcopalians who wish to remain a part of the Episcopal Church when diocesan leadership chooses to leave it?" on March 28, in Okatie.[178] Yet another telling sign was that *Jubilate Deo*, the diocesan newsletter, now edited by Joy Hunter with the assistance of Kendall Harmon, refused to print an article the Forum had submitted announcing the meeting. Moreover, the newsletter would not even post the Forum meeting in the list of events around the diocese such as tea rooms. Afterwards, *Jubilate Deo* gave no hint that the Forum had had a meeting. Communication in the diocese was now monopolized by the conservative leadership to the exclusion of the pro-Episcopal faction.

What effect the defeat of R–3 had on Lawrence was impossible to tell in the public records. He resumed his usual hectic schedule of traveling about the diocese building bonds with clergy and laity. He also resumed his frequent trips out of state, six in the next four months. From March 15 to 18, 2009, he attended the House of Bishops meeting in Kanuga, North Carolina. Talk of the upcoming General Convention would have been common. On March 30, he traveled to Bakersfield, California. The next day he apparently participated in his son Chad's ordination service in St. Paul's Anglican Church. He wrote in his diary: "9:30—11:30 Sermon Preparation (. . .). 2:30—4:30 Sermon Preparation. 5:00 Rehearsal for Ordination. 6:30 Chad's Ordination in St. Paul's, Bakersfield."[179] St. Paul's had earlier joined the secession of the majority of San Joaquin from the Episcopal Church and was at this time not an Episcopal Church. From April 15 to 17, Lawrence was in Houston for a meeting of the Anglican Communion Partners and the Anglican Communion Institute.[180] From May 13 to 16, he was in Ambridge, Pennsylvania, for a Trinity School Board of Trustees meeting and the graduation of his son, Chad.[181] May 18–21 he was in Lake Logan, North Carolina, for a meeting of the College of Bishops.[182] On June 2, he was back at Kanuga, North Carolina, for a three day meeting of the Province IV bishops.[183] On June 30 and July 1, he was in Kanuga again for

---

177. Ibid.

178. "Episcopal Forum of SC Sponsors Spring Conference on March 28." eNewsletter, Episcopal Forum of SC, March 13, 2009, http://www.mynewsletterbuilder.com/tools/view_newsletter.php?newsletter_id=1409870707.

179. *Journal of the Two Hundred and Nineteenth (. . .)* 2010, 41.

180. Ibid., 42.

181. Ibid., 45.

182. Ibid.

183. Ibid., 47.

a conservative gathering called the Renewal Conference.[184] The race to build bonds near and far had not slowed at all.

The April 15–17 meeting in Houston had an important outcome. It was a gathering of Communion Partner bishops, all traditionalists as Lawrence, sponsored by a highly conservative think tank called the Anglican Communion Institute whose *raison d'être* seemed to be to produce a stream papers relentlessly critical of the Episcopal Church. This time was no exception. On April 22, the ACI produced an article called "Bishops' Statement on the Polity of the Episcopal Church."[185] It was signed by Lawrence, ten other diocesan bishops, and four other bishops.[186] It was a thirteen-page treatise meant to demonstrate that individual dioceses were sovereign, not the central authority of the Episcopal Church. It argued that the bishop was the only authority in a diocese, that the Episcopal Church was a voluntary association, that dioceses were not subordinate to any hierarchy, that episcopal vows did not pledge obedience to a higher power, and that dioceses could maintain membership in the Anglican Communion. Local sovereignty was a theme Lawrence had established early on, even showing up in the Schofield protest just two months after his consecration. Once again, Lawrence did his best to publicize the ACI paper. On May 4, he published an essay in Virtue Online expounding on the points of the paper.[187] As we will see, Lawrence and the diocesan leadership would develop the idea of local sovereignty into one of the guiding principles of the schism. It is interesting to note the irony that conservatives supported independence for dioceses in the Episcopal Church but not for the Episcopal Church in the Anglican Communion. The Anglican Covenant was promoted by conservatives to force confessional uniformity on the individual Anglican provinces such as the Episcopal Church.

While the idea of local sovereignty developed, another far more fateful issue appeared in the spring of 2009, the control of local property. The diocese was still in the courts trying to enforce the Dennis Canon in the case of All Saints parish, Waccamaw. In May of 2009, St. Andrew's Church in Mount Pleasant appealed to the standing committee to approve a plan in which St. Andrew's would shift millions of dollars' worth of real estate into a special trust beyond the control of the diocese and national Church. The trust was to be governed by a board of trustees separate from the vestry. Bishop Salmon, for all his criticism of the Episcopal Church had been resolute in his enforcement of the Dennis Canon. St. Andrew's request would mean two points: the Dennis Canon would be ignored in the diocese, and a precedence would be set for other parishes to remove

---

184. Ibid., 49.

185. "Bishops' Statement on the Polity of the Episcopal Church." The Anglican Communion Institute, April 22, 2009, http://www.anglicancommunioninstitute.com/2009/04/bishops-statement-on-the-polity-of-the-episcopal-church.

186. Diocesan: Lawrence; Adams, Western Kansas; Beckwith, Springfield; Howe, Central Florida; Jacobus, Fond du Lac; Little, Northern Indiana; Love, Albany; MacPherson, Western Louisiana; Smith, North Dakota; Stanton, Dallas; Wimberly, Texas. Others: Frey, Rio Grande; Hathaway, Pittsburgh; Lambert, Dallas; Salmon, South Carolina.

187. Lawrence, (the Rt. Rev.) Mark. "South Carolina: Bishop Reflects on Bishops' Statement on Polity." Virtueonline, May 4, 2009, http://www.virtueonline.org/portal/modules/news/print.php?storyid=10376.

property from diocesan, and national Church, control. This matter would turn out to be far more important than anyone could have imagined at the time.

When St. Andrew's request arrived in the standing committee in May of 2009, Bishop Lawrence gave it at least tacit approval, perhaps much more. He was a non-voting attendant of the committee. The existing record showed no remark of Lawrence against the request in the standing committee. His motives for giving what appears to be support remained hidden. The significance of this matter could not have been lost on him. He must have known very well what it meant for the diocese and the Dennis Canon. It showed that less than a year and a half into his episcopacy he was ready to make a major move in disregard of the Dennis Canon of the Episcopal Church which was still the explicit law of the diocese. Moreover, the corporate charter at that time stated outright that the diocese operated under the Constitution and Canons of the Episcopal Church. The diocesan leadership would be going against diocesan law and national Church law and doing so, ironically, while the diocese was still in court enforcing the Dennis Canon on All Saints Waccamaw; however, they would now be acting under the secrecy of the standing committee.

With the request in hand, the Rev. Jeffrey Miller, chair of the Standing Committee, told the committee on May 26, 2009, that they should be prepared to vote on St. Andrew's petition at the upcoming committee retreat.[188] Three days later, the committee gathered at Camp St. Christopher.[189] On the afternoon of the 30th, it took up St. Andrew's property request. The parish asked approval of the transfer of a several pieces of its property to "an irrevocable charitable trust known as the St. Andrew's—Mt. Pleasant Land Trust" that had already been established.[190] The significance of this was lost on no one present. Indeed, the official minutes of the meeting stated: "there is a concern that this transfer, on the basis of fundraising limitations, will have long-standing ramifications for every church in the diocese."[191] The writer could not have known what an understatement that would turn out to be.

St. Andrew's request was no small amount. The properties had been assessed at $8,300,000, but reportedly had a market value of $5,300,000.[192] The sale price was given as $3,445,000.[193] St. Andrew's vestry was to be the seller while St. Andrew's Land Trust was to be the buyer. What this meant was that St. Andrew's was simply shifting the real estate from one part of the parish to another with the obvious aim being to secure local control over the property beyond the right of the diocese and national Church. After the committee discussed the rather complicated figures and legal aspects, Johnnie

188. "Minutes of the Standing Committee." [May 26, 2009].

189. Committee members present were: the Revs. Jeffrey Miller, Shay Gaillard, Patrick Allen, Anthony Kowbeidu, Jennie Olbrych, as well as Lydia Evans, Ann Dennis, Drak Drakeford, Frenchie Richards, William Clarkson, Johnnie Corbett. Also present were Bishop Lawrence, Chancellor Wade Logan, and retired Bishop Alden Hathaway of Pittsburgh. "Minutes of the Standing Committee." [May 29-30, 2009].

190. Ibid.

191. Ibid.

192. Ibid.

193. Ibid.

Corbett made a motion that the committee approve St. Andrew's request pending some slight clarification of the legal language with Drak Drakeford seconding the motion.[194] Concerned about the inadequacies of the legal wording, Lydia Evans made a motion to table Corbett's motion, seconded by the Rev. Patrick Allen.[195] Evans's motion was put to a vote, and failed to carry a majority.[196] Suddenly, and perhaps unexpectedly, there appeared the possibility the committee would split up over the matter, a rare occurrence. Perhaps sensing impending trouble, Bishop Lawrence spoke up and suddenly offered a prayer of "discernment" for the committee.[197] Immediately following this, the Rev. Jeffrey Miller made a motion to approve St. Andrew's request, seconded by Corbett.[198] The committee then voted approval. The properties were subsequently moved into the irrevocable trust. Apparently, the details of the Standing Committee vote on St. Andrew's property remained hidden until the committee minutes were turned over to lawyers as background of the circuit court trial of 2014.

The Standing Committee's approval of St. Andrew's request was of enormous importance in the history of the schism. It overturned the Dennis Canon as the policy of the diocese once and for all. The state supreme court soon returned its ruling on the *All Saints* case. Lawrence was to declare the Dennis Canon dead in the diocese. Actually, it had already died. The Standing Committee killed it on May 30, 2009 at Camp St. Christopher. Thus, by the late spring of 2009, the diocesan leadership had made two landmark stands: local sovereignty, and local ownership of property. It would not be long before they would move on to the next step, independence from the Episcopal Church. First would come the General Convention of the Episcopal Church.

The General Convention of 2009

It was with more than a little concern that the shrinking conservative minority of Episcopal bishops, now lacking the departed Schofield, Duncan, Iker, and Ackerman, journeyed to Anaheim, California, for the triennial General Convention of the Episcopal Church, July 7–18. They knew that, once again, the issue of homosexuality would be front and center and that they were in the minority. The last two general conventions had been a roller coaster ride for them. They had been outraged, to put it mildly, at the 2003 House of Bishop's affirmation of the first openly gay bishop. In 2006, they had breathed a slight sigh of relief at the overwhelming passage of B033 that favored the Windsor Report and the suspension of the consecration of homosexual persons as bishops. But they were all anxiously well-aware that there was more to come, much more.

Lawrence led the delegation from South Carolina for the entire eleven-day event, the last general convention of the Episcopal Church in which this would be true. The eight delegates, four clergy, and four lay, plus the bishop, represented part of the inner circle of

---

194. Ibid.
195. Ibid.
196. Ibid.
197. Ibid.
198. Ibid.

diocesan leadership.[199] All were close to Lawrence, and all but one would later play roles in the diocesan secession. Lawrence's diary shows that he spent almost all of his free time with like-minded friends and colleagues: the South Carolina delegation, the Anglican Communion Partners, Trinity School groups, Nashotah House friends, and conservative bishops. He gave one interview, and that was to the conservative outlet, Anglican TV. It was as if South Carolina had already set itself apart from the Episcopal Church.

The most important resolution passed in the 2009 General Convention was D025. It opened with a long pledge of fidelity to the Anglican Communion then turned to the issue of homosexual persons in the ministry: "God has called and may call such individuals [homosexuals] to any ordained ministry in The Episcopal Church."[200] *Any ordained ministry*. It passed overwhelmingly.[201] The Convention thus adopted a resolution that clearly approved in principle the ordination of homosexuals as deacons, priests, and bishops. In addition, the Convention passed another controversial resolution, C056 that called for theological studies about liturgical rites for the blessing of same-sex unions.[202] There was little debate in the House of Bishops on C056 perhaps reflecting a defeatist resignation on the right wing.

The conservative minority immediately charged that D025 revoked B033 of 2006 and that C056 meant rites for the blessing of same-sex unions. Actually, neither one did that explicitly, although one might argue about the overall intentions and meanings of the resolutions. The reality of the resolutions depended on how one interpreted the nuances of their wordings. Hoping they had stopped the hated issue of homosexuality in 2006 with B033, the frustrated traditionalist minority now raged in protest. The South Carolina delegation let their feelings fly to their followers back home. Typical was Kendall Harmon who shot back: "The passage of Resolution D025 by the General Convention of 2009 is a repudiation of Holy Scripture (. . .). It is a particularly ugly sight."[203] Perhaps more representative of the South Carolina delegation, Elizabeth Pennewill wrote in frustration "The Diocese of SC was, after all, a small but complete minority, practically impotent."[204] She fumed at the social gospel diversion: "The Episcopal Church has become, a cause-driven action-oriented political organization."[205] Perhaps sniffing an air of secession she revealed her hand: "I don't know what's going to happen with our Diocese and its relationship with TEC (. . .). I trust our leadership."[206] *I trust our leadership*. That

---

199. Clergy: Kendall Harmon, Steve Wood, Haden McCormick, John Burwell (Chair). Laity: Reid Boylston, Wade Logan, Elizabeth Pennewill, Lydia Evans.

200. *Journal of the General Convention of the Protestant Episcopal Church in the United States of America Otherwise Known as The Episcopal Church 2009*. New York, the church, 2009, 627–28.

201. Vote on D025 in House of Bishops: 104 yes, 30 no, 2 abstain. Vote in House of Deputies: Laity, 78 yes, 21 no, 9 divided; clergy, 77 yes, 19 no, 11 divided. Thus, D025 passed every voting assembly with at least 75% of the vote.

202. *Journal of the General Convention* (. . .) 2009, 780.

203. "Kendall Harmon on D025." Episcopal Café, http://www.episcopalcafe.com/lead/general_convention_2009_live/kendall_harmon_on_d025.html.

204. "SC Diocesan Delegates Frustrated at GC." eNewsletter, Episcopal Forum of SC, July 17, 2009, http://mynewsletterbuilder.com/tools/view_newsletter.php?newsletter_id=1409983085.

205. Ibid.

206. Ibid.

had to be reassuring to Lawrence and the standing committee. In one more way, he was bonding the majority of the diocese. Steve Wood was less restrained: "'The conservatives are treated more as zoological oddities. We're patted on the head, nice-nice, and then we get steamrolled.'"[207] He sounded the most ominous note from a South Carolinian: "[we] disavow this General Convention's actions. We will now prayerfully seek ways to be faithful to the Anglican Communion and to the mutual responsibility and interdependence to which we are called, no matter what the cost."[208] *No matter what the cost.*

Not one to sit by idly and accept defeat, Lawrence prepared an aggressive response to the General Convention's actions. On the last day of the meeting, July 18, he gave an interview to Anglican TV blasting away at the Episcopal Church.[209] It was promulgating a false gospel that would replace the Gospel of Jesus Christ, he declared. The House of Deputies was committing aggression against the Church by pressing its wrongful agenda of inclusivity, he charged. What was at stake was the very survival of the Anglican Communion, he proclaimed. What about changing the Episcopal Church from within? "We do not see ourselves as reforming the Episcopal Church," he retorted perhaps with an air of resignation if not with a veiled threat.[210]

Ever the man of action, not just word, Lawrence had been meeting intermittently with his fellow Communion Partner bishops, really a sub-set of the Convention, basically the same ones that had signed the April 22 "Bishops' Statement on the Polity of the Episcopal Church," throughout the eleven days of the Convention. On July 16, two days before the end, the Communion Partner bishops drew up a declaration called the "Anaheim Statement."[211] They styled it a minority report in opposition to the enacted resolutions, D025 and C056.[212] In it, they rejected the ordinations of non-celibate homosexuals and the blessings of same-sex unions and reiterated support for the various actions in the Anglican Communion that had called for a suspension of actions on those two matters: "We reaffirm our commitment to the three moratoria requested of us by the instruments of Communion."[213] They claimed that two of the moratoria had been ignored in the passage of D025 and C056. Bishop Lillibridge, of West Texas, read the Anaheim Statement aloud in the House of Bishops to a respectful and appreciative audience.[214] It was circulated among the bishops at the convention and eventually thirty-five signed it, some of whom had actually voted for one or both of the two denounced resolutions.

---

207. Goodstein, Laurie. "Episcopal Bishops Give Ground on Gay Marriage." *The New York Times*, July 16, 2009, http://www.nytimes.com/2009/07/16/us/16episcopal.html.

208. "Statement of South Carolina in Response to the Passage of Resolution C056." July 17, 2009, http://www.kendallharmon.net/19/index.php/t19/article/24284/.

209. "GC 2009: A Conversation with Bishop Lawrence." Video recording, Anglican TV, July 18, 2009, 28 minutes, http://www.YouTube.com.

210. Ibid.

211. *Journal of the Two Hundred and Nineteenth (. . .)* 2010, 50.

212. Thirty bishops had voted "No" on D025 and C056, although they were not the same thirty.

213. "Updated GC 2009: Minority Bishops Release 'Anaheim Statement.'" Virtueonline, July 17, 2009, http://www.virtueonline.org/ports/modules/news/article.php?storyid=10853. The three moratoria: ordinations of homosexuals, blessing of same-sex unions, cross-border incursions.

214. "Seven Diocesans Meeting with Rowan Williams." Episcopal Café, September 2, 2009, http://www.episcopalcafe.com/lead/anglican_communion/7_diocesans_meeting_with_Rowan.html.

The Anaheim Statement was an after-the-fact publicity show and not a plan of action. It had no teeth. It gained news attention, but had little effect afterwards. Lawrence's real concern was perhaps the impact of the Convention on the Diocese of South Carolina. Well before the end of the convention he started taking measures for it. He wrote and rewrote a letter to the diocesan clergy, finished and sent on July 18.[215] In it he announced that he had scheduled a meeting with the convocation deans, the standing committee, and others on July 28 because "we face significant challenges."[216] He slammed the controversial resolutions: "If blessing same-sex unions is morally wrong now, it will be morally wrong in the future."[217] To enhance the sense of urgency of the moment, he returned to the theme he had raised in his bishop's address back in the annual diocesan convention of March 2009, that the horizontal religion of the Episcopal Church must be stopped now before it spreads like a cancer through the whole worldwide Anglican Communion (he did not explain how such a phenomenon would actually happen in the fiercely socially conservative Global South). This was no longer a fight for true religion in America, he said. It was for no less than the world: "There is an increasingly aggressive displacement within this Church of the gospel of Jesus Christ's transforming power by the 'new' gospel of indiscriminate inclusivity which seeks to subsume all in its wake (. . .) imperialistic plans to spread throughout the Communion."[218] Alluding to a place apart for the diocese to fight this supposed impending cataclysm, he wrote: "This calls for a bold response. It is of utmost importance that we find more than just a place to stand."[219] If that would not rile up the communicants and clergy, what would? Lawrence could not have forgotten that only a few months earlier his clergy had shown that they were reluctant to walk apart from the Episcopal Church.[220]

The Aftermath of the General Convention of 2009

Even though Lawrence spent a few days after the Convention visiting family in Bakersfield, he remained busy making plans and communicating with people back in South Carolina. The South Carolina delegation returned home ready to spread their condemnation of the Convention. On July 19, Wade Logan, delegate and diocesan chancellor, addressed an assembly in St. Michael's of Charleston: "'It really is a political convention, that's what it turned into."[221] On his travel day to Charleston, on July 22, Lawrence busily made numerous phone calls to close allies such as Robert Duncan and Kendall

---

215. *Journal of the Two Hundred and Nineteenth* (. . .) 2010, 50.

216. Lawrence, (the Rt. Rev.) Mark. "Bishop Mark Lawrence Writes to the Clergy of the Diocese Regarding General Convention 2009." July 18, 2009, http://kendallharmon.net/t19/index.php/t19/article/24328/.

217. Ibid.

218. Ibid.

219. Ibid.

220. By defeating Harmon's resolution in the diocesan convention to suspend the General Convention.

221. Cowall, Alan. "Anglicans May Form 2 Tracks." *The Post and Courier* (Charleston, SC), July 29, 2009.

Harmon.[222] On July 23, his first full day back in Charleston, he had a two hour meeting with the deans certainly to discuss the Convention and his ideas of diocesan reaction.[223] From the 24th to the 28th he spent a good deal of time preparing for the meeting of July 28 that he had set up and announced before the end of the Convention. Lawrence later testified: "After the convention of 2009 I came back to the diocese, to a restless environment. I wrote a 10 or 11 page document which was addressed to the clergy of the diocese in which I articulated, as best I could, the theological, moral and polity challenges that were before us at the diocese with decisions of ultra vires ["beyond powers" or invalid] acts that The Episcopal Church's general convention had taken in 2009."[224]

The July 28 meeting was arguably the most important conference that Lawrence convened in his episcopacy. At 10:30 a.m., he brought together the power core of the diocesan leadership: deans of the convocations[225], the twelve-member Standing Committee,[226] and several other key figures as Kendall Harmon, Jim Lewis, the canon to the ordinary, and Wade Logan, the chancellor. They met privately at the Church of the Good Shepherd in West Ashley, across from Charles Towne Landing. Harmon, never one to understate matters, blogged at TitusOneNine: "You all know we are not gathering to have tea and crumpets. *There is no way we as a diocese can function in the way we have before* [sic]. How to move forward (. . .) is the issue."[227] If records existed of this meeting, they were not released to the public. Harmon reported that they started meeting at 10:30 a.m. and continued longer than anyone expected. They ordered dinner out and finally adjourned at 9:00 p.m., ending a ten and a half-hour marathon.[228] The only public report of the session came from Harmon who wrote: "The atmosphere was prayerful, focused, intense, deeply trusting of one another and the Bishop, and with a sense that the stakes are very, very high. There was broad general agreement about the basic direction the Diocese needs to take."[229] Three points he made were important to emphasize: a sense of crisis coming out of the General Convention, innate trust in the bishop, and agreement on direction. Events were soon to show that Harmon's assessment was completely on mark.

It soon became clear that Lawrence and the diocesan leadership core resolved in the meeting of July 28 to move farther apart from the Episcopal Church. Just how far to move was the lingering question. They agreed to call a special diocesan convention soon

222. *Journal of the Two Hundred and Nineteenth (. . .)* 2010, 50.

223. Ibid.

224. "Deposition Transcript—Mark J. Lawrence," 105.

225. John Barr, John Scott, Ed Kelaher, Peet Dickinson, Craige Borrett, Chuck Owens, and John Burwell.

226. Clergy: Jeff Miller, Jennie Olbrych, Anthony Kowbeidu, Shay Gaillard, Patrick Allen, David Thurlow; Laity: William Clarkson, Johnny Corbett, Drak Drakeford, Lydia Evans, Anne Dennis, Frenchie Richards.

227. Harmon, (the Rev.) Kendall. "Kendall Harmon: Your Prayers Requested for a Diocese of South Carolina Leadership Meeting Today." July 28, 2009, http://kendallharmon.net/t19/index.php/t19/article/24504/.

228. Harmon, (the Rev.) Kendall. "Update on Yesterday's South Carolina Standing Committee Meeting with the Bishop and Deans." July 29, 2009, http://kendallharmon.net/t19/index.php/t19/article/24518/.

229. Ibid.

and to present a list of resolutions to be approved. They drew up the resolutions for that convention, the precise wording of which must have been very time consuming. As we will see, the sum of these resolutions was to create a de facto separation of the Diocese of South Carolina from the Episcopal Church.

The meeting of July 28 did not occur in a vacuum nor was it a starting place. It was the logical sequence of the fundamental ideas, policies, and procedures that the diocesan leadership had been building for at least a year and a half. The diocesan convention of March 2009 had already shown a willingness to denounce the Episcopal Church and move away from it, if only slightly. It was the General Convention of 2009, however, that set the stage for the crucial meeting of July 28. The secretive meeting of some two-dozen people on that day was the crucial point of the whole Episcopal schism in South Carolina. From there, it was a one-way street to lead the diocese out of the Episcopal Church in all but name. Next, Lawrence would have to bring along the diocesan clergy, the very group that had shown reluctance only a few months before. Once again, he would follow his well-established pattern: make agreements with the standing committee for action, pass them along to the dependent clergy, and rubber-stamp them in a diocesan convention. A convocation day for bishop and clergy was set for August 13.

In the following weeks, Lawrence continued working hard on follow-up items from the July 28 meeting and on the upcoming clergy conference. On August 5, he held another long meeting, 10:30 a.m. to 6:00 p.m. with the deans and standing committee on the "Future of the Diocese."[230] There was no public information about this meeting, but one might safely assume that the attendees continued work on the wording of the resolution proposals. Even when he made a short driving trip to visit family in Maryland on August 7–8, he kept in communication with home. On August 10, Lawrence sent a formal letter to the clergy calling a "Post-Convention Clergy Day."[231] He assured them that they would not be asked to make any decision or vote on any resolution. He wished to show the "gravity" of the situation and to lay out the "direction" he believed the diocese should follow.

On the day Lawrence sent out his call for a clergy day, August 10, some of the most conservative parishes of the diocese felt the need to clarify their attitude toward the national Church. St. Helena's in Beaufort, Church of the Cross in Bluffton, and St. Luke's at Hilton Head issued a joint statement denouncing the General Convention:

> "we (. . .) disassociate ourselves from the actions of the 76th General Convention of the Episcopal Church held in July 2009. During its deliberations, that body denied the Lordship of Jesus Christ and the authority of Holy Scriptures (Old and New Testaments), overturned the sanctity of marriage between one man and one woman, and refused to abstain from the ordination of persons whose manner of life violates Christian tenets in practice for almost 2,000 years."[232]

230. *Journal of the Two Hundred and Nineteenth* (. . .) 2010, 51.

231. Lawrence, (the Rt. Rev.) Mark. "A Letter to the Active Clergy of the Diocese of South Carolina." August 10, 2009, http://www.episcopalforumofsc.org/Overview%20Documents/Letter_to_Active_Clergy_of_the_Diocese.pdf.

232. "A Statement from the Parish Church of St. Helena, Church of the Cross and St. Luke's Episcopal Church at Hilton Head Island." As quoted in Virtueonline, August 13, 2009, http://www.virtueonline.org/modules/news/print.php?storyid=11013.

The statement was signed by the vestries and clergy of the three parishes. No one could miss the very clear position of three important parishes in hostility to the Episcopal Church nor the word "disassociate."

The Rev. Jeff Miller, rector of St. Helena's, seemed concerned that the diocese should leave the Episcopal Church. Under questioning by Church lawyer Thomas Tisdale, the Rev. Dow Sanderson, rector of the Church of the Holy Communion in Charleston, testified in the circuit court trial on July 15, 2014, that Miller had called him on the telephone just before August 13, 2009, to complain that "Bishop Lawrence was not moving quickly to take the Diocese of South Carolina out of the Episcopal Church."[233] When Tisdale asked what Miller had said, Sanderson replied that Miller told him, "We elected him to take us out of the Episcopal Church."[234] Then Sanderson went on "The reason that I went directly to the clergy day is that Father Miller's passion was not his alone, it was shared by many at that clergy day."[235] Thus, according to Sanderson's testimony under oath, by August of 2009 there was a considerable movement among the clergy of the diocese to leave the Episcopal Church. Only a few months earlier, the majority of these same clergy had voted against suspending the General Convention.

Clergy Conference, August 13

The highlight of the clergy conference of August 13 at St. James Church on James Island was Lawrence's address that, at 6,000 words ran an hour and a half.[236] He started with raising the problem of discerning God's Will, then proceeded to interpret the same. In roughly the first half of the speech he laid out his by now all too familiar litany of complaints against the Episcopal Church under the general heading "The false Gospel of Indiscriminate Inclusivity": attacks on orthodox doctrines of the Trinity and the uniqueness of Christ, scriptural authority, baptism, human sexuality, and aggression against the historic faith. Roughly the second half of the speech was what to do about this repulsive "false Gospel." He announced a "Strategy" of four guiding principles: 1-a special convention of the diocese to be held on October 24 to take up resolutions in response to the General Convention of 2009, 2-partial withdrawal from the Episcopal Church, 3-engagement with other traditionalists inside and outside the Episcopal Church, and 4-evolving identity in South Carolina of Anglicanism. As for number two, he announced the blockbuster proposed resolution: "that this diocese begin withdrawing from all bodies of governance of TEC that have assented to actions contrary to Holy Scripture." In his concluding thoughts, Lawrence made the cryptic statement that "Should a parish find it needs to be served by alternative Episcopal care I will work with them toward that end."

---

233. "Transcript of Record," July 15, 2014, Vol. VI, 1312. Testimony of the Rev. Marshall (Dow) Sanderson.

234. Ibid., 1313.

235. Ibid.

236. Lawrence, (the Rt. Rev.) Mark. "We are Called to Stay and Fight in TEC, says Bishop Mark Lawrence." As quoted in Virtueonline, August 13, 2009, http://www.virtueonline.org/portal/modules/news/article.php?storyid=11015.

He finished by sounding a call to action in the deaneries and parishes: "mobilization of clergy, parishes, and laity."

Lawrence's long address left many clergy scratching their heads, bewildered and confused more than pepped up. The guessing game after the speech was: What did the bishop actually say and mean? The address was in reality a masterpiece of conflicting messages that boggled many minds. Lawrence himself admitted as much a few weeks later.[237] Would the diocese leave the Episcopal Church or not? Lawrence said they should stay in the Church but withdraw from the governing bodies. He did not elaborate on how this contortion would actually work. Is it possible for a diocese to stay in the Church and not participate in it? Anyway, what would be the point of such a thing? It was abundantly clear that the conservative minority in the Episcopal Church had shriveled into insignificance. Should the diocese make peace with the Church or wage war? Lawrence said they should honor the institution of the Church while waging a moral war against it. His address was full of martial metaphors: e.g. battle, mobilize, engage, call to action. Indeed, the address opened and ended with allusions to war, the American Revolutionary War. Should we condemn homosexuality or tolerate it? Under "false Gospel," Lawrence had given a short paragraph showing only moral outrage at the idea of marriage equality, then near the end declared "we are not to be in this Diocese about the business of encouraging prejudice [against homosexuals]." Should the diocese stay in the Episcopal Church or identify itself only as "Anglican?" While asserting they should stay in the Church, Lawrence spend a great deal of the speech outlining how they would partner with Anglicans overseas and develop an "Anglican" identity outside of the Episcopal Church. Lawrence spent the first half of the speech condemning the grievous errors of the Episcopal Church then said the diocese should stay in it. If it were so hopelessly in error, would not it be wrong to remain in it? Furthermore, he said the diocese should remain in the Church while developing ties to GAFCON and the Anglican Church in North America. In fact, both GAFCON and ACNA had repudiated the validity of the Episcopal Church. Moreover, Lawrence said the crisis caused by the General Convention of 2009 was so serious that the diocese needed a prompt special convention. They could not wait until the next regular convention a few months later. If the transgressions of the Episcopal Church were so wrong as to require urgent response, why remain in it at all?

The effect of Lawrence's address was to enhance the ever-escalating opposition in the diocese to the Episcopal Church. He was clear on his condemnation of the Church. Much of the speech, however, was his interpretation and opinion, some of which was highly controversial, if not misleading. He implied that D025 and C056 promoted homosexuals in the ordained ministry and sanctioned homosexual marriages. That those resolutions violated the Constitution and Canons of the Episcopal Church would have been hotly contested by the 70 percent of Episcopal bishops who had voted for them. But, Lawrence's speech was never debated publicly. There was no occasion for the pro-Episcopal side to present a differing opinion. His address was his traditionalist understanding of religion that was at variance from the mainstream of the Episcopal Church as shown in the resolutions

---

237. Lawrence, (the Rt. Rev.) Mark. "The Bishop's Address at the Synod or Special Convention of the Diocese of South Carolina, 24 October 2009." Audio recording, Diocese of South Carolina, October 24, 2009, http://www.diosc.com/sys/images/documents/Lawrence_conv_add_10_24_09_to_audio.pdf.

passed by the recent General Conventions. As the bishop, his thoughts carried the weight of authority in the diocese. Since there was no counter voice of any stature to defend the Episcopal Church in South Carolina, his address went entirely unquestioned and certainly not challenged in the diocese. The September/October 2009 issue of *Jubilate Deo* gave the full text of the bishop's address and no other comments.

The most puzzling part of the address was Lawrence's short remark near the end offering alternative episcopal oversight to parishes that wished it. That was commonly interpreted at the time to mean conservative parishes that wanted to leave the Episcopal Church. However, Lawrence said later that he actually meant this for the local pro-Episcopal churches.[238] Reactions to the address varied greatly even with differing opinions of the interpretations of the speech. The loyal Episcopalians of the diocese were concerned by the bishop's talk of "withdrawing" from parts of the Episcopal Church even if he did not call for a complete break. The Episcopal Forum sounded an alarm: "Diocese of SC Leadership Teeters on Verge of Schism from TEC. Convention Resolutions and SC Supreme Court Ruling Escalates Risk of Schism."[239] On the other side, the far-right seemed to be the most upset of all, disappointed that he had not called for outright secession as the fifth sister departing from the Episcopal Church. David Virtue wrote a scathing review of Lawrence's address on his website Virtue Online.[240] He quoted one unnamed priest, "'It was bizarre. People are trying to understand what the bishop really said.'"[241] He quoted another as saying, "'He is skating on very thin ice. He was pressed over and over, but would not reveal the deeper plan of the diocese.'"[242] Clearly disappointed that Lawrence had not broken completely with the Episcopal Church, Virtue concluded, "'The truth is the diocese is isolated with nowhere to go. It is surrounded by liberal and revisionist Episcopal dioceses.'"[243]

The Background of the Special Convention of October 24, 2009

Following this somewhat tumultuous clergy day, Lawrence had more than two months before the special diocesan convention was to meet on October 24 to approve the list of proposed resolutions he had presented on August 13. In the gap, he resumed his busy schedule of building bonds near and far. After a vacation to Vermont and Maine in August, Lawrence flew to London on August 31 to join six other Communion Partner

---

238. "S.C. Episcopalians Nearing Vote." *The Post and Courier* (Charleston, SC), October 11, 2009, http://www.postandcourier.com/apps/pbcs.d11/article?avis=CP&amp.date=20091011&amp.

239. "Diocese of SC Leadership Teeters on Verge of Schism from TEC." eNewsletter, Episcopal Forum of SC, September 19, 2009, http://www.mynewsletterbuilder.com/tools/view_newsletter.php?newsletter_id=1410041967.

240. Virtue, David. "South Carolina: Bishop's Address Leaves Clergy Bewildered as to Diocese's Future." Virtueonline, August 14, 2009, http://www.virtueonline.org/portal/modules/news/article.php?storyid=11020.

241. Ibid.

242. Ibid.

243. Ibid.

bishops.[244] They met with Rowan Williams, the Archbishop of Canterbury, at Lambeth Palace, on September 2 from 2:30 to 4:00 p.m.[245] The Archbishop's office refused to release any information about the conference. Not one of the seven visiting bishops issued a public report about it. Perhaps the most revealing statement came from Dan Martins who was closely connected to the seven bishops. Martins wrote on his blog: "they're talking about how Dr. Williams' 'two tier/two track' plan might actually get implemented (. . .) steps a diocese might take to remain on Tier/Track One even as TEC per se is assigned (consigned?) to Tier/Track Two."[246] In other words, the seven bishops were asking Williams to support a diocese's right to endorse and enact the Anglican Covenant even if its province refused to do so. Apparently, nothing came of this meeting since no public statement was ever released about it by the Archbishop or any of the seven bishops. Still, even without explicit help from the Archbishop of Canterbury, the conservative bishops in the Episcopal Church continued to put great hope in the soon to be released proposal of an Anglican Covenant that would presumably put pressure on the Episcopal Church to conform to the majority conservative opinion in the Anglican Communion.

Lawrence filled the remainder of the time before the special convention with business around the diocese, preparing for the convention, and a trip to Albany, New York, September 21–24. The bishop of Albany was one Lawrence's closest Communion Partner allies. As October 24 neared, Lawrence spent more and more time talking with core leaders, working on his address, and intensifying other preparations. He noted in his journal a meeting with Wade Logan, the chancellor, and Alan Runyan on October 20.[247] This was Lawrence's first mention in his diary of Runyan, the lawyer who would go on to become the zealous lead in the legal representation of the diocese against the Episcopal Church. In October, Lawrence also contacted Thomas Tisdale, former chancellor and prominent lawyer known to favor the national Church, and invited him to lunch in order to clear up some "misapprehensions."[248] This was Tisdale's first conversation with Lawrence. The two spent two and a half hours together bonding and discussing a wide range of issues.[249]

A month before the special convention was to meet, the South Carolina Supreme Court handed down its ruling in the *All Saints* case. It had a major impact locally and nation-wide. It was the final decision in this matter. A parish had succeeded in breaking away from an Episcopal diocese and keeping the property with the final sanction of a court of law. The anti-Episcopal elements declared a major victory and read into the decision what they wished. Clearly the most important point in the ruling was that of the quit claim deed. This issue had guaranteed All Saints' eventual success. Some conservatives extrapolated from the ruling that the Dennis Canon was ineffective everywhere in the state of South Carolina, although the court ruling was for only one parish. They

---

244. *Journal of the Two Hundred and Nineteenth* (. . .) 2010, 52. Lillibridge, West Texas; Little, Northern Indiana; Love, Albany; Smith, North Dakota; Stanton, Dallas; MacPherson, Western Louisiana.

245. Ibid.

246. "Seven Diocesans."

247. *Journal of the Two Hundred and Nineteenth* (. . .) 2010, 56.

248. Tisdale, interview with author.

249. Ibid.

also learned the importance of pressing litigation in the local state courts that follow the guide of "neutral principles." The implications of the *All Saints* decision was not lost on Bishop Lawrence.

The Special Convention of October 24

It would take some time for everyone to absorb the significance and meaning of the *All Saints* case. Meanwhile, the special convention for the diocese that Lawrence called in the aftermath of the General Convention met at Christ Church in Mount Pleasant on October 24, 2009, some three hundred delegates attending. Perhaps to heighten an atmosphere of crisis and urgency, the meeting was closed to all visitors and media in contrast to the usual practice of holding open conventions. By October 24, the proposed resolutions had been long announced and circulated. They were all people had talked about for weeks.

Lawrence gave an address to the assembly that was basically a reiteration of his presentation to the clergy of August 13, once again loaded with military metaphors. His opening theme sounded the tone for the whole meeting: "'When the foundations are being destroyed, what can the righteous do?'"[250] This implied that the Episcopal Church had turned unrighteous and that the diocese of South Carolina was "righteous" and had to "do" something about it. The first part of the address was yet another survey of Lawrence's well-established complaints against the Episcopal Church concluding with the puzzling statement: "I have not sought to make The Episcopal Church the problem. Rather, I have suggested it is the embrace of this false gospel of indiscriminate inclusivity which is the problem."[251] A few paragraphs later he said, "The General Convention has become the problem."[252] He did not explain what he meant by three "problems" [homosexuality?]. The second part of the speech, "Why Are We Here Today?" sought to clear up some of the admitted confusion from the August 13 address to the clergy. The next part he entitled, "What are we to do?"[253] Everyone knew what that meant, pass the resolutions. The last part he called "Finally, What difference will it make?" He was not clear, but seemed to imply that South Carolina's resolutions would have some impact on the direction of the Episcopal Church. Exactly how, he did not explain even as he warned that the next general convention would take up rights for homosexuals again. He did not deny that passing the resolutions at hand was going against the Episcopal Church: "if we are disloyal, it is the disloyalty of those who have loved what we believe is our best heritage."[254] He did not elaborate on the meaning of staying in the Episcopal Church and being disloyal at the same time. What about the oath of loyalty he took at his consecration? While this address was not as wordy as the lengthy presentation on August 13, it was scarcely any clearer. However, clarity was not really the point. As on August 13, the

250. Lawrence, "Bishop's Address."
251. Ibid.
252. Ibid.
253. Ibid.
254. Ibid.

apparent point was to energize an atmosphere in the diocese of differentiation from the Episcopal Church and to promote and justify action against it. This it achieved at least among his supporters. Al Zadig, the rector of St. Michael's gushed that it was the bishop's finest address.[255] *Jubilate Deo* printed the full text of the bishop's address and the five proposed resolutions but not a word elsewise in its November/December 2009 issue.

Five resolutions were proposed. Number One, entitled "The Lordship of Christ and the Sufficiency of Scripture"[256] stated that the Presiding Bishop and the general conventions had raised questions about the Episcopal Church's commitment to true religion and that "the Diocese of South Carolina (. . .) commits to exercising all such actions as the Bishop and Standing Committee may believe edifying."[257] It prescribed a revised Oath of Conformity to be taken at ordinations. This resolution passed by 86 percent.

The Second Resolution was the most important one, "Godly Boundaries." It authorized "the Bishop and Standing Committee to begin withdrawing from all bodies of the Episcopal Church that have assented to actions contrary to Holy Scripture."[258] It did not define which bodies and what criteria would be used to assess "contrary." Furthermore, it declared the 2009 General Convention's "Resolutions D025 and C056, to be null and void, having no effect in this Diocese."[259] It passed overwhelmingly.[260]

Resolution Number Three, "Domestic Engagement for Missional Relationships,"[261] called for the parishes of the diocese "to enter into their own Missional Relationships with orthodox congregations."[262] It passed by 85 percent.

Number Four, "Emerging 21st Century Anglicanism,"[263] declared that the diocese had "inherent sovereign authority" and that it endorsed the Ridley Draft of the proposed Anglican Covenant. This passed by 87 percent.

Numbers one through four sailed through easy passage. Not so for resolution number five, entitled "The Rubric of Love."[264] It stated: "this Diocese will not condone prejudice or deny the dignity of any person, including but not limited to, those who believe themselves to be gay, lesbian, bisexual or transgendered."[265] The operative word here was *believe*. Many conservatives asserted that homosexuality is a free choice. Therefore, people who practiced homosexual behavior only *believed* they were homosexuals. No one was born homosexual.

255. Parker, Adam. "Episcopal Diocese: Convention Oks 4 of 5 Resolutions." *The Post and Courier* (Charleston, SC), October 25, 2009, http://www.postandcourier.com/article.20091025/PC1602/310259906.

256. "Resolutions Offered at Special October 24, 2009, Convention." Diocese of South Carolina, http://www.diosc.com/sys/index/php?view+article&id=226%3Aresolution.

257. Ibid.

258. Ibid.

259. Ibid.

260. A call was made for a roll call vote. Clergy, 87 yes, 17 no, 1 abstention; parishes, 39 yes, 8 no; missions, 13 yes, 3 no, 2 divided, 1 abstention.

261. Ibid.

262. Ibid.

263. Ibid.

264. Ibid.

265. Ibid.

When the proposed resolutions were published, some people in the diocese were concerned about the wording and intent of Number Five, "The Rubric of Love." At Grace Church, in Charleston, a group of concerned communicants met with Tom Tisdale and asked him to confer with Wade Logan, the chancellor, about rewording the resolution. Tisdale met with Logan twice and then suggested a substitute resolution drawn from the baptismal service in the prayer book. When the resolution came up for consideration in the convention, however, the presiding officers refused to allow Tisdale's substitute. The Standing Committee's resolution alone was put forth for a vote.[266] Once again, the diocesan leadership exercised its monopoly of power.

Somewhat surprisingly, the bishop and the Standing Committee apparently were not of one mind on this resolution going into the convention as opposed to the first four. When the delegates took up Number Five, the committee revised the original proposal to sound more compassionate but the logistics of providing new copies and of entertaining a long string of amendments promised to send the convention into long and uncertain overdrive.[267] Rather than have the convention dissolve into wrangling over what the leadership considered by far the least important resolution, a motion was made to table the proposed resolution and pass it on to the next diocesan convention. The motion was approved 182–117. This maneuver averted a near-disaster for the diocesan leadership as the convention was heretofore almost perfectly united and might have dissolved into chaos thus endangering the solidity that Lawrence had worked so hard to form, negating the unifying effects of the earlier four votes. Still, it was somewhat ironic that the issue underlying all of the earlier resolutions proved to be the very one on which the convention could not agree. This might make one wonder whether the main issue at stake in South Carolina at the time was homosexuality, something on which they could not agree, or loyalty to the diocesan leadership, something on which they did agree. It seemed that the diocesan leaders had been using, and continued to use, homosexuality as a wedge issue to move the diocese away from the Episcopal Church without really intending to deal with the issue itself.

The sum of these resolutions showed that the Diocese of South Carolina all but declared its independence from the Episcopal Church. It remained in the Episcopal Church in name only. Harmon boasted to a reporter that the diocese had gone "about as far as you can get but still be in."[268] As the state of South Carolina had done long ago, the diocese declared itself sovereign and self-governing. Unlike the state before 1860, however, the diocese went a step farther in declaring a unilateral alteration of its alignment in the national government giving to itself the right to choose the governing bodies in which it would participate. Lawrence later testified that the diocese actually did not withdraw from any governing bodies of the Episcopal Church.[269] If the diocese did not,

---

266. Tisdale, interview with author.

267. Skardon, Steve. "The 2009 Special Convention." *South Carolina Episcopalians*, October 24, 2009, http://www.scepiscopalians.com/2009_Special_Convention.html.

268. Smith, Bruce. "Meeting to Consider Future of S.C. Episcopal Diocese." *Aiken Standard* (Aiken, SC), October 18, 2009, http://www.aikenstandard.com/news/meeting-to-consider-future-of-s-c-episcopal-diocese/article_4e769fc8-c33c-53d5-9406-e4524099d92b.html.

269. "Deposition Transcript—Mark J. Lawrence," 109.

in fact, enact the resolutions, that raised the question of why they were passed in the first place.

As important as the five resolutions were, the crucial story of October 24 garnered barely a glance from anyone including Lawrence's critics. Embedded in the language of Resolution Two was the provision to give the bishop and standing committee the right to make policy for the diocese *carte blanche*. They and they alone would decide forever the relationship between the diocese and the Episcopal Church. If anyone had any doubts about the power structure in the diocese, they could have them no longer. Decisions would be made at the top by the bishop and standing committee, passed on to a subservient clergy and perhaps on to an approving diocesan convention. In just seven months, the body of the clergy of the Diocese of South Carolina had changed from rejecting Harmon's proposed resolution to suspend the General Convention not only to overwhelmingly supporting it but also to handing over power of decision making in the future to the bishop and the standing committee. It was a stunning turnaround that went completely under the radar until it was too late for anyone to do anything about it. Therefore, following the terms of Resolution Two, Lawrence said on October 24 that the diocese would withdraw from the General Convention and the House of Bishops.[270] This monumental announcement was met with barely a nod from the special convention all but buried under the talk of the resolutions. As Steve Skardon, the leading pro-Episcopal pundit opined, "Saturday's Convention was a personal victory for Bishop Lawrence. As a political strategist he may have proven himself to be somewhat masterful."[271] Skardon did not know just how true these words would prove to be. Lawrence's long, hard work of bonding had worked perfectly.

The Episcopal Church leadership and local loyal Episcopalians viewed all of this with grave concern if not panic alarm. If South Carolina voted to leave the Church it would be the fifth, and largest, diocese to do so. Even before the special convention, Bonnie Anderson, the president of the House of Deputies, sent an open letter to the diocese giving her opinions on the proposed resolutions.[272] She expressed her fear that the resolutions were "steps preliminary in attempting to separate the Diocese from the Church" because they were strikingly similar to resolutions passed by some dioceses that had earlier voted to leave the Episcopal Church. She warned, "While individuals have left the Episcopal Church, dioceses have not, and to do so would require the permission of General Convention."[273] She showed great concern that the resolutions "contain misleading statements or assert positions that are in conflict with those of this Church," particularly on the oath in Resolution One. Moreover, she spent a good deal of space on the issue of nullification: "All dioceses must make an unqualified accession to the Constitution and Canons of the Episcopal Church (. . .) adoption of a resolution declaring an action of General Convention null and void is itself, a nullity (. . .). Actions of General

---

270. Parker, "Episcopal Diocese"

271. Skardon, "2009 Special Convention."

272. "Bonnie Anderson Writes the Diocese of South Carolina Deputies before Special Convention." [October 22, 2009?], http://www.kendallharmon.com/t19/index.php/t19/article/bonnie_anderson_writes_the_diocese_of_aouth_carolina.

273. Ibid.

Convention are binding on dioceses."[274] She pointed out that the Executive Council of the Episcopal Church, on June 14, 2007, had ruled that any amendment passed by a diocese to reduce its accession to the Constitution and Canons of the Episcopal Church is itself null and void. Therefore, the proposed Resolution Two was illegal. South Carolina did not have the right to declare any resolution of General Convention to be null and void in the diocese. Finally, she concluded: "It is my prayer that Resolutions 1–4 are not steps being proposed to move the Diocese away from The Episcopal Church and towards efforts by others to create an alternate Anglican structure in our midst."[275]

Local pro-Episcopal forces in South Carolina, weaker than ever within the structure of the diocese, also showed signs of clairvoyant gloom. Barbara Mann, a director of the Episcopal Forum wrote on the Forum website, "After all is said, what was accomplished by the October 24 special convention, except to accelerate the Episcopal Diocese of South Carolina on its slippery slide out of The Episcopal Church?"[276] Contrary to the rising tide of certainty in the diocese she insisted that there was no threat to the core beliefs of the Episcopal Church and that there was a broad range of scriptural understandings on subjects, points that had been loudly rejected by the special convention. In late 2009, it must have been clear to supporters of the Episcopal Church in South Carolina that they could not stem the tide. They were being swept away by a tsunami they were powerless to stop. Nevertheless, the Forum refused to surrender. On December 5, 2009, they held another symposium under the slightly desperate-sounding title of "I am Episcopalian," at the Harbour Club in Charleston.

The Aftermath of the Special Convention

Lawrence was clearly energized by the outcomes of the clergy conference in August and the special diocesan convention in October. After a brief vacation at Disney World, he returned to his pace of hard work with renewed vigor making his endless rounds of meetings, church visits, talks and the like. Wasting no time putting the newly passed resolutions in practice, he hosted a small group of his closest allied bishops to make a "Missional Relationship." On November 4 and 5, Lawrence led a meeting in Charleston of fellow conservative bishops Stanton (Dallas), Howe (Central Florida), MacPherson (Western Louisiana), Love (Albany), and Beckwith (Springfield). They agreed to set up a website for sharing materials and resources and to call a three-day conference in Dallas, September 23–25, 2010, "for the purpose of encouraging, empowering, emboldening and equipping missionally focused individuals, congregations and dioceses."[277] Meanwhile, the Anglican Communion Development Committee that Lawrence had set up earlier under Kendall Harmon, the Director, had organized and developed as another

274. Ibid.
275. Ibid.
276. Mann, Barbara. "A Brief History of the Ongoing Disassociation of the Diocese of SC from the Episcopal Church." November 3, 2009, http://www.episcopalforumofsc.org/Overview%20Documents/A%20Brief%20History%202011-3-09.pdf.
277. Lewis, (the Rev.) James. "Seven Dioceses Meet: Begin Missional Relationships." *Jubilate Deo* (Diocese of South Carolina), January/February 2010, 1.

way of expanding ties between the ultra-conservative diocese and like-minded Anglicans abroad.[278]

Other events occurred in 2009 that impacted on the Diocese of South Carolina. On June 22, 2009, the Anglican Church in North America was formally established at a meeting in Bedford, Texas, with Lawrence's old friend and ally Robert Duncan as its first archbishop. This was an outgrowth of the Common Cause Partnership in which Lawrence had been active. The common cause was to oppose equal rights for homosexual people. With the backing of GAFCON, the ACNA was created to provide a counter-revolutionary parallel church that intended to replace the Episcopal Church as the new Anglican entity in the U.S. recognized by the majority of the Anglican Communion. This was the conclusion of the drive to create a replacement church that the ultra conservatives had talked about at least since the Robinson affair of 2003. Now, it remained to be seen whether the replacement stratagem itself would succeed.

If the diocesan move of May 30 to allow St. Andrew's to transfer property to its own control was meant to appease the parish's anti-Episcopal Church attitude, it did not work. On September 4, 2009, the Rev. Steve Wood sent a letter to his congregation of St. Andrew's announcing a forty day "discernment" to decide if the parish should stay in the Episcopal Church which he called hopelessly in error. The discernment ended in a predictable vote announced on December 17: 838 to align with the ACNA, 58 to remain in the Episcopal Church, 4 votes nothing, and 2 abstain. Within a few months, Saint Andrew's would officially declare that it had withdrawn from the Episcopal diocese and by extension the Episcopal Church. If Bishop Lawrence had hoped that his support of St. Andrew's land transfer in May of 2009 would keep the parish in the diocese, he was to be disappointed. St. Andrew's hostility to the Episcopal Church was too far advanced in 2009 for Lawrence to counteract it enough to keep the parish in the diocese. Lawrence failed to keep his largest parish in his diocese, and in so doing set the precedent the diocese would follow from then on, that the properties belong to the local parishes. In the end, this was the issue that was to cause him to be declared in abandonment of the Episcopal Church, but it would take more than three more years for that to happen.[279]

St. Andrew's was the second parish to vote to leave the Episcopal Diocese of South Carolina (the first was All Saints, Pawleys Island, in 2004) and the first under Lawrence. In time, Bishop Lawrence would have no choice but to remove the clergy of St. Andrew's from the ministry of the Episcopal Church. He did so in 2010 and informed the presiding bishop by letter.[280] Lawrence did nothing to enforce the Dennis Canon as St. Andrew's made it plain to everyone that they were leaving the Episcopal Church and doing so with all the property in hand. Indeed, Lawrence kept a friendly stance to St. Andrew's writing "As for St. Andrew's Mount Pleasant, I will continue to be in communication with the leadership of the parish, ministering to all members of the diocese and parish

---

278. Lawrence, (the Rev.) Robert. "Anglican Communion Development Committee Surveys Parishes: Begins New Initiatives." *Jubilate Deo* (Diocese of South Carolina), January/February 2010, 3.

279. This was also an issue that contrasted him with his predecessor, Bishop Salmon, who took legal action to enforce the Dennis Canon against the breakaway parish of All Saints, Pawleys Island.

280. "Bishop Lawrence Removes Four from Episcopal Ministry." Episcopal Café, October 28, 2010, http://www.episcopalcafe.com/lead/episcopal_church/bishop_Lawrence_removes_four_f.html.

as seems appropriate."[281] Lawrence's attitude to parish property, showing up even in early 2009, was lost on neither the Episcopal Church leadership nor the other restive parishes in South Carolina.

Two other highly conservative parishes in the Diocese of South Carolina took steps to disassociate themselves from the Episcopal Church although neither followed through at this time. On December 1, the vestry and members of Saint Luke's on Hilton Head voted to remove all references to "'the Protestant Episcopal Church of the United States, the Diocese of South Carolina, and any Canons associated therewith.'"[282] The rector of St. Luke's, the Rev. Greg Kronz, Lawrence's old acquaintance from Pittsburgh days and chair of the search committee that recommended Lawrence for bishop, refused to comment publicly: "'It really is a St. Luke's matter.'"[283] Also in December, Trinity Church in Myrtle Beach voted to remove all references to the Episcopal Church in its bylaws. These actions, and Lawrence's inaction in the face of them, caught the attention of the Episcopal Church leadership who decided the time had come to take some action.

If the immediate problem tearing the counter-revolutionary minority from the majority revolutionary Episcopal Church was the interface of homosexuality and the Church, that issue suddenly bounded front and center again to everyone's attention in late 2009. On December 5th, the Diocese of Los Angeles elected the Rev. Mary Glasspool to be a suffragan bishop of the diocese. Glasspool was an open and partnered homosexual person. Conservatives had been outraged at Gene Robinson's consecration in 2003 as the first openly homosexual Episcopal bishop, but they had calmed somewhat on the hope that Robinson was a one-time event, that dioceses would willingly avoid electing another such person. Glasspool proved them wrong and the whole issue of homosexuals in the Episcopal ministry boiled up again. Glasspool would go on to get the necessary consents and to be consecrated a bishop in the Episcopal Church by Presiding Bishop Jefferts Schori before a crowd of three thousand people in Los Angeles. She was the second openly homosexual Episcopal bishop, and as everyone now knew, certainly not the last, much to the chagrin of the morally indignant ultra-conservatives across the Episcopal Church including the rebellious leadership of the Diocese of South Carolina.

As the second year of his episcopacy came to a close, it was clear that Bishop Lawrence had succeeded brilliantly in building bonds between himself and the majority of communicants of the Diocese of South Carolina as well as conservative bishops beyond in the Episcopal Church and the wider Anglican Communion. His tremendous capacity for hard work and his projecting personality had paid off. So far, at least, he had managed the tightrope walk of denouncing the Episcopal Church and keeping the diocese in it. He could claim with some justification that he was serving all the communicants of the diocese. He had lost only one parish, St. Andrew's of Mt. Pleasant. He had won over a slightly wary body of diocesan clergy to gain their trust and support. He had solidified his standing with the leaders of the diocese. He had formed a simple but highly efficient power structure: bishop—unified standing committee—dependent clergy—approving

---

281. Parker, Adam. "Parish Looks to Leave." *The Post and Courier* (Charleston, SC), December 19, 2009, http://www.postandcourier.com/news/2009/dec/19/parish-looks-to-leave/.

282. Ibid.

283. Ibid.

diocesan convention. He had no suffrragan bishop with whom he might have to share power. He had installed a dutiful canon to the ordinary and had reorganized the diocesan staff. The apparati of the diocese had turned completely to his side. *Jubilate Deo* and all the communications of the diocese did nothing but serve the bishop's, and the diocesan leadership's, interests, to the exclusion of any criticism or alternate viewpoints.

Now the question facing the Diocese of South Carolina at the dawn of Lawrence's third year was: Where do we go from here? While it was obvious that the solid majority of the diocese was devoted to Lawrence and the diocesan leadership, it was not obvious what this relationship meant or where it was going. The creative arrangements that Lawrence had made in the four resolutions of October 2009 were highly dubious at best and downright unworkable at worst. Even the bishop could not give a clear picture of the future. No other diocese had ever tried to formulate such a contorted unilateral arrangement with the national Church. Could South Carolina construct a new model whereby a dissident diocese could remove itself from the governing structure of the Episcopal Church in protest and remain in the Church? Even if it could, would the national church accept such a model? Did Lawrence really intend to stay in the Episcopal Church, or was he only leading it out in gradual phases? Could he continue to ignore the Dennis Canon without the intervention of the national Church? Could he keep parishes teetering on the edge of secession from following St. Andrew's? What about the rival self-proclaimed "Anglican" presences in the Low Country, the Anglican Mission in America at All Saints, Pawleys Island, and the Anglican Church in North America at St. Andrew's of Mt. Pleasant? How might these factors impact on his diocese? A great deal remained to be seen as 2010 arrived and Bishop Lawrence moved into his third year in South Carolina.

4

Storm Clouds, 2010–2011

2010

The Logan/Tisdale Affair, January-February

THE YEAR 2010 BEGAN with a sort of after-the-storm stillness in the Diocese of South Carolina. The landmark 2009 general convention and diocesan special convention were in the past. The four controversial resolutions had been enacted and put away with only one left to be resolved. The bishop and governing leadership of the diocese seemed confidently in control of matters. By all accounts, the diocese, if not completely unified, was overwhelmingly approving of its contentious bishop and standing committee. The jitters of the pro-Episcopal party in the diocese and the national Church leadership seemed minimal and inconsequential. The surface of the waters appeared more or less calm as Bishop Lawrence prepared to begin the third year of his episcopacy in South Carolina.

The annual conference of Mere Anglicanism met as usual at St. Philip's in Charleston, this year on January 21–23. The theme was "Human Identity, Gender, and Sexuality: Speculation or Revelation." If anyone had thought that homosexuality was only a side issue in South Carolina, he had only to pay attention to this conference. Conservative views on homosexuality monopolized the conference as one speaker after another with impressive credentials arose to "say same-sex marriages have no basis in biology, psychology, or sociology—spiritually, biblically or theologically."[1] One such speaker was Robert Gagnon, a professor of New Testament at Pittsburgh Theological Seminary, who had made a name for himself as a leading proponent of biblical condemnation of homosexuality. Bishop Lawrence was to rely on Gagnon's writings later.

Even before counter-revolutionary Episcopalians and Anglicans met to reinforce their own preconceived notions of human sexuality, the leadership of the Episcopal Church had already begun to stir with unease about South Carolina. They read several worrying signs there, particularly involving property. In the first place, Lawrence had shown no interest in appealing the *All Saints* decision of September 2009 to the U.S.

---

1. Virtue, David. "Charleston SC: Theologian and Psychiatrist Reject Gay Marriage and Homosexual Behavior." Virtueonline, January 25, 2010, http://www.virtueonline.com/portal/modules/news/article.php/storyid=11988.

Supreme Court. It was true that the Episcopal Church did not appeal the case either, but it could hardly have done so without the support of the local diocese. In the second case, Lawrence apparently had turned a blind eye as St. Andrew's of Mt. Pleasant transferred millions of dollars' worth of property into a land trust, even possibly approved of it in advance. Moreover, as St. Andrew's very publicly moved to break with the diocese and the Episcopal Church, Lawrence had done nothing about asserting the diocesan control over St. Andrew's property. By late 2009, Episcopal Church leaders were growing seriously concerned that Lawrence had abandoned the Church's Dennis Canon. His predecessor, Bishop Salmon, although conservative and critical of the Episcopal Church in many ways, had nevertheless always rigorously upheld the Canon and had fought for years in court to enforce it.

In regard to the *All Saints* case, there was talk about appealing to the United States Supreme Court the state supreme court ruling of September 18, 2009, in favor of the local breakaway parish as the property owners.[2] All Saints Episcopal Church of Pawleys Island, the minority of faithful Episcopalians from old All Saints parish, had been meeting separately after the majority enacted a break from the Episcopal diocese in 2004 and remained in occupation of the property. When the state supreme court ruled against them, the vestry of All Saints Episcopal resolved to pursue an appeal to the U.S. Supreme Court. They received no help from Lawrence in this. They found their own lawyers in Mobile, Alabama, and Washington, DC and got an extension of a deadline to file an appeal to February 15, 2010. On February 12, Guerry Green, on behalf of the vestry of All Saints Episcopal filed a thirty-three page "Petition for a Writ of Certiorari" with the Supreme Court of the United States.[3] Soon thereafter, the Anglican and Episcopal parishes began negotiating a settlement. The two parties announced a final agreement on March 25, 2010, before the Supreme Court could respond to the petition: the Anglicans would keep the old parish properties, worth at least ten million dollars, the Anglican congregation would give the Episcopal parish three hundred and seventy-five thousand dollars, the name All Saints would remain with the Anglicans, and the Episcopalians would find a new name.[4] This ended any attempt to have the U.S. Supreme Court rule on the *All Saints* case. The South Carolina Supreme Court ruling would stand as the final word in South Carolina. In this, the Episcopal Church suffered its first major loss regarding its Dennis Canon. The fact that this case ended on Lawrence's watch did nothing to reassure national Church leaders of Lawrence's dubious attachment to the Dennis Canon.

After it was clear in late 2009 that Lawrence had no intention of enforcing the Dennis Canon, the national Church leadership decided to move in order to assert the Church's trustee interest in the properties. Late in the year, David Booth Beers, the Presiding Bishop's chancellor, contacted his old attorney friend Thomas Tisdale in Charleston

---

2. There had been three court actions on All Saints, Waccamaw: a circuit court ruled in favor of the breakaway parish, a trial court ruled in favor of the diocese, and the state supreme court in favor of the breakaway parish.

3. "Petition for a Writ of Certiorari." Guerry Green v. W. Russell Campbell, In the Supreme Court of the United States, February 12, 2010, http://www.standfirminfaith.com/media/Petititon_for_Certiorari_01733358.pdf.

4. Swenson, Charles. "All Saints Groups Reach Accord on Land Dispute." *Coastal Observer* (Pawleys Island, SC), April 1, 2010, http://www.coastalabserver.com/articles/2010/040110/1.html.

and asked Tisdale to represent the national Church in South Carolina.[5] Shortly thereafter, Tisdale resolved to talk with Wade Logan, the diocesan chancellor, to ask that if the Diocese intended to assert its legal rights to the local properties; if not, would the Diocese agree to allow the national Church to do so?[6] On December 31, 2009, Tisdale met Logan for a lengthy and friendly conversation.[7] Logan said that Bishop Lawrence planned no action to protect the property of the Church and as far as he (Logan) was concerned the national Church could do so.[8] Tisdale said he needed documents from the diocese concerning certain local parishes whereupon Logan told Tisdale to send him letters describing what the national Church wanted and he would respond.[9]

Between January 25 and 29, 2010, Tisdale sent nine letters to Logan requesting information and documents from the Diocese, or at least access to the documents.[10] He called himself "South Carolina counsel for The Episcopal Church" and asked for the materials in the name of the Church, apparently to be forwarded to Beers and Jefferts Schori. One letter asked what action Lawrence planned to take to protect parish property. Another requested copies of oaths of conformity since last October 24. Another wanted transcripts of the special convention and copies of proposed resolutions for the upcoming diocesan convention. Yet another asked for changes to parish bylaws since 2006. One letter requested all the minutes of the standing committee since Lawrence's consecration. Others wanted specific records from four parishes: St. Luke's of Hilton Head, St. Andrew's of Mt. Pleasant, St. John's of Johns Island, and Trinity of Myrtle Beach. Upon receiving the letters, Logan telephoned Tisdale to say that he would first have to show the letters to Bishop Lawrence.[11] As soon as Lawrence read the letters everything changed.

Tisdale did not receive one item he had requested. What he did receive was a furious barrage of collective rage from the diocesan leadership, particularly the bishop. Even though it was Logan who had originally suggested the letters, he fired back an official response to Tisdale on February 5, not only denying the requests, but accusing the national Church leaders of trying to pick a fight with Lawrence and the diocese. "TEC is trying very hard to find reasons to involve either the Bishop or the Diocese, or perhaps both, in an adversarial situation."[12] He did not elaborate. Five days later, even though he had not been addressed, Alan Runyan, the Beaufort Lawyer that had been recently retained for the diocese, sent two letters to Tisdale. Runyan enhanced Logan's earlier charge. In one, "Information Requested of The Diocese of South Carolina," he dismissed the requests as irrelevant and sniffed they were a "breach of our sovereignty."[13]

5. Tisdale, interview with author.
6. Ibid.
7. Ibid.
8. Ibid.
9. Ibid.
10. "Diocesan Convention Postponed until March 26." Diocese of South Carolina, February 9, 2010, http://www.diosc.com/sys/index.php/view=article7catid=153Alatest-news7id=20953Aan-important-pastoral.
11. Tisdale, interview with author.
12. [Logan, Wade]. Wade Logan to Thomas Tisdale, February 5, 2010.
13. [Runyan, Alan]. Alan Runyan to Thomas Tisdale, "Information Requested of the Diocese of South Carolina," February 10, 2010.

In the other, entitled "Information Requested from the Diocese of South Carolina Concerning Diocesan Parishes," Runyan again dismissed the requests because, he said, the "Diocese of South Carolina is sovereign (. . .). There is no provision in the Constitution and Canons, which provides for this infringement on its authority."[14] He added that "None of these parishes have left the Episcopal Diocese (and consequently the Episcopal Church)."[15] That was technically true at the moment. Although St. Andrew's congregation had voted to leave the Diocese, it would be several weeks before the vestry would make it official. The other three parishes had only reworded their documents to drop all references to the Episcopal Church. The complaint most often repeated by the lawyers and by Lawrence himself was that the presiding bishop had not consulted Lawrence by phone or otherwise beforehand. Lawrence was apparently offended by this unexplained breach of courtesy. Within two weeks of the letters, Tisdale had received flat denials of all of his requests. In fact, the Diocese did not allow Tisdale access to one document. Tisdale did not press the matter. That was the end of that; or, was it?

The incident between the Episcopal Church lawyer and the diocesan lawyers could have been a simple and short one. Tisdale asked for a list of documents. Logan refused. Runyan refused. Lawrence refused. Tisdale dropped it. End of incident, at least on the Episcopal Church side. However, this was not to be the case on the diocesan side. Bishop Lawrence decided that this matter was far too important to be left alone. Even though not one of Tisdale's letters was addressed to him, Lawrence immediately took charge of the whole matter. His official bishop's journal shows that as soon as Logan received the letters in late January, Lawrence was on the phone often with Logan and Harmon. On February 1, he noted: "12:00—4:00 Counsel [sic] of Advice [Standing Committee]."[16] On February 2, he had a long conference call with Logan and Runyan that brought in Runyan as the Diocese's lead lawyer in the matter even though he was not the chancellor and had not been addressed in Tisdale's letters.[17] Lawrence resolved swiftly what he would do. On February 4, he wrote the first draft of a letter to the diocese.[18] On February 9, he met the Diocesan Council and called in the Standing Committee for another long session, from 11:45 a.m. to 3:30 p.m. in which he presumably presented to them the letter he had drawn up days earlier and got their unanimous approval.[19] His letter to the diocese was dated February 9, the day he met the Standing Committee and a day before Runyan sent his two letters to Tisdale.

Lawrence's response to the Tisdale letters was to declare a crisis: a hostile invasion of the sovereign Diocese of South Carolina designed to unseat the innocent bishop.

---

14. [Runyan, Alan]. Alan Runyan to Thomas Tisdale, "Information Requested from the Diocese of South Carolina Concerning Diocesan Parishes," February 10, 2010.

15. Ibid.

16. *Journal of the Two Hundred and Twentieth Annual Meeting of the Convention of the Diocese of South Carolina, Parish Church of St. Helena's, Beaufort, South Carolina, February 18 & 19, 2011.* Charleston, SC: the diocese, 2011, "Bishop's Journal 2010," 27. The Standing Committee also served as the Council of Advice.

17. Ibid.

18. Ibid.

19. Ibid.

His public letter of February 9 sounded an alarm to the whole diocese: "the Presiding Bishop's Chancellor, if not the Presiding Bishop herself, is seeking to build a case against the Ecclesiastical Authorities of the Diocese (Bishop and Standing Committee) and some of our parishes."[20] He implied that the Presiding Bishop was trying to build a case to have him removed on abandonment of communion. He continued with his sweeping accusations, "this action is an unjust intrusion" into a "sovereign diocese" and a "provocative interference." Moreover, he charged this "unprecedented incursion" showed "the apparent trajectory of the Presiding Bishop's Office to extend powers not attendant with the office." Again, perhaps implying that she was out to oust him. Once again, he did not offer evidence. Referring to the four parishes named in Tisdale's letters, Lawrence said, "these parishes have not made these changes with the intention of leaving the Diocese." That certainly was not true in regard to St. Andrew's of Mt. Pleasant. In fact, weeks earlier, St. Andrew's had voted with every intention of leaving the Diocese, had said so very publicly, and would soon make it official. Lawrence concluded his letter by saying that the urgency of the situation required the diocese to move the upcoming diocesan convention back by three weeks, to March 26, "in order for the Bishop, Standing Committee and Diocese to adequately consider a response." He did not explain what would happen in the extra three weeks; and he did not mention that his two lawyers were already settling the matter with Tisdale.

Buried in the letter was a cryptic phrase that must have given the national Church leaders pause. It perhaps went unnoticed by the public, but could not have been missed by Jefferts Schori and Beers. Lawrence wrote, "I have been working with their [four parishes in question] clergy and lay leaders to find appropriate ways to resolve their struggles with the recent decisions of the General Convention in ways consistent (. . .) with the canons of the Church and the laws of the state of South Carolina."[21] *The laws of the state of South Carolina.* Ever since the state supreme court's ruling in the *All Saints* case, conservative lawyers and others had insisted that the Dennis Canon was illegal in the entire state of South Carolina. If Lawrence were now agreeing that the Dennis Canon was dead in his diocese, this, combined with his inaction on recent property issues, would have turned the unease among the national Church leaders into alarm. Having completely failed in their Tisdale initiative, they must have wondered what to do next. They did not have long to wait long for the next crisis as the annual diocesan convention was bearing down.

One direct outcome of the Logan/Tisdale affair in South Carolina happened in the diocesan Board of Trustees and remained hidden from the public for years. Bishop Lawrence served as president of the Board. On March 17, 2010, the Board of Trustees made a formal lease agreement with Lawrence giving him the right to the diocesan-owned episcopal residence at 50 Smith Street, Charleston, for ten years whether he remained bishop or not.[22] The property included six bedrooms, four and a half baths, and 5,211

20. "Diocesan Convention Postponed."
21. Ibid.
22. "Lease agreement dated March 17, 2010, between Trustees of the Protestant Episcopal Church in South Carolina and Mark J. Lawrence." State of South Carolina, Court of Common Pleas, County of Dorchester, Case No. 2013-CP-18-00013, Transcript of Record, Exhibit DSC-28, July 8, 2014.

square feet of living space in a four-story house and separate apartment.[23] In December of 2016, the Zillow website valued this property at $2,137,454 with a monthly rent estimate of $9,166.[24] The Realtor.com website listed it at $1,424,510.[25] The lease agreement stipulated an annual rent of one dollar and was to run for five years with the option of another five years and held that he was entitled to use the property even if he were not bishop.[26] This meant Lawrence would have the bishop's residence virtually rent-free until the year 2020. When asked years later why he did this, Lawrence said in an official deposition that it was because the Presiding Bishop had acted in hostility to the diocese and she and her chancellor were regularly trampling on the constitution and canons of the Church.[27] He added that he was following the advice of his chancellor, Wade Logan.[28] Neither Lawrence nor Logan ever publicly clarified the connection between the Presiding Bishop and the ten-year lease on the official episcopal residence. What the deal implied was that the diocesan leaders intended to keep Lawrence as bishop and that Lawrence intended to remain as bishop even if he were removed from office by the Church authorities. For the time being, the lease remained a secret held among the diocesan power structure. It came to light in the circuit court trial in July of 2014.

On the same day as the lease, March 17, 2010, another important legal document was registered.[29] Bishop Lawrence and the Rev. Marshall Huey filed an amended copy of the By-Laws of the Trustees of the Protestant Episcopal Church in South Carolina. There were two diocesan entities that were registered as corporations with the South Carolina Secretary of State. The other was the "The Protestant Episcopal Church in the Diocese of South Carolina," or simply, the Diocese. The purpose of the Trustees was to manage the assets of the diocese. In the By-Laws, the Bishop of the Diocese was the president of the corporation of the trustees. This meant Bishop Lawrence would be head of both corporations, the diocese and the trustees of the diocese.

The break between the end of the Logan/Tisdale affair, on February 10, and the annual diocesan convention, on March 26, heightened the growing tensions between the diocese and the national Church. Presiding Bishop Jefferts Schori met the Executive Council of the Episcopal Church in Omaha on February 19–22, and stated the obvious: "things are heating up in South Carolina."[30] She said the reason for the Tisdale initiative was "to ascertain the diocese's plans for dealing with disaffected Episcopalians."[31] She seemed a bit offended at Lawrence's reaction saying he had delayed the annual con-

23. "50 Smith St., Charleston, SC 29401." Zillow, http://www.zillow.com/homedetails/50-smith-st-Charleston-SC-29401/10903300_zpid.

24. Ibid.

25. "50 Smith St." Realtor.com, http://realtor.com.

26. "Deposition Transcript—Mark J. Lawrence," 147.

27. Ibid., 149–51.

28. Ibid., 151.

29. "By-Laws of the Trustees of the Protestant Episcopal Church in South Carolina [March 17, 2010]." State of South Carolina, Court of Common Pleas, County of Dorchester, Case No. 2013-CP-00013, Exhibit DSC-16, July 8, 2014.

30. Schjonberg, Mary Frances. "Executive Council Begins Four-Day Omaha Meeting." Episcopal Life Online, February 19, 2010, http://www.episcopalchurch.org/7999901_119606_ENG_HTM.htm.

31. Ibid.

vention and blamed it on her: "'supposedly to my incursions in South Carolina.'"[32] She added, "'He's telling the world that he is offended that I think it's important that people who want to stay Episcopalians there have some representation on behalf of the larger church."[33] She did not suggest any further action in South Carolina.

The national Church leaders were not the only critics of Lawrence to see that things were "heating up." The Episcopal Forum placed a full-page ad in the Charleston *Post and Courier* inviting everyone to a conference in Charleston on March 6, entitled "Enthusiastically Episcopalian." The ad also listed characteristics of Episcopalians, "I am Episcopalian." After a talk by a noted pro-Episcopal Church professor, Frank Wade, the sold-out meeting settled into a panel discussion entitled "What in the World is Going on in the Episcopal Diocese of South Carolina?" That certainly was a question on many a mind. The ad and the meeting must have won some notoriety because Peter Moore, a retired dean from Trinity School and staff member at St. Michael's of Charleston felt the need to issue a strong denunciation of the meeting and the Episcopal Church in Virtue Online.[34]

The Diocesan Convention, March 26

Lawrence resumed his busy schedule of diocesan duties while remaining focused on the upcoming convention. He communicated with Harmon and his lawyers often in the interim. On March 17 came the news that made many a counter-revolutionary heart sink, Mary Glasspool received the necessary consents to approve her consecration as bishop. Lawrence noted simply in his diary: "(Glass Pool [sic] Consents Granted)."[35] Even though he had announced at the special convention last October that he was withdrawing from the Episcopal Church House of Bishops, he attended the meeting of the House of Bishops at Camp Allen, Texas, from March 19 to 24, perhaps to visit with his Communion Partner bishops with whom he had communicated several days beforehand. He left his diary blank on these days. An important study was presented in the House of Bishops meeting by its Theology Committee entitled "Same-Sex Relationships in the Life of the Church." It was an eighty-seven-page paper giving equal time to experts on the "traditionalist" and "liberal" sides of the issue. Lawrence never mentioned this substantial report showing both sides of the issue and no trace of it could be found in South Carolina.

It was also at the House of Bishops meeting that Lawrence first met Andrew Waldo, the bishop-elect of his neighboring diocese of Upper South Carolina.[36] The two of them

32. Ibid.

33. Ibid.

34. "South Carolina: Former Trinity Seminary Dean Blasts Episcopal Church Leadership." Virtueonline, March 17, 2010, http://www.virtueonline.org/south-carolina-former-trinity-seminary-dean-blasts-episcopal-church-leadership.

35. *Journal of the Two Hundred and Twentieth (. . .)* 2011, 30.

36. The Diocese of South Carolina Standing Committee denied consent to the election of Waldo as bishop of Upper South Carolina in its meeting of February 9, 2010. Bishop Lawrence was present at the meeting. The motion to reject was made by the Rev. Patrick Allen, seconded by the Rev. Shay Gaillard, and passed by a majority of the Committee. In the same session, the Committee denied every pending consent (Oregon, Louisiana, two for Los Angeles). "Minutes of the Standing Committee," February 9, 2010. In its subsequent meetings of almost three years, minutes showed that the DSC Standing

took a long walk and for an hour and a half discussed a wide range of issues getting to know each other and establishing a bond that was to endure. Waldo later reported that Lawrence was "gracious, honest, straightforward, and open in disagreement."[37] "Disagreement" was the key word, for Waldo recognized from the start that he and Lawrence were on very different theological paths. Still, Waldo thought it was important to do everything possible to bring peace and reconciliation in a situation that he knew well was moving in the opposite direction. He knew all along the odds were against him, but he was resolved to try anyway to do his best; and he did. Unfortunately for him, to have peace and reconciliation, both sides must be willing to give and take. As time and events would show, that would not be the case here. In the end, Waldo would not be able to achieve his goal, but this was not through any fault of his own. Meanwhile, he would spend the next several years building the closest bonds he could with his fellow bishop in the down-state.[38]

Sandwiched among these events, Lawrence worked hard on the upcoming diocesan convention meeting. He spent two weeks writing and rewriting his bishop's address. March 25, the day before the convention, he spent in frantic preparation. He revised his convention address, had a two-hour teleconference with his Council of Advice (Standing Committee), made numerous telephone calls, reworked convention agenda and his address, and got to bed at 1:00 a.m.[39] Apparently too keyed up to sleep, he was up from 2:00 to 3:00 a.m. "reviewing convention agenda."[40] He finally got to bed at 3:00 a.m. only to arise at 6:30 to head out to Diocesan House to revise his address yet again.[41] He arrived at St. Paul's of Summerville at 8:30 a.m., ready for a full day.

Amid rising tensions, the annual diocesan convention met at St. Paul's on March 26, following its three-week postponement. This was the third diocesan convention within thirteen months. Lawrence's "Bishop's Address" to the assembly was a six-thousand-word treatise given in forty-eight minutes. He reiterated the themes he had introduced a year earlier at the diocesan convention and had continued to expand ever since: The Episcopal Church had abandoned the traditional religion, a state of war existed between the Church and the Diocese, the Diocese was sovereign and autonomous, the Episcopal Church and its leaders had acted in an unconstitutional and non-canonical way, the Church had erred on issues of sexuality, and South Carolinians should think of themselves as "Anglicans" connected to a global Anglican Communion. In this speech, however, Lawrence went beyond his well-established themes to sound a new level of alarm on two recently occurring counts: "The Trajectory of The Episcopal Church Continues Unabated," that is, the Episcopal Church had willfully disregarded Scripture and the Anglican Communion by approving a second openly homosexual bishop [Glasspool], and "The Presiding Bishop's Incursion and Significance," that is, Jefferts Schori had violated her own constitution and canons by invading his diocese, meaning the Logan/Tisdale Affair.[42]

Committee denied every request for consent to the elections of Episcopal bishops except four cases.

37. Waldo, (the Rt. Rev.) Andrew. Interview with author, September 4, 2014.
38. Ibid.
39. *Journal of the Two Hundred and Twentieth* (. . .) 2011, 30.
40. Ibid.
41. Ibid.
42. *Journal of the Two Hundred and Nineteenth* (. . .) 2010, 22–28.

Not surprisingly, Lawrence spend about a quarter of his time on homosexuality, or what he liked to call "the false Gospel of Indiscriminate Inclusivity."[43] He denounced the Episcopal Church's stand on the ordination of homosexuals as "contrary to the received teaching of God's Holy Word, the trustworthy traditions of the Christian Faith, and the expressed will of the Anglican Communion."[44] He went on to make two serious accusations without any evidence to back them up: "the majority of the bishops would appear to be regarding same-sex blessings as marriages. I believe it is also the desire of many in TEC to bring the rest of the Anglican Communion to embrace this as well."[45] On the first point the fact was that the bishops had called only for considering liturgies for the blessings of same sex unions, nothing more. The second point was nonsense as the Episcopal Church had no right at all to impose anything on any one of the other thirty-seven independent provinces of the Anglican Communion. He even made a strangely cryptic warning about "an ever wider embrace of sexual understandings for those in ordained ministry."[46] He left that up entirely to the imaginations of his listeners. What he did make clear was a clarion call for war: "This is our battle to engage (. . .). This is our time to stand and be humbly counted among the faithful."[47]

With homosexuality out of the way, Lawrence next turned his ire on another favorite target, Presiding Bishop Jefferts Schori. He spent a third of his speech blasting her "non-constitutional and non-canonical incursion"[48] in the Logan/Tisdale affair. He went on darkly to impugn her motives: "The retaining of counsel now has all the signs of an adversarial relationship—one of monitoring (. . .) how a Diocesan Bishop and Standing Committee may choose to deal with its priests and parishes;"[49] and "The stated purposes for her incursion is the protection of Church property. Whether there are other more disruptive reasons for such non-canonical incursions can only be surmised."[50] *More disruptive reasons.* Then Lawrence got to the heart of the matter. In a statement that must have caught the attention of all of the Episcopal Church leaders, he said: "The Standing Committee, the Bishop and perhaps the Board of Trustees of the local diocese alone have charge in various ways over these matters of property."[51] In fact, the Episcopal Church Canon I.7.4 states "All real and personal property (. . .) is held in trust for this Church and the Diocese."[52] Lawrence boldly asserted that the Presiding Bishop had no right to protect the property of the Episcopal Church.[53] He demanded she remove her legal counsel in the Diocese.

43. Ibid., 24.
44. Ibid., 23.
45. Ibid., 24.
46. Ibid.
47. Ibid.
48. Ibid., 25.
49. Ibid.
50. Ibid.
51. Ibid., 26.
52. *Constitution and Canons, 2012, Together with the Rules of Order for the Government of the Protestant Episcopal Church in the United States of America Otherwise Known as The Episcopal Church.* New York: the church, 2012, 41. http://www.episcopalchurch.org/files/documents/2012_candc.pdf.
53. *Journal of the Two Hundred and Nineteenth* (. . .) 2010, 26.

Later in his address, Lawrence returned to a theme that he would increasingly emphasize in time, the myth of history. He claimed that the Diocese of South Carolina existed before the Episcopal Church, that it helped create the Church, and that it voluntarily joined the Church and by extension could voluntarily leave it. He said South Carolina "formed a diocese, elected a bishop, and helped form the Protestant Episcopal Church."[54] In fact, as we have seen the Episcopal Church began organizing first and invited the Anglicans of South Carolina to organize a state convention and to send representatives to a national Church convention. South Carolina's delegates to the 1789 national convention ratified for their state the Episcopal Church's new Constitution and Canons by signing them. Succeeding meetings in South Carolina affirmed this. Six years later, in 1795, South Carolina elected its first bishop and then could rightfully be called a diocese. Only years later did the South Carolinians draw up a full state constitution. The idea that a distinctly independent and sovereign Diocese of South Carolina existed before the Episcopal Church was a misconstruction of history.

Although Lawrence did not call for a complete break with the Episcopal Church, he stressed that the gulf between the Diocese of South Carolina and the Church was enormous and growing. His speech was a call for war that offered no concessions or backing away. It made only demands on the Church and offered no peace settlement. Quite the contrary, Lawrence indicated that the distance between diocese and national Church was now too wide to cross: "The Presiding Bishop and I stand looking at one another across a wide, deep and seemingly unbridgeable theological and canonical chasm."[55] *Unbridgeable.* One could only wonder if this meant Lawrence believed he could never be again, if he had ever been, on the same side as Jefferts Schori.

Lawrence also discussed the resolutions that were about to be put forth for vote. Then, toward the end of his talk he suddenly announced that he was calling yet another diocesan convention meeting on October 16, 2010. This would be the fourth diocesan meeting in the two years of 2009 and 2010. Surely this would heighten the sense of crisis and urgency that he had tried so hard to create in his address as if his declarations of invasions, call to arms and numerous military metaphors had not been enough. Then, it was time to move on to the new resolutions.

Lawrence said repeatedly from the start of his episcopacy that three issues divided the Diocese from the Episcopal Church: theology, polity, and sexuality. At first, sexuality had been given prominence as Lawrence and his allies denounced "The Gospel of Indiscriminate Inclusivity." As events had shown, however, it was much easier to unify the diocese on the first two issues than on the third. In early 2010, the diocesan leaders seized the Logan/Tisdale Affair as a convenient cause; they moved the topic of polity into the forefront. They claimed that the Presiding Bishop and her chancellor had violated their own constitution and canons, exceeded their authority, invaded the sovereign diocese of South Carolina, and menaced their innocent bishop. They declared that this grave crisis necessitated a greater differentiation of diocese from Church and therefore new resolutions should be passed to that effect. Four of the five proposed resolutions followed this path.

54. Ibid., 27.
55. Ibid., 26.

Five resolutions had been composed and published in advance, one by Kendall Harmon and four by the Standing Committee. They were the only resolutions presented to the convention. All were easily approved. The first resolution was drawn up by Harmon and co-signed by thirty-two priests and deacons of the diocese, the majority of which later broke with the Episcopal Church and were removed from ministry in the Church. It was a rewording of resolutions approved by the two preceding conventions. In March 2009, it was called the Uniqueness of Christ. In October 2009, it was labeled The Lordship of Christ and the Sufficiency of Scripture. In this third incarnation, Harmon once again stressed the vertical nature of faith: "a gospel diocese (. . .) an evangelical faith (. . .). Jesus came into the world to save the lost."[56]

The other four resolutions all dealt with the polity of the Episcopal Church and the diocese. Resolution Two denounced the "intrusions" of the presiding bishop: "the Presiding Bishop has no authority to retain attorneys in this Diocese."[57] It went on to say: "the Diocese of South Carolina demands that the Presiding Bishop withdraw and terminate the engagement of all such legal counsel in South Carolina."[58] An amendment was proposed to change the word *demands* to *requests*. It was overwhelmingly defeated.[59] This convention was in no mood to "request" anything.

Resolution Three stated that the ecclesiastical authority of the diocese was the bishop, and in his absence the standing committee. It declared that the ecclesiastical authority was the sole and final authority in all matters concerning the constitution and canons of the diocese. If the bishop ruled, his word could not be appealed. This resolution was important on several levels. It showed the fear promoted by the diocesan leadership that the Presiding Bishop was heading toward removing Lawrence from office. They had suggested as much during the Logan/Tisdale Affair. Moreover, and most importantly in the subsequent story of the schism, this resolution invested the bishop with the monolithic power of interpreting the governing documents of the diocese, a sort of absolute monarch or infallible pope. Moreover, under this resolution the bishop had the personal discretion of ignoring the Dennis Canon at will since he could interpret the constitution and canons and his word was "final and binding in all respects."[60] This alone had to give the Presiding Bishop and her chancellor cause for alarm.

If Resolution Three were cause for alarm, Four was even more so. It called for adding a section to the canons of the diocese: "It is within the power of the Ecclesiastical Authority [bishop] of this Diocese to provide a generous pastoral response to parishes in conflict with the Diocese."[61] *Generous pastoral response* would most certainly not be a

56. Ibid., 62.

57. Ibid.

58. Ibid.

59. Mann, Barbara. "Report on the 3/26/10 Diocesan Convention." Episcopal Forum of SC, April 9, 2010, http://www.episcopalforumofsc.org/Overview%20Documents/EFSC_Report_on_the_3-26-10_convention-Mann-4-9-10.pdf.

60. *Journal of the Two Hundred and Nineteenth* (. . .) 2010, 62. This resolution was to be crucial in the background of the schism. In September of 2012 it was the basis of Lawrence's declaration to the Standing Committee that they had the authority to remove the diocese from the Episcopal Church.

61. Ibid.

lawsuit to retain the property for the diocese and the Church under the Dennis Canon. Indeed, the "Explanation" given with the resolution denounced the presiding bishop for her litigation and even curiously enough denounced the "destructive force" of the lawsuits in the *All Saints* case which ironically the Diocese of South Carolina itself had initiated and pursued to the bitter end.[62] One could wonder if the delegates to this convention realized that by passing this resolution they were rejecting the work of their own diocese and its previous "ecclesiastical authority." Once again, the bishop was declared to be "the authority" to deal with the parishes. With such absolute power, Lawrence could give the property to the departing parishes at will. The significance of this resolution could not have been lost on either the national Church leaders or the local parishes that now had a bright green light to leave the Episcopal Church with the property in hand, something that St. Andrew's of Mt. Pleasant was to do soon after this resolution was enacted. It left with millions of dollars' worth of property and Lawrence's "generous pastoral response."

Right after all five resolutions passed by overwhelming numbers,[63] suddenly old Resolution Number Five from last October's convention, "The Rubric of Love," was presented to the convention without any fanfare. This was the resolution saying the Diocese would have no prejudice against homosexuals. It presented the three hundred delegates with the glaring contradiction between two decades of diocesan policy on homosexuality and "Love" for homosexuals. The conflict was too much to reconcile. It had caused a near collapse of the October 2009 convention as perplexed delegates wrangled over meaning and wording. To save unity, worried diocesan leaders scurried to have it tabled, left pending, and passed on to the next convention. The leaders had learned their lesson this time. There would be no danger of chaos in this convention now so well united against the presiding bishop. Suddenly a motion was made to "withdraw" "The Rubric of Love." A vote was taken; it passed by a majority.[64] Thus, the "Rubric of Love" disappeared forever. The one effort to introduce even a small horizontal facet to a fiercely vertical religion died an unceremonious death. South Carolina disposed of "Love."

The issue of homosexuality had proved too thorny for the diocesan leadership. It was easier to fan the flames of homophobia than to come to grips with the actual issue of homosexuality. The Diocese of South Carolina went on opposing the ordination of non-celibate homosexuals without ever coming to a consensus on the matter of homosexuality, indeed without ever publicly discussing it again. However, if homosexuality were to be downplayed, the two other issues of theology and polity would have to take up the slack; and this they did.

It is important to note that resolutions One through Four in the March 2010 convention derived from two of the three points of differentiation that the diocesan leadership saw with the Episcopal Church: theology and polity. Number One reasserted the vertical faith so dear to the hearts of the traditionalists. It also contained a scarcely veiled criticism of the Presiding Bishop's broader theology. Resolutions Two, Three, and Four declared virtual independence of the diocese from the Episcopal Church and gave to the

62. Ibid.
63. Resolution Five was relatively unimportant and dealt with only one parish.
64. Ibid., 18.

bishop authoritarian power over the constitution and canons of the Episcopal Church. There was no resolution presented at all on the third point of differentiation, the driving issue of homosexuality. Thus, by early 2010, the diocesan leadership had turned to emphasizing the differences with the Episcopal Church on polity first and theology second.

The close of the regular annual diocesan convention, on March 26, 2010, meant that three diocesan conventions had met within thirteen months, considered fourteen resolutions, and passed twelve of them. Only one had been defeated (March 2009, suspension of the General Convention). It was the last resolution to be voted down in a diocesan convention. Only one other had failed to pass; it had been tabled, (October 2009, no prejudice against homosexuals), only to be abolished by the subsequent convention. Three of the resolutions, one at each convention, were virtually the same proclaiming the vertical theology of salvation through Christ alone and the primacy of the Scriptures. Two of the votes were only local concerns. The rest, seven in all, half of all the resolutions offered, dealt with polity, or the government of Church and diocese. Together they asserted the sovereign independence of the diocese, denied the power of the central authority of the Episcopal Church in South Carolina, and promoted identity beyond the national Church with the conservative parts of the Anglican Communion. It was clear by now that although the trigger issue driving all this differentiation remained homosexuality, the battle lines were being drawn around other points that would rally the local diocese. The leadership had come to emphasize local rights, particularly the absolute power of the bishop of South Carolina to interpret for himself the Constitution and Canons of the Episcopal Church. This strategy worked very well. The Rev. Chuck Owens, of Church of the Cross in Bluffton said "the Diocese of South Carolina and The Episcopal Church are on opposite sides of a battle that will soon be engaged on several fronts. Theology and polity being the most obvious at the moment."[65]

It was also interesting to compare the reactions in the Diocese of South Carolina to the first and second openly homosexual bishops in the Episcopal Church. The first, Gene Robinson, prompted a major reaction in the Diocese of South Carolina in 2003. A special diocesan convention met urgently to denounce strongly his affirmation. The diocese went on to appeal for alternate primatial oversight beyond the Episcopal Church. Seven years later, the second, Mary Glasspool, did get a blast from Lawrence in his bishop's address to the March 2010 convention, but that was about the extent of the reaction.[66] No other mention was made in the diocesan convention. The resolutions offered in the March 2010 convention left an incongruous silence on Glasspool. While Robinson was followed by a bomb, Glasspool was followed by a firecracker. Once again, this indicated that in the intervening period, the diocesan leadership had put the issue of homosexuality on the back burner in favor of more actionable unifying factors, particularly local rights over national. The war had not changed but the campaigns and battles had, from stimulating the differentiation to enacting it. As if to emphasize the rising intensity of

---

65. Kwon, Lillian. "S.C. Diocese Engages in 'Battle' with Episcopal Church." *The Christian Post*, March 27, 2010, http://www.christianpost.com.

66. On July 16, 2010, the Diocese of South Carolina Standing Committee directed the Rev. Jeff Miller to draft a statement that the Committee would not recognize Mary Glasspool as a bishop of the Episcopal Church. "Minutes of the Standing Committee," [July 16, 2010].

the war, the convention voted to recess, not adjourn, and to reconvene on October 15, 2010, at St. Paul's of Summerville. This would be the fourth diocesan convention within nineteen months. The pace of action quickened.

Tensions

The diocesan convention had settled nothing with the national Church. Quite the opposite, the declaration of invasion, call to arms, passage of demanding, self-governing resolutions, and the refusal to adjourn all served to roil the already troubled waters. The diocesan leaders persisted in claiming they were still in the Episcopal Church, however tenuous that may be. Exactly what settlement they expected to make with the Presiding Bishop remained to be seen. She did not respond to their resolutions and demands, but she did not press the matter either. After Tisdale had dropped his requests in February, he said nothing more about them, nor did Beers, or the Presiding Bishop.

Although St. Andrew's of Mt. Pleasant had voted as a congregation to leave the Episcopal Church the previous December, the parish was still officially in union with the diocese when the convention met on March 26. However, just two days after the convention had met and had not broken completely with the Episcopal Church, all of this changed suddenly. On Sunday, March 28, 2010, the vestry of St. Andrew's met at 7:15 a.m. and unanimously passed a resolution: "to withdraw from and sever all ties with The Episcopal Church (. . .) and to transfer its canonical residence to the Anglican Church in North America." At 12:15 p.m. a special parish meeting convened to vote on the vestry's action. Of the 722 ballots cast, 703 were in favor.[67] The parish claimed some 2,800 communicants. The pertinent question was, what would Lawrence do about the property?[68]

In reality, it was not an open question. Lawrence had already signaled what he would do in his words and in the resolutions of the convention, *generous pastoral response*. There would be no repeat of All Saints, Waccamaw. There would be no attempt to enforce the Dennis Canon. There would be no claims on the property or other assets. There would be no litigation. All of this Lawrence had shown in advance. When the rupture occurred, he put all the blame for it on the Episcopal Church: "The departure of the Episcopal Church from the way of Christ and the biblically rooted teachings of the Church has become too discordant for them [St. Andrew's] to tolerate any longer."[69] In the end, Lawrence did nothing about St. Andrew's except to give his blessings to Wood and the parish. There was not even a provision made for the minority of St. Andrew's who wanted to remain in the Episcopal Church.

---

67. "St. Andrew's Parish Challenges Polity of the Diocese of SC and TEC." eNewsletter, Episcopal Forum of SC, March 30, 2010, http://www.mynewsletterbuilder.com/email/newsletter/1410254485.

68. Bishop Lawrence removed the clergy of St. Andrew's from the ordained ministry of the Episcopal Church by Declaration of Removal made on October 21, 2010 for Stephen D. Wood, Anthony K. Kowbeidu, Kenneth L. Alexander, and Brian C. Morgan. The Declaration was forwarded to the Presiding Bishop.

69. Schjonberg, Mary Frances. "South Carolina: Mount Pleasant Parish Members Vote to Leave Episcopal Church." Episcopal News Service, March 31, 2010, http://archive.episcopalchurch.org/81803_121208_ENG_HTM.htm.

Virtually ignoring St. Andrew's, Lawrence resumed his busy schedule of building bonds at home and abroad. In the seven months between the diocesan conventions of March and October of 2010, he made eight trips out of state totaling thirty-three days. Most of these travels were to strengthen ties with other conservative forces. The first trip was a nine-day journey to Singapore, from April 15 to 24, for the Fourth Anglican Global South to South Encounter. This was mainly a continuation of GAFCON from the Jerusalem meeting in 2008. Lawrence had also attended that gathering. Lawrence and John Howe (Central Florida) were the two Episcopal Church bishops that joined 128 other delegates for the Singapore meeting. As before, this conference also denounced the Episcopal Church: "we continue to grieve over the life of The Episcopal Church (. . .) and all those churches that have rejected the Way of the Lord as expressed in Holy Scripture."[70] It also bemoaned the affirmation of Mary Glasspool as a bishop. It went on to point out that many southern provinces had already broken communion with the Episcopal Church and called on others to follow. Moreover, it hailed the Anglican Church in North America as a "faithful expression of Anglicanism" and called on all provinces to be in full communion with ACNA.[71] Finally it promoted the Anglican Covenant as the new bond.

Following his return from Singapore, Lawrence made seven trips out of state in the next several months. From 12 to 14 May, he was in Sewickley, Pennsylvania, for the Trinity School for Ministry board meeting. May 19 to 21, he and Kendall Harmon were at Nashotah House in Wisconsin for commencement. There they met the Rt. Rev. Michael Nazir-Ali, retired bishop of Rochester, England, a man well-known for his outspoken conservative views. They discussed Nazir-Ali becoming a visiting bishop of South Carolina.[72] Lawrence was not present when Andrew Waldo was consecrated bishop of Upper South Carolina at Christ Church, Greenville, on May 22.[73] From June 28 to 30, Lawrence was at Kanuga, North Carolina, for summer camp. On August 25, he flew to Washington DC, to meet Bishop Michael Nazir-Ali at the right-wing think tank Heritage Foundation and to visit All Saints Church, Chevy Chase, Maryland.[74] From September 15 to 17, he was in Phoenix, Arizona, for the House of Bishops meeting. On September 29, Lawrence left for Cairo, Egypt, as the guest of the Most Rev. Mouneer Anis, the Bishop of Egypt with North Africa and the Horn of Africa and president bishop of the Episcopal Church in Jerusalem and the Middle East. He remained there until October 8. On October 11 and 12, Lawrence was at Sewanee, Tennessee for the installation of the new vice-chancellor of the University of the South.[75]

---

70. "Fourth Trumpet from the Fourth Anglican Global South to South Encounter." Global South Anglican Online, April 23, 2010, http://www.globalsouthanglican.org/index.php/blog/comments/fourth.

71. Ibid.

72. *Journal of the Two Hundred and Nineteenth* (. . .) 2010, 29.

73. The Standing Committee had voted "no" on consent to the election of Waldo.

74. In 2011, the Rev. Ed Kelaher became rector of All Saints. He had been the priest of the Episcopal congregation from All Saints Pawley's Island that made the settlement with the Anglican church and took the name Christ the King. The Episcopal Church of Christ the King adhered to Lawrence in the schism.

75. *Journal of the Two Hundred and Nineteenth* (. . .) 2010, 31–42.

While it was evident that Lawrence had succeeded well in solidifying the majority of the Diocese and in strengthening ties with reactionary forces beyond South Carolina, a minority of loyal Episcopalians in the Low Country grew ever more alarmed at the bishop's relentless actions to differentiate the diocese from the national Church. By 2010, the Episcopal Forum of South Carolina claimed six hundred members in two-thirds of the parishes and a mailing list of one thousand.[76] Although excluded from the official diocesan power structure and media, the Forum had tried its best to defend the Episcopal Church among the communicants. It held numerous public conferences including regional ones in April and May of 2010, in Johns Island, Summerville, Hilton Head, Florence, and Myrtle Beach. After three diocesan conventions in quick succession, however, it was clear to all that the tide was against them. By August of 2010, the leaders of the Forum believed that they had no choice but to appeal to the national church for help. The Forum sent a formal letter, dated September 22, to the Executive Council of the Episcopal Church and the House of Bishops requesting an investigation of the diocese. It said "recent actions and inactions (. . .) are accelerating the process of alienation and disassociation of the Diocese of South Carolina from The Episcopal Church;"[77] and added "we request that The Episcopal Church leadership investigate the situation in our Diocese."[78] The letter listed complaints as: inaction on St. Andrew's, inaction on other parishes moving to secession, the declaration of independent diocesan sovereignty, removal of references to the Episcopal Church from the diocesan website, failure to support a mission of loyal Episcopalians at Port Royal, and modification of the declaration of conformity made by new clergy. It concluded by asking for an investigation of: parishes moving to disassociation, withdrawal of St. Andrew's, and property titles and corporate documents of the parishes.

Appended was a copy of a letter of April 13, 2010, from Ross "Buddy" Lindsay, III, a lawyer in Myrtle Beach, to an unspecified parish advising them in detail on how to leave the diocese with the property. Lindsay had been involved in the *All Saints* case. One important point in Lindsay's letter read "Some parties are creating irrevocable land trusts to hold their property. The bishop and standing committee have to consent to such a transfer or sign a quit-claim deed first."[79] This would suggest that Lawrence and the Standing Committee must have either consented to a transfer or given a quit claim deed to St. Andrew's before it moved millions of dollars' worth of property into a separate land trust in July of 2009.

What the Forum was asking was essentially what Tisdale had tried to get a few months earlier. At that time, the diocese had absolutely refused to release any documents to him or anyone else, instead had gone on the offensive to demand the removal of the counsel. The Presiding Bishop and her chancellor did not remove the counsel but they

---

76. "Enthusiastically Episcopalian Conference & Forums—Spring 2010." eNewsletter, Episcopal Forum of SC, June 8, 2010, http:www.mynewsletterbuilder.com/email/newsletter/1410350025.

77. The Episcopal Forum to the Executive Council of the Episcopal Church and the House of Bishops, August 24, 2010, http://www.episcopalforumofsc.org/Overview%20Documents/EFSC%20Letter%20to%20HOB%20and%20EC%20with%20Attachments.pdf.

78. Ibid.

79. Ibid.

did not pursue the matter either. The Forum's appeal, however, was beyond the Presiding Bishop to the Executive Council and the House of Bishops.

Lawrence responded to the Forum's appeal immediately in an open letter of his own to the diocese dated September 23, 2010.[80] Not surprisingly he continued his long-held strategy that the best defense is a good offense. On the point about St. Andrew's, he did not deny the charge but fired back by attacking the Diocese of South Carolina's role in the *All Saints* case that "drained" away five hundred thousand dollars. He said that the state supreme court ruling in that case meant he would not "replicate" the All Saints experience. This clearly implied that he believed the ruling made the Dennis Canon invalid in the Diocese of South Carolina. On the second point, that the bishop had done nothing to stop other parishes from heading for exit, Lawrence again turned the tables: "What they [the Forum] and some of our Episcopal Church leaders ought to do is spend a bit more time listening to and seeking to understand what is motivating (. . .) the parishes." Again, he had not denied the point. On the third issue, that the bishop had declared the diocese "sovereign," yet again he did not deny it but in fact boasted of it. He cited as his authority a book by Powell Mills Dawley in the Church Teaching Series and asserted that South Carolina had long "affirmed this independent or sovereign character." There was clearly a difference on interpretation of the word sovereign. On the next point, that the diocese and many parishes had removed the word "Episcopal" from their websites, Lawrence once again did not deny it but turned the tables and accused the Forum of never using the term "Episcopal Diocese of South Carolina" in its letter, only "Diocese of South Carolina." On the next item, that he had not helped the loyal Episcopal mission at Port Royal, Lawrence continued his offensive strategy and blamed the people in the mission whom he called "disgruntled members of St. Helena's" who were acting in "a disappointing way (. . .) to repay my kindness." On the next point, the modification of the declaration of conformity made by new clergy, Lawrence correctly pointed out that the revision was only read aloud at the ordination. Nevertheless, he went on to challenge the Forum to refute any of the reading. Concerning the last point, that the bishop and Standing Committee proposed six new resolutions for the upcoming diocesan convention, Lawrence put all the blame on the Presiding Bishop: "The refusal of the Presiding Bishop to respond, along with the concerns we have discovered in the revised Title IV disciplinary canons is the reason for the continuation of the Annual Convention." In the conclusion of his letter, Lawrence returned to his war mode in phrases such as "we are engaged in a worldwide struggle," "this struggle," "a battalion in a military campaign which is ordered to hold a pass," "we are called to resist," "we are called to stand our ground," "this is not a time to give-in nor give up," and "let us hold fast." The one-sided war continued.

Lawrence's combative reply to the Forum gave no ground. It made no concession. It showed no regard, let along compassion, for the rising anxiety common among the loyal Episcopalian minority of the diocese who were now desperately pleading for help from the national Church. However, it may well not have been aimed at the Forum. As

---

80. "Bishop Lawrence Responds to Request for Investigation." Diocese of South Carolina, September 23, 2010, http://www.diosc.com/sys/index.php?view=article&catid=1%3Alatest-news&id=287%Abishop-lawrence-responds.

the first letter was addressed to the power structure of the Episcopal Church, Lawrence's was perhaps also aimed there and no doubt to the majority of the diocese. He may have been preparing a defense for what might develop into a serious move against him in time on the part of the Church constitutional structure. In that case, he would need the solid support of the majority in his diocese to which he had already well bonded and could disregard the powerless and marginalized minority represented by the Forum.

The Special Convention, October 15

The preparations for the October diocesan convention began weeks earlier. At a clergy conference on September 2, at St. Paul's in Summerville, diocesan lawyer Alan Runyan made a report on the revisions to the Title IV canons of the Episcopal Church dealing with discipline for bishops and priests. In his view, the revisions gave too much power to bishops, particularly the presiding bishop, and removed due process from the accused. They were unacceptable and must be addressed by new resolutions to be put before the upcoming diocesan convention. On September 9, Lawrence met with the Standing Committee from 10:30 a.m. to 3:00 p.m. The committee approved all proposed resolutions to be offered to the convention next month.[81] The six were published immediately, on September 9. The deaneries held meetings in September to review the resolutions.

Sandwiched among three out-of-state trips to Phoenix, Cairo, and Sewanee, and his spat with the Forum, Lawrence found time to prepare for the diocesan convention. However, he did not show the same tension or sense of urgency that he had shown at the diocesan convention in March of 2010. On Wednesday, October 13, two days before the convention, Lawrence wrote a letter to the Presiding Bishop. He later said: "I wrote directly to the Presiding Bishop (. . .) of my concerns and reminding her of the concerns of this Convention (. . .) that she remove the attorney unconstitutionally retained within this Diocese."[82] On October 14, Lawrence received an e-mail from the Presiding Bishop. He said she failed once again to address this issue and expressed "her fear about the havoc that she believes is likely to ensue if I keep on my present course."[83] Immediately thereafter, Lawrence wrote a letter to the Presiding Bishop, but did not send it.[84] Neither the contents of this letter nor the reason for not sending it have been revealed.

The "Reconvened" diocesan convention that met on October 15, at St. Paul's of Summerville, was a rather brief, predictable, opened-and-closed affair that ended just after 2:00 in the afternoon. This was the fourth diocesan convention led by Lawrence within twenty months. Perhaps the frequency of these meetings contributed to the lack of drama. Lawrence's address to the convention was another of his verbose, lengthy, and cloudy speeches although not so much as that of last March. In the first half of the address, Lawrence emphasized the "Anglican" identity of the diocese returning to his familiar theme "Making Biblical Anglicans for a Global Age." He talked of his visit to

81. *Journal of the Two Hundred Twentieth* (. . .) 2011, 39.
82. *Journal of the Two Hundred and Nineteenth* (. . .) 2010, 33.
83. Ibid.
84. *Journal of the Two Hundred Twentieth* (. . .) 2011, 39.

the Global South conference in Singapore and of the "Communion Partners." He also announced that he had arranged for the Rt. Rev. Michael Nazir-Ali to serve as the new "Visiting Bishop in South Carolina for Anglican Communion Development." Lawrence said Nazir-Ali was to make periodic visits to the diocese and to represent the diocese in the world, exactly how was left unspecified. Lawrence also announced the news that he had established a partnership between the dioceses of South Carolina and Egypt. The bishop of the latter was the Rt. Rev. Mouneer Anis who had become a close friend and ally of Lawrence. Again, Lawrence made no mention that this had been approved by anyone else in the diocese.[85]

Having expounded at length on the "Anglican" identity of the diocese outside of the Episcopal Church, Lawrence turned to the real cause for the special convention, the resolutions at hand. As background, he launched into a long and by now familiar denunciation of the Episcopal Church, particularly the Presiding Bishop. He blamed her for forcing this special convention: "Had she removed the attorney she had retained without the authorization of this church's polity we may have been able to adjourn this convention (. . .). But that has not been the case (. . .). The request this convention made of her to desist her unauthorized incursion has met with stony silence."[86] Next, Lawrence turned to the Title IV revisions that were to go into effect in 2011 that he claimed, "gives unconstitutional authority to the Presiding Bishop to intrude into a diocese without the Standing Committee's authority."[87] Again, he made sweeping generalizations with no specifics or details. He went on to make an astounding assertion that the revisions that had been worked out by the General Convention of the Episcopal Church were unconstitutional and that the Diocese of South Carolina alone knew the truth and had to act to save the Church. In other words, the consensus of the entire General Convention was in error and this one diocese had to show them so. He portrayed himself as the innocent victim: "The sad truth is that our theological commitments are seen by more than a few of the present leaders in this church as the enemy. We hold a position that needs to be purged or eliminated."[88] This was another sweeping and serious charge completely without substantiation or evidence. But he was not through with his victimization, far from it. He next turned to "The Gravity of the Moment That is Before Us."[89] His words turned ominous as he described how six bishops had received e-mails from the Presiding Bishop: "She was encouraging each of them to speak with me as 'the apparent focus of this diocesan gathering does not bode well for [Mark's] status as a bishop.' Perhaps she has forgotten it has not boded well for my status as a bishop since the first election."[90] One delegate, a lawyer, observed "That seemed to make a lot of members of the clergy

---

85. The Lawrence-Anis friendship was to prove crucial. Anis was the first to come to Lawrence's defense in the crisis of 2012. In Feb. of 2014 he led the establishment of an Oversight Primatial Council for South Carolina. This was ratified by the Diocese of South Carolina convention in March of 2014.

86. *Journal of the Two Hundred and Nineteenth* (. . .) 2010, 31. Actually, the March convention had used the word "demand" and had voted down a substitute word of "request."

87. Ibid.

88. Ibid.

89. Ibid.

90. Ibid.

more determined to vote defiantly on these resolutions."[91] This theme of victimization at the hands of the Episcopal Church and particularly the Presiding Bishop had appeared earlier but had never been emphasized so much as now. This was a theme that would continue to develop. Having already bonded well with the majority in the diocese, the majority of the diocesan clergy and lay leadership naturally rallied around its supposedly beleaguered bishop. As Lawrence ended his remarks, the crowd arose for a standing ovation, by now the standard response.

Lawrence's address was also remarkable for what else it contained and for what it did not contain. It did not contain the slightest hint of reconciliation or peace with the Episcopal Church. What it did contain was a continuation of the by now familiar military metaphors, e.g. "worldwide struggle," "a battalion in a military campaign," "hold a pass or a position against overwhelming odds," "we are called to resist," "to resist until it is no longer possible," "a sword in one hand and a trowel in the other," and "to guard the faith."[92] No one could have been surprised by this usual call to arms, however one may have been surprised by the total absence of the subject of homosexuality. Only last March, his bishop's address had contained long passages about fighting against "the false gospel of indiscriminate inclusivity." This address in October left a thundering silence on the topic. On reflection, it was not surprising because Lawrence had already been moving away from the third of the three points of differentiation with the Episcopal Church: theology, polity, and sexuality. One should recall that the only resolution to cause an uproar in a convention led by Lawrence was "The Rubric of Love," that had been tabled in 2009 and withdrawn in March of 2010. Apparently too dangerous and volatile, the subject of homosexuality had been moved to the sidelines in favor of theology and polity, or church government. Theological differences with the liberal leadership of the Episcopal Church had been rather well developed by this point but polity had not been. The resolutions arising would change that.

The six proposed resolutions to be taken up by the special convention in October of 2010 had already become well-known having been published on September 9 and discussed widely in the deaneries. Alan Runyan, by now the leading lawyer for the diocese, addressed the convention to "explain" the canons and revisions to the delegates.[93] He gave a dire prediction about the Title IV revisions. He said they would reduce safeguards, broaden offenses, increase the power of the Presiding Bishop, and allow her to "interfere" in a diocese. Although he did not say so directly, his implication may well have been that the Presiding Bishop would be free to remove Bishop Lawrence. He did not mention that defenders of the revisions had an entirely different view of them "as an effort to move from a court-oriented system toward one based on safety, truth telling, healing, and reconciliation."[94] On the topic of accession to the Constitution and Canons of the Epis-

---

91. Davies, Matthew and Mary Frances Schjonberg. "South Carolina: Convention Approves 'Protective Resolutions.'" Episcopal News Service, October 15, 2010, http://www.archive.episcopalchurch.org/81803_125222_ENG_HTM.htm.

92. *Journal of the Two Hundred and Nineteenth (. . .)* 2010, 32.

93. "DSC 2010 Convention: Alan Runyan Explains Canons." Video recording, Anglican TV, 11 minutes, http://www.YouTube.com.

94. Davies and Schjonberg, "South Carolina: Convention."

copal Church, Runyan said that accession did not apply to the founding dioceses, only to new dioceses. He claimed that twenty-seven dioceses in the Church had not acceded to the Church's Constitution and Canons. On the most important topic at hand, the Dennis Canon, Runyan declared that it had always been "optional" and that thirty dioceses had not listed it in their canons. The implication was that South Carolina was completely free to delete the Dennis Canon from its own Constitution and Canons. The available video showed a self-assured lawyer's presentation with no questions or discussions. There was obviously no counter-presentation giving the opposing viewpoints. In reality, Runyan's authoritatively-delivered assertions were all debatable and had already been rejected by official voices in the Episcopal Church, something that apparently was not mentioned in the convention. The assembly proceeded to vote on the proposed resolutions.

The first resolution, "R-6," was entitled "Amendment of the Constitution of the Diocese of South Carolina."[95] It provided for the Constitution of the Diocese to delete all references to the Canons of the Episcopal Church, that is, to withdraw the diocese's accession to all of the canons of the national Church. The accompanying "Explanation" asserted that the diocese must declare its sovereignty in order to resist the "legal threat" from the Presiding Bishop and Title IV's "infringement upon the rights to due process of all the clergy of this diocese." After some "good discussion"[96] the resolution passed by a majority vote.

The next resolution, "R-7," was called "Article XII—Of Altering the Constitution." It provided for changing Article XII of the diocesan constitution to remove the word "annual" before the word "Convention." This would mean that conventions could be called other than annually. There was more discussion on this proposal before it too passed by a majority vote.

The following resolution, "R-8," was called "Removal of Accession to the Canons of the Episcopal Church." R-6 had amended the Constitution of the diocese. This one changed the Canons of the diocese to remove the unqualified accession to the Canons of the Episcopal Church. This was aimed at nullifying the Title IV reforms that would go into effect in the Episcopal Church in 2011. The revisions in this resolution kept the 2006 standards, or pre-Title IV revisions language. R-8 passed overwhelmingly: clergy, 87 yes, 10 no; parishes, 40 yes, 7 no; missions, 14 yes, 1 no.[97]

The next resolution, "R-9," was entitled "Canon XXXVI." It amended the canon to remove the word "annual" before the word "Convention." R-7 had applied to the diocesan constitution. This one dealt with the diocesan canons. It also passed overwhelmingly. "R-10," provided that Section 5 of Canon XXIX of the diocesan canons be deleted. This section contained the Dennis Canon. The "Explanation" said "The ruling of the South Carolina Supreme Court has established that in this state there is not an implied

---

95. "Resolutions for Reconvened 219th Diocesan Convention." Diocese of South Carolina, September 9, 2010, http://diosc.com/sys/index.php?view=article&catid=1%3Alatest-news&id=286%3Aresolutions.

96. Mann, Barbara. "Observations about the Convention." eNewsletter, Episcopal Forum of SC, October 16, 2010, http://www.mynewsletterbuilder.com/email/newsletter/1410572025.

97. "Diocese Votes Overwhelmingly in Favor of Resolutions." Diocese of South Carolina, October 15, 2010, http://www.diosc.com/sys/index.php?view=article&catid=1%Alatest-news&id=298%3A219th-diocesan-convention.

trust in the property of the parishes of this diocese. Given that ruling, this Section no longer applies and should be removed."[98] The last resolution, "R-11," was called "Corporate Charter Purpose Statement." It revised the original corporate charter Bishop Temple had registered with the state of South Carolina on November 14, 1973, to change the purpose of the incorporation from representation of the Episcopal Church to that of the Diocese of South Carolina alone. It also passed by a large majority. All of the resolutions easily sailed through and the convention promptly adjourned shortly after 2:00 p.m.

A very important direct result of the convention was the alteration of the diocesan charter of incorporation. The original charter of 1973 had specified incorporation under the Constitution and Canons of the Episcopal Church. On October 19, 2010, Lawrence signed a new charter of incorporation to be officially registered with the state of South Carolina that removed any reference to the Episcopal Church.[99] It declared incorporation solely under the Constitution and Canons of the Diocese of South Carolina. Lawrence signed as the President of the Board of Trustees. When asked later in an official deposition by what authority he held that office, Lawrence could not provide an answer. Lawyer Thomas Tisdale asked Lawrence: "Can you point us to any authority in any constitution, canons, resolution or anything else that gives you such authority to sign a document to change the purpose of this corporation."[100] Lawrence responded, "No I cannot point to something."[101] This at the least cast doubt on the legality of the re-incorporation of October 19, 2010.

On October 21, 2010, the Standing Committee, sitting under a new designation as the Board of Directors, adopted a revised edition of the By-Laws of the corporation of the Diocese.[102] In one provision, the board said that in the event of a dispute over the identity of the bishop of the diocese, the Board alone would determine the identity of the bishop. In another, the Board said that if the diocese were without a bishop, the Board alone would appoint a President for the Board (Standing Committee). In yet another, the Board said that any removal of a member of the Board would be the sole right of the Board. In perhaps the most telling, if not provocative move, the revised By-Laws stated that the President (bishop) could be removed only by unanimous vote of the Board of Directors (Standing Committee). Many provisions provided in the revised By-Laws were directly contradictory to the Canons of the Episcopal Church. The diocesan convention, however, had just passed a resolution to end accession to all of the canons of the Church.

The special diocesan convention of October 1010 was the turning point, the point of no return for the Diocese of South Carolina in the run-up to the schism of 2012. Therefore, it is important to linger at this crucial place and emphasize several key factors.

98. "Resolutions for Reconvened."

99. "State of South Carolina, Secretary of State, Nonprofit Corporation, Articles of Amendment." October 9, 2010, State of South Carolina, Court of Common Pleas, County of Dorchester, Case No. 2013-CP-18-00013, Exhibit DSC-9, July 8, 2014.

100. "Deposition Transcript—Mark J. Lawrence," 127–28.

101. Ibid., 128.

102. "By-Laws of The Protestant Episcopal Church in the Diocese of South Carolina [October 22, 2010]." State of South Carolina, Court of Common Pleas, County of Dorchester, Case No. 2013-CP-18-00013, Exhibit DSC-6C, July 8, 2014.

In the first place, the convention acted on the unquestioned assertions of a well-known and influential lawyer of Beaufort, Alan Runyan, one of the most successful and respected lawyers in the Low Country. His word carried a great deal of weight in any assembly. Runyan gave an autobiography and personal testimony in 2014 that was recorded and posted on Kendall Harmon's blog, Titus One Nine.[103] He was born in 1951 in Nigeria, the son of Baptist missionaries, and lived there until the age of ten. He obtained a bachelor's degree from the University of South Carolina in 1973 and a law degree from the same in 1976. That year he was admitted to the bar in South Carolina and began serving as a law clerk. He was also a deacon and a Sunday School teacher in the First Baptist Church in Columbia. He became an associate and then a partner in a law firm in Columbia until he and a fellow attorney established a new firm, Speights and Runyan, in Beaufort, in 1987. In the late 1980s and the 1990s Runyan specialized in several areas of law, apparently successfully, particularly in issues of asbestos and liability.[104] In Beaufort, he joined the First Baptist Church, but, he said, it "didn't feel right."[105] In the spring of 2006 he first attended services at St. Helena's Episcopal Church in Beaufort and "heard the Gospel" from the rector, Jeff Miller.[106] Although a bit hesitant about the unfamiliar liturgies, he enthusiastically joined the Episcopal Church in his fifty-fifth year. He saw in this the hand of God: a "continuation of God's guidance," in "a path only He could have chosen."[107] The reason for this guidance became apparent, he said, in September of 2009, when Miller contacted him about the *All Saints* decision of the South Carolina Supreme Court. Runyan testified that he was suddenly overwhelmed and "driven by a desire God placed within me," to dwell on "these issues;" and it was all he thought about for a long while, asking himself "To what purpose?"[108] The purpose he came to see as helping the parish and diocese fight against the "spiritual darkness" of the "false gospel" that had consumed the Episcopal Church with "beliefs we never held."[109] Runyan became a devoted advocate for the conservative cause of the diocese against the Episcopal Church and made immediate contact with Bishop Lawrence who apparently bonded with him instantly. A few weeks later, in January of 2010, as we have seen, Runyan was already the leading lawyer of the diocese and handled the Logan/Tisdale affair even though Wade Logan remained the official chancellor of the diocese. After the Logan/Tisadle Affair, Runyan turned his attention to the Title IV revisions of the Episcopal Church which were to go into effect in 2011. It seemed that Runyan feared the presiding bishop would be empowered to override local rights of the dioceses.

103. "The Personal Testimony of Mr. Alan Runyan, Attorney for the Diocese of South Carolina." Audio recording, Christ/St. Paul's Church, Yonges Island SC, January 12, 2014, 11 minutes, http://www.kendallharmon.net.t19/index.php/t19/article/the_personal_testimony_of_mr_alan_runyan_attorney_for_the_diocese_ofsouth_carolina.

104. "C. Alan Runyan." Speights & Runyan, http://www.speightsandrunyan.com/attorneys-alan-runyan/.

105. "Personal Testimony."

106. Ibid.

107. Ibid.

108. Ibid.

109. Ibid.

In his presentation to the special convention that we have on video, Runyan made sweeping statements as background support for the resolutions at hand. These formed two general areas, the Title IV revisions and the diocesan accession to the Constitution and Canons of the Episcopal Church. The Title IV revisions had been approved by regular constitutional process in the General Convention in 2009 after a great deal of preparation. The proponents of the revisions argued that they actually improved the safeguards and pastoral care, the opposite of what Runyan claimed. Runyan also asserted that numerous dioceses had not given unqualified accession to the Constitution and Canon of the Church, the implication being that South Carolina did not have to accede to them either.

It was also in the special convention that Lawrence announced the creation of a new position in the diocese, that of "visiting bishop." The new Visiting Bishop, Michael Nazir-Ali was born in 1949 in Karachi, Pakistan. He was ordained an Anglican priest in 1976. From 1994 to 2009 he was the bishop of Rochester, in England. As bishop, he was an outspoken opponent of the ordination of openly homosexual persons and to the blessing of same sex unions.[110] He was one of the bishops who signed a letter protesting Archbishop Williams's decision not to block the appointment of Jeffrey John as Bishop of Reading in 2003.[111] He refused to attend the Lambeth Conference of 2008 because he could not approve of the American Episcopal Church's stand on homosexuality.[112] Instead, he was actively involved in the GAFCON I gathering in Jerusalem in 2008. He also cultivated friendly relations with the Anglican Church in North America.

The special convention of October 15, 2010, cast the die for the future of the Diocese of South Carolina. Having been confidently assured by their esteemed lawyer that the diocese was sovereign and self-governing, the delegates declared their virtual independence by casting off the canons of the Episcopal Church while retaining its constitution, nullifying national Church laws they did not like, and revoking the Dennis Canon. These changes would form the bases of some of the accusations against Bishop Lawrence when the Disciplinary Board for Bishops decided he had broken communion with the Church and the Presiding Bishop restricted him in the fall of 2012.

The actions of October 2010 prompted the question of why the diocese did not go all the way to total independence from the national Church at that time. When Lawrence raised this point himself in his bishop's address "Why Not Just Leave?" he replied "We still have a God-given vocation within this worldwide struggle (. . .) to resist until it is no longer possible and at the same time to help shape the emerging Anglicanism in the 21st century."[113] The meaning of this statement was anyone's guess.

---

110. "Michael Nazir-Ali," Wikipedia, http://en.wikipedia.org/wiki/Michael_Nazir_Ali.

111. Ibid.

112. Ibid.

113. *Journal of the Two Hundred and Nineteenth* (. . .) 2010, 32.

The Aftermath of the Special Convention

Apparently, many people were left guessing after the convention adjourned. Not surprisingly, reports of the meeting in print and online varied greatly. The Charleston *Post and Courier*, tried to put it in historical perspective: "Friday's vote was the latest development in a drawn-out disagreement between the diocese and the church leadership (. . .). The diocese has made efforts to distance itself from its parent church since the 2003 consecration in New Hampshire of Gene Robinson, who is openly gay."[114] As expected, *Jubilate Deo* led off with a glowing report by Joy Hunter: "Diocese Votes Overwhelmingly in Favor of Resolutions; Lawrence Remarks on Opportunities and Challenges."[115] She gave the full text of the bishop's address. The newsletter had long been an organ of the diocesan leadership which allowed no other opinions. This report was picked up and repeated by conservative online sites. Starkly different opinions appeared in Steve Skardon's web site, South Carolina Episcopalians. Skardon, an observer at the convention and outspoken critic of Lawrence, described the confusion: "Delegates left the convention unsure about exactly what they had done (. . .). Some thought they'd voted to leave the national Church. Others said they'd voted to leave the Church next February, while still others insisted they did nothing that would change the relationship of the Diocese to the Episcopal Church."[116] Reflecting this troubling confusion, Rob Wendt, a delegate and the senior warden at pro-Episcopal Church parish Grace Church of Charleston said "'It's clear that these resolutions are an implicit intent to separate from the Episcopal Church (. . .). It's a wait-and-see approach (. . .). The split has occurred, but when will it become a de facto split? We're just waiting so that we can move on.'"[117] Actually, the split was indeed de facto. The lingering question was, how and when would it become more than that?

The Presiding Bishop did not make a public statement concerning the convention. No doubt she had kept a close eye on it. Evidently, she was taken aback by Lawrence's hostile response to her efforts to reach him through several fellow bishops. She sent an e-mail to Episcopal News Service that was published on their web site: "'I grieve these actions [of the convention], but I especially grieve Bishop Lawrence's perception of my heartfelt concern for him and for the people of South Carolina as aggression. I don't seek to change his faithfully held positions on human sexuality, nor do I seek to control the inner workings of the diocese. I do seek to repair damaged relationships and ensure that this church is broad enough to include many different sorts and conditions of people.'"[118]

The Episcopal Forum of South Carolina made an astute public statement about the convention: "Today is a sad day in our Diocese. Ever since the 2003 'Chapman Letter' and the vote of the Diocese to join the 'Anglican Communion Network,' loyal

---

114. Parker, Adam. "Episcopalians Assert Authority." *The Post and Courier* (Charleston, SC), October 16, 2010, http://www.postandcourier.com/news/2010/oct/16/episcopalians-assert-authority/.

115. Hunter, Joy. "Diocese Votes Overwhelmingly in Favor of Resolutions; Lawrence Remarks on Opportunities and Challenge." *Jubilate Deo* (Diocese of South Carolina), Fall 2010, 2.

116. Skardon, Steve. "October 15, 2010." South Carolina Episcopalians, http://www.scepiscopalians.com/Chronology_since_2007.html.

117. Davies and Schjonberg, "South Carolina: Convention."

118. Ibid.

Episcopalians in South Carolina have feared today's actions."[119] The Forum would soon move to respond forcefully to the convention's, and the bishop's, controversial actions.

Another public reaction to Lawrence's moves came from the Rt. Rev. James R. Mathes, the bishop of San Diego. On October 15, the day of the convention, he posted a note on the Episcopal Café web site, "Nullification Revisited,"[120] in response to Lawrence's article of October 1 in *The Living Church* entitled "A Conservationist among Lumberjacks." Lawrence had lamented walking among the stumps of old-growth Episcopalianism. Too many trees had been chopped down, he said; and he was there to preserve the rest of the forest, hence his upcoming resolutions. Lawrence believed the Presiding Bishop was threatening the historic polity of the Episcopal Church in three ways: by retaining an attorney in South Carolina, by the Title IV revisions, and by the way in which the House of Bishops had dealt with the bishops who had left the Episcopal Church. Mathes went on to opine that all this was nothing more than a return of historic South Carolina attitudes: "An Episcopal diocese is no more independent of the Episcopal Church than a state is independent of the federal government." Mathes raised objections to Lawrence's charges: "there is no real threat from the presiding bishop (. . .). The Title IV revisions (. . .) are an effort to shift from a disciplinary model to a pastoral model (. . .) [and] it is rather silly to raise procedural objections to Bob Duncan's deposition." Mathes concluded with a plea to Lawrence: "no one cut them [deposed bishops] out. They were not the victim of lumberjacks; they uprooted themselves. We pray that you will not do the same (. . .). Please don't fire on Fort Sumter."

As we have seen, a month before the convention, the Episcopal Forum had appealed to the Executive Council of the Episcopal Church and the House of Bishops in the wake of the publication of the proposed resolutions. Perhaps Forum leaders hoped for some intervention or at least strong statements against the proposed resolutions from the Council or the bishops before the meeting of the special convention. If so, they would have been disappointed. There was no response before October 15. However, the Executive Council had long ago published a statement on the issues at hand. In July of 2007, it had declared that every diocese was required to give unqualified accession to the Constitution and Canons of the Episcopal Church and that any amendment to a diocesan constitution that attempted to change this was null and void. Thus, in the standing opinion of the Council, the resolutions passed in South Carolina on October 15 were all null and void. Ten days after the convention, the secretary of the Executive Council sent a letter to Barbara Mann, of the Episcopal Forum, giving the Council's response.[121] It was non-committal: "The Presiding Bishop's office is invested in responding in all the ways that are canonically and pastorally possible (. . .). The realities of our church polity

---

119. "The Episcopal Café Reports of the Convention." eNewsletter, Episcopal Forum of SC, October 16, 2010, http://www.mynewsletterbuilder.com/email/newsletter/1410572025#article_6.

120. Mathes, (the Rt. Rev.) James R. "Nullification Revisited." Episcopal Café, October 15, 2010, http://www.episcopalcafe.com/daily/episcopal_church/nullification_revisited.php.

121. [Straub, (the Rev.) Gregory]. Gregory Straub to Barbara Mann, October 25, 2010, http://www.episcopalforumofsc.org/Overview%20Documents/TEC_letter_to_EFSC_10-25-10.pdf.

mean that there are canonical limits to how her office and the Executive Council can intervene."[122] The Executive Council offered nothing new.

Having found no direct help from the Presiding Bishop or the Executive Council, the directors of the Episcopal Forum met and decided to appeal to the bishops of Province IV who were to convene soon in Miami. Province IV was the southeastern United States including South Carolina. On November 9, they sent a letter to the provincial bishops with attachments of the resolutions passed by the recent convention.[123] They mentioned the September 22 letter to the council: "The letter enumerated our observations, and our concerns, regarding the direction toward disassociation from TEC that has been pursued by the Bishop and the Diocese of South Carolina." They warned of dire consequences looming: "We have watched our diocese slide further and further away from TEC over the years. And it appears to us that the actions of this diocesan convention [Oct. 15] have triggered the final break, contingent on the constitutional ratifications next year." They concluded: "The purpose of this letter is to bring you, as Bishops of our Province, up to date on our situation (. . .) and to ask you for your support and guidance." Only time would tell whether this letter would get more response that that of September 22.

Lawrence returned to his busy schedule in the four months before the next diocesan convention would meet in February of 2011. Amid the usual rush of administrative duties and visits around the diocese, he met the standing committee for most of the day on October 21.[124] In the wake of the recent diocesan convention, the committee drew up new bylaws of the diocese, to be called officially "The Protestant Episcopal Church in the Diocese of South Carolina." References to the Episcopal Church were removed. Bishop Mark Lawrence was named the president of the corporation. The Standing Committee became the Board of Directors. As if anticipating the future, the bylaws sought to insulate the diocese from the Episcopal Church. The Board (Standing Committee) was given the sole right to determine the identity of the bishop. Moreover, the President (bishop) could not be removed except by unanimous vote of the Board (Committee). Also, members of the Board (Committee) could be removed only by action of the Board (Committee). All authority beyond the diocese was blocked: "No outside entity or persons claiming authority for removal shall have any standing or authority for such purposes."[125] All of these provisions were in direct violation of some of the canons of the Episcopal Church. It should be recalled that the diocesan convention of October 15 had resolved to remove accession to the Canons of the national Church.

On November 15, Lawrence drove to Orlando for a two-day Communion Partners gathering. He gave to the like-minded bishops a presentation on his Anglican Communion Development Committee.[126] On the 17th, he drove on to Miami for the Province IV bishops' meeting. In the afternoon session on November 18, Lawrence gave a "question

122. Ibid.

123. "The Episcopal Forum of South Carolina to The Province IV House of Bishops." November 9, 2010, http://www.episcopalforumofsc.org/Overview%20Documents/EFSC_to_PIV_HoB_11-09-10.pdf.

124. *Journal of the Two Hundred and Twentieth (. . .) 2011*, 42.

125. "Bylaws of The Protestant Episcopal Church." [October 22, 2010].

126. *Journal of the Two Hundred and Twentieth (. . .) 2011*, 42.

and answer session with the bishops regarding South Carolina."[127] On November 20, he returned to Charleston. While Lawrence was away, the Standing Committee met on November 18 accompanied by Wade Logan, Alan Runyan, and Jim Lewis. Toward the end of the meeting "Jeff Miller [chair of the Committee] emphasized our continuing vigilance and preparations during this period of inaction by those opposed to our direction; and that as leaders of the diocese we, the standing committee, must continue the work of preparing the diocese for the future."[128] The committee must have known exactly what Miller was talking about, but today one may be left wondering what he meant by *preparing the diocese for the future*. Miller's remark meant the leadership had something important in mind for the future of the diocese. Was that "future" outside of the Episcopal Church? Only time would tell.

Direction may well have been the impetus for a new revision of the corporate bylaws. On December 16, 2010, the Board of Directors (Standing Committee) changed the bylaws to clarify and expand the ones issued in October. The new bylaws stated explicitly that the Board (Standing Committee) alone had power to determine the identity and authority of the bishop: "In the event of a dispute or challenge regarding the identity of the Bishop (. . .) the Elected Directors shall have the sole authority to determine the identity and authority of the Bishop." The new bylaws went on to block any ultra-diocesan removal of members of the Board (Standing Committee) and the bishop. Members of the Board and the bishop could be displaced only by unanimous vote of the diocesan Board of Directors. The new bylaws also called for an employment contract with the bishop, a contract that could be ended only by unanimous vote of the Board (Standing Committee) and a two-thirds vote of each of the two houses of a diocesan convention.[129] An employment contract was given to Lawrence on February 1, 2011.

As Lawrence stood looking at the start of his fourth year as bishop of the Diocese of South Carolina, he could see behind him the crucial year of 2010. The basic change of the third year was to set aside the heretofore leading issue of homosexuality in favor of the other two of the three areas of differentiation that he had named with the Episcopal Church: theology and polity. The five resolutions passed in March and the six in October were all about theology and polity. There was not a hint of sexuality in any of them. Not even the consecration of Mary Glasspool would change that. The next most important issue to come out of 2010 was Lawrence's clear resolution to end the Dennis Canon in South Carolina. First, he apparently gave at least tacit approval of St. Andrew's transfer of property into a special trust. Then he ignored the canon when St. Andrew's left the diocese with its millions of dollars' worth of property. In October, the diocesan convention removed the Dennis canon from the diocesan documents. Another important development in 2010 was the continuous enlargement of the concept that the Episcopal Church, particularly the Presiding Bishop, was the enemy. From the Logan/Tisdale affair, the diocesan leaders built up the notion that the Presiding Bishop was

127. Ibid.
128. "Minutes of the Standing Committee." [November 18, 2010].
129. "Bylaws of The Protestant Episcopal Church in the Diocese of South Carolina [December 16, 2010]." State of South Carolina, Court of Common Pleas, County of Dorchester, Case No. 2013-CP-18–0013, Exhibit DSC-6A, July 8, 2014.

the aggressor out to remove the innocent victim who was the bishop of their diocese, South Carolina. This was greatly enlarged in the campaign against the Title IV revisions that was so cleverly and successfully led by a brilliant lawyer, Runyan. The resolutions of October were all based on the fear that the Presiding Bishop was out to take over the diocese that now must defend itself. Meanwhile, Lawrence capitalized on his earlier efforts to build up bonds abroad by hiring Nazir-Ali as the visiting bishop of the diocese in order to strengthen the ties between South Carolina and equally conservative Anglican entities at home and abroad. By the end of the year, Lawrence had all but broken off from the Episcopal Church. He led the diocesan convention in October that declared local sovereignty, nullified Episcopal Church laws it did not like, revoked accession to the Canons of the Episcopal Church, and revised the corporate charter to remove the Episcopal Church from it. The corporate charter was revised twice in late 2010 to try to prevent the national Church from removing the bishop and the standing committee. Yet, Lawrence claimed that he had not left the Episcopal Church because the diocese still acceded to the Constitution of the Episcopal Church. The Episcopal Forum had tried to stem the march away from the Episcopal Church but it was proved helpless under the circumstances. It was completely powerless within the diocese and its desperate pleas for help from the Church leaders beyond were all in vain. The diocesan leadership could only regard their adversaries' apparent impotence as encouragement in their march of differentiation. Lawrence's first two years of hard work of building bonds at home and abroad had paid off abundantly. At the same time, the Episcopal Church leadership had shown itself to be entirely ineffective at stopping the diocese's wayward movement.

2011

The Diocesan Convention, February 18–19

As 2011 began, the Diocese of South Carolina prepared for yet another convention meeting, this one just four months since the last. It would be the fifth diocesan session since Lawrence had begun presiding over the conventions in March of 2009. Five convention meetings occurred within a twenty-four-month period. In the first meeting, March 12–13, 2009, Lawrence had raised the issue that the diocese might not continue to be a part of the Episcopal Church. Every session afterwards added landmarks along that path until the last, October of 2010, declared the virtual independence of the diocese and kept attachment to the Episcopal Church in name only. It was to be the turning point. All the convention meetings after that one only consolidated what it had accomplished. Such was the case of the annual meeting in February of 2011.

The run-up to this convention lacked any drama at all. It was simply a foregone conclusion that the 2010 resolutions requiring more than one vote would be approved again. In his official bishop's diary, Lawrence showed no concern about the next convention. In January, he spent a good deal of time and attention on the annual Mere Anglicanism conference in Charleston that had become a major gathering of conservative leaders.[130]

---

130. *Journal of the Two Hundred and Twenty First Annual Meeting of the Convention of the Diocese of South Carolina, St. Philip's Church & The Cathedral of St. Luke and St. Paul, Charleston, South Carolina,*

Lawrence devoted a considerable amount of time to the Rt. Rev. Mouneer Anis and to his Visiting Bishop, Nazir-Ali. On February 7 and 8 he journeyed to Pennsylvania to address the clergy conference of the Diocese of Central Pennsylvania.[131]

Before leaving for Pennsylvania, Lawrence met the Standing Committee and signed an official agreement that guaranteed his continued employment in perpetuity in the diocese regardless of what happened with the Episcopal Church. On February 1, 2011, Lawrence and the Rev. Jeffrey Miller, president of the Standing Committee, signed a contract stating "If, for any reason beyond the employee's [Lawrence] control, the employee is prevented from continuing as employer's [Standing Committee] bishop, employee will continue to serve as employer's chief executive officer/chief operating officer."[132] The contract was open-ended and gave no time limit. Lawrence could be removed only by death, total disability, his own application, or the bylaws of the diocese. In other words, Lawrence would remain the chief authority of the diocese regardless of what actions the Episcopal Church might take, even his removal from the office of bishop. This implied an expectation among the diocesan leadership that the Church would remove Lawrence as bishop and that the diocese would reject that. With the ten-year lease on the episcopal residence of March 17, 2010, this employment contract all but guaranteed that Lawrence would remain the ecclesiastical authority of the diocese for the indefinite future even if he were removed and deposed by the Episcopal Church although how this could happen was not spelled out. Also, as with the house lease, this paper remained little-known outside the official circle for a long time to come. It was publicly revealed in the circuit court trial in July of 2014. The employment contract of February 1, 2011, showed that by this point, the bond between bishop and diocesan leadership was rock solid. With his employment, residence, and absolute authority to interpret the diocesan constitution and canons secure, Lawrence could approach the upcoming convention in a high level of certain confidence. He and the diocesan leadership were as one.

The 2011 annual diocesan convention met on February 18 and 19, at St. Helena's Church in Beaufort. It was another open-and-shut affair. Bishop Lawrence's address, at forty-one minutes, was not quite as long and nowhere nearly as tense, contentious, or strident as his earlier ones.[133] Gone were all the military allusions, the calls to arms. As in October 2010, there was not a word about homosexuality although Lawrence alluded to a discussion of sexuality to be held at the upcoming provincial bishops' meeting. Too, there was not a word about a reconciliation with the Episcopal Church. The tone of the message sounded as if the issues with the national Church had been settled. Lawrence began by saying: "It is my expressed hope that this year of 2011 will be free from constitutional and canonical challenges from the 'national' leadership of the Episcopal

---

March 8 & 9, 2012. Charleston, SC: the diocese, 2012, 37.

131. Ibid., 38.

132. "Bishop's employment agreement Dated February 1, 2011." State of South Carolina, Court of Common Pleas, County of Dorchester, Case No. 2013-CP-18-00013, Exhibit DSC-29, July 8, 2014.

133. "Bishop Mark Lawrence Address SC 2011." Video recording, Anglican TV, February 18, 2011, 41 minutes, http://www.YouTube.com.

Church."[134] If this were a sincerely held wish, Lawrence was to be disappointed as events would show that the year would be anything but "free" of "challenges."

Lawrence went on in his address to dwell on church growth within the diocese, as he put it, making new church plantings to lead the lost to salvation. However, when he arrived at St. Mark's chapel of Port Royal his attitude changed. St. Mark's was mainly composed of loyal Episcopalians from St. Helena's. Lawrence made the cryptic remark: "The presence of St. Mark's Chapel in Port Royal raises questions which need answering."[135] Indeed, but he offered neither questions nor answers. The bishop also took up the issue of stewardship and called for a true return to the 10–10–10 principle adopted in the 1990s, 10 percent individual giving to the parish, 10 percent parish to diocese, and 10 percent diocese to national church. This system had never really worked. The amount the diocese gave to the national Church fell drastically to the nominal amounts of $35,741 in 2010, $23,377 in 2011, and only $14,924 in 2012.[136] In the last year of its contribution, 2012, the pre-schism diocese gave the Episcopal Church just .007 % of its annual income.[137] Certainly, Lawrence's point was that the parishes should increase their contributions to the diocese. He gave statistics to support this, but his table of figures revealed an unintended fact: parish contribution to the diocese had reached a dollar-amount high in 2007, the year in which he had been elected bishop, and had declined every year since then.[138] Next, Lawrence turned to what he considered the good effects of the diocesan stand against the Title IV revisions: "Several other dioceses have followed our lead in expressing concerns with the Title IV revisions."[139] As for the Episcopal Church, he said simply "I have received no official comment from the Presiding Bishop regarding our Reconvened Convention in October."[140] As for the official structure of the Anglican Communion, he showed similar frustration: "The Instruments of Unity have proven inadequate to mend the net of Anglicanism."[141] He went on to outline plans for direct contacts with conservative Anglican provinces and dioceses. Nowhere in the address did he hint at the secret permanent employment contract he had just made with the Standing Committee. In comparison, this was a mild address which sought to present a business-as-usual scene as the diocese supposedly moved on with its mission of internal growth and development while enlarging its concept of global Anglicanism.

Three resolutions passed easily. The convention had an air of a return to normality. Its focus was on the internal growth and development of the diocese and on building ties in the Anglican world beyond. Lawrence had done his best to put the contentious issues behind him and to make the radical canonical changes simply part of the past. He downplayed as much as possible differences with the national Church while he completely

134. Ibid.

135. Ibid.

136. *Journal of the Two Hundred and Twenty-First (. . .)* 2012, 123.

137. Ibid.

138. "Bishop Lawrence Addresses 220th Diocesan Convention." *Jubilate Deo* (Diocese of South Carolina), Spring 2011, 8.

139. Ibid, 9.

140. Ibid.

141. Ibid.

avoided the issue of homosexuality. His whole focus, and that of the convention as well, was to move forward as if everything had been settled. This may have been his, and the convention's, fervent wish, but they were not the only actors on this stage. The Episcopal Church leadership had already sounded its warnings against the diocese. Matters may have been settled on the diocesan side, but time would tell if the national Church had the same response.

A Gathering Storm, March–September

If he were trying to present the appearance of a return to business as usual in early 2011, Lawrence could not have forgotten a looming date, July 1, 2011. On that day, the Title IV revisions were to go into effect in the Episcopal Church. The new rules under Title IV, Canon 17, Sections 3 through 6 of the Canons of the Episcopal Church, discipline in the Episcopal Church, set up a Disciplinary Board for Bishops to have jurisdiction over all matters concerning the rules for bishops.[142] The Board was to be composed of ten bishops elected by the House of Bishops, and four priests or deacons and four lay persons appointed by the president of the House of Deputies, for a total of eighteen board members. The canons continued that if a bishop should abandon the Episcopal Church by "renunciation of the Doctrine, Discipline or Worship of the Church," or admission into another religious body, or exercising episcopal acts for another religious body, the Board, by majority vote, would certify the charge of abandonment to the presiding bishop. The presiding bishop would then place a restriction on the bishop's exercise of ministry until the House of Bishops should act on the matter. The restricted bishop would then have sixty days to submit a written statement to the presiding bishop that the charges were false. If the presiding bishop should be satisfied that the statement made a good faith retraction or denial of the charges, the presiding bishop could, with consent of the Disciplinary Board, remove the restriction. If the bishop should fail to submit a statement or the presiding bishop should fail to restore the accused, the matter would then go to the House of Bishops. If the House should vote by majority against the accused, the presiding bishop would be required to remove that person from the ordained ministry of the Episcopal Church. Therefore, the assertion of the diocesan leadership that the Title IV revisions removed due process or safeguards and gave the presiding bishop too much power was highly dubious. The whole process rested on the Disciplinary Board for Bishops of eighteen people, not one of whom was appointed by the presiding bishop.

In addition to Title IV, Canon 17, there was another canon of the Episcopal Church that would come into play in the months ahead. It was Title III, Canon 12, section 7, "Release and Removal from the Ordained Ministry of the Church."[143] It read, "If any Bishop of the Episcopal Church shall express, in writing, to the Presiding Bishop, an intention to be released and removed from the ordained Ministry of this Church (. . .) with the advice and consent of a majority of the members of the Advisory Council, the Presiding Bishop may pronounce that person is released and removed from the ordained Ministry

---

142. *Constitution and Canons,* 2012, 152–58.
143. Ibid., 114–15.

of this Church."[144] Thus a bishop could be separated from the episcopacy either by a process beginning with the Disciplinary Board for Bishops or by voluntary renunciation. Both would eventually enter the story ahead.

In 2010, Lawrence and the other leaders of the diocese, particularly attorney Runyan, had made a major issue of the revisions of Title IV under the fear that they were directed at Lawrence. The October 2010 special convention had passed a resolution removing the diocesan accession to the Canons of the Episcopal Church. This had been aimed at nullifying the Title IV revisions made by the General Convention in 2009 in favor of a return to the 2006 disciplinary rules of the Church. In Lawrence's view, the Title IV changes that were about to go into effect in the Episcopal Church would not go into effect in the Diocese of South Carolina. By diocesan convention resolution, the 2006 rules on discipline were the only legal and legitimate ones in the diocese. With this disregard of the Episcopal Church's canonical changes in mind, Lawrence proceeded into his fourth year as bishop with his usual self-confidence and active and energetic hard work.

As soon as the diocesan convention concluded on February 19, Lawrence resumed his busy activities building bonds both within and without the diocese. This would be his focus for the next seven months. Inside the diocese, he resumed his frequent travels around the territory meeting as often as possible with clergy, vestries, deaneries, and congregations. On the diocesan level, he continued his practice of lengthy sessions with the Standing Committee, the Committee sitting as the Council of Advice, and the trustees of the diocese. During the seven months of March–September 2011, Lawrence made seven out-of-state trips as he continued to promote his conservative views in the Episcopal Church and to build relationships with like-minded elements. On March 17, he flew to Illinois to participate in the ordination and consecration of Daniel Martins as bishop of Springfield.

From March 25 to 30, Lawrence attended the House of Bishops meeting at Kanuga, North Carolina, except for a brief return trip to Charleston on the 27th.[145] It was reasonable to assume there were many conversations among Lawrence and his fellow bishops about the astounding recent events in South Carolina, particularly the highly controversial convention resolutions. Lawrence later said that he raised two issues with the bishops concerning the Title IV reforms: due process and constitutionality, that the bishops listened attentively, and that he spoke privately with the presiding bishop.[146] The website South Carolina Episcopalians reported on March 23, 2011, that "many, if not most, bishops are exasperated with Lawrence, who they say has been evasive and vague about what the Diocese wants." There were certainly many words about another big topic of the day, the Anglican Covenant, something Lawrence and the other conservatives were advocating strongly as a way of blocking future consecrations of openly homosexual bishops in the Episcopal Church. By his own account, Lawrence attended the long regular sessions of the House, but outside of them he spent most of his time with like-minded friends

---

144. Ibid.

145. *Journal of the Two Hundred and Twenty-First (. . .)* 2012, 41.

146. "Minutes of the Board of Directors [Standing Committee] for the Diocese of South Carolina." The Board of Directors [Standing Committee] of the Diocese of South Carolina [April 5, 2011].

such as the Communion Partners.[147] On April 13, Bishop Waldo traveled to Charleston to meet Lawrence for a LARCUM (Lutheran, Anglican, Roman Catholic, and United Methodist) bishop's conference. Waldo was accompanied by his ecumenical officer, the Rev. Furman Buchanan, and Lawrence by his, the Rev. Dow Sanderson.[148]

In May, Lawrence traveled to visit his two favorite seminaries, both bastions of traditional Episcopalian "orthodoxy", Trinity School for Ministry and Nashotah House. Perhaps the most important conference Lawrence attended in 2011 was the Province IV meeting of bishops at Kanuga, North Carolina, June 6–8. It was certainly the one for which he spent the most time in preparation. As early as April he had started working on his talk for the meeting. He entitled it "Sex and Salvation."[149] The main source of his talk was apparently *The Bible and Homosexual Practice*, a book by a leading advocate of scriptural condemnation of homosexuality, Robert Gagnon.[150] According to Lawrence, the provincial bishops held a meeting on June 6, from 1:30 to 9:30 p.m. It was in this session that Lawrence presented his prepared remarks on "Sex and Salvation." Even without a record of his words, it would not take much imagination to surmise his points. By then he had a well-established record of opposing the ordinations of non-celibate homosexual persons, an issue that had already been settled in the Episcopal Church.

If the diocesan leadership believed that all was settled, there were others, inside and outside the diocese, who were growing increasingly alarmed at the direction of the diocese in late 2010 and early 2011. Within the diocese, the Episcopal Forum still stood as the only internal organization unifying the pro-Episcopal Church parties. Even before 2011, however, it had been rendered completely powerless, even irrelevant, among the diocesan structure. The diocesan leadership increasingly regarded it as an adversary. Nevertheless, the Forum did not surrender to its official banishment. It called another, the defiantly entitled "Enthusiastically Episcopalian Conference" on March 12, at the North Charleston Convention Center. The theme of this gathering had the rather ominous, if not gloomy, title of "How Can We Flourish as Enthusiastic Episcopalians in the Diocese of SC?" The program featured Bonnie Anderson, the president of the House of Deputies of the Episcopal Church. Although the conference had no influence with the diocesan leadership, at least it boosted the sagging morale of the thousands of Episcopalians in South Carolina who wanted to keep the diocese in the Episcopal Church.

While the pro-Episcopal party in the diocese wished fervently to keep South Carolina in the Episcopal Church, by 2011 they had no opportunity to campaign for their program on the diocesan level. Well before 2011, the entire diocesan official apparatus had already become solidly conservative and hostile to the Episcopal Church. Diocesan committees routinely voted unanimously, apparently without a hint of dissent. Earth-shaking resolutions passed through conventions with hardly a bump. Secrecy prevailed throughout the power structure. Monthly meetings of the most important group, the standing committee, were private except for selected leaks. In almost every meeting, the committee went into separate "executive sessions" that were strictly off the record

---

147. *Journal of the Two Hundred and Twenty-First (. . .)* 2012, 41.
148. Waldo (the Rt. Rev.) Andrew. E-mail message to author, September 10, 2014.
149. *Journal of the Two Hundred and Twenty-First (. . .)* 2012, 41.
150. Ibid., 44.

and blanked out. Indeed, its minutes of June 14, 2011, recorded "the Committee was reminded and agreed that all of its discussions while in Executive Session are strictly confidential and not to be disclosed to or discussed with anyone else."[151] The diocesan leaders saw the Episcopal Forum as the internal nuisance, if not their nemesis, and often discussed such in the secret standing committee meetings. On March 1, 2011, Lawrence told the committee that the Forum had placed an ad in a local newspaper with false statements and misrepresentations whereupon the committee directed Lawrence to prepare a statement to be released after the Forum meeting of March 12.[152] There was no way the Forum, or any pro-Episcopal Church could influence or change the official diocesan structure which was rigidly set against them.

Frustrations, along with alarm, were mounting within the Forum by early 2011. Its devoted leadership, however, refused to quit, quite the contrary. On May 25, 2011, Melinda Lucka, a lawyer and member of the Board of Directors of the Forum, sent a letter to Katharine Jefferts Schori, the Presiding Bishop, Bonnie Anderson, the President of the House of Deputies, and Gregory Straub, Secretary of the Executive Council and of the General Convention.[153] The letter was co-signed by five other leaders of the Forum: Barbara Mann, David W. Mann, Lynn A. Pagliaro, Stephen L. Skardon, Jr., and Colton M. Smith III, a priest of the diocese.

Earlier letters of the Forum to church leaders had resulted in little or no response. This one would be different. Lucka's letter of May 25, 2011, was to become the effective starting place for the ensuing period of investigations that a year and a half later would end in Lawrence being restricted as a bishop in the Episcopal Church. Therefore, this correspondence merits close scrutiny. The letter itself was three pages while its attached "Addendum" contained sixteen pages. Although the letter was sent to the three recipients named above it was addressed to the members of the Executive Council under the leading "Request for consideration of Executive Council Resolution." Lucka asked the Council for one of two responses: that it pass a resolution nullifying the recent controversial resolutions of the diocesan conventions such as it had done for the first four secessionist cases in June of 2007, or that it modify its June 2007 resolution to include South Carolina. At any rate, Lucka was asking the Executive Council to overrule the controversial South Carolina resolutions. She went on to say, "Since 2004, the South Carolina Diocesan Convention has adopted Resolutions that have increasingly shown disloyalty to and disassociation with The Episcopal Church."[154] These resolutions, she added, violated the terms of the Constitution of the Episcopal Church that required dioceses to accede to the Constitution and Canons of the Episcopal Church.

In her letter, Lucka went on to lay out four specific cases of resolutions from the 2010 and 2011 diocesan conventions that "were clear and definitive" in violating the Constitution and Canons of the Church.[155] The first revised the official diocesan corpo-

---

151. "Minutes of the Standing Committee." [June 14, 2011].

152. "Minutes of the Standing Committee." [March 1, 2011].

153. [Lucka, Melinda}. Melinda Lucka to Katharine Jefferts Schori, Bonnie Anderson, and Gregory S. Straub, May 25, 2011.

154. Ibid.

155. Ibid.

rate charter on record with the state government to remove the terms "Episcopal" and "Protestant Episcopal Church" and keeping only "Diocese of South Carolina." The second removed accession to the Canons of the Episcopal Church. The next ended accession to the Constitution of the Episcopal Church where it was deemed to be inconsistent that that of the diocese. The fourth removed the Dennis Canon that required all property to be held in trust for the Episcopal Church and its diocese. Lucka and her so-signers asked that the Executive Council declare the enumerated resolutions to be null and void. The following Addendum gave fifteen examples of diocesan convention resolutions from 2006 to 2011 that they believed showed a willful, gradual, and illegal disassociation from the national Church.

Straub replied to Lucka's letter on June 16 to say that the Executive Council had met and agreed that its judgment enunciated in 2007 applied also to present-day South Carolina.[156] In June of 2007, the Executive Council had resolved that 1-dioceses are required to give unqualified accession to the Constitution and Canons of the Episcopal Church, 2-any diocesan amendment changing this is null and void, and 3-the amendments of the four dioceses purporting to change their constitutions are null and void.[157] "The Joint Standing Committee agreed that, while the Diocese of South Carolina is not named therein, the resolution covers the situation there without its being reconsidered by the Council."[158] The Council did not grant either of Lucka's original requests. It did not pass a new resolution declaring the South Carolina actions to be null and void; and it did not officially revise its June 2007 resolution to include South Carolina. However, it made the same point in declaring that the resolutions of the two recent diocesan conventions in South Carolina concerning the constitution and canons were all null and void and without any validity; and that was really the aim of Lucka's letter. Moreover, Straub promised to monitor developments in South Carolina.

On August 26, Lawrence and Jeff Miller, the president of the Standing Committee received copies of Straub's letter to Lucka of June 16.[159] Lawrence then requested of Straub a copy of Lucka's original letter; and Straub promptly sent one. Once she knew that the diocese had been informed of all the correspondence, Lucka sent a letter to Barbara Mann, chair of the Forum, on September 22, officially informing her of the Executive Council's response.[160] By then the news was public; and the ensuing public reactions online were predictable. The pro-Episcopal voices seemed glad that at least some clear stand had been taken by the national Church in opposition to the controversial diocesan moves. The pro-Lawrence side declared it to be another example of the Church's efforts

---

156. [Straub, (the Rev.) Gregory]. Gregory Straub to Melinda A. Lucka, June 16, 2011, www.diosc.com/sys/images/documents/exec_coun_corr_11_9_28.pdf.

157. San Joaquin, Pittsburgh, Quincy, and Ft. Worth.

158. [Straub], Gregory Straub to Melinda A. Lucka.

159. "Bishop and Standing Committee Respond to Actions of Executive Council." Diocese of South Carolina, http://www.diosc.com/sys/news-events/about-news/365-bishop-and-standing-committee-respond-to-actions-of-executive-council.

160. [Lucka, Melinda]. Melinda Lucka to Barbara Mann, September 22, 2011, http://www.episcopalforumofsc.org/Overview%20Documents/20110922_re_NAC023.pdf.

to drive out Lawrence. The website Virtue Online entitled its article on the news, "Episcopal Church Begins Campaign to Unseat South Carolina Bishop Mark Lawrence."[161]

A week after the letters were released to the public and well into a rising common discussion of them, Lawrence decided it was important to issue an official response. On September 28, Lawrence and Paul C. Fuener, the new president of the standing committee, sent a letter to Straub and promptly posted it and its accompanying documents on the diocesan website. Interestingly enough, however, Lawrence did not release Lucka's original letter of May 25, then or later. Lawrence's letter of reply was his standard procedure by this point: reject and deny all, give no ground, and find fault with the procedures as well as the substance.

It is important to look in some detail at Lawrence's letter to Straub of September 28 considering the events that would soon follow. It set structure of approach and arguments that would become more pronounced in time. The first half of the letter established a clear tone of hostility to the recipient criticizing the procedures, complaining of delays and gaps in time, and failing to provide what Lawrence considered to be all the appropriate documents. The second half laid out Lawrence's complete dismissal of the Executive Council's decisions. In the first place, he rejected the notion that South Carolina was bound by the Constitution and Canons of the Episcopal Church. He said the requirement of accession applied only to new dioceses, "It does not apply to this Diocese or to the other founding Dioceses."[162] In his view, South Carolina had never been required to adhere to the rules of the Episcopal Church. In the second place, Lawrence rejected the authority of the Executive Council to pronounce judgments for the Church, really another procedural point. Curiously enough he then cited a quote that directly contradicted his first point: "'Only General Conventions can pass resolutions that bind the Church.'"[163] Within two paragraphs, Lawrence said that South Carolina was not bound by the Constitution and Canons and that the Church was bound by resolutions of the General Convention. Perhaps Lawrence did not realize that in his effort to diminish the authority of the Executive Council he had actually made their point for them: *resolutions that bind the Church*. South Carolina was, after all, still in the Episcopal Church, however tenuously. Lawrence's third point would turn out to be the most fateful: "the actions taken by the Diocese of South Carolina at its convention (. . .) were, and are, consistent with the statutory and non-statutory law of the state of South Carolina."[164] The unmistakable implication in his statement was the he would follow the ruling of the state Supreme Court in its September 2009 judgment in the case of *All Saints*. Finally, in the end of his letter, Lawrence sweepingly rejected the Executive Council's judgments: "the Diocese of South Carolina does not agree with, nor does it recognize, the resolution

---

161. Virtue, David. "Episcopal Church Begins Campaign to Unseat South Carolina Bishop Mark Lawrence." Virtueonline, October 24, 2011, http://virtueonline.org/portal/modules/news/article.php?storyid=14922.

162. "Bishop and Standing Committee Respond to Actions of Executive Council." Diocese of South Carolina, http://www.diosc.com/sys/news-events/latest-news/365-bishop-and-standing-committee-respond-to-actions-of-executive-council.

163. Ibid.

164. Ibid.

and its attempted application to the Diocese of South Carolina."[165] Thus, once again, Lawrence closed the door on any thought of reconciliation with loyal Episcopalians within his diocese and with the national Church leadership.

The Lucka—Straub—Lawrence correspondence exchange went on for four months, May to September of 2011. On the surface, it appeared to end in a total victory for Lawrence. Lucka appealed to the national Church to intervene in South Carolina—the Executive Council had declared the South Carolina resolutions to be null and void—Lawrence had completely rejected both Lucka's and the Council's charges, authorities, and rights. He gave in not one iota. That was the end of that. Or was it? Times had changed. The new Disciplinary Board for Bishops could do far more than simply issue letters that could be easily discarded.

In the months between February and September of 2011, the life of the Diocese of South Carolina was playing out on two different levels. Lawrence and the diocesan leadership tried to project the image that all had returned to normal. On another level, however, there was plenty going wrong. Loyal Episcopalians had grown increasingly alarmed at the diocesan direction and had appealed once again to the national Church. This time the Church leadership decided to make an open judgment on South Carolina. They very publicly condemned the recent diocesan decisions. The alarm that was felt at the local level clearly moved to the national Church. Meanwhile all of this was happening at the very moment that the Title IV revisions went into effect setting up a new Disciplinary Board for Bishops. South Carolina's assertions of having removed itself from the Canons of the Episcopal Church was such a serious issue that it could not be safely ignored. The Episcopal Church would have to address the question of whether a diocese could by its own will withdraw accession to the Constitution and Canons of the Episcopal Church.

The Disciplinary Board for Bishops, September–November

If Lawrence and the other diocesan leaders thought all had returned to routine and unexceptional normality, they would be suddenly jolted back to reality on September 29, 2011. On that day, the entire future of the Diocese of South Carolina changed abruptly. Bishop Dorsey Henderson,[166] chair of the Disciplinary Board for Bishops, notified Lawrence that he was under investigation by the Board on charges of abandonment of communion.[167] This was a most serious turn of events for Lawrence and the diocese because, if the Board decided he should be charged with abandonment, he could face removal not

---

165. Ibid.

166. Henderson retired as bishop of Upper in South Carolina in 2010, to be replaced by Andrew Waldo.

167. The Board was composed of 18 persons: 10 bishops, 4 clergy, and 4 laypeople. Bishops: Ian T. Douglas of Connecticut; Robert Fitzpatrick of Hawaii; Dena Harrison of Texas; Dorsey Henderson of Upper South Carolina; Herman Hollerith of Southern Virginia; J. Scott Mayer of Northwest Texas; Thomas Shaw of Massachusetts; Prince Singh of Rochester; James Waggoner of Spokane; and Catherine Waynick of Indianapolis. Clergy: Marjorie Menaul of Central Pennsylvania; Jesus Reyes of El Camino Real; Angela Shepard of Maryland; Robert Two Bulls, Jr. of Los Angeles. Lay: Victor Feliberty-Ruberte of Puerto Rico; Christopher Hayes of California; Josephine Powell of Michigan; Diane Sammons of Newark. Dorsey Henderson was chosen as president of the Board.

only from the office of bishop of the Diocese of South Carolina but also from ordained ministry in the Episcopal Church. For now, Lawrence would have to wait until the Board completed its investigation and voted on whether to charge him with abandonment.

The Board's work on the Lawrence matter went on for several months. The charges and evidence originated with communicants of the Diocese of South Carolina. In May of 2011, a group of communicants led by Melinda Lucka compiled a set of evidence against Lawrence and sent it to the Bishop's Review Committee, the predecessor of the Disciplinary Board for Bishops.[168] The Committee passed it on to the Disciplinary Board for Bishops when it was established on July 1, 2011. The Board did not initiate the action. This was done by certain residents of the diocese; and under the canons the Board was required to consider the matter once it was brought to them. On September 29, the day Lawrence was first informed, the file was sent to him. It was a list of twelve enumerated charges each with supporting evidence. The whole package came to sixty-three pages.

The twelve accusations against Lawrence presented to the Disciplinary Board were apparently listed in order of importance. They fell into seven distinct categories. The first section of items 1 to 5 was basically the same information that Lucka had put in her letter of May 25 to the Episcopal Church authorities. In fact, the supporting evidence for items numbered One to Five given in "Tab 1" was a copy of Lucka's "Addendum" to her letter of May 25. Item number One, which the accusers presumably considered to be the most serious wrongdoing of Lawrence, described the alteration of the corporate charter to remove references to the Episcopal Church. It had been passed by the October 2010 convention. In the new wording, the diocese would be an independent local institution unattached to a larger body in the eyes of the state of South Carolina. This was at least statutory disassociation from the Episcopal Church on the state level. Item number Two on the list of twelve was removal of unconditional accession to the Constitution of the Episcopal Church. The third item on the list concerned the removal of accession to the Canons of the Episcopal Church. Item Four identified the resolutions declaring the authority of the bishop and standing committee. The last item in this section, number Five, related Lawrence's assertions that the diocese was a "Sovereign Diocese." No one could argue that these were not the most important charges against Lawrence supporting the accusation that he had abandoned the communion of the Episcopal Church.

The other seven sections of the list of twelve charges dealt with less serious issues, but still ones important enough to be included. The second section of the list was item number Six that pointed out the removal of the word "Episcopal" from virtually the entire diocesan website and from at least half of the parish websites. The third part, item Seven, complained that Lawrence had done nothing to keep parishes from leaving the Episcopal Church. As evidence for this, Tab 2 provided a letter from R.M. "Buddy" Lindsay, a lawyer working with All Saints of Pawleys Island to a parish on how to leave the Episcopal diocese. The fourth part was item number Eight which held that Lawrence had refused to support a loyalist Episcopalian community known as St. Marks in Port Royal. The fifth section of complaints was number Nine on the list. It showed a reference to Lawrence from an Anglican Church in North America conference. The sixth section was items Ten and Eleven that provided a litany of disparaging remarks Lawrence had made

---

168. Lucka, Melinda. Interview with author, September 3, 2014.

about the Episcopal Church from several of his diocesan convention addresses and a paper of 2006. The last section of the list was item number Twelve. It stated that Lawrence had ordained his son Chad Lawrence as a priest in the Episcopal Church when Chad had not been ordained a deacon in the Episcopal Church and had served in a non-Episcopal church. Tab 12 provided newsletter evidence of this. In fact, Chad Lawrence had been ordained an Anglican deacon in St. Paul's Anglican Church in Bakersfield when Mark Lawrence visited there from March 30 to April 1, 2009.

Exactly two months elapsed from the day Henderson informed Lawrence of the Board's investigation to the day Henderson informed Lawrence of the Board's decision, September 29 to November 28. The atmosphere conveyed by Lawrence and the diocesan leadership in these two months was grim and heavy if not quite panicked. Outwardly they tried to balance a sense of urgency with a steady and controlled appearance, but just beyond the public cover they were acting very differently. In his official diary, Lawrence showed time and again a growing strain and tension as the weeks passed. On October 3, he spent the day in bed with a fever and cancelled a planned trip to Egypt.[169] October 5 was so hectic and tumultuous that he fell in bed at midnight unable to sleep.[170] By October 19 things were so unsettled that Lawrence wrote a "draft of possible message to the diocese" that, apparently, he did not finish.[171] After weeks had gone by and after two days of clergy conference at Camp Saint Christopher, Lawrence went to bed on November 16 writing "Tired; heavy of heart."[172]

The Disciplinary Board for Bishops was about bishops and not dioceses. If the Board should finally charge a bishop with abandonment, the subsequent actions required in the canons would be with him alone and not the diocese. However, this was not the way Lawrence and his allies saw it, or the way they portrayed it to the public. They quickly made this into a case of Episcopal Church against the Diocese of South Carolina. One should recall that the Diocese of South Carolina by resolution of its convention in October of 2010 had withdrawn from the Canons of the Episcopal Church. It had unilaterally reverted to the canons of 2006 on issues of discipline. Therefore, from this aspect, Lawrence really had to do nothing in South Carolina because the diocese had already declared the Disciplinary Board for Bishops to be invalid in the Diocese of South Carolina. If he had wished, Lawrence could have declared, simply, the whole matter of the Board irrelevant and gone on about business as usual. Instead he set out to declare a crisis and rally the diocese in unity to defend him as their bishop.

The best evidence we have of Lawrence's life in these two months is the bishop's official diary that he published in the diocesan convention journal of 2012.[173] Lawrence apparently kept his regular schedule of official parochial visitations which, no doubt, had been arranged far in advance, but kept all to a minimum. His days became long and hectic with lists of meetings, phone calls, visits, and e-mails. He corresponded with and met his lawyers on numerous occasions, not surprisingly. A person appearing in the

169. *Journal of the Two Hundred and Twenty First (. . .)* 2012, 50.
170. Ibid.
171. Ibid.
172. Ibid., 52.
173. Ibid., 49–53.

record regularly, not surprisingly, was Kendall Harmon. Lawrence listed at least thirteen phone calls with Harmon and two in-office visits. No doubt there were many more times the two talked on other occasions of meetings. By all appearances, Harmon remained one of Lawrence's closest advisors, if not the closest.

Lawrence gave the thrust of his time and efforts in these two months to the diocesan leadership. When it came to a crisis, everything would have to rest on his relationship with the power structure of the diocese. This would have to be the bedrock of his support. He met with the leading diocesan committees often and in long sessions. Of all the groups in the diocesan structure, Lawrence relied most on the Standing Committee meeting as the Council of Advice. He met with them three times in person (September 30, October 6, October 31) and three times by conference call (October 10, October 20, November 4) for a total of eighteen hours. In addition, he conferred with the Standing Committee on three other occasions, October 4, November 1, and November 8 for a total of thirteen hours. Moreover, he talked with the Board of Trustees three times, October 6, November 3, and November 17 for four and a half hours altogether. He also met with the finance committee for two hours on November 10. In the end, no one would be able to say that Lawrence had not done his best to tie the diocesan leadership to himself, to make the cause of the bishop that of the diocese. The crisis mode served to further tighten the already strong bond among the diocesan leadership.

It is important to note that Lawrence did not summon a diocesan convention in the two months of the investigation. This was perhaps surprising given his record of frequent callings of convention. There was, however, a secret plan in place to call a diocesan convention in order to disassociate from the Episcopal Church.[174] At 10:30 a.m. on November 1, the Standing Committee met under the title of Board of Directors. Present were committee members: Paul Fuener, chair, John Barr, Reid Boylston, Ann Dennis, Jim Lewis, Lynda Richards, Suzanne Schwank, Greg Snyder, Ann Hester Willis. Also present were Bishop Lawrence, chancellor Wade Logan, and lawyer Alan Runyan. After consulting with the lawyers, the committee unanimously approved a motion to call a special convention of the diocese a month after any of the following actions concerning Lawrence: 1–the Disciplinary Board for Bishops certified abandonment, 2–declaration of Episcopal Church authorities that Lawrence had renounced his orders, 3–any restriction on the ministry of Lawrence. By a curious caveat, however, Lawrence was given the right to rescind the call of convention within twenty-four hours of any action against himself. Thus, the final authority to call a convention in this scenario remained with Lawrence. The one-page of official minutes of the Standing Committee meeting of November 1, 2011, was presented in the investigation of Lawrence by the Disciplinary Board for Bishops in 2012. It has been cited as evidence by those who charge that certain prominent leaders of the Diocese of South Carolina enacted a premeditated conspiracy to remove the diocese from the Episcopal Church and to retain control of the property.

---

174. "Episcopal Church Takes Action against the Bishop and Diocese of SC." Diocese of South Carolina [October 17, 2012?], http://www.diosc.com/sys/index.php?option=com_contents&view=article&id=452:the-episcopal-church-takes-action-against-the-diocese-of-south-carolina-special-convention-called&itemid=75.

The diocesan leadership was prepared to separate the diocese from the Episcopal Church nearly a year before the schism actually occurred.

Beyond the leadership, though, lay most of the diocese: the clergy and the communicants. Lawrence met with the deans of the convocations for four hours on September 29. When the news broke that he was under investigation by the Board, Lawrence immediately called a clergy day for October 11, at St. James's Church in Charleston. About one hundred priests and deacons converged on St. James's Church on Tuesday, October 11, to hear what their bishop had to say. The meeting was closed to the public; and the diocese did not release a transcript of it. Two reports did appear afterwards quoting participants. One came from the diocesan office and one from Steve Skardon, the well-known blogger and critic of Lawrence.[175] Not surprisingly, the reports described the meeting very differently. Regardless, it was clear that Lawrence gave a long, rambling discourse in which he apparently did not address the twelve accusations directly. He did not deny the charges. Instead, he portrayed the investigation of himself as an attack on the diocese since the diocesan conventions had passed the resolutions in question. He went on to denounce the whole process of the investigation, the Title IV revisions, the Board, and the anonymity of the accusers. In addition, he spent a great deal of time on what was by now his all too familiar theme of righteous differentiation with the Episcopal Church. However, in his talk, Lawrence pared down his earlier three points of theology, polity, and sexuality, to two: theology and polity. He had dropped the third issue of homosexuality months earlier. Influential speakers had apparently been set up to follow Lawrence. One was Alan Runyan, by now viewed as the diocesan authority on the law. In the diocese's own account, Runyan charged that the Church was out to get Lawrence and the diocese: "deposition of the bishop would be followed by attacks on diocese and the parishes."[176] Retired Bishop Allison also arose to add his voice. Jeffrey Miller, past president of the Standing Committee, said "'The question is not whether we can stay; it is whether they will let us stay and follow what we believe.'"[177] Clearly, the diocesan leadership were doing their best to unify the diocese against the supposed unwarranted aggression of errant Church leaders of suspect motive.

The attendant clergy who reported to Skardon had less than glowing remarks about the occasion. They said Lawrence gave a long, angry and rambling monologue "followed by a carefully-orchestrated series of speakers determined to put an hysterical spin on the inquiry."[178] Others complained that "the overall content of the presentations Tuesday as 'paranoid' and 'delusional.'"[179] Still other said the bishop showed no concern for the welfare of the clergy and their parishes. Another complaint was that the bishop seemed

---

175. "Bishop and Clergy of the Diocese Meet to Discuss 'Serious Charges' Made against Bishop Lawrence." Diocese of South Carolina, October 12, 2011, http://www.diosc.com/sys/index.php?view=article&catid=1%3Alatest-news&id=369%3Abishop-and-clergy-of-the.; Skardon, Steve. "Lawrence's Defense Does Little to Inspire Worried Clergy." South Carolina Episcopalians, http://www.scepiscopalians.com/Older_Posts_2011_2012.html.

176. "Bishop and Clergy."

177. Skardon, "Lawrence's Defense."

178. Ibid.

179. Ibid.

to lack focus and guidance. He told the group he was staying with the Episcopal Church for now but could not say what the future would bring.[180] Many clergy left the meeting wondering just what the bishop had said and just what he meant for the future which was, after all, their future too. The next month he led a clergy conference of two days, November 14-16, at Camp Saint Christopher. By this point, there was no doubt that the clear majority of the diocesan clergy were firmly attached to their bishop and agreed with him that an action against Lawrence was an action against their diocese.

At the same time that Lawrence hurriedly surrounded himself with the leadership, clergy, and laity, he also moved to strike back against the national Church. He repeated the strategy he had so well established by this point: take the offensive on points of policy and procedure rather than substance, reject and deny all charges, rally his friends at home and abroad, and refuse to give in a bit to his opposition. The function of the Board was to investigate the charges and vote yes or no that the bishop had abandoned the communion. If yes, the matter then went to the presiding bishop. If no, the case ended. The Board was only for investigation, not for prosecution. That would be handled in the canonical process allotted to the presiding bishop and the House of Bishops. Nevertheless, Lawrence and his allies immediately turned their attention to the Board to make it the public focus rather than Lawrence's guilt or innocence. This was true even though the diocese had already declared non-recognition of the Board, and in fact all the canons of the Episcopal Church, thereby giving Lawrence and the diocese a ready excuse to ignore the whole business of the Board if they wished.

From the moment the news of the investigation broke publicly, on October 5, Lawrence's allies on the Internet rushed to defend him and to denounce the Church and its process. Steve Skardon called it a media blitz. Kendall Harmon's website immediately started carrying notices about the investigation and posts from various conservative sources characterizing it as an illegal attack on the diocese. The very first blast from the right was one of the harshest. It was Ephraim Radner's essay on October 5, "A Response to the Reported Title IV Disciplinary Process Begun Against Bishop Mark Lawrence."[181] Writing for the highly conservative think-tank, Anglican Communion Institute, Radner led off with a bitter attack on the Episcopal Church and its leadership: "the allegations (...) are so absurd as to cross the line into deceit and malice. The fact that these allegations are being made and then taken seriously by the leadership of TEC in itself constitutes an affront to the commitments for which a Christian church stands."[182] He went on to say that the issues of sovereignty and hierarchy were all debatable and therefore Lawrence should not be disciplined because he kept one side of the debate: "It is morally repugnant to imagine Bishop Lawrence being disciplined, let alone deposed, because he has vigorously upheld one side of an (...) argument (...). The disciplinary procedure on this front not only smacks of, but is clearly reflective of coercive intolerance, once

---

180. Ibid.

181. Radner, Ephraim. "A Response to the Reported Title IV Disciplinary Process Begun against Bishop Mark Lawrence." Anglican Communion Institute, October 5, 2011, http://www.anglicancommunioninstitute.com/2011/10/1-response-to-the-reported-title-iv-disciplinary-process-begun-against-bishop-mark-lawrence.

182. Ibid.

associated with the worst of America's McCarthy era."[183] He was not through: "Presiding Bishop, you have bankrupted your apostolic office, broken your vows, and sullied this church."[184] Radner's shrill essay was immediately picked up and repeated in other right-wing websites. It set the stage for the furious barrage from like-minded pundits and commentators against the Episcopal Church that continued for two nearly two months until the Board closed the case.

Lawrence's supporters made a major media offensive effectively setting the public agenda for the debate. Even daily newspapers began reporting the inaccuracy that the Episcopal Church had charged Lawrence with abandonment. As the Church side was thrown on the defensive, the Church news service and Bishop Henderson, head of the Board, tried to get out information clarifying the process but found only mixed results that made the Church and the Board appear to be reactive and defensive. On October 5, the day the news broke, Episcopal News Service posted a long article giving details about the background and process of the matter.[185] On the same day, the online journal Episcopal Café carried an article about the Title IV process.[186] It included a memo from Henderson stating that information to the Board came from communicants of the diocese, not from the Presiding Bishop or the House of Bishops and that the Board will proceed under Title IV rules in confidentiality. These articles did nothing to deter the furious pro-Lawrence blitz. Henderson tried again a few days later with a tone of frustration: "Public media has recently reported that 'The Episcopal Church is alleging that Bishop Mark Lawrence has abandoned the church. That is incorrect."[187] He tried once again to explain the background, structure, procedures, and process of the Board. Henderson also provided a lengthy article to *The Living Church* in which he went into detail about the individual canons in Title IV, again trying to clear up misconceptions about the process.[188]

While the defenders of Lawrence were busy promoting public relations, they also found another issue with which they could criticize the Board and divert attention away from the question of Lawrence's abandonment, the matter of Josephine Hicks. When the Board had formed on July 1, it had hired Hicks as its attorney, a role that had been provided in the Church's canons. The Hicks affair started when she sent a letter on September 30 to the Rev. Paul Fuener requesting of the Standing Committee all documents concerning the ordinations of the Rev. Chadwick E. Lawrence, a son of Bishop Lawrence, and all documents concerning the resolutions of the diocesan conventions from

183. Ibid.

184. Ibid.

185. Schjonberg, Mary Frances. "South Carolina Bishop Investigated on Charges he has Abandoned the Episcopal Church." Episcopal News Service, October 5, 2011, http://archive.episcopalchurch.org/79425_130067_ENG.HTM.htm.

186. "Henderson Clarifies SC Complaint and Investigation." Episcopal Café, October 5, 2011, http://www.episcopalcafe.com/lead/episcopal_church/henderson_clarifies_sc_complaint.html.

187. "The Role of the Disciplinary Board Regarding the Bishop of South Carolina." eNewsletter of the Episcopal Forum of SC, October 13, 2011, http://www.mynewsletterbuilder.com/email/newsletter/1411073205.

188. "Bp. Henderson Explains Disciplinary Board's Duty." *The Living Church*, November 16, 2011, http://www.livingchurch.org/content/bp-henderson-explains-disciplinary-board%E2%80%99s-duty.

October 2009 to February of 2011. These documents obviously related to some of the charges against Lawrence that had been brought to the Board.

The diocesan leaders' reaction to Hicks's letter was similar to that in the Logan/Tisdale affair of early 2010. Instead of furnishing the materials asked, they launched a furious offensive against the sources of the letter. After all, she had asked for a long list of the minutes of the Standing Committee which had been secret heretofore. On October 7, Wade Logan, the chancellor of the diocese, sent Hicks a letter pointing out that she was listed as a member of the Board on its roster and that the canons prohibited a member from serving as the attorney for the Board. Hicks had indeed been listed as a member, but this turned out to be a clerical error as she should have been listed as attorney. The error was cleared up in the official record on October 12.[189] It did not matter at the time as news flew of Hicks's and the Board's supposedly illegal activity. The right-wing blogosphere went into high gear in full attack mode. Hicks herself unfairly became the center of the storm for the time being. Steve Skardon reported on his blog that Lawrence's supporters attacked her character and motives and "others reportedly put pressure on her law firm."[190]

Hicks had in fact a stellar past as a lawyer and active layperson in the Church leadership. She was a partner in the law firm of Parker, Poe, Adams & Bernstein, a major company with offices in six cities. However, it was her record in the national Church that bothered the conservatives the most. She had been a member of the Executive Council (2003–09) that had declared the moves of the four seceding dioceses to be null and void, the resolution that had been cited against South Carolina in 2011. Moreover, she had been a member of the Anglican Consultative Council and had opposed the Windsor Report and defended the rights of homosexuals in the Church.

For reasons that remained unclear, Hicks recused herself from the Lawrence case on October 14. On that day, Henderson sent the message of Hicks's withdrawal to each member of the Board and to news outlets such as *The Living Church* magazine. He gave a somewhat cryptic explanation: "unanticipated circumstances have created the possibility of a conflict arising regarding fiduciary responsibilities for members of her law firm (. . .) she is not at liberty to disclose any details concerning that possibility."[191] Henderson did manage to grant her a belated slight nod of approval: "Any apprehension, implication or suggestion that Ms. Hicks' work would not be impartial is unfounded, just as the claim that she served as a member of the Board is unfounded."[192] Three days later, on October 17, Henderson announced that Hicks was being replaced by Jack W. "J.B." Burtch, an attorney in the firm of Maccaulay & Burtch, of Richmond, Virginia. This was for the Lawrence case only as Hicks was to continue with the other matters before the Board. In the October 17 letter to the members of the Board, also released

---

189. "Bishop: Attorney Never on Disciplinary Board." *The Living Church*, November 16, 2011, http://www.livingchurch.org/content/bishop-attorney-never-disciplinary-board.

190. Skardon, Steve. "Diocese's Tactics Backfiring?" South Carolina Episcopalians, October 15, 2011, http://www.scepiscopalians.com/Older_Posts_2011_2012.html.

191. "Church Attorney Recuses Herself." *The Living Church,* November 16, 2011, http://www.livingchurch.org/content/church-attorney-recuses-herself.

192. Ibid.

to the media, Henderson made another puzzling statement: "[Burtch] did preliminary work on the Bishop Lawrence information, so he is already more than familiar with that information and the task which is now ours."[193] He inadvertently gave the Lawrence side new ammunition that they used immediately. Allegations swirled anew that the Church had been out to get Lawrence for a long time.

Amid the raging storm of hard feelings there were people trying to calm things down and smooth over the differences. Henderson did all that he could to keep Lawrence closely informed all along. Lawrence's official diary listed five phone calls from Henderson in this period.[194] In terms of peacemaking, however, no one came close to the role of Andrew Waldo, bishop of the Diocese of Upper South Carolina. He telephoned Lawrence at least every few days for a total of nine times.[195] Some of the conversations were lengthy. Waldo published an essay in Columbia's *The State* newspaper on October 19 trying to be the moderate conciliator. He gave a vote of confidence to this brother bishop: "I know him to be a loyal and faithful minister who seeks to raise valid and serious questions as to the theology, polity, and structure of the Episcopal Church."[196] Then Waldo tried to take both sides: "it is hard for me to see how the actions complained of against Bishop Lawrence rise to the level of an intentional abandonment of the communion of this Church."[197] On the other hand, he went on "I have felt grief over what certain recent actions in the convention (. . .) have done to our relationships (. . .). I do not understand or seek to judge the reasons for such disassociation. But I grieve the result: a fractured catholicity."[198] Waldo's point was that the Episcopal Church needed the diversity of differing parties, traditionalists and progressives.

A few days later, on October 22, the Diocese of Upper South Carolina, in its annual meeting, in Aiken, South Carolina, passed a resolution calling on Jefferts Schori and Lawrence to "'come together in person at a mutually convenient time and place in order to strengthen the bonds of our community' and 'engage in healing conversation regarding the ongoing tensions between The Episcopal Church and the Diocese of South Carolina.'"[199] The resolution also directed Waldo to hand-deliver the letter to both parties. He handed Lawrence's copy to him at their hour and a half luncheon meeting in Columbia on the 24th and Jefferts Schori to her when he was in New York on November 2. The resolution was certainly well-motivated and well-meaning but it lacked specifics. Lawrence had already made it clear that the gulf between himself and the Presiding Bishop was wide and "unbridgeable." Besides, the problem at hand was between Law-

---

193. Ibid.

194. *Journal of the Two Hundred and Twenty-First* (. . .) 2012, 49–53.

195. Ibid.

196. Waldo, (the Rt. Rev.) Andrew. "Unity, Diversity both Needed and Possible in Episcopal Church." *The State* (Columbia, SC), October 19, 2011; *The Post and Courier* (Charleston, SC), October 22, 2011.

197. Ibid.

198. Ibid.

199. *Journal of the Eighty-Eighth Annual Convention and the Eighty-Ninth Annual Convention of the Episcopal Church in the Diocese of Upper South Carolina, Trinity Cathedral, Columbia, SC, October 15–16, 2010, St. Thaddeus Episcopal Church, Aiken, SC, co-hosted by St. Augustine of Canterbury Church, Aiken, SC, October 22, 2011.* Columbia, SC; the diocese, 2012, 95.

rence and the Board. Under the rules, the presiding bishop was completely separate from the Board. Did the two meet as the resolution requested? There is no public record of an in-person meeting between Jefferts Schori and Lawrence for nearly a year afterwards. They did meet on October 3, 2012, and then it was under very different circumstances.

Two months of high tension elapsed before the Disciplinary Board for Bishops met by conference call on November 22 to vote that they could not certify that Lawrence had abandoned the communion of the Episcopal Church. The decision was based entirely on the information in the sixty-three-page file. The Diocese had adamantly refused to turn over any documents to the Board. Indeed, there was no public record that Burtch requested any documents from the Diocese. Henderson indicated that the committee could not conclude that actions by a diocesan convention could constitute abandonment by a bishop even if he supported the actions.[200] Speaking only for himself, Henderson said that he took Lawrence at his word that he did not intend to take the Diocese out of the Episcopal Church.[201] Henderson called Lawrence on November 28 to give him the news before it was officially announced on the 29th. On the 29th, Lawrence sent a letter to the diocese completely devoid of gratitude or goodwill toward the Board or the Episcopal Church let alone any hint of reconciliation with the Church, but also completely empty of boasting and gloating. He wrote, in a tone of hostility, that the Board's statement "appears to read like a complex statement of a complex decision in a complex time within a complex church."[202] Then he added, "I believe it is best to take it at face value (even while noting that this diocese has not recognized the constitutionality of the new disciplinary canon)."[203] *Jubilate Deo* gave only a brief announcement on its front page.[204] While Lawrence downplayed his exoneration, his supporters on the Internet seemed taken aback at the news and made a rather quiet celebration while continuing to take shots at the Church and the Presiding Bishop. David Virtue said: "It was a revelatory moment that most orthodox Episcopalians, including this writer, thought would never happen."[205] Lawrence's critics, certainly many with their high hopes of certification deflated, seemed equally stunned and would have remained glumly quiet except for an unexpected turn of events that changed everything, again.

---

200. Schjonberg, Mary Frances. "Abandonment Complaint against South Carolina Bishop Dismissed." Episcopal News Service, November 29, 2011, http://episcopaldigitalnetwork.com/ens/2011/11/29/disciplinary-board-dismisses-abandonment-complaint-against-south-carolina-bishop.

201. Ibid.

202. Lawrence, (the Rt. Rev.) Mark. "Bishop Lawrence Writes to the Diocese about Disciplinary Board Decision." Diocese of South Carolina, November 29, 2011, http://www.diosc.com/sys/news-events/latest-news/382-bishop-lawrence-writes-to-the-diocese-about-disciplinary-board-decision.

203. Ibid.

204. Hunter, Joy. "Majority of Disciplinary Board Unable to Certify Abandonment by Lawrence." *Jubilate Deo* (Diocese of South Carolina), Winter 2012.

205. Virtue, David. "South Carolina Bishop Mark Lawrence Walks, for Now." Virtueonline, November 29, 2011, http://virtueonline.org/portal.modules/news/article.php?storyid=15259.

Quit Claim Deeds, November–December

Ever since September of 2009, when the South Carolina Supreme Court had ruled that the Dennis Canon was invalid for the parish involved in the *All Saints* case, Lawrence and the diocesan leadership had evidently believed the ruling meant the Dennis Canon was dead in the diocese. Documents presented in the Board investigation of Lawrence in 2012 showed that Lawrence began granting quit claim deeds to diocesan parishes soon after the court decision.[206] A quit claim deed quit, or removed, any interest or claim the diocese had as a trustee of the local properties. The diocese issued five quit claim deeds to local parishes before October 19, 2010, when the diocese revised its corporate charter to remove references to the Episcopal Church. Before the revision, the charter stated that the Diocese of South Carolina was bound to the Constitution and Canons of the Episcopal Church, therefore to the Dennis Canon that was included therein. Four of the five were issued under the names of Mark J. Lawrence, bishop, and Jeffrey Miller, chair of the standing committee: St. John's of Johns Island (February 1, 2010), Church of the Holy Communion of Charleston (February 1, 2010), Church of the Cross of Bluffton (February 1, 2010), Christ/St. Paul's, of Yonges Island, (March 15, 2010). Two others were issued otherwise, one to St. Philip's of Charleston (July 11, 2011), and St. James of James Island (March 28, 2010). All these were recorded in the appropriate court houses between November 16 and 21, 2011. Fifteen more deeds were granted between October 19, 2010, the time of the charter revision, and November 16, 2011, the date that Wade Logan, the chancellor, sent a letter to all parishes granting them all quit claim deeds. These fifteen were: St. John's of Florence (October 28, 2010), St. Thomas and St. Denis, and Church of the Holy Cross of Sullivan's Island (November 22, 2010), Church of Our Saviour of John's Island (February 1, 2011), Church of the Good Shepherd of Charleston (July 11, 2011), Cathedral Church of St. Luke and St. Paul of Charleston (July 11, 2011), Trinity Church of Charleston (July 11, 2011), Christ the King of Pawleys Island (October 3 and 4, 2011), Church of the Resurrection of Surfside Beach (October 3, 2011), St. Paul's of Conway (October 4, 2011), Christ Church of Mt. Pleasant (October 4, 2011), St. Bartholomew's of Hartsville (October 4, 2011), St. George's of Summerville (October 4, 2011), St. Paul's of Bennettsville (October 4, 2011), St. Matthew's of Darlington (October 9, 2011), and St. Helena's of Beaufort (October 27, 2011).

Lawrence announced the issuance of the quit claim deeds to all parishes at the clergy conference held at Camp Saint Christopher on November 15. "As he woke up Nov. 16, after announcing the decision the previous evening, 'I thought, I feel like for the first time, I am the bishop of this diocese,' he said."[207] This is what he told others, but he wrote in his diary on that day of a very different feeling, "Tired; heavy of heart."[208] Lawrence was well aware of the gravity of his action and the serious consequences that were certain to come from the national Church. He was already under investigation on allegations of abandonment. He knew that outright and sweeping defiance of the Dennis

---

206. "Episcopal Church Takes Action," Exhibit A.
207. "The Bishop Brings the Crozier." *The Living Church*, November 23, 2011, http://www.livingchurch.org/bishop-brings-crozier.
208. *Journal of the Two Hundred and Twenty-First* (. . .) 2012, 52.

Canon could only strengthen the case against him, if not now, then in the future. Yet, there could be no turning back at this point. Outright defiance of a cardinal canon of the Episcopal Church gave the Church no choice but to act anew. Either sovereignty rested in the Episcopal Church as a whole or it did not.

On November 16, Wade Logan, the chancellor, sent a letter to every parish granting quit claim deeds to all. He wrote, "'For 190 years (1789–1979) there has never been any idea that somehow the parishes did not completely and fully own their property. Our Supreme Court has now said that the attempt to change that in 1979 by the General Convention was not binding on the parish of All Saints, Pawley's Island SC. In recognition of that ruling and in continued pursuit of our historic unity based on common vision rather than legal coercion, the Diocesan Convention removed the relevant section from our canons in October 2010.'"[209]

Six days after Logan's letter, the Disciplinary Board for Bishops met electronically to vote on the issue at hand. The members of the Board could not consider the quit claim deeds because they were bound entirely by the information presented in the original sixty-three-page report. News of the deeds came too late. Therefore, when word spread that the Board had failed to charge Lawrence with abandonment, the news was somewhat muted by the excited talk of the deeds that had been going on for days. Everyone knew that the Church could not ignore the quit claim deeds. Even Lawrence's supporters on the Internet were saying the bishop had walked only for now. Everyone expected that the quit claim deeds would provoke more action from the national Church.

Before that would happen, however, the bishops of Province IV, the southeastern United States, resolved to try to intervene with Lawrence. The provincial bishops met for their regular session November 29–December 1 in Memphis. When Lawrence did not go to them in their official meeting, some of the bishops decided to go to him. The bishops spent a good deal of time in Memphis discussing the quit claim deeds "'with some concern.'"[210] On December 5, the Rt. Rev. Clifton Daniel III, vice-president of the province and bishop of East Carolina, wrote to Lawrence asking for a meeting.[211] He said, "Since we have had no direct communication from you regarding these reported actions [deeds], we determined that it is our duty as bishops of this province to address these concerns in direct communication with you."[212] He went on, "What we seek is a face-to-face meeting with you."[213] Then he wrote, "We have heard and read reports that you have given a quitclaim deed to each congregation (. . .) under what canonical authority did you proceed?" He went on to request a copy of a deed and an explanation for it. Daniel

---

209. Anderson, (the Rt. Rev.) David C. "Weekly Letter from Bishop Anderson." American Anglican Council, November 18, 2011, http://www.facebook.com/notes-american-anglican-council/weekly-letter-from-bishop-anderson/10150407219289544.

210. Schjonberg, Mary Frances. "South Carolina Bishop asked to Explain Property Action." Episcopal News Service, December 5, 2011, http://episcopaldigitalnetowrk.com/ens/2011/12/05/provincial-colleagues-ask-south-carolina-bishop-to-explain-property-action.

211. "Province IV Bishops Publically Request Meeting with Bishop Lawrence." Diocese of South Carolina, n.d., http://www.diosc.com/sys/news-events/latest-news/384-province-iv-bishops-publically-request-meeting-with-bishop-lawrence.

212. Ibid.

213. Ibid.

asked for a meeting of several bishops and Lawrence. Lawrence agreed; and a date was set for December 14 at diocesan headquarters in Charleston.

Lawrence remained polite and courteous to his fellow bishops throughout the whole episode of the visit. This was the same way in which he had treated Bishop Waldo who had tried so hard during the Board investigation to calm down the crisis. In fact, Lawrence met Waldo in person, at least briefly, at a conference in Columbia on December 12, and talked with him on the phone on the 13th.[214] All signs indicated that the two maintained a good and friendly relationship. Behind the scenes, however, the diocesan leadership regarded the other bishops with anything but cordial feelings. On December 6, the day after Daniel called Lawrence and sent him a letter, Lawrence met the diocesan Standing Committee for six and one-half hours.[215] One can only surmise the conversation while recalling that this body had secretly voted unanimously to disassociate from the Episcopal Church only a month earlier. Lawrence also met with the diocesan Council for three and one-half hours and the deans of the convocations for two hours on December 13, the day before the bishops were to visit Charleston.

Three days after their long session with Lawrence, the Standing Committee issued a blistering and confrontational open letter to Daniel and his fellow bishops. They did this although Daniel had not addressed the committee, only Lawrence. It is difficult to imagine that the committee was doing anything but acting as Lawrence's surrogate here. Lawrence could keep a diplomatically polite public face while getting out his real message to the bishops and the public. True to form in the well-established strategy of the diocesan leadership, the committee directly attacked the bearer of the letter. This should bring back memories of Tisdale, Straub, and Hicks. "The Constitution of the Episcopal Church does not allow a bishop to act within any other Diocese" they proclaimed as they got started.[216] They continued, "the Synod [province] expressly lacks any 'power to regulate or control the internal policy or affairs of any constituent diocese.' Therefore, the bishops of Province IV have no constitutional or canonical grounds for these requests."[217] Making it even more personal, they added, "your inquiries into the affairs of this diocese, without constitutional or canonical support, are contrary to [your] oath."[218] As if that were not personal enough, they added "we are concerned about your motives" and left the interpretation of that open. It did not take much imagination to get their meaning.

While furiously rejecting the authority of the bishops and insulting their personal characters, the committee also portrayed Lawrence as the innocent victim of malicious out-of-control outside forces trying to run out Lawrence and take over the diocese that "grows weary of the constant interference in its internal affairs."[219] They gave a litany of

214. *Journal of the Two Hundred and Twenty-First (. . .)* 2012, 54.

215. Ibid.

216. "Standing Committee Responds to Province IV Bishops' Request to Meet with Bishop Lawrence." Diocese of South Carolina, December 9, 2011, http://www.diosc.com/sys/news-events/latest-news/385-standing-committee-responds-to-province-iv-bishops-request.

217. Ibid.

218. Ibid.

219. Ibid.

familiar complaints: the Presiding Bishop hiring counsel in the diocese, the Executive Council trying to nullify resolutions of the diocesan conventions, the investigation of Lawrence by the Disciplinary Board for Bishops on frivolous charges, and now "yet another attempt without canonical or constitutional support to inject others into the internal affairs of this autonomous diocese."[220] Why all this hostility to the Episcopal Church? The committee said it was righteous indignation over the Church's wrong policies on property, communion of the un-baptized, and "the practice of same sex marriage or blessings."[221] They were echoing Lawrence's oft repeated theme of theology, polity, and sexuality. If Daniel, Waldo, and the other bishops of the southeast had any doubts about where South Carolina stood, they could not hold them after this. The Standing Committee had shed all the famous genteel politeness of the Low Country to give bishops "from off" a most impolite in-your-face tantrum. The bishops could go to South Carolina but they had better not expect to change anything the diocese had done. The diocesan leadership was in no mood to give in an inch on compromise and reconciliation. It did not take much to predict how this meeting was going to turn out. If nothing else, the idea of separating Lawrence from his diocese was off the table.

On December 14, six bishops met Lawrence at 1:00 p.m. in the diocesan offices on Coming Street, Charleston. They were: Daniel; Waldo; Scott Anson Benhase of Georgia; Michael B. Curry of North Carolina (later the Presiding Bishop of the Episcopal Church); Don E. Johnson of West Tennessee; and G. Porter Taylor of Western North Carolina. They talked for two hours. The conversation was private and no record of it has been released. Afterwards, the seven bishops did issue a joint statement about the meeting. Through the polite and diplomatic language, it revealed that nothing changed. They reported: "Gracious hospitality and collegiality characterized the gathering during which we prayed and participated in open, honest, and forthright conversation. Probing questions were asked by all, and it is fair to say that we did not agree on all matters discussed. For the visiting bishops, the gathering particularly helped to clarify the context of the Diocese of South Carolina's quitclaim decision."[222] *We did not agree on all matters discussed.* What they did agree on, everyone wanted to know. It certainly was not apparent. In reality, the meeting changed nothing.

As Lawrence reached the end of his fourth year as bishop, matters within the Diocese of South Carolina were more settled but relations between the diocese and the Episcopal Church were more unsettled than ever. The diocese acceded only conditionally to the Constitution and not at all to the Canons of the Episcopal Church. The Dennis Canon was dead as far as the diocesan leadership was concerned. The Title IV reforms had been rejected and replaced by the old 2006 rules. An "Anglican" identity was rising to replace the old Episcopalian one. The Diocese of South Carolina had created a unique situation in which it claimed to be in but not of the Episcopal Church. The problem was

---

220. Ibid.

221. Ibid.

222. "Province IV Bishops Release Statement Concerning Meeting with Bishop Lawrence." Diocese of South Carolina, December 15, 2011, http://www.diosc.com/sys/news-events/latest-news/386-province-iv-bishops-release-statement-concerning-meeting-with-bishop-lawrence.

that this had been done unilaterally. The response from the national Church was yet to come.

In early 2011, Lawrence went about his episcopal duties as if everything had returned to normal. The diocesan convention in February carried only routine formalities following up on the groundbreaking work of the 2010 conventions. For months, Lawrence focused on a return to his busy schedule of building bonds at home and abroad. He resumed a crowded round of travels throughout the area while making numerous trips out of state.

Lawrence had displayed an adversarial tension if not a hostility to the Episcopal Church leadership from the start of his episcopacy. At first the bad relations were tolerable and could be put aside if not ignored. As time went by, though, the relations turned worse. By the end of 2010 they could no longer be put aside. The virtual declaration of independence by the diocese and its subsequent self-removal from the structure of the Episcopal Church meant that the Church and its supporters would have to act to preserve the integrity of the Church as a national institution. A diocese could not be allowed to withdraw from the constituted structure of the Church on its own terms. If it did, the whole structure would collapse. Sovereignty had to remain in the central authority for the Episcopal Church to survive. South Carolina's excuse that the founding dioceses were not subject to the laws of the Church because only newer ones were required to give unconditional accession to the Constitution and Canons of the Episcopal Church did not make common sense. No national institution could survive with a two-tier government, one for the founders and another for everyone else. The idea that the original thirteen states were not bound by the U.S. Constitution the way all the later ones were bound would have been equally absurd and unworkable.

To be sure, Lawrence and the diocesan leadership claimed that everything they were doing *vis-à-vis* the Church was entirely legal and legitimate. They claimed they were still in the Episcopal Church and had no intention of leaving it. As for the property, they said that the state Supreme Court had ruled that the local properties belong entirely to the congregations and therefore Lawrence had every right, even a duty, to issue quit claim deeds. On the diocesan side, whatever problems existed came from the national Church leadership, not from South Carolina. In their view, any move to discipline Lawrence was unconstitutional and vindictive. Thus, in Lawrence's mind, there was no problem with issuing any deeds to the parishes and the national Church had no right to interfere in his decisions.

On the Episcopal Church side, views were radically different. Quite simply, the Episcopal Church had to act regarding South Carolina's declaration of independence and sovereignty. It was not something the Church wanted or sought, yet it could not be ignored after 2010. Melinda Lucka's letter of May 25, 2011, started the ball rolling in a movement that had to be made. In response, the Church's Executive Council declared the controversial South Carolina convention resolutions null and void. Lawrence rejected all of this and denounced Lucka and the Council for their actions. He could not, however, rebuff the next challenge. He was formally investigated by the newly constituted Disciplinary Board for Bishops on accusations of abandonment of the Episcopal Church which he had vowed to support and obey in his consecration as bishop. In fighting back,

Lawrence did his best to diminish his accusers: Lucka, Straub, the Board, and the Board's attorney Josephine Hicks. The attack on Hicks worked and she was soon replaced as attorney on the case by a new lawyer who apparently demanded nothing of the Diocese. In the end, the Board backed off and declared that Lawrence had not met the requirement necessary to be charged with abandonment. It seemed that everyone wanted to give him one more benefit of the doubt for the sake of unity.

That last benefit of the doubt for Lawrence among the Church leaders vanished even before the Disciplinary Board could get out its vote of exoneration. A few days before he was cleared by the Board, Lawrence proudly announced that he had issued quit claim deeds to all parishes in the diocese. This was in open and defiant disregard of the Dennis Canon, a law that he knew very well the Episcopal Church held dear and would press against all odds. Near the close of the year, neighboring bishops made a last-ditch attempt to prevail on Lawrence to obey the Church he had taken an oath to uphold. It was of no use. Lawrence was adamant that he was the ultimate authority in his diocese and that the Diocese of South Carolina was an autonomous unit of the national Church free to ignore the canons of the Church.

Thus, the year 2011 ended with tensions between the Diocese and the Episcopal Church higher than ever. Options for settlement between the local diocese and the Episcopal Church were running out if they had not been exhausted already. With open defiance of the Dennis Canon, Lawrence crossed the line of toleration. He handed the Episcopal Church an offer it could not refuse. To maintain the integrity of the structure of the Episcopal Church that had built up for more than two centuries, the Church would have to enforce its rules in every diocese. It could not allow any one diocese to flout its laws with impunity. As the year 2012 dawned and Lawrence began his fifth year on the bishop's throne, it was clear that a major crisis was about to break between the Diocese of South Carolina and the Episcopal Church. The Disciplinary Board had said it could not be about diocesan convention resolutions. It would be about property. It would be about local rights against the national authority. It was as if everything old was new again in South Carolina.

5

The Crisis of 2012

THE BACKGROUND OF THE GENERAL CONVENTION, JANUARY–JUNE

The Return of the Issue of Homosexuality

As the year 2012 began, two critical issues overshadowed the relationship between the Diocese of South Carolina and the Episcopal Church: property and homosexuality. Each side had polar opposite views of each. Property was a major issue for the Church and a non-issue for the Diocese. Homosexuality was a major issue for the Diocese and a non-issue for the Church. On the first item, property, the diocese had already declared the Dennis Canon to be dead within the boundaries of the diocese. In fact, the diocesan convention had voted to revoke unilaterally its accession to the canons of the Episcopal Church. In the quit claim deeds, Bishop Lawrence had surrendered all diocesan interest in the local parochial properties. To the diocesan leaders, there was no longer anything to discuss about canons or property. The door was closed. The Episcopal Church leaders had the opposite view as they promoted on every turn the Dennis Canon and insisted that Church laws applied equally to all dioceses in the Church. On the second point of contention, homosexuality, there was a similar bi-polarity. The Episcopal Church had already settled its stand of the equality for homosexual persons. The acceptance of homosexuals in the life of the Church was no longer an issue in the national church as a whole. In South Carolina, however, homosexuality was still very much a live issue even though the diocesan leaders had set it aside for more than a year in favor of differentiation on polity and theology. The problems of property and homosexuality in the Church-diocese relationship would dominate the year 2012. Now, the extreme opposition that the two sides held on these critical matters would test to the outer limit the final tenuous ties holding together the majority in the Diocese of South Carolina and the Episcopal Church.

The matter of the interface between the Episcopal Church and homosexuality had different aspects. One dealt with the question of whether non-celibate homosexual persons should be ordained priests and bishops in the Church. Another aspect was whether the Church should allow the liturgical blessing of same-sex unions. This was the issue on center stage in 2012. In 2009, the committee of music and liturgy of the General Convention had started addressing the matter. As time for the General Convention of 2012 approached, everyone expected the committee to make a report presenting some sort of a liturgy of blessing and that the Convention would approve its recommendation. Once again, South Carolina would return to the issue of homosexuality in 2012 in anticipation of the response to actions of the General Convention.

As 2012 began and attention turned to the upcoming General Convention of the Episcopal Church that was to meet that summer, all the talk was about one aspect of the issue of homosexuality, liturgies for the blessings of same-sex unions. The conservatives had lost on the issue of ordination. The idea of alternate primatial oversight within the Church had also faded as neither the Anglican Network nor the Episcopal Church could come up with a mutually agreeable system. The Title IV reforms were firmly in place and had even worked in favor of Bishop Lawrence as the Disciplinary Board for Bishops rejected charges of abandonment of communion. The only real point of contention left in 2012 on the broad issue of homosexuality was the approval of new liturgies for the blessing of same-sex unions. The conservatives in South Carolina and everyone else knew all signs indicated that this too was probably a lost cause. No one had any real doubt that General Convention would approve some sort of services for the blessings. In South Carolina, diocesan leaders began girding early in 2012 for what was shaping up to be the final campaign in a long war they knew they had already lost.

The Annual Diocesan Convention, March 10

As the question of the liturgies loomed, Lawrence returned the issue of homosexuality to the public stage in early 2012 after a two-year absence. When the annual diocesan convention met on March 10, 2012, he took up the matter in his address to the meeting. Once again, he blasted the Episcopal Church for its stand on homosexuality. This time, however, he surprisingly added the ordination of women: "The commitment to understand the ordination of women and now the blessing of same-sex unions, as fundamentally issues of justice—and not theology—has likewise been and will continue to be destructive of our common life as Episcopalians."[1] Of the 151 names on the official clergy list of the pre-schism Diocese of South Carolina, in 2012, 19 were women, making just 8 percent of the total (nationwide one-third of Episcopal clergy were women).[2] Most of these 19 were deacons. No female priest was head of a medium or large parish. On the diocesan level, every committee and council was dominated and headed by men. Some were completely male. Apparently, there was not one woman among the inner-leadership circle of the Diocese.[3]

1. *Journal of the Two Hundred and Twenty-First* . . . 2012, 33.
2. Ibid., 11–19.
3. Post-schism figures are revealing. In the independent diocese, 11 of the 140 clergy listed in 2014 were women (8 percent of all): 6 deacons and 5 priests. Two priests were listed as serving churches in the independent diocese: Louise Weld associate at St. James, Charleston, and Janet Echols, priest-in-charge at St. Matthew's, Ft. Motte. Jennie Olbrych, a priest, was listed under both dioceses. She served St. James Santee, in the Episcopal diocese. In 2014: Standing Committee, 3 women in 12; Diocesan Council, 4 women in 12.

Lawrence did not mention the subject of women clergy again publicly. Many people were left puzzled as to why he felt the need to raise the matter at all.

Lawrence's goal in his bishop's address to the convention was to set the stage for a diocesan reaction to the upcoming General Convention. Besides, the issue of the ordination of women in the Episcopal Church had been settled long ago both in the nation and in the diocese. It was irrelevant at this point in South Carolina. Instead, it was the subject of homosexuality that he would emphasize now. He raised a dire warning about the impending move to approve rites for the blessing of same-sex unions: "The possible departure from Christian Teaching on Marriage is the most disconcerting of all."[4] Then, he suddenly left the door open as to a diocesan reaction to the new rites and moved on to other topics.

Lawrence's official address to the diocesan convention in March of 2012 was another of his long (6,000 words), rambling discourses to which his listeners had become accustomed. Once he had hung out the lantern of homosexuality, he turned to other subjects for lengthy thoughts. He started off the speech with the recent Disciplinary Board for Bishops episode and gave a backhanded compliment to his accusers for having proven the unbreakable bond between diocese and bishop: "we [bishop and diocese] hung together, with or without dreams, knowing, I suppose that if we didn't we would surely hang separately."[5] In fact, the experience of the investigation had proven that Lawrence had succeeded in welding himself to the majority in the diocese. In the future, he could remain confident that any move against him would be seen as a move against the whole diocese. Lawrence's words may have been a scarcely veiled warning to his critics that any effort to remove him as bishop in the future would result in diocesan secession. The rest of the address contained all familiar themes. He spent a lot of time on another long-standing favorite topic, developing the diocesan consciousness of being "Anglican" rather than Episcopalian. In the end, he wrapped up his address with a theological summary that was entirely vertical.[6] Outside of his strange remark on the ordination of women, there was really nothing new in the speech. Nevertheless, he succeeded in setting the diocesan stage for a new confrontation with the Episcopal Church on the issue of homosexuality.

As the earlier chapters revealed, Lawrence had spent the first few years of his episcopacy building bonds between himself and the majority in the diocese and between himself and conservative Anglican forces in the United States and abroad. These efforts had obviously succeeded very well. By 2012, no one could doubt that Lawrence and the majority of the diocese were as one. Even much earlier, Lawrence had taken up the routine use of unitary term "we" to describe himself and the diocese. The Disciplinary Board episode had tested that bond somewhat, and found it solid, but had not tested it to the limit because the Board dismissed the charges against the bishop after two months.

In the Episcopal Church diocese in South Carolina 85 clergy were listed in 2014, 13 women (15 percent of all): 8 priests and 5 deacons. The highest-ranking woman clergy was the Ven. Calhoun Walpole, archdeacon of the diocese. There were far more women priests serving in the Episcopal Church diocese than in the independent one. In 2014: Standing Committee, 5 women in 12; Diocesan Council, 4 women in 12.

4. *Journal of the Two Hundred and Twenty-First (. . .)* 2012, 33.

5. Ibid., 28.

6. Ibid., 34.

The case was closed. By the start of 2012, however, two stronger challenges were possibly, perhaps probably, looming that would indeed test the bonds to the last degree: the response to the expected approval in the General Convention of a liturgy for the blessing of same-sex unions, the clear possibility of a new investigation by the Disciplinary Board arising from the quit claim deeds. These would be much stronger threats to the union of bishop and communicants than had been seen before. In view of this, Lawrence's schedule in the first half of 2012 suggested that he resolved more than ever to shore up every bit of support within the diocese and without.

Preparations for a Crisis, March–July

Bishop Lawrence's official diary, published in the journal of the annual convention of the diocese, was the best source of information on the activities in the diocese in the run-up to the General Convention of 2012.[7] It revealed a great deal of activity on his part inside and outside the diocese in the six months prior the General Convention met in July of 2012. There was an atmosphere of unsettled, if not worried, expectation within the diocese. The shadow cast by events in the recent past, the Disciplinary Board and the deeds, was intensified by the shadow of anticipated events looming just ahead. Lawrence's schedule seemed busier than ever with hours in meetings of diocesan councils and committees, numerous clergy gatherings, several conferences with the delegates to the General Convention sandwiched in among dozens of local church visits, all topped off by more out-of-state travel than ever and by occasional restorative recreational breaks and vacations. The diary lists the usual long daily log of phone calls and visits with the well-known names of assistants and close advisors, lawyers and friends (but not the contents of the communications). The monthly meetings of the Standing Committee and Diocesan Council went on as usual, an average of five hours for the former and two and a half for the latter. Lawrence and the Standing Committee went on a retreat at Camp St. Christopher for two days, March 28 and 29. There was also a six-and-a-half-hour presentation on church pensions, meetings with the insurance and finance committees, and at least two long sessions with the Anglican Communion Development Committee all of which stressed the independence of the diocese from the Episcopal Church. The rather routine nature of the diocesan councils and committees meeting suggested the absence of any drama or differences therein.

There was more activity in Lawrence's meetings with the diocesan clergy. He met the deans for several hours on February 2 and March 29. Lawrence had appointed the deans, all six of whom were close allies of Lawrence and solidly loyal to him.[8] Lawrence met with the clergy on four occasions: May 9, on May 28 for an all-day picnic, May 31, and on June 12. He spent several hours with a deacon's class on June 9. At this point,

---

7. *Journal of the Two Hundred and Twenty Second Annual Meeting of the Convention of the Diocese of South Carolina, Francis Marion Fine Arts Center, March 8th and 9th, 2013, Hosted by St. John's, Florence, All Saints, Florence & St. Matthew's, Darlington.* Charleston, SC: the diocese, 2014, 28–51.

8. Deans in 2012: Charles Owens (Beaufort), vacant, then Peet Dickinson (Charleston), Craige Borrett (Charleston West), John Barr (Florence), Paul Fuener (Georgetown), David Thurlow (Orangeburg).

there was no doubt that the majority of the priests and deacons would automatically defend their bishop no matter what.

As always, Lawrence put thousands of miles on his car keeping an energetic round of episcopal visits to the parishes and missions scattered from Georgia to North Carolina that would have exhausted a less hardy person. His diary notes show that in these months he often lengthened his routine local visits, usually for confirmations, to provide time to talk at length with the congregations, vestries or other groups no doubt about the prevailing issues between diocese and Church. Since he would need all the parishes and missions as possible behind him, Lawrence seemed to put more time and energy into the local visits than usual. Within his dozens of episcopal visits, he delivered extra talks giving his views on the issues of differentiation between the diocese and the Episcopal Church on twenty-eight occasions speaking to what he called "bishop's forums," as well as Sunday School classes, vestry meetings, congregational meetings, retreats, special meetings, dinners, and the like.[9] As everyone knew, Lawrence could be a persuasive, dramatic, even charismatic, speaker at times. There was no doubt that he was widely admired and respected by most laypeople in the diocese who naturally valued him as their chosen leader and inclined to give him implicit trust and loyalty. When the crisis would come, no one could say that the bishop had not tried his best to win the support of most of the ordinary people-in-the-pews and that he had succeeded.

Lawrence was busy in many other ways in the months before the General Convention. In January of 2012, he was preoccupied with the Mere Anglicanism conference. He also met with the deputies to the General Convention three times for a total of seven hours, on May 2, June 14, and June 26.[10] He even found time to attend the Episcopal Forum's two-hour conference at Grace Church, Charleston, on April 15. His motive in making a surprise appearance at his strongest critics' gathering remained unclear: "Lawrence listened carefully sitting on the back row and did not respond to any of the speakers until the very end of the program, when he took issue with what he felt was the strident tone of comments of a final speaker. Speaking for less than a minute, Lawrence offered the Forum members an opportunity to engage with him in a more structured dialogue around these issues. He also offered a benediction."[11] He also offered a report on his visit in the next meeting of the standing committee on May 1. The committee secretary recorded: "They [Forum] seem to be at a loss about what to do since they have been unsuccessful at taking out Bishop Lawrence."[12] Lawrence also said he found Melinda Lucka to be "less acrimonious" than any of the other leaders and even Steve

---

9. Lawrence's diary January 1–July 1, 2012. *Journal of the Two Hundred and Twenty Second (. . .)* 2013, 28–40.

10. Lydia Evans, Reid Boylston, Jim Lewis, David Thurlow, Elizabeth Pennewill, John Burwell, and Lonnie Hamilton. All but the last one were close to Lawrence and all but the last remained with him after the schism.

11. Skardon, Steve. "SC Episcopalians—Episcopal Forum's Spring Meeting Highlights." Episcopal Forum of SC, April 15, 2012, http://www.mynewsletterbuilder.com/email/newsletter/1411306785.

12. "Minutes of the Standing Committee." [May 1, 2012].

Skardon "came across as reasonable."[13] Lawrence's tone in his report revealed he felt the Forum was no threat as an enemy.

Another curious incidence occurred in the Spring of 2012. Lawrence telephoned Thomas Tisdale, the attorney retained by David Booth Beers in late 2009 to represent the Episcopal Church in South Carolina, and invited him to lunch "to mend things."[14] It should be recalled that Lawrence had furiously demanded that the Presiding Bishop fire Tisdale after the Logan/Tisdale affair in early 2010. Soon after Lawrence's invitation, Tisdale drafted a letter to Lawrence stating that he could meet only if there were an understanding that they could not discuss legal matters except how to improve relations between the diocese and the Church.[15] Shortly thereafter, Lawrence e-mailed a response to Tisdale inexplicably withdrawing the invitation to meet.[16] That apparently ended Lawrence's effort to "mend things" with the Church until after the General Convention when he agreed to meet with Waldo and the Presiding Bishop.

Lawrence also found time in the first six months of 2012 to travel beyond South Carolina nine times on business, one of them overseas, and one for vacation, all totaling more than a month away. The one trip abroad was to England from April 23 to 27, to attend a conference of the Fellowship of Confessing Anglicans. While in England, he addressed the Guildford Diocesan Evangelical Fellowship on April 25. His speech was staple Lawrence criticizing and denouncing the Episcopal Church for its "indiscriminate inclusivity," accusing the Church of illegally interfering in South Carolina, and praising conservative Anglicans worldwide. He said, "The Episcopal Church could drop off the face of the earth and it would hardly be a blip on the radar screen of the Kingdom of God."[17] Instead, global Anglicanism he believed was the wave of the future. He received a warm reception, but one should wonder what the listeners thought of an American bishop speaking so disdainfully of his own Church, and in a foreign country to boot.

Lawrence's eight out-of-state trips within the continent in early 2012 covered a wide variety of venues. In February, he went for two days to the Virginia Theological Seminary to talk with faculty and students there.[18] Later that month he traveled to Pennsylvania to visit the Trinity School for Ministry at Ambridge.[19] In March, he spent a third of the month away on three big trips. First he traveled to Toronto as a guest of Ephraim Radner, a theologian and writer who had made a name for himself as a leading conservative critic of Episcopal Church policies.[20] Then, he went to Camp Allen, Texas, to attend the meeting of the House of Bishops, even flying home and back in the middle of the meeting to conduct confirmation in Beaufort.[21] The day after returning home from the bishops'

13. Ibid.
14. Tisdale, interview with author.
15. Ibid.
16. Ibid.
17. "Bishop Mark Lawrence's April [2012] Address Given in England—Transcript." http://www.kendallharmonnet/t19/index/php/t19/article/45594.
18. *Journal of the Two Hundred and Twenty Second (. . .)* 2013, 30.
19. Ibid., 31.
20. Ibid., 32.
21. Ibid., 32–33. Lawrence's granddaughter, Esther Lawrence was one of the confirmands.

meeting, he drove to Orlando, Florida, to participate in the consecration of the new bishop of the Diocese of Central Florida, Gregory Brewer. On May 22, Lawrence left for three days at Nashotah House, in Wisconsin, to attend the board of trustees meeting.[22] In June, the last month before the General Convention, Lawrence made three trips: to attend the Province IV bishops' synod at Kanuga, North Carolina, to attend a summit on immigration in Atlanta, and finally, toward the end of the month, to enjoy a four-day vacation to the mountains of Virginia and North Carolina.[23] Lawrence had not traveled so much in any comparable time since becoming bishop in 2008. As with his extra efforts to bond with the communicants in the parishes and missions, when the crisis should come, no one would be able to say that he had not done his utmost to shore up support for himself and the diocese, this time among bishops and others in America and abroad.

The public thrust of the opposition to the upcoming General Convention in South Carolina came from the Standing Committee.[24] It met seven times in the first six months of 2012.[25] As early as March, the committee apparently began preparing for a crisis. At that time, it discussed property insurance programs and pension plan options separate from the Episcopal Church while it directed the chancellor and counsel to join the lawsuit against the Episcopal Church on the side of the schismatic Fort Worth diocese. On March 27, the committee resolved "to communicate to parishes a plan for asset protection."[26] Most telling of all, at that same meeting the committee agreed to request a date for a special diocesan convention to respond to the anticipated actions of the General Convention.[27] Moreover, they passed a resolution calling for Lawrence to issue a pastoral letter opposing the same-sex blessings, for the preparation of a diocesan response to the blessings, and for the Rev. Thurlow to present a minority report in General Convention opposing the blessings.[28] Thus, more than three months before the Convention was to meet, the Standing Committee was already preparing a major diocesan reaction against the national Church. The existing record did not indicate the source of the request for a special convention or the purpose of such a meeting, whether to make a protest or to disassociate from the Episcopal Church. In its May 1 meeting, the Standing Committee passed a resolution directing the diocesan delegation to file a minority report, refrain from worship at the General Convention, and to leave the Convention immediately following the passage of the same-sex blessing rites.[29] At the same meeting, the committee discussed a booklet entitled "When Should We Divide?" that was distributed by the Rev. Greg Snyder.[30] Finally, on June 15, the Standing Committee published a public declaration regarding the General Convention expressing its opposition to the

22. Ibid., 37.

23. Ibid., 38–39.

24. Paul Fuener, president; Kenneth Weldon, Greg Snyder; Andrew O'Dell; Tripp Jeffords; Ann Hester Willis; William Lyles; Elizabeth Pennewill; John Barr; Suzanne Schwank; Ed. Mitman.

25. *The Journal of the Two Hundred and Twenty Second (. . .)* 2013, 58–59.

26. Ibid., 58.

27. Ibid., 59.

28. "Minutes of the Standing Committee." [March 27, 2012].

29. "Minutes of the Standing Committee." [May 1, 2012].

30. Ibid.

"inevitable outcome" of the Convention.[31] In a somewhat bitter tone, the declaration not only denounced in the sharpest terms the Episcopal Church but also sneered at homosexuals: "those who struggle with and act upon same-gender attraction." They went on to "repudiate, denounce, and reject any action of the Episcopal Church which purports to (. . .) bless same-gender unions" and finally fired a warning shot, "we will not walk with General Convention." It was remarkable for the standing committee of a diocese to repudiate in advance a measure that had not even been passed. What would be the purpose of such an unusual statement? It certainly would not be to influence the Episcopal Church. It was no doubt to rally the diocese and set the stage for what Lawrence and the committee had already planned long before, to call a special convention to further the separation of the diocese from the national Church. But what was left to separate? The only remaining tie was conditional accession to the Constitution of the Episcopal Church. If that were revoked, the break would be complete.

Another issue appeared, unexpectedly, on the eve of the General Convention in which the diocesan leaders could denounce the national Church. In late June, word broke that the former bishop, Edward Salmon, was one of nine bishops being considered for disciplinary actions by the Episcopal Church under Title IV of the Canons. The nine had intervened in court as friends of the parties opposing the Episcopal Church in Fort Worth, Texas, and Quincy, Illinois. The Standing Committee immediately released a statement, on July 3, denouncing the action and declaring it was another attempt to destroy the conservative forces in the Episcopal Church.[32]

By the time the Episcopal Church General Convention opened on July 5 in Indianapolis, Lawrence and the other diocesan leaders had had six months to prepare the Diocese of South Carolina to make a response. They made full use of the time. After the 2012 Convention, the issue of the interface of the Episcopal Church and homosexuality was likely to melt away. Thus, in early 2012, it looked as if this year would be the last time that the leadership in South Carolina could rally the diocese against the national Church on this subject of homosexuality.

While homosexuality was certain to function as a wedge issue in 2012, that of property was not. Lawrence's supporters had declared victory when the Disciplinary Board dismissed charges in 2011. It was clear then that the Board wanted to give Lawrence plenty of leeway so as not to alienate the teetering diocese. They cautiously differentiated between bishop and diocese so as not hold Lawrence accountable for the actions of the diocesan conventions. Even after Lawrence had shocked the Church by issuing the quit claim deeds, even at the very moment the Board was dismissing charges, months went by without any response at all from the Episcopal Church leadership. In early 2012, there was no sign that the Church was about to investigate Lawrence again although there was plenty of talk. Thus, the chance that the Disciplinary Board would act a second time

---

31. "Standing Committee Releases Statement Regarding General Convention." Diocese of South Carolina, June 15, 2012, http://www.diosc.com/sys/index.php?option=com.content&view=article&id=422:declaration-of-the-standing-committee&catid=1:latest-news&Itemid=75.

32. "Standing Committee Releases Statement, July 3, 2012." Diocese of South Carolina, July 3, 2012, http://www.diosc.com/sys/news-events/latest-news/426-standing-committee-releases-statement-july-3–2012. The nine bishops later settled this by signing an official statement following the Title IV rules.

could not be discerned at that time. The issue of the deeds was very much in the air but no one could tell where the national Church would go in forcing Lawrence to respect the Church canons. Lawrence could be investigated again by the Board but everyone knew this would probably provoke a secession crisis in South Carolina. The Church dilemma was whether to enforce the Dennis Canon on Lawrence and watch the loss of the majority in a fifth diocese, or ignore the Dennis Canon and keep South Carolina in the Church, however tenuously. In early 2012, the possibility that Lawrence could be removed as the bishop of South Carolina was there, but no one could say about the probability. Therefore, the diocesan leaders emphasized only the issue of homosexuality in the run-up to the General Convention. It was a sure bet to further differentiate the diocese from the national Church. Property was not.

THE GENERAL CONVENTION, JULY

The Controversial Resolutions

The General Convention of the Episcopal Church was set to meet in the Indiana Convention Center in Indianapolis, Indiana, from July 5 to 12. Bishop Lawrence led the delegation from the Diocese of South Carolina: Lydia Evans, Reid Boylston, Jim Lewis, David Thurlow, Elizabeth Pennewill, John Burwell, and Lonnie Hamilton. All but the last were well-known stalwart supporters of Lawrence who were to remain such through the schism. Lawrence decided to drive the 710 miles from Charleston to Indianapolis, a road trip of twelve hours. Having his own car would allow him to leave the meeting as he wished. On Tuesday, July 3, he left home early to collect riders Evans, Lewis, and Boylston. The group arrived at their hotel at 8:00 p.m. Burwell and Hamilton did not ride with Lawrence to Indianapolis. As we will see, they were the two deputies who would stay behind in the Convention after the rest of the delegation walked out. On the 4th, the group went through registration and met with the Anglican Communion Partners group in the evening.[33] Other than a dinner with the Trinity School for Ministry group on July 10, Lawrence and the delegation stayed to themselves during the Convention.[34]

Of the seemingly countless resolutions discussed in the Convention, Lawrence objected publicly to four of them in this order: A049, D002, D019, and C029. The first, A049, was most important. It was to "Authorize Liturgical Resources for Blessing Same-Gender Relationships."[35] This was the resolution that Lawrence had railed against for months all over South Carolina. This was the resolution that the Standing Committee had publicly blasted the month before. This was the focus of the whole 2012 campaign in South Carolina against rights for homosexuals in the Church. Lawrence had at least implied that the resolution meant the Episcopal Church's establishment of same-sex marriage. The resolution, as passed, authorized a provisional liturgy entitled "The Witnessing and Blessing of a Lifelong Covenant" to begin the first Sunday of Advent, 2012,

33. *Journal of the Two Hundred and Twenty Second (. . .)* 2013, 40.
34. Ibid.
35. *Journal of the 77th General Convention of the Protestant Episcopal Church in the United States of America Otherwise Known as The Episcopal Church.* New York: the church, [2013?], 565–67.

under the permission of the diocesan bishop. It would be an official liturgy for the blessing of a same-sex couple. It was not a marriage service.

D002 and D019 both dealt with rights for transgendered persons. D002, "Affirming Access to Discernment Process for Ministry," added gender identity and expression to the protected list under which persons could not be denied access to ordination.[36] The explanation read, "Gender identity (one's inner sense of being male or female) and expression (the way in which one manifests that gender identity in the world) should not be bases of exclusion, in and of themselves, from consideration for participation in the ministries of the Church." D019 was a corollary to change the canons of the Church accordingly: "As with D002, this proposed revision is based upon our increased understanding and practice to respect the human dignity of transgender people."[37] Both of these resolutions were meant to remove all discrimination in the Episcopal Church ordination process against transgendered people. The last of the four controversial resolutions was the least important: C029, "Access to Holy Baptism and Holy Communion."[38] It stated that baptism was the entry point for Holy Communion but also called for continuing study of the issue.

There was little opposition to these resolutions since by this point the conservative wing of the Episcopal Church had declined into a distinct minority. When the first resolution on equality for transgendered persons came up in the House of Bishops, it was reported that only Lawrence and his good friend, William Love, of Albany, spoke out on the floor against it.[39] When the corollary resolution to change the canons arose, Lawrence spoke out against it too. This time he was joined by Andrew Waldo, of Upper South Carolina.[40] Lawrence, and other conservative bishops, reportedly also spoke out against the liturgy for blessing same-sex unions. Then, just as the Standing Committee had predicted the month before, the House of Bishops easily passed the resolution on July 9 by roll call vote. One hundred and eleven bishops voted yea, 41 nay, and 3 abstained.[41] Edward Salmon and William Skilton joined Lawrence in voting against it as did some of the other bishops of Province IV such as Andrew Waldo. Some of the southeastern bishops who voted against the measure, as Waldo, went on to accept it and to develop ways of implementing the resolution in their dioceses. The proposed resolution moved to the House of Deputies the next day where South Carolinian David Thurlow delivered a minority report against the resolution on the floor of the House.[42] Upon Thurlow's wish, an addition was made to the original proposed resolution to allow any clergy or layperson to refuse to support the Church's action: "That this convention honor the theological diversity of this church in regard to matters of human sexuality, and that

36. Ibid., 512.
37. Ibid., 505.
38. Ibid., 728.
39. Mueller, Mary Ann. "GC2012: South Carolina's Actions: A Shot Heard around the Anglican Communion." Virtueonline, July 12, 2012, http://www.virtueonline.com/portal/modules/news/article.php?storyid=16301.
40. Ibid.
41. *Journal of the 77th General Convention*, 200–203.
42. Ibid., 562.

no bishop, priest, deacon or lay person should be coerced or penalized in any manner, nor suffer any canonical disabilities, as a result of his or her conscientious objection to or support for the 77th General Convention's action with regard to the Blessing of Same-Sex Relationships."[43] This was a provision in the final resolution. The diocesan bishop would have full discretion over the use of the liturgy in his or her own diocese. This meant, of course, that Lawrence could declare right off that he would not allow the liturgy in his diocese. That would be the end of the matter in the Diocese of South Carolina. Some diocesan bishops actually did this in the months ahead.

As one will see, Thurlow's influence in the Episcopal Church outlived the schism. In the General Convention of 2015, his same statement, word-for-word down to "the 77th" was placed in Resolution A054 that concerned same-sex marriage in the Church. In the question-and-answer period in the House of Deputies on July 1, 2015, a questioner, Deputy Wong, of Central Gulf Coast, asked about the process of making the proposed resolution. Brian Baker, the Chair of the Special Committee that made the proposed resolution, responded that paragraph 19 of A054 was suggested by Deputy David Thurlow three years earlier when the convention debated the resolution on the liturgy for the blessing of same-sex unions. The committee had decided to add the "Thurlow amendment" once again to the new resolution for the same reasons as before.[44]

Thurlow's provision allowing anyone to opt out of same-sex blessings was the major concession in the House of Deputies to the conservative side but it had no effect on the South Carolina delegation that had already decided how they would vote. As with the bishops, both orders of the House of Deputies easily approved A049. Among the laity, the vote was 86 yea, 19 nay, and 5 divided; among the clergy the vote was 85 yea, 22 nay, and 4 split.[45] This meant the final adoption of the resolution on the blessing of same-sex unions. After many years of controversy, the Episcopal Church finally settled this landmark reform and did so with overwhelming approval. In the end, it turned out to be not very controversial at all. This fact, however, did nothing to impress the implacable foes from South Carolina.

The several resolutions in question addressed two different facets of the larger subject of the interaction of the Church and sexuality: rights for homosexual persons and equality for transgendered persons in the life of the Episcopal Church. They were not the same issue, but Lawrence, and other like-minded conservatives opposed them both for the same reasons. They believed that God assigned gender and it was wrong for anyone to question that, let alone alter it. The resolutions that the Episcopal Church Convention adopted in 2012 simply tried to treat homosexual and transgendered people as everyone else, worthy children of God with the same rights in Christ's church as anyone else. It was clear that the Episcopal Church, once and for all, identified itself as a champion of

---

43. "2012–A049, Authorize Liturgical Resources for Blessing Same-Gender Relationships." Episcopal Church, General Convention 2012, July 12, 2012, http://www.episcopalarchives.org/cgi-bin/acts/acts_resolution.pl?resolution=2012-A049.

44. Episcopal Church. General Convention 2015. HOB 07-01-2015 Afternoon, @ 1:18, http://livestream.com/accounts/12656718/events/3897940.

45. *Journal of the 77th General Convention*, 562.

homosexual and transgendered rights at the time when most Christian churches were still adamantly refusing to do so.

Immediately after the resolution on the blessing of same-sex unions cleared final passage in the House of Deputies on July 10, the South Carolina delegation moved into pre-planned action. Lawrence and the delegation issued a public statement that they immediately posted on the diocesan website. It quickly spread to other outlets. It referred to the Standing Committee's declaration of June 15 "the clear position of our diocese on marriage."[46] It continued: "We grieve that General Convention has further departed from those values and adopted a resolution to permit pastoral license to violate the existing canons on marriage. We believe this decision will seriously wound the Church."[47] It was signed by the entire delegation. Lawrence and his delegation's bitter anger, hostility and resentment came through clearly even though the statement itself was inaccurate. The resolution had nothing to do with the traditional definition of marriage as they claimed. Back in South Carolina, Kendall Harmon unsurprisingly blasted the Episcopal Church on his website, Titus One Nine: "This General Convention action is unbiblical, unchristian, unAnglican and unseemly (. . .). The Episcopal Church moves further away from Jesus Christ and His teaching. It thereby makes it necessary for the Diocese of South Carolina to take further decisive and dramatic action to distance itself from this false step."[48] The problem was in deciding on "distance." There was almost none left.

The Walk-Out

The delegation went on to declare an action of protest: "The South Carolina deputation has concluded that we cannot continue with business as usual. We all agree that we cannot and will not remain on the floor of the House and act as if all is normal (. . .) our action is not to be construed as a departure from the Episcopal Church."[49] Burwell and Hamilton agreed to remain in the Convention to hold the diocesan place while the rest of the delegation conspicuously absented itself for the last two days. Not one other of the more than one hundred delegations at the Convention walked out. What was this protest meant to achieve? The resolutions were history. There was nothing to be accomplished by this in the Convention, but there was plenty to be gained back in the Diocese of South Carolina. Word spread like wildfire that the delegation had walked out of the General Convention in righteous indignation. It was all over the news at home.

Lawrence prepared for his next moves. He knew that time was of the essence as the Convention was set to adjourn on the day after next, July 12. On the evening of the day the despised resolution had been passed, July 10, he attended a dinner for his good friends from the Trinity School for Ministry and then met with the South Carolina

46. "S.C. Deputation Statement, July 10, 2012." Diocese of South Carolina, July 10, 2012, http://www.diosc.com/sys/news-events/latest-news/431-sc-deputation-statement-july-10-2012.

47. Ibid.

48. Mueller, "GC2012."

49. Hunter, Joy. "South Carolina Differentiates Itself from Actions of General Convention." Diocese of South Carolina, July 12, 2012, as quoted in Episcopal News Service, http://episcopaldigitalnetwork.com/ens/2012/07/12/south-carolina-differentiates-itself-from-actions-of-77th-general-convention.

deputies at 9:00 p.m.[50] No doubt Lawrence shared with the delegates what he planned to do the next day, and the next.

On the following day, July 11, deputies Burwell and Hamilton returned to their seats in the South Carolina section of the Convention alone as the scene at center stage turned from the House of Deputies to the House of Bishops. In the morning session, Bishop Michael Smith, of North Dakota, presented and read a minority report to the House condemning A049.[51] His report, called "The Indianapolis Statement," was a list of seven paragraphs that basically reiterated the points that Lawrence had been making for a long time, most importantly that same-sex union is the same as marriage and introducing a liturgy for the blessing of a same-sex union is the same as making a new marriage liturgy. After his presentation, Smith invited other bishops to sign. In all, twelve bishops signed the statement but not Lawrence. Strangely enough, he ignored this important declaration and did not give a reason in the public record of why he failed to sign it. Most of his close friends and philosophical allies did sign: Bill Love of Albany, Daniel Martins of Springfield, James Stanton of Dallas, Ed Little of Northern Indiana. Even Gregory Brewer of Central Florida signed along with Ed Salmon and Bill Skilton.[52]

Lawrence chose to go it alone in the House of Bishops. According to his own testimony, at 2:15 p.m., he arose, requested, and was granted a private session in the House as a point of Personal Privilege.[53] He addressed his fellow bishops for less than half an hour. After thanking them for their hospitality, generosity, and fairness, he turned to his point, to denounce the three resolutions on the blessing of unions and equality for transgendered persons. He did not hold back: "These resolutions in my opinion are disconcerting changes to the doctrine, discipline and worship of the Episcopal Church (. . .) a departure from the doctrine, discipline and worship of Christ as this Church has received them, therein making it necessary for me to strongly differentiate myself from such actions."[54] He made the same points his friends had made in the morning Statement. As he concluded, he told the bishops that he was leaving the Convention and leaving with the question of whether he could continue in the Episcopal Church.[55] Lawrence later recalled the incident:

> I said that the decisions of the general convention had changed the doctrine, discipline and worship of The Episcopal Church and that I could no longer seek to engage to conform to that. I told them that I would—I was presented with a profound moral—personal moral crisis. I asked them to pray for me, and I had told them I would pray for them, because I had some decisions to make.

50. *Journal of the Two Hundred and Twenty Second (. . .)* 2013, 40.

51. *Journal of the 77th General Convention*, 243.

52. "12 Bishops Submit Dissenting 'Indianapolis Statement.'" Episcopal News Service, July 11, 2012, http://episcopaldigitalnetwork.com/ens/2012/07/11/12-bishops-sumbit-dissenting.

53. *Journal of the Two Hundred and Twenty Second (. . .)* 2013, 40. The only record of this episode in the House of Bishops came from Lawrence himself. The Journal of the 77th General Convention states that the morning session on July 11 ended at 12:49 p.m. and the afternoon session started at 3:07 p.m. It made no mention of Lawrence. *Journal of the 77th General Convention*, 249.

54. Lewis, (the Rev.) Jim. "Bishop Seeks Direction for Self and Diocese." *Jubilate Deo* (Diocese of South Carolina), Fall 2012, 1.

55. Ibid.

I assumed I was working with a body that would give me time to sort through those questions. But they decided to attack.[56]

There was no record that any other bishop joined Lawrence in the walk-out. Some bishops implored him not to leave. The fact that none of his allies, whose supportive friendship he had cultivated for a long time, would join him in his dramatic gesture may explain why he had refused to sign their Statement of the morning. He was back at his hotel by 2:50.[57] He then visited a museum and met the delegation at 9:00 p.m.[58] One reporter wrote that Lawrence did not leave the Convention and was seen around in the evening.[59] He told another reporter, "'I am not leaving The Episcopal Church (. . .) but I need to differentiate myself.'"[60] He did not explain the difference. On the next day, Thursday, July 12, he checked out of his hotel at 7:00 a.m. He arrived home in Charleston at 9:00 p.m.[61] The 77th General Convention of the Episcopal Church adjourned on the same day.

The public records did not reveal the interactions between Lawrence and his fellow bishops during the days of the General Convention, but his diary showed no personal time with any other bishop. The fact that he did not sign the dissenting Indianapolis Statement drawn up by his good friends indicated he was keeping his distance from them. In his farewell statement in the House of Bishops he was alone; and apparently, he did not ask anyone to join him, or even to support him. Indeed, no other bishop and no other diocese would join the defecting South Carolinians. Lawrence's aim in his behavior, then, perhaps was not to impact on the bishops or the Convention. It was in South Carolina that the storm would hit; and it started on the very next morning after Lawrence's late-night return home.

THE AFTERMATH IN SOUTH CAROLINA, JULY–OCTOBER

The Declaration of a Crisis

As Lawrence returned to South Carolina, he faced several viable options available to him at that point. One option was to denounce the controversial resolutions, forbid the blessing of same-sex unions in his diocese, ignore the transgender issue and then return to business as usual within his insular diocese. Another was simply to resign from office and from the Episcopal Church. A third choice was to call a diocesan convention to declare null and void the hated resolutions within the diocese. A fourth was to lead the diocese completely out of the Episcopal Church with himself at its head and the property in hand.

The first option, to ignore the national Church and go about business as usual, was the choice of practically all the solidly conservative bishops of the Episcopal Church.

---

56. "Deposition Transcript—Mark J. Lawrence," 168.
57. Jim Lewis, "Bishop Seeks."
58. Ibid.
59. Mueller, "GC2012."
60. Mueller, Mary Ann. "SC: Bishop Mark Lawrence Leads his Delegation Out of General Convention." Virtueonline, July 11, 2012, http://www.virtueonline.org/portal/modules/news/article.php?storyid=16297.
61. *Journal of the Two Hundred and Twenty Second (. . .) 2013*, 40.

They announced immediately, as they had every right to do, that they would not allow the blessings of same-sex unions under any conditions in their dioceses and went on to ignore the issue of transgendered clergy and to run their dioceses as they had been doing. Although this was an obvious choice, signs indicated that this option was not a likely move in South Carolina as bishop, delegation, and leaders as Harmon all had said that business could not go on as usual between the diocese and the Episcopal Church although what that meant was not clear.

The second choice, to resign as bishop and leave the Episcopal Church, was even more farfetched. Over the years, several bishops had done such for one reason or another. However, Lawrence and the majority of people in his diocese had bonded as one. For a long time, he had thought of himself and his diocese as the same entity, "we." This was proven in 2011 when the Standing Committee resolved in secret to withdraw the diocese from the Episcopal Church if any action were taken by the Disciplinary Board against their bishop. There was no public record that Lawrence ever suggested his resignation and removal from the Diocese of South Carolina. His leaving the diocese seemed out of the question in the summer of 2012.

The third option, to call a special diocesan convention, was certainly a viable one. Lawrence had established a habit of calling conventions frequently to address critical problems. A new meeting could declare the hated resolutions "null and void" in the diocese, give everyone a chance to vent hostility against the national Church and reassert defiant local sovereignty. There were several problems with this course of action, however. In the first place, the resolution on the blessing of same-sex unions did not need to be nullified since the diocesan bishop already had the choice of forbidding it on his or her own. The resolutions on transgendered clergy were likewise non-threatening because ordinations of deacons and priests were always ultimately at the discretion of the bishop. Yet another consideration was that earlier conventions had left almost no room for more distancing from the mother Church. Thus, if a special convention were summoned, there would be a problem of exactly what it was supposed to accomplish.

The fourth option in view was to lead a complete separation of the majority of the diocese from the Episcopal Church. This had certainly been a big topic of discussion for a long time although Lawrence had protested repeatedly he did not "intend" to leave the Episcopal Church. Harmon hinted of separation in his public pronouncement of July 10. Lawrence also hinted as his departing shot in the House of Bishops on July 11. The obvious problem with this was how to leave with the diocesan and parish properties in hand. Declaring independence would be easy. Following it up with possession of the assets would not be so easy. Long, difficult, and expensive court battles between the diocese and the Episcopal Church would be a guaranteed certainty if Lawrence chose this option.

As events would soon show, at some point Lawrence chose to follow the last option although the existing public records do not reveal exactly when he and the diocesan leaders made their decision. He had prepared himself and the diocese for General Convention long in advance; and he knew what was almost certain to happen in it. It was entirely possible that he plotted out a course of action for himself well before July of 2012. He certainly had had plenty of time in which to do it. He got to work immediately on his return home. It was surely no coincidence that the first person he was to see on his first day back was

Kendall Harmon, at 9:30 in the morning on Friday, July 13.[62] From there, events moved quickly and decisively. It would soon become clear that a breaking point had been reached in the bishop's and in the diocese's relations with the Episcopal Church.

Lawrence lost no time in proceeding in his reaction to the controversial resolutions. First, though, he would need to set the stage to be sure that everyone understood his reasons for moving along. He needed to declare a diocesan crisis, explain the causes of the crisis supposedly thrust upon them by the national Church, and direct urgent action within the diocese to address the crisis. Strategy in place, this was the tactic he employed in the two weeks after the General Convention. He started right away, on his first afternoon back in Charleston when he wrote a two-page letter to the diocese laying out once again his views of the supposed fatal errors of the Episcopal Church. He required the clergy across the diocese to read it to congregations at Sunday services just two days later, July 15.

Lawrence's July 13th open letter to the diocese built upon his highly visible publicity campaign of the two previous months when before, then during, the General Convention he and the diocesan leadership had loudly denounced the Episcopal Church in the strongest possible terms for its reforms on sexuality. The bishop's departing dramatic scene in the House of Bishops and the delegation's flourishing walk-out from the House of Deputies were meant to draw as much attention as possible to South Carolina's dissent from the national Church. It was to be the icing on the cake. It worked. All the talk was about the conflict between the diocese and the national Church. If the atmosphere were not crackling enough with volatile electricity before the Convention, it definitely was afterwards, at least in South Carolina. As in 1860, everyone could sense an impending violent storm, and many people perhaps actually longed for it to arrive, whatever the consequences, anything to relieve the unbearable tension and stifling atmosphere that was smothering so many good church people in South Carolina.

Lawrence's letter to the diocese was meant to capitalize on the moment. The contents, however, really contained nothing new as they were only a reemphasis and summary of his already well-known public views.[63] The first paragraph declared a crisis, the next several gave the reasons for the crisis, and the last few revealed the justifiably urgent actions he planned to take in the near future to address the crisis. The crisis, he said, was that the Episcopal Church in its General Convention made "a significant and distressing departure from the doctrine, discipline and worship of Christ as this Church has received them." Then, he turned to the reasons for the crisis employing trigger words and phrases to set the mode of emergency: "distressing," "uneasiness," "the house is on fire," "conflict, "departs," and "jeopardy." All the reasons, he said, derived from the four controversial resolutions that stood "in direct conflict" with the historic religion of the Episcopal Church.

The largest part of Lawrence's letter to the diocese returned to his favorite whipping-horse of the day, homosexuality. There was nothing new here. He unleashed his harshest

---

62. Ibid.

63. Lawrence, (the Rt. Rev.) Mark. "Bishop Lawrence Addresses Diocese Following 77th General Convention." Diocese of South Carolina, July 15, 2012, http://www.diosc.com/sys/news-events/latest-news/433-bishop-lawrence-addresses-diocese-following-77th-general-convention.

words on the two resolutions concerning transsexual persons: "an even more incoherent departure from the teaching of Holy Scripture and from our Episcopalian and Anglican Heritage."[64] He said they opened the door to complete sexual anarchy, a fate he implied was even worse than homosexual marriage. Finally, the last two paragraphs of the letter laid out his plan of action in meetings with diocesan councils, the deans, and clergy within the next two weeks. He said that going about business as before the Convention was not an option. Finally, he concluded that he would ask the leaders and clergy what the diocese should do in view of the changes in the Episcopal Church. Although Lawrence left it at that, the implications of these final thoughts could not have been lost on anyone. He left dangling the unmistakable idea of secession from the Church. He would leave it at that for the people to mull over for the next few weeks. After reading the letter in church, the clergyperson was supposed to encourage everyone to take home a printed copy which were to be available. And, in case anyone missed it, the letter was reprinted on the front page of the next issue of *Jubilate Deo*.

Delivered as it was in the heat of the moment, the letter served to help further galvanize the majority of the diocese for some sort of drastic action although exactly what action was not spelled out. The majority of communicants certainly trusted their bishop implicitly. They took the letter at face value, but in retrospect the letter had numerous problems. In the first place, it all but declared the vast majority of bishops in the Episcopal Church heretics because of their support for the controversial resolutions. He indirectly accused more than one hundred fellow bishops of overthrowing the doctrine, discipline, and worship of the Episcopal Church. This was truly an astonishing charge. One can only imagine the reaction of the bishops to Lawrence's immoderate accusation, or at least implication. For the moment, they kept quiet no doubt in dismay over what was going on in South Carolina.

Lawrence said nothing in his letter to remind people of what the diocese had already done *vis-à-vis* the Episcopal Church. In view of the earlier resolutions of the diocesan conventions, there did not have to be a crisis at all. The diocese had clearly declared itself to be sovereign, that is, self-governing. It had said that it was not subject to the measures of the General Convention since it was a founding diocese of the Church, only later dioceses were. It had declared null and void General Convention resolutions it did not like. And, most importantly, it had repealed its accession to the canons of the Episcopal Church. Lawrence reminded the people of none of this. The majority of communicants dutifully and faithfully bought his story. A public sense of great crisis arrived.

Lawrence was not content to end his publicity campaign with a major blitz of the diocese. He decided to spread the word to the general public through public media. A week after the Convention, he gave an interview to NBC News charging that the "sexual and gender anarchy" in the Episcopal Church would doom it to greater decline.[65] On July 24, he wrote an article for the Charleston *Post and Courier*.[66] It was published in the paper on Sunday, July 29. It was essentially a condensed version of his July 13 letter to

---

64. Ibid.

65. Bratu, Becky. "Is Liberal Christianity Signing its own Death Warrant?" NBC News, March 27, 2013, http://www.NBCnews.com.

66. *Journal of the Two Hundred and Twenty Second (. . .)* 2013, 41.

the diocese.[67] Once again, he blamed it all on the resolutions of the General Convention: "the Episcopal Church was not content merely to change the standard of Christian marriage to include same-sex partners. It voted to step unreservedly into the normalization of transgender, transsexual, queer and questioning human self-understandings." Once again, he made shocking and sweeping accusations without evidence while omitting the actual resolutions themselves. Then he repeated his well-known beliefs about sexual identity and about marriage before ending with the same dangling thought: "the Diocese of South Carolina must distance itself" without any explanation of what that might mean. There was only one small tie left, accession to the Episcopal Church's Constitution. In case anyone missed it, this article was reprinted as the lead in the next issue of *Jubilate Deo*.

Not published in the next issue, or any issue, of *Jubilate Deo* was an article in the same *Post and Courier* (July 29, 2012) by Melinda Lucka, the head of the Episcopal Forum.[68] While it was clear that the majority of communicants in the diocese were duly aroused more than ever to oppose the Episcopal Church, there was still the irrepressible Forum, still the mouthpiece of the discarded minority that wanted only to keep the classical Anglican three-legged stool of Scripture, reason, and tradition. Its task was getting much harder. Lucka tried to set the record straight on what was actually in the resolutions. She also recounted the moves over the years of the diocesan leaders to pull the diocese away from the national Church and warned darkly of the obvious end of such a trend. Lucka's letter was all but ignored by the diocesan leadership which had long ago lost concern about the power of the Forum or any other group to stop its course of "differentiation." In fact, there was no powerful counter-voice to Lawrence and the diocesan leadership in South Carolina and had not been for years. There was really no one to challenge Lawrence let alone call him to account for his highly individualistic interpretation of the controversial resolutions and the errors of the Episcopal Church.

With the letter to the diocese and the article in the main Charleston newspaper, Lawrence had done about all he could do in July of 2012 to publicize his views on the Episcopal Church and the impending crisis in the diocese. There was no doubt that he succeeded well in claiming the field on his home turf. The letter was highly effective as it had been read in every local Episcopal church with hard copies spread about the diocese. No regular churchgoer could have missed it. The newspaper article was somewhat effective in setting out the position of the diocese among the general public although many non-Episcopalians would not have understood, or even cared about, the details of the issues or Episcopal Church government. They would understand us-against-them, local rule versus tyranny "from off."

Lawrence solidified the power structure of the diocese. On the third, fourth, and fifth days after his return to Charleston from Convention, he huddled with the entire

67. Lawrence, (the Rt. Rev.) Mark. "Church Needs to be Clear in Teaching What is Written." *The Post and Courier* (Charleston, SC), July 29, 2012, www.postandcourier.com/features/faith_and_values/church-needs-to-be-clear-in-teaching-what-is-writtensierra/article_521b7718-faa4-5847-8a14-dba0cd85a2a2.html.

68. Lucka, Melinda. "The Episcopal Church Remains Vibrant Amidst Controversy." eNewsletter of the Episcopal Forum of SC, August 2, 2012, http://www.mynewsletterbuilder.com/email/newsletter/1411423806.

diocesan leadership. All of the meetings were closed; and no report of any of them has ever been released to the public. He called first the Standing Committee to sit as the Council of Advice, on Monday, July 16. He spent the morning preparing for it and the afternoon in a four and one-half session with it.[69] The next day, he met the same committee again for three hours.[70] On the following day, he conferred with the deans of the convocations for two and one-half hours.[71] After consulting with the established leadership, he then turned to the clergy of the diocese. He called a clergy day at St. Paul's in Summerville on Wednesday, July 25.

Lawrence spent the morning of the 25th preparing for the clergy meeting and the afternoon (1:00—4:50) with the attending priests and deacons from across the diocese.[72] The veil of secrecy continued. Very few details have even been released about this clergy conference. Once again, the meeting was private and no record of Lawrence's remarks to the assembly has ever been made public. In fact, the only first-hand source of information on the meeting came from Lawrence's assistant, Jim Lewis, who posted a brief account on the diocesan website on July 30.[73] Lawrence related to the assembly his already well-known views on the controversial resolutions and the events that had happened in the General Convention. He clearly threatened to leave the Episcopal Church when he said that the Church had crossed a line that he could not cross. A newspaper source indicated Lawrence advocated schism: "At the 25 July meeting of the South Carolina clergy, Bishop Mark Lawrence said he longer sees a place for the diocese in the General Convention."[74] However, in his remarks, Lawrence apparently gave no hint that he would leave his position in the diocese. Quite the contrary, the language was all about Lawrence leading the diocese into the foreseeable future. He announced a vacation to go to mountaintops and deserts to seek discernment and said he would return to consult with the diocesan leadership on where to go from there. Finally, he asked the clergy to remain united; he need not have asked. The great majority of the clergy present were firmly bonded to their bishop.

In the two weeks after General Convention, Lawrence controlled the public message in South Carolina and easily reaffirmed his union with the diocesan leadership and clergy. He had created a sense of crisis greater than ever; and he raised the unmistakable idea of leaving the Episcopal Church. As he departed South Carolina for a nineteen-day absence, he left behind an atmosphere of tense drama in which the people of the diocese could brew in uncertainty for a while. He also left with confidence of unity; he could rest assured that whatever might happen, he and the majority of the diocese were one. As he

69. *Journal of the Two Hundred and Twenty Second (. . .)* 2013, 41.

70. Ibid.

71. Ibid.

72. Ibid.

73. Lewis, (the Rev.) Jim. "Bishop Lawrence Meets with Clergy of the Diocese of South Carolina Following General Convention." Diocese of South Carolina, July 30, 2012, http://www.diosc.com/sys/news-events/latest-news/435-bishop-lawrence-meets-with-clergy-of-the-diocese-of-south-carolina-following-general-convention.

74. "South Carolina Mulls Secession." *The Church of England Newspaper*, August 12, 2012, 5, as quoted in Conger, August 15, 2012, http://geoconger.wordpress.com/2012/08/15/south-carolina-mulls-secession-the-church-of-england-newspaper-august-12-2012-p-5.

promised, he went off to mountaintops and deserts, literally: California, Utah, Colorado and Nevada. Meanwhile, in his absence, speculation built steadily even well beyond South Carolina. In England, *The Church of England Newspaper* carried a story entitled "South Carolina Mulls Secession," that began "The Diocese of South Carolina is on the brink of secession from the Episcopal Church."[75] The whole world could see the obvious.

The Secret Plan, August

Lawrence returned to Charleston on August 18th as everyone eagerly awaited word on what he had discerned afar. If people expected their returning bishop to proclaim a grand revelation of what was to happen to the diocese in the near future, they were to be disappointed. Lawrence offered no great public pronouncement, no message to the people of what the discernment had brought. Instead, it was more of the same for the communicants who had now been on tenderhooks for a long time. While there was nothing new for the public, evidently matters were moving apace in the hidden world of the diocesan leadership.

On his third day back, August 21, Lawrence spent the day on very important business with the Standing Committee and his lawyers. The committee sat for four and one-half hours (10:30 a.m.–3:00 p.m.). Afterwards, he met with his lawyers for an hour, then talked on the phone again with Wade Logan, the chancellor, and Alan Runyan.[76] Signs suggested that August 21 was the defining moment for the diocese in the background of the schism. Almost nothing, however, has ever been publicly revealed about the events of that turning-point day. The participants said nothing at all about what happened, then or later. The diocesan leadership released only two very brief, cryptic messages to the public about the Standing Committee meeting. These are the only pieces of information about the fateful meeting of bishop and Standing Committee on August 21 that have ever been released publicly. The diocesan office posted one sentence that day on its website: "The Bishop met today with the Standing Committee, which unanimously approved the course of action he outlined for the Diocese of South Carolina."[77] This tantalizingly terse sentence revealed three truths: 1-a plan was presented to the Standing Committee, 2-Lawrence delivered it, and 3-the agreement was unanimous. Of course, everyone's next question was, "What was the plan?" For that they would have to wait. The next question was, "Why will not they reveal the plan now?"

Many weeks later, the "diocesan administrator" posted an after-the-fact time line of events on the diocesan website which included another puzzling sentence about August 21: "Lawrence meets with Standing Committee. They unanimously agree to allow him to seek to negotiate with the Presiding Bishop for a peaceful way forward."[78] This was an intriguing, and possible apocryphal, statement that begged for more explanation. "Allow;" what did that mean? Allow implied permission; why would Lawrence need permission to

75. Ibid.
76. *Journal of the Two Hundred and Twenty Second* (. . .) 2013, 42.
77. As quoted in Scepiscopalians.com, August 21, 2012.
78. "Timeline of Events." Diocese of South Carolina, January 3, 2013, http://www.diosc.com/sys/news-events/40-aboutus/forthemedia/486-timeline-of-events.

talk with the Presiding Bishop? What did "negotiate" mean? That word implies give and take on two or more sides of an issue. One should recall that the position of presiding bishop of the Episcopal Church is not one of policy making. All policy decisions along with rules and regulations are made by the triennial General Convention. The presiding bishop is an administrative position defined by strict terms in the Church's Constitution and Canons. What negotiation Jefferts Schori could do with Lawrence would be highly restricted. Certainly, the fundamental question prompted here was "What was the goal of the negotiation?" In other words, exactly what did the Bishop Lawrence and Standing Committee want from the presiding bishop? Besides, why did they need any negotiation since in their eyes the diocese was independent and self-governing?

Lawrence met his hand-picked deans on the next day, August 22, to inform them of his plan in a two and one-half hour meeting.[79] The absolute secrecy continued. No word ever leaked out from this meeting, not even a sentence from the diocesan office. When the deans spoke of the meeting at all, they did so in strictly guarded terms. One of them, John Barr, was reported as saying: "Bishop Mark has faithfully sought God's Leading and has been given a vision for the future of this Diocese."[80] What was this "vision"? On August 25, Lawrence attended the consecration of Steve Wood as the new bishop of the Diocese of the Carolinas in the Anglican Church in North America. Lawrence noted in his diary that he did not vest or process.[81] Wood remained the rector of St. Andrew's Anglican Church in Mt. Pleasant; and Lawrence kept up his friendly relations with him.

Six days after Lawrence's August 21st meeting with the Standing Committee and the agreement on the secret plan, he met Bishop Waldo in Columbia for a two-hour session.[82] Each bishop was accompanied by his chancellor. The four discussed the crisis in the Diocese of South Carolina and agreed to seek a meeting with the presiding bishop. Lawrence told Waldo it would be "really difficult" for the Diocese of South Carolina to stay in the Episcopal Church after the passage of the same-sex blessing resolution.[83] Afterwards, Waldo arranged with Jefferts Schori to meet with him and Lawrence in New York City on October 3. Still, it remained entirely unclear what Lawrence hoped to gain from such a meeting or what he saw as an acceptable negotiated settlement. Lawrence did not inform Waldo at the meeting on the 27th that he had a secret plan for the Diocese of South Carolina. When interviewed in 2014, Waldo said Lawrence had never informed him about the contents of the secret plan, not even about its existence.[84] It is safe to assume the Presiding Bishop likewise knew nothing of Lawrence's secret plan.

What we now know about August 21 is that on that day Lawrence finally presented a plan of action for the future of the diocese, the Standing Committee unanimously approved it, apparently, that plan was set firmly in place, and people were told there was a

---

79. *Journal of the Two Hundred and Twenty Second (. . .)* 2013, 42.

80. Skardon, Steve. "Post-Vacation, Bishop Dampens Speculation on 'Godly' Vision, Leaving the Episcopal Church." South Carolina Episcopalians, August 30, 2012, http://www.scepiscopalians.com/2012_Reports.php.

81. *Journal of the Two Hundred and Twenty Second (. . .)* 2013, 42.

82. Ibid.

83. Waldo, interview with author.

84. Ibid.

plan. The details of the plan were known only to the diocesan leadership. Everything that happened later occurred in the shadow of the landmark secret plan of August 21, 2012.

It seemed then, Lawrence had indeed used his pilgrimage to deserts and mountaintops in early August to "discern" a plan for the future of the diocese. By the time he returned home, apparently, he had decided on a clear-cut course of action for the diocese to take. There was never a hint that he would act alone without the diocese. He did not consult any known parties as he mulled over his plan while on vacation. He returned to Charleston to present it to his inner circle who wholeheartedly agreed to it. He gradually let the rest of the diocesan leadership in on his plan but everyone else would have to wait, how long no one knew. The wearing suspense did not abate.

Whatever the plan was, it must have been a very grave one because it hung over Lawrence like a heavy cloud for some time. On Friday, August 24, he spent the entire afternoon, three and a half hours in what he described as "prayer for Diocese/seeking God's guidance."[85] A few days after that, on August 29, he met the Diocesan Council for three and a half hours perhaps to talk with them about the plan.[86] How much he revealed of the content of the plan to them remained unclear. Contrary to the earlier leak-free meetings, this one had a participant who was willing to talk, at least according to one reporter.[87] The attendee related that Lawrence did not seem so sure of things after all when he told the council "'I did not bring back any tablets. I did not bring back any jewels.'"[88] The report went on that the bishop insisted he had no intention of resigning from office and had no plan to call a special convention as had been his habit. At least some people were left puzzling over the mixed messages and why Lawrence had not been so confidential with this group after he had been with the Standing Committee and the deans a few days earlier.

Although at present one cannot document the secret plan of August 21, 2012, judging from subsequent events, it is reasonable to assume it was an agreement that the diocese would secede from the Episcopal Church.

Outward and Inward Signs, September–October 2

With Lawrence's secret plan for the diocese firmly in place among the core diocesan leadership, with Waldo's efforts to intervene with the national Church, and with a date set for the two bishops to meet the Presiding Bishop in New York City on October 3, events picked up momentum in September. While there were outward signs of movement toward a negotiated, peaceful settlement with the Episcopal Church, events within the diocesan leadership indicated the opposite. On September 18, Lawrence met at 9:00 a.m. with lawyers Logan and Runyan, Paul Fuener (chair of the Standing Committee), and his assistant, James Lewis.[89] They then met with the Standing Committee from

---

85. *Journal of the Two Hundred and Twenty Second (. . .)* 2013, 42.
86. Ibid.
87. Skardon, "Post Vacation."
88. Ibid.
89. *Journal of the Two Hundred and Twenty Second (. . .)* 2013, 44.

10:30 a.m. to 3:00 p.m. The committee went into a discussion of disassociation from the Episcopal Church. They talked of the need to clarify provisions in the diocesan constitution and canons regarding the diocese's right to withdraw from the Episcopal Church. They resolved to seek an official, written clarification from the bishop who, according to the revised canons, had sole and final authority to interpret the diocesan constitution and canons. The committee resolved to ask of the bishop:

> (1)What is the meaning and function of Article 1 of the Diocese's Constitution, particularly the language that the Diocese "accedes to the Constitution" of the Episcopal Church? (2)Can the Diocese withdraw the accession referred to in Article 1 and/or its membership as a constituent member diocese of the Episcopal Church? (3)What are the procedures by which the accession and membership can be withdrawn, including whether such decisions can take effect without amending Article 1 and what diocesan bodies or offices are authorized to make such decisions? (4)Does the letter dated June 16, 2011 from the Secretary of the Executive Council of the Episcopal Church, subsequently copied to the Diocese, have any effect on the interpretation of the Diocese's Constitution and Canons?[90]

Two days after the Standing Committee meeting, Fuener, as chair of the committee, sent a formal letter to Lawrence requesting an official ruling on certain provisions. The origin of Fuener's letter of September 20 is unclear but it is interesting to note that he and Lawrence met with their lawyers, Logan and Runyan, just before the session that was to vote unanimously to send the letter, the lawyers were present in the Committee meeting, and the Committee went into executive session just before and just after it resolved to ask the questions of the bishop. There was no mention of such a notion in the public references of the Standing Committee before September 18. At any rate, it was clear from this that in September of 2012 the concern of the diocesan leadership was not how to stay in the Episcopal Church but how to leave it. Indeed, in the meeting of the 18th, Lawrence notified the committee that ordinations of candidates for the diaconate and priesthood were "problematical (. . .) because of the vow to conform to the doctrine, discipline and worship of The Episcopal Church."[91]

Fuener's letter of September 20 to Lawrence spelled out several questions that had been raised in the committee resolution of 18th. The first and most important was the meaning of Article One which read: "The Diocese of South Carolina accedes to the Constitution of the Protestant Episcopal Church (. . .) in the event that any provision of the Constitution (. . .) of the Protestant Episcopal Church (. . .) is inconsistent with, or contradictory to, the Constitution and Canons of the Protestant Episcopal Diocese of South Carolina, the Constitution and Canons of this Diocese shall prevail."[92] The next question was, "Can the diocese withdraw its accession and its membership in the Episcopal Church?" Then, how would the diocese go about doing this? Finally, did the

90. "Minutes of the Standing Committee." [September 18, 2012].

91. Ibid.

92. Lawrence, (the Rt. Rev.) Mark, to the Rev. Paul Fuener, Chair of the Standing Committee, October 2, 2013. "Episcopal Church Takes Action Against the Bishop and Diocese of South Carolina," Attachment C—Interpretation of Constitution and Canons. Diocese of South Carolina, October 17, 2012, http://www.diosc.com/sys/index.php?option=com_contents&view=article&id=452:the-episcopal-church-takes-action-against-the-diocese-of-south-carolina-special-convention-called&Itemid=75.

opinion of the Episcopal Church executive committee have any validity in the diocese? Thus, the entire letter was asking for the bishop's authoritative guidance on how to leave the Episcopal Church. It is hard to imagine that the committee did not know the answers in advance. These matters had been under discussion for a long time. A year earlier the Standing Committee had voted to leave the Episcopal Church if Lawrence were charged by the Disciplinary Board.

While working with the diocesan leadership, Lawrence could not forget his relations with Waldo and with the people of the diocese. Lawrence drove to Columbia on September 19 for a two-hour luncheon meeting with Waldo at Waldo's home in expectation of their meeting with the Presiding Bishop scheduled for October 3.[93] Upon his return to Charleston that day, the first person he talked with on the phone was Kendall Harmon.[94] For the public, Lawrence wrote a brief but tantalizing notice to the thousands of faithful communicants who had been left in the dark and were anxiously wondering what was going on. He wanted to let them know that he and the Standing Committee were at work without revealing any details. On September 22, he posted a terse comment on the diocesan website: "we announced last month on August 20th that the Standing Committee and I were in agreement on a course of action regarding the future (. . .) [it is] imprudent to reveal that course of action. Things are progressing—we have not stopped or dropped the ball (. . .). I will communicate to you the details at the very earliest moment such a communication is prudent."[95] The Rev. Paul Fuener, chair of the Standing Committee and rector of Prince George Winyah parish in Georgetown, echoed this in the September 2012 parish newsletter, *The Cross and Crown*: "This is one of those times in life where to announce in advance what you are going to do is foolish."[96] In an inadvertently poor choice of words, Fuener wrote: "bank robbers do not announce their intentions in advance."[97]

Lawrence dated his official letter of response to Fuener and the Standing Committee as October 2, two weeks after its request. It was a well-prepared, dense legal treatise of sixteen pages going into detail on the committee's questions. It had all the appearance of having been written over many hours by one or more lawyers. Lawrence made no mention of working on it in his diary. Indeed, he was away in Texas for four days of the period.[98] It was full of legalistic language sprinkled with court cases that a non-attorney would not have known readily. Regardless of who may have written it, the letter carried only one signature, Lawrence's. It certainly expressed his well-known personal beliefs and thoughts.

Lawrence addressed the questions raised by the Standing Committee then gave his answers and rationales. The basic point he made was that the Diocese of South Carolina was an independent and sovereign entity. It had existed before the Episcopal Church; and it had not surrendered its sovereignty when it acceded to the Constitution of the

---

93. Waldo, interview with author.
94. *Journal of the Two Hundred and Twenty Second (. . .)* 2013, 44.
95. "'Imprudent' to Disclose Secret Plan Now, says Bishop Lawrence." South Carolina Episcopalians, September 22, 2012, http://www.scepiscopalians.com/2012-Reports.php.
96. *The Cross and Crown*. Prince George Winyah Episcopal Church, Georgetown SC, September, 2012.
97. Ibid.
98. *Journal of the Two Hundred and Twenty Second (. . .)* 2013, 45.

Episcopal Church. The diocese was free to change its own constitution and canons at will including removing its accession to the Constitution of the Episcopal Church. Only later dioceses were required to give unqualified accession to the Constitution and Canons of the Episcopal Church. Too, he said, there were two glaring omissions in the Episcopal Church Constitution. It did not have a supremacy clause declaring the General Convention resolutions to be binding on the dioceses, and it lacked a provision prohibiting a diocese from leaving the Church.[99] In the end, Lawrence gave answers to the questions that had been raised. On accession, he declared "both withdrawal of the accession to the Constitution and withdrawal from membership in the association are permitted."[100] On how disassociation could be accomplished, Lawrence wrote "decisions concerning accessions, withdrawals of accession and decisions concerning association membership can be effected by any competent diocesan authority, including the Diocesan Convention, the Bishop acting as Ecclesiastical Authority of the Diocese, the Standing Committee."[101] On the subject of the Church's Executive Council, Lawrence declared, unsurprisingly, that its opinions had no effect in South Carolina.[102] In conclusion, he all but appealed for secession: " [the Diocese's] legal existence as a separate religious society incorporated in the state of South Carolina would continue uninterrupted if it elected to terminate its membership in that association [the Episcopal Church]."[103] Thus, at the very moment when Lawrence was publicly working with Waldo and Jefferts Schori supposedly to negotiate a peaceful settlement, he was clearly encouraging, if not urging, the diocesan leadership to remove the diocese from the Episcopal Church.

If Lawrence were pressing the suggestion of secession from the Episcopal Church, he was not to be disappointed. He presented his letter dated October 2 at the opening of the October 2 meeting of the Standing Committee sitting as the Board of Directors and attended by lawyers Logan and Runyan. They sat for three hours, from 9:30 a.m. to 12:30 p.m. with a full agenda of business. The members would scarcely have had time to read thoroughly, digest, and discuss Lawrence's lengthy and weighty letter and conduct all its other business. Nevertheless, they went into executive session then accepted the letter and directly moved to action. Ann Hester Willis offered a motion, seconded by Rev. Greg Snyder, for a resolution that sounded as if it had been prepared in advance rather than on the spot:

> The Protestant Episcopal Church in the Diocese of South Carolina, through its Board of Directors and its Standing Committee, hereby withdraws its accession to the Constitution of the Episcopal Church and disaffiliates with the Episcopal Church by withdrawing its membership from the Episcopal Church. This decision shall be effective immediately upon the taking of any action of any kind by any representative of the Episcopal Church against The Bishop, The Standing

---

99. From a literal standpoint, Lawrence was correct on these two points. By contrast, the U.S. Constitution does have a supremacy clause for laws of Congress. However, it too does not have a provision forbidding a state from seceding from the Union.

100. Lawrence to the Paul Fuener, 13.

101. Ibid., 15.

102. Ibid.

103. Ibid., 16.

Committee or any of its members or the Convention of this Diocese or any of its members (. . .). The Chancellor shall certify to the Ecclesiastical Authority and to the Board of Directors that such condition has occurred which certification shall be conclusive.[104]

The resolution passed unanimously. Within minutes after the meeting concluded, Lawrence left for the airport and a flight to New York City to meet with Waldo and Jefferts Schori. Outwardly he went to discuss ways to settle their differences and keep South Carolina in the Episcopal Church while inwardly he harbored the knowledge that his inner circle had just voted to leave the Episcopal Church as soon as the first opportunity arose.

The Standing Committee resolution of October 2 remained a secret tightly held by the diocesan leadership for the next two weeks. Lawrence revealed it to the Presiding Bishop only on October 17, then to the diocesan clergy on the 19th. Kendall Harmon announced it to the public on October 20. As it was publicized, it was declared to be the retroactive rationale for the *fait accompli* of disassociation. The resolution of October 2 stands as the "smoking gun" of a premeditated plan to remove the diocese from the Episcopal Church. It was a hidden trap set for the unaware presiding bishop.

Another area of evidence supporting the view that the diocesan leadership was planning a schism concerned the diocesan financial accounts. Nancy N. Armstrong, assistant diocesan treasurer, gave an official deposition to the Church lawyers on June 11, 2014, that was entered as evidence on day twelve of the circuit court trial, July 23, 2014. The lawyer asked Armstrong, "Tell me about what was done to move assets in anticipation of this disaffiliation."[105] She replied, "Accounts were opened up and old accounts were closed and the transactions, wire transfers, checks, or whatever needed to be done was done."[106] The lawyer asked, "Why were old accounts closed and new accounts opened?"[107] Armstrong replied, "We wanted to be assured that our assets were protected in an account that would not be subject to being frozen simply with an adverse claims letter. We wanted assurance that it would require a court order for our funds to be frozen."[108] Thus, Armstrong revealed that the diocesan authorities had moved around bank accounts to hide them from the Episcopal Church officers. In the deposition, however, she did not give specific dates and names of banks. One should recall that in the case of the Diocese of Quincy, in January of 2009, the Church lawyers had gone to the bankers holding the old diocesan accounts and convinced them to freeze the funds of several million dollars. Hiding the accounts in South Carolina would preclude the Church from freezing the monies the diocese would need to pay for the litigation after a schism.

By October of 2012, Lawrence had been fighting and losing in the Episcopal Church for more than two decades. He had opposed allowing homosexuals to be ordained as priests only to be swept away. He had fought against non-celibate homosexuals being consecrated as bishops only to see it happen, not once but twice. He had protested

---

104. "Minutes of the Standing Committee." [October 2, 2012].

105. "Deposition of Nancy Armstrong." State of South Carolina, Court of Common Pleas, County of Dorchester, Case No. 2013-CP-18-00013, Exhibit DSC-23, July 23, 2014.

106. Ibid.

107. Ibid.

108. Ibid.

against allowing the blessing of same-sex unions and had denounced the acceptance of transgendered people in the ordained ministry, only to be overwhelmed in the General Convention of 2012. What was there left for which to fight? He had fought the good fight. He had lost in the Episcopal Church on turn after turn. By July of 2012, he had apparently come to the last bridge to cross with the Episcopal Church. As a young man, Lawrence had not gone undefeated as a wrestler by giving in or giving up. If he believed in his cause enough, if he fought long and hard enough, in this case for what he considered true Anglicanism, he could still prevail even without the Episcopal Church. Meanwhile, the diocesan leadership claimed, and believed, they had every right to take the Diocese of South Carolina with them to the new Anglican Realignment, or to "make biblical Anglicans for a global age," as Lawrence had grown fond of saying.

Apparently, Lawrence never gave a second thought of going on alone without the diocese. He had spent too long, worked too hard, bonded too well to think of himself as separate from his diocese. Whatever he had envisioned, it would be as the bishop of the Diocese of South Carolina. On returning from General Convention, he had declared a crisis and rallied the diocese to respond anew. In a flourish, he had gone off to mountaintops and deserts to seek God's guidance in discerning a faithful way forward. Upon his return, he had delivered his lonely discernment to his inner circle. He had presented to them a secret plan of action for the future of the diocese. It had been unanimously and enthusiastically enveloped by the tight-knit, leak-proof dozen or so of the diocesan leadership. While publicly working with Waldo to pursue a peaceful settlement with the Episcopal Church, in private he had provided authoritative guidance to the Standing Committee that resulted in their secret vote on October 2 to withdraw the diocese from the Episcopal Church under certain circumstances. On the very day he had watched as his inner circle unanimously adopted a secret scheme to remove the diocese from the Episcopal Church, he left for New York to talk with the Presiding Bishop about staying in the Episcopal Church. Meanwhile, in the midst of all the post-General Convention drama in the Low Country, out of sight, and far from Charleston, the Disciplinary Board for Bishops had received a new complaint from a group of communicants in the Diocese of South Carolina who had also crossed their last bridge. In September, the Board voted on the complaint. In October, the hurricane hit.

THE EPISCOPAL CHURCH AND BISHOP LAWRENCE, SEPTEMBER–OCTOBER

The Episcopal Church leaders had been in a quandary for years about how to respond in the one-sided war of Bishop Lawrence and the Diocese of South Carolina. By the late summer of 2012, the wayward diocese was on the verge of severing the last small, tenuous tie with the national Church and everyone knew it. Options were running out.

The beginning of the end of the Episcopal Church's toleration of Lawrence came not from the Presiding Bishop, not from the Church leaders, not from the bishops, and not from the General Convention. It came from a group of twenty-four ordinary communicants at home, in the Diocese of South Carolina. Quietly, they gathered in the winter of 2012 under the representation of Charleston attorney Melinda Lucka, head of the Episcopal

Forum, and resolved that they had had enough of Lawrence's anti-Episcopal Church actions in the Episcopal Diocese of South Carolina. Once the diocesan convention of March 2012 had concluded, they decided to file a formal request with the national Church and drew up a letter of complaint against Bishop Lawrence dated March 23, 2012. Since the loyal Episcopalian minority in the diocese had long been cut off from the diocesan power structure, they had little choice but to appeal to the authorities beyond the diocese. The twenty-three signing Lucka's formal letter of complaint of March 23 were: Robert R. Black, Grace Church, Charleston; Barbara G. Mann, Grace Church, Charleston; David W. Mann, Grace Church, Charleston; Robert B. Pinkerton, St. Mark's Chapel, Beaufort; Mrs. Benjamin Bosworth Smith, St. Stephen's, Charleston; the Rev. Colton M. Smith, III; John L. Wilder, Grace Church, Charleston; Virginia C. Wilder, Grace Church, Charleston; Eleanor B. Koets, St. Paul's, Summerville; John Kwist, St. Paul's, Summerville; Margaret S. Kwist, St. Paul's, Summerville; M. Jaquelin Simons, St. Paul's, Summerville; Patricia P. Riley, St. Paul's, Summerville; Thomas W. Riley, St. Paul's, Summerville; Charles G. Carpenter, St. John's, Florence; Margaret A. Carpenter, St. John's, Florence; Frances L. Elmore, St. John's, Florence; Cynthia L. Harding, St. John's, Florence; Flint Harding III, St. John's, Florence; Dolores J. Miller, St. John's, Florence; Warren Mersereau, Church of Our Savior, John's Island; Eleanor Horres, Grace Church, Charleston; and the Rev. Roger W. Smith. Lucka sent the letter of Complaint with its twenty-three other signatures to the Rt. Reverend F. Clayton Matthews, Bishop for Pastoral Development, Episcopal Church Center, New York City who then passed it on to the Disciplinary Board for Bishops. Attached to the letter was a large collection of supporting documents.[109]

The Complaint of 2012 was quite different than that of 2011 even though many of the charges against Lawrence were the same. Accompanying Lucka's letter was a forty-eight-page attachment plus numerous additional pages of supporting evidence. The first part of the attachment was ten pages of "Factual Allegations and Background," a review of the history of Bishop Lawrence's words and actions against the Episcopal Church. The second part was the nucleus of the case, "Violations of Canon Law and Legal Basis to Support Charges." These would be the charges on which Lawrence would be judged. The Violations part was sub-divided into three large areas, all relating to the Constitution and Canons of the Episcopal Church in Title IV, Canons 3 and 4 and the so-called Dennis Canon (Title I, Canon 7, Section 4).[110]

The first of the three parts of the charges was "Failure to Safeguard Property." This centered on Lawrence's actions made in disregard of the Dennis Canon. This point would turn out to be the crucial difference in the first and second investigations of the Disciplinary Board. The second of the three parts of charges against Lawrence was entitled "Knowingly Violating Constitution and Canons, Directly or Through Acts of Another." It focused on the vows Lawrence had taken as he was admitted to Holy Orders of the Episcopal Church. He had solemnly pledged to conform to the Episcopal Church in his ordination as a bishop. The third part was "Conduct Unbecoming a Member of the Clergy." Title IV, Canon 4.1. (h) (8) held that a member of the clergy must not bring disorder or discredit upon the Church. Pages 10 to 21 of the attachment then spelled out

109. Lucka, Melinda. To (the Rt. Rev.) F. Clayton Matthews, March 23, 2012.
110. Ibid.

in detail how Lawrence had violated the Episcopal Church's Constitution and Canons in these three broad areas.[111]

In conclusion on pages 21–22, Lucka and the committee summarized the charges against Bishop Lawrence in a list of ten enumerated items. Number One was "Failing to retain property that was to be held in Trust for The Episcopal Church." This was the violation of the Dennis Canon, the first and most serious charge, and, as it turned out, the one that would carry the most weight. Number Two was allowing parishes to amend their by-laws to remove references to the Episcopal Church. Number Three was the issuance of the quit claim deeds. Number Four referred to the hiring of lawyers. The list went on: declaring the diocese to be "sovereign"; supporting diocesan removal of accession to the Canons of the Episcopal Church; changing the diocesan corporate charter to remove references to the Episcopal Church; modifying the Oath of Conformity; failing to conform to the vows of ordination and consecration; and refusing to administer Confirmation in a home church.[112]

Following the charges came sixteen items of exhibits and affidavits to provide substantiating evidence. First, and most important, was a detailed list of quit claim deeds that Bishop Lawrence had granted to the parishes. Most incriminating of all were the six known instances where Lawrence had issued the deeds while the Diocese of South Carolina was still under its original corporate charter recognizing the supremacy of the Constitution and Canons of the Episcopal Church. The charter was modified on October 19, 2010. Following that was a list of eighteen known parishes for which Lawrence had issued deeds between October of 2010 and November of 2011. This list of twenty-four cases where Bishop Lawrence had willfully violated the Canons of the Episcopal Church was to be convincing to the Board.[113]

Other exhibits included were resolutions of diocesan conventions, the revision to the corporate charter, the modified oath of conformity, the declaration of sovereignty for the diocese, an index of statements made by Lawrence, and changes in by-laws of several parishes. Then followed seven affidavits of personal witnesses by Virginia C. Wilder, Barbara G. Mann, Eleanor B. Koets, Warren Mersereau, Robert Pinkerton, Christina E. Wilson, and James E. Wilson. Finally, the attachment included the allegations considered by the Disciplinary Board in 2011 and the current diocesan Constitution and Canons.[114] In all, Lucka's letter and its attachments presented an impressive case against Bishop Lawrence.

According to a timeline provided later by the post-schism independent Diocese of South Carolina, the Board met in Salt Lake City on September 17, 18, and 19.[115] It made its decision by a vote on September 18.

There was a great contrast between the first Disciplinary Board investigation of Lawrence in 2011 and the second in 2012. The first episode occurred in the glare of the public spotlight. Bishop Dorsey Henderson, chair of the Board, started off trying to be as considerate, open, and fair as possible. As soon as he could, he informed Lawrence

111. Ibid.
112. Ibid.
113. Ibid.
114. Ibid.
115. "Episcopal Church Takes Action." Timeline.

of the Board's investigation, on September 29, 2011, and on that same day sent him the entire sixty-three-page file of evidence supporting the twelve accusations. Lawrence, the diocesan leadership and his allies and supporters beyond immediately launched a furious, all-out counter-attack against the Board and the entire structure of the Episcopal Church painting Lawrence and the Diocese of South Carolina as the innocent victims of wrong-thinking, liberal bullies from off. Lawrence busily huddled with his inner circle in the diocesan committees and councils and urgently called a clergy day. The Internet went wild in a frenzy of inflammatory posts from the popular anti-Episcopal Church blogs. The diocesan standing committee even unanimously, and secretly, resolved to call a special diocesan convention within thirty days if Lawrence should be formally charged by the Board with abandonment. By the time the Board voted to dismiss the accusations, on November 22, it was perhaps more out of relief than anything.

Henderson would not repeat the Disciplinary Board's unpleasant experience of 2011. When Lucka and the committee presented to him their accusations and evidence in 2012, he handled it all entirely differently. To begin with, there would be no public spotlight. Henderson made no public announcement. This time the Board conducted its work in private. There was no record that Henderson informed Lawrence that he was under investigation. He did not tell Lawrence of the accusations or send him the evidence. While there was no record of this, it was possible that rumors spread that Lawrence was under the Board's investigation again. The flurry of dramatic activity in the diocesan leadership in August and September certainly indicated an atmosphere of new urgency. The Standing Committee's resolution of October 2 to secede from the Episcopal Church must have been in reaction to some belief, at least strong suspicion, of an imminent move against Lawrence. Throughout the year 2012, there had hung over the diocese the dark cloud of the possibility, perhaps even probability, of a new investigation of Lawrence, and a far more serious one than had happened the year before.

On September 18, 2012, the Disciplinary Board for Bishops drew up a five-page "Certificate of Abandonment of The Episcopal Church and Statement of the Acts or Declarations which Show Such Abandonment."[116] By majority vote, the Board certified that Bishop Mark Lawrence had abandoned the Episcopal Church "by an open renunciation of the Discipline of the Church."[117] The certificate went on to list and describe three acts by which Lawrence had abandoned the Church. The first was to preside over the diocesan conventions in 2010 and 2011 that 1-gave only qualified accession to the Constitution of the Episcopal Church, 2-revoked diocesan accession to the Canons of the Church, and 3-altered the diocesan corporate charter to remove the Episcopal Church. "The failure of Bishop Lawrence to rule those resolutions out of order or otherwise to dissent from their adoption, and in fact his endorsement (. . .) violated his ordination vows to 'conform to the doctrine, discipline, and worship of The Episcopal Church' and to 'guard the faith, unity, and discipline of the Church,' as well as his duty to 'well and faithfully perform the duties of [his] office in accordance with the Constitution and Canons of this Church,' constituting abandonment of The Episcopal Church by an open renunciation of the

---

116. "Certificate of Abandonment."
117. Ibid.

Discipline of the Church."[118] The certificate went on to the second act showing abandonment, that Lawrence had signed, executed, and filed an amended official corporate charter that removed the Episcopal Church. The explanation said this contravened Article V, Section 1 of the Constitution of the Episcopal Church that required dioceses to give unqualified accession to the Constitution and Canons of the Episcopal Church. Again, the paper stated, Lawrence violated his ordination vows showing that he had abandoned the Church by an open renunciation of the discipline of the Church. The third act was Lawrence's issuance of the quit claim deeds in November of 2011. The Board declared this was an "effort to impair the trust interest of The Episcopal Church and of the Diocese of South Carolina in church property located in that Diocese."[119] In doing so, the charge went on, Lawrence once again violated his ordination vows and abandoned the Episcopal Church by an open renunciation of the discipline of the Church. Thus, the Board found that Lawrence had abandoned the Episcopal Church by violating his vows to uphold the Constitution and Canons of the Episcopal Church and he did so by issuing the quit claim deeds that directly contradicted the Dennis Canon, by presiding over the conventions that had voted to revoke unqualified accession to the Constitution and Canons of the Episcopal Church, and by revising the official charter to remove the Episcopal Church from the legal incorporation of the diocese under the state law.

The difference between the Board's first investigation, in 2011, and the second, in 2012, was more than just on the public face. The outcomes were opposite. In the first consideration, the Board had decided that the twelve charges and the accompanying sixty-three pages of evidence did not sufficiently support the grave accusation that Lawrence had abandoned the Episcopal Church. In the second hearing, the Board decided that there were three ways in which Lawrence had abandoned the Church. The first two had already been considered the year earlier and found to be too weak in and of themselves. The major difference was in the third issue, Lawrence's granting of the quit claim deeds. The Board obviously did not accept Lawrence's well-publicized rationale that he had to issue the deeds because the state Supreme Court had invalidated the Dennis Canon in the whole state of South Carolina. In fact, the state Supreme Court case had been for only one parish. The Disciplinary Board charged Lawrence with abandonment in 2012 because they believed he had violated his consecration oath of loyalty to the Episcopal Church by willful acts in contradiction of the Canons of the Church.

It is useful to revisit the Church canon under which the Disciplinary Board acted and the Presiding Bishop would go on to act. Canon 16 in Title IV of the Episcopal Church Canons is entitled "Of Abandonment of The Episcopal Church."[120] It provided three reasons for which a bishop could be removed: open renunciation of the doctrine, discipline, and worship of the Episcopal Church, admission into a religious body not in communion with the Church, and engaging in Episcopal acts for a body other than one in communion with the Church.[121] The Disciplinary Board agreed that Lawrence had

118. Ibid.
119. Ibid.
120. *Constitution and Canons*, 2012, 152–53.
121. Lawrence attended but did not participate in the consecration of Steve Wood as a bishop in the Anglican Church in North America in August of 2012. If he had been an active participant in the

violated the first provision. If the Board should agree on abandonment, it was required to certify such to the presiding bishop. The canon did not give a time frame for doing this. It is important to note that the Board was not a court and its actions were not a trial, only an investigation followed by an opinion to be sent to higher authorities for judgment and enforcement. It did not have to follow the usual procedures of civil law. Thus, it would be incorrect to say that Lawrence had been tried and convicted by the Disciplinary Board.

Upon receiving the certification of abandonment, Canon 16 required the presiding bishop to place a "restriction" on the exercise on the bishop's exercise of ministry. Again, no time frame was specified for imposing this. Under restriction, the bishop in question was forbidden from conducting any episcopal, canonical, or ministerial acts until the matter was taken up by the House of Bishops. Once the restriction was in place two options were open. In the first, the restricted bishop would have sixty days in which to make an official notification to the presiding bishop stating a good faith denial or retraction of the actions that had led to the charge of abandonment. Then, the presiding bishop would have discretion to remove the restriction and thereby restore the bishop to full rights. The other avenue was for the restriction to continue until the matter could be presented at the next meeting of the House of Bishops. By majority vote, the bishops could depose the restricted bishop or release and remove him or her. Failure of a majority on either would clear the restriction and restore the bishop's full rights in the Church. Thus, the decision to restore or remove the bishop rested with the presiding bishop and perhaps with the body of bishops.

Therefore, under the canons of the Episcopal Church, Presiding Bishop Jefferts Schori had to place a restriction on Bishop Lawrence. Once he was restricted, Lawrence would have two ways in which he could be restored as a bishop in the Episcopal Church. He could send a letter to the Presiding Bishop pleading his case. She would have the choice of exonerating and restoring him; or, he could plead his case before the House of Bishops who likewise could clear him. There was no reason in September of 2012 to think Lawrence did not have a good chance at both of these. After all, it was not in the Episcopal Church's interest to alienate a bishop who was so tightly wound up with his diocese. Everyone knew that if Lawrence bolted, the majority of his diocese would too. This would be the dreaded fifth secession. However, while Church leaders did not want another mass defection, at the same time they could not allow flagrant violation of the agreed-upon rules and regulations on which the whole structure of the institutional Church rested. After all, it was their sworn duty to uphold and defend the Episcopal Church.

The presiding bishop was not a member of the Disciplinary Board for Bishops but it was difficult to imagine that Jefferts Schori did not know something about the Board's proceedings. Even if she did know, she had no constitutional authority to respond until the Board presented to her its official certificate of abandonment which it did on October 10. She had no right in this matter until then. The flurry of activity around both Lawrence and Waldo in August and September suggests that they too may have had some inkling of an impending move regarding the bishop of South Carolina. Meanwhile the Disciplinary Board kept a seal on its deliberations and actions.

---

consecration he would have been in violation of this provision.

Lawrence left the fateful October 2 meeting with his lawyers and standing committee just after noon to catch a flight to New York City. At 9:30 a.m. on the next day, October 3, he met Waldo for coffee and at 10:00 a.m. the two of them were in the office of the presiding bishop at the Episcopal Church Center, 815 Second Avenue, a stone's throw from the Chrysler Building in Manhattan.[122] The conference among the three did not last more than two hours. Jefferts Schori and Waldo have not made public statements on the conversation, but in an interview with the author, Bishop Waldo revealed that Lawrence did not mention the resolution passed by his standing committee the day before (Waldo and Jefferts Schori learned of it on Oct. 17).[123] Instead, the three talked about "creative solutions" to make "peace in the conflict" in order to allow the Diocese of South Carolina to oppose measures of the Church while staying in the Church.[124] Since the focus was on keeping the relationship going, there was no specific proposal raised. The independent Diocese of South Carolina later issued a timeline of events leading up to the schism in which the meeting was described as one seeking creative solutions to avoid all-out war, but that the Presiding Bishop focused on how much longer Lawrence intended to remain as bishop and asked if five years were reasonable.[125] They left agreeing to meet next on October 11.[126] The only known outcome of the meeting was the agreement to meet again on the 11th. While Lawrence failed to mention the Standing Committee's resolution of "disassociation" of October 2, Jefferts Schori also apparently did not reveal to Lawrence in the meeting that he had been formally investigated again by the Disciplinary Board.[127] If neither side informed the other of what was happening in private, one should wonder what sort of creative solutions could possibly have overcome the obstacles that had already been set up on both sides.

Lawrence and Waldo had lunch together before Lawrence left at 1:30 for the airport to catch a flight to Pittsburgh.[128] While in LaGuardia waiting on the flight, Lawrence placed phone calls to Jefferts Schori, his lawyers Logan and Runyan, and then to some of his inner circle as Lewis, Fuener, Borrett, and Burwell.[129] That evening, he arrived in Pittsburgh. The next day, October 4, he spent a long day in the Trinity School board of trustees meeting and dinner with the board and some students.[130] The following day, he drove twelve and a half hours back to Charleston. Again that day, he placed phone calls with the presiding bishop's office as well as with Logan and Runyan.[131]

According to the independent diocese's timeline, on October 9, Presiding Bishop Jefferts Schori contacted Bishop Lawrence to request a private conversation in Atlanta on

---

122. *Journal of the Two Hundred and Twenty Second (. . .)* 2013, 45.
123. Waldo, interview with author.
124. Ibid.
125. "Episcopal Church Takes Action." Timeline.
126. Ibid.
127. Such an announcement at that point would have been outside the bounds of the canons.
128. *Journal of the Two Hundred and Twenty Second (. . .)* 2013, 45.
129. Ibid.
130. Ibid.
131. Ibid.

Saturday, October 13, when she would be there to preside at a consecration.[132] Lawrence's official bishop's diary, however, does not list a phone call from the Presiding Bishop on that day.[133] It does list phone conversations on the 9th with Logan, Runyan, and Waldo.[134]

Wednesday, October 10, 2012, was to be a fateful day for everyone concerned. On Lawrence's side, overnight he had resolved that he would not meet the Presiding Bishop in Atlanta on the 13th. At some time on the 10th, he informed Jefferts Schori that he could not meet her at that time.[135] Their meeting that had been originally set in their visit in New York for the 11th was moved to the 22nd. He gave as his reason for not meeting on the 11th as the funeral of Nick Zeigler, the highly esteemed former chancellor of the diocese. Zeigler had died on October 8; his funeral was set for St. John's in Florence on Thursday the 11th. Two weeks later, Lawrence told a "bishop's forum" at St. John's, Florence, that Zeigler's funeral was "providential" because it allowed him to avoid a scheduled meeting with the Presiding Bishop.[136] While the funeral explained missing the meeting set for the 11th, it did not explain his refusal to meet Jefferts Schori in Atlanta on the 13th. Lawrence had all day on the 12th and the morning of the 13th in which he could made the five-hour drive from Charleston to Atlanta. His diary showed nothing on these days that could not have been missed.[137] Lawrence's claim that pressing events precluded him from meeting Jefferts Schori in Atlanta on October 13 did not square with the public evidence. What Lawrence did on October 10th was to confer with the Standing Committee acting as his Council of Advice for two hours and forty-five minutes.[138] As of the end of the day on the 10th, the only scheduled meeting of Jefferts Schori and Lawrence was set to be held on October 22. Lawrence knew that he had only to wait for any Episcopal Church authority to take "any action of any kind" against him. All signs now indicated that moment was at hand.

The second fateful event on October 10 was the Presiding Bishop's reception in her office by U.S. mail of the Disciplinary Board's official certification that Lawrence had abandoned the Episcopal Church. The canon required the Presiding Bishop to issue a restriction on the accused bishop, but it did not specify exactly when she was to do this. While it did not set a certain time, the canon did imply expeditious action. Jefferts Schori was now under greater pressure than ever to deal with Lawrence and to do so at once. According to the independent diocese's timeline, on the next day, October 11, Jefferts Schori responded to Lawrence's notice that he could not meet her in Atlanta on the 13th.[139] At that time she told him, "'I do need to speak with you in the next few days"

---

132. "Episcopal Church Takes Action." Timeline. The ordination and consecration of the Rt. Rev. Robert Christopher Wright as the tenth bishop of the Episcopal Diocese of Atlanta, at Morehouse College, Atlanta, Oct. 13, 2012.

133. *Journal of the Two Hundred and Twenty Second (. . .)* 2013, 45.

134. Ibid.

135. "Episcopal Church Takes Action." Timeline. Bishop Lawrence's official journal did not mention contacting the Presiding Bishop on October 10th.

136. Author's notes. St. John's Episcopal Church, Florence, SC, October 28, 2012.

137. *Journal of the Two Hundred and Twenty Second (. . .)* 2013, 45–46.

138. Ibid, 45.

139. "Episcopal Church Takes Action." Timeline.

and requested a conference phone call including Logan, the chancellor, preferably on October 15, 16, or 17.[140]

On Friday, October 12, Lawrence and Jefferts Schori set a date and time for a conference call to be conducted on Monday, October 15 at 1:00 p.m. By this point it must have been obvious to Lawrence that the urgency on the Church side had moved to the highest level. Jefferts Schori had made it plain that she could not wait another week for their agreed-upon date of the 22nd to talk with him. It would not have taken much for anyone to surmise the reason for her sudden change in attitude. The gravity of the moment weighed in on Lawrence who took three hours on the afternoon of the 12th to "process/pray through decision."[141] This meant that a "decision" was on his mind. The first person he called after his meditation was Alan Runyan.[142] The trap that the leadership had secretly set up on October 2 was about spring shut.

Lawrence spent the weekend of October 13–14 in routine business without showing any agitation or even concern about the crisis.[143] On Saturday the 13th, he drove down to Beaufort to visit Jeff Miller and then over to Bluffton for a service at Church of the Cross. He had dinner with Chuck and Becky Owens and got to bed as his usual hour. On Sunday the 14th, he spent the morning at Church of the Cross for confirmation then drove back to Charleston where he called it a day at 4:00 p.m. to relax and get to bed at his usual time.

SCHISM

October 15

Monday, October 15, dawned. Lawrence spent a rather leisurely morning exercising, reading the Bible, writing in his diary, and arrived at the diocesan office at 10:30.[144] The Presiding Bishop moved the conference call time from 1:00 p.m. to 12:00 noon. At 12 started the "conference call w/PB, DBB, Wade L,"[145] that is, with himself, the Presiding Bishop, the Disciplinary Board for Bishops, and Wade Logan, the diocesan chancellor. Jefferts Schori talked; Lawrence listened. She announced that on October 10 she had received the certificate of abandonment from the Disciplinary Board and that she was following the Church canon that required her to place a restriction of Lawrence's ministry. She made it effective at 12:00 p.m. on that day, October 15. She added that she would be sending right away hard copies of this.[146] The restriction meant that he was not to perform any acts as an ordained person. Jefferts Schori told Lawrence that she would not make the news public until after October 22 when Lawrence, Waldo, and their chancellors were scheduled to have a confidential meeting with the Presiding Bishop in New

140. Ibid.
141. *Journal of the Two Hundred and Twenty Second (. . .)* 2013, 46.
142. Ibid.
143. Ibid.
144. Ibid.
145. Ibid.
146. "Episcopal Church Takes Action." Timeline.

York.¹⁴⁷ The Church's account said that Lawrence agreed to the confidentiality until that time.¹⁴⁸ Jefferts Schori still hoped that she and Lawrence could find a peaceful resolution privately that would allow her to remove the restriction without public fanfare. It should be recalled that under the canon, the Presiding Bishop had the discretion to lift the restriction if the accused presented a letter in good faith denying or retracting the offending actions. No doubt this is what Jefferts Schori wanted Lawrence to do at this time so that she could end the crisis quietly. Later that afternoon, Lawrence received by e-mail the hard copies of the Board's certification of abandonment and the Presiding Bishop's restriction.¹⁴⁹ Jefferts Schori ended the day with the expectation that Lawrence would keep the matter confidential and the two of them would meet the next Monday, October 22, to try to work out their differences.¹⁵⁰ Lawrence said later in his deposition that the Presiding Bishop never restricted him: "There came a time when the presiding bishop said (. . .) she needed to restrict my ministry, but she never did it (. . .). The reason why she never did it is because that canons state that I shall receive it in writing, which I never received."¹⁵¹

This telephone call turned out to be the climax of the crisis of 2012. Yet, neither a transcript of it nor a detailed account existed in the public record. Lawrence released only bits and pieces through the diocesan office. None of the other participants has ever produced a public accounting of it. Apparently, Lawrence listened to Jefferts Schori politely and said little in response. Although one can know little of what was actually said, one can surmise from the immediate aftermath what was not said. He did not dispute, let alone try to refute the charge of abandonment. It seemed he made no argument at all in reaction to the serious charge leveled at him by the Disciplinary Board. Lawrence did not tell the Presiding Bishop about the Standing Committee resolution of October 2 that he knew would instantly invalidate everything she said, at least in the diocese. Needless to say, he did not hint at exploring ways of lifting the restriction let alone solving the crisis at mutually agreed upon terms. Finally, Lawrence did not tell Jefferts Schori that he would discard everything she said as soon as he hung up the phone. All of this became clear within the first few hours after the call.

What were Bishop Lawrence's viable options at the moment he learned he had been restricted by Presiding Bishop Jefferts Schori? There were several possible credible choices he could have made in response to the not-unexpected news. In the first place, he could have accepted the restriction and worked with the Presiding Bishop to make a peaceful settlement. This was certainly her choice as shown in her appeal for confidentiality and expectation of a new private conference, and no doubt what she was trying to do. A meeting of the two was already awaiting on the 22nd. It was Lawrence who had

---

147. "Fact Sheet: The Diocese of South Carolina." The Episcopal Church, Perspectives, November 9, 2012, http://www.episcopalchurch.org/es/posts/perspectives/fact-sheet-diocese-south-carolina.

148. Ibid.

149. "Episcopal Church Takes Action." Timeline.

150. On July 25, 2014, Mark Lawrence testified in court that he never received an official restriction signed by the presiding bishop and likewise never received an official certificate of abandonment. "Transcript of Record," July 25, 2014, Vol. XIV, 2454.

151. "Deposition Transcript—Mark J. Lawrence,"169.

backed out of the possible meetings on October 11 and 13. There was every indication that Lawrence could have been cleared of the charge against him by the Presiding Bishop. One should recall too that the whole matter on the Church side concerned Lawrence and not the diocese. On this option, however, there was no evidence that Lawrence ever considered it.[152] A second choice would have been to resign as a bishop in the Episcopal Church. He would then be replaced by a like-minded bishop who could go on leading the Diocese of South Carolina in the path of non-conformity it had already chosen. Once again, there was no evidence that Lawrence ever considered this while there was plenty of evidence of the opposite. A third credible option would have been for Lawrence to declare the actions of the Disciplinary Board and the Presiding Bishop to be null and void in the diocese and without any effect. The diocese had already done such with earlier canons of the church. In fact, the diocesan convention had resolved to withdraw accession to the canons of the Episcopal Church. Under this provision, Lawrence would not even have had to recognize the Church's actions against him. He and the diocese could simply go on into the future conducting business as they had been doing for several years in virtual disregard of the national Church. The obvious holdback to this would be the defeat of those in the diocese who might have been urging a complete break from the Episcopal Church. Yet another option would have been for Lawrence to go back to the Standing Committee and ask for a revision of the October 2 resolution. It could have been changed in various ways such as declaring disassociation only after Lawrence had been removed as bishop. The obvious opposition to this would be the same as the option before. It would have defeated the forces that might have been pushing the diocese to leave the Church. Another possible choice was to call a special diocesan convention to have an open, full, and thorough discussion of the future of the diocese. Lawrence had already shown he was fond of declaring crises and calling special conventions. However, none of his conventions had been free and open affairs. They were all arranged to reach predetermined results. Finally, a choice would be simply to do nothing, leave the Standing Committee resolution of October 2 in place, and use it to declare unilaterally the absolute and irreversible diocesan secession from the Episcopal Church. This was the choice Lawrence and his immediate circle made and did so instantly.

As soon as Lawrence said goodbye to Jefferts Schori on the telephone, he swung into action. He called chancellor Logan right away.[153] Under the resolution of October 2, the chancellor would have to pre-approve the Standing Committee's action of disassociation. A conference call was then set up with the Standing Committee acting as the Council of Advice at 1:30 p.m.[154] Jefferts Schori's request for confidentiality lasted less than one hour. All the Presiding Bishop's fondest hopes of a quiet and private peaceful settlement suddenly vanished even though it would be two more days before she would know it. Apparently, chancellor Logan rendered his required opinion and the Standing

---

152. When asked in his official deposition of June 3, 2014 "Did you take advantage of the provisions of Title IV to declare that it was a false—that there were false allegations," Lawrence replied, "The diocese was already disassociated from The Episcopal Church by that time." "Deposition Transcript—Mark J. Lawrence," 170.

153. *Journal of the Two Hundred and Twenty Second (. . .)* 2013, 46.

154. Ibid.

Committee agreed in the conference call to enact its heretofore secret October 2 resolution to disassociate the diocese from the Episcopal Church. Soon thereafter, Lawrence consulted on the phone with Jeff Miller, Paul Fuener, chair of the Standing Committee, and Kendall Harmon.[155] Apparently, within a few hours of the Presiding Bishop's call to Lawrence, the entire diocesan ruling establishment of no more than two dozen people agreed in secret that the diocese had removed itself from the Episcopal Church as of the noontime phone call in which the Episcopal Church took "any action of any kind" against the bishop. By late afternoon, Lawrence had left for six hours on a previously scheduled bishop's visit to All Saints Church, Hampton. He returned home at 10:15 and to bed.[156] As far as the authorities of the diocese were concerned, the Diocese of South Carolina was now an independent entity completely separate from the Episcopal Church. Their next step was to decide how to relay this to everyone else.

The next day, October 16, Lawrence moved into action. In the morning, he assembled the deans of the convocations for a two-hour meeting. On this day, perhaps in this meeting, Lawrence resolved to call an assembly of all the diocesan clergy three days later, on October 19. St. Paul's of Summerville was to be the place. That afternoon he met with the Standing Committee sitting as the Council of Advice from 2:00 to 6:30 p.m.[157] Although there were no public minutes of this meeting, subsequent events would reveal this to be the time the diocesan leadership planned the arrangements of a special diocesan convention on November 17 necessary to change formally the canons of the diocese and finalize the break. Moreover, as the next day's events would show, someone spent a good deal of time preparing public press notices to be released on the afternoon of the 17th. That evening, his only phone conversation was with Kendall Harmon.[158] By bed time, Lawrence could go to sleep completely confident of his fateful action planned for the next day. He knew that everything had been settled among the diocesan leadership, that his bond with them remained as solid as ever, that everyone was in agreement and prepared to move forward. He knew it was time to play the final public act with the Episcopal Church.

October 17

On Wednesday, October 17, Lawrence arrived at the diocesan office at 10:00 a.m. prepared to act.[159] His first phone call of the day with Mouneer Anis, his closest ally in the Anglican world overseas.[160] He made several other phone calls, then one to Alan Runyan. Next, he called the Presiding Bishop to tell her he could not keep confidentiality because of the hitherto secret resolution of the Standing Committee of October 2,

---

155. Ibid.
156. Ibid.
157. Ibid.
158. Ibid.
159. Ibid.

160. Mouneer Anis, bishop of Egypt, was the first foreign Anglican to go to Lawrence's defense in 2012. In 2014, he apparently headed the effort of Global South to provide primatial oversight to the independent diocese; this was ratified by the diocesan convention in March of 2014.

2012. The resolution had stated explicitly that at the moment the Episcopal Church took "any action" against Bishop Lawrence, the sovereign Diocese of South Carolina would automatically "disaffiliate" and remove its membership in the Episcopal Church with himself as its bishop. Thus, Lawrence told her, the "disaffiliation" was a *fait accompli* as of noon, October 15. It could not be undone. The bishop, the standing committee, and the other authoritative bodies of the diocese had left the Episcopal Church. This meant he would no longer recognize her authority or the rights of the Episcopal Church in his diocese. Four and one half years after making a vow to adhere to the discipline of the Episcopal Church, he made it plain to the head of the Church that he had cancelled his vow. It must have been a breath-taking moment. Apparently, it was not a long conversation. Lawrence talked. Jefferts Schori listened, no doubt in stunned silence, if not quite disbelief. No transcript or detailed description of this phone call has ever been released, only excerpts provided by the diocese, but obviously, this was the point of the final break between Lawrence and the Episcopal Church. The meaning of the break would become the new problem instantly.

Lawrence's call to the Presiding Bishop must have been around noon on the 17th. As soon as he hung up the phone, he moved into what was clearly a pre-planned action. He immediately called Joy Hunter, his diocesan communications assistant, no doubt to tell her to proceed with the obviously pre-prepared public news releases.[161] Next, he called Bishop Waldo.[162] Waldo remembered later "I was surprised to learn of his Standing Committee's disaffiliation" and felt deeply sad at the news.[163] No one had worked harder to avoid this awful day than had the bishop of Upper South Carolina. Now, he could see that all of his toil had been for naught.[164] Next, Lawrence called to inform Bishop Salmon, Bishop Allison, John Burwell, Bishop Skilton, and interestingly enough, Michael Wright, the rector of the leading pro-Episcopal Church parish in the diocese, Grace Church of Charleston.[165] That evening, he once again talked with Waldo and Salmon.[166] In an interview with the author, Waldo said that he first learned of the Standing Committee's resolution of October 2 by phone on October 17 and that he expressed his disappointment to Lawrence for having kept this hidden from him all the while.[167] Lawrence responded that he saw no need to reveal the resolution ahead of time to others.[168] By then the news was everywhere having been released in the afternoon by the diocesan office and picked up and spread by Church news outlets and then by

---

161. *Journal of the Two Hundred and Twenty Second (. . .)* 2013, 46.

162. Ibid.

163. Waldo, (the Rt. Rev.) Andrew. E-mail message to author, September 12, 2014.

164. Ibid. Waldo later said that he knew from the start that the odds were against him, that he knew all along his efforts with Lawrence would likely fail. However, he went on, "I had to, for the sake of my own conscience and the life of reconciliation to which Christ calls us, work at every possible angle to discover an opening." In time, Waldo discovered there had been no opening all along. In retrospect, it is clear that it was Bishop Waldo who had acted in good faith and his ultimate failure was from no fault of his own.

165. *Journal of the Two Hundred and Twenty Second (. . .)* 2013, 46.

166. Ibid.

167. Waldo, interview with author.

168. Ibid.

countless other friends and foes on the Internet. It seemed the whole Episcopalian and Anglican world exploded with the electrifying news that the leadership of the Diocese of South Carolina had acted to declare the diocese's complete independence from the Episcopal Church. This was not just any schism. This was the self-proclaimed secession of one of the nine original bodies that had formed the Episcopal Church 223 years earlier. The gravity of this moment struck the Anglican world, the Episcopal Church, and the diocese with hammer force. Anglicanism could never be quite the same again. Indeed, it raised the question of whether the Episcopal Church as it had been known could survive. Of course, too, it meant that the diocese would have to find a new place in the world, no small matter.

One could argue that Lawrence's open defiance and outright rejection of the Presiding Bishop's constitutional authority proved conclusively that he had abandoned the Episcopal Church. At his ordination and consecration as a bishop he had made a sacred vow "I, (Mark Joseph Lawrence) (. . .) do solemnly engage to conform to the doctrine, discipline, and worship of The Episcopal Church."[169] At that time, the Diocese of South Carolina was still giving unqualified accession to the Constitution and Canons of the Episcopal Church and this fact was still included in its corporate charter. Moreover, one could reasonably say by declaring that the diocese had disassociated from the Episcopal Church and continuing to function as its bishop, Lawrence was also renouncing his orders in the Episcopal Church. Of the three reasons given in the Church canons for the removal of a bishop, one refers to joining a church not in communion with the Episcopal Church. Another refers to performing episcopal acts for a church not in communion with the Episcopal Church. If the diocese were independent as he claimed, then it was not in communion with the Episcopal Church. By serving as a bishop of a church not in communion with the Episcopal Church he met two of the three causes for the removal of a bishop in the Episcopal Church. Thus, after October 17, Episcopal Church leaders could make a reasonable case that Lawrence had both abandoned the Episcopal Church and renounced his orders in it. The Presiding Bishop, however, was far from ready to jump to any such dreadful conclusions on October 17. It would be seven more weeks before Jefferts Schori would finally reach the sad end of the rocky road with Mark Lawrence.

In retrospect, it was clear that the diocesan leaders spent the forty-eight hours between the two phone calls of October 15 and 17 getting well-prepared to launch a major public relations campaign in order to control the message in the massive public discourse that was certain to follow. On the afternoon of the 17th, soon after Lawrence's call to Jefferts Schori, the diocesan office posted the news on its website that the diocese had "disassociated" from the Episcopal Church and had called a special convention on November 17 to finalize it canonically. This was the announcement that carried the news instantly around the world that South Carolina had declared itself to be free of the Episcopal Church. The post was entitled "Episcopal Church Takes Action Against the Bishop and Diocese of SC."[170] It clearly had taken considerable time and effort to prepare in the previous forty-eight hours. First, it presented a cover letter announcing that the

169. *The Book of Common Prayer,* 513.
170. "Episcopal Church Takes Action."

Diocese of South Carolina had "disaffiliated" from the Episcopal Church and a special convention had been called for November 17 to make all the canonical changes to finish it up.[171] It went on to complain that the identity of the accusers had not been revealed.[172] The cover letter finished with an astounding paragraph: "We feel a deep sense of sadness but a renewed sense of God's providence that The Episcopal Church has chosen to act against the Diocese and its Bishop during a good faith attempt [to] resolve our differences peacefully. These actions make it clear that The Episcopal Church no longer desires to be affiliated with the Diocese of South Carolina."[173]

This statement established the public relations position of the diocese and provided its message well into the future. Several points in it should be reviewed. In the first place, it established the myth that the Episcopal Church "attacked" the diocese. In fact, there had been no "attack" on the diocese at all. What really happened was that Bishop Lawrence had been treated under the Constitution and Canons of the Episcopal Church with all due respect to his rights guaranteed therein. There was nothing illegal, illegitimate, or unscrupulous about his treatment. Moreover, all of this had nothing to do with the diocese, only with Lawrence. The charge of an outside "attack" on the diocese was certainly meant as a rallying cry to unite the communicants around the bishop, but it had no substance in fact. The second myth it set up was that Lawrence had been working to make peace with the Church and it was Jefferts Schori who sabotaged that. In fact, as we have seen, it was Lawrence who had backed out of the meeting that had been set up for the 11th citing a funeral. It was he who had refused to drive to Atlanta to see Jefferts Schori on the 13th when he certainly could have done so. And, it would be he who would refuse the scheduled meeting of the 22nd. The next misconception this statement perpetrated was that the Episcopal Church had caused the schism because it no longer wanted to be "affiliated with the Diocese." The idea that the Episcopal Church wanted to cast out one of its own dioceses, and a founding one at that, was too absurd to deserve attention. It is also important to recognize what the letter did not say. It did not try to refute the accusation that Lawrence was guilty of abandoning the Episcopal Church. Nevertheless, by getting out front with its version of the news, the diocesan leaders had set the agenda for the public debate to follow. It was a brilliant pre-emptive stroke of the sort that would be repeated.

Following the cover letter, the diocesan post provided fifty-eight pages that had been assembled to stake out the strongest position for the diocese.[174] First, it published five documents from the Episcopal Church that had been received in the forty-eight-hour gap between calls. One was the certificate of abandonment from the Disciplinary Board, another the restriction of ministry from the Presiding Bishop and the rest the collection of evidence from the Disciplinary Board.[175] Then it gave five documents from the diocese, a "timeline" that went to October 17, the Standing Committee resolutions to disaffiliate from the Episcopal Church of November 1, 2011, and October 2, 2012,

171. Ibid.
172. Ibid.
173. Ibid.
174. Ibid.
175. Ibid.

the first Disciplinary Board ruling, and Lawrence's sixteen-page interpretation of the diocesan canons of October 2, 2012.[176] This turned out to be a treasure trove of crucial documents most of which had been held in secret. If the aim of this website posting was to bolster the diocese's case, however, it could be argued that the revealing documents did not succeed. But then it was doubtful that many people read past the cover letter.

By late afternoon of October 17, the news had spread like wildfire that the schism had happened and the story moved on to the next stage where the two parts would claim to be the one and only legitimate diocese of South Carolina. But first, there was to be a great deal of recrimination as the old diocesan leadership still had to be sure that the majority of the diocese would go along and validate the break they had made. There would be another month before the special convention would do that.

THE CONTEST FOR LEGITIMACY, OCTOBER–DECEMBER

A War of Words

The shocking news the diocesan leaders posted on the website on the afternoon of the 17th to clear the ground was only the opening salvo in what would become an every-gun-blazing, full-scale, no-holds-barred fusillade against the Episcopal Church and her defenders, at home and beyond, that would continue unabated for many weeks. In the next few months, the diocesan leaders would make every effort to retain the legal and legitimate identity and rights of the old Diocese of South Carolina. In contrast, Episcopal Church leaders would do everything in their power to prevent that and to ensure that the diocese remain in the Church. For the moment, however, the powerful right of possession was securely in the hands of the remarkably well-prepared diocesan leaders.

The schism had been enacted in secret by a closed band of the diocesan leadership, perhaps no more than two dozen people. Their next job was to bring along safely the rest of the diocese; and this they had started right away with the news release on October 17. Although they must have been reasonably certain of it, they could never know for sure until the deed was done.

But first, it took some time for the shock of the news to settle down and people could process what had happened, or at least what they were told had happened. This was the first stage of the post-schism period. To be sure, on the diocesan side, the conservative websites lit up in a predictably furious response to the news. On the Episcopal Church side, news outlets tried to relay information, but it was largely an unprepared defense against a well-organized and well-prepared offense. They could do little but state what the Disciplinary Board had done and react to the sensational posting on the diocesan website with its fifty-three pages of documents. It was clear right off that the diocese controlled the public message and there was not much the pro-Church side could do but fight a rear-guard action. And this was only the beginning. The next week would see the full-frontal advance.

As soon as the diocesan news item appeared on its website on the afternoon of the 17th, a surprised Episcopal News Service scrambled to get a coherent story on

176. Ibid.

the Internet. The first reaction on the Church side, though, perhaps came from Steve Skardon, the longtime blogging watchdog critic of Lawrence from within the diocese. Skardon summarized the news.[177] The Episcopal Church website posted two articles. The first came from the Episcopal Church Office of Public Affairs.[178] It simply described the details of the Disciplinary Board action. The main article came from Mary Frances Schjonberg, of Episcopal News Service.[179] It was a long summary of the events of the past several years largely reactive to the diocesan news release and Skardon. The semi-official Episcopal magazine, *The Living Church*, also released a brief notice on the afternoon of the 17th summarizing the diocese's news release of that day.[180] As the news swirled in the afternoon, Melinda Lucka issued a press release giving the names of the members of the committee that had made the complaint to the Disciplinary Board. She had sent a copy earlier to Lawrence. The members had agreed to have their names released.[181] They all wanted to show that the complaint came from a broad committee, not from the Episcopal Forum.[182] By the end of the day, the news of the schism was everywhere, but the pro-Church side seemed to be caught completely off guard, stunned, reactive, defensive, and disorganized. As usual, the diocese ruled the field and controlled the message.

While it appeared later that a complete break had happened on the 17th, there were tantalizing hints that this may not have been quite the case. Adam Parker, a reporter for the Charleston *Post and Courier*, talked with Lawrence late on the 17th.[183] Parker reported the next day that "it is unclear what step they will take next. They could affiliate with another church body in the U.S., or abroad, or they could find a way to reconcile with The Episcopal Church. Lawrence said he's interested in finding a solution. 'We, on our end, are still open to negotiations,' he said. 'But it needs to be done with the diocese, Episcopal Church and larger Anglican Union, knowing what is at stake.'"[184] This begged the question, what "solution"? If the diocese had disaffiliated from the Episcopal Church,

---

177. Skardon, Steve. "Lawrence 'Restricted' as a Bishop and Priest." South Carolina Episcopalians, October 17, 2012, htto://www.scepiscopalians.com/2012_Reports.php.

178. "Disciplinary Board for Bishops Certifies that South Carolina Bishop has Abandoned the Church." Episcopal Church, Public Affairs Office, October 17, 2012, http://www.episcopalchurch.org/posts/publicaffairs/disciplinary-board-bishops-certifies-south-carolina-bishop-has-abandoned-church.

179. Schjonberg, Mary Frances. "Disciplinary Board Says South Carolina Bishop has Abandoned Church, Decision Prompts Diocese to Claim it has 'disaffiliated' with the Church." Episcopal News Service, October 17, 2012, http://episcopaldigitalnetwork.com/ens/2012/10/17/disciplinary-board-says-south-carolina-bishop-has-abandoned-episcopal-church.

180. "+Lawrence's Ministry Restricted." *The Living Church*, October 17, 2012, http://www.livingchurch.org/lawrence-ministry-restricted.

181. "South Carolina Episcopalians Explain Complaint against Bishop." Episcopal News Service, October 18, 2012, http://episcopalchurch.org/library/article/south-carolina-episcopalians-explain-complaint-against-bishop.

182. Schjonberg, Mary Frances. "South Carolinians Say Diocesan Actions were 'too far out of bounds.'" Episcopal News Service, October 18, 2012, http://episcopaldigitalnetwork.com/ens/2012/10/18/south-carolinians-say-diocesan-actions-were-too-far-out-of-bounds/.

183. Parker, Adam. "Bishop Mark Lawrence said to have Abandoned Episcopal Church." *The Post and Courier* (Charleston, SC), October 18, 2012, http://postandcourier.com/article/20121018%/PC16/121019254/1005/bishop-mark-lawrence.

184. Ibid.

what was the point of any negotiation with the Church? Lawrence did not elaborate. Besides, what was this unknown "larger Anglican Union" contained in this obtuse statement? If there were some possibility of a negotiated solution to end the schism at that point, it never developed.

On October 18, Jefferts Schori said in a news conference that she was "'still hopeful that we can find a way for South Carolina to remain part of the Episcopal Church.'"[185] She too did not elaborate. It was also a fact that Lawrence and Jefferts Schori talked on the phone at least three times in the few days after October 17. One was on October 19, at the end of his long clergy day meeting. The call was at 3:30 p.m. and may have lasted as long as forty-five minutes.[186] They spoke again on October 20, at 3:45 p.m.[187] It was either on the 19th or the 20th that Lawrence informed Jefferts Schori that he would not meet with her and Waldo in New York on the 22nd as had been planned.[188] Yet another phone call occurred on October 22, the date of their meeting that he had cancelled.[189] Interestingly enough, the call came after he had consulted with the Standing Committee acting as his Council of Advice and before he talked with his lawyers and Harmon.[190] According to Lawrence's official diary, that was the last time he spoke with the presiding bishop for several weeks. Neither Lawrence nor Jefferts Schori has ever revealed the contents of their three conversations after October 17. For some time to come, however, Lawrence remained vague when asked about his post-schism relations with the Episcopal Church.

Lawrence's official diary also revealed other hints of his uncertainty, or at least inner turmoil, after his dramatic declaration to the Presiding Bishop on October 17. For the next week, he clearly exhibited a certain amount of emotional distress. On the evening of the 17th he fell in bed at his usual time but found he was unable to sleep. At midnight, he arose, spent three hours in "night watch/prayer," and went back to bed at 3:00 a.m. to awaken at 7:00.[191] The next day, he spent the whole day talking with Logan, Runyan, Harmon, and others and meeting with the Standing Committee. That evening he went to bed at the usual time and once again found he could not sleep. At midnight, he arose, as the night before, to stay up until 3:00 a.m., to go back to bed and arise at 6:00 a.m.[192] On that day, the 19th, he spent the entire day preparing for the clergy conference, conducting the conference, and talking with Jefferts Schori, Harmon and others.[193]

The clergy conference, at St. Paul's in Summerville on the 19th was another of Lawrence's closed meetings. Contrary to past practice, the diocese released neither a transcript of Lawrence's address to the clergy nor an account of it. None of the participants made a public report. This indicated that the diocesan leaders intended the meeting to benefit the attending clergy only and not the communicants beyond. The schism would

---

185. Schjonberg, "South Carolinians."
186. *Journal of the Two Hundred and Twenty Second (. . .)* 2013, 46.
187. Ibid.
188. "Fact Sheet."
189. Ibid.
190. Ibid.
191. *Journal of the Two Hundred and Twenty Second (. . .)* 2013, 46.
192. Ibid.
193. Ibid.

not be canonically finalized until the special diocesan convention acted on November 17. The leaders would need all the clerical support they could muster to ensure a solid majority. The only public information on the conference came from Steve Skardon who reported some remarks from attending clergy.[194] Skardon's sources told him Lawrence announced the diocese had left the Episcopal Church, that the Presiding Bishop's "restriction" was "irrelevant," and that he had cancelled the scheduled meeting with Jefferts Schori on October 22.[195] Some attendees stood and cheered heartily, some sat in stunned bewilderment.[196] The schism of four days earlier was delivered to the collected clergy of the diocese as a *fait accompli*.

That evening, October 19, Lawrence collapsed exhausted in bed at 9:00 p.m. but once again found he could not sleep, "very sleepy and tired but hopeful."[197] Yet again he got up at midnight for "night watch/prayer" and went back to bed at 3:00 a.m. to arise at 8:00.[198] On October 20, Lawrence spent a less hectic day communicating with Logan, Runyan, Harmon and the like again, and once again talking with the Presiding Bishop on the phone.[199] That evening, for the fourth night in a row, he went to bed at his usual time and found that he could not sleep. Yet again he was up from midnight to 3:00 a.m., then went back to bed to arise for the day at 6:15 on Sunday, October 21.[200] That day, Lawrence went on as usual making a previously scheduled bishop's visit to Trinity Church in Pinopolis where he held a "bishop's forum" to tell the people there his view of recent events.[201] That evening he relaxed watching a football game and got to bed at midnight for, apparently, his first full night's sleep in five days.[202] The following day, Monday, October 22, was another crucial day. In the morning, he talked by conference call with the Standing Committee acting as the Council of Advice. Just after noon he went into prayer and then called the Presiding Bishop at 1:00 p.m. and spoke with her briefly.[203] Immediately thereafter he talked with his lawyers, Harmon, and others then went home to relax with a movie and get to bed on time.[204] On the next day, the 23rd, Lawrence met with the Trustees of the diocese and talked with Bishop Waldo twice before going to bed as usual, but once again unsettled, "confusion for me during the Trustees regarding AR [Alan Runyan]—'descent into hell.'"[205] *Descent into hell?* Thus, it was clear that Lawrence struggled personally through the week after his declaration of schism to the Presiding

---

194. Skardon, Steve. "Lawrence Quits the Episcopal Church; Tells Clergy He's Taking Them Out Too." South Carolina Episcopalians, October 19, 2012, http://www.scepiscopalians.com/2012_Reports.php.

195. Ibid.

196. Ibid.

197. *Journal of the Two Hundred and Twenty Second (. . .)* 2013, 46.

198. Ibid.

199. Ibid.

200. Ibid.

201. Ibid.

202. Ibid.

203. Ibid.

204. Ibid.

205. Ibid.

Bishop. Perhaps he lacked confident inner peace and calm, or perhaps he was simply exhausted.[206]

If there were any uncertainty on Lawrence's part, there was none at all among the other diocesan leaders. There was no mistaking the message in the remarkable public relations campaign the diocese and its philosophical allies carried out in the week following the 17th. It was an all-out offensive worthy of any Madison Avenue agency. It was also a continuation of the diocesan leaders' well-established practice of the-best-defense-is-a-good-offense approach. All of their guns now aimed squarely at their perceived enemies: the Disciplinary Board, the Presiding Bishop, the Episcopal Church, Lucka's committee, and the Episcopal Forum.

From October 19 to 25, the diocesan leaders made five major public relations initiatives that effectively controlled the message. The first was a newspaper advertisement that ran as a half-page article in the Charleston *Post and Courier* and in several other local newspapers. The second was a clergy conference where Lawrence gave a long, impassioned address to the diocesan clergy. The next was a news release from Harmon declaring the diocese's "disassociation" from the Episcopal Church. At the same time, Lawrence's assistant, Jim Lewis, published a denunciation of the Episcopal Forum. Finally, the diocesan website posted a long "Questions and Answers" giving the leaders' views of the recent events. It was all quite effective, at least to the majority of the communicants to whom it was all no doubt intended.

It should be recalled that the diocesan leaders had already established the public relations themes in their posting of October 17: the Episcopal Church attacked the diocese, Lawrence had been working to settle the crisis peacefully, and the Church deliberately drove off the diocese. These points would remain basic but would be embellished, enlarged, and compounded in the week afterwards through the five initiatives. The first public message following the October 17th announcement of the schism came in a paid newspaper article on October 19. This one set out a longer and clearer case than the brief statement of the 17th. The ad was entitled, "Episcopal Church Abandons Bishop and Diocese."[207] Its subdivisions laid out the general ideas: "An Assault on the Bishop," "An Assault on the Diocese," "Abandoned."[208] It held that the Episcopal Church had: illegally and wrongly attacked the bishop, inexcusably attacked the diocese and its parishes, and tried to capture the diocese in order to prevent its freedom of expression.[209] Thus, the Episcopal Church, which had gone off the deep end theologically and institutionally, was entirely guilty of causing the schism. The diocese was forced to leave the Church to maintain its freedom and integrity and practice the pure religion. The word "assault"

---

206. When this writer attended a "bishop's forum" in Florence a few days later, Lawrence appeared to this observer to be tired, irritable, and slightly distracted. His answers to questions were not very clear. He rambled some and seemed to be most interested in criticizing the acceptance of transgendered people. At one point, he grew quite testy with one questioner who did not want simply to accept his responses. Author's notes, St. John's.

207. "Episcopal Church Abandons Bishop and Diocese." Diocese of South Carolina, October 19, 2012, http://www.diosc.com/sys/news-events/latest-news/454-episcopal-church-abandons-bishop-and-diocese.

208. Ibid.

209. Ibid.

appeared five times, "freedom" five times, and "abandon" twice.[210] The ad concluded that the diocese rejected all the Church's malevolent actions, declared itself independent, and would go on in the future as it had in the past. In short, the ad gave the leaders' rationale for the schism; there was nothing subtle about it.

The next day, "the Rev. Canon Dr. Kendall S. Harmon, Canon Theologian," issued on the diocesan website a major article, "Diocese Releases Statement Regarding Disassociation from the Episcopal Church."[211] It was a reiteration of the themes in the ad of the day before, with elaboration and some new points. Actually, the official announcement of the "disassociation" had already been made three days earlier. Harmon's purpose in this piece was to build on that and more fully explain the reasons for the schism. He continued the same ideas: victimization (he used the word "attack" three times), purity, and self-defense. It was here that the leaders began to turn attention away from the issue of homosexuality to make it only one of three errors of the Episcopal Church: that it had abandoned the "uniqueness" of Christ as salvation, that it had abandoned the authority of Holy Scripture, and that it had replaced the traditional definition of marriage. In time, the leaders would drop the theme of homosexuality and eventually declare that the schism was not about homosexuality at all. Lawrence and other diocesan leaders had long followed a habit of reciting all three charges without giving much supporting evidence. It should be noted that Harmon, as in the earlier posts, did not dispute the charges of abandonment. He did not argue that Lawrence was innocent, much less that he should stay and fight the accusations in the Church venue. By this point, however, that did not matter to the leaders and the majority of communicants in the Diocese of South Carolina. Harmon's overall point was that the diocese was entirely justified in leaving the Episcopal Church and would go on as it had before.

On the same day, another item appeared on the diocesan website. This one, by the Rev. Canon Jim Lewis, assistant to the bishop, was entitled "Episcopal Forum Members Initiate Attack on Bishop."[212] It returned to the theme of illegal and wrongful attack on the bishop and diocese, this time placing the blame on a small group of dissidents whom he insisted did not at all reflect the general will of the communicants of the diocese. It should be recalled that right after the schism, Lucka had voluntarily released the names of the twenty-four persons who had made the case to the Disciplinary Board. Now, Lewis turned and accused them of being in fact the leaders of the Episcopal Forum charging that the whole thing had been generated by the Forum. For a long time, the diocesan leaders had sneeringly dismissed the Forum as a small band of chronic malcontents mainly based in one Charleston parish [Grace Church]. Lewis's approach was a continuation of a well-established policy in the diocese of making personal recriminations against their perceived enemies as evidenced in their treatment of the Presiding Bishop,

---

210. Ibid.

211. Harmon, (the Rev.) Kendall. "Diocese Releases Statement Regarding Disassociation from the Episcopal Church." Diocese of South Carolina, October 20, 2012, http://www.diosc.com/sys/images/documents/tec/dio_statement_10_20_12.pdf.

212. Lewis, (the Rev.) Jim. "Episcopal Forum Members Initiate Attack on Bishop." Diocese of South Carolina, October 20, 2012, http://www.diosc.com/sys/news-events/latest-news/458-episcopal-forum-members-initiate-attack-on-bishop.

Thomas Tisdale, and Josephine Hicks among others. Lewis's presentation, however, arrived at a new level of criticism such as some of the people on the committee were married to each other. But, Lewis's main point was that, once again, the Episcopal Church had acted illegally and wrongfully by defying its own canons. Therefore, he concluded, it was a good thing that he diocese left the Episcopal Church in order to retain canonical purity: "It is for good reason that the Diocese of South Carolina put in place the canonical and constitutional firewalls that now seal it off from such continued abuses."[213] In other words, Lewis made the contorted argument that the diocese had to leave the Episcopal Church in order to preserve within the diocese the Church's own canons which the Church itself had abandoned. The illogic did not matter. The point was made that a small group of people had forced the diocese to break off from the Episcopal Church. This continued a favorite broad theme of victimization. It is also important to note that Lewis, as Harmon, did not dispute the accusation that Lawrence had abandoned the Church.

The last public relations initiative in this period came on October 25 in the form of a long "FAQs" posted on the diocesan website under the title "Diocese Answers Questions about its Present and Future."[214] This article was meant to turn attention from the causes of the schism to its nature and the future course of the diocese as well as elaborate on the earlier themes. The first few questions focused on the Church's actions concerning Lawrence repeating the established assertions. They also reiterated the theme that the diocese was part of the wider Anglican Communion. The leaders would now emphasize to the faithful that they were the legal and legitimate Episcopal Church in lower South Carolina and that they were part of the Anglican Communion. The next few questions dealt with the meaning of "disassociation" and the reasons for calling a special convention. Another question dismissed the idea of the restriction on Lawrence, "his ministry will continue unabated."[215] The next question returned to the old claim that Lawrence had been trying to find a peaceful settlement with the Presiding Bishop when he was ambushed. The rest of the questions concerned the ongoing work of the diocese since it departed from the Episcopal Church continuing the idea that nothing would change. It was clear that the whole intent of these "FAQs" was to redirect attention from the causes of the schism to acceptance of the schism as a good thing bringing a bright future for the diocese.

Thus, within the first eight days after October 17, the diocesan leaders established very effectively the basic public themes they would use for the next two months. The general areas were the past, that is, the causes of the schism, the present, that is, the state of the diocese, and the future, or what would happen to the diocese in time to come. They completely ignored the question that had generated the crisis in the first place, the charge that Lawrence had abandoned the Episcopal Church. As in their past reactions against the Church, for instance the depositions of Schofield and Duncan, the diocesan leaders did not argue whether the actions were merited, only that the conduct of the actions was flawed. They argued process rather than substance. It was the same

213. Ibid.

214. "Diocese Answers Questions about its Present and Future." Diocese of South Carolina, October 25, 2012, as quoted in Virtueonline, October 25, 2012, http://www.virtueonline.org/portal/modules/news/article.php?storyid=16701.

215. Ibid.

here. For the past, the leaders insisted that the Episcopal Church had caused the schism. It did so by an unscrupulous, illegal, and illegitimate use of its own canons to attack Bishop Lawrence and the diocese and did so at the very moment Lawrence was trying to negotiate a peace settlement. The Church's goal was to take over the diocese in order to destroy the orthodoxy which the diocese maintained. The Church forced the diocese to declare its independence to preserve orthodoxy. The Episcopal Church had overturned the true religion of the ages primarily in three areas: theological change setting aside the uniqueness of Christ, removing the authority of the Holy Scriptures, and adopting a non-biblical interpretation of human sexuality. The diocese had to leave the Episcopal Church to preserve traditional religion in all of these. As for the present, the diocesan leaders asserted that the diocese was a sovereign entity, always had been, and had every right to leave the Episcopal Church if it wished. Its disaffiliation was perfectly legal. Regarding the future, the leaders insisted that the diocese would go on being the one and only legitimate Episcopal diocese in lower South Carolina and a part of the Anglican Communion. Nothing would change except that the diocese would no longer be affiliated with the Episcopal Church. These were the positions that the diocesan leaders clearly and strongly presented to the twenty-eight thousand members of the old diocese and to the world beyond immediately after the schism. Since there was little in the way of counter argument at this time, the overwhelming tendency was for the average churchgoers to believe what they were told. Surely the bishop and leading clergy would not lead them wrong. The concerted diocesan publicity campaign was overwhelmingly effective in South Carolina as events would soon show.

Awaiting the Special Convention

It was exactly one month between Lawrence's announcement of the schism to the Presiding Bishop on October 17 and the diocesan special convention on November 17. Until the convention validated the schism officially, the diocesan leaders could not rest easy that the deed had finally been done. Certainly, the aim of their public relations tsunami was to prepare the clergy and communicants to make the final break in the special convention. The leaders had known for a long time that they had the unqualified support of the majority in the diocese, they could not have known the exact amount of the support. After all, they would need all the numbers they could muster to build a strong base of operations to carry the diocese into the difficult days which everyone knew lay ahead. The majorities in four dioceses had left records to predict what would happen to South Carolina *vis à vis* the Episcopal Church. A great deal of expensive litigation was a guaranteed certainty. It was important to Lawrence and his inner circle that they have the solid support of as many local churches and communicants as possible.

The schism in South Carolina had been a long time in coming. Along the way, many local churches chose sides early on to become well identified partisans, perhaps more than half of the diocese. On the secessionist side, there had long been large and influential parishes such as St. Philip's, St. Michael's, St. James, and St. John's in Charleston, Trinity in Myrtle Beach, St. Helena's of Beaufort, Church of the Cross in Bluffton, and St. Luke's in Hilton Head, all highly conservative if not fundamentalist in outlook, and bitterly critical of

THE CRISIS OF 2012

the Episcopal Church. The pro-Episcopal Church side was not so numerous. St. Stephen's, Charleston, long ago had declared that it would not leave the Episcopal Church under any condition. Then there was the flagship of the pro-Church side, Grace Church in downtown Charleston. Calvary Church, the leading historically black congregation in Charleston also let it be known they were staying with the Church. Another question mark was the choice of the Anglo-Catholics who took their lead from Church of the Holy Communion in Charleston. Dow Sanderson, the rector there, had been a diocesan leader for years before Lawrence's arrival and for several years after. The Anglo-Catholics faced an unpleasant dilemma, whether to go along with their theological opposites, the fundamentalist-leaning evangelicals, or stay with their social opposites, the liberal Church. Although they were not very numerous in traditionally Low Church South Carolina, they still carried a certain importance in the diocese. Moreover, there was an undefined minority of non-partisan parishes and missions that were split and undecided. Indeed, well into the next year, twelve of them were still painfully trying to choose one of the two sides. Thus, while Lawrence and his close allies could count on a majority, they could not know the extent of the support beyond that until the special convention acted.

Earlier in the year Lawrence had summoned up every bit of his uncommon energy to prepare the diocese to meet the crisis around the General Convention in July. It had worked. However, what he did then, impressive as it was, paled in comparison to his activities in the month before the special convention. It is unimaginable that anyone could have worked any harder to prepare the clergy and communicants for the coming event. There were many days in which Lawrence did not get to bed before midnight, some afterwards.[216] In the month, he conducted six major clergy conferences, held six bishop's forums around the diocese, prepared one newspaper article, and made extensive preparations for the special convention.[217] All of this was in addition to his regular schedule of diocesan councils and committees and bishop's visitations to local churches scattered from Georgia to North Carolina. Whatever one may think about Mark Lawrence, one must give him credit for a truly impressive amount of stamina, energy, and devotion to duty. The marathon that Lawrence ran in that month would have left many another bishop in a collapsed heap on the roadside.

Lawrence's strategy in the month was to go to the clergy first, then to the communicants. The fastest and most efficient way to get the word to the people was through the clergy in the Sunday church services. His clergy day on the 19th for all the priests and deacons of the diocese was followed up by a meeting of the clergy of the west Charleston deanery at St. James Church on October 29 when he talked with them about the "current crisis."[218] A few days later he did the same at St. Matthias in Summerton.[219] Then came his most important outreach to the clergy, nearly three days in a clergy conference at Camp St. Christopher when he spent many hours talking with groups and individuals.[220] On

---

216. *Journal of the Two Hundred and Twenty Second (. . .)* 2013, 46–48.
217. Ibid.
218. Ibid., 47.
219. Ibid.
220. Ibid., 48.

November 11, Lawrence made a presentation at the deanery meeting in Trinity, Myrtle Beach.[221] Two days later he did the same at St. Bartholomew's in Hartsville.[222]

Sandwiched in among these numerous clergy sessions, Lawrence spent many hours in various bishop's forums, open meetings with the local communicants around the diocese, usually held in conjunction with confirmations. The first was at Trinity Church in Pinopolis.[223] The next was at St. John's in Florence. St. John's, the largest parish in the Pee Dee, was one of the few large churches that had not come out strongly partisan although it had been moving in that direction under its rector Ken Weldon. On Saturday, October 27, Lawrence spent three hours with St. John's vestry. They were committed to him. The next morning, he held a forum attended by one hundred people.

This author attended Lawrence's forum at St. John's on October 28.[224] While he cannot say for sure, he can only imagine this was typical of Lawrence's bishop's forums around the diocese at the time. Lawrence spoke briefly in a somber, serious tone appearing rather sad and tired. His speech was replete with military metaphors: e.g., the Episcopal Church had fired a "missile" that led to "all out war." It was clear that he saw this as the war of a lifetime, a life-and-death struggle between good and evil. He remarked the Nick Zeigler's funeral, which had been in St. John's, was "providential" because it kept him from having to meet with the presiding bishop. The following question-and-answer period went off on many different topics. At one point, Lawrence declared, "I am no longer an Episcopalian" to the murmuring approval of the audience. He spent a great deal of time on sexuality and seemed most concerned that he had met two transsexual priests at the Convention. Referring to the blessing of same-sex unions and equal rights for transsexual persons, Lawrence said "the canons of the Episcopal Church have gone where no civilization in history has ever gone." On one question about keeping the property, he said anyone could follow the buildings if they wanted. He did not guarantee them they could keep the property. When asked about ongoing negotiations with the Episcopal Church, Lawrence seemed evasive. He did not say that talks had broken off for good. It was clear from the audience reaction that this was a mostly supportive crowd, but not entirely. One person, Dolores Miller, arose to confront Lawrence.[225] She asked him on what authority he was acting since he had been inhibited. He corrected her that he had been "restricted" and added that he was there as a bishop in the one holy, catholic and apostolic church which no restriction could affect. When Miller remained standing and continued asking pointed questions, Lawrence grew annoyed and became short and testy. After the audience began to grow restless and murmur disapproval of Miller's persistent line, Haigh Porter arose to make a tearful appeal that they should love one another above all. It was clear that this group was in a good deal of emotional pain and anguish as longtime friends were about to part from one another. Lawrence looked on impassively. Finally, a man arose to ask of Lawrence the question on everyone's mind, "Shepherd, where will you lead us from here?" It was the best question of the day. The crowd fell hushed in eager anticipation. Lawrence

221. Ibid.
222. Ibid.
223. Ibid., 46.
224. Author's notes, St. John's. All the information in this paragraph came from the author's notes.
225. Miller was one of the committee that had made the complaint to the Disciplinary Board.

made a vague, rambling response, maybe here, maybe there. His lack of clear vision did not matter. Most of the crowd stood and clapped loudly in approval. It was clear that Lawrence did not have to worry about the loyalty of this parish.[226] Lawrence proceeded on to preside over confirmation for a large class without telling them they were not being confirmed in the Episcopal Church.

The events that occurred in the month between Lawrence's call to Jefferts Schori on October 17 and the diocesan convention on November 17 moved along on two separate trajectories originating from two very different views of what constituted "the Diocese of South Carolina." On the Lawrence side, the bishop and standing committee of the old diocese claimed that they had made the diocese a completely independent self-sustaining entity as of noon on October 15. Lawrence asserted he remained the one and only legal bishop of the diocese while the standing committee continued to operate as usual. They claimed complete ownership of the old legal diocesan structure. The Standing Committee, now regularly calling itself the Board of Directors, changed the Bylaws of the corporation of the diocese on October 29 to ban "Outside Influence. No Director shall be elected, appointed, designated, removed or suspended and no vacancy filled except in accordance with these Bylaws."[227] This was meant to prevent the presiding bishop from removing the standing committee. This was really a moot point because two weeks earlier the standing committee had declared complete separation of the diocese from the Episcopal Church.

Jefferts Schori and the national Episcopal leadership claimed on the contrary that a diocese could not leave the Church of its own will. People could leave the Church but dioceses could not. In their view, even though the entire institutional authority of the old diocese had quit the Episcopal Church, they did not take the institutional structure of the diocese with them when they left. Therefore, while the majority of the old diocese moved inexorably to their self-declared official break from the Episcopal Church, the national Episcopal Church leadership would not stand by idly. Lawrence's announcement to the Presiding Bishop on Oct. 17 that he had refused the discipline of "restriction" and that he and the Standing Committee had already declared "disassociation" from the Episcopal Church left a complete vacuum in the diocesan power structure. Lawrence's announcement to Jefferts Schori that he would not meet with her on the 22nd ended all hope of further negotiations. Thereupon, Jefferts Schori turned to the task of reorganizing the authoritative organs in what she considered to be the Diocese of South Carolina. It should be recalled that she had retained a lawyer, former chancellor Thomas Tisdale, in Charleston starting in late 2009, even over the loud protests of Lawrence and Runyan. It was under the authority of the presiding bishop that Tisdale began bringing together in late October a leadership group of loyal Episcopalians to start organizing a steering committee.[228] The group was meant to "begin the process of re-establishing an admin-

226. When St. John's later took a congregational vote on secession from the Episcopal Church, over eighty percent of the ballots were in favor.

227. "Bylaws of The Protestant Episcopal Church in the Diocese of South Carolina, a South Carolina nonprofit religious corporation." [October 29, 2012]. State of South Carolina, Court of Common Pleas, County of Dorchester, Case No. 2013-CP-00013, Exhibit DSC-6B, July 8, 2014.

228. Parker, Adam. "Breakaway Anglicans Forge New Path; Local Episcopalians Reorganize." *The Post and Courier* (Charleston, SC), November 11, 2012, http://www.postandcourier.com/article/20121111/PC1204/121119983.

istrative body in the continuing diocese."[229] "On Thursday, October 25, representatives of the Presiding Bishop met in Charleston with a small group of lay and clergy persons of the diocese of South Carolina to outline steps that could be taken by such a steering committee. Such a group would, among other things, also be in close communication with Presiding Bishop Jefferts Schori during the reorganization effort."[230]

By early November, a steering committee for the reorganization of the Episcopal Church diocese formed under the chairmanship of Hillery P. Douglas, senior warden of St. Mark's Church, Charleston. Erin E. Bailey, of Mt. Pleasant was to serve as secretary and the Rev. James E. Taylor, St. Thomas, North Charleston, treasurer. The other members were Holly H. Behre, of Charleston, William P. Baldwin, of McClellanville, Dr. Charles C. Geer, of Charleston, Lonnie Hamilton III, of Charleston, Margaret S. Kwist, of Summerville, the Rev. Richard C. Lindsey, of Hilton Head/Beaufort County, Rebecca S. Lovelace, of Conway, the Rev. Wilmot T. Merchant, II, of North Myrtle Beach, John O. Sands, of Pawleys Island, the Rev. Calhoun Walpole, of Charleston, and Virginia C. Wilder, of Summerville. The "Episcopal Advisors" were local retired bishops, the Rt. Rev. John Clark Buchanan, and the Rt. Rev. Charles vonRosenberg.[231]

It did not take long for the battle lines between the competing sides to appear. Although the thick of the fighting did not begin until after the convention on November 17, early skirmishes began immediately after Lawrence's call of October 17. They would grow in intensity as the weeks went along. On the day after Lawrence's call, the Standing Committee met for two and a half hours and, among other things, voted to amend the articles of incorporation to comply with IRS regulations for a tax-exempt organization, and voted to retain a company to administer a 403(b) plan for diocesan employees.[232] Six days later, October 24, they met again to confirm that no Standing Committee member had received any communication from the Episcopal Church and to pass "a resolution regarding the removal of members of the Standing Committee."[233] Presumably this resolution was to refuse any attempt by the Church to replace the Standing Committee. One might wonder about the purpose of such a resolution in light of the committee's declaration of having left the Episcopal Church as of October 15.

No doubt, word circulated back to the old diocesan office in late October that Jefferts Schori and Tisdale were busy organizing the remaining loyal Episcopalians. Lawrence and his allies grew alarmed at the prospect that the other group would challenge the old diocesan leaders for the legal identity of the old diocese. On November 3, two pro-Episcopal local churches, All Saints', Hilton Head, and St. Mark's Chapel, Port Royal, placed an advertisement in the *Beaufort Gazette* and the *Island Packet* using the diocesan shield declaring that the "'Episcopal Diocese of South Carolina (. . .) will continue'" in the

---

229. Ibid.

230. "Fact Sheet."

231. "Open Letter to Episcopalians in SC from the Steering Committee for Reorganization of Episcopal Diocese of SC." eNewsletter of the Episcopal Forum of SC, November 11, 2012, http://www.mynewsletterbuilder.com/email/newsletter/1411531562.

232. *Journal of the Two Hundred and Twenty Second (. . .)* 2013, 60.

233. Ibid.

Episcopal Church under "'new leadership and a new bishop.'"[234] By early November word had spread that the Episcopal Church claimed possession of the diocese and fully intended to reorganize it as a continuation of the legal entity of the old diocese. On November 6, Lawrence met with the Standing Committee for a long session, 10:30 a.m. to 4:00 p.m. They discussed at length with their lawyer, Runyan, the legal issues at stake. Bill Lyles made a motion, seconded by Ann Hester Willis "to authorize the lawyers for the Diocese and the Standing Committee to take whatever measures they deem appropriate and necessary to protect the Diocese and its property."[235] It passed unanimously. This was the initial resolution that led to Runyan's filing suit in the circuit court on January 5, 2013.

In the eleven days between the November 6 meeting of the old standing committee and the special convention on the 17th, events accelerated quickly as both sides maneuvered to secure the legal status of the old diocese and therefore block the other side. On the afternoon of November 7, the majority of the clergy of the old diocese received an anonymous e-mail bearing the seal and name of the diocese inviting them to a clergy day to be held at the Church of the Holy Communion in Charleston.[236] On learning of this, Lawrence immediately called Dow Sanderson, the rector of Holy Communion, who said he understood the meeting was to be for a small group of clergy who had already decided to remain with the Episcopal Church.[237] Sanderson went on to declare later, "'Neither I nor anyone at Holy Communion sent that email (. . .). I have notified the sender that we will not be hosts.'"[238] Right after his call to Sanderson, Lawrence called Jim Lewis, then his lawyers Logan and Runyan.[239] On the next day, the diocesan office issued an open letter angrily denouncing the whole business and projecting an unsubtle warning to the Episcopal Church about trying the use the legal apparati of the old diocese.[240]

Following more than three weeks in which the old diocesan leadership almost completely ruled the public relations field, the Episcopal Church finally issued a strong public statement called a "Fact Sheet" on November 9 giving its position on the issues at hand. After asserting that the Presiding Bishop "continues to encourage openness to various paths forward" with Lawrence, it proclaimed "Dioceses cannot leave the Episcopal Church. While some clergy and individuals may choose to leave, congregations and property remain in the diocese to be used for the mission of the Episcopal Church."[241] The Fact Sheet dropped some tantalizing hints that were not in the public record. One was that in the spring of 2010, at the time of the Logan/Tisdale Affair, "a private meeting was held in Charleston at the request of the Presiding Bishop to see if the trajectory that

234. Conger, George. "Presiding Bishop backs Ecclesiastical Coup in South Carolina." Anglican Ink, November 11, 2012, http://anglicanink.com/article/presiding-bishop-backs-ecclesiastical-coup-south-carolina.

235. "Minutes of the Standing Committee." [November 6, 2012].

236. "Group Attempts to Mislead Clergy; Unauthorized Use of Diocesan Seal and Name." Diocese of South Carolina, November 8, 2012, http://www.diosc.com/sys/news-events/latest-news/465-group-attempts-to-mislead-clergy-unauthorized-use-of-diocesan-seal-and-name.

237. Ibid.

238. Ibid.

239. *Journal of the Two Hundred and Twenty Second (. . .)* 2013, 48.

240. "Group Attempts."

241. "Fact Sheet."

was apparent could be changed."[242] This begged the questions: Meeting of whom? What did the meeting discuss? What was its outcome? The Sheet continued that also in 2010, Bishop Clifton Daniel, of East Carolina, head of Province IV, and Jefferts Schori "engaged in private conversations with Lawrence."[243] Again, this begged the questions: When were the conversations? What did they discuss? What were the outcomes? The Fact Sheet then spent a good deal of space on the Title IV proceedings. Finally, it described the Presiding Bishop's actions after October 17 and the present efforts to reorganize the Episcopal Church diocese. It was a useful and helpful review for loyal Episcopalians, but was really too little and too late to have any positive effect on anyone else.

As the time for the special diocesan convention on November 17 drew closer, the war of words between the two sides escalated. On November 11, a public relations initiative appeared from each of the opponents. On November 11, the new Steering Committee published an ad in major newspapers as "An Open Letter to Episcopalians in the Diocese of South Carolina."[244] It announced a reorganization of the old diocese, a diocesan convention for next March, and a website, episcopaldioceseofsc@gmail.com. It used the name of the Diocese of South Carolina and the official seal of the Diocese. The website, which began on November 11, included a list of questions and answers such as the claim that the upcoming special convention was not a legitimate convention of the diocese: "This is not a gathering of the Episcopal Diocese of South Carolina."[245] Meanwhile on the same day, the two sides traded shots in the Charleston newspaper, *The Post and Courier,* in an article by Adam Parker. Spokesperson for the independent side, Joy Hunter, said: "neither Bishop Lawrence nor the standing Committee have been informed that they have been removed as the ecclesiastical authority. Has that been done without our notification?"[246] Neva Fox, spokesperson for the Episcopal Church, shot back: "Lawrence was indeed informed of his restricted status, and those associated with the new corporate entity called the Protestant Episcopal Church in the Diocese of South Carolina have left the church, and, therefore, have neither ecclesiastical authority nor a right to dictate what those who remain in the church can do."[247]

The skirmishes on the 11th were nothing compared to what was to come. Three days later, Lawrence published a full-page newspaper ad entitled "A Message to the People of the Diocese of South Carolina."[248] It was endorsed by sixty-nine clergy of the old diocese. The list was actually less than half of the enumerated clergy of the pre-schism diocese and included many deacons and retired clergy. Steve Skardon said the list contained only

---

242. Ibid.

243. Ibid.

244. "An Open Letter." [November 11, 2012].

245. "FAQs from New Diocesan Website." eNewsletter of the Episcopal Forum of SC, November 11, 2012, http://www.mynewsletterbuilder.com/email/newsletter/1411531562#article_4.

246. Parker, "Breakaway Anglicans."

247. Ibid.

248. Lawrence, (the Rt. Rev.) Mark. "A Message from Bishop Lawrence to the People of the Diocese of South Carolina." Diocese of South Carolina, November 14, 2012, http://www.diosc.com/sys/news-events/latest-news/467-a-messgae-from-bishop-lawrence-to-the-people-of-the-diocese-of-south-carolina.

thirty-three of the seventy-five rectors of the old diocese.[249] Lawrence's letter was about as hard-hitting as he could get at that point. Unsurprisingly he started out by deriding the Episcopal Church which he said had caused the present crisis through its revision of the true faith.[250] Next, he insisted that his diocese was fully "Anglican" and recognized and supported by a majority of Anglicans around the world. Then he turned to his real business at hand, "the national leadership of TEC is taking steps to undermine this diocese. What we are faced with is an intentional effort by the ill-advised TEC organization to assume our identity."[251] He continued, "it is hard to imagine what would drive former parishioners to such lengths except an agenda put forward by TEC's national litigation strategy team which has been used in other locations in similar ways when faithful dioceses and parishes have left TEC."[252] Finally, he warned darkly "This misuse of the diocesan seal and the diocesan name (. . .). Not only is it morally questionable; it is something for which they can be held accountable."[253] *Held accountable.* It would not take much imagination to know what Lawrence meant by this phrase. In fact, he knew very well that eight days earlier the Standing Committee had directed Runyan to begin legal efforts against the Episcopal Church. While Lawrence had reiterated the standard talking-points of his side, he also raised a new threat of legal action against the other side. He did so in spite of the fact that there had been no hint of legal action by the Church against the independent diocese.

Lawrence's open letter in the newspapers was timed to appear one day before the clergy conference that the Church side had organized for November 15 at St. Mark's in Charleston. The attendees who assembled could not have missed Lawrence's dire warning in the newspaper of the day before. Reports on the meeting varied according to the source. Pro-Church sources reported between sixty and seventy clergy present while anti-Church sources said forty. At any rate, it was only a fraction of the resident diocesan clergy of the old diocese. The group celebrated Eucharist, retired bishop vonRosenberg preached a sermon of hope, and the assembly moved on to discuss a wide range of issues surrounding the reorganization of the diocese in the Episcopal Church. One attendee was the Rev. Canon Jim Lewis, assistant to Lawrence, who was there to prepare a report for Lawrence and the Standing Committee. Lewis said the clergy day was held by the steering committee which was being directed by Jefferts Schori.[254] He relayed back to the Standing Committee that there "were only about forty people, mostly retired clergy and representatives from the five parishes that have stated that they are remaining in the National Church."[255] He added that the meeting was "conducted" by Tom Tisdale, serving as legal counsel for the presiding bishop, and that Tisdale had listed an advisory committee for the steering committee: the Rt. Rev. John Buchanan, the Rt. Rev. Charles

249. Skardon, Steve. "Enthusiasm for Renegade 'Convention' Cools." South Carolina Episcopalians, November 16, 2012, http://www.scepiscopalians.com/2012_Reports.php.

250. Lawrence, "A Message from Bishop Lawrence."

251. Ibid.

252. Ibid.

253. Ibid.

254. "Minutes of the Standing Committee." [November 20, 2012].

255. Ibid.

vonRosenberg, Melinda Lucka, and the Rev. Michael Wright.[256] The Standing Committee seemed to be unconcerned about the clergy day, but on the Church side it served as a sort of framework for a reorganization that was now well underway and would culminate in a special convention two months hence.

On the same day as the clergy conference at St. Mark's and two days before the independent diocese's special convention, the presiding bishop issued a pastoral letter to the Episcopalians of South Carolina.[257] She repeated much of what was already in the earlier "Fact Sheet." For instance, "the Diocese has not left. It cannot, by its own action. The alteration, dissolution, or departure of a diocese of the Episcopal Church requires the consent of General Convention, which has not been consulted."[258] Even though Lawrence had made it plain to her that he and the entire constituted authority of the old diocese had left the Episcopal Church, Jefferts Schori was not quite ready to accept it. She wrote, "If it becomes fully evident that those former leaders have, indeed, fully severed their ties with The Episcopal Church, new leaders will be elected."[259] She did not elaborate on "fully evident" but one might imagine she was referring to the special convention to be held in two days. Jefferts Schori went on to remind everyone that Lawrence could still end the crisis rather simply: "Bishop Lawrence has an extended period (60 days) in which he can repudiate those charges, and I stand ready to respond positively to any sign that he has done so."[260] The presiding bishop's letter buoyed the battered morale of the faithful Episcopalians of South Carolina, but it apparently had no effect at all on Lawrence and his followers who were now well-prepared for the special convention they had been planning for at least a month.

Responses to the crisis of October–November among Episcopal and Anglican bishops varied greatly. The vast majority kept a hands-off attitude. To be sure, Lawrence's close friends in the Global South leadership immediately rallied to his side. Not all of Lawrence's close friends were supportive. Daniel Martins, bishop of Springfield, issued an appeal entitled "For the Love of God" on his website.[261] Lawrence was so close to Martins that he had participated in Martins's consecration, one of the very few consecrations Lawrence attended as bishop. Martins wrote, "In the Presiding Bishop's defense, there is solid evidence that she has been a good-faith participant, with Bishop Lawrence and Bishop Andrew Waldo of the neighboring diocese of Upper South Carolina, in discussions pointed in the direction of creative avoidance of the impasse that has, in fact, ensued."[262] He went on, "To my beloved brothers and sisters in the Diocese of South

---

256. Ibid.

257. Jefferts Schori, (the Most Rev.) Katharine. "Presiding Bishop issues Pastoral Letter to Episcopal Diocese of South Carolina." Episcopal Church, Office of Public Affairs, November 15, 2012, http://www.episcopalchurch.org/posts/publicaffairs/presiding-bishop-issues-pastoral-letter-episcopal-diocese-south-carolina.

258. Ibid.

259. Ibid.

260. Ibid.

261. Martins, (the Rt. Rev.) Daniel. "For the Love of God." November 15, 2012, http://www.cariocaconfessions.blogspot.com/2012/11/for-the-love-of-god.

262. Ibid.

Carolina (. . .). For the love of God, step back from the brink (. . .). I am begging you: Do not abandon us."[263] He ended, "I am reduced to tears, and they may yet flow."[264] Martins was not the only one reduced to tears.

The Special Convention

Despite the ever-escalating war of words, despite all the excited publicity and anticipation, despite all of the dramatic posturing, the special diocesan convention of November 17, 2012, was in a way an anti-climax. A month earlier, the diocesan authorities had declared the diocese to be legally "disassociated" from the Episcopal Church, according to their own words. Lawrence and the entire diocesan leadership had very loudly and publicly declared they had left the Church and taken the diocese with them, lock, stock, and barrel. All efforts, at least public ones, at peace and reconciliation between diocese and Church had evaporated long ago. The convention was called only as a formality to follow the letter of the law and affirm the changes that had already been made. Everyone knew what was going to happen. Everyone knew the outcome in advance. Nevertheless, the assembly in St. Philip's Church in Charleston on November 17 had a historic gravity of moment that was unmistakable. For some it was a great hour of joy and celebration for others a time sorrow and sadness. Although the voting was only going through the motions, there was still a sense of irreversible finality, a crossing of a bridge after a very long, and for some exhausting, journey that had lasted more years that most of them could remember. Perhaps the assembly in St. Philip's came close to feeling the crowd euphoria of the December 1860 secession convention that had met a few blocks away or the unbridled joy most Charlestonians felt at 4:30 a.m. on April 12, 1861, when thundering cannons aimed at Fort Sumter jolted the city awake and people gathered on the rooftops to cheer wildly in a release of long pent-up emotions. Others though, such as the great diarist Mary Boykin Chesnut, fell on their knees in the pre-dawn darkness with fearful and tearful appeals to Heaven. They were the ones who really understood the significance of what was happening and the catastrophic whirlwind they were likely to reap. Practically everyone attending the special convention in 2012 was a jubilant secessionist too. The others stayed away, perhaps, as Chesnut had been, on their knees and in tears.

The majority of the diocese was represented at the special convention. Seventy-four clergy[265] were present along with 170 lay delegates (52 with voting rights).[266] Of the 71 parishes and missions of the old diocese, 55 were represented at the convention.[267] Sixteen boycotted the meeting that was, after all, illegal in the eyes of the Episcopal Church. These 16 would form the nucleus of the Episcopal Church diocese that was still in the early stage

---

263. Ibid.

264. Ibid.

265. "Diocese Moves Forward after Disassociation from TEC." *Jubilate Deo* (Diocese of South Carolina), Winter 2013, 1.

266. At the convention to elect Lawrence bishop, September 16, 2006, there were 106 clergy, 223 lay delegates representing 71 local churches.

267. On Nov. 18, 2012, the diocesan website listed 75 parishes and missions. Approximately 24 of them were missions.

of reorganization. When it came time to vote on the resolutions, 6 local churches abstained from voting leaving 49 parishes and missions to vote.[268] When 49 voted, that meant that 22 local churches of the old diocese did not vote. Thus, the decisions in the special convention came from about two-thirds of the old diocese. Nevertheless, it was clear that a majority of local churches and clergy were ready to go with the purported legal changes at hand. For many of them, if not most, it was not a question of whether to leave the Episcopal Church. In reality, they had already declared their independence years earlier. Thus, the official proceedings of the special convention were undramatic and quick.

The most remarkable moment of the day came in Lawrence's address to the assembly. It was another of his typically long, rambling, and wordy discourses (5,400 words) full of astonishing and sweeping assertions and generalizations with little evidence, and with plenty of righteous indignation, and Bible verses sprinkled for supportive effect. However, this one was different. This time was different. Everyone listened in rapt attention for this was the first public speech Lawrence made after he had announced the diocese's departure from the Episcopal Church seven weeks earlier. The crowd in the assembly hung on every word as the historic address was recorded by audio and video.

The address was divided in halves, the past and the future. The first part was mostly a reiteration of familiar themes established long ago by the diocesan leadership. In the first paragraph, Lawrence depicted himself as the innocent victim hounded to death while he was "seeking a peaceable way through this crisis."[269] Next, Lawrence took up his oft-repeated and by now well-known criticism of the Episcopal Church on three major points: theology, morality, and polity. Although he had recently backed away from the wedge-issue of homosexuality, he could not resist one more swipe: "our understanding of human nature, the given-ness of gender as male and female, woven by God into the natural and created order, is now declared by canon law to be unacceptable."[270] In this speech, Lawrence came down hardest on polity: "it is the Disciplinary Board for Bishops misuse of the church's polity that has finally left us with no place to stand within the Episcopal Church."[271] Again, he did not elaborate on the "misuse." Thus, Lawrence claimed, the Episcopal Church's abandonment of the true religion was the cause of the schism. The diocese was rightfully leaving a church that had fallen hopelessly in error.

Following his placing the entire blame for the schism on the Episcopal Church, Lawrence declared independence from the Church: "We have withdrawn from that

---

268. Parker, Adam. "Convention Sets Majority in Diocese on New Anglican Path." *The Post and Courier* (Charleston, SC), November 18, 2012, http://www.postandcourier.com/article/20121118/PC16/121119275. An Episcopal News Service article had different figures. It gave a total of 78 parishes and missions in the old diocese with 54 present (42 parishes and 12 missions). If 6 local churches abstained from voting, then 48 voted. If 48 voted, then 30 did not vote. Thus, the resolutions were passed by 62 % of all the parishes and missions. See Young, Sarah Moise, "South Carolinians Affirm Decision to Leave Episcopal Church." Episcopal News Service, November 17, 2012, http://www.episcopalchurch.org/library/article/south-carolinians-affirm-decision-leave-episcopal-church.

269. "Bishop Lawrence's Address to the Special Convention of the Diocese of South Carolina." Diocese of South Carolina, March 15, 2014, http://www.diosc.com/sys/index.php?option=com_content&view=article&id=468:bishop-lawrences-address-to-the-special-convention&Itemid=75.

270. Ibid.

271. Ibid.

Church (. . .) we move on (. . .). We shall move on. Actually let me state it more accurately, We have moved on. With the Standing Committee's resolution on disassociation the fact is accomplished."[272] It is important to note his use of the word "we." That word included himself. This was the public declaration of the news he had first given the Presiding Bishop on the phone on October 17. Next, Lawrence went on to a couple of unintentionally revealing comments. In one, he said that for some time the diocese had been developing its own pension plan for clergy, property insurance coverage for parishes, and health insurance, all entirely separate from the Episcopal Church. This should leave one wondering why the diocese would move to such things if they had no intention of separating from the Episcopal Church and if the schism was forced on them by a surprise attack of the Disciplinary Board for Bishops. In another place, Lawrence lamented the loss of the African American, Anglo-Catholic, and multi-racial congregations yet he ignored the reasons these groups might want to remain in the Episcopal Church.

In the second half of his address, Lawrence turned to the future. This was the part of the speech that everyone was awaiting. "Shepherd, where will you lead us from here?" That was the question on every communicant's mind on November 17. We have cut our ties with the Episcopal Church, so what do we do now? Lawrence announced that the diocese would not affiliate with anyone, at least just yet. He used the divorce metaphor: "if you've been in a troubling, painful or dysfunctional relationship for a long period of time and then the marriage or relationship ends, you would be wise not to jump right away into the first one that comes along."[273] He lamented the multitude of overlapping "Anglican" jurisdictions in the state of South Carolina, and did so without a hint of irony that he had just added to it. One looming question was why the diocese did not immediately affiliate with the Anglican Church in North America. All the earlier four cases of separatist dioceses had joined ACNA; and its archbishop, Robert Duncan, was an old and close friend of Lawrence from the Pittsburgh days. Lawrence did not address that issue. Indeed, he left the question of future affiliation wide open: "as we await further guidance from God regarding future affiliation."[274] Meanwhile, Lawrence declared to the assembly, "we remain an extra-provincial Diocese within the larger Anglican Communion."[275] As Lawrence finished, the adoring audience in old St. Philip's arose in enthusiastic, loud, and sustained applause. Lawrence and his people were as one. The long course of bonding had worked almost perfectly. The assembly did not care that he was not leading them anywhere. He was their man and they had given themselves to him without question. They implicitly trusted in him to lead them into the future as they trusted in God. Indeed, the first resolution about to appear for a vote boldly declared: "God has sent Bishop Lawrence to be our Bishop, only He has the authority to declare otherwise."[276] It would not be possible to give Lawrence a greater stamp of approval than that.

272. Ibid.
273. Ibid.
274. Ibid.
275. Ibid.
276. "Proposed Resolution R-1, 2012, Special Diocesan Convention." Diocese of South Carolina, November 17, 2012.

Exactly what was an extra-provincial diocese in the Anglican Communion? In the official structure of the Anglican Communion, there were six dioceses outside of the jurisdictions of the thirty-eight provinces, or independent churches, of the Communion. All but one of these were directly under the Archbishop of Canterbury. The one exception was the Diocese of Cuba which was a unique case because of certain highly unusual circumstances. Cuba was overseen by a metropolitan council made up of the primates of the Anglican provinces in Canada, the West Indies, and the United States. In fact, there was no such diocese as Lawrence claimed, a free-floating independent entity completely removed from a primatial authority in the Anglican Communion. Too, he gave no definition or description of how such a diocese would exist and function in the context of the Communion. To be sure, Lawrence never alluded to the fact that the Anglican province that had once given him legitimate power had "restricted," or temporarily removed, that power. Moreover, he gave no explanation of why the Diocese would not join the other four seceding dioceses in uniting with the Anglican Church in North America which had been recognized by GAFCON as the legitimate Anglican province in the United States.

Lawrence had told the assembly they were there to "affirm" the actions the standing committee had already taken. Therefore, the business session was brief and to the point. It lasted ninety minutes with little fanfare.[277] The three proposed resolutions sailed through in a flash.

The first resolution, Proposed Resolution R-1, gave a long list of complaints against the Episcopal Church then offered two resolutions. The first point said: "we (. . .) declare that we concur in the decision of the Standing Committee that we are no longer in any relationship with TEC, including union or association with in any capacity, and we declare her rightful Bishop to be the Rt. Rev. Mark J. Lawrence."[278] It continued, "we declare that as God has sent Bishop Lawrence to be our Bishop, only he has the authority to declare otherwise."[279] The second point went on: "this Diocese repudiates the action of TEC purportedly taken against our Bishop and declare null and void any claim by any member or representative of TEC to have any authority whatsoever over this Diocese."[280] This was the most important resolution before the special convention; and to emphasize this, Lawrence provided a two-page legal rationale entitled "On The Diocese of South Carolina's Withdrawal from the Episcopal Church."[281] He issued it as "the final and binding interpretation issued by Bishop Lawrence in his capacity as Ecclesiastical Authority in the Diocese."[282] Moreover, the resolution was offered by thirty-seven clergymen (no female included) representing thirty-six parishes and missions.[283] Appropriately enough, the first name on the list was FitzSimons Allison. A voice vote of the convention was taken. Only one "Nay" vote

---

277. Skardon, Steve. "Renegade 'Convention' Votes to Try to Secede from the Episcopal Church." South Carolina Episcopalians, November 17, 2012, http://www.scepiscopalians.com/2012_Reports.php.

278. "Proposed Resolution R-1."

279. Ibid.

280. Ibid.

281. Ibid.

282. Ibid.

283. Ibid.

was heard.[284] Thus, by Resolution R–1, this assembly declared Mark Lawrence to be their bishop in disregard of the fact that a month earlier he had resigned from the Episcopal Church, the only institution that had ever ordained him as a bishop.

The second resolution, Proposed Resolution R–2, was offered by the Standing Committee. It amended the diocesan constitution to remove all references to the Constitution of the Episcopal Church. A voice vote was taken and only two "nay" votes were heard.[285] This ended the last tenuous tie to the Episcopal Church.

The third resolution, Proposed Resolution R–3, was also offered by the Standing Committee. It removed all references to the Episcopal Church from the diocesan canons. This one required a roll call vote by orders. Among the clergy, the vote was 71 in favor while 3 abstained.[286] Lawrence was among the ones in favor. In the lay order, 47 voted in favor and 5 abstained.[287] While it was obvious that the great majority of delegates were anxious to approve their leadership's actions, not everyone was so sure. Some harbored reservations such as the Rev. Daniel Hank, of Barnwell, who abstained and remarked "'The mother church is the flesh that bore us, brought us into this world as Christians. I have diligently searched Scriptures and prayer book and have found no ceremony where one can divorce one's mother.'"[288]

The second and third resolutions were unremarkable. They were necessary as routine formalities to change the constitution and canons of the diocese. The first resolution, however, stood as a strange and curious invention. In the first place, according to Lawrence and the Standing Committee, it was entirely unnecessary as they had the right to remove the diocese from the Episcopal Church. The reference to God and Lawrence was also interesting. If God chose Lawrence to be a bishop, he did so only through the Episcopal Church. Lawrence's ordination, consecration, and installation as a bishop was entirely within the Episcopal Church. His whole authority as bishop had been within the framework of the Episcopal Church. The resolution said that only God could remove Lawrence. Exactly how God was supposed to remove him was also curious, and left unexplained. Logically, however, if God made Lawrence a bishop through the Episcopal Church, could not He also remove Lawrence through the Episcopal Church? The resolution tested logic as it contained the contradiction of accepting the authority of the Episcopal Church on one hand and rejecting it on the other. The second point of the resolution, declaring null and void any action of the Episcopal Church, was redundant as the diocese had already voted to remove all accession to the Canons of the Episcopal Church. Thus, the first resolution was not necessary at all as a legal action. Its real purpose was to solidify the majority of communicants to the diocesan leadership as represented by Lawrence and the thirty-seven clergymen who presented it. In this it was a great success.

284. "Diocese Moves Forward."
285. Ibid.
286. Ibid.
287. Ibid.
288. Schjonberg, Mary Frances and Sarah Moise Young, "Continuing Episcopalians in South Carolina 'Looking to the Future.'" Episcopal News Service, November 19, 2012, http://episcopaldigitalnetwork.com/ens/2012/11/19/continuing-episcopalians-in-south-carolina-looking-to-the-future.

There was no doubt that the diocesan leadership had secured the strong support of the clear majority of the old diocese for the schism. However, the drive to secede from the Episcopal Church was not as overwhelming as they claimed or might have wished. Of the seventy-one local churches, forty-nine, a little more than two-thirds, had approved the final resolutions of independence in the special convention, and not all of these were rock-solid. Twenty-two local churches, slightly more than a third of the old diocese, either strongly opposed the secession or were undecided. Sixteen local churches had made it clear that they were remaining with the national Church. About ten local churches were wavering between the two sides; and that meant at least large local contingents in favor of remaining with the Episcopal Church. Thus, popular support for the break from the Episcopal Church was not as overwhelming as the leadership asserted.

With no more to be done, the special convention adjourned at 2:00 p.m. The diocesan public relations campaign began immediately. Upon the adjournment, media representatives were invited to a news conference presided over by Joy Hunter, diocesan communications director, and featuring Canon Jim Lewis, Lawrence's assistant, and Lawrence. Reporters at hand were Adam Parker, of the Charleston *Post and Courier*, Carolyn Click, of the Columbia *State*, Sarah Moise Young, for the Episcopal News Service, Mary Ann Mueller, for Virtue Online, and George Conger. Lawrence's remarks were mostly a reiteration of his well-known talking points. When asked substantial questions about his relations with the rest of the Anglican Communion, Lawrence sidestepped the issue: "Alignment is not something that at this time is on the table."[289] The news conference ended quickly. Conservative reporters gave extensive and glowing coverage to the convention. Others were not so inclined. According to one attendant, "Some reporters said they were offended by the open hostility and occasional paranoia among convention leaders. They also questioned the reasons for the highly-controlled access they were given to Bishop Lawrence, as well as the extensive and unnecessary security measures, including the presence of Charleston policemen."[290]

The Renunciation and the Release and Removal of Bishop Lawrence

The independent diocese's public relations initiative continued the next day, November 18, when Lawrence gave a forty-five-minute television interview on Anglican TV.[291] The friendly interviewer, Kevin Kallsen, gave Lawrence plenty of room to expound on his thoughts. In the entire first part, Lawrence talked at length on sexuality. Referring to the General Convention resolutions on the rites for the blessing of same sex unions and rights for transgendered clergy, he said the Episcopal Church led the charge for

---

289. Mueller, Mary Ann. "Charleston, SC.: Post Special Convention Internet News Conference." Virtueonline, November 17, 2012, http://www.virtueonline.org/portal/modules/news/article.php?storyid=16826.

290. Skardon, Steve. "Renegade 'Diocese' Struggling to Recover from Sputtering Launch." South Carolina Episcopalians, November 26, 2012, http://www.scepiscopalians.com/2012_Reports.php.

291. "Interview with Bishop Mark Lawrence." Video recording, Anglican TV, November 18, 2012, 45 minutes, http://anglican.tv/content/anglicantv-interviews-bishop-lawrence.

"subjective" identification of gender "contrary to the teachings of Scripture."[292] This, he said, "abandons all understanding of gender."[293] For Lawrence, this individualization of gender identity promoted by the Episcopal Church was "a place too far."[294] He had to leave a Church, he said, that had abandoned its own historic doctrine, discipline, and worship. The interview gave insight into Lawrence's thinking at the time. Months later, the diocesan leaders insisted that the break from the Episcopal Church had not been about sexuality, but about theology. Lawrence's interview of November 18 showed clearly that at that moment of the special convention it was very much about sexuality. That was the issue foremost in his mind; and that would be the subject he would continue to emphasize for the moment.

The diocesan leadership's actions for the past few weeks were primarily for local consumption. Beyond the diocese, they had little concern at the moment. There were few words of encouragement in the non-GAFCON Anglican world. Not one of Lawrence's close allies among the bishops of the Episcopal Church came to his aid publicly. Lawrence's closest ally in the southeast, Bishop Howe of Central Florida had retired and been replaced by Bishop Greg Brewer who was reported to have called Lawrence's action "'heartbreaking.'"[295] Not one diocese in the Episcopal Church publicly endorsed South Carolina's actions. Even among the conservatives who had formed the anti-Episcopal Church called the Anglican Church in North America and who had expected Lawrence to join them, there was more dismay than support for Lawrence. While breaking away from the Episcopal Church he had pointedly refused to join his philosophical allies in the ACNA. In reality, the diocese was an insular entity in isolation. For the moment, though, that did not concern the majority of communicants of the old diocese.

Nor was it the primary concern of the diocesan leadership who knew the war with the Episcopal Church was just heating up. Three days after the special convention, the Standing Committee met with Lawrence, Wade Logan, and Alan Runyan. Coming out of a secret executive session, the committee unanimously resolved to initiate a lawsuit against the Episcopal Church: "The Standing Committee hereby authorizes the lawyer for the Protestant Episcopal Church in the Diocese of South Carolina to file at a time and place of his choosing a lawsuit on behalf of the Protestant Episcopal Church in the Diocese of South Carolina against TEC for a declaratory judgment."[296] This movement would remain secret outside the diocesan leadership until January 4, 2013, when the news of the lawsuit would break. One might wonder why the resolution on November 20 was necessary in light of the Standing Committee's resolution just two weeks earlier, on November 6, that had authorized its lawyers to take whatever legal steps necessary to protect the Diocese and its property.

---

292. Ibid.

293. Ibid.

294. Ibid.

295. Virtue, David. "Charleston, SC: Parishes are Free to Choose their own Ecclesiastical Future, says Bishop." Virtueonline, November 17, 2012, http://www.virtueonline.org/portal/modules/news/article.php?storyid=16827.

296. "Minutes of the Standing Committee." [November 20, 2012].

Awaiting the lawsuit, the diocesan leadership concentrated on continuing to press the public relations initiatives they had long handled so well. When the lawsuit came, they would need to control the message, at least for the sake of the local churches in the fold and those wavering. On November 25, they placed a full-page advertisement in a major newspaper outside the diocese, *The State*, published in Columbia, in the Diocese of Upper South Carolina. It was mainly a reiteration of Lawrence's points in his special convention address, and nothing new, but was endorsed by eighty listed clergypersons representing thirty-seven local churches in the down-state. The ad was a surprise to Bishop Waldo, of Upper South Carolina. No doubt it was a surprise to others too especially considering Lawrence's record of objecting to bishops interfering in other dioceses. Lawrence did not tell Waldo in advance of the ad; and Lawrence never explained his reasons for it to Waldo, nor did the two of them discuss it in one of their numerous subsequent phone calls.[297] Asked about the ad later, Waldo said he was not offended by this initiative and "perceived it as a rhetorical escalation directed at disaffected Episcopalians across the state" and not meant for the Diocese of Upper South Carolina per-se.[298] Waldo added that, at any rate, the ad "did not have any substantial effect in Upper South Carolina."[299] Its effects were perhaps strongest among the Church people in the upper regions of the old Diocese of South Carolina where *The State* was the standard daily newspaper.

While Lawrence and the other diocesan leaders continued boldly and confidently on their new path staking out their complete independence with the diocesan legal identity and most of the properties in hand, the Episcopal Church leaders were in a quandary as to an appropriate response. The Constitution and Canons of the Episcopal Church had no provision that addressed precisely a situation such as the one presently occurring in South Carolina. After Lawrence informed Jefferts Schori of the diocese's removal from the Church on October 17, she continued to hold out hope for several weeks that somehow a final break could be avoided. In time, she came to realize this was not possible and to see that Lawrence, who knew the Constitution and Canons very well, would do nothing to facilitate the Church actions against himself.

Presiding Bishop Jefferts Shori decided she had to act. The special convention of November 17 was the last straw for her. In it, Lawrence had publicly proclaimed he had left the Episcopal Church and had gone on record as voting for the three resolutions of the convention severing all ties to the Episcopal Church. It should be recalled that he had announced his resignation from the Episcopal Church to her by telephone a month earlier and had proceeded to disregard all the rules and regulations of the Episcopal Church thereafter. He ignored the restriction. He refused to see her again. That gave her two choices, either act on her own perhaps around the margins of the rules, or await a trial by the House of Bishops. The problem with the second was that the House would not meet until March of 2013, some four months away. This would leave the Episcopal Church in South Carolina unattended for a long time. Seven weeks after learning

---

297. Waldo, (the Rt. Rev.) Andrew. Telephone conversation with author, October 31, 2014.
298. Ibid.
299. Ibid.

Lawrence's intentions of complete independence, Jefferts Schori resolved to act and to do so with dispatch.

Her problem at the moment was that the Constitution and Canons contained two roadblocks that she would have to avoid. One was Title III, Canon 12, Section 7, part a (page 110 in the 2012 canons) that required a bishop to declare, in writing, to the presiding bishop, a renunciation of the ordained ministry of the Episcopal Church in order for the presiding bishop to issue a release. The other was Title III, Canon 12, Section 7, part b (page 110 in the 2012 canons) that held a bishop could not renounce his ministry if he or she were under presentment for any canonical offense. In view of the situation in which Lawrence declared that as an independent bishop he would not abide by the rules of his former Church, Jefferts Schori decided that she too could not be bound literally by the canons. She was in a place that had been occupied by many U.S. presidents who found that certain urgent circumstances unforeseen by the writers of the Constitution required them to work around the edges. Lincoln was famous for this as was Jefferson, Franklin Roosevelt and others. The greater need of the moment trumped the literal interpretation of the Constitution. One can see in retrospect their wisdom.

Immediately after the special convention of November 17, Jefferts Schori proceeded to act. In the absence of a formal letter from Lawrence declaring his renunciation of orders, she interpreted his words and actions in the convention to be the equivalent, that is, a de facto renunciation. She consulted her Council of Advice which was composed of the presidents or vice-presidents of the nine provinces of the Episcopal Church plus two others.[300] The Council concurred with the Presiding Bishop. Jefferts Schori drew up the official documents accepting Lawrence's renunciation of Holy Orders in the Episcopal Church and releasing him from the ordained ministry.

On Wednesday, December 5, 2012, Lawrence was going about his routine business apparently unaware and certainly unconcerned about the doings of the Episcopal Church leadership. That morning he had a meeting at St. Paul's in Summerville. By noon he was back in his office at the diocesan headquarters on Coming Street. At 12:30, he entered a meeting of the Benefits Committee concerning the diocesan pension plan. At 12:45 p.m. he was summoned for an unexpected phone call. It was from the Presiding Bishop in New York. She told Lawrence that she had accepted his renunciation of ministry and had released him from his ordinations. She said she was sending hard copies by e-mail and mail. He listened politely, asked a couple of questions, did not argue or try

---

300. The Council of Advice: Bishops Steven Lane of Maine (Prov. I); Lawrence Provenzano of Long Island (Prov. II); Neff Powell of Southwestern Virginia (Prov. III), Dabney Smith of Southwest Florida (Prov. IV), Wayne Smith of Missouri (Prov. V); Rob O'Neill of Colorado (Prov. VI); Larry Benfield of Arkansas (Prov. VII); James Mathes of San Diego (Prov. VIII); Francisco Duque of Colombia (Prov. IX); Dean Wolfe of Kansas, vice-president of the House of Bishops; Clay Matthews of the Office of Pastoral Development. "Presiding Bishop Accepts Mark Lawrence's Renunciation." Episcopal Church, Office of Public Affairs, Episcopal News Service, December 5, 2012, http://episcopaldigitalnetwork.com/ens/2012/12/05/presiding-bishop-accepts-mark-lawrences-renunciation.

to rebut, then hung up.[301] Back in the committee meeting, he spent the next three hours sending out e-mails.[302]

The whole matter was short, business-like and to the point. The Presiding Bishop's official document, called "Renunciation of Ordained Ministry and Declaration of Removal and Release," declared tersely Lawrence "is therefore removed from the Ordained Ministry of this Church and released from the obligations of all Ministerial offices, and is deprived of the right to exercise the gifts and spiritual authority as a Minister of God's Word and Sacraments conferred on him in Ordinations."[303]

A new war of words began immediately on December 5. The Church public relations office tried to get out front on the story in the afternoon by publishing a defensive news article on the Church website entitled "Presiding Bishop Accepts Mark Lawrence's Renunciation." It was a long piece describing the presiding bishop's action, the Disciplinary Board's work, and the Presiding Bishop's pastoral letter of November 15. However, as usual this was no match for the furious barrage from the old diocesan leadership. Before nightfall on December 5, the diocesan office posted on its website a blazing article and an equally defiant letter from Lawrence. The article denounced the "lawless" Presiding Bishop for ignoring the canons that required a letter of renunciation from a bishop and prevented a release while a bishop was under a disciplinary process. It declared "Bishop Lawrence has never renounced his orders or expressed the desire to do so."[304] This was proof, the article said, of the moral bankruptcy of the Episcopal Church: "As surely as these same interpretive habits have created theological chaos within the Episcopal Church, these latest actions are further evidence of increasing canonical chaos and a leadership that has slipped all restraints in pursuit of its agenda and goals."[305] *Slipped all restraints in pursuit of its agenda and goals.* As usual, the "agenda" and "goals" were left unidentified, but did not take much imagination to get the meaning. Lawrence's letter was also bluntly defiant: "Quite simply I have not renounced my orders as a deacon, priest or bishop any more than I have abandoned the Church of Jesus Christ (. . .) the Diocese of South Carolina has canonically and legally disassociated from The Episcopal Church. We took that action before today's attempt to claim a renunciation of my orders, thereby making it superfluous."[306] He continued: "So we move on—onward and upward (. . .) and I remain the Bishop of the Diocese of South Carolina."[307] Then he concluded that with the support of "the vast majority" of the Diocese and "the majority of Anglicans around the world" he remained "an Anglican Bishop in good standing."[308]

---

301. "Diocesan Statement Regarding Claimed Renunciation." Diocese of South Carolina, December 5, 2012, http://www.diosc.com/sys/news-events/latest-news/477-diocesan-statement-regarding-claimed-renunciation.

302. *Journal of the Two Hundred and Twenty Second (. . .)* 2013, 50.

303. "Presiding Bishop Accepts."

304. "Diocesan Statement."

305. Ibid.

306. Ibid.

307. Ibid.

308. Ibid.

The question remained, did Mark Lawrence renounce his Holy Orders? The Episcopal Church leadership said he did. The old diocesan leadership said he did not. Lawrence said he did not. It all goes back to how one defines the word "renounce." A dictionary definition of the word renounce is to refuse to follow, obey, or recognize, as the authority of a church. That Lawrence did without question. He very publicly renounced the authority of the Episcopal Church. This was in contradiction of his consecration vow on January 26, 2008, to adhere to the discipline of the Episcopal Church. He cast off this ordination vow of obedience to the discipline of the Episcopal Church on October 15, 2012, reiterated this to the presiding bishop on October 17, and publicly proclaimed it in the convention of November 17. All of his ordinations had been in the Episcopal Church. All of his authority to be a bishop had come from the Episcopal Church. The fundamental question then was whether the Church that had conferred the orders on him had the right to revoke them. The Church said it did. Lawrence said it did not. Lawrence believed the Church had the right to confer authority on him but did not have the right to remove it since it had not followed the letter of the law. But then, if he were not in the Episcopal Church under what authority would he be acting as a bishop? What church would be recognizing him as a bishop? Lawrence's answer to that of one holy, catholic, and apostolic church is a concept, an idea, not a specific institutional reality. The idea that a person could renounce an institution and take with him the powers granted by that institution was not logical. Yet, Lawrence was correct to say that he did not submit a letter of renunciation to the presiding bishop as stated in the canon. Moreover, there was no record that he publicly stated explicitly such a renunciation of his orders. Thus, in a technical sense, Lawrence was correct to say that he did not renounce his ministry. He was correct that the presiding bishop did not strictly adhere to the letter of the law. However, the question of the renunciation was similar to the question of the restriction. In a strictly narrow sense Lawrence was right, but not in the broader world of reality. He could say on a technicality that he had not been restricted when he and everyone else knew that he had been. Too, he could say that he had not renounced his Holy Orders when he and everyone else knew that he had voluntarily resigned from the Episcopal Church, the very institution which had conveyed the Orders on him. Beyond the legal technicalities and narrow interpretations, the reality was that Lawrence left the Episcopal Church, the one and only church that had granted him ordination and episcopal authority. However, none of this mattered to the rank-and-file communicants who followed Lawrence. They fervently rallied around their leader who insisted he was still a bishop and the legitimate bishop of the diocese. As far as they were concerned he was right and the Episcopal Church was wrong.

The Episcopal Church's handling of Lawrence on December 5, 2012, was not unprecedented. In fact, several years earlier, four dioceses and their bishops had already done what South Carolina and Lawrence did in 2012. Two of those four bishops, Schofield of San Joaquin and Duncan of Pittsburgh were deposed after votes of the House of Bishops determined that they had abandoned the Episcopal Church. The two others, Iker of Fort Worth and Ackerman of Quincy were handled similarly to Lawrence's case. As Lawrence, they did not submit a written renunciation of their orders or a resignation from the Episcopal Church, but led the majorities in their dioceses out of the Church declaring by word and deed their, and their diocese's, complete separation from the Episcopal Church. Jefferts Schori and her Council then accepted the renunciation of orders from Iker and Ackerman and deposed them as ordained clergy.[309] She did the same with Lawrence.

The Eve of the Legal War, December 2012

Once the matter of Lawrence's release and removal was out of the way, the prevailing issue at hand was: Who owned the legal rights to the old diocese? Most importantly: Who owned the properties? Both sides claimed sole ownership and proceeded to act accordingly. The independent diocesan structure had an enormous advantage over the other side by possession and by a highly efficient in-place institutional organization. As we have seen, long before Lawrence was released and removed, the old standing committee had twice directed its lawyers to proceed with a lawsuit against the Episcopal Church to "protect" the legal rights including the property. Judging from the January 4, 2013, lawsuit, Runyan was already well underway with the preparation of the lawsuit. This was an advantage that was to pay off handsomely for the independent diocese in the months to come. It was clear from the start that the old diocese was well-prepared to take a pro-active, even aggressive, posture toward the Episcopal Church. They were not going to wait around for the Episcopal Church to drag them into court. Apparently, they had learned valuable lessons from the four earlier cases of secessionist dioceses. The South Carolinians would handle things differently.

On the Church side, matters were anything but the same. The entire governing structure had left the Church and the bishop had been removed. In the Church's view, after December 5, there was no ecclesiastical authority in the Diocese of South Carolina, no bishop, and no standing committee. There was a vacuum that needed to be filled, and soon. They did not know just how soon until they were suddenly and surprisingly hit with the diocesan lawsuit on January 4. By then, it was a little late. Meanwhile, the steering committee that had formed in October assembled on December 6, the day after Lawrence was officially removed as bishop. They immediately "voted to hold a special Convention in early 2013 for the purpose of electing a Standing Committee and other officers and a Provisional Bishop for the Episcopal Diocese of South Carolina."[310] The committee also announced that it was calling a meeting on health insurance coverage on December 13.

Events began to move apace on the Church side. Mindful of the urgency of the moment, the steering committee tried to act as quickly as possible. Two days after their December 6 meeting, they announced that the special convention would be held on January 25 and 26, 2013, at Grace Church in Charleston, to be presided over by none

---

309. Schjonberg, Mary Frances. "Lawrence Says He's Still Bishop, Calls Renunciation 'Superfluous.'" Episcopal News Service, December 6, 2012, http://episcopaldigitalnetwork.com/ens/2012/12/06/lawrence-says-hes-still-bishop.

310. "News from the Steering Committee, December 6, 2012." eNewsletter of the Episcopal Forum of SC, December 7, 2012, http://www.mynewsletterbuilder.com/email/newsletter/1411559727.

other than the presiding bishop.[311] Moreover, a nominating committee was at work with the presiding bishop to discern a nominee for provisional bishop.[312] Across the diocese, ordinary Episcopalians began collecting into informal worshipping communities as their parishes left the Episcopal Church and the non-Episcopalians continued to occupy the properties. The best known of these communities had actually been around for a long time. It was St. Mark's at Port Royal. Lawrence apparently had done little to help this fledgling community, perhaps not to offend his staunch allies at St. Helena's.[313] At the special convention in a few weeks, St. Mark's communicants would make a triumphal entry amid loud, enthusiastic, and long applause, to be proclaimed a mission of the diocese. In Florence, twelve communicants of St. John's met in a living room to continue the Episcopal Church. All of the parishes and missions of the Pee Dee had left the Episcopal Church. In time this group would grow rapidly to become St. Catherine's mission as it drew scores of loyal Episcopalians from miles around. Large and enthusiastic worshipping communities of devoted Episcopalians also formed on Edisto Island, and in Conway, Summerville, and Mount Pleasant. From the upstate, Bishop Waldo, still a friend to Lawrence, also sent his encouragement to the Episcopalians: "'choose a better way, a way that is neither dismissive of our own theological diversity nor the challenge Jesus has laid literally at the feet of his disciples as he washed them: to love and serve him in one another—together.'"[314]

Over on the independent diocesan side, the leadership continued to fight back strenuously against the Episcopal Church's claim to the legal status of the diocese. Upon release of the news of the special convention and the presiding bishop's visit, Lawrence posted on the diocesan website a strong statement: "They are certainly free to gather and meet, but they are not free to assume our identity."[315] He continued: "The Diocese of South Carolina has disassociated from the Episcopal Church (. . .) we continue to be the Diocese of South Carolina—also known, legally as the Protestant Episcopal Church in the Diocese of South Carolina and as the Episcopal Diocese of South Carolina, of which I remain the Bishop."[316] For good measure he offered advice to the Church steering committee: "select a new name or choose another Diocese with which to associate."[317] The committee would not take his advice. Jim Lewis and Kendall Harmon also added com-

---

311. Skardon, Steve. "Continuing Diocese of South Carolina to Elect New Bishop on January 25–26." South Carolina Episcopalians, December 8, 2012, http://www.scepiscopalians.com/2012_reports.php.

312. Schjonberg, Mary Frances. "Presiding Bishop to Visit South Carolina Diocese." Episcopal News Service, December 10, 2012, http://episcopaldigitalnetwork.com/ens/2012/12/10/presiding-bishop-to-visit-south-carolina.

313. Skardon, Steve. "Enthusiasm for the Continuing Diocese Builds as Election of New Bishop Approaches." South Carolina Episcopalians, December 18, 2012, http://www.scepiscopalians.com/2012_Reports.php.

314. Click, Carolyn. "Lowcountry Congregations Wrestle with Whether to Stay or Go." *The State* (Columbia, SC), December 11, 2012.

315. Lawrence, (the Rt. Rev.) Mark. "Diocese Responds to Announcement of January TEC Meeting." Diocese of South Carolina, http://www.diosc.com/sys/news-events/latest-news/479-diocese-responds-to-announcement-of-january-tec-meeting.

316. Ibid.

317. Ibid.

ments below Lawrence's on the posting. Lewis said: "A new entity will need to be created by those who choose to leave the Diocese and re-associate with the Episcopal Church."[318] Harmon added his opinion: "they run roughshod over their own constitution and canons. They have created a tails we win, heads you lose world where the rules are adjusted according to their desired outcomes—no wonder we disassociated from a community like that."[319]

If the pre-schism leaders were riled up at the news of the Church's special convention, they were doubly so when they learned on December 19 that the presiding bishop had issued an official call for a convention under the title of "the Diocese of South Carolina." The old diocesan leaders had no intention of giving up that title or the other official names. The next day, the diocesan authorities posted a statement on the diocesan website in the strongest terms possible. It said: "The Presiding Bishop has no authority to call any convention in the Diocese of South Carolina under its corporate bylaws and canons (. . .). Under South Carolina law, only Bishop Lawrence and the Standing Committee, acting as the Board of Directors can call a convention of the Diocese. 'We have not called any convention for January 2013,' explained Bishop Lawrence"[320] Lawrence insisted that the presiding bishop was setting up a new diocese: "'The name 'The [Episcopal] Diocese of South Carolina' is the registered property and identity of the Diocese.'"[321] Then Lawrence concluded with a dark warning to the Church side: "'This misuse of our name and identity by TEC is a violation of South Carolina law and can subject it to liability for treble damages and attorneys' fees (. . .). I call upon TEC to cease and desist from the continued misuse of our name and identity.'"[322] Lawrence's words fell on deaf ears.

As the year 2012 drew to a close, the two sides were at a stand-off as the war of words escalated. The division was complete. The two sides were separate. The independent diocese under Lawrence was on its own, unaffiliated with any larger group, while it stubbornly clung to the legal rights, titles, and properties of the Episcopal diocese. The Episcopal Church claimed possession of the old diocese too and continued using the official names in spite of Lawrence's warning. It had drawn up plans for a special convention in January to reorganize the Church diocese. Unknown to them, Logan and Runyan were well underway to take the Church to court long before the reorganization could take place. All things considered, the independent diocese was in the stronger position and was about to make that even stronger.

Mark Lawrence had every reason to close the year of 2012 in satisfaction even if it were in exhaustion. He had weathered the storm to hold the majority of the old diocese together. They were strongly bonded to him. He had led them out of what he saw as the errant old Episcopal Church with legal rights and property in hand. He had avoided punishment from the Episcopal Church by simply leaving the Church. He had a strong

---

318. Ibid.

319. Ibid.

320. "Diocese of South Carolina Only Authority to Convene Convention in the Diocese." Diocese of South Carolina, December 20, 2012, http://www.diosc.com/sys/news-events/latest-news/483-diocese-of-south-carolina-only-authority-to-convene-convention-in-the-diocese.

321. Ibid.

322. Ibid.

and devoted diocesan leadership around him and equally strong and resolute lawyers not to mention thousands of loyal communicants. On the whole, signs looked good and hopeful for the survival of the independent diocese. Lawrence was even beginning to get appreciative recognition outside the Anglican world. A highly socially conservative group calling itself the "Gay Christian Movement Watch" with "A Blog Upholding Biblical Standards of Sexuality," on the Internet named Lawrence one of its "12 Heroes of the Faith" for the year 2012.[323]

In the midst of all this, Lawrence received the sad news on December 10, that his beloved mother, Bertha Lawrence, was dying in California.[324] He left at once. The next day he was in Santa Margarita, California, at her side by 3:30 p.m. He talked with her for the last time. At 5:30 the next morning, his sister Pam called with the news that their mother had died. The funeral was held on December 15, at Trinity United Methodist Church in Bakersfield where his mother had been a fixture for decades. At that place and at that time in his life, Mark Lawrence could not have helped being overwhelmed by memories of the past, his mother, his father, growing up in Bakersfield, his religion, his ministry, and his very eventful life since leaving home. The frail newborn who barely survived birth had proved in the long run to be a tough survivor indeed. He must have felt some satisfaction in that even in the view that difficult challenges lay just ahead. The next day, Lawrence returned to Charleston to begin preparing for those hard days. December of 2012 had ended more than one phase of his life. The close of the year would prove to be both an end and a beginning of a new chapter for himself and the diocese he led.

323. "GCMW Releases its '12 Heroes of the Faith' List for 2012." Gay Christian Movement Watch, December 27, 2012, http://www.gcmwatch.com/tag/bishop-mark-lawrence.

324. *Journal of the Two Hundred and Twenty Second (. . .) 2013*, 50.

6

Two Dioceses, 2013 and After

CHARTING A NEW COURSE

THE YEAR 2012 ENDED with the old Diocese of South Carolina finally divided into two hostile camps, both calling themselves the Diocese of South Carolina and both claiming the rights and assets of the pre-schism diocese. The dispute between the two sets of former friends involved not just the names and insignia, but also an estimated half billion dollars' worth of assets in accounts, paraphernalia and real estate. The old diocesan officials insisted the diocese was an independent entity fully entitled to disassociate at will from the Episcopal Church and equally entitled to continue the form and substance of the pre-schism diocese through its two state-registered corporations, the Diocese and the Trustees of the Diocese. On the other hand, the Episcopal Church party of the old diocese demanded that it alone held the rights to the Episcopal diocese through the terms of the Constitution and Canons of the Episcopal Church. As all the earlier cases of dioceses claiming to secede from the Episcopal Church, this one too would inevitably go to the courts. Consuming litigation would dominate the lives of the two dioceses in the few years following the schism of 2012.

Legal actions were not new in the Diocese of South Carolina. The Diocese had recently spent nine years in court battling the breakaway parish of All Saints of Pawleys Island. However, since the *All Saints* case was a dispute between the diocese and a parish, it did not necessarily set the precedent to settle a dispute between the diocese and the Church which raised different issues. Nor could the two dioceses look to the four earlier cases of schisms for legal precedent. All four had been litigated, but the judges' decisions varied widely from one side to the other. No national standard had emerged, even after years of actions in various state courts. By the time of the South Carolina schism, only one of the four cases had been finally settled and that was because of a peculiar local circumstance unknown in the other cases. By the time of the South Carolina schism, the local courts across the nation had rendered widely divergent decisions, but none of the cases had been finally settled in court.

The two sides in South Carolina had no standard legal precedent to follow. None of the four earlier cases had been resolved in a state supreme court. Not one had been accepted by the United States Supreme Court. While the lawyers had no national law to follow, they did have five years of legal actions in the four earlier cases to study. As time would tell, it was evident that the lawyers on both sides were intimately familiar with the four earlier cases and patterned their strategies on lessons learned. The fifth case of a diocese disputing the national Church would turn out to be quite different than the earlier ones.

The basic difference between South Carolina and the earlier four was the proactive and preemptive strategy and tactics the secessionist diocesan lawyers took. Wade Logan remained the chancellor of the diocese, but the lead was taken by Alan Runyan, who had been hired in late 2009 as the attorney of the standing committee. As we have seen, well before the schism, the diocese had moved certain funds into hidden accounts according to the deposition of assistant treasurer of the old diocese, Nancy Armstrong, entered in the circuit court trial of 2014.[1] This would prevent the Church lawyers from freezing the diocesan funds as they had done in Quincy. We have also seen that the standing committee directed Runyan to prepare legal action soon after the schism occurred. In the first four cases, the Episcopal Church took the offense and forced the breakaway diocese to fight on the defense. This would not happen in South Carolina. The secessionist lawyers prepared well and carefully to strike first. This time it would be the secessionist diocese that would declare war forcing the Church to scramble and fight on the defensive. This would make the litigation in South Carolina strikingly different than that in all of the four previous cases.

As a last item of preparation before entering a lawsuit, the secessionists' lawyers registered a revised version of the corporate By-Laws of the Trustees of the diocese. On January 4, 2013, the new By-Laws changed the President of the corporation of the Trustees from "the Bishop" to "Mark J. Lawrence."[2] This guaranteed that Lawrence personally would remain the head of the Trustees' corporation whether or not he was the bishop of the diocese. Before going to court, the diocesan authorities and their attorneys had apparently done all they could to solidify and protect Lawrence's place as head of the diocese regardless of whatever actions the Episcopal Church, and possibly even the courts, might take. None of the earlier four cases of secessionist dioceses had gone to such lengths for its bishop.

TO STATE COURT, EARLY 2013

At 11:52 a.m. on Friday, January 4, 2013, Runyan led a team of five attorneys[3] representing the Diocese of South Carolina[4] to enter a lawsuit against the Episcopal Church in

1. "Deposition of Nancy Armstrong."

2. "By-Laws of the Trustees of the Protestant Episcopal Church in South Carolina." January 4, 2013. State of South Carolina, Court of Common Pleas, County of Dorchester, Case No. 2013-CP-18–00013, Exhibit DSC-17, July 8, 2014.

3. Runyan, Henrietta U. Golding, Charles H. Williams, David Cox, and Thomas Davis.

4. For simplicity sake, from this point on, the author will refer to this entity as DSC. The authorities and majority of the pre-schism diocese remained in possession of the institutional structure, the diocesan properties, and most of the local properties of the old diocese. In January of 2013, a circuit court gave legal rights of this group to the names: Diocese of South Carolina, The Protestant Episcopal Church in South Carolina, and the Episcopal Diocese of South Carolina. The author will also refer to Mark Joseph Lawrence from this point on as "Bishop Lawrence," although Lawrence had abandoned the

a local state court. The place they chose was the Court of Common Pleas of the First Judicial Circuit. There, Judge Diane Schafer Goodstein took the case.

The lawyers did not explain publicly why they chose this particular court. The state of South Carolina was divided into sixteen circuits for the basic court, called the Common Pleas. Eight of these were in the eastern half of the state, the area occupied by the diocese of South Carolina. Charleston and Berkeley counties composed District Nine, the largest set of courts in the low country. However, Runyan and the others entered their case not the expected site of Charleston, the seat of the diocese, but in District One which covered rural Dorchester, Orangeburg, and Calhoun counties and held only two judges, one being Goodstein. The lawyers entered their suit in Dorchester County where the court convened in the county courthouse in Saint George, a small town some forty miles northwest of Charleston.

There was one pre-existing tie between Runayn's law firm and Judge Goodstein. A lawyer in the Runyan firm had clerked for Judge Goodstein. Runyan and his partner Daniel A. Speights had established the law firm of Runyan and Speights in Beaufort in 1987. As of its website in 2016, it held four attorneys, Runyan, Speights, A.G. Solomons III, and Andrew Platte. Platte had been admitted to the South Carolina Bar in 2008 and had "Served as Law Clerk to the Honorable Diane S. Goodstein, Chief Administrative Judge, First Judicial Circuit."[5]

By the time of the schism in 2012, Runyan had gained a national, perhaps international, reputation as a highly successful litigator, particularly for environmental issues such as asbestos. Soon after establishing his own firm in Beaufort with Speights, Runyan was hailed by *The New York Times* "one of the nation's busiest asbestos property damage lawyers, persuaded a jury to award Clayton Center Associates nearly $17.9 million."[6] Runyan was quoted as saying, "'There are a lot of asbestos property damage cases out there with larger claims than this (. . .). I have some of them myself.'"[7] One witness wrote, "Since 1990, he has obtained verdicts or settlements for his clients in environmental property damage cases in excess of $150 million."[8] According to his website in 2016, Runyan's specialties were: "asbestos property damage, products liability, environmental litigation, computer software development suits and class actions."[9] Within a few weeks after the state supreme court's *All Saints* decision of September 2009, Runyan formed a close bond with Bishop Lawrence and quickly became the leading legal light of the diocese, as we have seen, playing a significant role in guiding the diocese on legal matters promoting the differentiation of the diocese.

Episcopal Church and the Church had removed him as a bishop. Lawrence and his followers insisted he was still a bishop. As a matter of convenience, the text will continue to refer to his as Bishop Lawrence.

5. "A Tradition of Advocacy and Success. Andrew Platte." http://www.speightsrunyan.com/attorneys/andrew-platte.

6. Feder, Barnaby J. "Making a Difference: Making a Mark in Asbestos." *The New York Times*, March 8, 1992.

7. Ibid.

8. Simons, Robert A. *When Bad Things Happen to Good Property*. Washington, DC: Environmental Law Institute, 2005, xix.

9. "A Tradition of Advocacy and Success. C. Alan Runyan." http://www.speightsrunyan.com/attorneys/c-alan-runyan.

Judge Goodstein had also become a well-known figure before the schism. She was born Diane Schafer in 1951, in Dillon, South Carolina. She was admitted to the South Carolina Bar in 1981 serving as an associate in the firm of Goodstein, Bowling, Douglas & Phillips until 1983 when she began sharing a law practice with her husband, Arnold Samuel Goodstein. Arnold Goodstein had been a member of the state senate from 1975 to 1980 and was at one time state highway commissioner. By the early 2000s, Arnold Goodstein had built a major construction company, Summerville Homes, eventually developing thirty subdivisions in the fast-growing Charleston suburbs.[10] After the housing crash of 2007–08, he declared bankruptcy owing about $63 million.[11] Diane Goodstein was not named as a party in the bankruptcy, but according to one report: "she was transferred unspecified property during or within a year of the bankruptcy filing. She's paying her portion of the settlement from annuity she owns."[12] The Goodsteins agreed to pay five hundred thousand dollars to settle a lawsuit that they improperly transferred real estate holdings involved in the bankruptcy proceedings.[13] Although agreeing to pay the sum, Diane Goodstein did not admit guilt in the matter and disputed the claim of impropriety.[14]

In 1998, Diane Goodstein left the law practice she had shared with her husband when she was elected by the state legislature to the post of judge for the Circuit Court of the First Circuit. In South Carolina, judges and justices were elected by the General Assembly upon recommendation of a commission. In 2007, Diane Goodstein was a candidate for justice of the state supreme court but failed to gain the post. Before the schism, she was in the news concerning accusations that she had colluded with Catholic Church authorities in a sexual abuse case. In June of 2008, a local newspaper reported that Gregg Meyers, an attorney for the abuse victims "is accusing the church of delaying payment of $1.375 million and colluding with class counsel and Diane Goodstein, the circuit court judge in Dorchester County who presided over the class-action case."[15]

On January 4, 2013, Runyan and his cohorts filed with Judge Goodstein "Complaint for Declaratory and Injunctive Relief" asking the court to declare the independent diocese to be the holder of the legal rights and assets of the pre-schism diocese and forbidding the Episcopal Church from doing so.[16] The lawyers argued in their sixty-five-page treatise that the diocese was an independent and self-governing body that had withdrawn from the Episcopal Church. Sixteen parishes joined in the suit.[17] Runyan, and

10. Stech, Katy. "Goodstein Details Downfall." *The Post and Courier* (Charleston, SC), July 24, 2010, http://www.postandcourier.com/article/20100724/PC05/307249990.

11. Ibid.

12. "Judge, Husband Settle Bankruptcy Dispute." Patch, March 15, 2013, http://patch.com/south-carolina/summerville/judge-husband-settle-bankruptcy-dispute.

13. Ibid.

14. Ibid.

15. Parker, Adam. "Charges Fly in Suit over Catholic Diocese Settlement." *The Post and Courier* (Charleston, SC), June 5, 2008, http://www.postandcourier.com/news/charges-fly-in-suit-over-catholic-diocese-settlement/article_61076476-Se27-Sdle-bb93-a7b0adc3271a.html.

16. "Complaint for Declaratory and Injunctive Relief." State of South Carolina, County of Dorchester, In the Court of Common Pleas for the First Judicial Circuit, Case No. 2013-CP-18-13, January 4, 2013.

17. Christ/St. Paul's of Yonges Island, Church of the Cross at Bluffton, Holy Comforter of Sumter,

Andrew Platte, Goodstein's former clerk, were listed as attorneys of six of the parishes. Binding local churches into the diocesan lawsuit was something new. None of the four earlier breakaway dioceses had done such. This combination would both strengthen the suit and solidify the local churches' stake in the diocesan schism.

The original lawsuit of January 4 included as co-plaintiffs only about a third of the local churches of the old diocese. Diocesan leaders aimed for as much unity and strength as they could muster for the war ahead against a Church they claimed was not only heretical but also an aggressive villain out to steal local property. As Bishop Lawrence told his followers: "'Legal action is necessary to protect our members from an organization that uses the threat of legal action as a cudgel to keep the parishes in line (. . .). We seek to be free from the national church's unorthodox theology which separates it from centuries of Anglican teachings and the fundamental beliefs of the global Anglican Communion.'"[18] Diocesan leaders spread the word that the lawsuit was necessary "to prevent The Episcopal Church (TEC) from hijacking local property."[19] The cry to circle-the-wagons-against-the-attacking-enemy, even if the supposed enemy was nowhere in sight, worked well. On January 22, diocesan lawyers entered an amended suit adding fourteen parishes as co-plaintiffs plus St. Andrew's Anglican Church of Mt. Pleasant.[20] On 28 February diocesan lawyers entered a second amendment to the original suit adding three more diocesan parishes as plaintiffs and naming the Episcopal Church diocese, called the Episcopal Church in South Carolina, as a co-defendant along with the original one, the Episcopal Church.[21] The second amendment ended the formation of the original lawsuit. As the suit finally stood, the corporation of the Diocese, the corporation of the Trustees of the Diocese, thirty-three parishes of the Diocese, and one parish in another denomination (St. Andrew's of Mt. Pleasant) were the plaintiffs bringing the suit while the Episcopal Church and the Episcopal Church diocese (the Episcopal Church in South Carolina), were the defendants responding to the suit. This was to set the stage for years of legal combat between the independent diocese and the Episcopal Church/Episcopal Church diocese.

As preparations for the reorganization of the Episcopal Church diocese continued apace, Bishop Lawrence and the other authorities of DSC feared that the Church entity

---

Church of the Redeemer of Orangeburg, St. Luke's of Hilton, Head, St. John's of Florence, St. Matthias of Summerton, Cathedral Church of St. Luke and St. Paul, Our Saviour of Johns Island, Good Shepherd of Charleston, St. Philip's of Charleston, St. Michael's of Charleston, Prince George Winyah of Georgetown, St. Helena's of Beaufort, St. Paul's of Summerville, and Trinity of Myrtle Beach.

18. "Another 15 Parishes Join the Diocese Suit to Block The Episcopal Church from Seizing Local Property." Diocese of South Carolina, January 22, 2013, http://www.diosc.com/sys/news-events/latest-news/495-another-15-parishes-join-the-diocese.

19. Ibid.

20. All Saints of Florence, Christ the King of Pawleys Island, Holy Trinity of Charleston, St. Matthews of Darlington, St. Bartholomew's of Hartsville, St. David's of Cheraw, St. James of James Island, St. Paul's of Bennettsville, St. Paul's of Conway, Epiphany of Eutawville, Resurrection of Surfside Beach, St. Matthew of Ft. Motte, Trinity of Edisto, and St. John's of Johns Island. St. Andrew's Anglican Church (ACNA) of Mt. Pleasant also joined the suit.

21. "Three More Parishes Join in Suit to Prevent TEC from Seizing Property." Diocese of South Carolina, February 28, 2013, http://www.diosc.com/sys/news-events/169-news/press-releases/502-three-more-parishes. The three parishes were: St. Jude's of Walterboro, Trinity of Pinopolis, and Holy Cross in Stateburg.

would assume the names, legal rights, and properties of the pre-schism diocese. In fact, Bishop Lawrence had given this as his reason for entering the lawsuit of January 4, 2013. In an open letter to DSC, he wrote: "We are saddened that we feel it necessary to ask a court to protect our property rights, but recent actions compelled us to take this action. As you know, The Episcopal Church (TEC) has begun the effort to claim the Diocese of South Carolina's identity."[22]

Runyan and his cohorts had already launched a preemptive strike against the Episcopal Church in entering the lawsuit of January 4, but that meant only a slow process in an undeterminable future. In December of 2012, the Episcopal Church had called a special convention to meet in Charleston on 26 January and continued using the names and insignia of the old diocese. Preparations were well underway for what the Church side represented as the continuation of the Diocese of South Carolina. The DSC attorneys decided to make a second preemptive strike against the Church, this time to stop the Church from using the names and symbols of the old diocese and reserve them for the DSC. On January 22, just four days before the Church's special convention, Runyan and the other four lawyers filed a motion with Judge Goodstein for a temporary restraining order.[23] They asked the court for an order "restraining the Defendants [the Episcopal Church] (. . .) from assuming, using, or adopting the names of the Diocese of South Carolina and its emblems as well as its registered names and seal."[24] Judge Goodstein responded immediately. The next day, January 23, at 5:11 p.m., she issued a Temporary Restraining Order *ex parte*,[25] that is, without allowing the Church lawyers a chance to challenge it beforehand.[26] She declared that DSC was the owner of the names Diocese of South Carolina, Protestant Episcopal Church in the Diocese of South Carolina, and the Episcopal Diocese of South Carolina and that no other party would be allowed to use the names and seal. For good measure, Goodstein finished by listing the names of persons allowed to use the name and seal.[27] The judge also called for a hearing on 1 February at the Richland County Courthouse in Columbia to determine whether the Order would be extended or turned into an injunction. This was all the DSC lawyers could have wished. The next day and the day after (Jan. 24–25) the Restraining Order

---

22. Lawrence, (the Rt. Rev.) Mark. To the Diocese of South Carolina, January 4, 2013, http://www.diosc.com/sys/images/documents/bishop_ltr_1_4_13.pdf.

23. "Motion for the Entry of a Temporary Restraining Order." State of South Carolina, County of Dorchester, In the Court of Common Pleas for the First Judicial Circuit, Case No. 2013-CP-18-00013, January 22, 2013.

24. Ibid.

25. A legal term meaning from, by, or for, the party. It is a legal proceeding brought by one party without notification or representation of the other parties.

26. "Temporary Restraining Order, Issued at 5:11 P.M., January 23, 2013." State of South Carolina, County of Dorchester, In the Court of Common Pleas for the First Judicial Circuit, Case No. 2013-CP-18-00013.

27. Mark Lawrence, James B. Lewis (Lawrence's assistant), John Wallace (DSC Treasurer), Nancy J. Armstrong (DSC Assistant Treasurer), Joy Hunter (DSC Director of Communications), the DSC Standing Committee acting as the Directors: Paul Fuener, John M. Barr, J. Reid Boylston, Ann Hester Willis, Julian Jeffords, William G. Lyles, Ed Mitman, Andrew O'Dell, Elizabeth Pennewill, Suzanne Schwank, Gregory A. Snyder, A. Kenneth Weldon; and the DSC Trustees: Craige Borrett, Jeffrey Miller, Robert Horn, Robert Kilgo, Robert Kunes, Glynn Watson, and Ivan Anderson.

was served to twelve people prominent on the Church side.[28] The lawyers did not explain why they thought it necessary to serve the Order to the individuals when it was known to everyone the instant it was issued.

Perhaps caught off guard by the swift and unexpected preemptive moves of the assertive DSC lawyers, attorney Thomas S. Tisdale, Jr. and the other Church lawyers scrambled to build a response. Rather than going to the hearing scheduled for 1 February, they decided to proceed with an agreement on 31 January. On that day, Judge Goodstein issued a Temporary Injunction extending the January 23 Restraining Order indefinitely.[29] An important caveat in the Injunction was the provision that one party could petition the Court for an order modifying or ending the Injunction. This meant that upon fourteen days' notice, the Church side could get the Court to reconsider the Injunction at any time indefinitely into the future. At least this bought time for the Church lawyers to prepare for a hearing on the injunction. Once again, even though the news of the deal flashed immediately, the DSC leaders felt it necessary to have the Injunction served personally to three people on 31 January and 1 February: the Rt. Rev. Charles vonRosenberg, the Rev. Michael Wright, and Melinda Lucka.[30]

Thus, within two months' time, by the end of February of 2013, the stage was set for the litigation between the two opposing dioceses. Although other courts, and other issues, would be involved along the way, the fundamental differences between the two sides would play out primarily in the South Carolina state courts. Beyond the circuit court would lie the state appeals court and the state supreme court. One could not help but being impressed by the brilliantly successful maneuvers of the DSC lawyers. Runyan and his committee of attorneys were well-planned, well-prepared, well-connected, focused, aggressive, and relentless. Their accomplishments for DSC in January and February of 2013 were nothing less than stunning to every observer. The Church side was left reeling on its heels and wondering whatever next. If this were a forecast of things to come, the Church would inevitably fall in a withering onslaught from a team of first-rate lawyers led by a man who for years had sharpened his singular litigation skills by taking on giant corporations and their legions of high-paid lawyers and bringing them to their knees under colossal sums they had to pay. After the first two months of litigation, the future of legal actions seemed only bright for the independent diocese and just the opposite for the Church side.

---

28. Two bishops, Charles vonRosenberg and John Buchanan; three priests: Callie Walpole, James E. Taylor, and Michael Wright; and seven lay people: George Hawkins, Virginia Wilder, Lonnie Hamilton, Erin Hoyle, Barbara Mann, Melinda Lucka, and Steve Skardon.

29. "Temporary Injunction (Consent)." State of South Carolina, County of Dorchester, In the Court of Common Pleas for the First Judicial Circuit, Case No. 2013-CP-18-00013, January 31, 2013.

30. DSC had other rounds of serving papers. After 28 February, they had the Second Amended Complaint (the second amendment to the original suit of 4 January) delivered to: Thomas S. Tisdale, chancellor of the Church diocese; the Rt. Rev. Charles vonRosenberg, bishop provisional of the Church diocese; and Virginia Wilder. Thus, in January and February of 2013, DSC had three legal papers served eighteen times, to thirteen different people prominent on the Church side, the Temporary Restraining Order, the Temporary Injunction, and the Second Amended Complaint.

THE EPISCOPAL CHURCH IN SOUTH CAROLINA

Rebuilding the Diocese

The position of the Episcopal Church leaders was that a diocese could not leave the Church by its own will. Dioceses were required to accede to the Constitution and Canons of the Episcopal Church which provided terms under which dioceses could join, divide, and depart from the Church. This was akin to a contract whereby two parties were bound and one side could not unilaterally revoke the agreement. Therefore, in the Church's view, the five dioceses that voted to leave the Church did not take the dioceses with them. This meant that in each of the five cases, the Church leaders had to step in and help the minority of loyal Episcopalians who refused to go along with the secessions to reorganize the Church dioceses. This was true in South Carolina just as it had been in San Joaquin, Pittsburgh, Quincy, and Fort Worth.

The Episcopal Church started work on rebuilding its diocese as soon as Bishop Lawrence announced the schism. By January of 2013, 10 of the 38 parishes of the old diocese moved to the Church side along with 8 missions. The parishes were: All Saints of Hilton Head, Calvary of Charleston, Grace of Charleston, St. George's of Summerville, Holy Communion of Charleston, Holy Cross/Faith Memorial of Pawleys Island, St. Mark's of Charleston, St. Stephen's of Charleston, St. Stephen's of North Myrtle Beach, and St. Thomas of North Charleston. The missions were: Holy Communion of Allendale, Christ Church of Denmark, St. Philip's, Voorhees College, of Denmark, Heavenly Rest of Estill, All Saints of Hampton, St. Alban's of Kingstree, St. Stephen's of St. Stephens, Epiphany of Summerville, and St. Augustine's of Wedgefield.[31] Among the dozen undecided local churches, one later joined the Church diocese, St. James, Santee, of McClellanville. One other mission, Good Shepherd of Sumter, originally went along with the Lawrence side, then rejoined the Episcopal Church diocese by the summer of 2013.[32] In addition, a half-dozen worshipping communities of loyal Episcopalians began meeting in places such as Florence, Conway, Summerville, Myrtle Beach, Edisto, and Mt. Pleasant.[33] By May of 2016, the Church diocese contained eleven parishes, nineteen missions, and one worshipping community, for a total of thirty-one local churches.

Before the schism, the 21 local churches that were to remain in the Episcopal Church listed 5,781 baptized members, about a fifth of the of the pre-schism diocese. By 2015, the Church diocese reported 6,706 members, a gain of 16 %. A few churches saw dramatic gains in membership: St. George's of Summerville (324 in 2011 to 488 in 2015, or +50%), Grace Church of Charleston (1,718 in 2012 to 2,177 in 2015, or +27%), Holy Cross/Faith Memorial of Pawleys Island (450 to 525, or +17%), St. Thomas of North Charleston (235 to 261, or +11%), St. Stephen's of Charleston (521 to 575, or +10%),

---

31. St. Mark's, of Port Royal, was admitted as a mission on March 9, 2013, and a parish on November 14, 2015. St. James Santee, of McClellanville, later voted to remain with the Church. This brought to 11 the number of missions in 2013.

32. vonRosenberg, (the Rt. Rev.) Charles. Email message to author, June 21, 2016.

33. There were eventually nine worshipping communities: Mt. Pleasant, Edisto Island, Summerville, Myrtle Beach, Ridgeland, Conway, Florence, West Ashley, and Cheraw. As of May 2016, all except the last were missions of the Church diocese.

and Holy Communion of Charleston (523 to 553, or +6%). The new parish, St. Mark's of Port Royal, counted 220 members and an income of $214,000 in 2015. The nine new worshipping communities/missions ranged from a size of 110 members in Conway to a dozen in Cheraw. A few churches saw dramatic rises in Sunday attendance, most notably Grace Church Cathedral of Charleston, where the Average Sunday Attendance grew from 692 in 2011 to 819 in 2015. Loyal Episcopalians flooded into Grace from downtown schismatic churches, as St. Philip's and St. Michael's. Some 60 new members joined Grace in the first two months of 2013.[34] In fact, of all the 71 local churches of the pre-schism diocese, Grace Church had the largest membership three years after the schism. The Average Sunday Attendance of all the local congregations in the Church diocese grew from 2,527 in 2011 to 2,922 in 2015, a gain of 16 %.[35]

On 10 January 2013, the steering committee overseeing the rebuilding of the Church diocese announced its unanimous choice as candidate for bishop provisional, the Rt. Rev. Charles Glenn vonRosenberg, retired bishop of East Tennessee and resident of Charleston.[36] His name would be put forth for vote in the special convention of 26 January. VonRosenberg was well-known and highly regarded in South Carolina. Born in Fayetteville, North Carolina in 1947, he had served churches in Upper South Carolina and was canon to the ordinary in that diocese from 1989 to 1994. From 1999 to 2011 he served as bishop of the Diocese of East Tennessee after which he retired to Daniel Island in Charleston. Following the schism, he became an advisor to the parties working for the reorganization of the Church diocese. Now retired at the age of sixty-five and set to enjoy a leisurely life with his family, which included six grandchildren, vonRosenberg unhesitatingly agreed to serve as bishop provisional, a daunting responsibility in a commitment that customarily lasted several years.

Presiding Bishop Jefferts Schori and the Rev. Gay Clark Jennings, president of the House of Deputies of the General Convention, led the special convention of the January 26, 2013. At 4:00 p,m, on the day before, a welcoming reception for them was held at Grace Church attended by four hundred appreciative people and another reception at Bishop Gadsden retirement home on James Island. Also attending the special convention were eight bishops and several other Church notables.[37] Approximately five hundred people registered for the special convention. Perhaps another two hundred joined them to attend the Festival Eucharist in Grace Church on the morning of the 26th, so many that the

---

34. "Easter Arrives Early for South Carolina Episcopalians." South Carolina Episcopalians, March 4, 2013, http://www.scepiscopalians.com/2013_News.html.

35. The Episcopal Church in South Carolina. [Diocesan statistics, 2013–2015], provided to author, August 16, 2016.

36. "Charles vonRosenberg Nominated as South Carolina Bishop Provisional." Episcopal News Service, January 10, 2013, http://episcopaldigitalnetwork.com/ens/2013/01/10/charles-vonrosenberg-nominated-as-south-carolina-bishop-provisional ; "The Right Reverend Charles G. vonRosenberg." The Episcopal Church in South Carolina, n.d., http://www.episcopalchurchsc.org/the-bishop.html.

37. Bishops: John C. Buchanan, provisional of Quincy; Rogers S. Harris, retired of Southwest Florida; Robert H. Johnson, retired of Western North Carolina; Dabney T. Smith, of Southwest Florida; Andrew Waldo, of Upper South Carolina; George D. Young, III, of East Tennessee; Dorsey F. Henderson, Jr., retired of Upper South Carolina; Henry I. Louttit, Jr., retired of Georgia. Others: Angela Daniel, President of Province IV; Kathleen Wells, Chancellor of Fort Worth.

Church was filled to overflowing. An atmosphere running high on the mixed emotions of loss, exhaustion, relief, exhilaration, triumph, and hope settled over the whole weekend when many an attendant let out the raging emotions in tears. After years of being neglected and maligned by the diocesan power structure and enduring endless denunciations of their beloved Church in their own diocese, the Episcopalians of the old Diocese of South Carolina at long last found their moment to celebrate their resurrection.

The special convention of 26 January started with a festival choral Eucharist beginning at 9:30 a.m.[38] Presiding Bishop Jefferts Schori was the officiant and preacher in the nearly two-hour long service. Not surprisingly there was great expectation at what she would have to say in her sermon about the situation of the diocese. She started by relating a story of a pilot who was unjustly jailed, briefly, by authorities who in fact had no justification to do that, then said "I tell you that story because it's indicative of attitudes we've seen here and in many other places. Somebody decides he knows the law, and oversteps whatever authority he may have to dictate the fate of others who may in fact be obeying the law, and often a law for which this local tyrant is not the judge." She continued, "Most human communities, from churches to governments to families, function more effectively in response to shared decision-making (. . .). Power assumed by one authority figure alone is often a recipe for abuse, tyranny, and corruption." She finished by calling for a compassionate inclusiveness: "What are those of you in this Diocese going to do in your interactions with those who've departed? Are they law-breakers who should be shot down or thrown in jail? Do we see them as vigilantes? Neither is going to produce more abundant life, my friends. When you meet them out there in the pasture, consider that some of the sheep may think they're listening to the voice of the Good Shepherd. Some are simply exhausted." It was a message of hope, toleration, reconciliation, and peace.[39]

Jefferts Schori's detractors did not see her sermon as one of reconciliation, quite the opposite. Peter T. Mitchell, a vestryperson of Prince George Winyah of Georgetown, wrote a scathing letter to the Charleston *Post and Courier*: "I was sickened and appalled, but not surprised by the vindictive and mean-spirited language Episcopal Church Presiding Bishop Katharine Jefferts Schori used in her sermon on Saturday."[40] He continued, "Alluding to Bishop Mark Lawrence as a 'tyrant' and comparing him to 'citizens' militias deciding to patrol (. . .) the Mexican border for unwelcomed visitors' was unconscionable."[41] Mitchell's letter sparked a response from a person who was actually in attendance at the convention, the Rev. John C. Fisher, of Edisto Island. Fisher wrote the *Post and Courier*, "I and the hundreds of loyal, God-fearing Episcopalians in attendance at that event heard no such language. We heard a profound, loving, inspirational

---

38. "Convention: The Episcopal Church in South Carolina, January 26, 2013." Video recording, YouTube, 1 hour and 56 minutes, http://www.youtube.com/watch?v=zo6GVOJ5mfc.

39. "The Presiding Bishop's Sermon." The Episcopal Church in South Carolina." [January 26, 2013], http://www.episcopalchurchsc.org/presiding-bishops-sermon.html.

40. Mitchell, Peter T. Letter to the editor, *The Post and Courier* (Charleston, SC), as quoted in "Ugly Sermon Preached by Jefferts Schori," Virtueonline, February 1, 2013, http://www.virtueonline.org/portal/modules/news/articles.php?storyid=17159.

41. Ibid.

call from the leader of our church for unity and comity in the face of a very painful rift (. . .). We did not hear any personal reference to former SC diocesan bishop Mark Lawrence. The 'allusion' the letter writer refers to is his own."[42] In her sermon, the Presiding Bishop did not, in fact, name Lawrence or mention his office. Whether she was referring to Lawrence at all would be in the mind of the listener. Jefferts Schori's sermon in the Eucharist was a message to the Episcopalians of South Carolina, a call for understanding and compassion, not for revenge.

After Eucharist, the special convention continued with a long list of business that had to be conducted. There was much to be done. Since the entire slate of office holders of the old diocese had left the Episcopal Church, all official positions of the dioceses had to be filled from the bishop down. In addition, all of the resolutions passed over the years by the old diocese purporting to repeal its accession to the Constitution and Canons of the Episcopal Church would have to be reversed. For this, thirty-six clergy were present along with fifty-three lay delegates.[43] One visitor in attendance was the Rev. James Lewis, assistant to Bishop Lawrence. The Rt. Rev. Charles vonRosenberg was elected by acclamation of the convention the bishop provisional and installed in office by the Presiding Bishop. In his address to the convention, vonRosenberg echoed the themes that the Presiding Bishop had set for the day, understanding, tolerance, and compassion with hope of reconciliation with those with whom we may disagree. He said, "As followers of Jesus, we need to recognize that other sincere Christians-former Episcopalians-have chosen a different path from ours. Theirs is a path committed to faith in Jesus, as they understand that faith."[44] In a later press conference, vonRosenberg elaborated on his theme: "'My hope is that as people realize that the ones who are perhaps on a different side at this time are not demonic, are not unchristian but have chosen a different way (. . .). As we come to that point and confront each other as people, that's where our hope lies and where, I believe, reconciliation begins.'"[45]

In following business, the convention approved attorney Thomas Sumter Tisdale as the chancellor, elected by acclamation a new standing committee,[46] and approved likewise a diocesan council.[47] Along with the festival Eucharist and installing a new bishop, another

42. Fisher, (the Rev.) John C. Letter to the editor, *The Post and Courier* (Charleston, SC), February 6, 2013, as quoted in South Carolina Episcopalians, February 6, 2013, http://www.scepiscopalians.com/2013_News.html.

43. "Minutes of the Episcopal Church in South Carolina Special Convention, January 26, 2013." The Journal of the Episcopal Church in South Carolina Special Convention, January 26, 2013. http://www.episcopalchurchsc.org/uploads/1/2/9/8/12989303/journal_of_the_special_convention_1-26-2013.pdf.

44. "Bishop vonRosenberg's Address to the Convention, January 28, 2013." The Episcopal Church in South Carolina, [January 26, 2013], http://www.episcopalchurchsc.org/bishop-vonrosenbergs-address.html.

45. Schjonberg, Mary Frances. "South Carolina Continuing Episcopalians Meet to Plan their Future." Episcopal News Service, January 26, 2013, http://episcopaldigitalnetwork.com/ens/2013/01/26/south-carolina-continuing-episcopalians-meet-to-plan-future.

46. Clergy: Richard Lindsey, David Williams, Colton Smith, Michael A. Wright, Wilmot Merchant, and Calhoun Walpole; Laity: Virginia C. Wilder, Melinda Lucka, Hillery P. Douglas, Rebecca Lovelace, Erin Elizabeth Bailey, and Lonnie Hamilton III.

47. Clergy: Mark Brinkmann, Roy Hills, Wil Keith, Jeff Richardson, John Zahl, George Tompkins; Laity: Nancy Bailey, Holly Behre, Alesia Rico Flores, Mary Ann Foy, Charles Geer, and Barbara Mann.

emotional high point of the convention was the revocation of thirteen resolutions that had been passed by earlier conventions of the Diocese of South Carolina. These were declared "Null and Void" by the convention. From the special diocesan convention of October 24, 2009, came two resolutions, one to change the Oath of Conformity at ordinations, and one authorizing the diocese to begin withdrawing from the bodies of the Episcopal Church. From the diocesan convention of March 26, 2010, came the resolution declaring the diocese to be sovereign. The longest list of past resolutions declared null and void came from the diocesan convention of October 2010: removal of accession to the Canons of the Episcopal Church, removal of the requirement that changes to the diocesan Constitution could be made only in annual conventions, adopted the 2006 rather than the 2009 Constitution and Canons, abolition of the Dennis Canon, and amendment of the corporate charter to remove reference to the Episcopal Church. Two resolutions from the February 2011 diocesan convention were revoked: removal of accession to the Episcopal Church Constitution except when consistent with the diocesan Constitution, and second reading of the abolishment of the requirement of annual convention. Three resolutions were overthrown from the special convention of November 17, 2012: concurrence with Standing Committee's resolution of October 2, 2012, to disaffiliate with the Episcopal Church, removal of all references in the diocesan Constitution to the Episcopal Church, and removal of all references in diocesan Canons to the Episcopal Church.[48] The passage of the resolution to revoke the thirteen earlier resolutions was the emotional watershed of the special convention because it meant the complete restoration of diocesan accession to the Constitution and Canons of the Episcopal Church, the full reunion of the diocese with the mother Church. Grasping the gravity and importance of the moment, the whole convention instantly arose in loud applause, cheers, and many attendees shed tears of joy. For many intrepid, longsuffering Episcopalians of eastern South Carolina, the long night was over. Their diocese had come home, bruised, wounded, and diminished, but alive. At the end of the day, the special convention adjourned as hundreds of delegates and visitors filed out of that beautiful 1840s Gothic church in old Charleston emotionally exhausted and full of hope.[49]

Outside of peninsular Charleston, membership movement from one diocese to the other was often not easy, particularly in the small cities and towns inland that might not offer a choice. Even before the institutional structure of the Church diocese was reorganized, local congregations had already begun reforming informally as the schism occurred. Before the end of 2012, several collections of displaced Episcopalians began organizing worshipping communities in living rooms. If one counts the original, St. Mark's of Port Royal, there were to be ten of these spontaneous house churches in the diocese. In Conway, two dozen Episcopalians from St. Paul's began meeting in living rooms in the autumn of 2012 calling themselves the "Conway Worship Group." Within

48. "Minutes of the Episcopal Church."

49. For newspaper accounts of the special convention, see: Parker, Adam. "Episcopal Church in S.C. Reforms Leadership." *The Post and Courier* (Charleston, SC), January 27, 2013, and "Continuing S.C. Episcopalians Install New Bishop, Welcome Leader of Church, Look to Rebuild." *The Post and Courier* (Charleston, SC), January 27, 2013; Click, Carolyn. "Lowcountry SC Episcopalians Rally, Elect Leader." *The State* (Columbia, SC), January 27, 2013.

a few months, they had grown into a vibrant, thriving church of 120 members meeting in the Lackey Chapel of the Coastal Carolina University under the name of St. Anne's. In Florence, a dozen Episcopalians from St. John's, All Saints, and nearby places as Hartsville and Darlington, began meeting in living rooms in December of 2012. Soon, they began holding services in the Cross and Crown Lutheran Church of Florence and became part of the ministry of the Rev. Jeff Richardson, priest at St. Alban's of Kingstree and St. Stephen's of St. Stephen. They too became a healthy and vibrant community meeting at the old Back Swamp School, just north of Florence before returning to Cross and Crown. Early on they took the name of St. Catherine's in honor of St. Catherine of Alexandria. On Edisto Island, a group of Episcopalians first met in January of 2013 in the home of Gretchen Smith. They then became perhaps the only Episcopal congregation in the nation to meet in a bar-be-que restaurant when they began holding services in Bobo's Po Pigs Bo-B-Q on Edisto. The 20–40 regular churchgoers affectionately called the place "St. Bobo's Cathedral." Afterwards, the group met in the New Missionary Baptist Church as the Episcopal Church on Edisto. In Summerville, Episcopalians from St. Paul's began meeting in a Methodist church as the Continuing Episcopal Church of Summerville. As the others, it grew large and energetic. They found their own quarters in Jan Waring Wood's CPA building as Church of the Good Shepherd. In the Mount Pleasant area, loyal Episcopalians formed the East Cooper Episcopal Church and met in the Hibben United Methodist Church. On the other side of downtown Charleston, Episcopalians, mainly from old St. Andrew's of West Ashley, formed a community called West Ashley Episcopalians in March of 2013. Soon they formed St. Francis Church while meeting in the Stuhr's funeral home chapel on Glenn McConnell Parkway in West Ashley. In Myrtle Beach, local Episcopalians formed the Episcopal Church in Myrtle Beach first meeting in homes, then, by August of 2013, holding weekly services in a university building. In time, they began meeting in St. Philip Lutheran Church of Myrtle Beach under the name of the Episcopal Church of the Messiah. At Okatie, near Hilton Head and Bluffton, a group of Episcopalians met on Easter Sunday of 2013 on a dock at the Chechessee River. For a while, the Episcopal Church in Okatie continued meeting on various local boat docks, perhaps the only Episcopal Church in the nation to do so, before moving into the Saint Luke Baptist Church of Okatie. In time, they found a permanent home in the Hazzard Creek Village in Ridgeland. Finally, Episcopalians in the remote northern edge of the diocese at Cheraw began meeting informally. In 2016, they were known as the Episcopal Worship Group of Cheraw and were holding services regularly in the Community Events Room of the First Bank of Cheraw.[50] The coordination of clergy visits to the worshipping communities was managed by Bishop vonRosenberg and the new Archdeacon, the Rev. Calhoun (Callie) Walpole. By 2015, all the worshipping groups, except the last, had been officially admitted as missions of the Church diocese.

By the time of the annual meeting of the convention, March 8–9, 2013, the turmoil of the schism had begun to settle. The Executive Council of the Episcopal Church did its part to help the struggling reorganized diocese in South Carolina. At its winter meeting

---

50. Parker, Adam. "Finding the Current: Small Episcopal Worship Groups Form in Wake of Theological Storm." *The Post and Courier* (Charleston, SC), March 3, 2013, http://postandcourier.com/apps/pbcs.d11/article?AID=/20130303/PC1204/130309908/1165/finding-the-current.

in 2013, the Council approved a grant to the diocese of up to $185,000 and a line of credit for legal fees of $250,000.[51] The annual meeting of the convention, coming so soon after the special convention, also helped to tie up loose ends and put the reorganized diocese on more solid footing. A joyous moment in the meeting was the entrance of the first mission admitted to the diocese since the schism, St. Mark's of Port Royal. St. Mark's had begun in 2003, nine years before the schism, mostly by communicants of St. Helena's of Beaufort who no longer felt welcomed in the parish that was growing increasingly hostile to the Episcopal Church. St. Mark's was incorporated by the state of South Carolina on February 24, 2005. The group worshipped in homes, then a motel, a Masonic lodge, and finally in the old Union Chapel in Port Royal. By late 2012, St. Mark's Chapel counted one hundred regular attendees. Bishop Lawrence twice rejected the group's petition to be recognized as a mission, first of St. Helena's then of All Saints of Hilton Head. In 2011, Lawrence refused to conduct confirmation in St. Mark's but he did attend once and celebrate the Eucharist.[52] In one of his first official acts as provisional bishop, vonRosenberg visited St. Mark's on 3 February and confirmed five people, his first confirmations as provisional bishop, and the Chapel's first confirmations ever. It was a great moment for a community that had endured so much for so long.[53]

The business of the annual meeting of the convention, 8–9 March, was mainly to confirm the measures taken in January to reestablish all ties between the diocese and the Episcopal Church. Seated in the meeting were 42 clergy and 62 lay delegates from the 10 parishes[54] and 10 missions[55] in union with the Church diocese plus 28 representatives from 8 churches of the old diocese not in union. In addition, five worshipping communities were represented. Nine resolutions were offered and approved, the most important being R–6, "A Resolution Modifying Certain Constitutional and Canonical Changes." This one returned to the resolutions of the January special convention that nullified the acts of the conventions of 2009, 2010, 2011, and 2012 that had violated accession to the Constitution and Canons of the Episcopal Church. R–6 restored the language in the 2007 diocesan Constitution and Canons to make it consistent with the Church's Con-

---

51. "Email News from the Diocese, March 4, 2013." Episcopal Church in South Carolina, http://us6.campaign-archive2.com/u=dc801ce41dd668e19fb313b7a&id=c7a033f9d8&e=97fa51dc8f. On June 10, 2013, the Executive Council increased the line of credit to ECSC by $300,000 to a total of $550,000; Schjonberg, Mary Frances. "Council Members Expand Support to South Carolina, San Joaquin." Episcopal News Service, June 10, 2013, http://episcopaldigitalnetwork.com/ens/2013/06/10/executive-council-members-expand-support-to-south-carolina.

52. "A Brief History of St. Mark's Episcopal Chapel, Revised December 5, 2012." http://www.stmarks.org.

53. Stice, Allison. "St Mark's Chapel Visited by New Episcopal Bishop." *The Island Packet* (Hilton Head, SC), February 3, 2013, http://www.islandpacket.com/2013/02/03/2366629/st-marks-chapel-visited-by-new.html.

54. All Saints of Hilton Head, Calvary of Charleston, Grace of Charleston, St. George's of Summerville, Holy Communion of Charleston, Holy Cross/Faith Memorial of Pawleys Island, St. Mark's of Charleston, St. Stephen's of Charleston, St. Stephen's of North Myrtle Beach, and St. Thomas of North Charleston.

55. All Saints of Hampton, Holy Communion of Allendale, Heavenly Rest of Estill, Christ Church of Denmark, Epiphany of Summerville, St. James Santee of McClellanville, St. Augustine's of Pinewood, St. Stephen's of St. Stephen, St. Alban's of Kingstree, and St. Philip's Chapel of Voorhees College.

stitution and Canons.[56] Another important measure of business was to name a board of the Trustees of the Diocese.[57] The meeting also approved a budget for 2013 of $378,000. This included the Church grant of $175,000. The diocesan contribution to the national Church was restored to $39,500 after having been gradually reduced to almost nothing before the schism. Thus, within the first several months after the schism, the Church diocese was reorganized, reinvigorated, and firmly reestablished even though on the legal front it had been thrown back on the defensive by the independent diocese and its assertive lawyers.

Having reestablished the structure of the diocese in the bishop, standing committee, council, and board of trustees, repealed the resolutions separating the diocese from the Episcopal Church, and formed a budget, the next issue to address was the status of the clergy of the old diocese, all of whom held Holy Orders in the Episcopal Church. Who among the priests and deacons would remain with the Episcopal Church and who would depart with Bishop Lawrence? Only about a third of the old clergy, fifty-eight to be exact, were listed in the official list of the convention in March of 2013. More than a hundred remained to be accounted for. This was the problem Bishop vonRosenberg addressed on 7 April 2013, when he sent a registered letter to the clergy of the old diocese who had not already declared their desire to remain part of the Episcopal Church.[58] He told them that if they chose not to remain in the Episcopal Church, they had two options. First, they could put in writing their desire to renounce the ministry of the Episcopal Church upon which the Bishop would issue a release from ordination. Second, if they chose not to respond within two weeks, the Bishop would consult with the Standing Committee to restrict, and then to depose, or remove, the clergyperson. Letters were sent to 140 priests and deacons of the old diocese.[59] After two weeks, the Bishop sent a second registered letter to each of those who had not responded warning them that the diocese would act on the canons to restrict and depose them.[60] He gave a deadline for response of 14 June. The standing committee was scheduled to meet on 21 June. Only a few clergy who received the letters responded.

The process of restriction and deposition began in June of 2013. On June 21, 2013, ECSC published a list of clergy in good standing with the diocese.[61] It contained the names of 63 priests and 11 deacons for a total of 74 clergy in ECSC. There were a few surprises on the list including the Rev. Daniel Clarke, rector of Holy Cross Church of

56. "Journal of the 222nd Annual Meeting of the Convention, The Episcopal Church in South Carolina, Grace Church, Charleston, March 8–9, 2013." Appendix IV, 18–29, http://www.episcopalchurchsc.org/uploads/1/2/9/8/12989303/journal_of_222nd_annual_convention_march_2013.pdf.

57. The Revs. Bruce Evenson, Jack Neitert, James Taylor; Jan Gilbert, Bob Pinkerton, Betsy Walker, Charles Carpenter, Robert Moffit.

58. vonRosenberg, (the Rt. Rev.) Charles. Letter, April 7, 2013, as quoted in Anglican Ink, http://www.anglicanink.com.

59. "Bishop Writes to Clarify Relationships with Clergy." The Episcopal Church in South Carolina, April 11, 2013, http://www.episcopalchurchsc.org/news-release-april-11-2013.html.

60. Ibid.

61. "Clergy in Good Standing in The Episcopal Church in South Carolina as of June 21, 2013." The Episcopal Church in South Carolina, June 25, 2013, http://www.episcopalchurchsc.org/clergy-in-good-standing.html.

Stateburg, the Rev. Matthew Schneider, associate at Prince George Winyah, the Rev. Ladson Mills III, a contributor to Virtue Online, and Dr. Robert Munday, former dean of Nashotah House. Two weeks later, the Church diocese issued an updated list of clergy in good standing containing 77 priests and 11 deacons for a total of 88.[62] In October, the diocese listed 91 clergy in good standing including 80 priests and 11 deacons.[63] It was curious to note that at that time, the names of 9 priests and 3 deacons appeared on both lists of DSC and ECSC clergy in good standing. As of November 2016, the diocese listed 90 priests and 11 deacons for a total of 101 clergy in good standing.[64]

On June 25, 2013, upon unanimous vote of the standing committee, Bishop vonRosenberg issued an official release to 104 priests and deacons of the old diocese who had not responded affirmatively to his earlier letters.[65] He sent to each of the 104 a Notice of Restriction and a warning that he or she had 60 days "'to transmit to the Bishop a retraction or denial, indicating your intention to abide by the promises made at ordination, which could lead to the withdrawal of this notice and restriction on ministry in The Episcopal Church.'"[66] If there were no response in 60 days, the clergyperson would be subject to deposition from ministry in the Episcopal Church. On August 30, 2013, the Church diocese announced that the 104 clergy had been removed from the Holy Orders of the Episcopal Church. Bishop vonRosenberg sent a "Notice of Removal" to each removing him or her from the ordained ministry of the Episcopal Church. However, to facilitate a reconciliation, he issued to the former clergy a "release and removal" rather than the harsher deposition on the grounds of abandonment of the Church.

After the schism occurred, the old diocesan office holders, all of whom abandoned the Episcopal Church, remained in physical possession of all the old diocesan assets, properties, possessions, records, papers, and archives. This was legally validated by circuit court judge Goodstein in an Injunction of January 2013. This meant that the personnel files of the nearly one hundred clergy of the pre-schism diocese who remained with the Episcopal Church were in the possession of Bishop Lawrence and his staff. Bishop vonRosenberg telephoned Bishop Lawrence and asked that these files be handed over to the Church diocese. Lawrence refused but said he would give the files to the priests individually upon their requests. When some Episcopal clergy did ask Lawrence for their files, he refused to surrender them. The Church diocese then had to start from scratch to develop personnel files on all of its clergy.[67] This was indicative of the reality that the independent diocese saw itself only as an adversary of the Church diocese.

62. Ibid., July 10, 2013.
63. Ibid., October 10, 2013.
64. Ibid., November 20, 2016.
65. "The Episcopal Church in South Carolina, Notice of Restriction." The Episcopal Church in South Carolina, June 25, 2013, as quoted in Virtueonline, http://www.virtueonline.org/south-carolina-rump-episcopal-diocese-deposes-103-priests-and-deacons.
66. "List Published to Clarify Standing of Local Clergy." The Episcopal Church in South Carolina, July 10, 2013, http://www.episcopalchurchsc.org/news-release-july-10–2013.html. The published list contained 103 names. One other was added.
67. vonRosenberg, telephone conversation with author.

Concerning the clergy of the old diocese, the schism did not force a complete separation into two hostile groups. Of the three former bishops of the pre-schism diocese, only one, Allison, fully supported the secession. However, apparently, he did not renounce his orders in the Episcopal Church; and has not been deposed by the Church. Edward Salmon remained an active resigned Episcopal bishop, served as head of Nashotah House, and participated in the Church's General Convention of 2015. Of the three former bishops, William Skilton tried the hardest to bridge the gap and minister to both sides of the divide. This, however, proved to be a problem. The Canons of the Episcopal Church forbade a bishop from administering ordinations and confirmations in a non-Episcopal Church. Skilton was careful to abide by this, but did administer sacraments such as the Eucharist in the non-Episcopal churches. Bishop vonRosenberg told him this would cause confusion. In March of 2013, Presiding Bishop Jefferts Schori asked Skilton to refrain from administering the sacraments on both sides at least temporarily. Apparently, Skilton told the assembled bishops at that time he felt he had to continue celebrating the Eucharist among the former Episcopalians.[68] Therefore, on 2 December 2014, vonRosenberg sent a letter to Skilton directing that he not function sacramentally in the Episcopal Church diocese and not represent the Episcopal Church in the diocese.[69] Skilton agreed and remained in the Episcopal Church, attending the General Convention of 2015, but also continuing his warm relations with the independent diocese which continued paying his annual stipend.

Since Bishop vonRosenberg had released and removed the 104 priests and deacons rather than deposing them, he left the door open for their reconciliation and reinstatement in the Episcopal Church. One priest returned in 2014, another in 2015, and another in 2016. On September 16, 2014, the Rev. H. Dagnall Free, Jr., reaffirmed his vows of ordination before the bishop and returned to the Episcopal Church.[70] He had been an assistant at St. John's on Johns Island, a parish that been actively critical of the Episcopal Church. In May of 2015, Free became rector of St. Mary's Episcopal Church, Staten Island, New York. On March 24, 2015, the Rev. H. Jeff Wallace, reaffirmed his vows and returned to the Church. He had been an associate at Christ the King, Waccamaw, at Pawleys Island, then served a Lutheran congregation in Texas. In January of 2016 Wallace became rector of Calvary Episcopal Church in Americus, Georgia. On November 11, 2016, a third priest of the pre-schism diocese returned to the Episcopal Church, the Rev. Matthew Wright McCormick.[71] Immediately thereafter the became the rector of Messiah Episcopal Church in St. Paul, Minnesota.

68. Skilton, (the Rt. Rev.) William J. "Open Letter to the Faithful Anglicans/Episcopalians in Lower South Carolina, December 12, 2014." http://www.diosc.com/sys/images/documents/tec/skilton_vonrosenberg.pdf.

69. vonRosenberg, (the Rt. Rev.) Charles. To (the Rt. Rev.) William J. Skilton, December 2, 2014. http://www.diosc.com/sys/images/documents/tec/skilton_vonrosenberg.pdf.

70. "Returning Priest Welcomed and Reinstated through New Path for Reconciliation." The Episcopal Church in South Carolina, September 18, 2014, http://www.episcopalchurchsc.org/2014-09-18-returning-priest-reinstated.htm.

71. "The Episcopal Church in South Carolina Welcomes Back a Priest through Reinstatement." The Episcopal Church in South Carolina, November 11, 2016, http://www.episcopalchurchsc.org/news-blog/the-episcopal-church-in-south-carolina-welcomes-back-a-priest-threough-reinstatement.

The reinstatement of clergy who had been released and removed had proved something of a problem in the Church diocese since there were no canons covering the matter. The diocese essentially developed a new structure for reinstatement. At the General Convention of 2015, South Carolina's plan was incorporated into a resolution that was passed by the Convention, A120, to amend the canons concerning the return to the ordained ministry of the Episcopal Church after release and removal. This gave a streamlined, and uniform standard for all dioceses to follow when deacons, priests, and bishops sought reinstatement in Holy Orders.[72]

As the year 2013 progressed, the reorganized Church diocese rebounded rather quickly from the trauma of the schism. The special convention in January and annual convention meeting in March advanced greatly the morale of the shell-shocked Episcopalian minority of the old diocese. The experienced new bishop and resolute new decision-making committees provided a strong and steady hand in reorganization. All the local churches finalized their choices of which diocese to follow as all the last of the dozen in discernment made their decisions and the new worshipping communities crystalized. Moreover, almost all the clergy completed their difficult decisions of which of the two bishops to follow.

In June of 2013 came another major morale boost for the still-rebuilding diocese, the semi-annual gathering of Province IV of the Episcopal Church.[73] On 25–27 June, twenty-five bishops and one bishop-elect, led by the President, Bishop Dabney Smith of Southwest Florida, met at Grace Church in Charleston to worship together, learn about the Episcopalians' recent experiences, and offer support and encouragement.[74] Retired suffragan bishop of South Carolina, William Skilton was one of the attendees. Another was Bishop Greg Brewer of Central Florida, the regional diocese that had been closely aligned with the pre-schism Diocese of South Carolina. Brewer's predecessor, John Howe, had been Lawrence's usual ally in the region in the run-up to the schism. Bishop Michael Curry, of North Carolina, and future presiding bishop, also attended the meeting. The meeting ended with the bishops issuing "An Open Letter to The Episcopal Church in South Carolina from the Bishops of Province IV." It was a warm message of approval and support for the intrepid Church people of eastern South Carolina. While commending the faithful for their hard work, the bishops also took pains to praise their attitude: "neither vengeance nor bitterness has any place with you."[75] Twenty-three bishops signed the letter.[76]

---

72. "2015–A120, Amend Canon III.7 to Add 7.11; Amend Canon III.9 to Add 9.12 and 9.13; and Amend Canon III.12, to Add 12.8 and Renumber 12.8, 12.9, and 12.10." The Episcopal Church, General Convention of 2015, http://www.generalconvention.org/gc/2015-resolutions/A120/current_english.text.

73. Province IV is the largest province of the Episcopal Church. It covers the southeastern U.S.: AL, FL, GA, KY, LA, MS, NC, SC, and TN.

74. "Episcopal Bishops from Across the Southeast Gather in Charleston." The Episcopal Church in South Carolina, June 26, 2013, http://www.episcopaldigitalnetwork.com/ens/2013/06/26/episcopal-bishops-from-across-the-southeast-gather-in-charleston.

75. "An Open Letter to The Episcopal Church in South Carolina from the Bishops of Province IV, June 27, 2013." The Episcopal Church in South Carolina, June 27, 2013, http://www.episcopaldigitalnetwork.org/province-iv-bishops-meeting.html.

76. Three did not sign: vonRosenberg, William Skilton, and Charles Duvall, retired of Central Gulf Coast.

Rebuilding the diocesan structure and morale continued in numerous ways in the following years. In 2014, there were three invigorating conventions, the annual meeting of the convention in February, another in November, and a special conference in May. On 21–22 February 2014, the diocesan convention met at All Saints Church in Hilton Head. The convention meeting of the year before had essentially returned the diocese to the 2007 level, before the revisions removing the diocese from the Church. The February 2014 meeting approved a new Constitution that brought the diocese up to date. It would have to be approved a second time to become effective. The assembly also adopted a new set of Canons that became effective immediately.[77] The preacher at that meeting was Bishop Michael Curry. Five worshipping communities were admitted to the diocese as missions: the Episcopal Church on Edisto, St. Francis of West Ashley, St. Catherine's of Florence, St. Anne's of Conway, and Good Shepherd of Summerville. In addition, the convention adopted a budget for 2014 that showed substantial gains from the year before. Contributions from parishes and missions nearly doubled. 2013 income was $203,000 from parishes and mission and $175,000 from the Episcopal Church. In 2014, local parishes and mission contributed $400,000, making the diocese self-supporting. The contribution to the national Church rose from $39,650 to $53,210. The total budget jumped from $378,000 to $400,000.[78]

On May 3, 2014 came the Enthusiastically Episcopalian in South Carolina conference at Holy Cross/Faith Memorial Church in Pawleys Island. It was led by Presiding Bishop Jefferts Schori, President of the House of Deputies, the Rev. Gay Clark Jennings, and Bishop vonRosenberg. After the opening festival Eucharist, the leaders gave talks on the state of the Church and the diocese. In the afternoon, workshops featured rebuilding after schism and featured speakers from the Pittsburgh diocese who were led by the Rt. Rev. Kenneth L. Price, Jr., former bishop provisional of Pittsburgh.[79]

To adjust the usual time of the annual meeting of the convention, another meeting was held 14–15 November 2014, in Charleston hosted by Church of the Holy Communion and Calvary Church. This assembly made the final approvals of the resolutions restoring the diocesan Constitution and Canons to full agreement with the Episcopal Church Constitution and Canons. Three worshipping communities were welcomed into the diocese as missions, the East Cooper Episcopal Church of Mt. Pleasant, the Episcopal Church in Okatie, and the Episcopal Church of the Messiah in Myrtle Beach. The preacher for the occasion was the Rt. Rev. James Tengatenga, Chairman of the Anglican Consultative Council. The meeting adopted a budget for 2015 that showed significant gains once again. The diocese was fully self-supporting with $435,500 in income and expenses. The contribution to the national Church went up once again, to $58,900.[80]

77. "Report from the Convention." The Episcopal Church in South Carolina, February 24, 2014, http://www.episcopalchurchsc.org/223rd-annual-diocesan-convention-february-2014.html.

78. "Journal of the 223rd Annual Diocesan Convention, The Episcopal Church in South Carolina, All Saints Episcopal Church, Hilton Head, February 21–22, 2014." Appendix VIII. http://www.episcopalchurchsc.org/uploads/1/2/9/8/12989303/journal_of_223rd_annual_convention_february_2014.pdf.

79. "Enthusiastically Episcopalian in South Carolina Conference, May 3, 2014." The Episcopal Church in South Carolina, May 5, 2014, http://www.episcopalchurchsc.org/enthusiastically-episcopalian.html.

80. "Journal of the 224th Annual Diocesan Convention, The Episcopal Church in South Carolina,

The 2015 annual meeting of the convention was held at Holy Cross/Faith Memorial Church in Pawleys Island on 13–14 November. For the first time, no resolution had to be passed to bring the diocesan Constitution and Canons into full compliance with the national Church. That had been finished in the last meeting. In a poignant moment, St. Mark's of Port Royal was admitted as a parish of the diocese. This was a time to celebrate a long and sometimes difficult journey of a dozen years. The assembly also voted to designate Grace Church, on Wentworth Street in Charleston, as the diocesan cathedral, to be known as Grace Church Cathedral. Mindful of the recent tragedy of the massacre at Emanuel A.M.E. Church in Charleston, the convention passed resolutions to develop measures to combat racism. Once again, the budget showed healthy growth, now at $457,000, a 14.4 percent increase over the budget of 2013.[81]

Announcement was made in the convention that Presiding Bishop Michael Curry, installed in office at the Washington National Cathedral only a few days earlier, on 1 November, would be visiting Charleston on 8–10 April 2016. Not only was the Church diocese rebuilding after the trauma of the schism but a much worse tragedy had recently occurred in Charleston in the massacre of nine people at Emanuel A.M.E. Church on June 17, 2015. Charleston, and South Carolina, were very much in need of his special kind of joy, faith, hope, and healing. The Episcopal Forum of South Carolina and all five Episcopal churches of downtown Charleston sponsored the activities and festivities of Curry's visit, of which there were many.

The reception the diocese gave the new presiding bishop in Charleston was the exact opposite of that the old diocese had given to another new presiding bishop, Jefferts Schori in February of 2008. It was as if life had replaced death, joy had vanquished despair. On Friday, 8 April, St. Stephen's Church, on Anson Street, hosted an ecumenical service featuring Curry and Dr. Betty Deas Clark, pastor of Emanuel Church, and unforgettable music that brought the house down. That evening, Grace Church held a youth lock-in. On Saturday, 9 April, a conference was held, "Spirituality, Evangelism, and Justice" followed by a Solemn High Mass at Holy Communion and a neighborhood block party at Calvary Church. The next day, Sunday, 10 April, Presiding Bishop Curry celebrated Eucharist at St. Mark's on Thomas Street, then preached at the Choral Eucharist in Grace Church Cathedral. Also there was the Very Rev. Robert Willis, the Dean of Canterbury Cathedral. When a no doubt exhausted Presiding Bishop Curry departed Charleston, the pain of the schism and the murders did not hurt quite as much.[82]

Hanging over all the reorganization and rebuilding was the reality that provisional bishops, usually retired bishops, typically serve only a few years. By mid-2015, the questions of the future of the diocese and the bishop's retirement needed to be addressed.

Church of the Holy Communion, Charleston, November 14–15, 2014." Appendix IV. http://www.episcopalchurchsc.org/uploads/1/2/9/8/12989303/journal_of_the_224th_annual_convention_november_2014.pdf.

81. "Proposed Budget for 2016." The Episcopal Church in South Carolina, http://www.episcopalchurchsc.org/uploads/1/2/9/8/12989303/final_amended_budget_2016.pdf.

82. "Presiding Bishop Michael Curry's Visit to Our Diocese, April 8–10, 2016." The Episcopal Church in South Carolina, http://www.episcopalchurchsc.org/presiding-bishop-currys-visit-2016.html ; "Celebration and a Call to Love Mark Presiding Bishop's Visit to Charleston." The Episcopal Church in South Carolina, April 13, 2016, http://www.episcopalchurchsc.org/2016-04-13-presiding-bishops-visit.html.

On September 10, 2015, Bishop vonRosenberg held a joint meeting of the Standing Committee, the Diocesan Council, and the Trustees to begin planning for the future of the diocese.[83] One outcome of the meeting was the creation of the Diocesan Future Committee on November 5, 2015.[84] By March of 2016, the committee settled on four feasible options for the future: a full-time bishop, a part-time bishop, continue a part-time provisional bishop, and merge with the Diocese of Upper South Carolina.[85] The last one seemed most unlikely. The first was questionable too as a full-time bishop would require a diocesan budget twice as large as the present one.

While the Future Committee was busy working on the future, Bishop vonRosenberg gave them more reason to do so. On January 14, 2016, he announced that he would retire from the office of bishop provisional after June 26, 2016.[86] The Standing Committee went to work on finding a replacement. On April 20, 2016, the committee announced its search subcommittee had interviewed candidates and was compiling a financial package to offer the next provisional bishop.[87] The committee said it would vote on a candidate, announce the choice, and call a special convention to formally elect the next bishop. On June 30, 2016, the diocese announced the nomination of the Rt. Rev. Gladstone B. "Skip" Adams III, to be the next bishop provisional. Adams was about to retire as bishop of Central New York. On September 10, 2016, a special meeting of the convention of the diocese was held at Grace Church Cathedral to elect and witness the installation of Adams as its new bishop provisional.

The Issues of Homosexuality and Racism

As we have seen, the issue of rights for homosexuals and transgendered people was the immediate, or direct, cause of the schism in South Carolina. After General Convention approved of the blessing of same-sex unions and rights for the transgendered in 2012, the old diocesan leadership began preparing in earnest to "disassociate" the diocese from the Episcopal Church. This was true even though the Church had agreed to give bishops the option of whether to allow same-sex blessings in their dioceses. South Carolina was not going to be forced to accept what it did not want.

The Episcopal Church in South Carolina had to decide whether to allow the blessings in the diocese. Once the repopulation of the diocesan governing bodies was finished in early 2013, the diocese could turn to the matter at hand. In 2013, the standing committee spent several months considering the issue and studying the materials from

---

83. "Diocesan Future Committee Seeking Input." The Episcopal Church in South Carolina, March 16, 2016, http://www.episcopalchurchsc.org/futures-committee.html.

84. Ibid. Members: Mark Szen, Bob Pinkerton, Emily Guess, Lonnie Hamilton, Jeremy Cook, Betsy Walker, Ginga Wilder, Jo Ann Ewalt, Bill Lonax, Doug Roderick, Lucille Grate, and the Rev. Jeff Richardson.

85. Ibid.

86. "South Carolina Charles conRosenberg to Retire as Provisional Bishop." The Episcopal Church in South Carolina, January 14, 2016, http://www.epicopalchurchsc.org/2016-01-14-bishops-retirement.html.

87. "Leadership Transition Information." The Episcopal Church in South Carolina, May 5, 2016, http://www.episcopalchurchsc.org/leadership-transition.html.

the General Convention.[88] In September of 2013, it voted unanimously to recommend the bishop move ahead with developing policy and process for the blessings of same-sex unions in the diocese.[89] A Diocesan Committee on Blessings was set up, led by the bishop, to adapt materials from General Convention for diocesan use.[90] It worked on the issue for fifteen months. By July of 2014, more than sixty of the 110 dioceses of the Episcopal Church had adopted liturgies for the blessings of same-sex unions. In Province IV, the southeast, fifteen of the twenty dioceses had established the liturgies.[91] Most importantly, Bishop Andrew Waldo, of Upper South Carolina, who had voted "No" on the resolution in the General Convention to allow the blessings, also set up a diocesan task force that spent a great deal of time and effort on the issue. On May 8, 2014, Waldo announced that the blessings would begin in the diocese and released a personal "Reflection" on the subject that was impressive in its rationale. The diocese released a model eighty-six-page guide for the interface of diocese and the blessing of same-sex unions.

Bishop vonRosenberg issued his diocesan policy on the blessing of same-sex unions on July 8, 2014. He opened the option for the services in the diocese but left the decisions on whether to allow them locally to the parish/mission governing bodies and clergy. In his announcement to the diocese, the Bishop said, "I am requiring that the appropriate vestry or mission committee give its approval."[92] He said the clergy too could decide: "I do want to be clear that this permission does not define an expectation for clergy."[93] For the church services, the diocese was to use the liturgy entitled "The Witnessing and Blessing of a Lifelong Covenant" that had been approved by the Diocesan Committee on Blessings.

Although the Episcopal Church's establishment of the blessing of same-sex unions was a major accomplishment for equal rights for homosexual persons, it was not the end of the issue. By the time Bishop vonRosenberg published the diocesan policy on the blessings of same-sex unions, more than half of the states in the U.S. had legalized same-sex marriage and the number was growing rapidly. The issue of the legality of same-sex marriage in the nation inevitably went to the United States Supreme Court. There, it was encapsulated in the case of *Obergefell v. Hodges* which was argued before the justices on April 28, 2015. In a 5–4 split, the majority ruled, on June 26, 2015, that same-sex marriage was legal in all of the United States settling the issue once and for across the nation. The decision was the culmination of a decades-long struggle for equal rights of homosexual persons in America.

The day before the Court issued its decision, the triennial meeting of the General Convention of the Episcopal Church had begun in Salt Lake City. When news arrived

---

88. "South Carolina: Bishop Permits Blessings of Same-Sex Relationships." The Episcopal Church in South Carolina, July 8, 2014, as quoted in Episcopal News Service, July 8, 2014, http://episcopaldigitalnetwork.com/ens/2014/07/08/south-carolina-bishop-permits-blessings-of-same-sex-relationships.

89. Ibid.

90. Members: Ellen Dooley, Carol Grish, Cornelia Pelzer, Bill Warner, Andrea McKellar, the Revs. Chris Huff, Wil Keith, Rick Lindsey, Michael Wright, and John Zahl.

91. Ibid.

92. vonRosenberg, Letter to the diocese, July 8, 2014.

93. Ibid.

of the Court ruling, applause spread across the meeting.[94] Most of the assembled Episcopalians, but certainly not all, greeted the news with joy as they too were working on resolutions that would have the Episcopal Church accept the right of same-sex couples to marry in the Church. Churches in America were split on their stands regarding same-sex marriage. Most still opposed it: Roman Catholic, Southern Baptist, United Methodist, the Mormons, Lutheran-Missouri Synod, but several denominations had already adopted it: the Presbyterian Church (U.S.A.), the Evangelical Lutheran Church, United Church of Christ, Unitarian/Universalists, Quakers, Reformed Judaism.[95] Same-sex marriage was the overwhelming issue of the day in the General Convention that met in Salt Lake City from June 25 to July 3. Bishop vonRosenberg led the South Carolina deputation whose members were clergy: the Revs. James Taylor, Wilmot Merchant, Richard Lindsey, and Michael Wright, and laity: Thomas Tisdale, Lonnie Hamilton, Mary Ann Foy, and Andrea McKellar. The retired South Carolina bishops Edward Salmon and William Skilton were also present. This was the first General Convention after the schism; and the delegation's attitude, congeniality, and participation was strikingly different than that of every contingent from the diocese in the past two decades. The Church diocese of South Carolina rejoined the mainstream of Episcopalians in America.

The moment of high drama in the General Convention came on 1 July, five days after the Supreme Court decision. The Special Legislative Committee on Marriage presented in the House of Deputies two proposed resolutions that would establish same-sex marriage in the Church, one by liturgies, and one by canonical change. It was reported that the House of Bishops had debated the issues for five hours before making compromises. The first of the two was A054, "Adopt Resources and Rites from 'Liturgical Resources I: I Will Bless You and You Will Be a Blessing, Revised and Expanded 2015.'"[96] This would essentially change the prayer book marriage liturgies to allow same-sex marriage. The committee spokesman presenting the proposal made an observation in recognition of South Carolina. He said that one part of the resolution was called "the Thurlow Amendment" in honor of the Rev. David Thurlow,[97] a deputy from South Carolina in 2012 who had promoted the local option provision in the blessing of same-sex unions. The Thurlow Amendment from 2012 was repeated here: "That the convention honor the theological diversity of this Church in regard to matters of human sexuality; and that no bishop, priest, deacon or lay person should be coerced or penalized in any manner, nor suffer any canonical disabilities, as a result of his or her theological objection to or

---

94. Schjonberg, Mary Frances. "Supreme Court Marriage Ruling Draws Applause in Salt Lake City." Episcopal News Service, June 26, 2015, http://episcopaldigitalnetwork.com/ens/2015/06/26/supreme-court-marriage-ruling-draws-applause.

95. Masci, David. "Where Christian Churches, Other Religions Stand on Gay Marriage." Pew Research Center, July 2, 2015, http://www.pewresearch.org/fact-tank/2015/07/02/where-christian-churches-stand-on-gay-marriage.

96. "2015–A054, Adopt Resources and Rites from 'Liturgical Resources I: I Will Bless You and You Will Be a Blessing,' Revised and Expanded 2015." The Episcopal Church, General Convention, July 1, 2015, http://www.generalconvention.org/gc/2015-resolutions/A054/current_english_text.

97. The Rev. David Thurlow was rector of St. Matthias Church, in Summerton. He left the Episcopal Church in the schism of 2012 to remain with DSC.

support for the 78th General Convention's action contained in this resolution."[98] The vote was taken by clerical and lay orders, by diocese. In the tally, the clergy voted 94 in favor, 12 against, and 2 divided while the laity voted 90 for, 11 against, and 3 divided.[99] Thus, the resolution was adopted with about 90 percent approval.

The second proposed resolution was the most profoundly serious of all resolutions offered in the 2015 General Convention. "A036 Amend Canon I.18 Marriage" would change the canonical description of marriage from the Solemnization of Holy Matrimony to the Celebration and Blessing of Marriage to allow for the usage of the new gender-neutral liturgies.[100] In other words, it would change the canons of the Episcopal Church to permit same-sex marriage in the church. Once again, in the spirit of the Thurlow Amendment, whether to allow same-sex marriage on the local level would be left to the discretion of the clergy. The vote on A036 was clergy: 85 for, 15 against, 6 divided, and laity: 88 in favor, 12 against, and 6 divided.[101] The resolution passed with about 80 percent of the vote. The deputies from South Carolina voted in favor of both resolutions.

The gravity of the moment was apparent to all, but the historical significance of the passage of the two resolutions may not have been clear to everyone at the Convention. In fact, this ended a thirty-nine-year course in which the Episcopal Church had wrestled with the issue of homosexuality. The question had first appeared in the General Convention of 1976. By 1990 the Church was generally divided into thirds, one in favor of equality for homosexuals, one against, and one neutral. In the next few years, however, the pro side carried the day by removing the barriers against the ordinations of gays. Still, as late as 1997, the conservatives were able to muster a majority vote to block the blessing of same-sex unions. It was not until 2012 that the Church adopted the liturgical blessing of same-sex unions. Now, only three years later, the Church established same-sex marriage in the church. This meant the complete removal of discrimination against homosexuals and their full inclusion in the official life of the Episcopal Church, an astonishing achievement in four decades.

The conservative opponents of gay rights were still around but their numbers and influence had declined drastically from the dominance they had in the 1970s and 1980s and the third in the 1990s. If nothing else, the votes on the two resolutions showed that reality. From about one hundred bishops opposing equality for homosexuals two decades earlier, now only twenty bishops could be found to make a statement in protest. On July 2, the day after the passage of the two resolutions, a conservative coalition of bishops issued the "Communion Partners Salt Lake City Statement." It strongly disagreed with the two resolutions and insisted that marriage must be between a man and a woman. However, absent was any threat to bolt the Church. Indeed, the dissenters vowed, "We are committed to the Church and its people, even in the midst of painful disagreement."[102]

98. Ibid.

99. Author's notes, Episcopal Church, General Convention, livestream, July 1, 2015.

100. "2015–A036, Amend Canon I.18 Marriage." The Episcopal Church, General Convention, July 1, 2015, http://www.generalconvention.org/gc/2015-resolutions/A036/Current_english_text.

101. Author's notes, Episcopal Church, General Convention, July 1, 2015.

102. "The Salt Lake City Statement." *The Living Church*, July 2, 2015, http://livingchurch.org/salt-lake-city-statement.

Signing the statement were the seven remaining of the dozen ultra-conservative "Communion Partners" bishops.[103] Five others had departed the Episcopal Church.[104] In all, twenty bishops signed including most of those from Latin America. Two of the bishops to sign were retired South Carolinians Edward Salmon and William Skilton.

The House of Bishops, no doubt relieved there were no new schisms on the right and perhaps trying to stave off any that might be ahead, heaped only praise on the grieving minority of bishops. Immediately after the twenty dissenters issued their Statement, the House published its own statement called "Communion Across Difference." It was filled with laudatory remarks meant to salve the wounds of the ultra-conservatives such as: "The equanimity, generosity, and graciousness with which the Communion Partners have shared their views on Christian marriage and remain in relationship is a model for us."[105] Whether the House's "Mind" made any difference, there was to be no new diocesan defection on the far right of the Episcopal Church. The crisis of the issue of homosexuality was over. Of all the contentious issues of the last half century including civil rights, women's ordination, and new prayer book, that of equality for homosexuals had been the most contentious. It took the longest to resolve, at thirty-nine years, and witnessed the most loss and disruption in the Church, but in the end the reforms were completed and a far more just and equitable Church survived largely intact.

Since the Episcopal Church was the first, and only, of the thirty-eight provinces of the Anglican Communion to establish same-sex marriage, the rest of the Communion could only stand and take notice, some with great dismay if not alarm. Indeed, one of the dissenters' complaints was the disruption this would cause in the Communion, many of whose Third World churches, particularly in Africa, were adamantly opposed to equal rights for homosexuals. The Archbishop of Canterbury, Justin Welby, lost no time in worrying aloud about the tumultuous effects of the American decision in the highly diverse and far flung Communion, a byproduct of the once global British Empire. On June 30, the Archbishop's office sent out a press release: "The Archbishop of Canterbury today expressed deep concern about the stress for the Anglican Communion following the US Episcopal Church's House of Bishops' resolution to change the definition of marriage in the canons so that any reference to marriage as between a man and a woman is removed."[106]

The dissenting bishops and the Archbishop of Canterbury may have had concerns that same-sex marriage in the Church was not the right thing to do, but the bishop provisional of South Carolina had no such hesitation. On July 21, 2015, Bishop vonRosenberg sent a message to his diocese that same-sex marriage would begin in South Carolina on the earliest possible date: "Our current policy involving 'blessings' remains in place until Advent I (November 29, 2015). At that point, the liturgies for marriage will

103. Tennessee, Central Florida, Dallas, Northern Indiana, Albany, Springfield, North Dakota.

104. San Joaquin, Pittsburgh, Fort Worth, Quincy, South Carolina.

105. "Mind of the House of Bishops Statement: 'Communion Across Difference.'" July 2, 2015, http://episcopaldigitalnetwork.com/ens/2015/07/02/mind-of-the-house-of-bishops-statement.

106. "Response to the US Episcopal Church Resolution on Marriage." The Archbishop of Canterbury, June 30, 2015, http://www.archbishopofcanterbury.org/articles.php/5581/response-to-the-us-episcopal-church.

be appropriate to use, as authorized rites of the Church."[107] As promised, the Episcopal Church diocese of South Carolina began conducting same-sex weddings after November 29, 2015. At long last, the issue of homosexuality was put to rest. It had roiled and embroiled the diocese for well over thirty years, at least since Bishop Allison had arrived in 1982. The end came with a whimper, not a bang. Over the years and along the way there had been plenty of fireworks, but in the end, the issue of homosexuality was put to bed and the lights turned out with hardly a notice.

Racism was another issue still hanging over South Carolina, arguably the American state with the deepest history of racial animosity. After centuries of slavery, after Reconstruction and a century of Jim Crow, the Civil Rights movement finally came to South Carolina in the 1950s and 1960s. The Episcopal diocese, which had been part and parcel of the state's racist past, finally turned to full equality and integration in the civil rights period. After 1980, however, the diocese virtually ignored the subject of racism in favor of other social and cultural issues the leaders considered to be more pressing, namely promoting the conservative evangelical cause and resisting other social reforms in the Church. This was essentially the history of the Diocese of South Carolina from 1982 to 2012. After the schism, the Episcopal Church diocese could return to work on combatting racism in its region.

The adoption of the two resolutions establishing same-sex marriage was not the only dramatic work of the General Convention of 2015. Another was the overwhelming election on the first ballot of the first African American Presiding Bishop of the Episcopal Church. Bishop Michael Curry, of North Carolina was elected on June 27, 2015, by a vote of 121 of the 174 in the House of Bishops and 800 of the 812 in the House of Deputies of the General Convention.[108] Curry was a dear friend to the Episcopal diocese of South Carolina. He had been the preacher at the annual meeting of the convention on Hilton Head in February of 2014. The office of Presiding Bishop was passed from Katharine Jefferts Schori to Curry as he was installed on November 1, 2015, in an elaborate and joyous service in the Washington National Cathedral.

On June 17, 2015, a few days before Curry was elected presiding bishop, one of the worst apparently racially-motivated crimes of South Carolina history occurred. A white man attended an evening Bible study class at the historic Emanuel African Methodist Episcopal Church, on Calhoun Street, in Charleston, and in a six-minute period, shot to death nine people, all African Americans. The victims included the Rev. Clementa Pinckney, the pastor and a state senator. The suspect, a twenty-one-year-old white man, Dylann Storm Roof, was soon arrested and charged with nine counts of murder; he reportedly said he was trying to start a race war.[109] There would be no race war. Times had changed in South Carolina and the overwhelming opinion among whites and blacks

---

107. vonRosenberg, (Rt. Rev.) Charles. "A Message from Bishop vonRosenberg." The Episcopal Church in South Carolina, July 21, 2015, http://www.episcopalchurchsc.org/2015-07-21-message-following-general-convention.html.

108. McCombs, Brady and Rachel Zoll. "Episcopal Church Elects Michael Curry, Its First Black Presiding Bishop." Huffington Post, June 27, 2015, http://www.huffingtonpost.com/2015/05/27/episcopal-church-michael-curry-black.

109. "Charleston Church Shooting." Wikipedia, http://en.wikipedia.org/wiki/Charleston_church_shooting.

in the state was horror and disgust at the murders and their apparent motivation. In the most touching moment of the nightmarish event, two days after the massacre, when Roof appeared for bond hearing in a teleconference with the court, several relatives of the victims tearfully forgave him to his face and assured him of God's forgiveness.[110] World-wide attention turned to Charleston and South Carolina. The funerals lasted several days. That of the Rev. Pinckney was held in the arena of the College of Charleston on June 26 before five thousand people and a global television audience. President Obama and dozens of top political leaders from Washington and Columbia attended. In Charleston and in the state, there was almost universal call for racial harmony. This came to focus on a demand for the removal of the Confederate battle flag from the state house ground in Columbia. The governor, Nikki Haley, the state's two senators, and numerous other officials demanded the flag be removed. The state legislature agreed; and the flag was removed to a museum on July 10, 2015.

As all the other religious leaders in the state, Bishop vonRosenberg immediately called for prayers and support. He also took money from the diocesan budget to contribute to the Mother Emanuel Hope Fund and made other contributions to the Lowcountry Ministries Reverend Pinckney Fund. Moreover, he led the diocese to develop a program on anti-racism training, something that was actually in the works before the Emanuel Massacre. In September of 2015, the diocese held four workshop sessions in Charleston, Hilton Head, Conway, and North Charleston featuring a documentary video "Traces of the Trade: A Story from the Deep North," the story of the slave trading DeWolf family of Rhode Island. Discussion was facilitated by Constance and Dain Perry. Local leaders were required to attend, but many others did too for three-hour sessions exploring ways to end the sin of racism.[111] The explorations continued after the training, at least in ongoing conversations of communicants of Calvary Church and the East Cooper Episcopalians.

Thus, as Bishop vonRosenberg's tenure began to near its end in early 2016, he could look back with satisfaction that two of the most difficult problems in the history of the diocese were much closer to being resolved than ever. In fact, one issue, homosexuality, was closed. Openly gay persons had been given full access to the offices of the Episcopal Church. Same-sex couples could now marry in the Episcopal Church by canon law and the official liturgies. Another issue, racism, was still alive, but was much closer to resolution than ever before. The Emanuel massacre had proven that the people of South Carolina, and of the Episcopal Church diocese, no longer saw society divided into hostile races. As it had been in the Civil Rights movement, the diocese was committed to ending racism.

---

110. The jury in the federal trial, Dec. 7–15, 2016, found Roof guilty of all counts, and on Jan 10, 2017, they recommended the death penalty. On Jan. 11, 2017, federal Judge Gergel sentenced Roof to death by lethal injection. On April 10, 2017, Roof pled guilty in state circuit court in Charleston thus ending the litigation. See: "Dylan Roof," Wikipedia, https://en.wikipedia.org/wiki/Dylann_Roof.

111. "Traces of the Trade: A Story from the Deep North." The Episcopal Church in South Carolina, http://www.episcopalchurchsc.org/anti-racism-training.html.

THE DIOCESE OF SOUTH CAROLINA

The Search for Meaning

Once the Diocese of South Carolina declared its "disaffiliation" from the Episcopal Church, its primary need was to define its meaning and mission and next to establish an identity of itself. If it were not to be a part of the Episcopal Church, then what was its character, its purpose, and its place in the world? Along with the ongoing litigation, the search for meaning and identity was to be the fundamental concern driving the work of the independent diocese for the next few years.

To give itself meaning, the diocese had to explain its reasons for leaving the Episcopal Church. Even well before the schism, the diocesan leaders had established the theme of three causes: theology, morality, and polity. As Bishop Lawrence and the other leaders had gone about the diocese in 2012, this was the consistent message. It would remain so in January and February of 2013 as the last few parishes and missions went through their decision processes. It was in one of these parishes that Lawrence gave a lengthy and full explanation that now stands as the best record of his public rationale for the schism. It was the only publicly available full transcript of Lawrence's remarks to a parish in discernment at this time. It is well worth a close consideration.

On 10 February 2013, Lawrence addressed a parish meeting at Old St. Andrew's, in West Ashley. St. Andrew's was a divided parish and would soon vote on which bishop to follow. A verbatim transcript of his remarks was published as a fifteen-page article.[112] He opened as usual with the theme of the three differences between the diocese and the Episcopal Church. On theology, he said the Episcopal Church had moved away from reliance on the Scriptures and belief in the uniqueness of Christ. As for the classical Anglican model of the three-legged stool of Scripture, reason, and tradition, Lawrence said that it was really a one-legged stood, Scripture. Reason and tradition came from Scripture: "The traditional way of understanding tradition is that it is 2,000 years of God's people reflecting on Scripture. Reason is the Scripture-guided mind inspired by the Holy Spirit to reasonably digest, read, mark, learn, and try to understand Scripture."[113] On the issue of the uniqueness of Christ, Lawrence questioned whether the leaders of the Episcopal Church still believed that: "the presiding bishop of the Episcopal Church and many other bishops have made statements that would seem to imply that the uniqueness of Jesus Christ is questionable."[114] Lawrence spent about fifteen percent of his time talking about how the Episcopal Church had abandoned the traditional interpretation of Scripture.

Lawrence also spent about fifteen percent of his time talking about polity. On this he focused on the Church's changes in Title IV of the canons and "intrusions" in the diocese which he called unconstitutional. He said the dioceses were autonomous of the national Church, but that the Church had made changes to give the presiding bishop

---

112. "Remarks by the Right Reverend Mark Lawrence, Bishop of the Diocese of South Carolina, to the Parishioners of St. Andrew's Parish Church, February 10, 2013." Unpublished transcription, St. Andrew's Church [Old St. Andrew's], Charleston, SC.

113. Ibid.

114. Ibid.

authority over the dioceses: "We made some changes to our diocesan Constitution and Canons because of intrusions by the presiding bishop that were unconstitutional and because The Episcopal Church in 2009 approved a Title Four canonical revision that was contradictory to the Constitution of The Episcopal Church. Which gave the presiding bishop unconstitutional authority, which the Constitution protects dioceses from." The average parishioner, who probably had little idea what Title IV was much less the fine points of the powers of the presiding bishop, would have had no way of seeing this differently. Regardless of the details, or lack thereof, they could not miss Lawrence's point that the Episcopal Church had acted unconstitutionally while the diocese had acted constitutionally.

Theology and polity were important to Lawrence but they paled in comparison to his concern for the second of the three issues, "morality." He spent a full third of his time on this, more than on theology and polity combined. By morality, Lawrence meant homosexuality and its associated topics of gender identity and marriage. He made it entirely clear that he believed God assigned gender to everyone, made everyone male or female, and instituted marriage as the union of a man and a woman as embedded in the Scriptures. In this scenario, the very existence of homosexuality would be problematical because it would be inconsistent with this creation narrative and any kind of sexual relations outside the bonds of Holy Matrimony would be unacceptable. Lawrence seemed unable to believe that people could really be homosexual. At one time he said: "If a person has homosexual proclivities, or what they perceive as orientation, and they are willing to live a celibate life, they may be ordained."[115] Another time he referred to a gay priest as "a person who struggles with same-sex attractions."[116] As he did in his talk at St. John's of Florence in October of 2012, Lawrence expressed his greatest concern at transgendered clergy which he believed the Church was forcing on everyone: "But this is the reality in the Episcopal Church today. If someone comes to the conclusion that he's a female in a male body (. . .) that's her gender identity now."[117] Later he said, "No religion in the history of the world that we know of has embraced that sort of understanding of gender. No civilization has. Now we have a church that's leading the way (. . .) I just don't want that world. If you want it, that's fine. It's in The Episcopal Church, you're there."[118] Lawrence insisted about the blessings, "there's no common meeting ground. Somebody's right and somebody's wrong. There is no way to make them both say the same thing. Now can we learn to live together? Well I suppose some people can, but not if I have to do it and approve it. I believe it is wrong to take what God has blessed and change it."[119] Lawrence glossed over a crucial fact in all of this, that the Church had indeed found a common meeting ground in the provision that allowed bishops the local option of whether to allow same-sex blessings in their dioceses. Similarly, on the issue of transgendered clergy, Lawrence implied that the Church was forcing this on the dioceses: "They [TEC] then passed two canons and because they're canons, everybody has to subscribe

115. Ibid.
116. Ibid.
117. Ibid.
118. Ibid.
119. Ibid.

to them. The first canon goes like this: no one shall be deprived of ordination in The Episcopal Church because of gender identity or gender expression. Canon two: no lay person shall be kept from any order or aspect of congregational life or ministry because of gender identity or gender expression."[120] Actually, ordination was always up to the local bishop as San Joaquin, Quincy, and Fort Worth had demonstrated for many years. Besides, the diocese had revoked its accession to the canons of the Church.

On the subject of women clergy, one questioner asked Lawrence, "Is there any difference between The Episcopal Church and the Diocese of South Carolina if a woman wants to become a priest?"[121] Here the normally verbose and animated Lawrence became curt: "No, we have women priests in this diocese, and so does The Episcopal Church." The questioner went on, "'And will you continue to ordain women?" Lawrence answered quickly, "As far as I can see. I can't speak for a bishop that would come after me." The questioner and Lawrence both ignored the fact that Lawrence had never ordained a woman to the priesthood and had ordained only two women among many men, to the diaconate. His answers, however, might leave one thinking Lawrence was completely in favor of the ordination of women. The record suggested differently.

From the amount of time spent on the three causes of theology, morality, and polity, one could conclude that to Bishop Lawrence the issue of morality was by far the most important cause of the schism. However, entwined in his discussion were several other factors that Lawrence emphasized. The most important of these was his victimization. He depicted himself as the innocent victim of a malevolent national Church. He believed this started before he became bishop: "I'm the only person in The Episcopal Church elected twice, and then went through two election processes and two deposition processes. Because they couldn't get rid of me on the first try, they had to make another try."[122] He did not define who "they" were. He did not explain what "get rid of" meant. He insisted that he had done all he could to avoid a schism: "For well over five years, maybe six, or maybe even seven, I have sought to avoid this day that you all are in, I was not able to do that."[123] Later he still insisted, "But I had sought to keep the Diocese of South Carolina intact and in The Episcopal Church."[124] In his victimization theme, Lawrence often used the "us" against "them" analogy. For instance, he said: "It's God's call on our lives. Frankly, we are more connected to the culture of South Carolina than is The Episcopal Church."[125]

Along with victimization was the recurring theme of fear of a conspiratorial national Church. After "they" had failed to keep Lawrence from become bishop, they tried to take control of the diocese through "intrusions" by a lawyer they hired. According to Lawrence, Presiding Bishop Jefferts Schori was overbearing by telling him she did not trust him and asked him why he stayed in the Episcopal Church. He insisted he had worked hard to prevent a schism by meeting with the Presiding Bishop on 3 October

120. Ibid.
121. Ibid.
122. Ibid.
123. Ibid.
124. Ibid.
125. Ibid.

2012. Curiously enough, Lawrence did not deny to his listeners the charge that he had abandoned the Episcopal Church. His main concern was that the Presiding Bishop had not told him about the investigation when he talked with her on 3 October. Actually, as we have seen, Jefferts Schori did not receive official notification from the Disciplinary Board until October 10. As we know now, Lawrence had not told the Presiding Bishop, or, apparently, anyone outside his narrow circle, about the Standing Committee's pending secret resolution of 2 October to "disassociate" the diocese from the Episcopal Church. It was in the area of the relation of events in the weeks around the schism of 15 October 2012 that Lawrence was the least forthcoming to the parishioners of St. Andrew's.

Mixed into Lawrence's remarks to the parishioners of St. Andrew's were references to the recurring theme of fear of the Episcopal Church. It was on the property issue that this fear was most developed. Concerning the parish property, Lawrence told the assembly, "The Episcopal Church will tell you, you own your property, but you hold it in trust for the diocese and the national church. You have all the financial responsibility for the upkeep of the buildings, insurance, protection, litigation, that come your way, but you don't own it, except in trust for them. We say no, in the state of South Carolina, you own your property if you own your deed."[126] The parishioners might conclude from this that if they stayed with the Church they would not own the property, but if they went with Lawrence, they would own it. In fact, the Dennis Canon, which the diocese had followed for years without any complaint about it, said that the local parish would own the property but in trust for the diocese and Church. As a practical matter, all this meant was that a local congregation could not sell the property without the permission of the diocese and Church.

Fear of the Episcopal Church as the dark "they" against "us" cropped up in other places in Lawrence's talk. At one point, Lawrence implied that St. Andrew's would wind up paying more to the diocese if it stayed with the Church: "I don't know what the newly forming diocese [i.e. Church diocese] is going to ask, but throughout most of The Episcopal Church, there are assessments. I don't know what they'll do, so I won't speculate on that. What you have is what you'll get from us."[127]

Perhaps it was not difficult to cultivate the dichotomy of "us" against "them." As evidence of how well this strategy of separation worked, there was not a single question, and certainly not a word voluntarily from Lawrence, about the reactions of other dioceses even the adjacent ones. If the Episcopal Church were so wrong on theology, morality, and polity as to require the diocese to break away from it, why were not other dioceses doing the same? In fact, not one bishop had followed Lawrence out of the Episcopal Church. Not one diocese had followed the Diocese of South Carolina in voting to leave the Episcopal Church. Could it be that only the Church leaders in eastern South Carolina understood true religion and all the other 110 dioceses did not? South Carolina was one of twenty dioceses in Province IV of the Episcopal Church, the area covering the southeastern United States, one of the most socially and culturally conservative regions of America. Not one of the bishops or dioceses of South Carolina's home province supported South Carolina's schism. No one in the assembly at St. Andrew's thought to ask

126. Ibid.

127. Ibid. Old St. Andrew's was contributing about 2% to the diocese.

about this obvious problem. South Carolinians' ancient penchant for localism remained strong.

Perhaps even more misleading than fear of the remote Church were Lawrence's words and implications about the future relationship of the Diocese of South Carolina and the Anglican Communion. The listeners might have drawn the conclusion from what Lawrence said that the diocese would remain a part of the worldwide Anglican Communion through some sort of Anglican provincial arrangement. Lawrence told the crowd: "At some point, we will become affiliated with a province somewhere."[128] He repeated the words "province" and "provincial" thirteen times and "Anglican" and "Anglicanism" fifteen times in his talk. The Anglican Church in North America, which the first four earlier secessionist groups had joined was in fact not a province of the Anglican Communion; nevertheless, Lawrence called it a "province of the Anglican Communion": "The Anglican Church in North America is recognized by the Global Futures, Global South, as a province of the Anglican Communion."[129] He went on that "The primates, the representatives of over 50 million Anglicans, have written to me to say that they recognize me as a bishop in good standing, and they recognize the Diocese of South Carolina as a diocese in the Anglican Communion."[130] He did not explain what "recognize" meant; as he failed to explain that Global Futures (GAFCON), and Global South were self-made alliances with no official status in the Anglican Communion and no right to declare anyone to be in the Anglican Communion. Asked again whether a new province of the Anglican Communion was being created in the United States, Lawrence replied, "There is already the Anglican Church in North America, which is a province that is recognized by 22 provinces of the Anglican Communion."[131] While speaking on affiliation, Lawrence chose his words carefully and remained technically accurate. It was not surprising then, that after the schism many people in Bishop Lawrence's diocese mistakenly believed they remained in good standing in the Anglican Communion and would inevitably be in a province of the Communion. In fact, by leaving the Episcopal Church, the diocese left the only official province of the Anglican Communion in the United States. Any role the diocese would play in the Anglican Communion after that would be an informal relationship among supportive friends at home and abroad.

Altogether, Bishop Lawrence did an impressive and obviously highly effective job in his presentation to Old St. Andrew's. He was decisive in dividing the dark force of "them," the Episcopal Church afar, against the shining force of "us," the local people of eastern South Carolina. This was truly remarkable considering that the diocese had been part of the Episcopal Church for 224 years, except for the 4 years of the Civil War, and the Episcopal Church was embedded in the culture of the elites of South Carolina. It was even more remarkable in Old Saint Andrew's. The parish was originally established in the Church Act of 1706; and its building was first constructed around 1708 making it the oldest extant church south of Virginia still holding regular services. Lawrence depicted himself and the diocese as innocent victims striving only for "orthodoxy" against

128. Ibid.
129. Ibid.
130. Ibid.
131. Ibid.

the menacing villains pushing non-Scriptural revisionism and sexual immorality. He brought up the three causes of the schism, but lingered only on the most emotionally arousing issue of homosexuality. Listeners could reasonably conclude from his words that the parishes would control themselves and the diocese would always be a part of the Anglican Communion. Apparently, most of the audience left the meeting confident and secure that following Lawrence and the majority of the old diocese was the right thing to do.

Bishop vonRosenberg also visited Old St. Andrew's, on 17 February, to discuss the issues and answer questions of the congregation. He tried his best to present the Church's views and to dispel some of the misunderstandings floating about, but no doubt by then the majority of parishioners had already made up their minds. He addressed the main issues of the day, the place in the Anglican Communion, same-sex blessings in the Episcopal Church, property rights, and the uniqueness of Christ.[132] The questions from the audience to vonRosenberg were overwhelmingly hostile, as opposed to the "softballs" generously lobbed to Lawrence; and some of the questioners were not members of St. Andrew's.[133] The next day, the Rev. Marshall Huey, the rector of St. Andrew's, told the vestry that he would follow Lawrence; he mailed a nine-page letter to his parishioners making his case.[134]

Huey's lengthy letter to his parishioners essentially restated the case Lawrence had made to the parish.[135] He too gave the three standard reasons for the schism, theology, morality, and polity. Moreover, he echoed the themes of Lawrence's victimization and fear of the Episcopal Church: "If Old St. Andrew's aligns with TEC, we will be forever subject to the Dennis Canon." He neglected to mention that Old St. Andrew's had been subject to the Dennis Canon for decades before the schism without a problem. While mostly repeating Lawrence's assertions, Huey added two new points. In one part labeled "Historical" Huey said that all the colonial Anglican parishes still in existence were going along with the secession and that Old St. Andrew's should not break this union. Perhaps he was not aware, but two surviving colonial churches were remaining with the Episcopal Church: St. James Santee and St. Stephen's of St. Stephen. He was certainly aware that one of the colonial parishes, All Saints Waccamaw, had declared its independence and had seen this ratified by the state supreme court in 2009. In another section, he called "Practical," Huey said the Church diocese would be very small and this could mean St. Andrew's would wind up being forced to pay much more money to support the needy diocese. In fact, the Church diocese was as large if not larger than many dioceses in the Episcopal Church and within a year was entirely self-supporting without forcing parishes to pay large new assessments. The fear that if they stayed with the Church the parish would lose in two ways, its property and high payments to the diocese, was not well grounded. Regardless, the rector's last-minute lawyerly plea for secession from the Episcopal Church must have been influential in the subsequent vote.

132. vonRosenberg, (the Rt. Rev.) Charles. "Presentation at Old St. Andrew's Church." [February 17, 2013]. Unpublished transcription, St. Andrew's Church, Charleston SC.
133. vonRosenberg, (the Rt. Rev.) Charles. Email message to author, June 22, 2016.
134. Porwoll, *Against All Odds,* 323.
135. Huey, (the Rev.) Marshall. Letter to Old Saint Andrew's Parish, [February 19, 2013?].

At the parish vote on February 24, 2013, 184 sided with Lawrence and 60 with vonRosenberg as the parish cast its lot with the independent diocese. Upon this, many of the loyal Episcopalians left St. Andrew's to form a worship community in West Ashley that eventually became a mission of the Church diocese called St. Francis. The annual journals of the diocese showed that communicant numbers at Old St. Andrew's parish in West Ashley declined from 962 in 2011 to 529 in 2013 and 509 in 2014.

By the time of the diocesan conventions, in early March of 2013, almost all of the seventy-one parishes and missions of the old diocese had chosen sides. Indeed, on the independent diocesan part, almost all the parishes had been locked into the lawsuit against the Church. The time of choosing, the time of discernment, was over. Having accomplished the schism, the reasons for the break began to change on the independent side. Before this point, Lawrence and the other diocesan spokespersons had talked of the three reasons of theology, morality, and polity, but gave overwhelming attention to morality, particularly to homosexuality and transgender. These were the emotional "hot button" issues to which everyone could relate and react instead of the more esoteric and arcane nuances of theology and church government. However, once the schism was done and set, Lawrence went almost silent on the subject of the causes referring to it only when required in legal settings. The diocesan spokespeople immediately began giving a revised explanation of the reasons for the schism.

In the revised explanation, the schism was all about theology and not at all about homosexuality or even "moral" issues. By March of 2013, Jan Pringle took the job of Director of Public Relations for the independent diocese. She immediately took to task a reporter for *The Charlotte Observer* by email that he was "confused" on his "facts" about the diocese. To set him straight she directed: "You say that we disassociated from TEC 'in disputes over ordaining gays and other issues.' This continues to be reported and I respectfully ask that you halt using this suggestion that we left TEC over sexual preferences. The fact is that we left because TEC has rejected the fundamental theology of the Anglican Church."[136] This became the new line. DSC did not leave the Episcopal Church over sexual issues. It left over theology. This not so subtle attempt to manipulate the media into a new explanation did not escape the notice of Steve Skardon who wrote a lengthy and stinging retort to Pringle on his blog.[137]

It took time for the independent diocese to publish its revised official version of the causes of the schism, but it did appear on October 2, 2013, in an article by the Rev. James Lewis, assistant to Bishop Lawrence, in the *Charleston Mercury* entitled "The Real Story Behind Our Split with The Episcopal Church."[138] This article has been reprinted, as in the diocesan newspaper, *Jubilate Deo*, of November 2013. Lewis summarized the new explanation in the phrase, "It's about God, not gays." He said, "Virtually all the ar-

---

136. "The Not-So-Gentle Art of Ecclesiastical Hectoring: Imaginary 'Diocese' Launches New Charm Offensive." South Carolina Episcopalians, March 26, 2013, http://www.scepiscopalians.com/Hectoring.html.

137. Ibid.

138. Lewis, (the Rev.) Jim. "The Real Story Behind Our Split with The Episcopal Church." *Charleston Mercury* (Charleston, SC), October 2, 2013, http://www.charlestonmercury.com/index.php/en/lifestyle/religion/129-the-real-story-behind-our-split-with-the-episcopal-church.

ticles suggest our diocese left because TEC ordained a gay bishop. That's just not true."[139] What was true, he insisted, was that the Episcopal Church abandoned historic faith for a "pluriform" religion and the diocese was forced to leave after the "modernist" Church leaders tried to remove the "orthodox" bishop of the diocese. Lewis barely alluded to sexuality, using the word "gay" only a few times at first, and never using the words "homosexual" or "transgender." Apparently, he meant to convey the message that the schism had nothing to do with homosexuality. He maintained, "We believe the decision [of the Disciplinary Board for Bishops] stemmed from the bishop's consistent efforts to protect traditional voices and beliefs. The charges laid against him were for actions taken by our Diocesan Convention and its duly-elected leaders."[140] Actually, as we have seen in the previous chapters, the charges against Lawrence came from his flagrant disregard of the Dennis Canon. Lewis then concluded with a wildly unhistorical assertion: "Bishop Lawrence spent years trying to keep us within TEC—only to be found guilty of abandonment while in the very midst of attempting negotiation. We were effectively fired upon under a flag of truce."[141]

Lewis's article became the official diocesan explanation of the causes of the schism of 2012: the break was entirely caused by the first of the three reasons, theology. It was the result of the diocese's resolution to defend "orthodox" religion against an heretical Church. The schism had nothing at all to do with issues of sexuality. All of a sudden, homosexuality was banished into nothingness, as if it had never existed. Having used it successfully for their own purposes, diocesan leaders no longer had any need for it. This was truly a breathtaking lurch away from an overwhelming historical record that was readily available to everyone. The trigger of the break was the Church's clumsy attempt to remove the "orthodox" bishop and flip the diocese to the new modernism. As sidelines, Lewis continued the old themes of Lawrence's victimization and the Church's greed for local property. Critical bloggers wasted no time in taking Lewis's new historical narrative to task. Steve Skardon wrote a lengthy scathing review on his blog South Carolina Episcopalians.[142]

As far as the diocesan leadership was concerned, the issue of the meaning of the schism was resolved before the end of 2013. They said the schism had been caused by theological differences. After that, they said little publicly about why the diocese left the Episcopal Church except for the depositions and court testimony in the circuit court trial of July 2014. Even then, they had nothing new to say. Beyond meaning came another question, identity. This would be another matter entirely, and one that was far more difficult and complicated. It would require much more time and attention and would go on for years after the schism.

---

139. Ibid.

140. Ibid.

141. Ibid.

142. Skardon, Steve. "The Real 'Real Story': It's Not about God or Gays. It's about Fear." South Carolina Episcopalians, November 3, 2013, http://www.scepiscopalians.com/jim_lewis_2013.html.

The Search for Identity

As the Diocese of South Carolina searched for meaning after the schism, it also looked for identity. How would it identify itself at home, in the United States, and in the world since it was neither part of any larger entity nor a part of the Anglican Communion? It was its own independent Christian denomination. It declared itself to be an "Anglican" diocese but in what sense could it be "Anglican" outside of the Anglican Communion? If it were not part of the Anglican Communion, what would be its relationship to the Communion? Institutional identification was to be a perplexing problem consuming much of the time, attention, and energy of the Diocese for years to come.

As for identity, the Diocese of South Carolina had two general options, go it alone, or join a larger group. Bishop Lawrence made it clear he wanted to go it alone at least at first. At the schism, he had declared the diocese to be an extra-provincial diocese of the Anglican Communion, something that was meaningless in the structure of the Communion. From the start of his episcopacy, Bishop Lawrence had devoted a great deal of energy and attention to the Anglican Realignment movement. Early on he had adopted the slogan, "Making Biblical Anglicans for a Global Age." It was difficult to see how the diocese could go it alone and be part of a global age.

If South Carolina joined any larger group, the logical choice seemed to be the most successful of the American groups that had peeled off the Episcopal Church, the Anglican Church in North America. GAFCON/GS had recognized ACNA as a province and its archbishop as a primate. One obvious problem of joining ACNA, however, was that just before the schism of 2012, ACNA had set up a Diocese of the Carolinas under Bishop Steve Wood, rector of St. Andrew's of Mt. Pleasant. Exactly how the Diocese of South Carolina would relate to the overlapping Diocese of the Carolinas remained to be seen. The leaders of ACNA were understandably desirous of South Carolina to join them, but Lawrence only bided his time for the few years after the schism refusing to make a commitment to any larger group. The lack of affiliation, however, left the Diocese of South Carolina in limbo in regard to the Anglican Communion. It called itself Anglican, but it was not part of the Anglican Communion.

The independent diocese's pursuit of new identity manifested itself in the few years after the schism primarily in three ways: the development of ties with conservative Anglicans abroad, the search for common ground with various conservative non-Episcopal "Anglican" churches in the United States, and the move toward affiliation with a larger entity. In what sense it would be "Anglican" remained to be seen. As far as the Anglican Communion went, it also remained to be seen how the rest of the Communion would interact with the Episcopal Church given the Americans' unique strand on homosexuality. The Diocese of South Carolina's identity would be something that would have to work itself out over a long period of time.

Diocesan leaders approached the first issue, developing ties with conservative Anglicans abroad, primarily through three avenues, building personal relationships with African bishops, bonding with the Global African Futures Conference (GAFCON), and making ties with GAFCON's associated alliance, Global South. The common element among all these forces was "Biblical" Christianity, translated as condemnation of homosexuality as immoral and unchristian.

Equatorial African bishops were natural allies of the Diocese of South Carolina. Several Anglican provinces in Africa had broken off recognition of the Episcopal Church after the Robinson affair of 2003. The bishops in countries such as Nigeria, Kenya, Uganda, and Rwanda were particularly strident in their stand against homosexuality. Their cultures traditionally condemned homosexuality, most treating homosexual acts as serious crimes to be punished under the law. The bishops themselves were in competition for believers against both a surging wave of Islam advancing from traditional Muslim areas of northern Africa southward and a host of other Christian denominations.

From the very start, the diocese worked to build ties with African bishops and would continue to do so for years. What the diocese needed from the Africans was recognition of legitimacy and support. What the African bishops needed was an American ally in their campaign against rights for homosexuals in their own countries and the Anglican Communion. On April 9, 2013, the Diocese of South Carolina sponsored a visit of four African bishops to Charleston. Speaking to a sparse crowd in the Cathedral of St. Luke and St. Paul, four bishops from Sudan, Rwanda, Tanzania, and Kenya heaped praise on Bishop Lawrence and condemnation on the Episcopal Church all while boasting of the true, "Biblical" practice of their kind of Anglicanism. They moved about the diocese speaking in various churches accompanied by the conservative Irish bishop, Ken Clarke, and Bishop Lawrence's close ally, Mouneer Anis.[143]

There were to be other visits from African bishops to the diocese, most notably for a symposium that diocesan leaders called "Voices of the Anglican Communion," held at the Cathedral of St. Luke and St. Paul on 11 April 2016. Of the ten bishops making presentations, seven were from equatorial Africa, and five of those were from Uganda. Homosexuality was a major issue in Uganda which had recently passed a draconian law, supported by some of the Anglican bishops, imposing sweeping punishments for homosexual acts. The law had been overturned by the high court, but replacement laws were reportedly in the works. One of the "Voices" was Ugandan Bishop Joseph Abura who, in 2009, had publicly denounced homosexuality and advocated for the punitive laws: "Ugandan Parliament, the watch dog of our laws, please go ahead and put the anti-Gay laws in place."[144]

Besides showcasing anti-homosexual-rights African bishops, diocesan leaders worked to build other ties to conservative Anglicans abroad through several means, particularly by participating in GAFCON II (Global Anglican Future Conference), in 2013, setting up an oversight scheme with Global South in 2014, and sponsoring Bishop Zavala's visit in May of 2015. Bishop Lawrence, who had attended the GAFCON I conference in Jerusalem in 2008, led a delegation from his diocese to the GAFCON II

---

143. "Anglican Bishops Express Strong Support for Bishop Lawrence and Diocese of South Carolina." Diocese of South Carolina, April 9, 2013, http://www.diosc.com/sys/news-events/latest-news/511-anglican-bishops-express-strong-support-for-bishop-lawrence-and-diocese-of-south-carolina.

144. "For Some Anglicans, Vices are Now Virtues." Spero News, November 25, 2009, http://www.speroforum.com/a/23193/for-some-anglicans-vices-are-now-virtues.

meeting which was held in Nairobi, Kenya, 21–26 October 2013.[145] The 1,300 attendees included 331 bishops.[146] This represented about 40 percent of the bishops in the Anglican Communion. The Archbishop of Canterbury, Justin Welby addressed the conference by video to chastise the group for its hardline against rights for homosexuals, "We all live in different contexts" and for uniformity, "It doesn't mean being unanimous."[147] At the end of the meeting, the conference, clearly unimpressed by Welby, issued "The Nairobi Communiqué" of October 26, 2013, that expanded on the original Jerusalem statement of 2008. As before, the new document condemned homosexuality right away: "a false gospel (. . .). It promoted homosexual practice as consistent with holiness, despite the fact that the Bible clearly identifies it as sinful."[148] It added, "We want to make clear that any civil partnership of a sexual nature does not receive the blessing of God" and "Marriage is a life-long exclusive union between a man and a woman." While superficially claiming to remain faithful members of the Anglican Communion, the GAFCON leaders came close to schism from the Communion. The Communiqué denounced the traditional Four Instruments of the Anglican Communion and set up a new GAFCON "Primates' Council" to work "beyond existing structures" of the Communion. Moreover, the document said, "We ask provinces to reconsider their support for those Anglican structures that are used to undermine biblical faithfulness." Without mentioning South Carolina directly, the Communiqué signaled support for the schismatic diocese: "in providing oversight in cases where provinces and dioceses compromise biblical faith," a plain reference to the American Episcopal Church. The South Carolina delegation had reason to return home with high hopes of foreign support in their new quest for meaning and identity.

GAFCON's promise of providing oversight for "orthodox" dioceses breaking away from the "false gospel" Episcopal Church was not long in coming to fruition. When GAFCON's overlapping and closely allied association called "Global South" held its primates' meeting in Cairo, 14–15 February 2014, the "Steering Committee" issued a statement including: "We decided to establish a Primatial Oversight Council, in following through the recommendations taken at Dromantine in 2005 and Dar es Salam in 2007, to provide pastoral and primatial oversight to dissenting individuals, parishes, and dioceses in order to keep them within the Communion."[149] The Steering Committee was

---

145. "Diocese of South Carolina Participates in GAFCON II." Diocese of South Carolina, October 22, 2013, http://www.diosc.com/sys/news-events/latest-news/540-diocese-of-south-carolina-participates-in-gafcon-II.

146. Virtue, David. "Nairobi: GAFCON Anglican Bishops Say They Will Cross Boundaries in Defiance of Any Archbishop." Virtueonline, October 25, 2013, http://www.virtueonline.org/portal/modules/news/article.php?storyid=18181.

147. "Archbishop's Message to GAFCON 2013: Seek Holiness and Unity." The Archbishop of Canterbury, October 23, 2013, http://www.archbishopofcanterbury.org/articles.php/5163/archbishops-message-to-gafcon-2013-seek-holiness.

148. "GAFCON 2013: The Nairobi Communiqué." October 26, 2013, http://www.gafcon.org/resources/nairobi-communique-2013.

149. "Statement from the Global South Primates Steering Committee, Cairo, Egypt, 14–15 February 2014." Global South Anglican, http://www.globalsouthanglican.org/index/php/blog/comments/statement_from_the_global_south_primates_steering_committee_cairo_egypt_14.

headed by Lawrence's longtime staunch ally Mouneer Anis, bishop of Egypt. The Committee offered oversight to the Diocese of South Carolina.

Timing was of the essence as the diocese was about to convene its annual meeting of the convention. The diocesan leaders would have to rush through a resolution to establish the oversight. This they did. Three weeks after the Steering Committee established the Primatial Oversight Council, the diocesan Anglican Communion Development Committee, that had been set up in 2009 under Kendall Harmon,[150] drew up Resolution R–3 to present for passage in diocesan convention of 13–14 March, 2014. The Resolution stated:

> Recognizing the generosity of spirit and faithful concern for the Anglican Communion represented by the Global South Primates Steering Committee in offering a means for bodies such as the Diocese of South Carolina to have a formal ecclesiastical connection to the larger Communion and the consequent relationship,
>
> Be it resolved that the Diocese of South Carolina accept the offer of the newly created Global South Primatial Oversight Council for pastoral oversight of our ministry as a diocese during the temporary period of our discernment of our final provincial affiliation and
>
> Be it further resolved that in this period of fluidity in the Anglican Communion we reserve the right to revisit this decision, as a convention, should it be necessary during this temporary discernment period, however long it may last.[151]

Thus, the diocese would have "pastoral oversight" provided by an unspecified committee of Global South primates, but this could be terminated at any time by choice of the diocese. The proposed resolution gave no description of the nature or character of the "oversight" nor of the membership of the Oversight Council. The term "formal ecclesiastical connection to the larger Communion" could be interpreted to mean a legitimate role in the Anglican Communion, something that was untrue. Nevertheless, Bishop Lawrence apparently suggested the oversight would give the diocese an official status in the Anglican Communion: [It] "will give us what some might term an extra-provincial diocesan status with an ecclesial body of the larger Anglican family."[152]

To encourage an easy passage in the annual convention meeting, just one week after the proposed resolution was released, the "Rationale" accompanying the resolution declared it to be God's will: "We believe the timing Providential to add this resolution as a third resolution from the floor of the current Convention (. . .). We choose to see it as a providential provision."[153] The authors of the resolution, and Lawrence, need not have worried about passage. The resolution sailed through the convention without a single

---

150. In 2014, the Rev. Bob Lawrence was chair of the Anglican Communion Development Committee. Harmon was listed "Anglican Communion Development Coordinator."

151. "Bishop Lawrence's Message Regarding Resolution R–3." Diocese of South Carolina, March 7, 2014, http://www.diosc.com/sys/php?option=com_content&view=article&id=557bishop-lawrences-message-regarding-resolution-r-3&catid=1:latest-news&Itemid=75.

152. Ibid.

153. Ibid.

vote in opposition.¹⁵⁴ This left one delegate complaining about the rush. Scott Harvin, of St. Jude's of Walterboro, said, "There was no time to sit and have an examination with the laity of the whole diocese. Most folks are not even aware of the situation."¹⁵⁵

The issue of identity still loomed large in the life of the diocese nearly a year and a half after the schism. Indeed, Bishop Lawrence devoted a third of his bishop's address of 2014 to this matter. He pressed the point that the diocese remained both Episcopalian and Anglican even though it had left the Episcopal Church and, since leaving the only legitimate province of the Anglican Communion in the United States, was not part of the Anglican Communion. He said, "But, yes, we can and have referred to ourselves as 'Episcopalians' (. . .) one mighty also say we are 'Anglicans.'"¹⁵⁶ The new oversight, he said, "strengthens our Anglican or Episcopal identity."¹⁵⁷ Lawrence declared to the convention: "This Primatial Oversight will bring us an extra-provincial diocesan status with an ecclesial body of the larger Anglican family."¹⁵⁸ Once again, as he had done since the schism, Lawrence at least implied that the Diocese of South Carolina was an extra-provincial diocese of the Anglican Communion. Lawrence may have dealt in insinuation but the official report on the convention issued by the diocesan office was anything but subtle as it loudly trumpeted to the world: "The Diocese of South Carolina has been formally recognized as a member in good standing of the Global Anglican Communion" and "this formal primatial oversight arrangement makes clear that the Diocese is officially part of the greater Anglican Church."¹⁵⁹ For its part, the Global South primates did not join in the unwarranted declarations, writing simply, "the Global South welcomes them as an active and faithful member within the Global South of the Anglican Communion, until such time as a permanent affiliation can be found."¹⁶⁰ No matter what Lawrence and the report said, in fact, the Diocese was not officially part of the Anglican Communion and the new oversight scheme did nothing to alter this truth. All of this showed that diocesan leaders went to great lengths to convince their communicants that the diocese was really Anglican. In time, they came to repeat the word "Anglican" even to excess while gradually reducing use of the word "Episcopal" except in legal matters. When Bishop Lawrence addressed the annual diocesan convention of 2016, he did not utter the word Episcopal, or any version of it, one time while he said the terms Anglican and Anglicanism twenty-five times.¹⁶¹

154. Hawes, Jennifer Berry. "Diocese of South Carolina Accepts Provisional Oversight from Global South Primates." *The Post and Courier* (Charleston, SC), March 15, 2014, http://www.postandcourier.com/features/faith_and_values/diocese-of-s-c-accepts-provisional-oversight-from-global-south/article_ce81c581–6f28–52ae-a33e-b54724bb3858.html.

155. Ibid.

156. "Bishop Lawrence's Address to the 223rd."

157. Ibid.

158. Ibid.

159. Ibid.

160. "Announcement Regarding the Diocese of South Carolina." The Global South of the Anglican Communion, August 21, 2014, http://www.globalsouthanglican.org/index.php/blog/comments/announcement_regarding_the_diocese_of_south_carolina.

161. "Bishop Lawrence's Address to the 225th Convention of the Diocese of South Carolina." Diocese of South Carolina, March 14, 2016, http://www.diosc.com/sys/ourbishop/bishops-messages/725-bishop-lawrence-s-address-to-the.

Another way in which diocesan leaders hoped to strengthen ties to conservative Anglicans abroad was through the visit to South Carolina of the Most Rev. Hector "Tito" Zavala, bishop of Chile and primate of the Anglican Church of South America, formerly known as the Southern Cone, on May 19 and 20, 2015. Zavala was one of the seven members of the primates' Steering Committee of Global South. He and his province were well-known advocates of the American schismatic dioceses and long term outspoken critics of the Episcopal Church. Zavala was elected primate of the Anglican province of the Southern Cone in November of 2010.

Before the visit, diocesan leaders touted Zavala's sojourn in South Carolina as validation of their claim of identity in the Anglican Communion: "Bishop Zavala will be in South Carolina specifically to encourage and support fellow Bishop, The Rt. Rev. Mark J. Lawrence, and the clergy and lay people of the Diocese of South Carolina."[162] Zavala's remarks turned controversial as he said, "'I'm here with you with the consent of the Archbishop of Canterbury.'"[163] He went on that the Archbishop "was with the Global South Primates 'Steering Committee' in a meeting in Cairo, Egypt in 2014 when 'we decided to establish a Primatial Oversight Council to provide pastoral and primatial oversight to some dioceses in order to keep them within the Communion.'"[164] By this, Zavala seemed to imply that the Archbishop of Canterbury had endorsed Global South's oversight of South Carolina. In fact, the Archbishop of Canterbury had attended only the very end of the Steering Committee meeting in Cairo and had not endorsed any primatial oversight plan.

If the Archbishop of Canterbury had thrown his weight behind a primatial oversight scheme, it would be major news indeed. This author, who was at the time maintained a web log on the schism in South Carolina, sent an email to the Archbishop's office at Lambeth Palace on May 21, for clarification of the Archbishop's position. On May 25, Ed Thornton, Senior Press Officer to the Archbishop of Canterbury, responded:

> A Lambeth Palace spokesperson said: "The Global South Primates Steering Committee announced in 2014 the establishment of Primatial Oversight for the Protestant Episcopal Church in the Diocese of South Carolina, which had seceded from the Episcopal Church, in order to keep the diocese within the Anglican Communion. The steering committee informed Archbishop Justin of their decision when he joined them for the final day of their meeting in Cairo.
>
> Archbishop Justin has since had discussions about how the arrangements will work, exploring the exercising of pastoral, not episcopal, oversight by Bishop Zavala. Archbishop Justin has discussed these developments with the Presiding Bishop of the Episcopal Church, Katharine Jefferts Schori."[165]

---

162. "Archbishop [sic] Tito Zavala Visiting Diocese, May 20." Diocese of South Carolina, May 7, 2015, http://www.diosc.com/sys/news-events/latest-news/654-archbishop-tito-zavala-visiting-diocese-May-20.

163. "Presiding Bishop of Anglican Province of South America Reassures Diocese that It's Part of Anglican Communion." Diocese of South Carolina, May 22, 2015, http://www.diosc.com/sys/news-events/latest-news/658-presiding-bishop-of-anglican-province-of-south-america-reassures-diocese-that-its-part-of-anglican-communion.

164. Ibid.

165. Thornton, Ed. Email message to author, May 25, 2015.

A few days later, this response was published in *Church Times*, the Church of England newspaper. Several points stood out in the Lambeth Palace statement of 25 May, most notably that the Archbishop had not approved of episcopal oversight and had not given any authorization to Zavala to represent him in South Carolina. Any statement or implication by Zavala otherwise had now been squashed by the Archbishop of Canterbury's office. Zavala's visit turned out to be an embarrassment as it called into question the credibility of his assertions; and it remained to be seen whether his appearance had advanced the diocesan leaders' goal of establishing legitimate identity in the Anglican Communion.

While diocesan leaders worked to build bonds with anti-Episcopal Church "orthodox" Anglicans abroad, they also sought to make closer ties with other dissident former Episcopalians within the United States. This, however, was problematical in the quest for Anglican identity since none of the many "Episcopal" and "Anglican" splinter groups in America was officially part of the Anglican Communion. The Anglican Church in North America styled itself a "province in formation," a status that did not exist in the Anglican Communion. Thus, it remained to be seen how joining ACNA or any other splinter group in the U.S. would further the diocesan quest for identity in the Anglican Communion. Nevertheless, Bishop Lawrence and other diocesan leaders met several times with independent groups' bishops after the schism. In June of 2013, Lawrence attended the Provincial Council meeting of the Anglican Church in North America where he inexplicably appeared to back away from any implication that the diocese was part of the Anglican Communion. He told the assembly: "We are presently an 'extra-provincial' diocese, not in any formal or officially ecclesial way, but as a fact rooted in our relationship with provinces and dioceses within the Anglican Communion. So we are a diocese without provincial affiliation—we are so provisionally but not, I believe, precariously."[166] Exactly what this meant remained undetermined. In fact, after the schism, the Diocese of South Carolina was not in a province of the Anglican Communion and was not an extra-provincial diocese of the Anglican Communion. It was a separate Christian denomination, albeit with friends in the Anglican Communion.

In September of 2013, Archbishop Robert Duncan, of the ACNA, called a sort of summit conference of Anglican splinter groups in South Carolina. He brought together representatives of PEARUSA (The North American Missionary District of Province de l'Église anglicane au Rwanda), the Reformed Episcopal Church, the Diocese of the Holy Cross, the ACNA, and the Diocese of South Carolina. Most notably absent, however, was Chuck Murphy and any representation of Anglican Mission in America, the original Anglican Realignment movement in the Low Country. The eight bishops present ended their meeting by issuing an innocuous statement whose only important point was the in future, Bishop Lawrence would convene any such meeting.[167]

---

166. "Diocesan Delegation Observers at ACNA's Provincial Council." Diocese of South Carolina, June 21, 2013, http://www.diosc.com/sys/index.php?option=com_content&view=article&id=519:diocesan-delegation-observers-at-acnas-provincial-council&catid=1:latest-news&Itemid=75.

167. "Statement from the Anglican Bishops with Jurisdiction in South Carolina." Virtueonline, September 11, 2013, http://www.virtueonline.org/portal/modules/news/print.php?storyid=18012.

Perhaps the most important meeting between diocesan leaders and a splinter group occurred at Camp Saint Christopher on 28–29 April 2015. This appeared to be a high-level and serious conference of representatives of the Diocese of South Carolina and the ACNA to address possible affiliation. There will be more about this meeting later. A few months afterwards, Archbishop Foley Beach, of the ACNA, returned to Camp St. Christopher to address the diocesan clergy conference, in October of 2015.[168] A few months after that, the ACNA convened its Provisional Council and College of Bishops at St. Andrew's Church of Mt. Pleasant, suburban Charleston, in late June of 2016.

By the spring of 2014, it was clear that DSC would go for affiliation with a larger body. The same diocesan convention meeting, in March of 2014, that passed the resolution setting up the temporary oversight plan with Global South also adopted a resolution creating a process to decide on permanent affiliation. "R-2 Discernment of Provincial Affiliation," authorized Bishop Lawrence to name a committee to study affiliation and make a report at the next convention. Lawrence chose the twelve members of the committee called the "Task Force for Provincial Affiliation" in April of 2014. It represented the governing core of the diocese, four from the Standing Committee, four from the Diocesan Council and four others. Seven were clergy. Ten were men and two women. Most of the names had been prominent in the direction of the diocese in the run-up to the schism. Kendall Harmon's cohort at Christ/St. Paul's, Craige Borrett, was chosen as the chair.[169]

At the next annual meeting of the diocese, in March of 2015, the Task Force announced it was not ready to make a recommendation on affiliation. It was in the following month that the crucial meeting between diocesan officials and ACNA authorities at Camp St. Christopher occurred. Bishop Lawrence led the diocesan delegation which came, apparently, from his inner circle including Wade Logan, the chancellor, Alan Runyan, the lead lawyer, Craige Borrett, Kendall Harmon, Jeffrey Miller, Elizabeth Pennewill, and Jim Lewis. The ACNA side, led by Archbishop Foley Beach, included Scott Ward, chancellor of ACNA, John Guernsey, a bishop, Bill Atwood, a bishop, Terrell Glenn, a bishop, Phil Ashley, CEO of the American Anglican Council, Jack Lumanog, CEO of ACNA, Ted Brenner, chancellor of Diocese of Quincy. Curiously absent from this high-level conference was the local ACNA bishop, Steve Wood, or anyone with authority in his diocese. The presence of so many lawyers in the meeting indicated substantial legal discussion, presumably about the responsibilities and liabilities involved in a union of the diocese and the ACNA. The subsequent diocesan report on the conference revealed little about what happened in the meeting. One phrase in the summary, "frank exchanges," could easily be construed to mean major differences.[170] The absence of Steve

168. "Archbishop Beach Speaks at Diocese of South Carolina Clergy Conference." Diocese of South Carolina, October 25, 2015, http://www.diosc.com/sys/news-events/latest-news/700-archbishop-beach-speaks-at-diocese.

169. "Task Force for Provincial Affiliation." Diocese of South Carolina, June 8, 2014, http:www.diosc.com/sys/index.php?view=article&catid=172%3Aprovincial-affiliation&id=580%3Atask-force-for-provincial-affiliation. Members: Clergy—Borrett, Peet Dickinson, Tripp Jeffords, Jeffrey Miller, Ken Weldon, John Foster, David Thurlow. Laity—Bruce McDonald (senior warden, St. James' of James Is.), Elizabeth Pennewill, John Benson (senior warden, Prince George Winyah), Karen Kusko, Julius Pinckney Thompson.

170. "Leaders from the Diocese of South Carolina and Anglican Church in North America Meet at

Wood, and the report's phrase "challenges posed by overlapping jurisdictions in South Carolina," may well indicate discussion of how to handle the existing ACNA diocese of the Carolinas, under Wood, and the Diocese of South Carolina, under Lawrence. Both covered the eastern half of South Carolina.

If there were serious differences between the two sides in the conference of April 2015, they must have been resolved because in the next annual diocesan meeting, in March of 2016, the Task Force recommended joining the ACNA. They concluded that the ACNA was the only logical choice for affiliation. In their report to the convention, they repeatedly called the ACNA a "province," as if to imply it was a province of the Anglican Communion: "the province called the Anglican Church in North America (ACNA)," "our best opportunity to have an influence in the wider Anglican Communion is also within this province," and "Having a formal affiliation with a province also gives us an identity beyond ourselves."[171] Meetings were to be held across the diocese for public discussion of the move to affiliation.

With the Task Force report of 2016, it was a foregone conclusion that the diocese would join the ACNA. However, joining ACNA was not as simple as one might think at first glance. The diocese would not just be sliding from one Anglican province, the Episcopal Church, to an equal. The repeated suggestion the diocesan leaders made that the ACNA was a province of the Anglican Communion was flatly untrue. It was correct to say that the ACNA was "recognized" and supported by some Anglican primates, but was not the same as saying it was a province of the Communion. Moreover, the Task Force report had completely avoided addressing the obvious problem of how the Diocese of South Carolina would relate to the already existing ACNA Diocese of the Carolinas that included South Carolina. Would the two dioceses be left to overlap each other? Would the two unite into one diocese? If so, who would be the bishop? What would happen to the other bishop? How would the money and other assets be combined?

The Anglican Church in North America had been set up in 2009 with the support of GAFCON to be the replacement province of the Anglican Communion, in the U.S., for the supposedly heretical Episcopal Church. When Foley Beach was consecrated archbishop of ACNA in 2014, the service was conducted by seven Anglican primates, all from GAFCON, and most from its core in equatorial Africa. Throwing cold water on the theory of ACNA's legitimacy was none other than the Archbishop of Canterbury. A few days before Beach's consecration, a reporter asked Archbishop Justin Welby, "Exactly what is the standing of the Anglican Church in North America?"[172] Welby replied: "ACNA is a separate church, It is not part of the Anglican Communion. (. . .)

St. Christopher Camp and Conference Center." Diocese of South Carolina, April 30, 2015, http://www.diosc.com/sys/index.php?view=article&catid=1:latest-news&id=652:leaders-from-the-diocese-of-south-carolina-and-anglican-church-in-north-america-meet-at-st-christopher-camp-and-conference-center.

171. "Report from the Task Force for Provincial Affiliation." Diocese of South Carolina, March 24, 2016, http://www.diosc.com/sys/affiliation/729-report-from-the-task-force-for-provincial-affiliation.

172. Ellis, (the Rev. Canon) Ian. Interview with Archbishop Justin Welby, October 3, 2014, *Church of Ireland Gazette*, as quoted in "Justin Welby on ACNA—What is an Anglican Church?" In a Spacious Place, October 8, 2014, https://inaspaciousplace.wordpress.com/2014/10/08/justin-welby-on-acna-what-is-an-anglican.

the definition of being part of the Anglican Communion is being in Communion with Canterbury."[173] This inconvenient fact had been entirely neglected by the diocesan Task Force in its recommendation of affiliation with ACNA. The unwelcomed truth avoided by the diocesan leaders was that joining ACNA would not make the diocese part of the Anglican Communion.

There were other undisclosed problem points that the diocese, if it joined ACNA, would have to confront in time. The ACNA had a Constitution and Canons which was readily available on the Internet. It was considerably different from what the diocese had known in the Episcopal Church. The diocese would not simply be substituting one equal for another, far from it. The ACNA rules would mean some important considerations for the diocese in the future. The Constitution and Canons presented a peculiar combination of local rule and centralized authoritarianism. Dioceses were expressly allowed to leave the ACNA at will. However, while in the ACNA, they had to submit to an archbishop and a centralized system largely controlled by the bishops. The laity were virtually excluded from power. As an important practical matter for the diocese, when it would elect a new bishop, he (women were not allowed to be bishops in ACNA), would have to be approved by two-thirds of the ACNA House of Bishops. This gave a virtual monopoly over the choice of a new bishop to the House of Bishops. In the Episcopal Church, bishops were normally chosen by a majority of the diocesan standing committees. Ironically, Mark Lawrence, and many others, would not have become bishops under the ACNA canons. Thus, the communicants of the Diocese of South Carolina had a great deal to consider in affiliating with ACNA; and much more than their leaders presented to them in 2016.

In a highly-charged atmosphere crackling with hostility against America, the Archbishop of Canterbury bravely called a conference of the thirty-eight primates, or heads, of the provinces of the Anglican Communion. In order to encourage the GAFCON contingent to attend, he invited their American ally, the ACNA archbishop, Beach, to attend the gathering. He would be a non-official participant.[174] GAFCON/ACNA declared a moral victory and journeyed to Canterbury for the meeting that the Archbishop refused to call a meeting (a "gathering").

The primates' gathering of 11–15 January 2016, proved to be the turning point in the nearly two-decades-long fight within the Anglican Communion over homosexuality. The Archbishop managed to establish the overriding theme of the conference as unity ("walk together"). The primates agreed that they must preserve the integrity of the old Anglican Communion. This, of course, would mean that GAFCON would have to give a great leeway to the Episcopal Church; and that proved to be the immediate challenge of the meeting. The GAFCON hardliners, led by Archbishop Stanley Ntagali, of Uganda, demanded that the pro-homosexual-rights Episcopal Church and the Anglican Church

173. Ibid.

174. "Statement on Votes Given to Primates at the Meeting in Canterbury." Primates 2016, January 17, 2016, http://www.primates2016.org/articles/2016/01/17/statement-votes-given-primates-meeting. Owing to conflicting claims about Beach's role in the gathering, the officials managing the meeting issued a statement on January 17, 2016, clarifying his role: "Apart from when the meeting agreed the agenda at the start, it was made clear to Archbishop Foley Beach that it would not be appropriate for him to take part and he was not invited to do so."

of Canada voluntarily withdraw from the Communion. They refused and the assembly refused to force them to withdraw. Therefore, at the end of the second day, Ntagali bolted the meeting to return home. Apparently, the next day, Wednesday, a vote to suspend the two churches for three years failed narrowly. Facing the impending dissolution of the meeting, the rest of the GAFCON primates decided to remain and get the best deal they could to chastise the Americans. At that point, power turned and the GAFCON/ACNA front against the Episcopal Church collapsed. As Beach looked on, the primates drew up a statement imposing "consequences" (the Archbishop adamantly refused to call them punishments) for the Episcopal Church: for three years the Episcopal Church could not represent the primates on ecumenical and interfaith bodies, should not be appointed or elected to an internal standing committee, and while participating in bodies of the Communion not take part in decision making on any issues of doctrine or polity.[175] As for the issue of the admission of the ACNA to the Anglican Communion, the primates said that belonged with the Anglican Consultative Council but discouraged admission: "such an application, were it to come forward, would raise significant questions of polity and jurisdiction."[176] Finally, the primates agreed to meet again, in 2017 and 2019, and to hold the Lambeth Conference in 2020. In a sudden sweep, not only did the GAFCON/ACNA alliance collapse, but the goal of ACNA replacing the Episcopal Church vanished, and the nineteen-year crusade to stop equal treatment for homosexuals in the Anglican Communion moved to a downward slope. It was a truly astonishing, even breath-taking, turn of events in what history may see as the conference that saved the Anglican Communion.

Both sides could claim some sort of face-saving victory. However, the "consequences" for the Episcopal Church were really meaningless. The problem was that the primates were only one of the Four Instruments of Communion. They really had no authority to impose anything on any church of the Communion or on any other one of the Four Instruments. Some of the GAFCON primates railed out that the consequences were punishments that must be enforced. They demanded the other three Instruments carry out the consequences. Meanwhile, the Americans proceeded on undeterred. It became clear early on that the effect of the "consequences" amounted to nothing significant. The real news from the primates' gathering was that, in all likelihood, ACNA was not going to be admitted as a province of the Anglican Communion. Admission would be up to the Consultative Council which was set to meet a few weeks later.

The Anglican Consultative Council, one of the Four Instruments of the Anglican Communion, met in Lusaka, Zambia, 8–20 April 2016. The American delegation participated fully in the meeting. The primates' "consequences" turned out to be irrelevant, at least in this conference. The delegates voted to receive the report on the consequences from the Archbishop of Canterbury but not to endorse the consequences.[177] Only three

---

175. "Walking Together in the Service of God in the World." Primates 2016, January 15, 2016, http://www.primates.2016.org/articles/2016/01/15/communique-primates.

176. Ibid.

177. Schjonberg, Mary Frances. "Anglican Consultative Council Declines to Go Along with 'Consequences.'" Episcopal News Service, April 18, 2016, http://episcopaldigitalnetwork.com/ens/2016/04/18/anglican-consultative-council-declines-to-go-along-with-consequences.

of the GAFCON provinces boycotted the meeting. Although most GAFCON provinces sent delegates, no one proposed the admission of the ACNA to the Communion as the primates' statement from their gathering had said they could do.

GAFCON's sudden abandonment of the ACNA meant the effective end of the replacement stratagem. It was no longer reasonable to believe that the Anglican Communion would admit the ACNA as a province or that the ACNA would ever replace the Episcopal Church as the legitimate Anglican province in the United States. The long-held replacement stratagem of GAFCON/ACNA died in the primates' gathering of January and the Consultative Council meeting of April 2016. How the GAFCON/ACNA alliance would function after this remained to be seen. Whether the GAFCON primates would continue to "walk together" with the traditional Anglican Communion also remained to be seen although after the primates' gathering of January 2016, it looked less likely that they would split the old Communion into two separate bodies along the lines of favor and opposition to homosexual rights.

GAFCON appeared strikingly weaker, perhaps even in disarray after the double blows of the January and April meetings in the Communion. When the GAFCON primates met in Nairobi, Kenya, immediately after the Consultative Council conference, 18–21 April, only ten provinces sent representatives, and most of those were from equatorial Africa, the core of the anti-homosexual-rights region. At the end of the meeting, the primates issued a communiqué that was remarkable for its muted tone.[178] Gone was any dire threat of schism in the Communion. It made only sad lamentations of the failure of the "consequences" and omitted any mention of ACNA. Whether the people in South Carolina realized it or not, for the Diocese of South Carolina, all of this meant the end of the hope that ACNA would be a province of the Anglican Communion and the decline of expectation of support from GAFCON. Nevertheless, the diocesan leaders proceeded on with their plans for affiliation with the ACNA. On March 11, 2017, the annual diocesan convention meeting voted unanimously to affiliate with the Anglican Church in North America.

Membership and Income

While the Diocese of South Carolina conducted its war against the Episcopal Church in the courts and sought meaning and identity in the few years after the schism, it also had to be concerned about its own internal status, specifically the impact of the break on membership and budgets. What effects did the schism have on the numbers of members in the diocese and on the diocesan income? Fortunately, we have the statistical tables published by the diocese in its annual journals for the years to 2015 (except 2012) showing the detailed figures of membership and budget.

The diocese's statistical tables showed the effects of the schism on the membership of the diocese. The last figures before the schism were for the year 2011. The diocese did not publish parochial statistics for the year of the schism, 2012. In 2011, the pre-schism

---

178. "Nairobi Communiqué 2016." GAFCON, April 22, 2016, http://gafcon.org/2016/04/22/nairobi-communique-2016.

diocese reported 29,643 "baptized members" and 27,003 "communicants."[179] Of the two categories, "communicants" was the more useful as it showed attendance at least once a year whereas "baptized" counted everyone baptized in the church regardless of whether he or she ever attended another service. "Communicants" meant active membership.

The pre-schism Diocese of South Carolina reported 27,003 communicants in 2011, the last figures before the schism of 2012. Of the 71 local churches listed that year, 21 remained with the Episcopal Church after the break of 2012. Those 21 parishes and missions accounted for 5,781 of the 29,643 baptized membership, and 5,010 of the 27,003 communicants reported in 2011.[180] The 50 local churches that went along with the schism reported a total of 21,993 communicants in 2011.[181] Those same churches listed 17,999 communicants in 2013, a decline since 2011 of 3,994 people, or-18%.[182] The next year, 2014, they reported 16,361 communicants, a fall of 26% since 2011.[183] The following year, 2015, they reported 15,556 communicants, a decline of 29% since 2011.[184] The 50 local churches of the Diocese of South Carolina lost 6,437 active members in 4 years. As of this writing (January 2017), 2015 was the last year of published statistics for the Diocese. Thus, a diocese that had counted 27,670 active members when Bishop Lawrence arrived in 2008, held 15,556 in 2015, a decline of 44%. As for the net immediate effect of the schism on membership in the Diocese of South Carolina, diocesan parochial statistics revealed that it lost a quarter of its active membership as a result of the schism. This was in addition to the loss of the 21 local churches that remained with the Episcopal Church. Altogether, the Diocese of South Carolina went from 27,003 communicants in 2011, to 15,556 in 2015, an overall decline of 42% in active membership. In other words, three years after the schism, the active membership of the Diocese of South Carolina amounted to 58% of that of the pre-schism Diocese.

The diocesan statistical tables from 2011, before the schism, to 2013, after the schism, and 2015, also revealed that most local churches which followed Bishop Lawrence in the schism lost significant numbers of active members. The largest declines in reported communicant numbers were at Holy Cross of Sullivans Island (2,540 in 2011, to 1,204 in 2013, to 1,354 in 2015, or-47% from 2011 to 2015), St. Michael's of Charleston (1,847–1,196–1,351, or-27%), Old Saint Andrew's of West Ashley (962–529–546,

---

179. *Journal of the Two Hundred and Twenty Second (. . .) 2013*, 128–29. In comparing the statistical tables of 2008, the year Lawrence became bishop, and 2011, one sees a decline in diocesan membership and income. In 2008, baptized membership stood at 31,559, and communicants at 27,670. By 2011, the last year before the schism, baptized membership had declined by 6 percent and communicants by 2 percent. The diocesan budget of 2008 stood at $2,995,289. The budget of 2012 was $2,311,184, a decline of 23% in four years.

180. Ibid.

181. Ibid.

182. *Journal of the Two Hundred and Twenty Third Annual Meeting of the Convention of the Diocese of South Carolina, March 14th and 15th 2014, Christ Church, Mt. Pleasant, South Carolina*. Charleston, SC: the diocese, 2015, 128–29.

183. *Journal of the 224th Convention of the Diocese of South Carolina, March 13 and 14, 2015, held in The Cathedral/Charleston Music Hall, Charleston, South Carolina*. Charleston, SC: the diocese, 2016, n.p.

184. *Journal of the 225th Convention of the Diocese of South Carolina, March 11 & 12, 2016, The Church of the Cross, Bluffton, South Carolina*. Charleston, SC: the diocese, 2016, 142–43.

or-43%), St. Helena's of Beaufort (1,737–1,334–951, or-45%), Holy Comforter of Sumter (525–399–271, or-48%), St. John's of Florence (652–375–417, or-36%), Trinity of Myrtle Beach (595–383–298, or-50%), St. Luke's of Hilton Head (951–939–644, or-32%), St. Philip's of Charleston (2,677–2,321–1,974, or-26%), St. James of James Island (612–500–500, or-18%), Christ Church of Mt. Pleasant (925–829–780, or-16%), St. Paul's of Conway (270–175–207, or-23%), Trinity of Edisto Island (183–137–155, or-15%), Good Shepherd of Charleston (302–290–202, or-33%), and the Cathedral of St. Luke and St. Paul of Charleston (305–189–200, or-34%).[185] Only a few local churches showed membership gains in the period 2011–15, most notably Church of the Cross in Bluffton (1,701–1,800–1775, or +4).[186] The diocesan parochial statistics made it clear that the schism had a major negative impact on the size of the active membership of the Diocese.

The statistics for Average Sunday Attendance in each of the fifty diocesan churches revealed a less sharp decline in the numbers of people attending services in these churches. Their cumulative ASA in 2011, before the schism, was 9,670. In 2015, it was 9,085, a drop of a modest 6 percent. Most local churches kept about the same numbers in Sunday attendance but some did suffer double-digit declines: Trinity of Edisto (189 in 2011 to 127 in 2015, or-33%), St. Paul's of Conway, (234 to 161, or-31%), St. David's of Cheraw (84 to 56, or-33%), St. Michael's of Charleston (531 to 505, or-5%), Trinity of Myrtle Beach (381 to 325, or-15%), St. John's of Johns Island (281 to 230, or-18%), Christ/St. Paul's of Yonges Island (228 to 193, or-15%), St. Helena's of Beaufort (739 to 636, or-14%), St. Matthew's of Darlington (102 to 90, or-12%), and Holy Cross of Sullivans Island (923 to 623, or-33%). Numerically, the largest declines were at St. Helena's of Beaufort (-103), Holy Cross of Sullivans Island (-300), Trinity of Myrtle Beach (-56), St. Paul's of Conway (-73), and Trinity of Edisto (-62).[187]

By 2015, the diocese counted several new missions but these had little impact on the overall membership figures. The old St. James' mission in Blackville revived as St. James' Anglican Church and rejoined the diocese. In North Myrtle Beach, a worshipping community that left the local Episcopal church formed as Grace Parish. Another worshipping community that left the Episcopal church in North Charleston took the name of the Church of the Resurrection. At Moncks Corner, a mission from St. Paul's of Summerville appeared as St. Timothy's of Cane Bay.

Diocesan budget figures seemed to show less of a negative impact. The last budget before the schism, 2012, was for $2,311,184.[188] In 2013, the budget was $2,091,165, a decline of 9%.[189] That of 2014 was $2,173,711, a slight increase.[190] In 2015, the actual

---

185. *Journal of the Two Hundred and Twenty Second* (. . .) 2013, 128–29; *Journal of the Two Hundred and Twenty Third* (. . .) 2014, n.p.; *Journal of the 224th* (. . .) 2015, n.p.; *Journal of the 225th* (. . .) 2016, 142–43.

186. Ibid.

187. Ibid.

188. *Journal of the Two Hundred and Twenty Second* (. . .) 2013, n.p.

189. *Journal of the Two Hundred and Twenty Third* (. . .) 2014, 111.

190. *Journal of the 224th* (. . .) 2015, n.p.

budget was $2,224,121, another small increase.[191] The final proposed budget for 2016 was $2,282,193, yet another slight rise.

A major question concerning the Diocese of South Carolina after the schism was how much money it raised and how much it spent for legal expenses. Unfortunately, this is impossible to know with the existing public evidence. Diocesan leaders have indicated they have spent two million dollars on such costs, but have given no details. The annual budget is not of much help in this matter. The budget line "Legal Expenses" posted $50,000 in 2008 and $35,000 in 2009.[192] The year 2010 was the first full year in which attorney Alan Runyan was employed by the diocese as the lawyer for the Standing Committee. That year, $50,000 was budgeted but the diocese actually spent more than five times as much, $266,567.[193] The next year, 2011, the diocese again budgeted $50,000 for legal costs but wound up paying $169,963.[194] In 2012, the diocese raised the budget level to $110,000 and actually paid out $198,228.[195] Thus in the pre-schism years of Lawrence's episcopacy, 2008–2012, the diocese publicly admitted to spending $719,758 in legal expenses.

Legal income and expenditure of the diocese after the schism was even more difficult to ascertain. The numerous court-related actions and reactions after January of 2013 soared, and so must have the legal expenses. The 2013 budget listed an unrealistically low figure of $147,000, but the diocese admitted to paying out $286,250 that year.[196] In 2014, the diocese said it budgeted $150,000 and actually paid $152,957.[197] This figure strains believability because this was the year of the three-week trial in the circuit court, in July, that involved more than 40 lawyers on the diocesan side. In 2015, the diocese budgeted $150,000 and claimed it spent only $96,333, another sum that seems unimaginably low given the fact that the state supreme court held a hearing on the church case in September of that year.[198] In 2016, the diocese once again budgeted $150,000 for legal expenses.[199] Thus, since the schism, the official budgets of the diocese show a total expenditure of $685,540 on legal costs, an amount that seems incredibly low considering the number of lawyers and the amount of legal work they have done in four different courts.

Giving credence to the thought that the official diocesan budget did not reveal all about the legal income and expenses was a diocesan public relations campaign to raise money for legal costs that moved into high gear in late 2013. According to one report,

191. "The Protestant Episcopal Church in the Diocese of South Carolina, 2016, Proposed Budget, 2nd Draft, February 11, 2016." Diocese of South Carolina, http://www.diosc.com/sys/images/documents/conventions/225_proposed_budget.pdf.

192. *Journal of the Two Hundred and Seventeenth* (. . .) 2008, 103; *Journal of the Two Hundred and Eighteenth* (. . .) 2009, 117.

193. *Journal of the Two Hundred and Twentieth* (. . .) 2011, 124.

194. *Journal of the Two Hundred and Twenty First* (. . .) 2012, 127.

195. *Journal of the Two Hundred and Twenty Second* (. . .) 2013, 126.

196. "Episcopal Diocese of South Carolina, 2015 Proposed Budget, February 10, 2015." The Diocese of South Carolina, February 10, 2015.

197. Ibid.

198. "The Protestant Episcopal Church in the Diocese."

199. Ibid.

Alan Runyan told communicants at St. Michael's of Charleston, on November 3, 2013, that they needed to come up with another $150,000 for legal fees even though they had already paid $50,000.[200] Meanwhile, in the late summer of 2013, the Diocesan Council and Bishop Lawrence set up the diocesan "Legal Defense Fund" "to assist the Diocese in raising $2 million to underwrite the cost of litigation against The Episcopal Church (TEC)."[201] In the diocesan newspaper's article introducing the Fund, Bishop Lawrence went so far as to call his courtroom opposition evil: "our legal suit is a tempestuous battle against '*the spiritual forces of evil* [sic].'"[202] The Fund appeared to be an independent entity under a Legal Defense Fund Committee,[203] but an advertisement for the Fund said "make your checks out to The Diocese of South Carolina, noting 'Legal Defense Fund' in the memo line."[204] This indicated the Fund was an element of the diocese. In December of 2014, the Fund committee announced: "The Diocese's special legal fund initiative, TAKE YOUR STAND, is raising $1.5 million from our churches, but will also need to raise an additional $500,000+ from loyal members of our Diocese and others."[205] Since the Fund was not listed in the publicly released diocesan budget, even though it was a function of the diocese, it is impossible to know at this point how much money it raised and how much it spent.

Apparently, the Fund did not raise all that the diocese needed for legal fees. After Judge Goodstein issued her favorable ruling on February 3, 2015, Peter Mitchell, the Fund Committee chair, announced the establishment of "The 1785 Society." He said the Fund had already raised $2 million but needed an additional $300,000 to fight the appeal.[206] He called for 168 people to join the society at a donation of $1,785 each in return for a lapel pin and a dinner with Bishop Lawrence. Again, in the annual meeting of the convention on March 14, 2015, Mitchell repeated his appeal for an addition $300,000 for legal fees "for the next period," presumably the next year.[207] And, once again, checks for the 1785 Society could be made out to the Diocese of South Carolina.

While the Legal Defense Fund raised money for lawyers, the lawyers advocated for the diocese in court, and the diocesan ruling establishment went on making governing decisions, the annual meetings of the convention continued as usual. As of this writing (March 2017), four annual meetings of the convention have transpired since the schism. On the whole, they have been unremarkable in their nature and conduct. They

---

200. "Lawrence 'Diocese' Stokes Imaginary Fears to Raise Funds for Quixotic Lawsuit." South Carolina Episcopalians, November 3, 2013, http://www.scepiscopalians.com/2013_News.html.

201. "Diocese Establishes Legal Defense Fund." *Jubilate Deo* (Diocese of South Carolina) [November 17, 2013].

202. Ibid.

203. Peter Mitchell, chair, John Barr, Haden McCormick, Jeffrey Miller, Myron Harrington, Elizabeth Pennewill, Charles Waring, Jim Lewis, and Bishop Lawrence.

204. "News from the Diocese of South Carolina." December 4, 2014, http://us1.campaign-archive2.com/?u=4961327fa871e140b6aecfe0e&id=c62711e0d67e=e0f4c5e6d5.

205. Ibid.

206. "1785 Society: Funding Legal Defense for the Defense of South Carolina." The Diocese of South Carolina, February 17, 2015, http://www.diosc.com/sys/149-donatenow/donatetodiocese/640-1785-society.

207. Author's notes, 224th Convention of the Diocese of South Carolina, March 14, 2015.

met mostly to approve decisions already made and to advertise the various programs of the diocese. This author was allowed to attend the annual meeting of 2015 but was barred the next year and the next.

While they were mostly humdrum sessions, on rare occasions the annual meetings displayed small flashes of independence, questioning of authority, and meaningful discussion. This usually happened around resolutions being offered. Normally the resolutions were handed down from the diocesan committees to be simply rubber-stamped by the usually robotic delegates. The meeting of 2014 was a case in point. The representatives unanimously passed the two resolutions to set up a task force on discernment and to accept the oversight of Global South, but then other proposed resolutions appeared, some of which were quite important and controversial. One, "C–5, Of Worship in the Diocese," required that only the Episcopal Church prayer books of 1979 and before could be used in services. This meant the new liturgies recently put forth by the Anglican Church in North America could not be used, a curious point. It passed easily. Then appeared "C–3 Authority of the Rector," offered by the Standing Committee and the Diocesan Council. It would give control of parish property to the rector: "the Rector shall have authority for all spiritual matters of the Parish (. . .) and for the use and control of the church, real and personal parish property and parish records."[208] The rector alone, who served at the will of the bishop, would have the "authority" to "control" "real and personal parish property" rather than the parish vestry. In other words, if the vestry voted to return to the Episcopal Church, the rector could block the church land and buildings from being returned to the Church, or could even presumably sell the property on his own. This was obviously strikingly incongruous with the whole theme of the diocese in the schism and the purpose of the litigation, that local property would remain entirely in local hands. Evidently, this proposed resolution ran into a brick wall in the meeting, a very rare event. It had been many years since the power structure had been denied their wish in an annual diocesan convention meeting. The proposed resolution was suddenly withdrawn ("tabled") without a vote. For the first time in many years, the ruling establishment retreated from the battlefield. Then, they killed their own measure. It was not brought back from the table the next year, 2015, or the following, 2016. Apparently giving the rector dictatorial rights over their local property was a bridge too far.

As we have seen, homosexuality had been a critical issue in South Carolina for three decades before the schism. Opposition to equality of homosexuals in the Church had risen to a crescendo in the Lawrence years, 2008 to 2012, when diocesan leaders used the issue to unify, energize, and motivate the majority of communicants in the diocese to differentiate themselves from the Episcopal Church. Once the schism occurred, the leaders no longer had any need of the issue. In 2013 and 2014 they said little about homosexuality. That inexplicably changed in 2015, when in the annual meeting of the convention, the leadership suddenly and surprisingly presented three proposed resolutions involving opposition to homosexuality. The first, "R–2 A Resolution Tasking the Standing Committee to Adopt Marriage and Employment Policy," called on the Standing Committee to work with the Task Force on Marriage to develop policies and

---

208. [Proposed resolutions, 2014]. Diocese of South Carolina, March 7, 2014, http://www.diosc.com/sys/images/documents/conventions/223_conv_resolutions.pdf.

rationales, and to prepare canonical changes to guarantee traditional marriage.[209] This passed quickly on a vote of 226 to 4.[210] The next, "R–3 A Resolution Directing the Task Force to Develop Parish Resources," declared that America was in "unparalleled confusion" about marriage and gender identity and called on the Task Force on Marriage to develop resources for parishes for the promotion of traditional marriage.[211] This too passed quickly, on a vote of 235 to 1.[212]

Then appeared a third proposed resolution on the issue, "R–4 A Resolution to Adopt a Standing Resolution on Marriage." This one not only demanded only traditional marriage, it condemned transgender: "God wonderfully creates each person as male and female. These two distinct, complementary genders together reflect the image of God. (Gen 1:26–27). Rejection of one's biological sex runs the grave risk of rejecting the image of God within that person."[213] The last sentence proved to be a stumbling block for some delegates who thought it was perhaps unsupported by scripture, unnecessarily harsh, alienating, or simply unnecessary. The Rev. Marshall Huey, of Old St. Andrew's, moved that the sentence be struck from the resolution. This produced a moment of unexpected drama in the convention as everyone knew that Bishop Lawrence had been a critic of transgender rights and presumably wanted to keep the sentence. Lawrence slipped away from the dais and strode around the aisles to get in line for the microphone. All eyes and ears turned to him as he reminded the assembly of why he had walked out of the House of Bishops in 2012. He said God created male and female "to protect us from confusion"[214] and asked the delegates to keep the sentence in the resolution. He boldly put his leadership and reputation on the line. The vote was then taken on whether to remove the sentence: 31 "Yes" and 155 "No." Between 44 and 50 delegates abstained. Lawrence carried the day with the support of about two-thirds of the assembly, a clear-cut but not overwhelming number.[215] The delegates then voted to reword the sentence to read a more moderate: "Rejection of one's biological sex opposes God's purpose in creation."[216] The Resolution went on to say "The term 'marriage' has only one meaning: the uniting of one man and one woman in a single exclusive union."[217] Even more explicitly, it said "The Diocese will only recognize and solemnize marriages between a biological man and a biological woman, that is between two persons whose birth gender identities were respectively male and female."[218] Why the diocese needed to pass these resolutions was never clarified. Whether the diocese would ever allow same-sex marriage was never in doubt. It was interesting to note that the revived campaign against

209. *Journal of the 224th (. . .) 2015*, 54.
210. Author's notes, 224th.
211. *Journal of the 224th (. . .) 2015*, 54–55.
212. Author's notes, 224th.
213. "Floor Resolutions for Consideration, 224th Annual Meeting of the Convention of the Diocese of South Carolina, March 14, 2015." Diocese of South Carolina, March 14, 2015.
214. Author's notes, 224th.
215. Ibid.
216. *Journal of the 224th (. . .) 2015*, 55.
217. Ibid.
218. Ibid.

homosexuality came at the same time the diocese was trying to raise a great deal of new money for legal fees.

Curiously enough, even as the leadership was preparing to return the diocese to opposing and denouncing equal rights for homosexuals, it promoted the visit to the diocese of an openly gay man. But, this was not just any gay man. He was Dr. Wes Hill, Assistant Professor of Biblical Studies at Trinity School for Ministry, in Ambridge, Pennsylvania. Hill was well-known as a leading evangelical advocate for the school of thought that homosexuality was innate, but that people who were homosexual by nature should not engage in homosexual acts. Instead, they should remain single and celibate. Conventional wisdom among the religious right was that homosexuality was not inborn but was learned in life. This came from the firm belief that God assigned gender and that people should not question that, let alone try to alter God's assignment. This view was very much in the spirit of the three resolutions that passed in the convention meeting of 2015. Promoted by the diocesan leadership, Hill presented a talk at St. John's of Johns Island on December 12, 2014, entitled "Spiritual Friendship: Ministering to Same Sex Attracted Christians." His theme was that the Church should promote celibate "friendship" among gay and lesbian Christians.[219] Judging by the resolutions passed just three months after his visit, Hill had no influence on softening the diocesan hard line on the issue of homosexuality. The possibility that the diocese would ever recognize its homosexual communicants, let alone promote friendship among them, seemed remote at best.

The resolutions passed in March of 2015 came in a growing public expectation that both the Episcopal Church and the United States Supreme Court would legalize same-sex marriage in the immediate future. This happened. On June 26, 2015, the Supreme Court ruled that same-sex marriage was legal in the United States. On the day the Supreme Court ruled, diocesan leaders issued a press release declaring, as if it were necessary, that the Diocese of South Carolina would not allow same-sex marriages: "The Diocese of South Carolina continues to affirm the historic position of the Christian Church: that God has ordained two states of life for His people, singleness or Holy Matrimony—the joining together of one man and one woman into a holy union."[220] Having reestablished its anti-homosexual stance in 2015, the diocese then returned to ignoring the issue, at least for the moment.

Women's ordination was another social reform issue that the diocese had faced warily for decades. On the whole, conservative Episcopalians had grudgingly accepted the ordination of women into the diaconate and priesthood of the Church starting in the 1970s. South Carolina began ordaining women in the 1980s, but without any enthusiasm. By the time Lawrence became bishop, the diocese had a handful of women clergy but none heading any medium-sized or large parish and none heading any important diocesan institution. Lawrence came from a diocese that was adamantly opposed to women's ordination; and, he showed little interest in the subject after he arrived in South Carolina. In time, he did ordain two women to the diaconate before the schism. Finally,

---

219. "Dr. Wes Hill to Speak on 'Spiritual Friendship: Ministering to Same Sex Attracted Christians.'" Diocese of South Carolina, December 10, 2014, http://www.diosc.com/sys/index.php?view=article&catid=1:latest-news&id=630:dr-wes-hill-to-speak-on.

220. "Statement from the Diocese of South Carolina." Diocese of South Carolina, June 25, 2015.

more than seven years after he was consecrated a bishop, Lawrence agreed to ordain a woman as priest, one of the two women he had ordained to the diaconate, Martha Horn, the wife of the Rev. Robert Horn, a priest of the diocese. Martha Horn was battling a serious case of cancer and undergoing chemotherapy. On October 10, 2015, bishops Lawrence and Alex Dickson ordained Horn to the priesthood in St. Luke's of Hilton Head. The Rev. Martha Horn died on December 28, 2015. Since then, Lawrence has ordained two more women to the diaconate, albeit it the "vocational diaconate," that is, not in line for the priesthood. On June 11, 2016, in a group of seven, Lawrence ordained Joyce Harder, of Christ Church, Mt. Pleasant, and Barbara Holliman, of All Saints, Florence. On March 17, 2017, Bishop James Hobby, of the Anglican Diocese of Pittsburgh, ordained to the priesthood the Rev. Catharine Moore Norris, at Holy Cross, Sullivans Island. Lawrence celebrated the Eucharist. Norris was the second woman to be ordained in the Diocese of South Carolina after the schism.

Thus, several years into the schism, the entity still calling itself the Diocese of South Carolina survived largely intact with about three-fifths of the active membership of the pre-schism diocese and still firmly governed by the fervently evangelical ruling clique that had guided it through its break from the Episcopal Church. It was in fact an independent Christian denomination. Although it insisted it was "Anglican," it was not officially part of the Anglican Communion and had no reasonable prospect of being part of it. Nevertheless, considering the number and magnitude of its internal and external challenges, its leaders and communicants had reason to give thanks that the diocese was in as good a shape as it was.

The schism was the result of a negative, that is, opposition to equal rights for homosexuals, and, in the broader picture, opposition to the horizontal, or social, trajectory of the Episcopal Church of the last half-century. The greatest challenge of the diocesan leadership was to sculpt out a positive purpose for the schism beyond the vague notion of the Anglican Realignment. For this, they sought meaning and identity for the diocese. They tried to give the diocese purpose, definition, and mission in the period after the schism. They tried to find a place for the diocese in the worldwide Anglican Communion. Although they developed strong and friendly ties with some conservative Anglicans abroad, they could not find a way to become truly a part of the Communion. The broad Anglican Realignment movement failed to move the whole Communion rightward or to break up the old Communion into two units on the issue of homosexuality. By 2016, the idea of replacing the Episcopal Church by a conservative new entity tied to GAFCON no longer appeared plausible. By then, the Diocese of South Carolina's place in the Anglican Communion was more problematical than ever.

Internally, the diocese struggled in the first few years after the schism to adjust to a declining membership and at best a near-flat-lining budget. What made these conditions all the most alarming was the rising need for money to pay the ever-mounting legal fees. Fewer communicants had to be pressed for more and more donations to pay two sets of lawyers, parochial and diocesan. Under the circumstances, it was remarkable that a diocese of its size, perhaps sixteen thousand active members, rather quickly came up with two million dollars and then another three hundred thousand dollars for lawyers. This was on top of what the parishes were already paying for their own local attorneys.

The three resolutions adopted by the March 2015 convention meeting may have finally revealed the leaders' aims in the schism. Following the resolutions, Bishop Lawrence named a Marriage Task Force of clergymen Kendall Harmon, Peter Moore, former dean and chair of the trustees of Trinity School for Ministry, Ted Duvall, Greg Snyder, Tyler Prescott, and Jim Lewis, Lawrence's assistant. The purpose of the Force was to enact the terms of the three resolutions. The committee drew up four documents for the diocese: "A Statement of Faith," a parish template for adopting the Statement, a diocesan employment policy, and a facilities use policy. The Standing Committee adopted the Statement of Faith and the employment policy on October 6, 2015, and the facilities policy on November 3, 2015. Altogether, the four documents established a clear expression of the beliefs, policies, and procedures for the diocese, really for the first time since the schism.

The Statement of Faith clarified the theological identity of the diocese as at least highly evangelical and vertical religion based entirely on a literal interpretation of the Bible and personal salvation. It went on to denounce homosexuality and transgender as against God's creation and to demand that marriage could only be between a man and a woman. It also declared the bishop to be the final authority and to require that all employees and "leaders" in the diocese make an oath of obedience to the Statement. The second document, the parish template, provided a form for all local parishes to adopt the Statement. The third paper, the employee policy, required all employees and "leaders" of the diocese to sign an oath of allegiance to the Statement. It said that the bishop could terminate any employment at any time. The last document, a facilities use policy, required anyone seeking to use church properties, such as for weddings, to sign a form of compliance with the Statement. This would prevent any diocesan church from being used for same-sex weddings. The Marriage Task Force made a report of its work to the March 2016 convention. The Force's rationale and its four documents revealed a diocese characterized by literal interpretation of the Bible, intolerance and authoritarianism, and adherence to social conservatism. This landed far right on the Protestant spectrum, some might say highly evangelical, others fundamentalist, or at least fundamentalist-leaning. The Diocese of South Carolina three years after the schism was strikingly different than it had been only a few decades earlier when it was in the mainstream of the Episcopal Church.[221]

TO FEDERAL COURT, 2013+

The legal war between the Diocese of South Carolina and the Episcopal Church began on 4 January 2013 when DSC brought a lawsuit in state circuit court against the Episcopal Church, and later the Episcopal Church in South Carolina. The Diocesan lawyers asked the court to declare that it alone owned the legal rights, properties, and other assets of the pre-schism diocese. Once entered, this lawsuit was set to work its way through the state courts. This, however, was not to be the only legal course after the schism. Two months after the Diocese filed suit, the Church side entered a suit in federal court against them. This meant legal action between the competing parties would move along two avenues, state and federal. Perhaps motivated by the belief that federal courts would be friendlier to

---

221. *Journal of the 225th (. . .)* 2016, 56–70.

the Episcopal Church side, the Church diocese brought three separate actions in federal courts within the few years after the schism. The first two of these were attempts to get the federal courts to take over the litigation of the dispute between the two dioceses. The first of the two was a lawsuit of Bishop vonRosenberg against Bishop Lawrence. The second was an attempt to move the proceedings already underway in state court to the federal court. The third was somewhat unrelated to the first two. It was an effort to have the Church Insurance Company help pay the legal fees of the Church diocese.

vonRosenberg v. Lawrence

On March 5, 2013, Charles vonRosenberg entered a lawsuit against Mark Lawrence in the United States District Court for the District of South Carolina, Charleston Division.[222] This began a legal action in which vonRosenberg essentially asked the federal court to declare him, and not Lawrence, to be the rightful bishop of the Episcopal Diocese of South Carolina. In time, vonRosenberg's suit would go down a long and winding path that included a hearing in the District Court in Charleston, an order from the judge, an appeal of the judge's decision to the U.S. Court of Appeals, a hearing in the Appeals Court, an order of the Appeals Court, a remand to the District Court in Charleston, a new hearing and a new order from the judge there, a new hearing of his new decision to the U.S. Court of Appeals, and a second remand to the District Court. And, after four years of such, the suit was no nearer closure than when it started.

In his action of March 5, vonRosenberg asked the court to declare him to be the rightful bishop of the Episcopal diocese and to grant "injunctive relief" which would prevent Lawrence from acting as the Episcopal diocesan bishop, have Lawrence pay for vonRosenberg's legal fees, and order Lawrence to make an accounting of all profits made as the illegal bishop.[223] As an earlier federal case in Texas, this one was also based on one federal law, the Lanham Act. This Act, signed into law in 1947, had been meant to protect trademarks. vonRosenberg's lawyers emphasized one particular part of the Act called Section 43 (a) that said: "any (. . .) false or misleading representation of fact which is likely to cause confusion (. . .) shall be liable in a civil action by any person who believes that he or she is or is likely to be damaged by such act."[224] The Church attorneys claimed that only vonRosenberg was the legitimate Episcopal bishop of South Carolina and, therefore, Lawrence was causing confusion by falsely representing himself to be the Episcopal bishop, in violation of the Lanham Act. If the court should agree with this claim, it would, in effect, be ruling in favor of the Church against the breakaway diocese.

As a matter of record, for many years, federal courts had been overwhelmingly favorable to Episcopal dioceses against breakaway congregations, but no federal court had gone so far as to render a decision on a dispute between the national Church and a diocese. If the federal judge in Charleston should choose to do so, he would be the

---

222. "Complaint." In the United States District Court for the District of South Carolina Charleston Division, March 5, 2013.

223. Ibid., 20.

224. "Lanham Act." Wikipedia, http://en.wikipedia.org/wiki/Lanham_Act.

first federal judge to rule on the legal relationship between the Episcopal Church and a diocese, the gravity of which could not be lost on him or anyone else.

In March of 2013, the federal court fight between one bishop and the other started a long, contentious, and tortuous course that defied resolution time and again. The case was taken by a senior judge of the District Court in Charleston, Charles Weston Houck, who was in his eightieth year. Houck had practiced law in Florence, South Carolina, for two decades before being appointed to the federal bench by President Carter in 1979. Chief judge of the District Court from 1993 to 2000, Houck assumed senior judge status in 2003.[225]

The case before Judge Houck continued for five months before he issued a decision. Two days after entering their lawsuit of 5 March, Church lawyers made a second request of Judge Houck asking him to grant a preliminary injunction preventing Bishop Lawrence from acting as the Episcopal bishop of South Carolina.[226] For this, they presented a forty-four-page brief and eighteen supporting exhibits of 229 pages. One was an affidavit of historian Dr. Walter Edgar, who emphasized the historical union of Episcopal Church and diocese. Another affidavit came from the eminent church historian, Dr. Robert Bruce Mullin, who argued for the unitary, not federal nature, of an hierarchical Episcopal Church where authority rested in the General Convention. Thus, within two days, the Church lawyers asked Judge Houck to declare vonRosenberg to be the legal bishop, grant injunctive relief, and issue a preliminary injunction against Lawrence. This was a tall order indeed. For the moment, Judge Houck bided his time.[227]

Having already jumped out on a strong footing in the state court, the DSC's panel of lawyers did not hesitate to spring into action again. Three weeks after the Church side entered its suit, their attorneys countered by presenting to Judge Houck two papers, one a motion to dismiss or stay proceedings and the other a collection of supporting evidence for this.[228] They asked Judge Houck to dismiss the Church's suit, or at least to put it on hold until the earlier state court action was finished. Perhaps the strongest arguments they made were that the state court had a parallel case between the two dioceses and had been adjudicating the case for two months, and that the Church diocese had agreed to an injunction keeping it from holding itself out as the legal Episcopal Diocese.

The Church lawyers responded to the independent diocese's arguments in Judge Houck's court on 22 April.[229] This time they emphasized the hierarchical nature of the

---

225. "Charles Weston Houck." Wikipedia, http://en.wikipedia.org/wiki/Charles_Weston_Houck.

226. "Plaintiff's Motion for a Preliminary Injunction." In the United States District Court for the District of South Carolina Charleston Division, March 7, 2013.

227. For newspaper reports on the Church diocese's lawsuit of March 2013 see: Smith, Bruce, "Preliminary Injunction Sought in SC Case." *Florence Morning News* (Florence, SC), March 7, 2013; Parker, Adan, "Episcopal Countersuit Filed." *The Post and Courier* (Charleston, SC), March 16, 2013; Parker, Adam, "Local Episcopal Officials Seek Injunction." *The Post and Courier* (Charleston, SC), March 8, 2013; Smith, Bruce, "Episcopal Diocese: Suit Undermines SC Court." *Florence Morning News* (Florence, SC), March 13, 2013; Parker, Adam, "Diocese Responds to Church's Federal Suit." *The Post and Courier* (Charleston, SC), March 14, 2013; Parker, Adam, "Countersuit Filed in Episcopal Dispute." *The Post and Courier* (Charleston, SC), March 17, 2013.

228. "Motion to Dismiss or in the Alternative to Abstain or Stay Proceedings." In the United States District Court for the District of South Carolina Charleston Division, March 28, 2013.

229. "Reply to Defendant's Response to Plaintiff's Motion for a Preliminary Injunction." In the United States District Court for the District of South Carolina Charleston Division, April 22, 2013.

Episcopal Church and the principle of the separation of church and state embodied in the First Amendment of the U.S. Constitution. These were the bedrock arguments of the Church lawyers that they advanced time and again in virtually all of the legal proceedings to come. If the Church were hierarchical, constituent dioceses would always be subject to the higher authority of the Church, in fact the General Convention. Moreover, if this were true, the civil courts would have to defer from interfering in the internal affairs of the Church. Following the arguments of hierarchy and institutional independence, vonRosenberg would have to be recognized as the legitimate Episcopal bishop of South Carolina. Lawrence would have to be declared as acting fraudulently and treated accordingly.[230]

As we will see, Judge Houck had already been moving away from federal court resolution of the problem between the two competing dioceses when he held a formal hearing on the case of *vonRosenberg v. Lawrence* on August 8, 2013. The two sides presented their best arguments to the Judge in the hour-long proceeding attended by the two bishops (who shook hands afterwards). Apparently, Judge Houck found Lawrence's lawyers to be more persuasive, especially on the point of the parallel and pre-existing adjudication in state court. At one point in the hearing, Houck told a Church lawyer: "'When I look at the act of trying this case in the shadow of the state court case, I can't figure it out.'"[231]

What Judge Houck did figure out was that he could abstain from adjudicating the case under the guidance of the *Brillhart/Wilton* principle that allowed, under certain provisions, a federal court to refuse to hear cases involving federal law if a parallel case was already under way in state courts. Therefore, on August 23, 2013, Houck issued an "Order" granting Lawrence's motion to dismiss the case and denying vonRosenberg's motion to grant a preliminary injunction: "The Court dismisses Bishop vonRosenberg's claim without prejudice in favor of the related state court proceeding pursuant to *Wilton/Brillhart* abstention to enable the parties to fully litigate all issues pertaining to this dispute, including those presented in the action, in the state court action."[232] In conclusion, Houck deferred to the state court: "The sum of all disputes and conflicts arising in the wake of the Diocese's estrangement from TEC are more appropriately before, and will more comprehensively be resolved, in South Carolina state court."[233] However, Houck did make one caveat, that he would reinstate the case if the state court failed to resolve all the issues at hand. With this, the Church's attempt to get the federal court to resolve the dispute between the two parties collapsed, at least for the moment. At that point, it looked as if the locally-oriented state circuit court would keep jurisdiction and move the case along to resolution without any interference from the federal courts. This was a major legal victory for DSC.

On 16 September 2013, Church lawyers asked Judge Houck to reconsider his decision. Their essential argument was that the Judge had used the wrong principle for

---

230. See also, "Legal Response Makes First Amendment Case for Injunction against Mark Lawrence." The Episcopal Church in South Carolina, April 24, 2013, http://www.episcopalchurchsc.org/news-release-april-24-2013.html.

231. "Judge Hears Arguments in U.S. District Court." The Episcopal Church in South Carolina, August 8, 2013, http://www.episcopalchurchsc.org/news-release-august-8-2013.html.

232. "Order." In the United States District Court for the District of South Carolina Charleston Division, August 23, 2013, 22.

233. Ibid.

abstention, *Brillhart/Wilton*, and should have used the more restrictive *Colorado River* guide.[234] On 14 January 2014, Judge Houck issued his answer. He denied the motion to reconsider and maintained that that he had used the relevant principle for deference, the *Brillhart/Wilton* standard.[235]

The question at hand was essentially which of the two standards for deference should be applied in this case, *Brillhart/Wilton* or *Colorado River*. In short, the former allowed considerable latitude to federal judges who wished to defer to state courts with parallel litigation while the latter still allowed deference but only under certain narrow "exception circumstances." Judge Houck apparently felt completely comfortable with the former while the Church side sought to employ the latter with its much stricter window of use. Perhaps reducing the scope of opportunity for deference would force federal judges to decide to adjudicate the cases regardless of the state court actions. The presumption underlying this was that federal courts would be more favorable to the Church as a national institution while state courts would be more favorable to local entities under local laws. All along, Church lawyers wanted the dispute to be seen as a religious issue with the expectation that federal courts would ultimately defer to a religious institution under the First Amendment requirement of the separation of church and state. On the contrary, the independent diocesan lawyers wanted the dispute to be seen as a property issue with the expectation that state courts would follow "neutral principles" and protect the local entities' claims to rights and properties under state laws. Thus, the whole course of litigation rested upon which approach the courts would take, a religious or a property dispute.

Again, the Church lawyers had no intention of leaving the matter after Houck's denial for reconsideration. On 5 February 2014, they gave notice of an appeal of Houck's Order to the United States Court of Appeals for the Fourth Circuit.[236] On 7 April, they submitted to the appeals court their opening brief containing their arguments of why Houck's Order should be reversed.[237] The Church attorneys argued several points: that the case in state court was not parallel to the federal case, that Houck used the wrong standard for abstention, he should have used *Colorado River* instead of *Brillhart/Wilton*, but that neither standard was applicable in this case. The federal court should not defer to the state court. They insisted this was a religious issue and not a property one: "So-called 'neutral principles of law' that states may use to resolve disputes over 'ownership of church property,' (. . .) have no bearing on the fundamentally religious dispute at issue here."[238]

---

234. "Plaintiff's Motion for Reconsideration." In the United States District Court for the District of South Carolina Charleston Division, September 16, 2013.

235. "Order." In the United States District Court for the District of South Carolina Charleston Division, January 14, 2014.

236. "Notice of Appeal." In the United States District Court for the District of South Carolina Charleston Division, February 5, 2014.

237. "Opening Brief of Appellant." In the United States Court of Appeals for the Fourth Circuit, April 7, 2014.

238. Ibid., 48.

As to be expected, the independent diocesan lawyers[239] countered with a stout defense of Judge Houck's decision. They argued that the state court action was essentially the same, that "neutral principles" must be applied, and that Houck had properly followed the *Brillhart/Wilton* standard for deference.[240] Shortly thereafter, the Church attorneys[241] filed a response with the appeals court arguing that the state and federal cases were not parallel, and that the federal court must address federal law.[242] Having filed their briefs with their best arguments, the two sets of lawyers could only wait until the appeals court would hold a hearing and render a judgment.

The Fourth Circuit Court of Appeals was one of twelve regional federal appeals courts in the United States. Sitting in Richmond, Virginia, it heard cases on appeal from the nine federal courts in Maryland, Virginia, West Virginia, North Carolina, and South Carolina. It had one Chief Justice, fourteen other judges, and two "senior judges." It was no stranger to Episcopal Church cases. In 2002, it had upheld Bishop Jane Holmes Dixon's victory in lower court recognizing her authority as bishop (*Dixon v. Edwards*). The three-judge panel making that unanimous decision was led by Judge Robert B. King and included Judge Roger Gregory and Judge Diana Gibbon Motz. Gregory and Motz would be two of the three judges to sit on both appeals from South Carolina.

In December of 2014, the Fourth Circuit Court announced that the hearing in the case of the appeal of Judge Houck's decision would be held in the court on January 28, 2015. Judge Diana Motz was to be the chair of the three-judge panel including Judge Roger Gregory, and Judge James A. Wynn, Jr. Motz and Gregory were choices of President Clinton, Wynn of President Obama.

The hearing before the three judges on 28 January 2015 lasted approximately thirty minutes.[243] Church lawyer Tisdale spoke first, then diocesan attorney Runyan. The presiding judge, Motz, asked the most questions while Wynn also spoke frequently. As the lawyers made their predictable pitches, the judges were almost entirely concerned with whether Houck had used the correct standard for abstention. They implied that he had not and should have used the more restrictive *Colorado River* principle. Judge Motz showed concern that *Brillhart/Wilton* should not have been used in a "mixed" case seeking declaratory and non-declaratory relief. The tone of the hearing and the judges' questions indicated their disagreement with Houck's use of the broad standard for abstention.[244]

Judge Motz wrote an opinion that was joined by Gregory and Wynn and published on 31 March 2015.[245] It followed closely the judges' thoughts and remarks in the hearing.

---

239. C. Alan Runyan, Henrietta U. Golding, Charles H. Williams, and David Cox.

240. "Brief of Appellees." In the United States Court of Appeals for the Fourth Circuit, May 12, 2014.

241. Thomas S. Tisdale and Jason S. Smith.

242. "Reply Brief of Appellant the Right Reverend Charles G. vonRosenberg." In the United States Court of Appeals for the Fourth Circuit, May 27, 2014.

243. Audio recording of the hearing was made available on the Court's website, www.ca4.uscourts.gov/oral-argument/listen-to-oral-arguments .

244. Author's notes, U.S. Court of Appeals, hearing, livestream, January 28, 2015.

245. "Appeal from the United States District Court for the District of South Carolina, at Charleston." United States Court of Appeals for the Fourth Circuit, March 31, 2015.

The judges said that the *Colorado River* rule was the proper standard in this case that involved declaratory and non-declaratory relief: "We now join several of our sister circuits in holding that *Colorado River* and not *Brillhart/Wilton*, must guide a court's decision to abstain from adjudicating mixed complaints alleging claims for both declaratory and nondeclaratory relief."[246] The judges overturned Houck's Order and sent the case back to Charleston for reconsideration following the Colorado standard: "Because the district court did not apply this abstention standard, we must vacate its stay order and remand for a determination whether such 'exceptional' circumstances are present in this case."[247] While it demanded that he follow the *Colorado River* principle, it left the door open to him to abstain again if he could demonstrate the required "exceptional circumstances" allowed by this standard.

Attorney Runyan and his cohorts were not ready to concede. Two weeks after the ruling, they filed a petition with the Fourth Circuit Appeals Court for a rehearing *en banc*, that is, before all the judges of the court.[248] This was allowed in certain circumstances of great importance. A majority of judges had to agree in order to hold a hearing before the entire court. Upon circulating the request for rehearing, not one judge would sign on. Thus, on 29 April 2015, the Appeals Court formally denied the independent dioceses petition for a rehearing.[249] This meant the case would return to the district court in Charleston without delay.

In light of the appeals court's remand, Judge Houck reopened the case of *vonRosenberg v. Lawrence* in June of 2015. All eyes turned to him as a moment of drama developed. Only a few months earlier, Judge Goodstein had issued her sweeping judgment in favor of the independent diocese; and now everyone was eagerly awaiting the hearing on the appeal of her decision that was scheduled in the state Supreme Court for September 23, 2015. The two sets of attorneys presented their best arguments once again to Judge Houck. On 30 June, the diocesan lawyers presented their brief arguing that the judge could follow the *Colorado River* standard and still abstain because of the nature of the parallel litigation in the state courts.[250] Since the argument of pre-existing parallel litigation in state courts had worked well before, there was no reason to think it would not again. The lawyers asked Houck to dismiss the case or issue a "stay." The Church lawyers argued that the case in the state courts was not parallel, mainly because the federal case was based on the federal Lanham Act, and that the *Colorado River* principle demanded federal adjudication except in a rare circumstance which they said did not occur here.[251]

---

246. Ibid., 10.

247. Ibid., 11–12.

248. "Defendant/Appellee's Petition for Rehearing and Rehearing En Banc." In the United States Court of Appeals for the Fourth Circuit, April 14, 2015.

249. "Order." United States Court of Appeals for the Fourth Circuit, April 29, 2015.

250. "Memorandum in Support of Defendant Lawrence's Supplemental Motion to Dismiss or in the Alternative to Stay Proceedings." In the United States District Court for the Diocese of South Carolina Charleston Division, June 30, 2015.

251. "Plaintiff's Memorandum in Opposition to Defendant's Supplemental Motion to Dismiss or in the Alternative to Stay the Proceedings." In the United States District Court for the District of South Carolina Charleston Division, July 15, 2015.

As in the first instance of the case, in August of 2013, Judge Houck seemed impressed by the independent diocesan lawyers' arguments and unmoved by the other side, and in this instance by the pressure plainly exerted by the appeals court.[252] As before, he insisted the cases in state and federal courts were essentially the same: "the Court notes that the state court action and the instant federal court action are parallel."[253] He continued that the special factors in this case provided the "exceptional circumstances" allowed by the *Colorado River* standard to permit him to abstain. He ended by placing all in the lap of the state Supreme Court. Houck issued a "stay" putting vonRosenberg's suit on hold pending the outcome of the South Carolina Supreme Court litigation.

Once again, as two years earlier, the independent diocese rejoiced at the federal judge's ruling. And, once again, the opposition was crestfallen, even more so now since the federal appeals court had raised hopes of success in the federal court of Charleston. Even so, the Church attorneys resolved to keep fighting. On 19 October 2015, Church lawyers Tisdale and Smith submitted a notice of appeal in Houck's court.[254] On February 22, 2016, they filed a new brief in the federal Fourth Circuit Appeals Court, in Richmond, once again complaining about Houck's inaction.[255] They insisted the two avenues of litigation, state and federal, were not parallel and that the federal Lanham Act demanded federal adjudication. Moreover, they held that Houck had not met the criteria for abstention under the terms of the *Colorado River* standard. On December 9, 2016, the Appeals Court held a hearing on the Church lawyers' appeal. On February 21, 2017, the Court agreed with the Church lawyers and ruled, unanimously, to remand the case to the District court with direction to follow the *Colorado River* standard. Judge Houck died on July 19, 2017, at age eighty-four. He was replaced by Judge Patrick Duffy, the one who had handled the Church Insurance Company matter.

Other Actions in Federal Courts

While the Episcopal Church diocese pressed its long-term lawsuit of *vonRosenberg v. Lawrence*, it also entered into two other actions in federal courts soon after the schism. One of these was an attempt to move the earlier litigation from state court to federal court. The other was to get the Church Insurance Company to pay for the Church's legal expenses.

The Episcopal Church and its diocese wanted the federal courts, rather than state courts, to resolve the disputes between the national Church and the breakaway dioceses. Conventional wisdom held that national courts would more be more likely to side with

---

252. "Order." In the United States District Court for the District of South Carolina Charleston Division, September 21, 2015.

253. Ibid., 11–12.

254. "Notice of Appeal." In the United States District Court for the District of South Carolina Charleston Division, October 19, 2015.

255. "Opening Brief of Appellant the Right Reverend Charles G. vonRosenberg." In the United States Court of Appeals for the Fourth Circuit, February 22, 2016.

a national institution whereas local courts would be more apt to side with local entities. On the whole, federal courts had indeed sided with the Church dioceses against the secessionist parishes all around the country. This was not a hard and fast rule, however, because as we have seen, some state courts, notably in Texas and California, had ruled in favor of the Episcopal Church. In some cases, state courts had declared the Episcopal Church to be hierarchical and had ruled in favor of the Church even while using the "neutral principles" standard. Still, Church authorities understandably preferred that federal courts handle the Church cases.

Along this line, the Church diocese in South Carolina attempted to move the litigation, already underway in the state circuit court, into the United States District Court in Charleston for federal adjudication. On 3 April 2013, a month after filing the *vonRosenberg v. Lawrence* lawsuit, and before its litigation gained steam, lawyers[256] for the Episcopal Church and the Episcopal Church in South Carolina entered into the U.S. District Court in Charleston a "Notice of Removal."[257] This removed the state court action, underway in the circuit court in Dorchester since January 4, to Judge Houck's District Court mainly because the dispute involved two large factors that belonged in federal court, the First Amendment to the U.S. Constitution and the Lanham Act.[258]

If the DSC attorney Alan Runyan and his team were thrown off balance by this ploy, they did not show it. They hastily scrambled to counter with a strong response in defense of the state court litigation. A week after the Church lawyers submitted their Notice of Removal, Runyan et al. submitted to Judge Houck a motion to send the case back to the state court.[259] They accompanied this with a 28-page brief with 4 exhibits.[260] The diocesan lawyers made the obvious argument that the Episcopal Church and its diocese had been actively involved in the state court action from the start three months earlier. The Church side had given at least de facto recognition of state jurisdiction. In their response, the Church lawyers disagreed with this contention and held that their action in state court did not demonstrate an intent to remain in that court.[261]

On 6 June 2013, Judge Houck held a hearing on whether to continue the case in the federal District Court or remand it to the state court. The courtroom was packed for the forty-five-minute hearing. The two bishops attended with a gaggle of lawyers, four on the Church side and around thirty on the diocesan side. This was the first courtroom meeting of the two bishops. Judge Houck may have been a bit overwhelmed by it all. He said at one point, "'When I first got this case, I was somewhat confused as to who was

---

256. TECSC: Thomas S. Tisdale, Jason S. Smith; TEC: Palmer C. Hamilton, George A. LeMaistre, Jr., David Booth Beers, and Mary E. Kostel.

257. "Notice of Removal." United States District Court for the District of South Carolina Charleston Division, April 3, 2013.

258. Ibid., 3.

259. "Plaintiff's Motion to Remand." In the United States District Court of South Carolina Charleston Division, April 10, 2013.

260. "Plaintiff's Memorandum of Law in Support of Motion to Remand." In the United States District Court District of South Carolina Charleston Division, April 10, 2013.

261. "Defendant's Response to Plaintiff's Motion to Remand." In the United States District Court for the District of South Carolina Charleston Division, April 29, 2013.

who.'"²⁶² Alan Runyan spoke first arguing for the state's right to litigate this dispute in state court under "neutral principles." It belonged in state court, he said, because it involved corporate and property issues. The main lawyer for the Church, Matthew McGill, of Washington D.C., argued the Church's basic position, that this was a First Amendment issue, a religious dispute, and that the state should not meddle in an hierarchical church.

Four days later, Judge Houck issued his decision.²⁶³ He ordered the case back to the state court. In his twenty-page ruling, he essentially agreed with Runyan's arguments. He downplayed the role of the First Amendment in this particular case and agreed that the state could and should continue to adjudicate the dispute under the established "neutral principles" standard. To be sure, the diocesan side rejoiced at the news of the judge's decision. The Church side had to recognize a major and disappointing setback. Houck's rejection meant they probably could not rely on the federal courts to settle this dispute, although the *vonRosenberg v. Lawrence* lawsuit before Houck was still active, and would have to endure the litigation in the state court and follow "neutral principles" that would probably favor the secessionist cause. Perhaps what made this defeat even harder to take was Houck's declaration in his Order that the Episcopal Church was hierarchical: "TEC is a hierarchical religious denomination (. . .). Each diocese is a subordinate unit of TEC and is bound by the provisions established in its Constitution, Canons, and Prayer Book."²⁶⁴ The Church side could only wonder wistfully from this whether Judge Houck would have ruled in favor of the Episcopal Church if he had litigated the case.²⁶⁵ Like it or not, the Church lawyers had to prepare to resume the case in Judge Goodstein's courtroom.

In addition to the *vonRosenberg v. Lawrence* lawsuit and the attempt to move the state court litigation to the federal court, the Church lawyers went to federal court on a third matter in an effort to get insurance coverage for legal costs. The Church Insurance Company of Vermont issued a policy to the Episcopal Church in South Carolina effective January 1, 2013. The Church diocese's chancellor, attorney Thomas Tisdale, requested the Insurance Company to honor the insurance policy and pay for some of the legal costs the diocese incurred. In August of 2013, the Company decided it was not contractually obligated for this coverage and informed Tisdale of its denial of his claim.

---

262. "Federal Judge Says He Will Soon Rule on Where Breakaway Group's Lawsuit Will be Heard." The Episcopal Church in South Carolina, June 6, 2013, http://www.episcopalchurchsc.org/news-release-june-6–2013.html.

263. "Order." In the United States District Court for the District of South Carolina Charleston Division, June 10, 2013.

264. Ibid., 4.

265. For commentary on Houck's decision to remand see: Parker, Adam, "Federal Judge Remands Episcopal Church Case Back to State Court." *The Post and Courier* (Charleston, SC), June 10, 2013; for reactions on the Church side, see "Federal Judge Remands Lawsuit to State Court." The Episcopal Church in South Carolina, June 10, 2013, http://www.episcopalchurchsc.org/news-release-june-10–2013.html; and "Federal Court Allows Lawrence's Lawsuit to Proceed to State Court." South Carolina Episcopalians, June 10, 2013, http://www.scepiscopalians.com/2013_News.html.; for reactions on the diocesan side, see "Court Finds that 'tacit' First Amendment Issues not in the Diocese's Complaint are not a Basis for Federal Court Jurisdiction." Diocese of South Carolina, June 10, 2013, http://www.diosc.com/sys/news-events/latest-news/517-federal-judge-remands-diocese-of-sc-case-to-state-court; and "Federal Judge Returns South Carolina Case to State Court." Anglican Curmudgeon, June 10, 2013, http://accurmudgeon.blogspot.com/2013_06_01_archive.html.

Two Dioceses, 2013 and After

In September of 2013, Tisdale filed an action in the U.S. District Court of Charleston against the Company essentially claiming breach of contract.

Judge Patrick Michael Duffy, a fellow judge of C. Weston Houck in the U.S. District Court in Charleston, took the case. Duffy ruled on January 6, 2014, that the Company was contractually obligated to pay.[266] He essentially granted Tisdale's claim and rejected the Company's motion to dismiss. The policy included coverage for up to one million dollars for certain liability. The Insurance Company then filed a motion with Duffy for reconsideration. On 4 March 2014, the judge denied the motion leaving the January 6 Order standing.[267] Then, on 22 September 2014, Judge Duffy ruled yet again in favor of the Church diocese on a supplemental complaint against the Company.[268] This was the third and last Order from Judge Duffy in this matter, all directing the Company to accept the coverage in question for the Church diocese. The dispute between the Episcopal Church in South Carolina and the Church Insurance Company of Vermont ended as the Company agreed to fulfill the coverage. On 3 December 2014, the two sides announced that they had reached a "confidential" settlement.[269] Although the details of the agreement were not released, one may imagine this will pay at least a large part of the Church diocese's legal expenses.

THE WAR IN STATE COURTS, MARCH 2013+

The Preparation for the Circuit Court Trial

The legal war between the Diocese of South Carolina and the Episcopal Church in South Carolina was to be fought out in the state courts. The case was first established in the circuit court in January of 2013 with the likelihood of many months or even years of back and forth in this court. Above that would be the South Carolina Appeals Court; and above that would be the South Carolina Supreme Court. The two parties looked into a long time of grinding, contentious, expensive litigation, all with an uncertain future. This was not a happy prospect for either side.

On 19 March 2013, Runyan and his large team of lawyers entered two motions in Judge Goodstein's court. One was a request for a partial judgment to recognize the control of the Episcopal Diocese of South Carolina to be in the hands of the Board of Directors (the Standing Committee) and the Officers.[270] The other was to ask for a contempt of court citation against the Church diocese.[271] The lawyers charged that the

---

266. "Order." In the United States District Court for the District of South Carolina Charleston Division, January 6, 2014.

267. "Order." In the United States District Court for the District of South Carolina Charleston Division, March 4, 2014.

268. "Order." In the United States District Court for the District of South Carolina Charleston Division, September 22, 2014.

269. "Settlement Reached in Insurance Lawsuit." The Episcopal Church in South Carolina, December 3, 2014, http://www.episcopalchurchsc.org/news-release-december-3-2014.html.

270. "Motion for Partial Summary Judgment." State of South Carolina, County of Dorchester, In the Court of Common Pleas for the First Judicial Circuit, March 19, 2013.

271. "Motion for Contempt on Behalf of the Plaintiffs in the Protestant Episcopal Church in the

Church diocese had continued to hold itself out as the Episcopal Diocese even after the restraining order and the injunction, both of which the Judge had issued in January. The Church side's lawyers, having just opened a major campaign front in federal court, were in no mood to vacate the field in the circuit court. Nine days after Runyan et al. entered their motions for judgment and contempt of court, they delivered to Judge Goodstein their own pleas.[272] The Church and Church diocese's lawyers asked the court to dismiss the Lawrence faction's claims and to recognize the Church diocese as the legal owner of the rights and properties of the pre-schism diocese. This clarified the lines of combat in the state court as both sides asked the judge for the same thing, sole recognition as the legal and legitimate Episcopal Diocese of South Carolina with all that entailed in rights and property.

With the case back in state court, Judge Goodstein held a hearing on July 11, 2013, to set up a schedule in preparation for a trial. She and the lawyers agreed on ninety days, to October 11, for "paper discovery," that is the collection of written documents and information from the other side. Then, they set another 120 days, to early February of 2014, for the taking of depositions, or sworn testimonies of persons who may be important to the issues at stake. After that, the judge said she would set a date for the formal courtroom trial of the lawsuits at hand.[273] With the agreements settled, the two sides began the months-long process of collecting the information and documents necessary for the trial in state court.

The process of preparing for the trial turned out to be longer and much more eventful than anyone imagined it would be at the hearing of July 11, 2013. The process that was supposed to last a few months, actually lasted three days less than a full year from the hearing. The actions of the three parties, the judge, the Church lawyers and the diocesan attorneys, took numerous unexpected twists and turns that would take them all beyond the bounds of this court. Before it was over and a date was set, both the state appeals court and supreme court would get involved as would numerous individuals, some to their surprise. The year of preparation for the trial, July of 2013 to July of 2014, involved five major movements: an attempt of the Church side to overturn the injunction against it, a move of the Church lawyers to broaden the case to certain individuals on the diocesan side whom they accused of conspiracy, a drive of the Church attorneys to obtain the correspondence between Bishop Lawrence and the lawyer Alan Runyan, the depositions of individuals on both sides, and final settlement on a date for the trial.

Diocese of South Carolina, and the Trustees of the Protestant Episcopal Church in South Carolina, a South Carolina Corporate Body." State of South Carolina, County of Dorchester, In the Court of Common Pleas for the First Judicial Circuit, March 19, 2013.

272. "Answer, Affirmative Defenses, and Counterclaims of the Episcopal Church in South Carolina to Second Amended Complaint for Declarative and Injunctive Relief." State of South Carolina, County of Dorchester, In the Court of Common Pleas for the First Judicial Circuit, March 28, 2013; "Answer and Counterclaim of the Episcopal Church to Second Amended Complaint for Declaratory and Injunctive Relief." State of South Carolina, County of Dorchester, In the Court of Common Pleas for the First Judicial Circuit, March 28, 2013.

273. "Transcript of Record." July 11, 2013, In the Court of Common Pleas, First Judicial Circuit, 2013-CP-18-00013, St. George, South Carolina.

Although Judge Goodstein did not respond to Runyan's requests of March 19, 2013, for a judgment and a contempt of court citation against the Church side, she did go on to rule repeatedly in his favor during the run-up to the trial. Time and again, she overruled Tisdale and his side. The first major occasion of this happened soon into the preparation period. On 30 September 2013, Tisdale entered two motions before Goodstein, a request to "vacate," or remove, the Injunction she had imposed on January 23, 2013, and another for an injunction to prevent the Lawrence faction from assuming the identity of the Episcopal Diocese.[274] On 11 October, Goodstein announced in court: "'I'm not going to disturb the injunction.'"[275] The Injunction of January 23, giving the legal rights of the pre-schism diocese to DSC, remained in place indefinitely.

Church lawyers also worked for months to expand the case to include numerous individuals who had been prominent on the diocesan side during the time leading up to the schism. On 2 October, Goodstein denied Tisdale's motion of May 2, 2013, to expand the case to add as defendants twenty-three people of the pre-schism diocesan standing committee and trustees. The Judge said: "'This court finds that the individual leaders whom Defendants seek to join as Counterclaim Plaintiffs are entitled to immunity.'"[276] Moreover, she said, "'adding the additional defendants would be futile.'"[277]

Personalizing the case may have seemed "futile" to the judge, as it no doubt was to the diocesan lawyers, but it certainly was not to Tisdale and the other Church attorneys. Having failed in state court to add individuals as defendants and to charge Bishop Lawrence in Houck's federal court, at least so far, Tisdale moved to an even more aggressive stance. In a blockbuster court action that shook up the entire legal scene, Tisdale boldly accused Lawrence and several of his close allies of a conspiracy. Conspiracy can be defined as a secret movement among a group to do something unlawful or harmful. Tisdale charged that Lawrence and four others conspired to remove the Diocese of South Carolina from the Episcopal Church. This was the most serious legal charge so far against Lawrence and one that potentially could have devastating consequences for him.

On the 25th of November of 2013, Tisdale delivered two motions to Judge Goodstein, one to "join," or add, Mark Lawrence, James Lewis, Jeffrey Miller, and Paul Fuener as parties in the case.[278] The other was a thirty-seven-page rationale and explanation

---

274. "Motion Filed to Have Injunction Lifted on Use of Diocesan Name." The Episcopal Church in South Carolina, October 7, 2013, http://www.episcopalchurchsc.org/news-release-october-7-2013.html.

275. "SC Judge Rejects TEC's Request to Remove Injunction Protecting Diocesan Names and Seals." Diocese of South Carolina, October 11, 2013, http://www.diosc.com/sys/news-events/latest-news/539-sc-judge-rejects-tecs-request-to-remove-injunction-protecting-diocesan-names-and-seal. See also Hawes, Jennifer Berry, "Breakaway Group Retains Right to Use Names and Seal of Diocese of SC." The Post and Courier (Charleston, SC), October 11, 2013.

276. "Judge Denies TEC Request to Expand Lawsuit." Diocese of South Carolina, October 3, 2013, http://www.diosc.com/sys/index.php?option=com_content&view=article&id=534:judge-denies-tec-request-to-expand-lawsuit&catid=344&Itemid=75.

277. Ibid.

278. "TECSC's Notice and Motion to Join Additional Parties." State of South Carolina, County of Dorchester, In the Court of Common Pleas for the First Judicial Circuit, November 25, 2013.

for adding the four.²⁷⁹ Tisdale charged that these men had willfully acted in illegal ways to harm the Episcopal diocese. He said that in or around 2006, a cabal formed among Lawrence and the members of the diocesan standing committee and bishop's search committee "to withdraw the Diocese from The Episcopal Church in return for their votes electing him Bishop of the Diocese."²⁸⁰ This was, in other words, a *quid pro quo*, or exchange of one favor for another. The ruling clique would make Lawrence bishop. In return he would grant them their wish of separation from the Episcopal Church. Moreover, Lawrence's ordination vows were fraudulent: "Lawrence made false assurances orally and in writing that he would conform to the doctrine, discipline, and worship of The Episcopal Church."²⁸¹ In addition, in or around 2009, these four parties "began executing a conspiracy to take away the Diocese's assets and deprive Episcopalians loyal to The Episcopal Church of their property rights by manipulating the Diocese's corporate entity and The Trustees."²⁸² Tisdale asserted that time and again, this group had acted *ultra vires*, that is, beyond the law, most notably in issuing the illegal quit claim deeds to the local parishes. Tisdale concluded by asking, essentially, for the court to recognize these acts as illegal and to restore the Episcopal Church parties as the legitimate authorities of the Episcopal Diocese of South Carolina.²⁸³

To bolster his sweeping charge and influence the judge to accept it, Tisdale submitted another bombshell to Goodstein. On 18 December 2013, he produced an affidavit of the Rev. Thomas M. Rickenbaker, made that day, affirming the charge of conspiracy.²⁸⁴ Rickenbaker said that when he was a priest in Edenton, North Carolina, in or around 2005, he was approached by the Rev. Greg Kronz, head of the bishop's search committee, and the Rev. Paul Fuener, a member of the committee. He said their first question to him was "'What can you do to help us leave The Episcopal Church and take out property with us?'"²⁸⁵ He went on that Fuener said, "'We are looking for a bishop who will or is willing to lead us out of the Episcopal Church and take our property with us.'"²⁸⁶ Rickenbaker said he told the two he was not interested in such. This abruptly ended his part in the

---

279. "TECSC's Claims Against Additional Parties." State of South Carolina, County of Dorchester, In the Court of Common Pleas for the First Judicial Circuit, November 25, 2013.

280. Ibid., 3.

281. Ibid.

282. Ibid.

283. For comments on Tisdale's legal action regarding conspiracy see: Hawes, Jennifer Berry, "Episcopal Church in SC Claims Breakaway Leaders Conspired to Leave National Church." *The Post and Courier* (Charleston, SC), November 26, 2013. For the Church side: "Actions Taken to 'Withdraw' from the Episcopal Church Violated State Laws, According to New Motion." The Episcopal Church in South Carolina, November 25, 2013, http://www.episcopalchurchsc.org/news-release-november-25-2013.html.; and "Courtroom Shocker!" South Carolina Episcopalians, November 25, 2013, http://www.scepiscopalians.com/2013_News.html. For the diocesan side: "Rump Diocese Tries 'Hail Mary' Pass in South Carolina." Anglican Curmudgeon, November 26, 2013, http://accurmudgeon.blogspot.com/2013/11/rump-diocese-tries-hail-mary-pass-in.html.

284. "Affidavit of Thomas M. Rickenbaker."

285. Ibid.

286. Ibid.

search. Shortly after Rickenbaker's statement, Fuener denied his account: "'I am confident that his recollection of our interview is seriously in error, if not worse.'"[287]

Apparently, Tisdale tried as hard as he could to turn the court proceedings into a trial about conspiracy. On 27 December of 2013, he presented to Judge Goodstein a fourth legal paper pressing the matter, this one an argument in support of his motion of 25 November.[288] Once again, Tisdale argued mainly that the four parties' actions were *ultra vires*. Alan Runyan and his team were certainly not going to let Tisdale's stunning charges go unanswered. On 30 December 2013, they submitted to Judge Goodstein, their official response.[289] It ridiculed Tisdale's arguments, e.g., "pounding the table," and suggested ulterior motives, e.g., "stalling the progress of this case."[290] On the same day as Runyan's response, Judge Goodstein held a hearing in her courtroom summarily dismissing Tisdale's motion to join the four parties, and denying two other motions of Tisdale's to boot. She said, in essence, that the four had already been charged as part of the larger group.[291]

The failure on Tisdale's part was not from want of trying. Despite the Judge's rebuff of 30 December, attorney Tisdale kept pressing his attempt to make the state case personal, all to no avail. On May 16, 2014, Judge Goodstein issued an order denying his motion to join the four individual parties to the case.[292] Tisdale then entered a motion before Goodstein for a reconsideration of her order. A few days later, on 6 June, she officially denied his request.[293] A couple of weeks after that, Tisdale appealed Goodstein's order of denial to the South Carolina Court of Appeals.[294] The Appeals Court summarily dismissed Tisdale's appeal as not immediately appealable and added that the circuit court could proceed immediately with the trial.[295] This ended Tisdale's efforts to charge Lawrence, and others, personally in the state case. This effectively meant that the

---

287. Hawes, "Judge Impedes."

288. "TECSC's Memorandum in Support of Its Motion to Join Additional Parties." State of South Carolina, County of Dorchester, In the Court of Common Pleas for the First Judicial Circuit, December 27, 2013.

289. "Plaintiff's Response to Defendant The Episcopal Church in South Carolina's Notice and Motion to Join Additional Parties." State of South Carolina, County of Dorchester, In the Court of Common Pleas for the First Judicial Circuit, December 30, 2013.

290. Ibid.

291. "Affidavit Shows Long-Held Plan to Leave The Episcopal Church." The Episcopal Church in South Carolina, December 30, 2013, http://www.episcopalchurchsc.org/news-release-december-30-2013.html.; and "Diocese of South Carolina Wins Again Against Episcopal Church." Diocese of South Carolina, December 31, 2013, http://www.diosc.com/sys/index.php?view=article&catid=1:latest-news&id=548:diocese.

292. "Order Denying TECSC's Motion to Join Additional Parties." State of South Carolina, County of Dorchester, In the Court of Common Pleas for the First Judicial Circuit, May 16, 2014.

293. "Order Denying TECSC's Motion to Reconsider the May 20, 2014 Order Denying TECSC's Motion to Join Additional Parties." State of South Carolina, County of Dorchester, In the Court of Common Pleas for the First Judicial Circuit, June 6, 2014.

294. "Notice of Appeal." The State of South Carolina in The Court of Appeals, Appeal from Dorchester County Court of Common Pleas, June 23, 2014.

295. "Order." The State of South Carolina in The Court of Appeals, July 3, 2014.

litigation in state court would proceed only as an institutional conflict, the independent diocese on one side and the Episcopal Church and its diocese on the other.

At the same time as Tisdale worked tirelessly, and ultimately unsuccessfully, to expand the case to include certain individuals, he also worked tirelessly, and ultimately unsuccessfully, to obtain the correspondence between Bishop Lawrence and attorney Alan Runyan. Lawrence's official diary listed numerous phone calls between himself and Runyan, perhaps more than with anyone else beyond his immediate staff with the possible exception of Kendall Harmon. It was the collection of emails between Runyan and Lawrence that Tisdale wanted, some one thousand. Runyan, however, refused to hand over the emails claiming attorney-client privilege. As with the campaign to add the individuals to the case, Tisdale entered into another year-long, and equally bruising fight to secure the emails in questions. These documents could be, obviously, crucial evidence in this case.

As with the individuals, Tisdale worked as hard as he could to get the emails, only to be blocked once again on every turn. Tisdale first requested the emails on March 27, 2013. Runyan refused but did produce a log of the emails numbering about one thousand.[296] On 19 September 2013, Tisdale entered a motion in Goodstein's court to compel Runyan to release all correspondence, including emails, between Lawrence and Runyan before November 17, 2012, concerning the relationship between the Diocese and the Episcopal Church. On 18 November 2013, Goodstein issued an order denying the motion on the grounds of attorney-client privilege.[297] Tisdale asked Goodstein to reconsider her decision, but on 31 December she dismissed that too. Two weeks later, on 13 January 2014, Tisdale appealed Goodstein's denial to the state Court of Appeals.[298] The diocesan lawyers countered by asking the appeals court to dismiss Tisdale's petition. Then, soon after that, Runayn et al. decided to go over the head of the appeals court and straight to the state Supreme Court to take over the appeal. On 7 February 2014, they asked the state's highest court to assume jurisdiction of the appeal thereby bypassing the mid-level state appeals court. Tisdale did not oppose this action.

Awaiting a reply from the South Carolina Supreme Court, the appeals court proceeded to issue a decision. On 18 March 2014, it dismissed Tisdale's appeal as not immediately appealable.[299] Tisdale quickly asked the appeals court for a rehearing.[300] A few days after that, the state Supreme Court entered the picture and issued its answer to Runyan's request to the Court of 7 February. On 4 April 2014, it announced it would indeed assume jurisdiction over the appeals.[301] At that time, the only pending action in

---

296. "The Episcopal Church in South Carolina's Return to Motion to Dismiss Appeal." The State of South Carolina in The Court of Appeals, January 24, 2014.

297. "Order Denying the Defendant TECSC's Motion to Compel Dates September 19, 2013." State of South Carolina, County of Dorchester, In the Court of Common Pleas for the First Judicial Circuit, November 7, 2013.

298. "Notice of Appeal." The State of South Carolina in The Court of Appeals, January 13, 2014.

299. "Order." The State of South Carolina in The Court of Appeals, March 18, 2014.

300. "The Episcopal Church in South Carolina's Petition for Rehearing of the Order Dismissing the Appeal." The State of South Carolina in The Court of Appeals, March 25, 2014.

301. "Order." The Supreme Court of South Carolina, April 4, 2014.

the appeals court was Tisdale's petition for a rehearing of the court's denial. Finally, on 7 May 2014, the state Supreme Court issued a brief order denying Tisdale's petition without explanation.[302] Interestingly enough, the order was signed by four of the five justices who would later hold the hearing in this court on the Church case: Jean Toal, Costa Pleicones, John Kittredge, and Kaye Hearn. This ended Tisdale's ultimately unsuccessful quest for the thousand emails between Runyan and Lawrence. As in the matter of joining the individuals to the case, Tisdale was frustrated on every turn in trying to obtain the crucial evidence in the treasure trove of emails between Lawrence and Runyan, in this case by the circuit court, the appeals court, and the state supreme court. If he were discouraged by all this, he did not reveal it.

The preparation process for the great circuit court battle between the two rival dioceses encountered other delays. Judge Goodstein had originally planned to have the lawyers finish their preparations by February of 2014, and hold the trial soon thereafter. However, the complications of the numerous motions, countermotions and appeals on both sides forced extensions in the original schedule. Nevertheless, by the end of 2013, Judge Goodstein had set time for the trial in July of 2014. Even this was not certain, however, because of the pending appeals to the appeals court and the state supreme court in early 2014. Trial could not begin until all extraneous issues were settled on both sides.

In early 2014, the biggest issue complicating matters was the taking on depositions, or individuals' sworn testimonies that could be entered as evidence in the trial. Both camps of lawyers planned to take numerous depositions from the principal figures on the other side. The taking of depositions itself became a problem in light of the appeals that were going on in early 2014. On March 18, 2014, the diocesan lawyers issued subpoenas for fourteen people on the Church side to make depositions in April and early May.[303] They were: Holly Behre, the communications officer of the Church diocese; Melinda Lucka, the leader of the complaint to the Disciplinary Board for Bishops; Robert Black, the husband of Melinda Lucka; Bishop John C. Buchanan, an advisor to the reorganizing Church diocese; Lonnie Hamilton III, a leader in the transition; George M. Hearn, Jr.; Bishop Dorsey Henderson, the head of the Disciplinary Board for Bishops; Presiding Bishop Katharine Jefferts Schori; Barbara Mann, a leader of the Forum and the transition; Steve Skardon, the pro-Church blogger; James E. Taylor, a clerical leader of the transition; Bishop Charles G. vonRosenberg; Callie Walpole, a leader of the transition and now archdeacon of the Church diocese; and Michael Wright, a leader of the transition and rector of Grace Church of Charleston. Most of these choices were self-evident and their testimonies would be of obvious importance. The choice of one, however, raised a lot of eyebrows and questions, George Hearn. Hearn and his wife Kaye Hearn were members of the loyalist Episcopalian contingent in Conway. More importantly, Kaye Hearn was one of the five justices on the South Carolina Supreme Court. Inevitably, she would sit in judgment on the church case. George Hearn had been neither a leader in the reorganization of the Church diocese nor an officer in it. The wisdom of DSC lawyers subpoenaing the husband of a supreme court justice, and a man who had

---

302. "Order." The Supreme Court of South Carolina, May 7, 2014.

303. "TECSC's Notice and Motion for Immediate Hearing." State of South Carolina, County of Dorchester, In the Court of Common Pleas for the First Judicial Circuit, April 8, 2014.

no discernable role in the schism, eluded many people. The Church lawyers too took many depositions, the most important of which was that of Bishop Lawrence. It was entered as evidence in the trial.

Judge Goodstein set a date for the trial to begin on July 7, 2014. Given the number of depositions both sides wanted to take and the off and on timing of the depositions during the appeals of early 2014, the Church lawyers asked the judge to postpone the start of the trial. On May 21, 2014, they entered a motion before Goodstein for a "continuance," or delay of the start date.[304] On July 2, the diocesan lawyers submitted their counter argument to deny the motion for continuance.[305] The next day, Judge Goodstein issued an order for the trial to begin as scheduled on July 7. On that very day, attorneys Tisdale and Smith rushed to the state appeals court a request for that court to overrule Goodstein.[306] On the same day, the appeals court denied their request and directed the circuit court to proceed with the trial immediately.[307] Judge Goodstein did allow the Church lawyers an extra day. She ruled that the trial would begin on July 8.

At long last, on July 3, the trial was finally set, once and for all, to start in five days. Both sides entered the last-minute phase of preparation and prayer. Bishop Lawrence sent a pastoral letter to be read in all of his churches on Sunday, July 6. He reminded them of why the diocese was going to court: "The path that has brought us as a diocese to this hour has been long and winding. Yet through it all we have been guided by a desire to be faithful to the doctrine, discipline and worship of Christ as we have received it ever striving to be mindful that we have been entrusted with this Truth."[308] This time Lawrence did not refer to the opposition as "the spiritual forces of evil" as he had done in the defense fund letter of 2013. Instead, he adapted an earlier prayer of the Rev. John Barr: "Enable us to bless and not curse those on the other side of this conflict."[309]

The preparation for the circuit court trial took a year and a half. The two sides handled the preparation period differently. The diocesan side sought to get the trial as soon as possible on the terms of the original lawsuit which they had brought on January 4, 2013. They struggled all the while to prevent the other side from changing the nature of the original suit. The Church lawyers, on the other hand, tried various maneuvers to avoid the circuit court or at least to give themselves a stronger hand in that court. They sought to get the case moved to federal court only to be rebuffed by the federal judge. They opened a second front in the legal war by having vonRosenberg sue Lawrence, but that suit only languished in the various federal courts. The Church attorneys also tried to make Lawrence and several of his allies parties of the circuit court case but they failed

---

304. "Plaintiffs Response to the Episcopal Church's Motion for Continuance." State of South Carolina, County of Dorchester, In the Court of Common Pleas for the First Judicial Circuit, July 2, 2014, 7.

305. Ibid.

306. "Petition for Supersedeas Relief with Request for Expedited Decision." The State of South Carolina in The Court of Appeals, July 3, 2014.

307. "Order." (. . .) July 3, 2014.

308. "A Pastoral Letter from Bishop Lawrence Regarding Upcoming Trial." Diocese of South Carolina, July 6, 2014, http://www.diosc.com/sys/news-events/latest-news/589-a-pastoral-letter-regarding-trial-from-bishop-lawrence.

309. Ibid.

in that too. Tisdale fought hard to obtain the thousand emails between Lawrence and Runyan but was turned away on that as well. The Church lawyers even failed to get the court date moved back.

Judge Goodstein denied most of the requests of the Church lawyers in the year and a half of preparation. On the other hand, she gave Runyan and his cohorts most of what they requested in this time. On the eve of the trial, the diocesan lawyers could rest confident that they held the commanding high ground of the battlefield. Their original lawsuit finally did come to trial unchanged. In fact, along the way the diocesan lawyers strengthened their hand such as in obtaining the Injunction in which the court unilaterally gave de facto recognition of the essential claim of the suit, that the independent diocese was the legal continuation of the pre-schism diocese. On the morning of Tuesday, July 8, 2014, Runyan and his team had every reason to feel confident while Tisdale and his side had every reason to feel anxiety as they traveled to the little town of St. George to begin the long-awaited showdown between the two competing dioceses.

The Circuit Court Trial, July 8–25, 2014

When Judge Diane Goodstein took the bench in the courtroom of the Dorchester County courthouse on that sultry summer day, the room was packed with lawyers, clergy, and spectators. The two bishops sat on opposite sides surrounded by their teams of attorneys. Bishop Lawrence was flanked by thirty-three lawyers representing the diocese and the individual parishes. The head of this large team was Alan Runyan who was to direct the presentation of the diocesan case. With Runyan was his fellow attorney Andrew Platte, Goodstein's former clerk. Another notable lawyer who was to participate a great deal in this trial was Henrietta Golding, of the McNair Law Firm of Myrtle Beach. In this context, she was perhaps best known as the attorney who had represented the secessionist congregation of All Saints of Pawleys Island all the way to its stunningly successful conclusion in the state supreme court in 2009. Bishop vonRosenberg was accompanied by seven lawyers, four for the Episcopal Church, and three for the Church diocese. Thomas Tisdale was the lead for the local diocese while David Booth Beers and Mary E. Kostel were prominent for the Church. In all, forty attorneys crowded the front of the room.

For the next fourteen days, each team of attorneys tried to steer the trial in the path of its own interests. The diocesan lawyers wanted the case to be conducted strictly under "neutral principles" where the two sides would be regarded as equal under state law, and to make the dispute one about corporate rights and property. This meant the case had to be interpreted as essentially secular rather than religious. They insisted the Diocese of South Carolina had always been an independent and self-governing entity fully protected by the state laws on corporations and property ownership. If they could succeed in establishing these as the parameters for the court, they were likely to prevail in the judge's eventual decision.

On the contrary, the Church lawyers tried to make the case that this was essentially a religious dispute. They insisted that the diocese was a dependent part of a larger national church. They said the First Amendment to the U.S. Constitution prevented a secular court from interfering in the internal workings of a religious institution. The

Episcopal Church must be left alone to settle its own internal dispute. They asserted, therefore, that the court should defer to the religious body even if the court adhered to neutral principles. If they could succeed in establishing these points as the parameters for the court, they were likely to prevail.

What all this came down to was whether the Episcopal Church was an hierarchical institution. Regardless of neutral principles, the judge would have to decide whether the Church was an hierarchy, that is, ruled from the top down. Was the Diocese of South Carolina a dependent part of a large institution or an independent entity? If dependent, the weight of decision would be on the Church side. If independent, the power would be on the local diocesan part. Thus, what was happening in South Carolina was nothing new. It had been the same fundamental issue in all the earlier court cases that came out of the first four movements of dioceses to leave the Episcopal Church with the property in hand.

The circuit court trial in St. George, South Carolina, went through three phases. On days one to six, July 8–14, the Diocese of South Carolina and the individual parishes produced their case and witnesses. On days six to twelve, July 15 to 23, the Episcopal Church and the Church diocese, made their arguments and presented their witnesses. The last phase, days thirteen and fourteen, July 24 and 25, was a time of rebuttal and conclusion.

In the first phase, days one to six, Runyan's team essentially tried to demonstrate that the diocese and parishes were self-governing entities independent of the Episcopal Church. They did this by keeping the focus almost entirely on the rights of corporations and property ownership. Early in the trial the Church lawyers put this to the test. On the second day of the trial, the Episcopal Church's lead lawyer, Beers, tried to move the subject to the religious nature of the dispute. Beers asked witness Rev. James Lewis, assistant to Bishop Lawrence, about a statement in a resolution passed by the special diocesan convention of 17 November 2012, holding that actions by the leadership and General Convention of the Episcopal Church were "repugnant to the plain teaching of scripture."[310] Beers asked Lewis to describe what actions of the General Convention were contrary to the teachings of scripture. When Lewis began to answer, he was interrupted by Runyan who protested to the judge: "He's asking him about religious beliefs, which just simply don't belong here."[311] Beers went on, "there is a doctrinal dispute here, and there is a dispute over the governance and polity of the Episcopal Church that the Court is going to, in our view, will have to wrestle with, and that's why we're trying to get the facts out."[312] Judge Goodstein overruled Beers: "The determinations that I will make (. . .) will be on the basis of, as you say, corporate governance, our corporate law, and not with regards to the ecclesiastic or doctrinal beliefs."[313] Beers, however, was not through making his point: "in disputes of this kind this Court is required by the First Amendment to defer to decisions made by the national church, even as they affect the property of the church."[314] As a parting shot, he told Goodstein: "this is a profound breach, a profound

---

310. "Transcript of Record," State of South Carolina (. . .) July 8–25, 2014, July 9, 2014, Vol. II, 253.
311. Ibid., 254.
312. Ibid., 255.
313. Ibid., 256.
314. Ibid., 257.

moment in the course of this litigation."[315] Goodstein ruled any testimony from Lewis on religious beliefs would be irrelevant. This exchange made it clear that the Church lawyers would be left to fight on the opposition's ground.

Now in firm control of the battlefield, Runyan et al. paraded in forty witnesses to testify for their side. First they presented three speaking for the diocese, Wade Logan, the diocesan chancellor, the Rev. James Lewis, and Robert M. Kunes, a lawyer representing the diocesan Board of Trustees. They emphasized the independence of the diocese and the propriety of its actions regarding corporate and property matters.

Once the diocesan witnesses were through, Runyan et al. brought in thirty-seven spokespersons for the parishes that were parties in the lawsuit, a mixture of clergy and lay people. It quickly became obvious that the parish representatives were prepared to follow a pre-set agenda on the stand. This "Ground Hog Day" pattern soon became tiresome. First the person was sworn in, then he or she described their role in the parish, produced documents relating to corporate and property law, described the corporate changes made in the schism, presented what turned out to be a uniform resolution passed by the seceding parishes called "Commitment to Continue Diocesan Relationship," which apparently had been urged on them by the diocese at the time of the schism, claimed that the parish owned the property, and denied that the parish had had any dealings with the Episcopal Church.[316] The last point caused the witnesses to stretch far, sometimes to humorous lengths. How could an Episcopal church claim not to be an Episcopal church? What about church names, advertisements, signs, symbols, flags, General Conventions, pension funds, and the like? Perhaps a little frustrated by the Church lawyers' relentless jabbing along this line, the witness for St. Bartholomew's of Hartsville declared: "We don't believe we were ever connected to the Episcopal Church."[317] The spokesperson on the stand for St. Michael's of Charleston offered in all seriousness: "St. Michael's has never been a member of the national Episcopal Church."[318] Perhaps to emphasize her point, she added without a hint of irony: "I don't know that anyone in leadership at St. Michael's even has read the canons and constitution of the national church."[319] The witnesses seemed to agree that Bishop Lawrence had been mistreated by the Episcopal Church. After thirty-seven repetitions of essentially the same points, the court certainly got the message the lawyers were making. Actually, the diocesan lawyers were not through presenting their witnesses. On the last two days of the trial they brought in their last five witnesses, with the very last being Bishop Lawrence.

Outside of the occasional eyebrow-raising and unintendedly humorous exaggerations of some of the witnesses, most of the diocesan testimony was unexciting, often uninteresting. There were, however, a couple of significant revelations in the testimony that were certainly of interest. When the senior warden of St. John's of Florence was on the stand, she was asked about the existence of the Douglas Trust. This was the trust of

---

315. Ibid.

316. "Reports from the Trial in the Circuit Court in Dorchester County." The Episcopal Church in South Carolina, July 11, 2014, http://www.episcopalchurchsc.org/july-2014-trial-in-state-court.html.

317. "Transcript of Record," July 11, 2014, Vol. IV, 782.

318. Ibid., July 14, 2014, Vol. V, 999.

319. Ibid., 1006.

William Douglas, then valued at $2,700,000. The Trust stipulated that St. John's would be a beneficiary so long as it remained an Episcopal Church in communion with the Church of England. Apparently, St. John's continued to take money from the Trust after the schism. The witness said she believed St. John's was in communion with the Church of England because her rector and bishop had told her so.[320] In fact, when St. John's voted to leave the Episcopal Church it also left the Anglican Communion and communion with the Church of England and the Archbishop of Canterbury.

Another surprise from the stand caused everyone to take notice. This one involved the Church of the Good Shepherd in West Ashley, Charleston, and appeared in the cross-examination of the church's rector, the Rev. Samuel Porcher Gaillard, IV. As it turned out, the deed from the landholder in 1996 giving the property to the church stipulated that the church agreed to be subject to the constitution and canons of the Episcopal Church.[321]

The first five and a half days of the trial were mostly humdrum. Witnesses came and went quickly, with as many as thirteen in one day. There was remarkably little in the way of interruptions or objections, or challenges. This was the first phase in which the diocesan side made its case and brought in its witnesses to take the stand.

On day six, all of this changed. The second phase of the trial was the turn of the Episcopal Church and the Episcopal Church in South Carolina to make their case and to bring in their witnesses. In contrast to the first phase, days six to twelve of the trial were to be remarkably tumultuous. The highest number of witnesses presented on any one day was four. On two days, only one witnesses took the stand. One day, a witness, Robert Klein was disqualified from testifying.[322] Interruptions, objections, questions, disagreements, delays became the order of the day. This was particularly true for three witnesses, Armand G. Derfner, Martin C. McWilliams, and Walter Edgar.

The first witness called by the Church side was Armand Derfner, a highly-credentialed specialist in constitutional law, particularly in the First Amendment. The trial transcript showed that during attorney Tisdale's questioning of Derfner, Runyan interrupted 11 times, his colleagues Golding broke in 2 times, and Andrew Platte 5 times. The judge herself spoke 59 times during the testimony.[323] This was mild compared to what happened during Martin McWilliams's testimony on day seven. McWilliams was a professor in the University of South Carolina law school and an expert in South Carolina corporate law. During the Church's questioning of McWilliams, the transcript showed that Golding spoke out 62 times making 19 formal objections.[324] The judge overruled not one of these. Runyan broke in 24 times making 6 objections, only one of which the judge overruled. During McWilliams's time on the stand, Judge Goodstein spoke 141 times. It was no wonder that he was the only witness that day. He did get to give his opinion that the diocesan bishop and officers had not followed corporate law and that the purported change in the corporation's charter in 2010 was invalid.[325]

320. Ibid., July 10, 2014, Vol. III, 678.
321. Ibid., July 14, 2014, Vol. V, 962.
322. Ibid., July 17, 2014, Vol. VIII, 1518.
323. Ibid., July 15, 2014, Vol. VI, 1241–67.
324. Ibid., July 16, 2014, Vol. VII, 1338–428.
325. Ibid., 1351–52.

Two Dioceses, 2013 and After

Then there was the case of Walter Edgar, the renowned dean of the historians of South Carolina. On day ten, he was the sole witness. He took the stand at 10:20 a.m. ready to go into detail about the long historical tie between the diocese and the Episcopal Church. He actually started testifying in earnest at 1:45.[326] Until then, the two sides of lawyers and the judge discussed at length just how far the witness could go into the relationship between the Church and the diocese. Edgar started out as a "factual" witness. Right away, Runyan reminded the court that as a fact witness, "He cannot offer opinion testimony."[327] Then, Tisdale offered him as an "expert" witness and therefore allowed to give opinion. However, the court blocked this relegating the leading historian of South Carolina to "factual" witness status. Shortly thereafter, Judge Goodstein cut off any potential discussion of hierarchy: "What I don't want—and if he's being offered for the proposition of hierarchical, let's play like he did that because I don't want to hear it because I've got that. You all know I've got that and where I am about that. I don't want to hear it."[328] Although he was subjected to numerous interruptions, Edgar did succeed in giving several hours of compelling testimony giving specific and relevant details of the history of the Diocese of South Carolina.

Amid, or perhaps in spite of, the numerous disruptions and limitations on testimony in the second phase, this part of the trial was notable for several points. On the Church side, the testimonies of the Revs. Dow Sanderson[329] and Thomas Rickenbaker[330] substantiated the theory of a conspiracy between the anti-Church party in the diocese and Mark Lawrence to exchange the office of bishop for diocesan secession from the Episcopal Church with property in hand. Rickenbaker was not present in the courtroom but his deposition was read aloud. On the diocesan side, Runyan did an effective job in pressing a strict construction approach to the Church's Constitution and Canons showing that they that lacked an explicit supremacy clause giving the Church authority over the dioceses and a non-secession clause. In one dramatic moment, when Bishop Clifton Daniel was on the stand, Runyan handed him a copy of the Episcopal Church Constitution and Canons and asked him to find to find the place where they said a diocese could not withdraw from the Church. Daniel said he could not find such a place.[331]

As interesting as the second phase of the trial was in courtroom drama, it was nothing compared to the third, and final phase, the last two days. Runyan and his team had done an impressive job of dominating the entire proceedings so far, but it was in the last two days that their brilliance really came through even though it may not have been recognized at the time. On the next to the last day, with the Church side's witnesses finished, the diocesan lawyers returned to presenting their last group of witnesses. They called to the stand as an expert witness, Allen C. Guelzo, a noted historian and writer on church history at Gettysburg College, the Rev. Robert Lawrence, the director of Camp St.

---

326. July 21, 2014 (Day 10)." The Episcopal Church in South Carolina, July 22, 2014, http://www.episcopalchurchsc.org/july-2014-trial-in-state-court.html.

327. "Transcript of Record," July 21, 2014, Vol. X, 1765.

328. Ibid., 1796.

329. Ibid., July 15, 2014, Vol. VI, 1312–13.

330. Ibid., July 22, 2014, Vol. XI, 2042–64.

331. Ibid., July 18, 2014, Vol. IX, 1737–38.

Christopher, Wade Logan, the chancellor who had testified on the first day, and Nancy Armstrong, the diocesan assistant treasurer. Apparently, Guelzo was there to rebut Walter Edgar's testimony for the Church side. Throughout the trial, the diocesan lawyers had made a major point was that this was a secular case to be decided on corporate and property laws under neutral principles. Judge Goodstein had repeated many times that under neutral principles she had to avoid the question of hierarchy because that was a religious matter. However, when Guelzo got on the stand, Runyan asked him, "Dr. Guelzo, is the Episcopal Church organized in a hierarchical religious structure?" Guelzo answered, "No."[332] Two Church lawyers immediately sprang to their feet to object. Then followed a long discussion between the Church lawyers and the judge about the hierarchical issue. Finally, Runyan said he would restate the question. He said, "Dr. Guelzo, is the Episcopal Church organized in such a fashion that its governance controls the dioceses and the parishes." Answer, "No."[333] After the court had avoided the issue of hierarchy for twelve days, Runyan succeeded in injecting testimony that the Episcopal Church was not hierarchical.

As the conduct of the long trial began to tire toward its end, tensions arose and broke open in the testimony of the second witness on the thirteenth day, Wade Logan. Mary Kostel, a lawyer for the Church, and Judge Goodstein had a contretemps over the appropriateness of a document being presented by attorney Golding, the certificate of abandonment made by the Disciplinary Board for Bishops against Bishop Lawrence. Goodstein finally burst out at Kostel. According to one eyewitness account: "The judge's face became beet red. Goodstein then focused her eyes squarely on Kostel, rose up in her chair, and shrieked at the astonished lawyer, threatening to have her sanctioned and removed from the courtroom."[334] At that, "Goodstein then abruptly spun around in her chair and bolted out of the courtroom, slamming the door in her wake.[335] "After about five minutes, the still agitated judge returned to the stunned courtroom, loudly closing the door and slamming her papers on the desk. 'Let me see that exhibit,' she snapped. The courtroom froze as she took a few moments to review the certificate."[336] She then told Golding to proceed with the questioning. A shaken Kostel dropped the matter. Goodstein soon announced that she had a commitment at 2:00 p.m.; the court adjourned at lunch to reconvene the next day.

The next day was the fourteenth, and last, day of the trial. The diocesan lawyers had reserved as their only witness of the day, Bishop Lawrence. If one expected the great fireworks of the trial to burst out in the star witness's testimony, he was to be disappointed. The pent-up emotions had exploded the day before. After that, everyone involved seemed only exhausted and ready to wrap it up and leave. For the most part, Lawrence's testimony on the stand was unremarkable. The opposition lawyers allowed him to speak freely, raising only two objections, one of which they withdrew. On cross-examination,

332. Ibid., July 24, 2014, Vol. XIII, 2336.

333. Ibid., 2342.

334. "Day 13: Enraged Judge Goes Ballistic, Threatens Church Attorney, the Storms Out of her own Courtroom." South Carolina Episcopalians, July 24, 2014, http://www.scepiscopalians.com/2014.php.

335. Ibid.

336. Ibid.

Church attorney Beers had only a few questions, and Tisdale none. There were several interesting points that Lawrence made. One time he was asked "Did you intend to take the Diocese of South Carolina out of the Episcopal Church?" He answered, "No."[337] Another time he was asked if he had been served with a signed restriction of ministry and with a certificate of abandonment with its attachments. He answered in the negative.[338]

Everything seemed to be going along smoothly as Lawrence was finishing his testimony and the court was preparing momentarily to close the trial when suddenly, and seemingly out of the blue, Runyan raised the issue that the Church's efforts to remove Lawrence as bishop may have been the result of collusion or fraud on the Church's part.[339] Church lawyers immediately protested to the judge that this issue had not been introduced before and if it were to be injected into the proceedings, it would require virtually a whole new trial to resolve. When Judge Goodstein seemed to agree, Runyan apparently realized the implication of his raising the issue and tried to back down and withdraw it.[340] Judge Goodstein, however, was not so quick to drop the matter. "When you raise the issue of fraud and collusion, my ears perk up," she told Runyan.[341] This led Goodstein into a question that was really at the heart of the Church's case, whether Lawrence had the authority to act as the bishop of the diocese after his open renunciation of November 17, 2012. She asked Runyan: "Are there any documents that were executed or actions that were taken on November the 17th, 2012, or beyond that you believe have an effect on your argument that the diocese could and did end its accession with the national church?"[342] At that point, the diocesan lawyers' entire case teetered on the edge of derailment. Runyan must have realized this and quickly changed the subject to emphasize to the judge again, essentially what he had been saying for thirteen days, that the diocese was always an independent and self-governing entity. Therefore, it did not matter what measures the national church took in regard to the diocese. Runyan withdrew the question that had started the whole brouhaha. That was the end of that. What actually happened was that Runyan had introduced the idea that Lawrence had been the victim of Episcopal Church officers' fraud and collusion without having to present evidence or to defend it against the other side. As it turned out, it was a risky maneuver because it came close to exploding the whole trial which, so far, the diocesan lawyers had nearly perfectly conducted with almost certain victory within their grasp. At any rate, Runyan again showed his courtroom brilliance. He had made three master stokes in the last two days, getting in the record testimony from an expert that the Episcopal Church was not hierarchical, injecting the idea, or at least suspicion, that Lawrence had been the victim of fraud, and presenting the most anticipated witness, Bishop Lawrence, to give testimony that went virtually unchallenged by the other side. It was as strong a finish for the diocesan side as anyone could have imagined.

337. "Transcript of Record," July 25, 2014, Vol. XIV, 2446.
338. Ibid., 2454.
339. Ibid., 2476.
340. Ibid., 2477–78.
341. Ibid., 2478.
342. Ibid., 2479.

After briefly teetering on the edge, the trial stayed on course after all. Shortly after Runyan introduced and then withdrew the issue of fraud, Judge Goodstein finally ended the trial on July 25, 2014, as she told the assembled lawyers: "And it has been one of the joys of my life to have spent this time with you, and I look forward to the study and the review that I get to embark upon, and I'll miss you while I do it."[343] With that the judge gaveled the end of the circuit court trial in the case of the Diocese of South Carolina and its parishes against the Episcopal Church and the Episcopal Church in South Carolina.

Even though the circuit court trial approached nowhere near its potential to be the great debate on the monumental issues at hand, it still produced a massive amount of legal work. In the course of the fourteen days, there were 61 witnesses to take the stand and 1,342 pieces of evidence to be entered into the record. The transcript of the trial eventually reached 2,523 pages. And, since there was no jury, all this massive amount of material would have to be judged by one person, Judge Diane Goodstein. In the end, she alone would make the entire decision determining the outcome of the trial.

When Judge Goodstein did issue her opinion six months later, on February 3, 2015, no one could have been surprised that she found entirely in favor of the diocese. Some people were surprised, however, at how far she went to favor the diocese. Runyan could not have asked for more. Both he and the Church lawyers submitted their "orders," or requests for judgment, to Judge Goodstein on December 10, 2014. Since these were not open to the public, we can know neither their contents nor how closely the judge may have followed Runyan's request in her decision. Goodstein handed Runyan and his fellow lawyers a sweeping and stunning victory. Only time would tell whether the public, and more importantly, the higher courts, would agree with her.

Judge Goodstein released her decision, called the "Final Order," on Tuesday, February 3, 2015 at 5:18 p.m.[344] In it, she declared that the Diocese and its parishes were the owners of the rights, property, and insignia of the old diocese and rejected all the claims of the Church side. It was a total victory for the Diocese of South Carolina. She followed exactly the arguments that Runyan and his colleagues had put forth in the trial. She claimed to follow "neutral principles" only: "When a church dispute can be completely resolved on neutral principles of law, it must be."[345] Moreover, she said the same issues were involved here as in the *All Saints* decision, corporate rights and property: "Just as in *All Saints*, the two primary legal issues here are 'church property and corporate control' (. . .). These issues can be completely resolved using neutral principles of law."[346] Goodstein assumed throughout her decision that the diocese was an autonomous entity operating under state corporate and property laws.

The fundamental issue that had to be addressed was hierarchy. Was the Episcopal Church an hierarchical institution or not? Throughout the trial, Goodstein had made a point repeatedly that she would not allow it to get into religious questions even though she permitted Guelzo to testify that the Church was not hierarchical. The Church

---

343. Ibid., 2521–22.

344. "Final Order." State of South Carolina, County of Dorchester, in the Court of Common Pleas for the First Judicial Circuit, Case No. 2013-CP-18-00013, February 3, 2015.

345. Ibid., 24.

346. Ibid.

witnesses, as Edgar, were routinely blocked from giving their opinion on the issue. In her Order, however, Goodstein solved the problem of hierarchy, at least to her satisfaction. She boldly proclaimed the Episcopal Church to be a congregational institution: "TEC is not organized in a fashion that in governance controls the Dioceses or the parish churches. Authority flows from the bottom, the parish churches, up."[347] She gave no evidence, authority, or even witness testimony to substantiate this astonishing claim.

Goodstein ruled that the Diocese of South Carolina was an autonomous and self-governing entity that had acted properly under the law. She said the Episcopal Church and its local province had no right to interfere in the internal working or the decisions of the autonomous diocese.[348] Moreover, she held that a diocese could leave the Episcopal Church at will: "The Constitution and Canons of TEC have no provisions which state that a member diocese cannot voluntarily withdraw its membership."[349] Even if there had been such a provision, the diocese could have withdrawn anyway under the principle of freedom of association. All along, Goodstein insisted that the Diocese had properly amended its corporate documents to withdraw from the Episcopal Church, e.g., "The Diocese withdrew its association from TEC in October 2012,"[350] "The Diocese clearly had the authority to amend its articles of incorporation, so the act of amending is not outside its power,"[351] and "There is no basis to claim that the Diocese did not validly exercise its legal and constitutionally-protected right to disassociate from TEC in October 2012."[352]

Goodstein also made several other sweeping judgments. As for the Dennis Canon, she dismissed any legal power it might have and made *All Saints* a blanket rule for all local church properties. Moreover, she agreed with the many parish witnesses who insisted that their churches had never been part of the Episcopal Church: "None of the Plaintiff parish churches have ever been members of TEC or TECSC."[353] As for Bishop Lawrence, Goodstein was sure he intended to be a loyal Episcopalian: "Mark Lawrence was not elected Bishop of the Diocese with the intent on either his part or on that of the Diocese to lead the Diocese out of TEC. From 2009 until October 2012, his intent was to remain 'intact and in TEC.'"[354] Also, Goodstein singled out one witness for the Church side and curiously went to considerable length to discredit him and even imply doubt about his motives. She pointed out he was a member of the Episcopal church and had been a legal advisor to the bishop of Upper South Carolina. As for his expert opinion on state corporate law, Goodstein declared: "the court finds this opinion incorrect. Mr. McWilliams' opinions lack factual support."[355]

347. Ibid., 22.
348. Ibid., 21.
349. Ibid.
350. Ibid., 14.
351. Ibid., 27.
352. Ibid., 32.
353. Ibid., 17.
354. Ibid., 14.
355. Ibid., 28.

Goodstein's decision was now part of the public record. It was a document remarkable in two ways, its profound, some might say simplistic, declarations on some highly controversial, and to many people complex and complicated issues, and its lack of strong supporting rationale and documentation, and in some cases any explanation, for these declarations. The higher judges were bound to take a long and hard look at both the decision and the way the judge had gone about reaching her decision.

Even though everyone knew Judge Goodstein's order would be appealed, it still stood as a powerful landmark in the long road of litigation. After two years of wrangling in the courts, a judge had finally handed down a definitive decision. The diocesan side had every reason to be elated, as they were. Conversely, the Church side had every reason to be disappointed and concerned for the future, as they were. Goodstein's order would stand as the law until and unless it was overturned by a higher court, at this point a dubious prospect. In an appeal, the burden of proof was always on the appellant to demonstrate why the lower ruling should be changed.

The immediate reactions to the news of the decision were remarkably subdued, perhaps because of the common expectation of the outcome. The diocese issued a low-key press release with a straightforward announcement. Absent was any hint that the other side was "evil," or that this was the work of God's will. Bishop Lawrence said simply, "'Our churches, our diocese are open to all. It's about the freedom to practice and proclaim faith in Jesus Christ as it has been handed down to us. We're ready to move forward and grateful to Judge Goodstein's handling of the case.'"[356] On the Church side, Bishop vonRosenberg tried to be philosophical as he sent out a letter reminding his flock of a long journey that may be filled with difficulties.[357] The Church diocese's lead lawyer, Thomas Tisdale, said he was not surprised by the decision and looked forward to an appeal: "'The result of the recent trial was not unexpected and road ahead in the judicial system is clear to us.'"[358]

The appeal of Goodstein's decision was certain. The next question was how well her judgments would withstand the careful scrutiny of the judges in the higher courts, the state appeals court and the state supreme court. The fate of the decision was uncertain and could take several paths. In general, the advanced judges could, on one hand uphold the decision, or on the other hand dismiss it. If rejection, they would have either to write a whole new decision or to send it back to Goodstein for re-adjudication. In the middle, they could accept parts and reject other sections of the decision. The only surety on February 3, 2015, was that the Church side would appeal.

As soon as it was clear that the Church lawyers would appeal and the legal war would escalate, the diocesan attitude changed markedly from low-key to strident. Three days after the decision, Bishop Lawrence sent a new letter calling on the faithful to

---

356. "SC Circuit Court Rules Diocese Keeps Historic Property." Diocese of South Carolina, February 3, 2015, http://www.diosc.com/sys/index.php?option=com_content&view=article&id=636:sc-circuit-court.

357. "A Pastoral Letter from Bishop vonRosenberg." The Episcopal Church in South Carolina, February 4, 2015, http://www.episcopalchurchsc.org/2015-02-05-pastoral-letter.html.

358. "Ruling Issued in Dorchester County Case." The Episcopal Church in South Carolina, February 4, 2015, http://www.episcopalchurchsc.org/news-release-febraury-4-2015.html.

prepare for the next round of legal warfare: "You may have read in the local media that the national Episcopal Church and its local diocesan representatives have already signaled their intention to appeal Judge Goodstein's ruling. So please note: There is a need for us to persevere."[359] Three times he mentioned the role of God: "Most grateful for the Mighty Hand of God throughout the whole ordeal (. . .) our God-given dreams and missions (. . .) grateful for God's grace, and seeking that God's love '*be poured into our hearts through the Holy Spirit which has been given to us.* [sic] '"[360] At the same time, the Rev. Jim Lewis, sent out a statement likewise calling on the diocese to rally for the new round of litigation: "We have every reason to be confident that South Carolina courts will continue to do so through the appeals process." As the bishop, Lewis also saw the hand of God: "It is God's grace that has brought us to this day. Legal counsel has affirmed repeatedly that they have experienced God's grace at work in this litigation from start to finish."[361]

The Church attorneys prepared for an appeal, but first had to go through the established process. Ten days after the decision was issued, they filed with Judge Goodstein the required request for a reconsideration.[362] Considering the short time period, their 182-page document was a *tour de force* that could easily be used as the model for all appeals of Goodstein's forty-six-page order. It was a detailed list of what the lawyers considered the sins of commission and omission in the judge's order. In one important point, the lawyers asked the court to declare that all property of the thirty-six parishes in question was held in trust for the Episcopal Church and the Church diocese.[363] On 23 February 2015, ten days after the Church lawyers filed their motion for reconsideration, the diocesan lawyers submitted a response answering some of the complaints.[364] A few hours later on the same day, Judge Goodstein denied the Church lawyers' motion for reconsideration.[365] This formal denial meant that the Church side then had thirty days in which to file an appeal of the February 3 order with the state court of appeals.

On 24 March 2015, Church lawyers filed a "Notice of Appeal" with the South Carolina Court of Appeals, in Columbia.[366] The paper was filed by attorney Blake Hewitt, of the law firm of Bluestein, Nichols, Thompson, Delgado, in Columbia. He was a former clerk of the state Supreme Court Chief Justice, Jean Toal, and was to be the Church's lead

---

359. Lawrence, (the Rt. Rev.) Mark. "Grateful: Bishop Lawrence Writes the Diocese Following Ruling." Diocese of South Carolina, February 6, 2015, http://www.diosc.com/sys/index.php?option=com_content&view=article&id=638:bishop-lawrence-writes-the-diocese.

360. Ibid.

361. Lewis, (the Rev.) Jim. "What It Means: Understanding Judge Goodstein's Ruling." Diocese of South Carolina, February 6, 2015, http://www.diosc.com/sys/index.php?view=article&catid=1%Alatest-news&id=637%3A.

362. "Defendants' Notice and Motion for Reconsideration of Final Order." State of South Carolina, County of Dorchester, In the Court of Common Pleas for the First Judicial Circuit, February 13, 2015.

363. Ibid., 176.

364. "Plaintiffs' Response to Defendants' Rule 59e Motion to Reconsider." State of South Carolina, County of Dorchester, In the Court of Common Pleas for the First Judicial Circuit, February 23, 2015.

365. "Order Denying Motion for Reconsideration." State of South Carolina, County of Dorchester, In the Court of Common Pleas for the First Judicial Circuit, February 23, 2015.

366. "Notice of Appeal." The State of South Carolina in The Court of Appeals, March 24, 2015.

lawyer in the hearing before the state Supreme Court. Immediately thereafter, Hewitt filed with the Supreme Court of South Carolina, in Columbia, a motion for the high court to assume the case, in other words, to bypass the appeals court.[367] Having the state Supreme Court take the appeal directly would save both parties a great deal of time and expenditure. On 15 April 2015, the Supreme Court issued an official consent to take the case directly, that is, to supersede the appeals court.[368] In its order, the Court noted that the diocesan side had filed a motion to expedite the matter and that the Church side had filed a counter motion not to expedite. The court denied the diocese's motion and ordered the hearing to be held in the supreme court on September 23, 2015, without the possibility of postponement. Thus, the date was fixed for the grand showdown in the highest court in the state. The lawyers had five months to prepare for what was likely to be the most important case they would ever present in their careers.

The Supreme Court of South Carolina

With the date for the hearing finally set for 23 September, the lawyers for both sides went to work preparing for the day. Usually, the hearing would be expected to last an hour, with each side getting equal time presenting their arguments to the assembled five justices. One side would make its case, and then the other, and perhaps a rebuttal. However, the justices could interrupt the presenting lawyer freely at any time to ask questions, request explanations, or make comments among themselves. This could take up the bulk of the time so that a lawyer might not get far in his prepared remarks. Lawyers appearing before the high court knew they had to be well prepared to promote and defend the case extemporaneously. In a usual case, the courtroom appearance required a great deal of hard work in preparation, but this was not the usual case. This one was bound to test the mind and will of any attorney.

While the teams of lawyers on both sides and the justices were busy preparing for the supreme court hearing of 23 September, an announcement suddenly appeared that caught everyone completely by surprise except those who were in on it. It was almost as astonishing as Goodstein's decision which was not at all a surprise. This announcement had the potential of blowing up the entire case and ending all the litigation that had been going on for two and a half years. It was the offer of a negotiated settlement.

On June 11, 2015, Bishop vonRosenberg sent an e-mail to the clergy and lay leaders of his diocese informing them that the Church side had made an offer of a settlement with the other side that "we and the Episcopal Church will relinquish any claim to that property of departed parishes and, in return, all the property of the diocese now claimed by those who departed will be returned to us."[369] He said the proposal had been under consideration by Episcopal Church and diocesan officials for over a year, that representatives of the mission churches had been involved, and that Presiding Bishop Jefferts

---

367. "Motion to Certify." The State of South Carolina in the Supreme Court, Appeal from Dorchester County Court of Common Pleas, March 24, 2015.

368. "Order." The Supreme Court of South Carolina, April 15, 2015.

369. vonRosenberg, (the Rt. Rev.) Charles. Email message to the clergy and lay leaders of the Episcopal Church in South Carolina, June 11, 2015.

Two Dioceses, 2013 and After

Schori had consented to it. Finally, he asked the e-mail recipients to keep this private until there was an official announcement. The e-mail was immediately leaked and the news of the offer appeared on the Internet on June 12. Word spread quickly that the Church had made a dramatic offer of a compromise settlement to end all litigation.

As it turned out what had happened was that Thomas Tisdale, the Church diocese's chancellor and lead lawyer, had sent a letter on June 1 to attorney Henry E. Grimball, who was representing St. Michael's of Charleston against the Church side. Tisdale told Grimabll he was making an offer "for the purpose of negotiating a settlement of all claims between the parties in all the pending litigation."[370] The offer was simple and straightforward. The Church and its diocese would relinquish all claims to the properties of all of the parishes involved in the lawsuit if the independent Diocese would release to the Church diocese claims to the rights, titles, and properties of the pre-schism diocese. This would mean that the Episcopal Church would be willing to recognize the independence of the parishes in the suit. In return, the secessionists would recognize the Church diocese as the legitimate Episcopal Diocese of South Carolina with all that that entailed, most notably the legal rights and outstanding assets as Camp St. Christopher, the Diocesan House on Coming Street, and financial accounts from the pre-schism diocese. In short, they would swap the parishes for the diocese. This offer was truly remarkable in numerous ways not the least of which was that the Church was willing to waive the enforcement of the Dennis Canon for the first time. On June 3, Tisdale sent letters to the attorneys for all the parishes involved making the same offer.[371] The letter gave a date for response as 15 June, or the parties might withdraw the offer.

The Episcopal Church in South Carolina made an official announcement of the offer on its website on 15 June.[372] It added a few more details. It said the internal negotiations to arrive at the offer had been going on for more than two years. A key issue was whether the local missions of the Church diocese would give up their claims to the properties held by the secessionist parishes. The report said diocesan authorities had worked with local leaders: "Most have moved ahead and created new Episcopal congregations, and gave their blessing for the settlement offer to be made."[373] Thus after lengthy negotiations, the local missions, the diocesan authorities, and Presiding Bishop Jefferts Schori were all finally in agreement that the offer be made. The announcement also said that no word had been received from the independent diocese since the offer was made on 1 June.

The deadline for response had been set in Tisdale's letter at 15 June. On that afternoon, the diocese gave its response in a posting on its website. It was a furious barrage against the officers waving the flag of truce.[374] The statement from the Rev. Jim Lewis

---

370. Tisdale, Thomas S. To Henry E. Grimball, June 1, 2015.

371. "Churches in Diocese of South Carolina Reject Episcopal Church's 'Spurious' Offer to Settle." Diocese of South Carolina, June 15, 2015, http://www.diosc.com/sys/351-communications/press-releases/664-churches-in-diocese-of-south-carolina-reject.

372. "Hoping for Reconciliation, Episcopalians Offer to Settle Lawsuit." The Episcopal Church in South Carolina, June 15, 2015, http://www.episcopalchurchsc.org/news-release-june-15-2015.html.

373. Ibid.

374. "Churches in Diocese."

flatly rejected the offer which it called "spurious," that is, false or fake. Lewis declared, "It was not a legitimate offer of good faith negotiation and never was intended to be."[375] He said the parishes had unanimously rejected the Church's offer. Lewis gave four "Reasons" for the rejection. The first was that the letter had not come from someone "with authority to bind all the parties on the Episcopal Church side."[376] The meaning of this was not clear. The second was that the letter should have gone to the Diocese's lead attorney (Runyan). If the letter went out to all lawyers representing the parishes, it went to Runyan. The third reason was that it should have been done in confidence. In fact, it was leaked to the public on June 12, three days before the deadline. The fourth reason was that it gave only fifteen days for a response, not adequate time. Thus, Lewis concluded this was not a real offer. As to the motives for this "deceitful imposter," Lewis posited four. The first he said was to disrupt the diocesan lawyers' preparation of a reply brief for the state Supreme Court that was due on June 15. The next was that the Church was trying "to create division between the Diocese, Trustees and the Parishes."[377] The third motive Lewis ascribed was publicity, that is, the Church was trying to appear reasonable and conciliatory when it really was not. The last motive, according to Lewis, may have been more revealing than he realized. He projected that the Church would lose in the state Supreme Court: "This is not an attempt to end the litigation but rather to disrupt it—and to do so when we are only one hearing away from its final conclusion."[378] Speaking more to the Diocese's motive, Lewis said, "We are part of a larger conflict in which the outcome here may significantly benefit other parishes and Dioceses wishing freedom from TEC."[379] This certainly implied that the Diocese expected to prevail in the state Supreme Court and may have suggested that the motive for the schism and for the litigation was to break up the Episcopal Church. Thus, The Diocese completely spurned the Church's offer of a settlement and even the offer to open negotiations. The "Reasons" Lewis gave were neither strong nor convincing. The tone of Lewis's press release of June 15 was that the Diocese was fully confident that Goodstein's decision would be upheld by the state Supreme Court. This was perhaps the real reason the Diocese rejected the compromise settlement to end all litigation.[380]

The two sides' preparations for the Supreme Court hearing mainly took the form of a brief presented to the Court by the Church lawyers, a counter brief from the diocesan

---

375. Ibid.
376. Ibid.
377. Ibid.
378. Ibid.
379. Ibid.

380. For reports on the Church's offer and its rejection, see: Hawes, Jennifer Berry, "Episcopal Church Makes Settlement Offer to Let Parishes Take $500 Million in Property." *The Post and Courier* (Charleston, SC), June 15, 2015; Heffernan, Ashley, "Breakaway Churches Reject Settlement from National Episcopal Church." *Charleston Regional Business Journal* (Charleston, SC), June 16, 2015, http://www.charlestonbusiness.com/news/54796-splinter-churches-refuse-offer-from-national.; "Breakaway Group Rejects Offer to Settle South Carolina Property Lawsuit." Episcopal News Service, June 15, 2015, http://episcopaldigitalnetwork.com/ens/2015/06/15/breakaway-group-rejects-offer-to-settle.; and "Lawrence 'Diocese' Rejects Settlement Offer on Behalf of Silent Parishes." South Carolina Episcopalians, June 15, 2015, http://www.scepiscopalians.com/2015_Archives.php.

lawyers, and a response from the Church side to the counter brief. These came in May and June of 2015. On 15 May 2015, Church lawyers Blake A. Hewitt and Allan R. Holmes, submitted to the Court their initial brief.[381] The fifty-one-page document laid out the framework for their presentation to the Court. They related what they saw as the errors of the circuit court trial, the issues involved, their main arguments, and their request to the court. In errors, they said the court had misused the neutral principles rule to disregard issues of church governance and hierarchy and by so doing excluded key evidence from the Church side. The issues that they put forth were basically the same as the Church side had argued from the start, this was an ecclesiastical dispute, the Episcopal Church is a hierarchy, and state laws do not allow a corporation to act in contravention to its charter at incorporation. The lawyers' primary arguments were that civil courts must defer to religious institutions, that the *All Saints* decision of 2009 was not appropriate to this case, the Dennis Canon imposed a trust, and the diocesan incorporation of 1973 explicitly bound the diocese to the Episcopal Church. The attorneys spent more space on the Dennis Canon than on any other pointing out the numerous state supreme court decisions based on it. In the end, the Church lawyers asked the Court not to reverse and remand but to make a new decision. The diocesan lawyers then had thirty days in which to make a counter brief.

Diocesan lawyers Runyan, Golding, and C. Mitchell Brown presented their fifty-nine-page counter brief to the state Supreme Court on 15 June 2015, the same day on which the diocese announced its rejection of the compromise settlement.[382] Basically, they asked the Court to expand its 2009 *All Saints* decision into this case. Chief Justice Jean Toal had written that decision; and it was expected that she would preside over the hearing in this case on 23 September. If *All Saints* were followed it would be to the advantage of the diocesan side because that decision found that the parish had revised its corporate documents properly to withdraw from the diocese and that the Dennis Canon could not be applied because the diocese had earlier issued a quit claim deed to the parish. The lawyers spent a great deal of space in their counter brief promoting the supposed precedence of the 2009 decision. They also emphasized two other points, that the recently settled Diocese of Quincy case established the legal standard that a diocese could leave the Episcopal Church and that the Dennis Canon was inoperable in South Carolina because state law required the property title holder to establish a trust. On the whole, the diocesan lawyers defended Goodstein's ruling. They said it properly followed neutral principles and overruled questions of hierarchy.

Ten days later, Church attorneys Blake and Holmes filed a response to the diocesan counter brief.[383] They asked the court to reverse Goodstein's ruling and to issue a new judgment on the case *de novo*, or anew. They asked the Court to recognize the Church diocese as the legitimate Episcopal Diocese of South Carolina and to declare the Dennis

---

381. "Initial Brief of Appellants." The State of South Carolina In the Supreme Court. Appeal from Dorchester County Court of Common Pleas, May 15, 2015.

382. "Brief of Respondents." The State of South Carolina In the Supreme Court, Appeal from Dorchester County Court of Common Pleas, June 15, 2015.

383. "Initial Reply Brief." The State of South Carolina In the Supreme Court, Appeal from Dorchester County Court of Common Pleas, June 25, 2015.

Canon to be in force. The lawyers also pointed out that Goodstein had made a sweeping judgment declaring the Episcopal Church to be congregational in structure in violation of her own stated guideline that excluded consideration of the institutional nature of the Episcopal Church. As for the Quincy case from Illinois, the lawyers dismissed its relevance to state laws in South Carolina. The lawyers renewed their pleas that the Episcopal Church was hierarchical, that neutral principles must be adjusted to this, and that the Dennis Canon established a trust.

With this, the two sides established their respective battle lines before the state's highest court. The diocese would argue that Goodstein properly followed neutral principles and that the *All Saints* decision must be the deciding precedent for this case. The Church would make the case that Goodstein's decision was so flawed in preparation and execution that it had to be discarded and replaced with an entirely new ruling, that hierarchy must be considered with neutral principles, that the diocese had violated corporate law, and that the Dennis Canon established a trust for the Church which meant that the local properties were held by the Church and the Church's diocese. Meanwhile, the five justices of the Court were busy studying the briefs, Goodstein's decision, and perhaps the mountain of documents produced by the trial.

As the two sides prepared to head for Columbia and the hearing, it would be fair to say that the diocesan side had the advantage and the momentum. If the diocesan authorities had rejected Tisdale's offer of a negotiated settlement in June because they believed they would prevail in the high court and the Church side was only acting in desperation, they had reason to hold such feelings. In the first place, at that point the cases of the first four dioceses that voted to leave the Episcopal Church had broken largely on the diocesan sides. Only in the unique case of Pittsburgh had the Episcopal Church prevailed. In the second place, the case before the Supreme Court was an appeal of a lower court order. The burden would be on the Church side to prove the inadequacies and errors in that decision. In the third place, the Court could be expected to honor its own unanimous decision in the *All Saints* case. Moreover, the author of that decision would be the head of the court to make the new ruling, and one of the attorneys who had successfully argued that case, Henrietta Golding, would be back to argue for the diocesan side. The South Carolina Supreme Court was already on record supporting local corporate rights and denying the power of the Dennis Canon. This was why the diocesan lawyers had made such a major point of pressing the *All Saints* decision in the run-up to the hearing. Apparently, they were banking on the Court simply extending the ruling in that decision to the whole diocese. It was perhaps from confidence that the diocesan office issued a call for prayers on 2 September: "Recognizing that divine favor which has overshadowed us from the beginning (. . .). Speak your words alone through Alan Runyan and the other attorneys who represent us."[384]

Although the diocese held the distinct advantage on the eve of the hearing, the Church side was not entirely without hope. The lead lawyer to present the Church case before the Court would be attorney Blake Hewitt. He was well known to the court as a

---

384. "Prayers Requested for South Carolina Supreme Court Hearing, September 23, 2015." Diocese of South Carolina, September 2, 2015, http://www.diosc.com/sys/news-events/latest-news/674-prayers-requested-for-south-carolina.

former clerk to Chief Justice Toal. Moreover, one of the five justices, Kaye Hearn, was an active member of St. Anne's Episcopal Church in Conway. It should be recalled that her husband, George Hearn, had been inexplicably subpoenaed by the DSC lawyers to give a deposition in early 2013 for the circuit court trial. St Anne's had been formed by loyal Episcopalians who fled from St. Paul's of Conway, a parish that followed Bishop Lawrence. Not one of the justices on the state Supreme Court held membership in a church of the Diocese of South Carolina. They were all of other denominations, Roman Catholic (Toal), Greek Orthodox (Pleicones), and Presbyterian (Kittredge). Hearn did not recuse herself; and there was no record of Runyan or anyone else asking her to withdraw from the case. Why the diocesan lawyers did not press Hearn to recuse herself from this case remained to be seen.

The five justices on the Supreme Court of South Carolina were Chief Justice Jean Hoefer Toal, and Justices Costa M. Pleicones, Donald W. Beatty, John W. Kittredge, and Kaye Hearn. All of them were graduates of the University of South Carolina School of Law. Toal was the first woman to serve as a justice on the state Supreme Court. She had been Chief Justice since 2004, and Justice since 1988. As her ten-year-term as Chief Justice was coming to an end in 2014, she decided to run for the office again even though she could serve only one more year because of the age restriction. The legislature chose her over Pleicones. The next year, it elected Pleicones to succeed her even though he could serve only one year, to the end of 2016. In the context of the Church case of 2015, Toal was most important as the author of the *All Saints* decision of 2009.

Chief Justice Toal was known for her sharp and quick intellect and forceful personality. Attorney Blake Hewitt, said of her: "'She was truly a force of nature. She never stopped. I have never known such persistent diligence, such serial focus and such relentless determination to succeed.'"[385] Another witness said her "specialty is framing issues in such a way that people come to agree with her."[386] Toal described her own temperament as "'controlled aggression.'"[387] As she prepared to retire at the end of 2015, a group of admirers issued a book about her, *Madame Chief Justice, Jean Hoefer Toal of South Carolina*. It was a collection of twenty-three essays including ones by Ruth Bader Ginsburg and Sandra Day O'Connor. Blake Hewitt contributed one. Walter Edgar co-wrote another.

Justice Pleicones served as a public defender then as a circuit court judge from 1991 to 2000, when he was elected to the Supreme Court. Justice Beatty served in the state legislature before he became a circuit court judge in 1995 and then an Appeals Court judge in 2003. In 2007, he was elected to the Supreme Court. Of the five justices to hear the Church case in 2015, he was the only one to have signed Toal's *All Saints* decision of 2009. Justice Kittredge, Phi Beta Kappa from the University of South Carolina, was elected circuit court judge in 1996, Appeals Court judge in 2003, and justice of the Supreme Court in 2008. Justice Hearn was a family court judge then a judge on the state Court of

---

385. Monk, John. "'Force of Nature,' SC Supreme Court Chief Jean Toal Strode Through History." *The State* (Columbia, SC), December 5, 2015, http://www.thestate.com/news/local/article48242630.html.
386. Ibid.
387. Ibid.

Appeals for fifteen years, ten of those as Chief Judge.[388] All five of the sitting justices had had long and distinguished careers as outstanding lawyers and judges in South Carolina.

At long last, the much-anticipated day arrived, Wednesday, September 23, 2015, and the host of lawyers, clergy, media, and other spectators crowded into the courtroom of the imposing Supreme Court building across Gervais Street from the state house in Columbia and a stone's throw from the cathedral of the Diocese of Upper South Carolina. The hearing was scheduled to start at 10:30 a.m., but actually began at 10:55. It lasted fifty-seven minutes.[389] Blake Hewitt spoke first for twenty minutes for the Church, then Alan Runyan, twenty minutes for the Diocese of South Carolina. Hewitt returned for a brief rebuttal. The hearing was streamed live on the Internet and a video copy was later posted on the Court website.

The structure of the South Carolina Supreme Court was similar to that of the United States Supreme Court in that decisions were made be by majority votes of the justices, in the state case, five justices instead of the federal nine. Therefore, it really mattered little what the lawyers said in court. It mattered a great deal what the justices said in court, for they alone would decide the outcome of the case. According to the South Carolina Bar Association handbook in the state Supreme Court, the process of the Court was this: a justice was assigned a case and that justice's assistant lawyer, called a "clerk," prepared an in-depth review of the case. The five justices normally used the hearing to ask the lawyers questions they have about the case. In the hearing, the appellant lawyer(s) made a presentation to the justices, the respondent lawyer(s) follows. Then, the appellant got to make a brief rebuttal as the last word. Soon after the hearing, perhaps on the same day, the justices met in private to discuss the case and make a decision by a preliminary vote. Then the assigned justice drew up a written opinion. Since decisions were by majority vote, it took three, four, or five votes to make a majority opinion. The minority justice or justices could write dissenting opinions either together or separately. The opinions were circulated for editing until all justices were satisfied at a settlement. Along the way, justices might change their votes on the outcome. Only when all justices were satisfied were the written opinion(s) released to the public. The majority opinion had the weight of law.[390]

If Runyan and his team were confident of a smooth victory in the Court, they were soon to be in for an unpleasant surprise. Hewitt barely got out his first comment before the justices lit into the shortcomings of the Goodstein trial and decision. In the course of the hearing there was to be plenty of criticism of Goodstein's work and not a word of support. Not one of the five justices had anything positive to say about the Goodstein decision. Two justices in particular, most importantly Chief Justice Toal, returned time and again to this subject. Apparently, Toal had assigned herself this case as she completely dominated the entire hearing, asking more questions, making more comments,

---

388. "Judicial Department Supreme Court." State of South Carolina, http://www.judicial.stste.sc.us/supreme/displayJustice.cfm.

389. The hearing was livestreamed on the Internet. A video recording was made available at: South Carolina. Supreme Court. Video Recording, hearing, 2015–000622–Protestant Episcopal Church v. Episcopal Church, September 23, 2015, http://www.judicial.state.sc.us/scvideo/indexarchived.cfm.

390. "The South Carolina Supreme Court." South Carolina Bar Association, http://www.scbar.org/Portals/1/Documents/LRE?COURTS?narrative%20ch%203.pdf?ver=2014-11-13-143159-677.

and speaking longer than any other justice. True to her self-described reputation of controlled aggression, she dominated the entire room for the entire time of the hearing. Toal was also the most critical of Goodstein. One time she said to Hewitt, "It may have been very unbalanced to have made the rulings that were made below that allowed one side's experts (. . .) to testify very fulsomely and forbade your side's two experts getting at all in the issue of lens through which we should look at this dispute, hierarchical versus congregational."[391] Later she leveled this withering blast at Runyan:

> This case was tried in a rather one-sided way on that particular issue [Church structure]. You all were allowed to put in an expert to discuss in detail his opinions about whether hierarchical matters (. . .). Now, the other side had Dr. Walter Edgar and Professor McWilliams for two that were prepared to delve into specifically matters of hierarchy and so forth and they were completely stopped from arguing that, from presenting evidence about that and then because the judge said we are not going to make a finding about hierarchical and then the order comes out and it finds that this church is a congregational church. How did all that happen with the way this case was tried?[392]

She was not through. When Runyan tried to make a comeback, she pushed him back on his heels again:

> They [Church] argued that [Church authority], but they were not permitted to put in any evidence on that point (. . .). And then, and the judge said I'm not getting into that, she termed it we are not a hierarchical state as a kind of odd thing because we discussed both those principles in *All Saints*, but she said this, none of this information is going to be considered by me because we are neutral principles. How in the world if that is the framework that was used was a finding made specifically that this is a congregational, that the Episcopal Church is a congregational church?[393]

Also highly critical of Goodstein's trial and order was Justice Hearn. Hewitt had barely opened his presentation when she interrupted him: "But didn't she [Goodstein] also disallow you, and I know you were not trial counsel, from introducing evidence that would tend to show that it was not a congregational church?"[394] Shortly thereafter she added, "But of course in this case Judge Goodstein wouldn't even let counsel for the national church bring in what had been done as far as disciplining Bishop Lawrence. In fact, she threatened to revoke his pro hoc vici statute if he didn't stop talking about that."[395] When Toal finished excoriating Runyan about Edgar and McWilliams, Hearn dug in the knife deeper:

> Yes, Mr. Runyan, and I would point out echoing the Chief's concern, this was a non-jury trial and yet I counted over twenty-five objections to Professor McWilliams' testimony in a non-jury trial. You all tried so hard to keep any of that

---

391. Author's notes, South Carolina Supreme Court, hearing, livestreamed, September 23, 2015.
392. Ibid.
393. Ibid.
394. Ibid.
395. Ibid.

evidence out, and then the order is issued and low and behold there is a finding that this church is a, controlled by the bottom, that the parishes are really in charge rather than the national church, so help us with that.[396]

By the end of the hearing, Goodstein's Order of February 3, 2015, seemed to lie in shreds.

All the justices spoke out in the hearing. Toal led with forty-one interjections. She gave the longest speeches of the hearing. Hearn was next with thirty-seven comments, several lengthy. Justice Kittredge interjected fourteen times, mainly trying the clarify the issues. Justice Pleicones spoke four times, and Justice Beatty two times. Toal and Hearn agreed that Goodstein's trial and decision were faulty. Beyond that they took very different paths in their questions and comments. Toal was primarily concerned about corporate law, property, the *All Saints* decision, and the authority of Bishop Lawrence. She seemed to focus on the right of the local entity to control itself through the state laws on corporations. After throwing Runyan back on the defensive, she brought him back to apparently what she saw as the basic issue at stake:

> Exactly, and particularly after the non-profit acts are, were changed the, all these organizations started to file articles of incorporation with the secretary of state including this diocese and there is nothing in those articles that are filed that forbids the corporation that we are talking about, which is your client, from disassociating or deaccessioning from the national church their corporation, they legally changed their purpose. They withdrew their accession to the national church and as a corporation they had the authority to do that, that's your argument, isn't it?[397]

When Runyan agreed, Toal went on: "If we see it as a matter of corporation law, and don't get tangled up in all the doctrinal issues, as a matter of corporate law they legitimately filed papers accomplishing that, that's your argument?"[398] In Hewitt's rebuttal, Toal returned to the same issue: "But Mr. Hewitt, there is nothing in the corporation law of this state that forbids a corporation, if it does it correctly and according to the law, from changing its purpose, is there?"[399] When Hewitt tried to answer, she asked somewhat incredulously, "So once the, let me see if I get you, you want us to declare that the corporate law of South Carolina is that once you put a purpose clause in your charitable corporation you are forever bound to that purpose clause and, it can never be changed even if your constitution and other operational documents are properly amended to do so?"[400] Finally, Toal said to Hewitt: "And you are saying that the national church, once you join it, you can never unjoin it, unless the national church lets you unjoin it? Alright, what principle governs that, the Dennis Canon?"[401]

If Runyan expected the Court simply to apply the *All Saints* to the whole diocese, he was to be in for a shock. Indeed, he opened his remarks to the court with this: "May it please the court, Madame Chief Justice, justices, I want to try and focus on what I think,

396. Ibid.
397. Ibid.
398. Ibid.
399. Ibid.
400. Ibid.
401. Ibid.

what I have heard that suggests that *All Saints* does not apply here. There really is no legal or factual distinction between *All Saints* and the facts of this case."[402] Toal was ready to have none of this as she launched into her longest speech of the hearing:

> Remember, recall Mr. Runyan that in *All Saints* there wasn't any dispute about the bishop's control (. . .). No question about the bishop's authority, Serbian church no question about the bishop's authority. Here big question about the bishop's authority (. . .) but also big questions about whether the diocese, whether the bishop, has any ownership interest at all to deal with because of the Dennis Canon, so big difference between this case and *All Saints* where they wasn't any question about the bishop's ability to quit claim, would you agree?[403]

Runyan did not agree and fumbled to make an explanation that apparently did not satisfy the court. Toal's forceful rejection of the precedence of *All Saints* was the defining moment of the hearing. The author of that very decision had spoken. No one could argue with her. Runyan and his fellow lawyers had based their entire case on *All Saints* only to watch as the Chief Justice withdrew it as an issue. The collective heart on the diocesan side must have sunk into disappointment. Any expectation of sailing through this Court evaporated.

Hearn advocated for the Church position, that the Episcopal Church was an hierarchy, that this was an ecclesiastical matter, that neutral principles could be compatible with hierarchy, that the Dennis Canon was effective, and that the *All Saints* decision was not the precedent for this case. During Hewitt's presentation, she sometimes made his points for him, but she saved her sharpest remarks for Runyan. Immediately after Toal had demolished the relevancy of the *All Saints* decision, Hearn entered into a back-and-forth with Runyan on the Dennis Canon. After nine exchanges, she snapped:

> Stop there just a minute (. . .). The Dennis Canon was in effect here for about thirty years, until this brouhaha happened, and in fact the diocese adopted its own version of the Dennis Canon. What I want to direct your attention to, what about Section 3331–180 of our own non-profit corporation act that said if religious doctrine governing the affairs of a religious corporation is inconsistent with the provisions of this chapter on the same subject, the religious doctrine controls? Why isn't that saying, why isn't that South Carolina General Assembly saying something like the Dennis Canon would trump any suggestion of state law?[404]

By the end of the hearing, the Church side was feeling encouraged and the diocesan side must have felt disappointed. It was obvious that the Court was not going to decide to uphold the Goodstein decision. This, and the criticism against the trial, must have been disheartening. The mastery that Runyan et al. had had over the circuit court trial disappeared in the Supreme Court. What decision the Court was going to make remained entirely unclear. Perhaps even more importantly, not one justice arose to agree with Runyan's position on his key argument for the *All Saints* decision. As for the Dennis Canon, there was a great deal of discussion about it but no clear position except for

402. Ibid.
403. Ibid.
404. Ibid.

Hearn who strongly supported it. As for direction toward a decision among the justices, the hearing seemed to suggest two paths, one led by Toal to recognize the corporate rights of the diocese, and the other led by Hearn to recognize the hierarchical rights of the Episcopal Church.[405]

On August 2, 2017, the South Carolina Supreme Court released its decision, twenty-two months after the hearing. Reflecting the difficulty and complexity of the case, the justices issued a sharply divided ruling that mostly sided with the Episcopal Church. In a 3–2 decision, the justices ruled that, of the 35 parishes in the lawsuit, the 28 that had acceded in writing to the Dennis Canon were subject to the Canon while the 7 that had not adopted the Canon were not subject to it. The majority also ruled that the Episcopal Church was hierarchical. As for the issues deriving from which of the two dioceses was legally entitled to assume the place of the old diocese, the majority deferred to the pending litigating in Judge Duffy's U.S. District Court. On the whole, the state supreme court overthrew most of Judge Goodstein's Order of February 3, 2015, recognized the Episcopal Church diocese's rights over the majority of the parishes, and left the ultimate decision of diocesan legality to the federal court. In general, this left the Episcopal Church and its diocese in the stronger position pending the outcome of the lawsuit in the U.S. District Court.[406]

---

405. For reports on the hearing see: Hawes, Jennifer Berry, "S.C. Supreme Court Hears Arguments in Episcopal Church Breakup Saga." *The Post and Courier* (Charleston, SC), September 23, 2015; Hawes, Jennifer Berry, "Questions Raised Over Justice's Impartiality in Episcopal Lawsuit." *The Post and Courier* (Charleston, SC), September 26, 2015. For reports from the diocesan side see: "Diocese of South Carolina Defends Its Property Against Another Episcopal Church Appeal," Diocese of South Carolina, September 23, 2015, http://www.diosc.com/sys/news-events/latest-news/689-diocese-of-south-carolina-defends.; "On the Oral Arguments in South Carolina," Anglican Curmudgeon, September 24, 2015, http://accurmudgeon.blogspot.com/2015/09/on-oral-arguments-in-south-carolina.html.; "Blatant Bias on Display in ECUSA's South Carolina Case," Anglican Curmudgeon, September 24, 2015, http://accurmudgeon.blogspot.com/2015/09/blatant-bias-on-display-in-ecusas-south.html.; Mills, Ladson, III, "SC Supreme Court Justice has Deep Ties to National Episcopal Church." Virtueonline, September 24, 2015, http://www.virtueonline.org/sc-supreme-court-justice-has-deep-ties-national-episcopal-church. For reports from the Church side see: "Supreme Court Hears Oral Arguments in Appeal," The Episcopal Church in South Carolina, September 24, 2015, http://www.episcopalchurchsc.org/news-release-september-23-2015.html.; "State Supreme Court Rips Goodstein Ruling, Questions Lawrence's Actions, Authority as Bishop," South Carolina Episcopalians, September 23, 2015, http://www,scepiscopalians.com/2015_Archives.php.

406. "The State of South Carolina, In the Supreme Court, Appeal from Dorchester County, Diane Shafer Goodstein, Circuit Court Judge, Opinion No. 27731, Heard September 23, 2015-Filed August 2, 2017."

7

Conclusion

THIS BOOK BEGAN BY posing an historical problem: What were the causes and origins of the Episcopal Church schism of 2012 in South Carolina? What was its nature? And, what effects did it have on South Carolina, the Episcopal Church and the world beyond? Having examined the evidence of the schism in the previous six chapters, one can now proceed to draw conclusions to solve the original problem.

There was a great deal of documentary evidence relating to this problem, much of it freely available on the Internet. Most useful were the journals of the annual meetings of the diocesan convention. These included the resolutions presented to the meetings and the detailed diary of the bishop. Also important were the records of the General Convention and other parts of the Episcopal Church. The diocesan offices issued innumerable press releases and statements, many concerning official functions of the diocese. Also invaluable were the hundreds of documents produced in and by the legal proceedings after January 4, 2013.

Unfortunately, a good deal of documentary evidence remained hidden from the public. Church diocesan attorney Thomas Tisdale tried his best to obtain the thousand or so emails between lawyer Alan Runyan and Bishop Lawrence in the run-up to the schism, but to no avail. Unavailable too were the minutes and other records of the bishop's search committee of 2004–2007. The diocesan standing committee did turn over its minutes to lawyer Tisdale, but they were heavily redacted. These records went blank whenever the committee went into "executive session" which was apparently anytime they wished to discuss controversial issues. Nevertheless, the body of existing evidence still dwarfed the void of missing material. The vast body of available public documents allows one to draw informed conclusions about the overriding problem at hand. From what one has seen in the preceding six chapters, he or she may proceed to answer the question of the causes, nature, and results of the schism.

CAUSES

Great problems of history always have three aspects of origins: underlying causes, direct causes, and initiating events. This was true for the schism of 2012.

A History of the Episcopal Church Schism in South Carolina

The underlying cause of the schism in South Carolina was a difference in the understanding of the meaning and purpose of religion. The Episcopal Church and the Diocese of South Carolina came to have fundamentally oppositional viewpoints on this. After the Second World War, the Episcopal Church resolved to do its part to right the wrongs in contemporary American society, that is, to champion human rights for African Americans, women, and homosexuals. The church resolved to give full inclusion to these long-maligned or neglected social elements. This meant the development of a horizontal religion that emphasized action for social reform. Along with this came a new prayer book that added another dimension of democratization to the ancient liturgies. On the other hand, conservative Episcopalians wanted to preserve the pre-Second World War traditional vertical religion of salvation between one person and one God. While neither side excluded the other, each side believed its view more important. The divergence of the Diocese of South Carolina from the national Church began in 1982 with the episcopate of Bishop Allison and developed in fits and starts for the next thirty years. The leadership of the diocese became increasingly defensive of the vertical religion and critical of the national Church that it considered too liberal, even heretical. They came to see the Episcopal Church as the erroneous other, then the adversary, and finally the enemy. The schism formally occurred in 2012, but it had been three decades in arriving. It was a schism in increments. No one person can be singled out as causing the schism. Presiding Bishop Jefferts Schori did not cause it. Bishop Lawrence alone did not cause it. Indeed, he arrived twenty-five years after the diocese had started on its path of divergence from the mainstream of the Episcopal Church.

The direct cause of an historical event always derives from the underlying cause. It cannot exist separately, in and of itself. The issue of homosexuality was the direct cause of the schism in South Carolina. There was no other matter that remotely rivaled this as the determinative force delivering the break. Full equality for and inclusion of non-celibate homosexuals was the last of the four great reform movements pressed by the Episcopal Church in the post-Second World War period, after civil rights, women's equality, and new prayer book. This issue, however, differed from the earlier ones in that it operated on two levels, polity and morality. With the Episcopal Church roughly divided into thirds, the left wing defined the issue as one of human rights while the right defined it as one of morality. Given the state of the sweeping movement of human rights for African Americans and women, the left prevailed in its campaign to define the issue as a continuation of a larger reform movement. The majority of the Episcopal Church agreed to full rights and inclusion of gays in the life of the church. Beginning in the early 1980s, the leadership of the Diocese of South Carolina, mostly devoted evangelicals, opposed with rising vigor the Church's majority trajectory on homosexuality and fanned the flames of anti-homosexual sentiment within the conservative and traditionalist-minded diocese. With every major decision of the Episcopal Church in favor of homosexuals, the majority of the diocese increased its hostility to, and distance from, the Church: opening of ordination, approval of a non-celibate gay man as a bishop, choosing a pro-gay presiding bishop, and establishment of a liturgy for the blessing of same-sex unions. When it came time to choose a new bishop to replace retiring Bishop Salmon, the diocesan leadership selected three finalists well-known to be highly critical of the Episcopal Church's social reforms, thus guaranteeing a continuation within the diocese of its crusade against equality for non-celibate homosexuals in the church. Now, the question may arise of whether the leadership's use of the issue of homosexuality was a cause or a result, that is, whether homosexuality itself drove them to turn against the Church or whether they deliberately used it as an issue to rile up the communicants against the Church for other reasons. The presently available documents did not answer this question; thus, one is left to take at face value the existing evidence that the issue of homosexuality was the cause, not the result. Regardless of motivation, the issue of homosexuality was indisputably the direct cause of the schism of 2012.

In South Carolina, the anti-homosexual rights stance, rising for more than two decades, reached a crescendo in the episcopate of Mark Lawrence starting in 2008. The increments of schism continued in reaction to the Episcopal Church's steps in favor of homosexuals. The diocesan leaders used the Church's General Convention of 2009, which created the path for a liturgy for blessing same-sex unions, to capitalize on a wave of riled-up hostility and call a reactive special convention to make a declaration of independence from the Episcopal Church by revoking accession to the canons of the Church. Three years later, the diocesan leadership used the General Convention of 2012, which approved the liturgy for same-sex blessing and defended the rights of the transgendered, to ride an even higher wave of popular opposition to the Episcopal Church to cut the final tenuous thread of allegiance, accession to the constitution of the Episcopal Church. In the wake of the Convention of 2012, a band of perhaps two dozen diocesan leaders confidently met in secret to draw up the final separation from the Episcopal Church knowing they could enact it with the resolute support of the incited anti-homosexual rights majority of the communicants. For years before the schism, the diocesan leadership was dominated by clergy alumni of Trinity School for Ministry, and their allies, all following a highly evangelical, fundamentalist-leaning theology.

Given the underlying and direct causes of the division between the Diocese of South Carolina and the Episcopal Church, the events that made the schism of 2012 derived from the purposeful acts of the leaders of diocese. However, the events that initiated the schism of 2012 came primarily not from issues of scripture or morality but from polity, or church government. Having solidified the majority against the Church on homosexuality, the leaders rallied the diocese to unite around its most visible official, Bishop Lawrence. They promoted an assertion, that soon became a popular assumption, that the Church was acting to remove the bishop from the diocese in order to flip the diocese from "orthodox" to liberal. This became the victimization theme, that is, that Bishop Lawrence was the innocent victim of the dark liberal forces from off controlling the errant Episcopal Church. This author found no documentary evidence to support this belief.

The specific act that set up the chain of events leading to the schism of 2012 was the issuance of the quit claim deeds. In late 2011, Bishop Lawrence delivered these to all of the parishes of the diocese relinquishing any and all claims the diocese had in the local properties. This was in direct and open disregard of the Dennis Canon of the Episcopal Church creating the real possibility, perhaps probability, that Lawrence could be charged with abandonment of the Episcopal Church by the Disciplinary Board for Bishops in 2012. The diocesan leaders prepared for such an event. With the majority of the diocese long-enflamed against the Episcopal Church on the issue of homosexuality, certain diocesan figures met with the standing committee to formulate a secret plan to ride the final tsunami of anti-Church sentiment to schism. The Church charge against Lawrence would create the rationale for the break. After thirty years of hostility to the Church and years of bonding between bishop and communicants, the leadership was confident in the moment. On October 2, 2012, the Standing Committee, upon approval of Lawrence, resolved in secret to separate the diocese from the Episcopal Church if a Church official took any action of any kind against Lawrence. Surely enough, this happened soon thereafter. On October 15, the presiding bishop placed Lawrence under restriction and the committee declared its heretofore secret plan to be enacted. The diocesan leadership then made the surprising announcement of the complete independence of the diocese to the presiding bishop, the clergy, and the public. The diocesan leadership then rejected all efforts at a peaceful settlement with the Episcopal Church and directed their lawyers to prepare legal actions against the Episcopal Church. As fully expected, the majority of the diocese, meeting in a special convention a month later, easily affirmed the previously enacted separation. Although the schism was enacted by no more than two dozen people, it was instantly and overwhelmingly accepted by the clear majority of the diocese. The schism by increments had finally run its course. Fundamental disagreement on the nature and purpose of religion, opposition to equal rights for and inclusion of homosexuals in the church, and a diocesan leadership committed to relentless hostility to the national Church finally produced a schism after thirty years. It was a counter-revolutionary movement from the top down.

The question of inevitability always rises with historical problems. Looking back in history, it often seems that a certain event that occurred was always inevitable, that is, bound to happen and nothing could have prevented it. Thus, the question arises, was the schism of the Diocese of South Carolina from the Episcopal Church inevitable? The problem with inevitability is that it presumes, or at least implies, lack of human control over contemporaneous events. People may simply be pushed along unable to decide for themselves the choices they can make. This cannot be the case. Every human being makes countless choices every day even if these are influenced by variable conditions. And, given the knowledge of good and evil since the days of the Garden of Eden, every decision has a moral dimension. The Christian concept of free will holds that human beings can choose to do good and to do evil. This means that nothing in history is really inevitable. People in South Carolina made choices for thirty years that finally wound up in schism but those were choices that they made freely and willfully. Faced with similar circumstances, the majority of the dioceses that joined the Anglican Communion Network chose to remain with the Episcopal Church. In the southeastern United States, every other diocese remained in the Episcopal Church. The majority in South Carolina, however, chose to follow their leadership and the leaders chose to break away from the Episcopal Church. These were free choices freely made. The people of the Diocese of South Carolina could have chosen to remain in the Episcopal Church. The schism of 2012 was not inevitable.

Another question that arises about the schism was whether it was a conspiracy. In the run-up to the circuit court trial, Church lawyer Thomas Tisdale charged that it was a conspiracy among a small group of diocesan leaders in a *quid pro quo* deal with Mark Lawrence: bishop's office in exchange for diocesan secession from the Episcopal Church with property in hand. Tisdale said the conspiracy was to defraud the Episcopal Church of its rightful assets. It is clear that the schism was a premeditated, secret agreement among a group to break the diocese away from the Church. The question is whether this was illegal or harmful. The diocesan leaders would argue that the schism was neither illegal nor harmful, but just the opposite, perfectly legal and actually good for the diocese. The diocesan lead lawyer, Alan Runyan, had spent a great deal of time and effort making the case convincingly to the majority of the diocese that they had every legal right to be free and independent of the Episcopal Church. Thus, what may be a conspiracy to the Church side would not be such to the diocesan side.

Documents showed that a pre-meditated secret agreement among a group to make a schism existed as early as October 2, 2012, thirteen days before the schism occurred. Existing evidence did not reveal how much earlier the final event of the schism may have been planned. It did show that a similar set-up had been made in 2011 when Lawrence was under his first investigation by the Disciplinary Board. That plan was not enacted since he was not charged by the Board at that time. Before that, there were only two clear pieces of hard evidence of a secret deal, both of which support the claim of a *quid pro quo*. Both were presented in the circuit court trial. One was the affidavit of the Rev. Thomas Rickenbaker who said that two members of the bishop's search committee had told him they were looking for a new bishop who would take the diocese out of the Episcopal Church. The other was the testimony of the Rev. Dow Sanderson who said that the Rev. Jeff Miller, head of the Standing Committee, had told him the diocese had chosen Lawrence to lead the diocese out of the Episcopal Church. Whether these pieces of evidence prove a conspiracy must be left to the judgment of the reader.

Aside from the hard evidence, there was a vast amount of documentation one may interpret as circumstantial evidence that the schism was the result of a long course conducted by the diocesan leadership to deliberately escalate the differences between the diocese and the Episcopal Church. This circumstantial evidence clearly pointed to a relentlessly escalating adversarial interface of the diocese and the Episcopal Church. This progression became very serious in 2003 on the heels of the Robinson affair, critical after the 2009 General Convention, and fatal after the 2012 Convention.

Reviewing the circumstantial evidence that appeared in the previous six chapters, the following areas stood out as most important:

1. *Hostility.* The standing committee and the diocese moved into a permanently hostile attitude toward the Episcopal Church in the wake of the Robinson affair of 2003.

    The diocesan deputies to the General Convention of 2003 refused to accept the pro-homosexual decisions of the Convention and returned home to reject the legitimacy of the acts of the national Church. On August 18, 2003, the Standing Committee declared that the acts in question were null and void in the diocese. This established permanently the principle that the diocese could nullify acts of the national Church. Moreover, the committee established itself as the power center for all diocesan actions in the future. From then on, all decisions would be made by a group of no more than two dozen people at the top of the diocese and relayed downward to the rest of the diocese. In the run-up to the schism, there was not to be a public discussion or debate of the merits of schism. There was to be no "discernment" among the people of the diocese. When the schism came, it was the work of a relatively small group of diocesan leaders, mostly clergy, who presented it as a *fait accompli* to the rest of the diocese.

In the special convention of October 2, 2003, the leadership only barely missed getting the delegates to declare the Episcopal Church "apostate." However, they overwhelmingly defeated an affirmation that the diocese would participate in the Episcopal Church. If the diocese was not to participate in the national Church, the only logical outcome would be separation from it.

2. *The bishop's search.* The conservative bishop's search committee of 2005–2007 chose as the three finalists men known to be highly critical of the recent trajectory of the Episcopal Church. No other nomination was allowed in the diocese. The committee sought Mark Lawrence's candidacy for the office of bishop. He was known through his writings and his role in the 2003 General Convention. This guaranteed the continuation of the already established stance of hostile differentiation from the Episcopal Church.

The Episcopal Church came close to rejecting Mark Lawrence as a bishop. It consented only on the benefit of the doubt after Lawrence announced his "intention" of staying in the Church. This came after he had issued two essays supporting diocesan disassociation and submission of the Episcopal Church to the Anglican Communion.

3. *Adversarial actions.* The diocesan leadership increasingly developed an adversarial relationship between the diocese and the Episcopal Church. There was a long list of evidence that could be included here. Some of the most significant would be:

   a. Role in the Anglican Communion Network. The diocesan leaders played a major role in the ultra-conservative ACN. This was the nucleus of the "Anglican Realignment" movement in the United States. Out of its core came the "replacement" stratagem of replacing the Episcopal Church as the legitimate province of the Anglican Communion in the U.S. The four most conservative dioceses of this group, supported by anti-homosexual rights GAFCON primates, formed the Anglican Church in North America explicitly to replace the Episcopal Church.

   The diocesan leaders appealed to foreign Anglican primates for "oversight." The Episcopal Church made several offers of alternate oversight. The diocese rejected all of them.

   b. Mark Lawrence's consecration as bishop set the tone for an episcopate that was decidedly hostile to the Episcopal Church from the start. The presiding bishop, who routinely presided over consecrations, was pointedly not invited to this one.

c. Presiding Bishop Jefferts Schori's visit to the diocese in February of 2008 was a set-up in which the diocesan leadership made an opportunity to differentiate the diocesan clergy from the national Church. She was subjected to shameful disrespect.

d. Bishop Lawrence participated in the GAFCON initial meeting of July 2008 that drew up the Jerusalem Declaration denouncing homosexuality and rejecting the authority of the Episcopal Church. From then on, he was active in building ties with GAFCON and Global South bishops. GAFCON eventually helped set up the Anglican Church in North America as a replacement for the Episcopal Church. On November 6, 2008, the diocesan Standing Committee endorsed the Jerusalem Declaration.

e. Bishop Lawrence spent several years building bonds with the communicants, particularly the conservative ones, in the diocese, and with other ultra-conservative forces in the U.S. and GAFCON/Global South bishops abroad. The bonding worked very well. In time, he referred to the diocese and himself as "we." When the schism came, the diocesan leadership instantly translated the Church's attempt to discipline the bishop as an act against the diocese. Immediately after the schism, the Global South made an "oversight" arrangement for the independent diocese.

f. Diocesan leaders long promoted the idea that the diocese was "Anglican" rather than Episcopalian. Bishop Lawrence promoted this diocesan identification. Upon returning from the GAFCON and Lambeth meetings of 2008, Lawrence told the clergy to "prepare for the emerging Anglicanism of the future." He likened the Episcopal Church to a cancer of the Anglican Communion as he told the diocesan convention in March of 2009: "Either Episcopalianism will repent of its unscriptural autonomy or it will spread its splintering tentacles of the last forty years throughout the Anglican Communion." He also established a new motto for the diocese: "Making Biblical Anglicans for a Global Age." Moreover, the diocese set up a commission for Anglican Communion development and named the Rt. Rev. Michael Nazir-Ali as "Visiting Bishop in South Carolina for Anglican Communion Development." By the time of the schism the diocesan identity as Episcopalian was all but non-existent.

g. The diocesan leaders used the decisions of the Episcopal Church General Convention of 2009 as rationale for a virtual declaration of independence from the Church. This was formulated in a marathon secret session of the diocesan leadership on July 28, 2009. Bishop Lawrence held a clergy conference on August 13, 2009 to prepare the clergy. The special convention of October 24, 2009, declared the sovereignty of the diocese and called for withdrawing from the governing bodies of the Church. This was the diocese's de facto declaration of independence from the Episcopal Church. Every subsequent event derived from this.

h. After the South Carolina Supreme Court ruled in 2009 that All Saints parish of Pawleys Island had legally separated from the diocese and was the owner of the local properties, Bishop Lawrence reversed a decade-long diocesan policy of enforcing the Dennis Canon. He refused to appeal the verdict to the United States Supreme Court and he gave no help to the local Episcopal congregation of All Saints which did make an appeal to the Court. All alone, the congregation soon decided on a negotiated settlement.

i. Following its declaration of independence, the diocese in its convention of October 15, 2010, removed its accession to the canons of the Episcopal Church. It also authorized the bishop to revise the terms of the state charter of incorporation. On October 19, 2010, Lawrence filed a revised charter removing diocesan recognition of the Constitution and Canons of the Episcopal Church. The Standing Committee began calling itself the Board of Directors and declared that it alone could determine the identity of the bishop of the diocese and the membership of the Board.

4. *Anti-Church monopoly.* The minority pro-Episcopal Church elements in the diocese were ignored, marginalized, ostracized, and finally declared the enemy by the hostile diocesan leadership which held a virtual monopoly of all the diocesan ruling apparati. With only rare exceptions, the anti-Episcopal Church ruling establishment controlled the diocesan power structure such as the standing committee, diocesan council, trustees, bishop's search committee, deans, and public relations.

    The Episcopal Forum tried and failed to make a positive presence for the Episcopal Church in the diocese. Time and again, it sought help from the national Church, to no avail. With every attempt, the Forum was dismissively maligned by the diocesan leadership. Eventually the Standing Committee defined the Forum as the enemy within. In time, the diocesan media refused to carry any news of the Forum. At the schism, the leadership blamed the Forum for the Church's "attack" on Lawrence.

    The reason the twenty-four complainants in 2012 went to the national Church was that there had been no way to make their voices heard within the power structure of the diocese. They had been frozen out. Their only recourse was to go to the Church authorities beyond the diocese.

5. *Promotion of the power and authority of the bishop.* The diocesan leadership built up both the power and the image of Bishop Lawrence as the local counter poise to the national Church.

    The power of the bishop was enhanced primarily in three ways. In the first, in March of 2010, the diocesan convention gave to the bishop the right to the sole and final interpretation of the diocesan constitution and canons. His decision was non-appealable. Afterwards, he alone could determine the course of the diocese by declaring his indisputable interpretation of the constitution and canons. The most important occurrence of this came in September and October of 2012 when he delivered a lengthy document to the standing committee advising them that they could break the diocese away from the Episcopal Church. In an earlier instance, on March 17, 2010, the diocesan Board of Trustees secretly made a lease agreement with Bishop Lawrence giving to him the official bishop's residence virtually rent-free for ten years regardless of his position as bishop. Along the same line came the third instance, a lifetime employment contract. On February 1, 2011, the Standing Committee secretly gave to Mark Lawrence what amounted to full salary for the rest of his life. Even if removed as bishop, he would remain employed as the diocesan "chief operating officer." As with the residence, the employment contract showed that the diocesan leadership fully intended to keep Lawrence as bishop regardless of what the Episcopal Church might do.

While promoting the power and solidifying the position of the bishop, the diocesan leadership also developed the claim of Lawrence's victimization. They said he was treated unfairly by the Episcopal Church authorities, the implication being they were trying to "take over" the diocese to rid it of its "orthodox" religion. Victimization was to become one of the most powerful themes in the schism and its aftermath.

The victimization theme arose at least three times. In the first, Lawrence and his lawyers claimed that the presiding bishop was trying to interfere in the internal workings of the diocese through the lawyer Thomas Tisdale in early 2010. The leadership loudly and dramatically demanded she cease and desist this "intrusion." In the second, the diocesan leadership denounced the Title IV reforms, that were to go into effect in the Episcopal Church in 2011, claiming these gave the presiding bishop the unconstitutional right to interfere in the diocese. In the third, the diocesan leadership made Lawrence out to be the victim of the Church through the supposedly unfair treatment of the Disciplinary Board for Bishops. The charge of victimization was to be a recurrent theme among the diocesan witnesses in the circuit court trial. This author found no documentary evidence to support the belief that Lawrence was a victim of the Episcopal Church.

6. *Property.* Bishop Lawrence's issuance of the quit claim deeds was the specific cause of the Disciplinary Board's charge of abandonment in 2012. However, from the start of his episcopacy, Lawrence showed no interest in enforcing the Dennis Canon.

The diocesan leadership showed disregard of the Dennis Canon in several ways. On May 30, 2009, three months before the *All Saints* decision and while the diocese still adhered to the Dennis Canon, the Rev. Jeff Miller, chair, led the Standing Committee, in the presence of the chancellor Wade Logan and Bishop Lawrence, to approve a request from St. Andrew's of Mount Pleasant to move several millions of dollars' worth of property into an irrevocable trust away from the diocese and Church. Miller made the motion which Lawrence at least tacitly supported for passage. Moreover, after St. Andrew's voted to leave the diocese on March 28, 2010, Lawrence apparently did nothing to enforce the Dennis Canon on the parish.

Bishop Lawrence issued five quit claim deeds under his own name (and Jeffrey Miller's) from February 1 to March 10, 2010, while the diocese still explicitly acceded to the Episcopal Church Constitution and Canons in both the diocesan Constitution and Canons and the corporate charter.

Lawyer Alan Runyan told the diocesan convention of October 15, 2010, that accession to the Dennis Canon was "optional." The convention proceeded to pass a resolution deleting the canon from the diocesan constitution and canons.

7. *Declarations of crises.* The diocesan leadership in Bishop Lawrence's tenure had a habit of declaring crises that invariably rallied the diocese against the Episcopal Church. There were three outstanding ones that finally created the schism. The first was in the aftermath of the General Convention of 2009 that set up a path for the blessing of same-sex unions. Diocesan leadership declared a crisis and called a special convention to begin making the canonical changes to remove the diocese from the Episcopal Church. That convention resolved to withdraw from the governing bodies of the Church. A year later, the convention voted to end its accession to the canons of the Episcopal Church. This was de facto secession from the Episcopal Church.

    The second major crisis was in January and February of 2010 in the Logan/Tisdale affair. Lawrence delayed the March 2010 annual meeting of the convention by three weeks heightening the drama.

    The third, greatest, and final crisis came in 2012 around the Church's General Convention that adopted a liturgy for the blessing of same-sex unions and defended rights of the transgendered clergy. Diocesan leaders, particularly the standing committee, worked steadfastly for six months before the Convention to prepare the diocese. Immediately after the convention, they successfully created a major crisis atmosphere in the diocese and used that sensationalized setting to put into effect a final chain of events that produced the schism of October 15, 2012.

8. *Rejections of settlements.* While the leadership developed diocesan hostility against the Episcopal Church, made adversarial actions against the church, and declared crises, they apparently did nothing to make a peaceful settlement with the Church or to accept peace overtures from the Church officials. Church leaders made numerous attempts to settle down the eroding relationship between the diocese and the Episcopal Church, all to no avail. Before Lawrence's time, the Church offered several plans for alternate primatial oversight. The diocese rejected all of them. In another instance, a group of bishops went to Charleston in December of 2011 to talk with Lawrence about his issuance of the quit claim deeds, a deed that was likely to get him charged with abandonment of communion. Diocesan leaders loudly objected to this "interference." Nothing came of the meeting.

    Church leaders tried to appease Lawrence and the rest of the diocesan leadership in other ways. The General Convention resolution of 2012 adopting a liturgy for the blessing of same-sex unions included a local option, the Thurlow Amendment, under which the diocesan bishop could refuse to allow the liturgy in his or her diocese. Diocesan leaders all but ignored this in their campaign against the Church.

    The most serious rejection of peaceful settlement came in 2012 in the run-up to the schism. Bishop Andrew Waldo, of Upper South Carolina, worked long and hard to end hostilities, all for naught. On the very day after the standing committee secretly resolved, upon Lawrence's authoritative permission, to "disassociate" the diocese from the Episcopal Church, Lawrence and Waldo visited the presiding bishop in New York. Lawrence failed to mention the committee's action as he discussed the idea of "creative solutions" to deescalate the crisis. Apparently, he made no proposal for a settlement. Afterwards, he refused every offer of the presiding bishop to meet for negotiations. After the schism, diocesan public relations insisted, incorrectly, that the Episcopal Church had "attacked" Lawrence while he was trying to make peace with the Church. In fact, this author found no documentary evidence that the diocesan leadership in the Lawrence years ever made an offer of a peaceful settlement with the Church. They spurned many peace offers from the Church, but apparently made none of their own.

Having reviewed the main elements of the circumstantial evidence of a premeditated plan to remove the diocese from the Episcopal Church, one should recall that Bishop Lawrence always maintained he tried, to the end, to keep the diocese in the Episcopal Church, as he often said, "intact and in TEC." The available public evidence showed that Lawrence's claim was literally true. This author found no document in which Lawrence explicitly called for schism. Although there was little hard evidence of an explicit conspiracy, there still may well have been an implicit conspiracy that was unwritten, perhaps even unspoken, in which the participants understood that they would escalate their hostility to the Episcopal Church, the logical eventual conclusion of which would be schism.

If there were a *quid pro quo* deal, as attorney Thomas Tisdale charged in the circuit court, Lawrence perhaps got the better part of it. The secessionists got, eventually, the diocesan separation from the Episcopal Church, but Lawrence got the bishop's throne, authoritarian power over the constitution and canons and, arguably over the institutional diocese, virtual lifetime employment whether or not he remained bishop, an annual compensation package worth around a quarter of a million dollars, virtually rent-free use of the million dollar, diocesan-owned bishop's residence in downtown Charleston until the year 2020 whether or not he remained bishop, and personal authority in the Board of Trustees.

In the available public record, the strongest evidence that Lawrence advocated schism came in his secret direction to the Standing Committee of October 2, 2012. On September 18, 2012, Lawrence met privately first with Alan Runyan and others, then with the Standing Committee which discussed the diocese's right to withdraw from the Episcopal Church. On September 20, 2012, the committee sent a private letter to Lawrence requesting an interpretation of the committee's rights. On October 2, 2012, Lawrence, accompanied by Runyan, delivered his sixteen-page response in a closed meeting of the committee. One may suspect that this long, legalistic paper was actually written by one or more lawyers, but it carried only one signature, that of Mark Lawrence. In it, he declared that the committee had the right to withdraw the diocese from the Church. Upon receiving this, the committee immediately voted to remove the diocese from the Episcopal Church if any action of any kind were taken against the bishop, something everyone knew was possible, if not probable, in the wake of the quit claim deeds. Technically, Lawrence did not make the schism, the Standing Committee did. However, the committee's action was a direct result of Lawrence's authoritative letter of permission to the committee.

Before leaving the causes of the schism, one may consider several other aspects of this issue. Why did not the diocese leave the Episcopal Church completely in 2009–2010 when it declared its sovereignty and revoked its accession to the Church canons? The available documents did not answer this. When asked about it, Bishop Lawrence gave only a vague answer. One may theorize that the diocesan leadership was trying to create a new model under which an ultra-conservative diocese could stay in the Episcopal Church by giving nominal but not substantial allegiance to the Church. Local autonomy would be the key. What threw doubt on this theory was the diocesan leadership's later repudiation of the principle of local autonomy. They refused to accept the approval of same-sex blessings in 2012 even though this was left to local discretion. The issue had not been about local autonomy all along.

Another question that has been asked was: why did not the Episcopal Church act sooner? The diocesan convention nullified acts of the national Church in 2003, declared sovereignty in 2009, and revoked its accession to the Church canons in 2010. In 2011, the Disciplinary Board for Bishops set aside a large amount of incriminating evidence against Bishop Lawrence to exonerate him in November. Time and again, the Forum appealed to the Church for intervention. Again, the existing evidence did not answer the question of why year after year the Episcopal Church did nothing about the defiant diocese. In the end, Lawrence's flagrant disregard of the Dennis Canon forced the Church to act.

Thinking about causes of the schism in South Carolina inevitably raises comparisons with the Civil War, or what many South Carolinians still like to call the War Between the States (civil would mean war within a union). Without carrying the analogy too far, one can see curious parallels. In 2003, the diocese established the principle of nullification, that is, it could set aside national decisions within its boundaries. In 2009 and 2010, it declared states' rights, that is, that sovereignty rested in the diocese; and it had the right to remove unilaterally its accession to the part of the national compact called the canons. The Standing Committee of October 2, 2012, was the secession convention. On October 15, the *Star of the West,* the presiding bishop's restriction, arrived to be repulsed. The firing on Fort Sumter began on October 17, in the diocese's open repudiation of the Church authority. Full-fledged war began on January 4, 2013 in the courts. To quote William Faulkner on Southerners and their history, "The past is never dead. It's not even past."

As a final consideration of the causes, one can see clear underlying, direct, and initial events of the schism of 2012. On the issue of whether the schism was a pre-planned move of the diocesan leadership, there was a limited amount of hard evidence and a great mass of circumstantial evidence. A reasonable conclusion to draw is that the leadership of the Diocese of South Carolina willfully moved the diocese in increments away from the Episcopal Church. This reached a logical conclusion in schism whether or not there was an explicit long-term plan for it.

NATURE

If the issue of the causes of the schism was complicated, that of it its nature was not. It was a rather simple and clear-cut occurrence easily described from its initiating events.

The schism happened at noon on Monday, October 15, 2012. That was the moment in which Presiding Bishop Jefferts Schori informed Bishop Mark Lawrence that she had restricted him from exercising ministerial rights in the Episcopal Church. According to the diocesan leadership, this immediately enacted the Standing Committee's October 2 secret resolution withdrawing the diocese from the Episcopal Church. As Lawrence regarded himself an integral part of the diocese, he too left the Episcopal Church. In his consecration oath of January 26, 2008, he had vowed to respect the discipline of the Episcopal Church. It should be noted, however, that Lawrence did not submit a formal written renunciation of his orders in the Episcopal Church. The leadership spent the rest of that day and all of the next preparing a public declaration. On October 16, Lawrence gave the news of the schism to the deans of the convocations.

On Wednesday, October 17, 2012, Lawrence called Jefferts Schori and informed her that the diocese had disassociated from the Episcopal Church as of October 15. This meant that Lawrence, no longer in the Episcopal Church, would not recognize the authority of the Church. Apparently, he refused to have any more relations with the Episcopal Church. Immediately thereafter, the diocesan leadership announced to the world that the diocese had separated from the Episcopal Church and was now an independent entity.

On November 17, 2012, the majority of the diocesan convention met and passed resolutions changing the constitution and canons of the diocese to remove all references to the Episcopal Church. Lawrence announced that the diocese had already disaffiliated from the Episcopal Church. The independent diocese reaffirmed Lawrence as the bishop. Lawrence declared the diocese to be an extra-provincial diocese of the Anglican Communion. This was a self-declaration that had no validity in the official structure of the Anglican Communion. The diocese was, however, supported unofficially by the conservative primates of GAFCON/Global South.

In the view of the Episcopal Church leaders, the institutional diocese of South Carolina did not leave the Church. It continued, momentarily vacant of all office holders. At that point, the Presiding Bishop had two choices. She could accept his words and deeds as his renunciation and release and remove him or she could hand the matter over to the House of Bishops that would meet in March of 2013. The latter would leave the loyal Episcopalians in South Carolina in limbo for four months. She decided on removal. After consulting with her council of advisors, she interpreted Lawrence's public statements of November 17 as his renunciation of his ordination vows in the Episcopal Church. One could not leave the Church and retain the rights of ordination in the Church. On December 5, 2012, Jefferts Schori officially removed and released Mark Lawrence as the bishop of the Episcopal Church diocese. Since he had left the Church on October 15, he dismissed her order as "superfluous."

The majority of the parishes, missions, and communicants of the old diocese went along with the schism and continued to recognize Lawrence as the bishop. The minority remained in the Episcopal Church and began reorganizing the Church diocese under a steering committee. The Church diocese reconstituted on January 26, 2013, by electing a new bishop and filling the offices of the diocesan governing bodies. By then, there were two separate and distinct dioceses, each claiming to be the legitimate heir of the pre-schism Diocese of South Carolina.

RESULTS

Immediately following the schism, the independent diocese was in the much stronger position. Not only was it in physical possession of all the diocesan rights and properties, it also had the majority of local churches. It was served by a well-organized, well-established, and prominent public relations operation that almost completely controlled the local field of public opinion. Too, it had a successful, highly capable, devoted, and aggressive lawyer in the person of Alan Runyan. From early November of 2012, he and his team prepared to take all the necessary legal actions to guarantee the success of what the independent diocese claimed.

For two and a half years after the schism, the diocesan lawyers held the upper hand in the courts. The state circuit court came down entirely on the side of the diocese while the federal courts largely shirked off the case. Perhaps given this background, the diocesan side refused a compromise offered by the Church to exchange the diocese for the local churches.

Not long after the schism occurred it became readily apparent that the diocesan leadership had no plan for the future. Apparently, all their focus had been on leaving the Episcopal Church with little thought of what to do afterwards. Lawrence offered only vague platitudes about making biblical Anglicans for a global age, or for the twenty-first century. Global South made an ill-defined "oversight" scheme supposedly giving the diocese a place in the Anglican Communion, but this was only an informal and temporary arrangement. After four years, the diocesan convention voted to join the Anglican Church in North America even though this too would not make the diocese officially part of the Anglican Communion. The ACNA was supported by GAFCON/Global South but not recognized by the traditional structure of the Communion.

The schism came at a heavy cost to the independent diocese. It lost twenty-six percent of its active members (communicants) in its first few years. At the same time, legal costs soared. As for the immediate cause, the diocese put homosexuality aside for the first two years, then brought it back in 2015 to pass three resolutions defending "traditional marriage" at a time when it was trying hard to raise new money. It established a Marriage Task Force, whose members were chosen by Bishop Lawrence and were led by Kendall Harmon and Peter Moore. This Task Force drew up a "Statement of Faith," an official and very explicit declaration of faith, policy, procedure, and morality to be imposed on the whole diocese. It was adopted by the standing committee and virtually forced on the parishes and employees. It may well be that this document was the long-awaited declaration of meaning for the schism. If so, it finally identified the Diocese of South Carolina as a narrowly-defined evangelical, fundamentalist-oriented "Anglican" sect but one clearly out of the mainstream of classical Anglicanism.

The Church diocese struggled to survive and develop too although it did not have problems of meaning and identity. Under provisional bishops, it slowly and surely regained strength after the trauma of the rupture. It had invaluable aid, encouragement, and support of the Episcopal Church which meant it was a part of the Anglican Communion. Led by Grace Church of Charleston it made a solid recovery. Across the diocese, ten new worshipping communities rallied the loyal Episcopalians displaced from the schismatic churches. In the first few years, the Church diocese showed a sixteen percent gain in membership. As for the direct cause of the schism, the United States Supreme Court and the Episcopal Church established same-sex marriage in 2015 and the Church diocese initiated it at the first opportunity. Ironically, as with the 2012 blessing of same-sex unions, the Thurlow Amendment applied. The local diocesan bishop had the option of refusing this in his or her diocese. If Bishop Lawrence had stayed in the Episcopal Church he could have blocked both same-sex blessings of 2012 and same-sex marriage of 2015 in the entire diocese of South Carolina.

The effects of the schism on the Episcopal Church and on the world beyond were not entirely clear. In 2015, the Episcopal Church completed its course of equal rights and inclusion of homosexuals by adopting same-sex marriage. This concluded its sixty-year period of dynamic social reform. The election of a new presiding bishop in 2015, Michael Curry, signaled a possible movement back to a more vertical posture in his call for the Church to be the Jesus Movement. The five diocesan schisms made the liberal leaning majority of the Church more sensitive to the thoughts and needs of the minority conservatives. How all this would translate in the future remained to be seen. However, the schism movement in the Episcopal Church appeared to have ended. The problem that must be solved by the courts is whether sovereignty rests in the Episcopal Church or in the local dioceses, that is, whether the Church is hierarchical or not. If the courts rule the Episcopal Church is hierarchical, the Church will maintain its integrity as a unitary institution. If, on the other hand, the courts rule that sovereignty rests in the dioceses, the Church may well disintegrate, or at least change drastically over what has been known.

The issue of homosexuality divided the Anglican Communion beginning in 1997. The ensuing Anglican Realignment movement threatened to rend worldwide Anglicanism into two separate parts, one under the old Communion structure, the other under upstart GAFCON. Primates from Third World countries, primarily equatorial Africa, hostile to rights for homosexuals, led the campaign against the pro-homosexual Episcopal Church. They created GAFCON and Global South to rally their like-minded forces of the Anglican Communion. The four secessionist dioceses in the United States and GAFCON created the Anglican Church in North America in 2009 to be the replacement of the Episcopal Church in the Anglican Communion. The anti-homosexual movement in the Anglican Communion reached a crisis and turning point in 2016. In the primates' gathering in January of that year, the anti-Episcopal Church forces failed to get significant punishment for the Americans and abandoned their replacement stratagem. They agreed that if ACNA wanted to join the Anglican Communion it would have to go through the Anglican Consultative Council. It was the kiss of death for the possibility of ACNA's inclusion as a province of the Anglican Communion. When the Council met shortly thereafter, it did not mention the ACNA. As more provinces took up rights for homosexuals, the opposition declined. The Anglican Communion survived intact as the divisive issue of homosexuality faded to be left, as before 1997, to the discretion of each of the thirty-eight independent churches.

In the run-up to the schism, the diocesan leaders in South Carolina increasingly supported and promoted the Anglican Realignment movement. They broke the diocese away from the Episcopal Church to make it a part of what they believed to be a better way for the future, a surging new worldwide Anglican movement of "orthodox" religion. They used the emotional issue of homosexuality to do this. The problem for diocesan leaders was that, after the schism, they could not find a viable place in the Realignment. After four years of going it alone, they turned to the Anglican Church in North America even though it was not in the Anglican Communion and most likely would not be in the future. In the end, the Diocese of South Carolina was left without an official place in the Anglican Communion, or even a meaningful role in the fundamentalist-oriented Anglican Third World sub-set.

In South Carolina, the litigation in state court has ended. The state supreme court ruled mostly in favor of the Episcopal Church. However, as of this writing (August 2, 2017), legal actions continue in the federal court. It is possible that DSC will appeal the state supreme court decision to the United States Supreme Court. If so, there is a reasonable chance the Court will take the case in order to clarify First Amendment issues. In recent years, the Court has established two approaches to civil courts dealing with religious institutions, one to defer to an hierarchical church to settle its own internal disputes and the other to follow "neutral principles," that is, to judge between two religious parties when the disputes are over property. As we have seen, the difficulty of all this was shown very well by the state courts in Illinois and California that arrived at diametrically opposed decisions following "neutral principles" on the same issues. Only a ruling from the national Supreme Court can end this confusion.

As seen today, the best-case scenarios for the future of both sides are far apart. For the independent diocese, hope rests in the Anglican Realignment in which the most conservative provinces in some way will reform the majority of worldwide Anglicanism into a confessional, authoritarian, and socially conservative religion. This new confessional Anglicanism varies significantly from the broadly tolerant classical Anglicanism of history. The diocese has chosen to cast its lot with the Anglican Church in North America which is closely attached to the most important institutional aspects of the Anglican Realignment, GAFCON and Global South. The diocesan leaders insist this makes the diocese a part of the Anglican Communion. In sum, the Diocese of South Carolina has remade itself into a conservative, authoritarian, fundamentalist-oriented independent church claiming Anglican identity, but really existing on the fringe of the Anglican world, and supported by like-minded friends in America and abroad.

On the other side, the best-case scenario is a reunion of the two major parts of the old diocese. The Episcopal Church and the Episcopal Church in South Carolina would like very much for the two parts of the old diocese to rejoin and move forward together. At this moment, such a possibility seems remote. In 2015, the independent diocese scornfully spurned the offer of a compromise peace settlement in which the Church would grant the local properties to the parishes in return for the diocesan rights and assets. If this could not happen, any greater agreement would be even more unlikely. Today the independent diocese seems resolute in its bitter opposition to the Episcopal Church. As time goes by, there will be two factors that may affect this. The leaders and most of the followers who made the schism of 2012, and are emotionally committed to it, will gradually leave the scene. Also, in the years ahead, the social sensibilities of most South Carolinians will shift, as they are doing, to favor equal rights for and full inclusion of homosexual persons in all areas of life. A change of leaders and followers and the local social ethos will erode the foundations of the schism and the *raison d'être* of the independent diocese. If the diocese does return to the Episcopal Church, it will have to come from the shifting understandings of the leaders and people of this diocese. If the schism were caused by changing social factors, it stands to reason that it could be resolved by changing social factors.

The story of the Diocese of South Carolina for the last thirty-five years has been one of division. It all began in the 1980s as the diocesan leadership established the guiding principle that theological purity, as they defined it, must take precedence over institutional integrity. The course of schism in lower South Carolina began in earnest in 1997 with First Promise and grew from there. In 2000, its outgrowth, the Anglican Mission in America, established foreign Anglican primatial intervention. In 2004, All Saints of Pawleys Island, the home base of First Promise and AMiA, broke away from the Church and the diocese and then won its case in court. In 2010, another large parish, St. Andrew's of Mt. Pleasant, also bolted the Church and diocese, property in hand. In 2012, the diocese itself declared its separation from the Episcopal Church. The direct cause of the three schisms in South Carolina, 2004, 2010, and 2012, was the issue of homosexuality. To the people making the schisms, their views of theological purity had to take precedence over institutional integrity. To them, the schisms were entirely justified. Thus, within about a decade, the old Episcopal Diocese of South Carolina dissolved into four parts. The largest surviving section now counts for a less than three-fifths of the pre-schism diocese.

The schisms of 2004–2012 were incongruous with the long and glorious history of the great Episcopal Diocese of South Carolina. Since 1785, its whole life had been devoted to strengthening its innate bond with the Episcopal Church: organizing a state structure on national invitation, choosing a bishop against its will and only for the sake of the unity of the Church, sponsoring General Theological Seminary, rebuilding after the Civil War, and embracing the great democratic social reforms of the late twentieth century. This was the main course of the history of the Diocese of South Carolina; and it benefited the diocese immeasurably.

If the past is any guide to the future, we must end this story of the schism of 2012 on the expectation of diocesan reunification. The Diocese of South Carolina was the very last of the 111 dioceses of the Episcopal Church to integrate its convention racially. For a shamefully long time, South Carolina was arguably the most racist diocese in the Church. When the Schism of 1887 occurred, it seemed unthinkable that the diocese would ever treat its African American members with anything resembling dignity and respect. It seemed out of the question then and for many years to come. Even a bishop's hint of racial equality ended up with his murder. Yet, racial integration did come, however painfully and slowly. It did finally arrive. It took sixty-seven years after the Schism of 1887 for the convention to admit its first historically black congregation. It took a century for the diocese to place a person of African descent into a position of leadership. What seemed utterly unthinkable in 1887 did, in fact, happen in time. There was a similar story with rights for women. The diocese was also the last one in the Church to give equality and inclusion to women. Both racism and sexism seemed intractable at first in the diocese, but proved not to be so in the long run, even if it were an exceedingly long run. Another social prejudice, homophobia, may seem permanently embedded today in the majority diocese, but judging from history, it is not. It too will fade just as racism and sexism did. When that happens, South Carolinians will look back in dismay at the self-created diocesan tragedy of the schism of 2012 just as they now look back in regret on their wrongs of racism and sexism. In the end, we must believe there will be a better world, a place of equal rights and inclusion for all of God's children regardless of race, gender, or sexual orientation, a place of healing, peace, and unity. Such would be true to the historical legacy of the Episcopal Diocese of South Carolina.

Index

Abbey at Pawleys Island, 140
Abura, Joseph (Rt. Rev.), 436
Accord, January 2013, 206, 211
Ackerman, Keith Lyon (Rt. Rev.), 68, 82, 98, 234; *see also* Quincy, litigation, schism
Adams, Gladstone B. "Skip" III, (Rt. Rev.), 420
"An Affirmation in Response to the Proposed Pastoral of the House of Bishops Concerning Human Sexuality," 66–68
African Methodist Episcopal Church, 17
Ahmanson, Howard and Roberta, 72
Akinola, Peter (Most Rev.), 98, 115, 142, 146
Alexander, J. Neil (Rt. Rev.), 149
All Saints Church, Florence, 47, 404
All Saints Church, Hampton, 407
All Saints Church, Hilton Head, 111, 114, 380, 407, 418
All Saints Church, Pawleys Island, 17, 59, 73, 78–80, 85, 140; after disassociation, 137–40; appeal to U.S. Supreme Court, 138, 276; First Promise, 58, 78–80; litigation, 87, 137–38; property issue, 85–87; separation from diocese, TEC, 113–14; settlement of 2010, 138, 276
All Saints decision, 138, 266–67, 276, 291, 487–94
Allen, Patrick (Rev.), 84, 256–57, 261
Allin, John M. (Rt. Rev.), 43, 61
Allison, Christopher FitzSimons (Rt. Rev.), 139, 145, 149, 152, 184, 234, 316, 366, 416; after retirement, 57–60, 66; before election, 44; and Bishop John Spong, 55, 58; censure of, 2004, 60; and Denver ordinations, 2001, 59; episcopacy of, 43–57; election of, 43; First Promise, 79–80; and homosexuality issue, 48–57; and ordination of women, 46–47; retirement, 56; *Sexuality: A Divine Gift*, 50–54; and Singapore ordinations, 2000, 58, 85; and Trinity School for Ministry, 44–45; writings, 57
Allston, Robert Francis Withers, 16
Alternate primatial oversight, 129–30, 149–51, 154–58, 191
American Anglican Council, 71–72, 76, 78, 82, 104, 116, 122, 124–25, 127, 129–32, 140–41, 146, 157, 190, 200
American Episcopal Church, 41
American Revolutionary War, 3–5
Amsterdam Consultation, 86
Anaheim Statement, 2009, 259–60
Anderson, Bonnie, 185, 270–71
Anderson, David C. (Rev.), 72, 116–17, 121, 140–41, 157
Anderson, Dorothy M., 21
Anderson, Ivan, 405
Anglican Catholic Church, 41
Anglican Catholic Church of Canada, 41
Anglican Church in colonial South Carolina, 2–5
Anglican Church in North America, 141, 435, 441–46; establishment, 200–201, 250, 272
Anglican Church of Canada, 245
Anglican Coalition in Canada, 200
Anglican Communion, 119–20, 375, 388, 424, 431, 435, 437, 439, 444–46, 454
Anglican Communion Development Committee, 253, 271, 438
Anglican Communion Institute, 134, 254–55, 317
Anglican Communion Network, 121, 125–26, 131–32, 134–37, 140, 146, 151, 192, 200, 250, 500

Index

Anglican Communion Partners, 254
Anglican Consultative Council, 119, 135, 145, 201, 445
Anglican Covenant, 141, 151–52, 154, 247, 254–55, 266, 268
Anglican Jurisdiction of the Americas, 41
Anglican Life and Witness Conference, 77
Anglican Mission in the Americas, 59, 79, 86–88, 114, 139–41, 200, 441
Anglican Network in Canada, 200
Anglican Province in America, 141
Anglican Realignment movement, 41, 435, 454
Anis, Mouneer Hanna (Most Rev.), 116, 289, 293, 365, 438
Appeals Court, federal, *see* Court of Appeals, United States, Fourth Circuit
Archbishop of Canterbury, *see* Williams, Rowan; Welby, Justin
Archer, Richard (Rev.), 62
Armstrong, Don, 98
Armstrong, Nancy N., 353, 401, 405, 478
Ashley, Phil, 442
Atonement Church, Walterboro, 23
Atwood, Bill (Rt. Rev.), 76, 442
Avera, Mack, 144

Bailey, Erin Elizabeth, 380, 410
Bailey, Nancy, 410
Bakersfield, CA, 218–21, 230–31
Baldwin, William P., 380
Barfoot, Allison (Rev.), 98, 137
Barfoot Memo, 137
Barnum, Thaddeus R. (Rt. Rev.), 59, 85, 88
Barnwell, W.H. (Rev.), 20
Barr, John (Rev.), 137, 240, 261, 315, 331, 334, 405, 450
Barrow, Christine, 206
Barth, Karl, 44
Bates, Stephen, 131
Battle, Michael, 94
Batts, Robert, 144
Beach, Foley (Most Rev.), 201, 442, 443, 444–45
Beatty, Donald W., 489–94
Beckwith, Peter (Rt. Rev.), 206, 250, 271
Beers, David Booth, 234, 276, 473–74
Behre, Holly H., 380, 410, 471
Belin, Allard H., 14
Bell, Robert S., 100–105
Belmore, Constance D.S. (Rev.), 46
Belser, Richard (Rev.), 50, 62, 83, 87, 105, 112
Bena, David (Rt. Rev.), 127
Benfield, Larry (Rt. Rev.), 393
Benhase, Scott Anson (Rt. Rev.), 325
Benitez, Maurice M. (Rt. Rev.), 60, 68

Benson, John, 442
Bills, Jim (Rev.), 109, 114
Bishop Gadsden retirement community, 241
Bishops of Province IV, Dec. 14, 2011, 323–25
Bishop's Search Committee, 160–70
Black, Andy, 112
Black, Robert, 355, 471
Black Awareness Coordinating Committee, 28
Black Economic Development Conference, 28
Blankingship, A. Hugo, Jr., 124–25
Blessing of same-sex unions, in Episcopal Church in South Carolina, 420–21; in General Convention, 336–37; issue in Diocese of South Carolina, 328–54
Blossom, John (Rev.), 206
Board of Directors, *see* Standing Committee
Board of Trustees, 279–80, 315
Bolton, Charles, 3
Book of Common Prayer, The, revisions, 31–33
Borrett, Craige (Rev.), 105, 109, 135, 163, 167, 253, 261, 331, 405, 442
Bowden, John, 163
Bowen, Nathaniel (Rt. Rev.), 14
Boylston, Reid, 258, 315, 336, 405
Brenner, Ted, 442
Brewer, Gregory (Rt. Rev.), 98, 334, 340, 391, 417
Brillhart/Wilton principle, 458–62
Brinkmann, Mark (Rev.), 410
Brisbane, William, 9–10
Brookhart, Frank (Rt. Rev.), 157
Browning, Edward Lee (Most Rev.), 61–62, 64, 68–69
Bruno, Jon (Rt. Rev.), 145
Brust, Ellis English (Rev.), 167
Buchanan, Furman (Rev.), 308
Buchanan, John Clark (Rt. Rev.), 203, 380, 383, 406, 408, 471
Burroughs, Clayton, 125, 136
Burrows, William Ward, 9
Burtch, Jack W. "J.B.", 319–20
Burwell, John B. (Rev.), 75, 87, 100, 125, 167, 244, 258, 261, 336, 340, 366
By-Laws of the diocese, 296, 301–2, 379
By-Laws of the trustees, 280, 401

Calvary Church, Americus, Georgia, 416
Calvary Church, Charleston, 17–18, 22–23, 31, 377, 407, 418–19
Calvary Church, Pittsburgh, 198–99
Cambridge Accord, 81–82
Cantier, James (Rev.), 109
Carey, George (Archbishop of Canterbury), 65

514

"Caring for all the Churches: A Response of the House of Bishops of the Episcopal Church to an Expressed Need of the Church," 129
Carpenter, Charles G., 355, 414
Carpenter, Margaret A., 355
Carruthers, Thomas (Rt. Rev.), 23
Carter, Dorothy, 143
Cathedral Church of St. Luke and St. Paul, Charleston, 25, 39, 61, 233, 322, 404, 436, 448
Causes of schism, 495, 506; direct, 496–97; initiating events, 497–98; underlying, 496
"Certificate of Abandonment of the Episcopal Church and Statement of the Acts or Declarations which Show Such Abandonment," 357, 361
Chapman, Geoffrey (Rev.), 80, 98, 130, 140, 229
Chapman Memo, 128–32
Charismatic movement, 225
Charleston Hospital Workers' Strike, 27–28
Charleston Mercury, The, 433
Charlotte Observer, The, 433
Charry, Ellen, 94
Cheraw, SC, 412
"Choose this Day," 146
Christ Church, Denmark, 407
Christ Church, Mt. Pleasant, 252, 267, 322, 448
Christ/St. Paul's Church, Yonges Island, 108, 322, 403, 448
Christ the King Church, Pawleys Island, 140, 322, 404, 416
Christ the King-Grace Church, Pawleys Island, 140
Church Insurance Company of Vermont, 464–65
Church of England, *see* Anglican Church
Church of England Newspaper, The, 346–47
Church of Our Saviour, Anglican, Florence, 42
Church of St. Luke and St. Paul, Charleston, *see* Cathedral Church of St. Luke and St. Paul
Church of the Advent, Brookline, PA, 202
Church of the Atonement, Carnegie, PA, 202
Church of the Cross, Bluffton, 262, 322, 376, 403, 448
Church of the Epiphany, Summerville, 407
Church of the Good Shepherd, Charleston, 261–62, 322, 404, 448, 476
Church of the Good Shepherd, Hazelwood, PA, 202
Church of the Good Shepherd, Summerville, 412, 418

Church of the Good Shepherd, Sumter. 23, 407
Church of the Heavenly Rest, Estill, 407
Church of the Holy Comforter, Sumter, 25, 63, 403, 448
Church of the Holy Communion, Allendale, 407
Church of the Holy Communion, Charleston, 49, 83, 322, 377, 381, 407, 418–19
Church of the Holy Cross, Stateburg, 404
Church of the Holy Cross, Sullivans Island, 322, 447–48, 454
Church of the Redeemer, Orangeburg, 404
Church of the Resurrection, North Charleston, 448
Church of the Resurrection, Surfside Beach, 322, 404
Church Times, 441
Circuit Court, litigation in, 401–6, 465–84; appeal, 2015, 482–84; background of trial, 465–73; decision, Feb. 3, 2015, 480–82; lawsuit of Jan. 4, 2012, 401–4; trial, July 8–24, 2014, 473–80
Civil Rights Movement, 24–31
"Clarity Ensued," 237–41
Clark, Anthony J. (Very Rev.), 100, 232
Clark, Betty Deas (Rev.), 419
Clark, Daniel (Rev.), 84
Clark, Holland (Rev.), 62
Clarke, Daniel (Rev.), 414
Clarke, Ken (Rt. Rev.), 436
Clarkson, William, 256, 261
Clement, James (Rev.), 206
Clergy day, Aug. 13, 2009, 263–65; Oct. 11, 2011, 316–17; Oct. 19, 2012, 371
Click, Carolyn, 390
Coleman, James M. (Rt. Rev.), 68
Coleridge, Clarence (Rt. Rev.), 157
Colorado River principle, 458–62
Committee on Negro Work, 23, 26
Committee to Reorganize the Diocese of Quincy, 203
Common Cause Partners, 141
"Communion Across Difference," July 2, 2015, 424
"Communion Partners Salt Lake City Statement," July 2, 2015, 423–24
Complaint for Declaratory and Injunctive Relief, January 4, 2013, 403
Conger, George, 390
"Consequences," *see* Primates' gathering, January, 2016
Conspiracy charge in court, 467–70, 498–99
Conspiracy, issue, *see* Bishop's Search Committee

Index

Constitution and Canons, 9–11, 14, 187, 206, 244–45, 285–87, 295, 306, 309–11, 322, 351–52, 358–59, 367–68, 392–93, 407, 428, 481
Continuing Anglican movement, 41
Convocation of Anglicans in North America, 200
Convocation of Negro Churchmen, 23, 26
Cook, Jeremy, 420
Cooperman, Alan, 131
Corbett, Johnnie, 256, 261
Council of Advice, 393
Countryman, William L., 63
Court actions, *see* Circuit Court; Court of Appeals; District Court, United States; Supreme Court, South Carolina; Supreme Court, United States
Court of Appeals, United States, Fourth Circuit, 460–62; decision, Mar. 31, 2015, 460; decision, Feb. 21, 2017, 462; hearing, January 28, 2015, 460; hearing, December 9, 2016, 462
"A Covenant on Episcopal Pastoral Care," 129
Cox, William (Rt. Rev.), 60
Curry, Michael B. (Most Rev.), 325, 417–18; election as presiding bishop, 425; visit to Charleston, April 8–10, 2016, 419
Cutler, Howard (Rev.), 29

Dalcho, Frederick, 5–10
Daniel, Angela, 408
Daniel, Clifton, III (Rt. Rev.), 234, 323, 325, 382, 477
Daniels, Theodore A. (Rt. Rev.), 94
Dar es Salaam Communiqué, 156–57
Dator, James, 12
Davids, Peter Hugh (Rev.), 228
Davis, Thomas F. (Rt. Rev.), 16
Dawley, Powell Mills, 291
"The Decision," 147
Dedmon, Robert (Rev.), 206
Dehon, Theodore (Rt. Rev.), 11, 13
Deimel, Lionel E., 176, 179
Delany, Henry B. (Rt. Rev.), 20
Demby, Thomas (Rt. Rev.), 20
Dennis, Ann, 256, 261, 315
Dennis Canon, 42, 43, 86–87, 137–38, 255, 257, 272, 276, 279, 288, 291, 295, 302, 310, 322–23, 356, 430, 432, 434, 481, 488–94
Derfner, Armand G., 476
DeWolf family, 426
Dickinson, Peet (Rev.), 261, 331, 442
Dickson, Alex (Rt. Rev.), 58, 60, 74, 79, 454
Diocesan Commission on Human Sexuality, 50

Diocesan Committee on Blessings, 421
Diocesan Convention, meeting of: 1785, 6; 1786, 7–8; 1787, 9; 1789, 9; 1790, 10–11; 1794, 10; 1795, 11; 1804, 11, 13; 1806, 14; 1807, 11; 1839, 14; 1840, 14; 1866, 16; 1887, 17; 1911, 20; 1945, 22; 1946, 22; 1949, 22; 1951, 22; 1953, 22; 1954, 22; 1955, 22; 1956, 22; 1960, 23; 1960 special convention, 25; 1965, 26; 1966, 26; 1967, 34, 38; 1969, 32; 1970, 29–30; 1971, 30; 1973, 38; 1975, 35; 1977, 35, 37; 1979, 33; 1980 special convention, 43; 1980, 31, 43; 1985, 48; 1987, 49, 52; 1988, 51; 1989 special convention, 61; 1990, 62; 1992, 65; 1997, 73–74; 2001, 83; 2002, 84; 2003 special convention, 109–13; 2009, 252–54; 2009 special convention, 267–71; 2010, 281–87; 2010 special convention, 292–98; 2011, 303–6; 2012, 329–31; 2012 special convention, 385–90; after schism, 439, 450–53
Diocesan Future Committee, 420
Diocese of Christ the King, 41
Diocese of South Carolina, after schism, 427–55: affiliation issue, 388, 390, 438, 446; and the Anglican Church in North America, 431, 435, 446; bishops visiting, 436; budgets, 48–49; disaffiliation from TEC, 365–66; and issues of homosexuality, 428–29, 451–53; legal expenses, 449–50; marriage policies, 451–53; membership in, 446–48; relations with the Anglican Communion, 431, 435, 438; special convention, Nov. 17, 2012, 385–90; Statement of Faith, 455; Task Force on Marriage, 451–53; and Women's Ordination, 429, 453–54
Diocese of South Carolina, before schism: accession to TEC Constitution and Canons, 9–14, 295; and All Saints Church, Pawleys Island, 85–87, 113–15, 137–38, 291; alternative primatial oversight, 110, 123–27, 154–59; Anglican Communion Network, 123–27, 134–37; and the Civil War, 15–16; consecration of Bishop Lawrence, 233–36; Dennis Canon, 255–57, 272, 279, 288, 295, 302, 322–23; early 19th century, 13–15; and election of Jefferts Schori, 2006, 152; establishment of, 5–10; first bishop, 11; General Convention of 2009, aftermath, 260–74;

General Convention of 2012, reaction to, 341–62; homosexuality issue, in 1980s, 48–54, in 1990s, 61–70, 77–80, in 2000s, 81, 84–85, in 2009–10, 257–60, 263–65, 267–70, 282–83, 286–87, in 2012, 328–85; incorporation change, 2010, 296; and Jerusalem Declaration, 2008, 245–46; membership statistics, 13, 17, 19, 22–23, 39, 56, 188–89; Negro Suffragan Bishop movement, 20–21; nullification, 107; prayer book reform, 31–33; and pro-TEC minority, 111–12, 133–34; racial integration, 22–23, 26–31; racism after the Civil War, 17–27; resolutions on sovereignty, 107; resolution on withdrawal from bodies of TEC, 268; resolution on withdrawal of accession to canons of TEC, 295; and the Righter affair, 68–70; and the Robinson affair, 104–15; role in TEC Constitution and Canons, 1789, 8–10; and St. Andrew's of Mt. Pleasant, 272–73, 288; Schism of 1887, 17–19; Schism of 2012, 362–65; search for new bishop, 2005–07, 159–89; and Title IV, 305–7; and Trinity School for Ministry, 44–45; visit of Jefferts Schori, 2008, 236–42; Windsor Report, 141–53; women's ordination, 33–35, 46–48, 329–30

Diocese of the Holy Cross, 441

Disaffiliation resolution, October 2, 2012, 352–53

Disciplinary Board for Bishops, 306, 312–21, 355–59, 362

District Court, United States (Charleston), 456–65: appeal to U.S. Court of Appeals, 2014, 459–61; appeal to U.S. Court of Appeals, 2015–16, 462; ECSC Lawsuit, Mar. 5, 2013, 456–57; hearing, Aug. 8, 2013, 458; insurance case, 464–65; Order, Aug. 23, 2013, 458–59; Order, Sept. 21, 2015, 462; removal to District Court, 462–64

Division of the Diocese of South Carolina, 1922, 20

Dooley, Ellen, 421

Douglas, Hillery P., 380, 410

Douglas, Ian T. (Rt. Rev.), 94, 312

Douglas, William, 475–76

Douglas Trust, 475–76

Drakeford, Drak, 256–57, 261

Drayton, Herbert, III, 112

Dromantine Communiqué, 145

Duffy, Patrick Michael, 465

Duncan, Robert (Rt. Rev.), 97–98, 101, 118, 122–26, 139, 141, 146, 154–55, 229, 244, 248–49, 272, 441; *see also* Pittsburgh, litigation, schism

Duque-Gomez, Francisco (Rt. Rev.), 149, 393

Duvall, Charles (Rt. Rev.), 455

East Cooper Episcopal Church, Mt. Pleasant, 412, 418, 426

Ecclesiastical Constitution, 7–8

Echols, Janet (Rev.), 329

Edgar, Walter B., 3–4, 457, 477

Edisto Island, 412

Ekklesia Society, 76, 78, 82

Elmore, Frances L., 355

Emanuel A.M.E. Church, Charleston, 419, 425

Enthusiastically Episcopalian conference, May 3, 2014, 418

Epiphany Church, Eutawville, 404

Episcopal Church: antebellum, 5–16; and civil rights, 24–31; and Civil War, 15–16; early counter-revolution in, 39–43, 76–77; establishment of, 5–9; government of, 12; homosexuality issues, 36–39, 61–70, 257–60, 336–41, 421–24; and prayer book reform, 31–33; women's equality issues, 33–35

Episcopal Church, conventions in Philadelphia: 1784, 5; 1785, 6–7; 1786, 8–9; 1789, 9–10

Episcopal Church in Okatie, 412, 418

Episcopal Church in South Carolina: churches of, 407; in circuit court, 401–6; Clergy in Good Standing, 414–15; convention, Mar. 8–9, 2013, 413–14; convention, Feb. 2014, 418; convention, Nov. 2014, 418; convention, Nov. 2015, 419; Enthusiastically Episcopalian conference, May 3, 2014, 418; membership, 407–8; Province IV meeting, June 2013, 417; and race, 425–26; release of clergy, 414–15; reorganization in 2012, 379–85, 396; reorganization in 2013, 407–20; return of clergy, 414, 416–17; same-sex marriage, 424–25; same-sex unions, blessings, 420–21; special convention, Jan. 26, 2013, 408–11; visit of P.B. Curry, Apr. 2016, 419

Episcopal Church on Edisto, 412, 418

Episcopal Church of the Messiah, Myrtle Beach, 412, 418

Index

Episcopal Forum of South Carolina, 133, 142, 158–59, 175, 186–87, 250, 254, 271, 281, 290, 299, 308, 332, 345: denounced, October 2012, 374; and election of bishop, 177; letter to Executive Council, Sept. 22, 2010, 290; letter to Province IV, Nov. 9, 2010, 301; letter to TEC, June 2007, 286–87

Episcopal Society for Cultural and Racial Unity, 25

Episcopal Synod of America, 55, 64, 71, 79

Episcopal Worship Group of Cheraw, 412

Ervin, Bill, 136

Establishment Acts of 1704, 1706, 3

Evans, Lydia, 100, 105, 125, 136, 163, 167, 186, 256–58, 261, 336

Evenson, Bruce (Rev.), 414

Ewald, Todd (Rev.), 225

Ewalt, Jo Ann, 420

Executive Committee, Council, Episcopal Church, 52, 59, 88, 145, 187, 271, 280, 290, 300, 309–12, 352, 412–13

Extra-provincial diocese, Anglican Communion, 387–88

Fairfield, Andrew (Rt. Rev.), 69

Fairfield, Leslie Parke (Rev.), 228

"The False gospel of indiscriminate inclusivity," 263–65, 267

Federal Court, *see* District Court, United States (Charleston), and Court of Appeals, United States

Feliberty-Ruberte, Victor, 312

Fellers, Gayle, 134

Fellowship of Concerned Churchmen, 41

Fellowship of Witness, 41, 45

Fielding, Herbert, 105

Final Order, Feb. 3, 2015, 480–82

First Promise, 58, 78–80, 85

Fisher, John C. (Rev.), 409

Fitzpatrick, Robert (Rt. Rev.), 312

Fleming, Samuel C.W. (Rev.), 48–49

Flores, Alesia Rico, 410

Flowers, Martha, 163

Forsythe, W.E. (Rev.), 26

Fort Worth, litigation, 209–15; schism, 207–9

Forward in Faith North America. 55, 82, 141, 200, 202

Foster, John (Rev.), 442

Four Instruments of Communion, 445

Foy, Mary Ann, 410, 422

Free, H. Dagnall, Jr. (Rev.), 416

Fuchs, Frances, 162, 167

Fuener, Paul (Rev.), 163, 170–71, 229, 311, 315, 331, 334, 365, 405, 467–69

Gadsden, Christopher (Rt. Rev.), 13–14

GAFCON (Global Anglican Future Conference), 115, 201, 248, 272, 443–46

GAFCON I conference, 245–46

GAFCON II conference, 436–37

GAFCON Primates' Council, 437

Gagnon, Robert, 308

Gaillard, Samuel Porcher, IV, 143, 256, 261, 476

Geer, Charles C., 380, 410

General Convention: 1865, 16; 1904, 20; 1955, 25; 1958, 25; 1964, 26. 32; 1967, 27, 32–33; 1969, 28; 1970, 34; 1973, 34; 1976, 35–36; 1979, 32, 37, 48, 61; 1982, 48, 50; 1985, 48; 1991, 53–64; 1994, 65–68; 1997, 74–77, 94; 2000, 81–82; 2003, 95–104; 2006, 147–54; 2009, 257–60; 2012, 336–41; 2015, 421–25

General Convention 2009, boycott resolution, 253

General Convention Special Program, 27–31

General Theological Seminary, 13

Gervais, Paul T., 14

Gibson, Eleanor, 30

"The Gift of Sexuality: A Theological Perspective," 94

Gilbert, Jan, 414

Gilchrist, Barbara, 105

Ginsburg, Ruth Bader, 489

Glasspool, Mary (Rt. Rev.), 273, 281

Glenn, Terrell (Rt. Rev.), 75, 77, 442

Global South, 73, 123, 248, 250, 289, 435, 438–39: meeting in Cairo, February 14–15, 2014, 437; Primates' Steering Committee, 437–38, 440; Primatial Oversight Council, 438

Golding, Henrietta U., 170, 473

Gomez, Drexel (Most Rev.), 98, 135, 146

Goodman, Mark (Rev.), 110, 165

Goodstein, Arnold Samuel, 403

Goodstein, Diane Schafer, 402–3; *see also* Circuit Court

Grace Anglican Church, Pawleys Island, 139–40

Grace Church, Charleston, 17, 29, 34, 46, 114, 269, 377, 407–8, 417; cathedral, 419–20

Grace Parish, North Myrtle Beach, 448

Grafe, Rob (Rev.), 139

Grant, Henry L. (Rev.), 26

Grate, Lucille, 420

Green, Guerry, 276

Green, Michael (Rev. Canon), 125

Gregg, William O. (Rt. Rev.), 94

Grifiss, James E., 94
Grimball, Henry E., 485
Grish, Carol, 421
Griswold, Frank Tracy (Most Rev.), 76, 79, 111, 117, 129–30, 154
Guelzo, Allen C., 477–78
Guernsey, John (Rt. Rev.), 442
Guerry, Edward (Rev.), 29
Guerry, William Alexander (Rt. Rev.), 19–21
Guess, Emily, 420
Guildford Diocesan Evangelical Fellowship, 333
Gulick, Edwin F., Jr. (Rt. Rev.), 149, 210

Hafer, Joel (Rev.), 109
Haines, Ronald H. (Rt. Rev.), 63–64
Haley, Nikki, 426
Halkward, Ted, 186
Hamilton, Lonnie, III, 100, 143, 186, 336, 340, 380, 406, 410, 420, 422, 471
Hane, Doris E., 47
Hank, Daniel (Rev.), 389
Harder, Joyce (Rev.), 454
Harding, Cynthia L., 355
Harding, Flint, III, 355
Harmon, Kendall S. (Rev.): 1980s, 53–55, 57; 1990s, 62–63, 75, 77; 2009, 253–54, 258, 261, 269; 2010, 285, 289; 2011, 315, 317; 2012 before schism, 339, 343; 2012, Nov., 397; 2015, 442, 455; AAC, 122–23; ACN, 125–26, 135; and Barbara Harris, 54–55; bishop's search, 182, 184, 186; GC 2006, 148; Hope and a Future, 2005, 146–47; in October 2012, 365–76; PB visit 2008, 239, 241–42; A Place to Stand 2003, 117–18, 2004, 140–41; Plano East 125; reaction to Robinson affair, 104–15, 136; and Robinson affair, 97–104, 127–28; and *Sexuality: A Divine Gift*, 53–54; and Windsor Report, 142–44
Harrington, Ann, 136
Harrington, Myron, 450
Harris, Barbara (Rt. Rev.), 54–55
Harris, Roger S. (Rt. Rev.), 408
Harrison, Dena (Rt. Rev.), 312
Harvin, Scott, 439
Haskell, Louis A. (Rev.), 22, 25
Hathaway, Alden (Rt. Rev.), 165, 196, 228–29, 234, 256
Hawkins, George, 406
Haworth, Janna, 206
Hayes, Christopher, 312
Haynsworth, George Edward (Rt. Rev.), 61, 66
Hayson, Lynn, 134
Hearn, George M., Jr., 471
Hearn, Kaye, 471, 489–94

Henderson, Dorsey (Rt. Rev.), 145, 157, 312–21, 356–59, 408, 471
Henning, William D., Jr., 228
Hewitt, Blake A., 483–84, 487–94
Hey, Sarah, 137
Heyward, Thomas, 105
Hicks, Josephine, 318–19
High, Rayford B., Jr. (Rt. Rev.), 210
Hill, Wesley, 453
Hills, Roy (Rev.), 109, 410
Hines, John F. (Rt. Rev.), 26
Hobby, James (Rt. Rev.), 201, 454
Hodgson, Gregory (Rev.), 109
Hollerith, Herman (Rt. Rev.), 312
Holliman, Barbara (Rev.), 454
Holmes, Allan R., 487
Holmes, David L., 15
Holy Cross Faith Memorial Church, Pawleys Island, 23, 114, 140, 407, 418–19
Holy Family Church, Fresno, CA, 225
Homosexuality: issue in equatorial Africa, 115–16; issue in Episcopal Church, in 1970s, 36, in 1980s, 61–62, in 1990s, 61–70, 2000–09, 95–104, 149, 258–60, 2012, 336–39, 2015, 421–23; issue in South Carolina, in 1970s, 37, in 1980s, 40, in 1990s, 61–82, in 2000s, 82–88, 2009, 258–60, 263–65, 267–71, 2010, 282–83, 286, 2011, 308, 2012, 328–69, after 2012, 428–29, 451–53
Hope and a Future, conference, 146–47
Hopkins, John Henry (Rt. Rev.), 16
Horn, Martha (Rev.), 454
Horn, Robert (Rev.), 405
Horres, Eleanor, 355
Houck, Charles Weston, 457
Houghton, Alanson (Rev.), 109
House of Bishops, 10, 57, 60, 64, 66, 94, 145, 156, 289, 307, 333:2003, 129; 2008, Mar., 243; 2008, Sept., 248; 2009, Mar., 254; 2010, Mar., 281; 2011, Mar., 307; and Dar es Salaam Communiqué, 156–57; and Windsor Report, 2005, 142–45
Howe, John W. (Rt. Rev.), 68, 91, 94, 121, 157, 271, 289
Howe, William (Rt. Rev.), 17–18
Hoyle, Erin, 406
Huey, Marshall (Rev.), 452; letter to the parish, February, 2013, 432
Huff, Christopher M. (Rev.), 421
Huff, William, 28
Huguenots, 2–3
Hulsey, Sam (Rt. Rev.), 208
Hunter, Joy, 248, 254, 299, 366, 382, 405

Index

Ihloff, Robert W. (Rt. Rev.), 94
Iker, Jack L. (Rt. Rev.), 68, 82, 98, 123, 150, 154–55; *see also* Fort Worth, litigation, schism
Incorporation, 38
Incorporation, Certificate of (1973), 38
"The Indianapolis Statement," 340
Injunction, *see* Temporary Injunction
Institute on Religion and Democracy, 71, 72, 127

Jecko, Stephen H. (Rt. Rev.), 68
Jefferts Schori, Katharine (Most Rev.), 1, 154, 186, 188, 471:2010, 280, 283, 292, 299; and Bp. Skilton, 416; and call from Lawrence, Oct. 17, 2012, 365–66; and Disciplinary Board for Bishops, 2012, 365–66; election as presiding bishop, 149–50; and Fort Worth, 208, 210; invitation to SC, 236; and Lawrence's Renunciation, 392–93; Oct. 3, 2012 meeting, 360; Oct. 3–15, 2012, 360–62; and Pittsburgh, 199–200; and Quincy, 203; and reorganization of diocese, 2012, 379–85, 408–11; removal of Lawrence, 392–94; restriction on Lawrence, Oct. 15, 2012, 362–64; and San Joaquin, 194; visit to Charleston, 2008, 236–42; visit to SC, Jan. 2012, 408–11; visit to SC, May 3, 2014, 418
Jeffords, Julian, III (Tripp) (Rev.), 334, 405, 442
Jenkins, Charles E., III (Rt. Rev.), 149
Jenkins, Edward (Rev.), 11
Jennings, Gay Clark (Rev.), 408, 418
Jerusalem Declaration of 2008, 245–46
Johnson, Don E. (Rt. Rev.), 325
Johnson, Edward (Rev.), 26
Johnson, Robert C., Jr. (Rt. Rev.), 69
Johnson, Robert H. (Rt. Rev.), 200, 408
Jones, Edward W. (Rt. Rev.), 69
Jones V. Wolf, 42
July 28, 2009 meeting, 261–62

Kaeton, Elizabeth (Rev.), 180
Kallsen, Kevin, 390
Kearon, Kenneth, 154–55
Keith, Wil (Rev.), 410, 421
Kelaher, Ed (Rev.), 261
Kelshaw, Terence (Rt. Rev.), 68
Kilgo, Robert, 405
Kirkland, Cecil, 136
Kittredge, John W., 471, 489–94
Knippers, Diane, 71–72, 98, 118, 122, 125
Koets, Eleanor B., 355–56

Kohne, Frederick, 13
Kolini, Emmanuel (Most Rev.), 58, 98
Kostel, Mary E., 473, 478
Kowbeidu, Anthony (Rev.), 163, 186, 256, 261, 288
Kronz, Gregory (Rev.), 162, 169–71, 229, 273, 468
The Kuala Lumpur Statement on Human Sexuality, 73–74, 79
Kunes, Robert M., 405, 475
Kusko, Karen, 442
Kwist, John, 355
Kwist, Margaret S., 355, 380

Lachicotte, Martha, 140
Lackey, Keith, 163
Lambeth Conference of 1998, 76–77, 81
Lambeth Conference of 2008, 246–47
Lane, Steven (Rt. Rev.), 393
Lanham Act, 456
LARCUM (Lutheran, Anglican, Roman Catholic, and United Methodist) conference, 308
Lawrence, Bertha Ann Coombs, 220–21, 399
Lawrence, Chadwick E. (Rev.), 254, 314, 318
Lawrence, Leo Douglas, 219–20
Lawrence, Mark Joseph (Rt. Rev.), 1, 405, 438–39, 450, 454: abandonment charge, 357–59; ancestry, 218–21; advertisement, Nov. 14, 2012, 282–83; and Archbishop of Canterbury, 265–66; at St. John's of Florence, Oct. 28, 2012, 378–79; at Old St. Andrew's, 427–32; authority of, resolution, Mar. 2010, 285–87; and background of General Convention, 2012, 328–36; before Lambeth 2008, 243–46; and Bishop's Search Committee, 165–75; and Board of Trustees, 279, 401; and Clergy Conference, Oct. 19, 2012, 371–72; and Clergy Day, Aug. 13, 2009, 263–65; and Clergy Day, Oct. 11, 2011, 316–17; and Clergy Day, July 25, 2012, 346; convention of Mar. 2009, 252–54; conversion, 222–23; and Dennis Canon, 255–57, 272, 302; disaffiliation declaration to presiding bishop, 365–66; and Disciplinary Board for Bishops, 2011, 312–21; and Disciplinary Board for Bishops, 2012, 355–59; early ministry, 225–33; employment agreement, Feb. 1, 2011, 304; failure of first consents, 182–83; first consent process, 175–85; first election, 169; GAFCON I, 2008,

245–46; and General Convention of 2009, 257–60; and Global South, 289; and House of Bishops, 243–44, 248, 254, 281, 289, 307, 333, 340; in Bakersfield, 230–33; in General Convention of 2012, 336–41; in McKeesport, Pennsylvania, 225–30; and Jefferts Schori after the schism, 365–85; Lambeth 2008, 246–47; lease agreement, 279–80; letter, Mar. 7, 2007, 182; letter, Sept. 23, 2010, 291; letter, Sept. 28, 2011, 311–12; letter of July 13, 2012, 343; letter to Standing Committee, Oct. 2, 2012, 351–52; and Logan/Tisdale affair, 277–80; meeting July 28, 2009, 261–62; Oct. 16–17, 2012, 365–69; Oct. 17–Nov. 17, 2012, 365–85; ordination and consecration as bishop, 233–36; and Presiding Bishop's visit 2008, 236–42; and quit claim deeds, 322–27; reaction to General Convention of 2009, 260–74; reaction to General Convention of 2012, 341–54; removal and release, 392–96; renunciation issue, 394–96; request from Standing Committee, Sept. 20, 2012, 350–51; restriction, 362–63; and Robinson Affair, 100, 232; schism, Oct. 15, 2012, 362–65; second consent process, 185–88; second election, 186–87; and special convention, Nov. 17, 2012, 385–90; and Trinity School for Ministry, 45, 249, 289, 308, 360; writings, 172–73; youth, 221–25; *see also vonRosenberg v. Lawrence*; litigation

Lawrence, Robert (Rev.), 477
Lawsuit of January 4, 2013, *see* Complaint for Declaratory and Injunctive Relief
Lee, Peter James (Rt. Rev.), 102–3, 154
Legal actions, *see* Circuit Court; Court of Appeals; District Court, United States; Supreme Court, South Carolina; Supreme Court, United States
Legal Defense Fund, 450
Leigh, Tobyn, 206
Lewis, James B. (Rev.), 261, 302, 315, 336, 349, 373–74, 383, 390, 397, 405, 409, 433, 442, 450, 455, 467, 474–75, 483, 485–86
Lichtenberger, Arthur (Rt. Rev.), 25
Lillibridge, Gary (Rt. Rev.), 157, 259
Limehouse, Frank (Rev.), 84, 87, 105, 144, 162
Lindsay, Richard C. (Rev.), 109, 111–12, 313, 380, 410, 421–22
Lindsay, Ross "Buddy" III, 290
Lipscomb, John (Rt. Rev.), 154

Litigation, *see* Circuit Court; Court of Appeals; District Court, United States; Supreme Court, South Carolina; Supreme Court, United States
Little, Edward (Rt. Rev.), 380
Logan, Wade H., III, 100, 244, 256, 258, 260–61, 266, 259, 302, 315, 319, 322–23, 347, 349–50, 360, 362, 364, 391, 401, 442, 475, 478; Tisdale, dispute of 2010, 275–81
Lomax, Bill, 420
Louttit, Henry I., Jr. (Rt. Rev.), 408
Love, William H. (Rt. Rev.), 271, 337, 340
Lovelace, Rebecca S., 380, 410
Lucka, Melinda, 313, 332, 345, 374, 384, 406, 410, 471; complaint of Mar. 23, 2012, 354–56; letter, May 25, 2011, 309–12
Luke, Betsy, 134
Lumanog, Jack, 442
Lumpkin, Mike (Rev.), 105, 110, 168
Lusaka, Zambia, 445–46
Lyles, William G., 334, 381, 405

McAlpine, Laurie A. (Rev.), 47
McConnell, Dorsey (Rt. Rev.), 200
McCormick, J. Haden (Rev.), 87, 137, 162, 181, 183–84, 236, 258, 450
McCormick, Matthew Wright (Rev.), 416
McCrady, Edward, 16
McCrady, Edward, Jr., 17
McDonald, Bruce, 442
McGill, Matthew, 464
McIntosh, Mark, 94
McKeesport, PA, 226–27
McKellar, Andrea, 421–22
Mackey, Stephen (Rev.), 26
McPhail, Donald (Rev.), 109
MacPherson, D. Bruce (Rt. Rev.), 206, 271
McWilliams, Martin C., 476, 481
Madden, Robert F. (Rev.), 228
"Making Biblical Anglicans for a Global Age," 253
Malone, Michael T. (Rev.), 100, 168
Mann, Barbara, 133–34, 271, 300, 310, 355–56, 406, 410, 471
Mann, David W., 355
Marriage Task Force, 455
Martin, Bill, 143
Martin, William E. (Gen.), 16
Martins, Daniel (Rt. Rev.), 266, 307, 340, 384–85
Mason, Bruce, 132
Masters, John E., 100, 232
Mathes, James R. (Rt. Rev.), 300, 393

Index

Matthews, Clayton (Rt. Rev.), 160, 355, 393
Mayer, J. Scott (Rt. Rev.), 210, 312
Meace, Eric, 136
Melango, Bernard (Most Rev.), 98, 116
"Memorandum of Agreement on Establishing a Network of Confessing Dioceses and Congregations in the Episcopal Church," 123
Menaul, Marjorie (Rev.), 312
Merchant, Wilmot T., II, 380, 410, 422
Mere Anglicanism conferences, 135, 275
Mersereau, Warren, 355–56
"A Message to the People of the Diocese of South Carolina," November 14, 2012, 382
Messiah Church, St. Paul, MN, 416
Meyers, Gregg, 403
Middleton, N. Russell, 14
Millard, Jonathan (Rev.), 201
Miller, Dolores J., 134, 143, 355, 378
Miller, Jeffrey (Rev.), 84, 144, 162, 171, 256–57, 261–62, 302, 304, 310, 316, 322, 365, 405, 442, 450, 467
Mills, Ladson, III (Rev.), 415
Minns, Martyn (Rt. Rev.), 98, 115, 121, 125, 136
Missionary Convocation of Kenya, 200
Missionary Convocation of the Southern Cone, 200
Missionary Convocation of Uganda, 200
Mitchell, Edward, 8
Mitchell, Peter T., 409, 450
Mitman, Edward, 334, 405
Moffit, Robert, 414
Moore, B. Allston, 29
Moore, Peter C. (Rev.), 229, 281, 455
Moore, William Moultrie, Jr. (Rt. Rev.), 46
Moriarty, Pete (Rev.), 78
Morris, Lewis, 9
Mpalanya Nkoyoyo, Livingstone (Most Rev.), 116
Mueller, Mary Ann, 390
Mullin, Robert Bruce, 457
Munday, Robert S. (Very Rev.), 126, 415
Murphy, Charles H., III (Rt. Rev.), 58, 62, 65, 73, 78, 82, 85–88, 113, 139–41, 441
Murray, Tom (Rev.), 84
Myers, Tom, 133–35

Nairobi, Kenya, 437, 446
"The Nairobi Communiqué," October 26, 2013, 437
Nashotah House, 45, 188, 245, 289, 308, 334
Nassau conference (2000), 82
Naughton, Jim, 71–72
Nazir-Ali, Michael (Rt. Rev.), 289, 292
Network of Confessing Dioceses and Parishes, 122–23
Neutral principles, 42
Nietert, Jack (Rev.), 109, 112, 143, 414
Noll. Stephen, 77, 228
Norris, Catharine Moore (Rev.), 454
"Notice of Removal," Episcopal Church in South Carolina, 415, 463
Ntagali, Stanley (Most Rev.), 444–45
Nullification, 268, 271
Nunley, Jan, 131

Obama, Barack, 426
Obergefell v. Hodges, 421
O'Connor, Sandra Day, 489
October 3, 2012, meeting, 360
October 15, 2012, schism, 362–65
October 17, 2012, 365–69
O'Dell, Andrew (Rev.), 334, 405
Ohl, Wallis (Rt. Rev.), 210
Okatie, SC, 412
Olbrych, Jennie C. (Rev.), 47, 100, 105–6, 125, 179, 256, 261, 329
Old St. Andrew's, *see* St. Andrew's Church (West Ashley)
O'Neill, Rob (Rt. Rev.), 393
"An Open Letter to The Episcopal Church in South Carolina from the Bishops of Province IV," June 27, 2013, 417
Orangeburg Massacre, 27–28
Owens, Chuck (Rev.), 137, 261, 331

Pagliaro, Dottie, 133–34
Pagliaro, Lynn A., 133–35, 159, 186
Parker, Adam, 370, 390
Parker, John, 8
Parsley, Henry N. (Rt. Rev.), 94, 149–50
Patterson, Donis D. (Rt. Rev.), 69
Pearson, Andrew (Rev.), 125
PEARUSA, 441
Pelzer, Cornelia, 421
Pennewill, Elizabeth, 258, 334, 336, 405, 442, 450
Perry, Constance, 426
Perry, Dain, 426
Petigru, James L., 14
Philadelphia conventions, *see* Episcopal Church, conventions in Philadelphia
Pinckney, C.C., 16
Pinckney, Charles, 7
Pinckney, Clementa (Rev.), 425
Pinkerton, Robert B., 355–56, 414, 420
Pippin, J. Edwin (Rev.), 47

Pittsburgh, litigation, 200–202; schism, 196–200
Place, Geoff, 143
"A Place to Stand: A Call to Action," 118–19
A Place to Stand, Declaring, Preparing, 116–19
Plano/Dallas conference, 2003, 116–19
Plano East, 125
Platte, Andrew, 402, 473
Pleicones, Costa M., 471, 489–94
Porcher, Philip (Rev.), 109
Porter, Haigh, 378
Poston, Jonathan, 134, 143
Powell, Josephine, 312
Powell, Marilyn (Rev.), 109
Powell, Neff (Rt. Rev.), 393
Prayer Book, see *Book of Common Prayer*
Prayer Book Society, 82
Prescott, Tyler (Rev.), 455
Price, Kenneth L., Jr. (Rt. Rev.), 200, 418
Primates' gathering, January 2016, 201, 444–45
Primates' meeting, Oct. 14–16, 2003, 120–21
Primatial vicar plan, 155
Prince Frederick's Church, 17
Prince George Winyah Church, Georgetown, 6, 230, 404
Prince William's Church, 7–8
Pringle, Jan, 136, 433
"A Prognosis for This Body Episcopal," 172
Progressive Episcopalians of Pittsburgh, 199
Provenzano, Lawrence (Rt. Rev.), 393
Purcell, Henry (Rev.), 6–7

Quincy, litigation, 204–7; schism, 202–4
Quit Claim Deeds, 322–27, 497–98; *see also* Disciplinary Board for Bishops, 2012

Radner, Ephraim, 98, 135, 317–18, 333
Ratzinger, Joseph Cardinal, 118
Read, Jacob, 7
"The Real Story Behind Our Split with The Episcopal Church," 433
Redeemer Church, Pineville, 23
Redeemer Movement, 18–19
Redman-Gress, Warren, 134
Rees, John, 124
Reformed Episcopal Church, 17, 141, 200, 441
Release and Removal from the Ordained Ministry of the Church, 306–7
"Remaining Anglican: In Defense of Dissociation," 173
Reno, Russell, 94
"Renunciation of Ordained Ministry and Declaration of Removal and Release," December 5, 2012, 393–94
Resolution 1.10 (1998), 81, 247

Restraining Order, *see* Temporary Restraining Order
Restriction on Bishop Lawrence, October 15, 2012, 362–63
Reyes, Jesus (Rev.), 312
Richards, Frenchie, 256, 261
Richards, Lynda, 315
Richardson, Jeff (Rev.), 410, 412, 420
Rickenbaker, Thomas M. (Rev.), 170, 477; Affidavit, 170, 468–69
Righter, Walter Cameron (Rt. Rev.), 63–64; Presentment, 68–69
Riley, Patricia P., 355
Riley, Thomas W., 355
Rivera, Victor (Rt. Rev.), 225
Robertson, Marcus B., 167
Robinson, Vicky Gene (Rt. Rev.): confirmation, 99–101; consecration, 127–28; election, 95; foreign reactions to, 115–16; in General Convention of 2003, 99–104; opposition to, 96–102; reactions to, in SC, 104–15; reactions to, in U.S., 115–27; vote on, 100–101
Roderick, Doug, 420
Rodgers, John Hewitt, Jr. (Rt. Rev.), 43, 45, 59, 82, 86, 88, 117, 139, 228
Roof, Dylann Storm, 425–26
Roseberry, David H. (Rev.), 117
Roskam, Catherine S. (Rt. Rev.), 94
Rothermel, Peter, 137
Rubric of Love, 268–69, 286
Rules and Regulations, 10–11, 14
Runyan, C. Alan, 266, 277–78, 302, 315–16, 347, 349–50, 360, 365, 442, 449–50; background, 297; in aftermath of schism, 372, 381, 391, 401; in background of circuit court trial, 401–4; in circuit court trial, 465–84; in SC Supreme Court. 484–95; in United States courts, 456–65; suit in circuit court, 401–6; Title IV, 292, 294, 297–98; *see also* Litigation

St. Alban's Church, Kingstree, 407, 412
St. Andrew's Cathedral, Singapore, 58
St. Andrew's Church, Mt. Pleasant, 236, 288, 414; real estate trust, 2009, 255–57; realignment, 272–73, 288
St. Andrew's Church (West Ashley), 17, 29, 447; Bishop Lawrence's visit, February 10, 2013, 427–32; Bishop vonRosenberg's visit, February 17, 2013, 432; discernment, 427–33; parish vote, February 24, 2013, 433

INDEX

St. Andrew's, Mt. Pleasant, Land Trust, 256
St. Anne's Church, Conway, 412, 418
St. Augustine's Church, Wedgefield, 23, 417
St. Bartholomew's Church, 6–8
St. Bartholomew's Church, Hartsville, 322, 404, 475
St. Catherine's Church, Florence, 397, 412, 418
St. Charles' Church, Paulsbo, WA, 147
St. Christopher's Camp and Conference Center, 27, 39
St. David's Church, Cheraw, 404, 448
St. Francis's Church, Charleston (West Ashley), 412, 418, 433
St. George, South Carolina, 402
St. George's Church, Dorchester, 6
St. George's Church, Summerville, 322, 407
St. Helena's Church, Beaufort, 6, 144, 262, 304, 322, 376, 404, 448
St. James' Anglican Church, Blackville, 448
St. James Church, Charleston (James Island), 186–87, 263, 316, 322, 376, 404, 448
St. James Church, Goose Creek, 6–8
St. James Santee Church, 6, 47, 407
St. John's Church, Berkeley, 6–7, 17
St. John's Church, Charleston (Johns Island), 29, 322, 376, 404, 416, 448, 453
St. John's Church, Charleston (mission), 30
St. John's Church, Colleton, 6
St. John's Church, Donora, PA, 202
St. John's Church, Florence, 322, 361, 378–79, 397, 404, 412, 448, 475–76
St. Jude's Church, Walterboro, 404, 439
St. Louis Congress, 41
St. Luke and St. Paul, Charleston, *see* Cathedral Church of St. Luke and St. Paul
St. Luke's Church, Columbia, 18
St. Luke's Church, Hilton Head, 229, 262, 273, 376, 404, 448
St. Mark's Church, Charleston, 17–18, 22–23, 383–84, 407, 419
St. Mark's Church, Port Royal, 291, 305, 380, 397, 407, 413, 419
St. Mark's Church, Shafer, CA, 225
St. Mary's Church, Charleroi, PA, 225
St. Mary's Church, Staten Island, NY, 416
St. Matthew's Church, Darlington, 322, 404, 448
St. Matthew's Church, Ft. Motte, 404
St. Matthias Church, Summerton, 404
St. Michael's Church, Charleston, 6–8, 17, 260, 376, 404, 447, 475
St. Michael's Church, Wayne Township, PA, 202
St. Paul's Church, Bakersfield, CA, 196, 231–33, 254
St. Paul's Church, Bennettsville, 322, 404
St. Paul's Church, Charleston, 17
St. Paul's Church, Conway, 322, 404, 411, 448
St. Paul's Church, Orangeburg, 22–23
St. Paul's Church, Summerville, 47, 109, 248, 282, 292, 371–72, 404
St. Paul's Church, Visalia, CA, 225
St. Paul's Episcopal Cathedral, Peoria, IL, 202–3
St. Philip's Chapel, Voorhees College, 407
St. Philip's Church, Charleston, 6–8, 17, 38, 169, 236–37, 322, 376, 385, 404, 407, 448
St. Philip's Church, Denmark, 23
St. Stephen's Church, Charleston, 112, 114, 377, 419
St. Stephen's Church, McKeesport, PA, 226
St. Stephen's Church, North Myrtle Beach, 407
St. Stephen's Church, Oak Harbor, WA, 147
St. Stephen's Church, St. Stephen, 6, 407, 412
St. Thomas's Church, North Charleston, 61, 407
St. Thomas and St. Denis Church, 6–8, 322
St. Timothy's Anglican Catholic Church, Charleston, 42
St. Timothy's mission of Cane Bay, 448
St. Vincent's Cathedral, Bedford, TX, 209
Salmon, Edward Lloyd, Jr. (Rt. Rev.), 60–217, 234, 335, 337, 340, 366, 416, 422, 424; and the Anglican Mission in America, 86–87; and Bishop John Spong, 80–81; Bishop's Search Committee, 160–63; death, 188; early years, 60–61; election and consecration, 61; and First Promise, 79–80; homosexuality issue, 61–88; retirement, 188–89, 206, 211; and Rev. Chuck Murphy, 73–74; and Righter case, 69–70; and Robinson affair, 97–115
Same-sex marriage, issue, in General Convention, 2015, 421–23; in ECSC, 424–25
"Same-Sex Relationships in the Life of the Church." (2011), 281
Sammons, Diane, 312
San Joaquin, litigation, 194–96; schism, 192–94
Sanderson, M. Dow (Rev.), 1980s, 51; 1990s, 75, 78–80, 83–84; 2003, 105; 2005, 143–44, 161, 164; 2006, 168–69, 171; 2008, 240; 2009, 263; 2010, 308; 2012, 377, 381; 2014, 477
Sands, John O., 134, 380
Sauls, Stacy F. (Rt. Rev.), 149
Schism of 1887, 17–18
Schjonberg, Mary Frances, 370
Schneider, Matthew (Rev.), 415
Schofield, John-David (Rt. Rev.), 68, 243–44; *see also* San Joaquin

Scholarly Engagement with Anglican Doctrine, 73, 82, 134
Schwank, Suzanne, 315, 334, 405
Scott, John (Rev.), 163, 261
Search Committee, *see* Bishop's Search Committee
Second Anglican Encounter in the South, 73
Secret plan of August 21, 2012, 347–49
Seitz, Christopher (Rev.), 98, 135
Settlement offer, June 1, 2015, 484–86
1785 Society, 450
Sexuality: A Divine Gift, 50–54
Shand, P.J. (Rev.), 16
Shaw, M. Thomas (Rt. Rev.), 58, 312
Shepard, Angela (Rev.), 312
Shuler, Jon (Rev.), 78
Simmons, Ned, 136
Simons, James (Rev.), 162, 165, 200
Simons, M. Jaquelin, 355
Singapore consecrations, 58, 85
Singh, Prince (Rt. Rev.), 312
Skardon, Steve, 112, 186, 299, 316, 332, 370, 372, 406, 433–34, 471
Skilton, William J. (Rt. Rev.), 61, 97, 105, 125, 134, 137, 145, 152, 161–62, 337, 340, 366, 416–17, 422, 424
Smith, Benjamin Bosworth (Rev.), 44, 109, 143
Smith, Benjamin Bosworth, Mrs., 355
Smith, Colton M., III (Rev.), 109, 143, 355, 410
Smith, Dabney T. (Rt. Rev.), 393, 408, 417
Smith, Gretchen, 412
Smith, Michael (Rt. Rev.), 157, 340
Smith, Robert (Rt. Rev.), 6, 8–11
Smith, Roger W. (Rev.), 355
Smith, Wayne (Rt. Rev.), 393
Smith, William, 9
Snyder, Gregory (Rev.), 21, 315, 334, 352, 405, 455
Society for the Advancement of Christianity in South Carolina, 13
South Carolina Supreme Court, *see* Supreme Court, South Carolina
Sovereignty issue, 215–16, 255, 268, 291, 351–52
Spong, John S. (Rt. Rev.), 49, 62, 64, 66, 69; ordinations, 55; *Twelve Theses*, 58, 80
Standing Committee, Diocese of South Carolina, 285, 302, 304, 308–9, 315, 324–25, 350–51, 361, 451, 455; and alternative primatial oversight, 153–54; before the General Convention of 2012, 331–36; and Bishop's Search Committee, 160–68; and by-laws, 301–2; disaffiliation resolution, Oct. 2, 2012, 352–53; in aftermath of schism of Oct. 15, 2012, 371, 379–83, 387, 389, 391; and Jerusalem Statement, 249; meeting, July 28, 2009, 261–62; meeting, Sept. 18, 2012, 349–50; reaction to General Convention of 2012, 346–47; reaction to Robinson affair, Aug. 18, 2003, 105–7; reaction to Windsor Report, 142–43; resolution on disassociation, Nov. 1, 2011, 315; and St. Andrew's property transfer, 256–57; schism, Oct. 15, 2012, 364–65
Standing Liturgical Commission, 32, 74–75
Stanton, James M. (Rt. Rev.), 68, 71–72, 82, 105, 116, 123, 135, 152, 154, 157, 271, 340
State court, *see* Circuit Court
"A Statement in Koinonia," 66–68
"A Statement of Faith," 455
Steenson, Jeffrey (Rt. Rev.), 79
Steering committee for diocesan reorganization, 380, 382, 396, 408
Stipulation agreement, 198–99
Stopfel, Barry (Rev.), 63, 69
Stoudenmire, Joseph (Rev.), 109
Straub, Gregory, 310–12
"Supplemental Episcopal Pastoral Care," 129
Supreme Court, South Carolina: background of hearing, 484–90; hearing, September 23, 2015, 490–93; justices of, 489–90
Supreme Court, United States, 453; All Saints appeal, 138, 276; Texas appeal, 213–14
Surratt, Tim (Rev.), 140
Szen, Mark, 420

Tanner, Kathryn, 94
Task Force for Provincial Affiliation, 442–43
Task Force on Marriage, 451–53
Task Force on Property Disputes, 200
Taylor, Cynthia Nan (Rev.), 47
Taylor, G. Porter (Rt. Rev.), 325
Taylor, James (Rev.), 380, 406, 414, 422, 471
Temple, Gray (Rt. Rev.), 25–39; and development of diocese, 38–39; episcopacy of, 25–39; election of, 25; and homosexuality issue, 36–37; and incorporation, 38; and prayer book reform, 31–33; and race issues, 25–31; retirement of, 39, 43; and women's ordination, 33–35
Temporary Injunction, January 31, 2013, 406
Temporary Restraining Order, January 23, 2013, 405–6
Tengatenga, James (Rt. Rev.), 418
Tennis, Cabell (Rt. Rev.), 69

Index

Texas court of appeals, 211, 215
Texas supreme court, 211–13
Theuner, Douglas E. (Rt. Rev.), 69
Thomas, Albert Sidney, 5, 13, 20
Thomasson, Richard, 136
Thompson, Julius Pinckney, 442
Thompson, Richard (Rev.), 109
Thornton, Ed, 440
Thurlow, David (Rev.), 163, 168, 261, 331, 334, 336–37, 422, 442
Thurlow Amendment, 337–38, 422–23
Tillman, "Pitchfork Ben", 19
Tindall, Byron (Rev.), 109
Tipton, Tommy (Rev.), 109
Tisdale, Thomas Sumter, 21, 262, 266, 269, 333, 406, 422; in ECSC reorganization, 379–82, 383, 410; Logan, dispute of 2010, 275–81; *see also*, Litigation.
Title IV, 292–94, 298, 305–7, 428
Title IV Review Committee, 209
Toal, Jean Hoefer, 471, 489–94
Tompkins, George (Rev.), 109, 410
"Traces of the Trade: A Story from the Deep North," 426
Trapier, Paul (Rev.), 16
Trawick, Bill, 241
Trinity Anglican Church, Bakersfield, CA, 232–33
Trinity Church, Charleston, 322, 404
Trinity Church, Edisto Island, 404, 448
Trinity Church, Ft. Worth, TX, 209
Trinity Church, Myrtle Beach, 47, 84, 273, 376, 404, 448
Trinity Church, Pinopolis, 378, 404
Trinity Episcopal Cathedral, Pittsburgh, PA, 202
Trinity Episcopal Church/Cathedral, Columbia, 25
Trinity School for Ministry, 44–45, 58, 77, 196, 225, 228, 230, 235, 245, 249, 254, 289, 308, 453
Truro Episcopal Church, 72, 98, 122
Truro Statement, 99
Trustees of the Protestant Episcopal Church in South Carolina, *see* Board of Trustees
"Truth in Cold Blood," 21
Turner, Philip (Rev.), 49, 98, 126, 135
Two Bulls, Robert, Jr. (Rev.), 312

United Episcopal Church, 41
United States District Court, *see* District Court, United States (Charleston)
United States Supreme Court, *see* Supreme Court, United States

University of the South, Sewanee, TN, 22, 250, 289
Upper South Carolina (diocese of), 20, 281, 320, 392

Van Norte, Jan, 134
Venables, Gregory (Most Rev.), 98, 146
Via Media, 134, 176, 180, 208
Virtue, David, 265
Voices of the Anglican Communion symposium, 436
vonRosenberg, Charles (Rt. Rev.), 243, 380, 384, 406, 408, 410, 420–21, 426, 471
vonRosenberg v. Lawrence, 456–62
Voorhees College, 20, 28

Waggoner, James (Rt. Rev.), 312
Waldo, Andrew (Rt. Rev.), 281, 308, 320, 324–25, 337, 348, 351, 360, 366, 384, 392, 397, 408, 421
Walker, Betsy, 414, 420
Walker, Peter, 135
Wallace, H. Jeff (Rev.), 416
Wallace, John, 405
Walley, Kent, 143
Walmsley, Arthur E. (Rt. Rev.), 69
Walpole, Calhoun (Rev.), 21, 330, 380, 406, 410, 471
Walsh, Marcy, 133–34
Walsh, (Mrs.) Norman, S., 47
Walton, Charles (Rev.), 84, 165
Wantland, William C. (Rt. Rev.), 60, 68
Ward, Scott, 442
Ward, Steve, 134
Waring, Charles, 450
Warner, Bill, 421
Watson, Glynn, 405
Waynick, Catherine (Rt. Rev.), 312
Weaver, William C. (Rev.), 26
Welby, Justin (Most Rev.), 437, 440–41, 443
Weld, Louise (Rev.), 329
Weldon, Kenneth (Rev.), 334, 378, 405, 442
Wells, Kathleen, 408
Wendt, Rob, 299
White, Donald, 29
White, Roger J. (Rt. Rev.), 69
White, William (Rev.), 5
Whitmore, Keith (Rt. Rev.), 203
Wilder, John L., 355
Wilder, Virginia C., 355–56, 380, 406, 410, 420
Wilkins, Christopher, 176
Williams, David (Rev.), 143, 410
Williams, Robert (Rev.), 62

Williams, Rowan (Most Rev.), 124, 151–52, 157, 246–47, 266; reaction to Robinson, 119–20
Willis, Ann Hester, 315, 334, 352, 381, 405
Willis, Robert (Very Rev.), 419
Wilson, Christina E., 356
Wilson, George, 136
Wilson, James E., 356
Wimberly, Don (Rt. Rev.), 105
Windsor Report, 141–45
"The Witnessing and Blessing of a Lifelong Covenant," 336
Wolf, Geralyn (Rt. Rev.), 157
Wolfe, Dean (Rt. Rev.), 393
Women's ordination, 33–35, 454
Wood, Stephen D. (Rt. Rev.), 125, 167, 258–59, 272, 288, 348, 435, 442
Woodward, James Herbert (Rev.), 20
Wragg, Samuel, 14
Wright, Michael (Rev.), 366, 384, 406, 410, 421–22, 471
Wright, Robert Christopher (Rt. Rev.), 361

Yong Ping Chung, Datuk (Most Rev.), 98
Young, George D., III (Rt. Rev.), 408
Young, Sarah Moise, 390
Young, Thomas J., 14

Zadig, Al (Rev.), 98, 242, 268
Zahl, John (Rev.), 410, 421
Zavala, Hector "Tito" (Most Rev.), 440–41
Zeigler, Nick, 61, 65, 73, 80, 87, 105, 361, 378

www.ingramcontent.com/pod-product-compliance
Lightning Source LLC
Chambersburg PA
CBHW080530300426
44111CB00017B/2665